Illuminati Unmasked
Everything you need to know about the
"New World Order" and how we will beat it.

Johnny Cirucci

Cover art: High Five, the Egyptian Liberal

Copyright © 2015 Johnny Cirucci

All rights reserved.

ISBN: 1506156290
ISBN-13: 978-1506156293

"Therefore do not fear them, for there is nothing concealed that will not be revealed, or hidden that will not be known." ~ Matthew 10:26

Table of Contents

Acknowledgements..ix

Introduction...xi

Preface..xii

Chapter 1—America Is a Captured Operation, But By Whom?........1
    Libya...4
    All Roads Lead to Rome..7
    Free Traitors..10
    Free Boarders...11
    Secret Subversives...19

Chapter 2—The Manchurian Messiah of Mystery........................33
    Barry Soetoro..34
    The Man of Many Names..35
    Where's the Birth Certificate?..38
    A Closer Look..41
    Barack Obama's Mystery Religion..42
    Barry's Catholic Mentor...44

Chapter 3—"Vatican Assassins"..53
    The "War Between the States"..55
    The Precedent for Injustice...60
    Wild Knight In Malta..62
    Character Assassination...65
    Calling All Deviants..67
    Federal Bureau of Obfuscation...70
    Missing Evidence..71
    Qui Bono? "Who Benefits?"..72
    Dr. Mary's Monkey...74
    How to Keep a Secret..75
    Assassination Central...75

Chapter 4—War: What Is It Good For?..87
    The Best Enemies Money Can Buy..87

Follow the Money..89
We Have Met the Enemy and He Works on Wall Street................91
Skull & Boned..92
The Fourth Reich...96
Interlocked..100
Ratlines...101
From Rome to Rio..102
Free Reign...103
Dull-es a Knife in the Back..104
Cardinal Spellman's War..106
Commiserating Catholic Communists In Castro's Cuba............109
The Jesuits and 9/11..111
"Something Far Worse"...112
Commissioned..112
Not Very Intelligent...113
"Freedom of Religion?"...115
"Freedom of Speech?"..115
"Freedom to Vote?"..116
Pre-Planned..116
Why 9/11?..118

Chapter 5–A Sovereign Unto Itself..130
"We Run The Pope"..132
Reformed..137
In the Sign of the Cross Shall You Conquer..............................138

Chapter 6–From Christ to Cromwell:
The Battle Against Tyranny..145
"Us" Verses "Them"..145
Religion: the Chains that Bind...147
William Tyndale...149
Vicious, Vindictive Vatican..150
Still Saving..152
Brother Against Brother...152
Lord Protector..154

Chapter 7–The Company..158
Covert Catholic Convert...161
A Dish Best Served Cold..168
Jesuitical...173
Banged Up..178

Just the Facts, Ma'am..178
Vatican II..179
The Fourth Beast...180
Ruptured..182
"Take Up Your Cross And Follow Me"..................................189

Chapter 8—A Good Jesuit Education..................................196
Society of Spies..196
Get Fluked...197
The Teleprompter In Chief..199
Three Ways To Sunset...202
Secret Secular Jesuits: Campions of the Catholic World Order...............202
Priests Without Collars...204
Jesuit Agent Resurrected...205
Top Man at the Pentagon...208
Speaking in Unison...209
The Catholic Intelligence Agency..210
Behind the All-Seeing Eye..214
Good Ole Georgetown...216

Chapter 9—The Clinton Years:
When the False Flag Was Perfected..................................226
On the Power of the Banking Family Cartels........................226
On the Secret Control of Nations by Central Banks..............226
On the Existence of Secret Societies Which Subvert Democracy...........227
On Political "Choice"...227
Kill the Messenger..228
His Fate Was Sealed..230
Little Rock Candy...234
They're All In It Together...234
The Making of a President...238
Flagged..239
August 21-31, 1992: Ruby Ridge...242
The First World Trade Center Bombing...............................244
Controlled Opposition..246
April 19th, 1993: Waco..246
Oklahoma City..251
Not a Truck Bomb..251
Loose Ends..254
The Jesuit Communist Powers that Molded Bill Clinton.......257
Un-American in the House..259

Chapter 10—Flagged 272
- Day of Infamy 272
- Hooked 273
- The Land of Make-Believe 282
- The Catholic Connection 284
- Down the Rabbit Hole 286
- You've Got Anthrax Mail 287
- Patriot's Day 291
- Ricin Shine 293

Chapter 11—The Fall and Rise of Saint George, the Dragon-Slayer 309
- Eternal Enemies 310
- Reduced 313
- Saint George and the Dragon 317
- Company Playground 319
- "Chairman Mao" 326
- "The Perestroika Deception" 327
- A Convenient Distraction of Death 330
- Constantine Rising 335
- Man of the Decade 339
- Putin's Russia 347
- A Look Inside Putin's Brain 352
- Saint George's Lance 355
- The Eye of Sauron 358
- Living Clean 361
- "The" Ukraine 363
- Bankers' Holiday 366
- Where There Is Unrest, There Is the CIA 370
- Agent Provocateured 371
- MH-17...Or Was It MH-370? 372
- The Rise of Saint George 376

Chapter 12—Movie Magic & Media Menageries 395
- Prison Planet 396
- Controlled Conspiracy 398
- Action Assassinated 406
- Crusin 407
- Controlled Opposition 409

Chapter 13—Boiling Frogs 418
    Vaccine Vectors 418
    Fatal Fluoride 421
    The Love of Money is the Root of All Evil 423
    Going Viral 424
    EboLie 425
    Clipboard Guy 426
    International Cartel of Malignancy 428
    Satan In Charge 429
    What In the World Are They Spraying? 437
    Geoengineering 440
    TED 442

Chapter 14—The Eaters of Children:
Sex Slavery is a Government Industry 451
    The Franklin Coverup 454
    Boys Town 457
    Nationwide 460
    Going the Extra Mile 461
    House of Horrors 461
    Satanic Panic 471
    Disney's Nightmare 476
    Hypno-tarts 479
    The Groves of Molech 480
    Generational Curse 481
    Presidential Model 484
    Turn On, Tune In, Drop Out 488
    It Takes a Village to Steal Your Child 489
    Controlled 491
    Two-Card Monte 493
    Don't Give Up Yet! 495

Chapter 15—The Light of Lucifer:
How the Devil Gives Nations He Rides Their Edge 503
    The Nazificaiton of American Technology 503
    Satan's Army 508
    Satan's Society 511
    "Mr. Crowley" 512
    Dumble-dalf 007 516
    Aeon of Horus 517

Secret Agent 666...519
On Her Majesty's Secret Service...521
The Watchers...523
JPL...527
Treasonous Intelligence..529
Porn Nation...537
Crushed Dreams..538

Chapter 16— Ancient Hate:
Pagan Mysticism Behind The One World Order..................549
Fallen Ones..549
Drawn to Power...552
Bohemian...552
Who "They" Are..555
Isis Unveiled..560
Illuminating...566
Perverse Prophecy..568
Rose & Cross...572
Enlightened..581
Looking Behind the Curtain..585
A Sign..595
National Treasure...598
Shrine On You Crazy Diamond...600
Washington: Demonically-Controlled..602
Tolerating Treason..603
Protesting...605
A Walk Around the Park..606
Moths to the Flame of "Knowledge"..610
Send In the Marines...611

Chapter 17—It's the Jews!..620
"Christian Zionists"...620
"Anti-Zionists"...620
Israel and the Jews: a Balanced Perspective...622
Promised..622
A Captured Operation...623
The Protocols of Zion..629
The Rothschilds...631
Even When Facts Bear It Out, Bigotry Isn't the Answer........................636

Chapter 18—From Nimrod to al Ilah...643
- The Goddess of Wisdom..646
- Barbarism In Common...648
- The Beast Behind Christian Persecution...649
- Inquiring Minds...655
- The Queen of Heaven..657
- Apparition Apprehensions...662
- "Miracle of the Sun" 666
- The Blue Army..668
- Alberto...669
- A Whore Rides the Beast...672
- The Purse of Satan...676

Chapter 19—The Golden Rule:
He Who Owns the Gold, Makes the Rules.........................682
- Year of Infamy..682
- Dr. Dino...686
- From Freedom to Fascism...687
- Banksters' Rule...687
- The First and-not-the-Last Central Bank.......................................690
- Old Hickory..691
- Supremely Subverted...699
- "It's the Jews!"...702
- The Creature from Jekyll Island...705
- The Great Panic..709
- Bureaucratic Brutality..713
- The "Aldrich Plan"..715
- A Rigged Game...719
- The First Sphere of Influence...722
- The Seed of the Serpent..726

Chapter 20— King Ghidorah: the Dragon from Outer Space.......732
- The Devil Will Have His Due..732
- "Stop and be Friends!"...733
- Zeta Homunculi..736
- "And There Were Giants In The Land...".......................................737
- The "Gift" of Technology...744
- "Brother Astronomer to Brother Alien...Come In!".....................745
- The Light Bearer..750
- Baptizing ET...752

    Check Your Brain..752
    Beast Forgotten?...754
    Setting the Stage...756
    One World Religion...758
    The Return of the Archons...764

Chapter 21—#ResistanceRising......................................771
    Nimrodded..772
    Full Spectrum Christianity..775
    Dominion Theology...777
    Resistance Rising..782
    "Be Strong and of Good Courage!".....................................784
    Magnificent Conclusion..785

Appendix A: The Secret Jesuit Leadership Oath..........................791

Appendix B: Correspondence Between Reverend George Washington Snyder and President George Washington................796

Appendix C: A Defense of Intelligent Design.............................800

About the Author and Contact Info..807

Acknowledgments

"No man is an Iland." ~ Meditation XVII:
Devotions upon Emergent Occasions, John Donne, 1624

If there's one thing I've learned, it's that someone can move you or teach you earth-shattering things because they're good at what they do and may even have great values, yet they are sometimes odd or even abrasive in person.

When you need help, rarely do they respond and rarer still are they helpful.

This is even more disturbing when you realize that so many of them are professing Christians.

All the more wonderful are those who were responsive and even encouraging.

Thanks to Doc Burkhart of TruNews for always being an encourager.

Julian Charles is the ultimate Christian Red Pill talk show host who lives his walk with Christ. One of the few whose heart matches how much he feeds you.

I remember with dear fondness our beloved Patrick Heron who corresponded with me like I was his friend. I will see you again, Patty.

Special thanks to attorney Jesse C. Trentadue for all of the help he rendered to me in seeking justice for his brother, Ken; murdered by the FBI.

Walid Shoebat is the kind of guy that hugs people in person—and a darn insightful writer, too.

On a personal level, I want to thank my mother-in-law and father-in-law for their repeated help in allowing us to pay our bills. They were there when no-one else was.

Most of all, I give thanks to my best friend; my wife. At every turn in the struggle to write this book and keep paying the bills, she was there helping, encouraging, making it possible.

The passion, the anger, the inspiration and the gifts I credit to the King of kings; the hardest and the easiest Mentor I've ever had.

Introduction

America needs answers.

Our nation is rushing towards a self-imposed implosion at break-neck speed.

Unspeakable treasons and blatant lawlessness prevail and, though it be broadcast on the evening news, no one in power lifts a finger to stop it.

Are they all asleep? Clearly, there are men who are privy to the knowledge of who America's real enemies are, yet they remain silent and complicit in her destruction.

This implies a "conspiracy"—a secret compact to destroy America from within.

Who has enough influence to infiltrate and control the most powerful intelligence agencies and financial institutions in the world (for, surely, that is where power resides)?

In order to answer these questions, I must take you at break-neck speed across history with reputable citations shotgunned across these pages to back up assertions that will chill you to the bone—there is, indeed, a conspiracy and its source is an ancient hatred for mankind and his best chance at freedom; the United States.

Each stop along the way can be researched far beyond what I have done and many good men and women have already done so. A modest amount of their works can be found in my endnotes.

An exhaustive approach to the symptoms is not my desire. My goal is to convince you of both the conspiracy and the identity of the conspirators, in the short time that we have, so that you will be prepared, when the time comes, to stamp them out like the serpents they are.

~ JC

Preface

This is not a book where the author bloviates endlessly—it is a collection of news, quotes and citations from the best sources I could find and put together to prove to you my shocking contention—that America has been captured by a malignant, foreign entity.

It may be unlike most anything you've ever read before in content and format.

As the saying goes, "Opinions are like [bodily orifices]." Instead of my opinion, I have a direction that I want to go and I let *other* people, whom you likely respect, take you there.

By the end of the book I hope to prove to you beyond a shadow of doubt exactly who that entity is as well as give you the roadmap for how we will beat them...and we will.

If you wish to follow any of my leads (and that is why I wrote the book), I've made it as easy for you as possible. Even if a news source has been taken down, I have given you information that can take you to wherever that same story has been archived (if it has).

My original manuscript I wrote to myself, rife with sarcasm and cynicism. I have labored through some 6 re-writes since then. I've left some of that original sarcasm in the copious end notes as a "treat" for anyone courageous enough to follow my leads.

Being human, I'm sure I've made a mistake or two (but I doubt it). I've noticed that, if I was able to quote a book by finding a digital copy, often the pages in the digital version do not match up with the original. Please keep that in mind if you find page references are incorrect.

Most of all, this book is designed to not only educate the reader but give them the tools to prove what I have written for themselves. If there are citations that lead to a broken link or dead end, I've done what I can to leave enough clues to find other locations where that particular item may still hang resident or have been reposted.

Fasten your seat belts and put your seat-backs and tray-tables in their upright positions.

Chapter 1

America Is A Captured Operation

America is on the verge of collapse.

Inexplicably, the United States is under a co-ordinated assault of unprecedented ferocity from her own institutions.

At every level of government, individuals and groups are making decisions and enacting policies that are causing America great harm, and they do so with impunity.

Patriotic citizens are seeing organizations who have claimed to be on their side repeatedly betraying them, adding aid and comfort to the very forces destroying the United States from within.

Their news media refuses to report these critical issues and individual journalists who do are dealt with in ways that echo the harsh methodologies of a banana republic.

The IRS has targeted political enemies for persecution and prosecution. When queried by Congressional committee about correspondence between conspirators, IRS Director of Exempt Organizations Lois Lerner said they "lost" the e-mails[1]...and then said they lost some more.[2]

Government agencies use online back-up services such as the one the IRS had via companies like Sonasoft but the IRS further claimed that their back-up service was cancelled before they could've helped track down the criminal behavior.[3]

When asked about resident files on individual computer hard drives, Legislators were told that those hard drives had all crashed.[4]

The most shocking aspect of the entire scandal has been the fact that it was bold, open lawlessness by a Democrat administration and there have been no substantive consequences levied by the Republican Party, the "Opposition Party".

During the 2008 Presidential election, armed black men from the New Black Panthers—a racist organization akin to the KKK—dressed in paramilitary garb, intimidated voters at a polling location.

Charges were brought and ignored. As further action was about to be taken, the entire case was dismissed by Justice Department officials. It was an unbelievable act of politically-driven lawlessness that went unaddressed by any other government agency. The one good man who was pursuing the case was forced to resign in disgust and despair.[5]

In 2011, Americans learned that the Bureau of Alcohol Tobacco Firearms and Explosives, the Drug Enforcement Agency and the Justice Department had been caught giving automatic weapons[6], handgrenades[7] and rocket launchers[8] to a bloodthirsty Mexican Drug cartel.

The rationale they used was that they were conducting a "sting" to track where the fully-functioning weapons ended up but, when queried further, admitted that there was no specific tracking method or technology that was used and assault weapons, .50 caliber sniper rifles and explosives were all "lost".[9]

Those same weapons soon started showing up as the cause of carnage on both sides of the border.

A Romanian AK-47—a true "assault rifle" that was fully automatic[a]—was found after a massive shootout that claimed the life of Mexican beauty queen Maria Susana Flores Gamez in Guamúchil, Mexico[10]. How is the United States government able to deal in automatic Romanian assault weapons?

Chihuahua City lawyer Mario Gonzalez Rodriguez was found in a shallow grave after being forced to conduct an al Qaeda-style "confession" video. Two more "Operation: FAST AND FURIOUS" AK-47s were found after a shoot-out with cartel members nearby.[11]

During another firefight, a Federal Police helicopter was downed injuring the two crew members and a massive cache of weapons was found, many of them were "Fast and Furious" weapons[12]. The name of that cartel, the "Caballeros Templarios"—the Knights Templar—speaks to an eerie higher power behind the drug ring. Why would Mexican drug lords make such an association?

More Fast and Furious weapons were found at the scene of the attempted assassination of Tijuana Municipal Secretary of Public Safety Julian Leyzaola.[13]

Hostotipaquillo, Mexico police chief Luis Lucio Rosales Astorga was

---

[a] "Black rifles" available to the common American are semi-automatic only; one trigger pull = one round.

murdered with a "Fast and Furious" sniper rifle.[14]

Perhaps worst of all are the American deaths, at least the ones we know of to date: Border Patrol Agent Brian Terry[15] along with Immigration and Customs Enforcement Special Agent Jaime Zapata[16] have both fallen to "Fast and Furious" weapons.

When the son of Sinaloa drug cartel leader Ismael "El Mayo" Zambada, Jesus Vicente Zambada-Niebla, was arrested by Drug Enforcement Agency officials in Chicago, it was disclosed[17] that he, his family and the entire Sinaloa cartel were on the U.S. government payroll. As long as they delivered information on rival gangs, they were free to distribute narcotics throughout America and receive deadly weapons in return.

Even more incredulous, Department of Justice officials knowingly conducted these operations with the ulterior motive of exploiting the bloodshed with new, stricter gun control legislation in the United States.[18]

A single reporter, Sharyl Attkisson, covered the story and she was immediately isolated. She was refused admittance to press conferences[19] and both her work and personal computers were hacked[20] so that important information could be wiped and classified documents planted that could have been used to prosecute her.[21]

Attkisson realized both CBS and the Obama administration were behind the tactics and she resigned as a result.[22]

The President of Mexico, Felipe Calderón, took to the floor of the United States Congress to implore legislators to re-enact the Clinton/Feinstein "Assault Weapons ban"[23]. Many saw this as an overtly subversive act, but one that was likely co-ordinated by American insiders.

U.S. citizens got no help from the Republican Party. Rep. Darrell Issa (R-CA), Chairman of the House Oversight and Government Reform Committee told Attorney General Eric Holder that he "owned" the Fast and Furious scandal[24], yet he refused to even ask Holder to resign[25], no less seek his criminal prosecution.

4 years later, instead of prosecutions, firings and resignations, supervisors within the ATF got promoted[26], just as the IRS official who oversaw political-oriented persecution, Steven Miller, was promoted to oversee America's new socialized healthcare, the "Affordable Healthcare Act".[27]

Barack Obama has been a thorough disappointment to anti-war activists who had heard him rail against the war in Iraq[28] and solemnly vow to close the international detention facility at Guantanamo Bay, Cuba[29]. The "War on Terror" rages on now, more than ever and "Gitmo" still has a steady stream of prisoners going in and coming out. Many are thoroughly perplexed at how seamless Obama policies have taken over from George W. Bush with so little change.

It is almost as if a higher authority guided them both toward the same end...a poisonous one.

Libya

In 2003, Libya's ruler, Muammar Gaddafi, had gone to excessive lengths to show then President George W. Bush that he wanted to be a respected member of the "fraternity of nations" and turned over all of Libya's weapons of mass destruction.[30]

Previous to that, when Pan Am flight 103 was destroyed over Lockerbie, Scotland killing 270 passengers, Gaddafi turned suspects over for prosecution. Such unprecedented co-operation saw then Secretary of State Condoleezza Rice remove Libya from the list of state sponsors of terrorism in 2007.[31]

Libya would receive her citizen-suspect back a few years later. After being convicted of murdering 270 people, Abdelbaset Ali Mohmet al-Megrahi was released from prison by United Kingdom authorities in Scotland after being diagnosed with prostate cancer.[32]

It was disclosed that Al-Megrahi had $4 million in a Swiss bank account which suspiciously spoke of having very powerful backing. Citizens were assured that Britain's MI6 was investigating,[33] but, to date, nothing has been disclosed.

Even more suspicious, it was later disclosed that Britain's most notorious muslim "hate preacher" Abu Hamza, was on the MI5 payroll.[34]

Were Western nations actively courting radical Islamists to destabilize their own countries?

Because of, or perhaps in spite of Muammar Gaddafi's co-operation, "al Qaeda" vowed to overthrow him that very same year; 2007.[35]

The man who made that threat, Ayman al Zawahri, was accused by Osama bin Laden's personal bodyguard of taking orders directly from

Washington, DC.

In an interview via Lebanon's Asian News Agency, Nabil Na'eem Abul Fattah claimed that both al Qaeda and Islamic "rebels" in Syria were controlled by the CIA.[36]

Foreign policy experts surmised that Gaddafi knew this and began acting accordingly.

First he pulled out of Western oil contracts.[37]

Then Gaddafi began to divest the U.S./Saudi Petro-Dollar and cut off "investments" of the International Monetary Fund[38], replacing the indebted fiat currency with a gold Libyan Dinar.

Gaddafi then utilized his nation's wealth to create irrigation that had been termed "the 8th wonder of the world".[39]

This was the beginning of his end.

In February of 2011, Barack Obama initiated military action in Libya without a formal declaration. The conflict endured for 8 months and culminated in a vicious public torture and execution of Muammar Gaddafi.[40]

An immediate and key target of NATO bombing runs was Libya's man-made river.[41]

A handful of Representatives gave easily-defeated resistance. A lawsuit lead by Dennis Kucinich (D, OH) and Walter Jones (R, NC) tried to stop Obama on a clear violation of the "War Powers Act". Unbelievably, judge Reggie Walton ruled

---

What is "fiat currency"?

"Fiat Currency" is a note of financial transaction that is not backed by any specie; a commonly recognized form of value e.g. precious metals such as gold or silver.

American currency continues to have worth only as long as those who use it believe America will not go bankrupt. After generations of debt-spending by both Parties, this is now guaranteed and international entities are rushing to use or create alternate forms of currency.

"Fiat currency" is what you have in your pocket right now. You can not exchange your "Federal Reserve Note" $1 bill for a dollar's worth of gold or silver.

Richard Milhous Nixon is credited with taking the dollar off the gold standard by issuing "Executive Order" 11615.

The "Executive Order" in and of itself has become a tool of tyranny, far removed from George Washington using it to procure china for the Capital.

they had no standing and threw it out.[42]

Later, Congressman Ron Paul (R, TX) would join Kucinich in calling for Obama's impeachment[43], but the effort immediately stalled. All key leaders inside the Republican Party fully support both Barack Obama and his policies.

Not only did the upstarts have no allies in Congress, the Republicans sent out a coalition of familiar names to celebrate what the Obama administration had done. United States Senators Mark Kirk (R, IL), Lindsey Graham (R, SC), Marco Rubio (R, FL) and John McCain (R, AZ) ran to get a quick photo op[44] with Islamists who were pulling Christians from their homes[45] and committing atrocities on them and their families.

Then Secretary of State Hillary Clinton, was asked about her reaction to the destabilizing of Libya and execution of that nation's sovereign. Her response was completely disconnected from reality and compassion; "We came, we saw, he died."[46]

Clinton, herself, had had an inexplicable and meteoric rise to power with no political experience. She became a United States Senator representing a state she never lived in, New York.

Clinton's past is a sordid one; she personally ruined the lives of women who accused Bill Clinton of sexual harassment and rape[47], she would be given access to FBI dossiers on key Republican political enemies to be used for blackmail[48], today she is shadowed by an assistant who is almost certainly an agent for the Muslim Brotherhood—Huma Abedin.[49]

Is this is a planned agenda?

"Inflation" will continue to devalue Middle Class buying power until it equals the Weimar Republic chaos of 1924 Germany.

In reality, it was Franklin Delano Roosevelt who took the power of privately-owned gold from the American people with *his* "Executive Order" 6102, confiscating personal gold from citizens in supposed reaction to the "Great Depression".

Americans willingly accepted it as did poor American citizens of Japanese descent.

It is a little-known fact that the cause of so much defamation of America via her "institutionalized racism" was done with a stroke of Roosevelt's pen: via Executive Order 9066, Roosevelt imprisoned an entire race of people, based solely upon their ethnicity.

Since then, an unaccountable Central Bank—our "Federal Reserve"—has been recklessly printing money completely disconnected to

Is there something to be learned from Clinton's sociopath response to Muammar Gaddafi's death?

It was Roman conqueror Julius Caesar who wrote to the Senate after defeating Pharnaces II, "*Veni, vidi, vici*" — "I came, I saw, I conquered." Was she acting on behalf of today's Roman authority?

> any worth.
>
> Is this agenda being pushed by a higher power that desperately seeks the destruction of the American Middle Class?

All Roads Lead To Rome

How is it possible that America could so repeatedly be ruled and governed by one Party that openly hates her and another Party that subversively enables them behind closed doors?

Not a judge, not a general, not even "Conservative" pundits speak of this conspiracy.

> *con·spir·a·cy: a secret plan made by two or more people to do something that is harmful or illegal*
> ~ Merriam-Webster

Many nations hate America...many more individuals do. But who has the power and reach to do so much harm with so little resistance?

To explain their behavior, Senators Kirk, Graham, Rubio and McCain were given an op-ed in the Wall Street Journal which they used to proclaim a "Promise of a Pro-American Libya".[50]

Less than a year later we would see the fruit of what they had all sown in "Pro-American Libya".

On September 11th, 2012, radical jihadists who had been running Libya since the overthrow of Muammar Gaddafi, raping, murdering and enslaving[51] innocents there, stormed what mainstream media called an "embassy[52]" in Benghazi and killed the United States ambassador.

Immediately, the Obama Administration stated that this was a "spontaneous[53]" conflagration as a result of outrage over a YouTube video that no one had ever heard of called "The Innocence of Muslims".

But, just as quickly, the story began to fall apart.

The apparent producer of the film disappeared and was later arrested.

Nakoula Basseley Nakoula was labeled as the Christian behind the film yet one of the actresses in it claimed the redundantly-named director professed to be a muslim.[54]

The quality of the film was less than amateur.

Mainstream media unquestioningly accepted the Obama Administration story but independent journalists found that the Canadian company that built the "Obamacare" website was the parent corporation for one of the outlets that helped promote "The Innocence of Muslims".[55]

The mistress of former CIA Director David Petraeus, Paula Broadwell, leaked during a speech at her alma mater, the University of Denver[56], that Benghazi was actually a CIA way-station used for interrogating prisoners.

More than that, Benghazi had become a funnel for weapons being taken from chaos-filled Libyan armories and secreted out to jihadists in Syria to help destabilize that nation as well. Saudi Arabia and Turkey were disclosed as helping British and American Intelligence (MI6 and the CIA) accomplish this agenda.[57]

The transfer of small arms to radical muslims from the CIA is a generational operation but when this transfer included man-portable SA-7 surface-to-air missiles stolen from Libyan armories, personnel at the State Department decided to intervene.[58]

Ambassador Christopher Stevens was dispatched to work with the jihadists, the Turks and the CIA. It later raised eyebrows to learn that the ambassador was reputed to have lived a homosexual lifestyle when he was in Chicago[59]. The Chicago homosexual connection would later be levied at Barack Obama, his former Chief of Staff Rahm Emanuel and other key figures.[60]

According to CIA insider Clair Lopez, the Turkish Consul General Ali Sait Akin conveniently slipped out of his meeting with ambassador Chris Stevens just before the ambush started[61]. Leading some to believe the adage "once in the Firm, always in the Firm," Lopez would later vehemently deny that the CIA was helping Libyan Islamists when interviewed by Christian news broadcaster Rick Wiles.[62]

With these facts in place, it becomes clear that powerful people in the CIA decided to counter Christopher Stevens' mission by selling him out— and they used the authority of Barack Obama to accomplish treason. Getting "MANPADS" (MAN-Portable Air Defense Systems) in the hands of reckless Islamists was so important to them it was worth being exposed as subversives in the highest offices of American government.

Then Secretary of State Hillary Clinton implicated her involvement by slashing the security at Benghazi before the September 11th attack. [63]

American personnel in Libya were distressed by her actions and asked that they be rescinded but they were repeatedly denied.[64]

Not only was the "consulate" under-protected, the attackers had inside information including where to find Chris Stevens in order to torture and execute him, even though he had what he thought was a secure location to retreat to.[65]

Guantanamo Bay detainee Sufyan Ben Qumu was released[66] in order to plan this event, along with U.S.-trained Muslim Brotherhood agent Mohsen Al-Azazi[67]. They joined a coalition of international[68] Islamists in Libya.

But the betrayal goes even further.

The tiny security detail at Benghazi held off the attackers for 13 grueling hours[69]. Everyone in Washington DC who needed to know, knew what was going on almost instantaneously[70]. With Predator drones overhead and security teams within a very short distance all ready to go[71], the message from Washington was "stand down".[72]

As the besieged Americans cried out for help hour after hour, military commanders in-theater broke ranks and readied to send help. They were relieved of duty.

AFRICOM commanding officer, General Carter Ham, and the theater Carrier task force commander, Admiral Charles M. Gayouette were both fired from their commands and investigative journalist Dave Hodges says at least Ham, for sure, was *arrested* by a CIA mole, his Executive Officer.[73]

Such a CIA-planted Executive Officer would've had some difficulty trying to arrest George Patton (who kept a Model 51 Remington .380 tucked in his belt at all times) or to stop him from rescuing Americans besieged at Bastogne. Patton would later be assassinated by the OSS because of his Patriotism and indomitable leadership.

How can American Intelligence be run by such poisonous power and remain unopposed?

How can Barack Obama's aberrant lifestyle be completely covered up?

As weak as the resistance was from those two flag officers, it was enough to cause fear in the Obama administration and a massive purge has been initiated by Obama's Iranian-born Senior Advisor Valerie Jarrett.[74]

As a result of the role she plays, Jarrett receives full protection from the Secret Service.[75]

Two former Navy SEALs, Glen Doherty and Tyrone Woods, disobeyed orders to do what no other military commanders had the integrity to do and brought help to the besieged Americans. They paid for their Patriotism with their lives.[76]

Although hard-Left pundits like Eleanor Clift put out stories that Ambassador Christopher Stevens died of smoke inhalation from a fire[77], it was clear that he was alive when the CIA-enabled Islamists tortured and murdered him.[78,79]

That was September 11th, 2012. *Two years later*, Speaker John Boehner, in charge of the Republican-controlled House of Representatives, would pick South Carolina firebrand Trey Gowdy to lead the Benghazi investigation[80] but while meaningless memes permeate social networking regarding the toughness of Gowdy and his qualifications to take over the House, there hasn't been a single subpoena.

As Gowdy remained quiet, the Republican Chairman of the Permanent Select Committee on Intelligence, Mike Rogers, issued a statement[81] and a report that there was no stand-down and no wrong-doing by the Obama administration on September 11th, 2012.[82]

As America slowly devolves into a complete Orwellian Police State where innocent citizens are watched and recorded without warrants or proof of wrongdoing, it is the Republican Party that leads the way.

In 2013, Republican Mike Rogers was lobbying hard for massive internet control and shutdown via "CISPA"; the Cyber Intelligence Sharing and Protection Act.

It was later disclosed that Rogers' wife, Kristi Clemens-Rogers, former president and CEO of the military contracting firm Aegis LLC, was helping funnel billions in taxpayer dollars toward her former company.[83]

Free Traitors

One of the most powerful weapons employed against the American Middle Class is "free trade".

America has been bereft of her best manufacturing jobs as both Democrats and Republicans (with "Conservatives" like Rush Limbaugh trumpeting the way) walk in lock-step to this agenda.[84]

Sick with Battered Wives Syndrome, organized unions consistently get out the vote each year for Democrat candidates who consistently support "free trade" agreements that obliterate tens of thousands of manufacturing jobs.[85]

Bush, Clinton, Bush, Obama—how can their trade policy be perfectly aligned if not because it's being managed by a higher power bent on *breaking* the American Middle Class?[86]

In Oregon, a woman opened up a Halloween costume for her child that she bought from Kmart and found a heart-breaking note in English begging for help from a slave laborer making $1.61/month.[87]

As Free Traders like Rush Limbaugh light another cigar on the golf course, Chinese peasants are chaining their toddlers outside their sweatshops because both parents are forced to work 12 hour days for pittance.[88]

Limbaugh's dutiful acceptance of both Barack Obama's Constitutional eligibility and the government narrative of the bin Laden execution have perplexed fans.

The Apple factory in China forces their Communist peasants to work 24 hour shifts while being exposed to a toxic environment. Conditions are so bad, workers were jumping off roofs to commit suicide. Nets were installed to save them...and send them back to their work stations.[89]

The founder of Apple, Steve Jobs, was an excellent example of the modern task master. Jobs drove his $250,000 Mercedes[90] without license plates and parked it in handicapped spots.[91,92]

Steve Jobs: dead at 56 of pancreatic cancer.

Free Boarders

But there's another agenda of self-destruction even more obvious than "Free Trade" and that's America's open borders.

The purposeful mismatching of disparate peoples has been a method of control by the Elite over the masses for thousands of years. Samaritans were maligned by ancient Hebrews because, after an Israeli civil war, the nation of Assyria later conquered the northern kingdom of Israel (the southern kingdom was known as "Judah"). Those conquered Jews were forcibly mixed with pagans that were brought in from as far as Babylon [II Kings 17:24]. Their capital, Samaria, became synonymous with their new religion; a syncretistic mix of Judaism and paganism, much as Rome mixes Christianity and paganism.

This forced intermingling, however, has met some resistance.

In Italy, tens of thousands of citizens marched in protest of a massive forced influx of immigrants—mostly illegal—into their nation, bringing disease, terror risk and a destruction of their culture and national identity.[93]

In Britain, roving gangs of muslim men are raping and enslaving white teenagers, at will, with no response from law enforcement. Inexplicably, the reason some agencies have given for their refusal to reign in the chaos and outrage is that they didn't want to be accused of racism.[94]

America is one of the only nations in the world who has left her borders wide open to pandemic disease, Islamic jihad and weapons of mass destruction.

Megacorporations and governments at all levels kowtow to Spanish-speaking aliens to insure they have no need to assimilate.

While illegal drunk drivers are slaughtering Americans by the bushel, when they are exposed to the government, they receive perks to go out and kill again.[95]

The reason for this agenda is to destabilize America and destroy her national identity and it's working.

In Sacramento, a tattoo-ridden alien and his wife killed two sheriff's deputies. Luis Enrique Monroy-Bracamonte had already been deported for possession and distribution of narcotics once before. He had returned and was using a different name.[96]

The state of California has seen the most concentrated influx of Hispanic illegal immigrants and they have empowered Leftist politicians at every level. Gun rights have been particularly targeted. If a retired soldier expresses emotional distress for any reason, they can easily be adjudicated "at risk" and law enforcement quickly shows up at the soldier's door to confiscate his firearms.[97]

Bureaucrats in California are exploiting every possible law and regulation to send SWAT teams to take *thousands* of privately-owned California weapons.[98]

No due process is required for gun confiscation in California[99,100] and provisions in the "Affordable Healthcare Act" (also known as "Obamacare") open *all* Americans to an unannounced visit from a "healthcare agent" if your family uses tobacco, your kids don't make straight A's or there's a veteran in the home.[101]

Criminal mayors use "sanctuary city" policies to deposit illegals on neighboring towns.[102]

California's political landscape has been carefully manipulated by an Unseen Hand via this illegal invasion.

> *California gave America two of its five most recent Republican presidents. But the state party has fallen on hard times since the days of Nixon and Reagan. After having fallen for decades, the number of registered Republican voters in California now stands at just 30% (see chart). With the number of voters expressing no party preference rising fast, the party is in danger of slipping into third place in the state.* ***No Republican holds statewide office in California, and the Democrats enjoy wide majorities in both chambers.*** *~ Fading Into Irrelevance*, the Economist [emphasis mine][103]

They are being openly enabled by Democrat politicians who vehemently push to grant illegals "citizen" status.[104]

Barack Obama has acted unilaterally via "Executive Order" to provide five million illegal immigrants with work permits and amnesty. Former Republican Florida governor and Presidential contender Jeb Bush is in full support.[105]

Inexplicably, this suicidal policy is being followed by both of America's political parties.[106]

They have a surprising ally behind them.

> *A coalition of religious leaders including San Francisco Archbishop George Niederauer led some 10,000 protesters Sunday in demanding Congress enact more immigrant-friendly policies. ~ Archbishop Joins Immigrant Rights Rally*, Associated Press[107] [quite a slanted headline]

Many Americans are ignorant of the Vatican's promotion of this agenda but there has been perfect continuity regardless of who is the Holy See.[108,109]

With such strong synergy between Washington and Rome, does this cooperative effort to harm America prove the existence of an Unseen Hand?

> *Illegal aliens are being allowed to fly on commercial airliners without valid identification, according to the National Border Patrol Council (NBPC). "The aliens who are getting released on their own recognizance are being allowed to board and travel commercial airliners by simply showing their Notice to Appear forms," NBPC's Local 2455 Spokesman, Hector Garza, told Breitbart Texas.* ~ Brandon Darby, Breitbart.com[110]

As these efforts become more powerful, the legitimization for them becomes more questionable.

Currently, Americans have been told that Mexican families are recklessly throwing their children aboard planes, trains and automobiles headed for America with no idea whose hands they will fall in to.

At best, such children are in grave danger of being sold into slavery for sexual abuse.

At worst, they aren't children at all.

> *Following reports that soldiers were booted from their barracks at an Oklahoma Army base to make room for a wave of illegal immigrant minors, the Obama administration is refusing to give the federal lawmaker who represents the state in Congress access to the facility.*
>
> *Could it be that the administration is hiding something? The facility, Ft. Sill, is located in Lawton about 85 miles southwest of Oklahoma City. It serves as the United States Army and Marine Corps' Field Artillery School and houses nearly 9,000 soldiers along with 62,621 family members, according to its official Army website. Last week Judicial Watch received reports that single enlisted soldiers were transferred from their barracks to tents in order to accommodate the flood of Unaccompanied Alien Children (UAC) coming from Central America.* ~ *Lawmaker Denied Ft. Sill Entry After Reports of Displacing Soldiers to Accommodate Illegal Aliens*, Judicial Watch[111]

In all of this, Barack Obama is a powerful conduit. While Americans of all stripes seek desperately to pull their nation out of economic malaise, Obama is using every means (most of them quite unconstitutional) to legalize illegal aliens.[112]

Catholic organizations wield shocking power in this effort with little media scrutiny.

> *Catholic Charities USA has taken on a major role in helping the federal government find temporary housing for the droves of Central Americans illegally crossing the border into the United States.*
>
> *And it's also helping finance the operation. ...*
>
> *NBC4 News in Los Angeles reported Thursday that St. Joseph's Catholic Church in Fontana, California, was receiving daily busloads of illegal immigrants and housing them in a former convent that is not even zoned for overnight stays. The report opens with concerns about whether the church's helping hand for the illegals "is even legal."*
>
> *John Andrews, communications director for the Catholic Diocese of San Bernardino, told WND that the diocese is working directly with the Department of Homeland Security to temporarily house the illegal immigrants. A DHS busload of 46 Central American women and children arrived Thursday. They are being housed in a former convent until they can be transported to various communities around the U.S., mostly by Greyhound bus.*
>
> *Andrews said the church was told by the government to expect a new busload of illegal immigrants every 72 hours. He said the initiative grew out of a meeting last week with a representative of U.S. Immigration and Customs Enforcement.* ~ Leo Hohmann, WorldNetDaily[113]

Large, Left-leaning Protestant organizations have joined in as well. They are so determined to inundate America with unassimilated illegal immigrants that they have found a powerful wedge to augment their efforts: refugee status.

> *Thousands of Central American children crossing the border illegally could soon turn into asylum seekers armed with immigration lawyers provided by church groups and paid for by federal tax dollars. ...*
>
> *Alexandria, Va.-based Catholic Charities USA reported receiving $1.7 million in government grants in 2012, according to its IRS Form 990.*
>
> *But one of the largest recipients of government funds to resettle*

immigrant children is the U.S. Conference of Catholic Bishops. The USCCB helps resettle not only unaccompanied alien children, or UACs, who enter the country illegally but also refugees fleeing persecution overseas who enter through legal channels.

The USCCB is one of nine agencies that receive hundreds of millions in tax dollars to resettle refugees and asylum seekers in the U.S. under contract with the federal government. Six of the nine contractors are religious groups, WND has learned, including the Lutheran Immigration and Refugee Service, Episcopal Migration Ministries, the Hebrew Immigrant Aid Society, the Church World Service and World Relief Corp., which includes a plethora of evangelical groups.

The Catholic Bishops alone received $65.9 million in federal grants to care for unaccompanied alien children and refugees, according to its 2012 annual report. ~ Hohmann[114]

The Episcopal Church is the best example of an institutionalized religion that is "Christian" in name only and does all it can to blaspheme everything held sacred by Christendom.

Episcopal "bishops" are women and open homosexuals. Episcopal "bishop" Gene Robinson has publically married another man and just as publically divorced him.[115]

The "Presiding Bishop of The Episcopal Church", a woman with two last names (Katharine Jefferts-Schori), has stated that the sinner's prayer of Salvation to Jesus Christ is a "great Western heresy".[116]

Bishop Jefferts-Schori has also stated that Paul's exorcism of the demon-possessed soothsaying girl in the Book of Acts was "mean spirited and bigoted", and that diversity is "the only road to the Kingdom of God".[117]

These are the custodians of the Washington National Cathedral in Washington DC.

... it is the sixth-largest cathedral in the world, the second-largest in the United States,[3] and the highest as well as the

Presiding Bishop of The Episcopal Church; Katharine Jefferts-Schori

Wikimedia Commons: Ozma1981

fourth-tallest structure in Washington, D.C. The cathedral is the seat of both the Presiding Bishop of the Episcopal Church, Katharine Jefferts Schori, and the Bishop of the Diocese of Washington, Mariann Edgar Budde. ~ Wikipedia[118]

In November of 2014, this icon of Christianity in the heart of the nation's capital invited a delegation of muslim worshippers who laid out prayer rugs that literally set their backs against the altar. A woman protested by loudly proclaiming that only Jesus Christ is Savior. She was man-handled off the premises.[119]

Clearly, however, inundating America with illegal immigrants has been a Catholic agenda with hard-Left Catholic Democrat politicians like the late Edward M. "Teddy" Kennedy and former Senator now Vice President Joe Biden pushing legislation to make it happen. They have successfully turned generous Welfare states like Minnesota into Little Somalia—and Minnesotans pick up the tab as their neighborhoods devolve around them into a muslim 3rd world.

> *Over the course of two decades, the federal government's Refugee Resettlement Program has forcibly infused the Minneapolis-St. Paul area of Minnesota with a large dose of Somali culture, and the transition has not always been smooth. ...*
>
> *Two Somali men from Minneapolis-St. Paul have died recently fighting for ISIS, and several Somali women have reportedly left their homes in the area to join ISIS. The FBI says up to 25 Somalis have left to fight with Islamic militants in the Middle East since 2007. ...*
>
> *The resettlement program gets its authority from the Refugee Act of 1980, sponsored by the late Sen. Ted Kennedy and former Sen. Joe Biden, and is overseen by the U.S. Department of State. The act allows the refugees to become U.S. citizens within five years. Once here, the refugees are allowed to bring in extended family members through the State Department's Family Reunification program. ...*
>
> *Debra Anderson, a working mother employed in the health-care industry in Minneapolis, said she became concerned two years ago after she bought her house in the northeast quadrant of the city and found out a second mosque was proposed nearby.*
>
> *"I basically live and work in the heart of the beast, and shortly after I moved in there was a proposal for another mosque in my neighborhood," said Anderson, who is a member of American*

Congress for Truth. "There are parts of southern Minneapolis that look like Somalia. We have one district in south Minneapolis that was estimated to be 40 percent east African, and they have a pretty strong political hold here." ~ Hohmann[120]

There are surprising advantages to being labeled a "refugee" in America and organizations like the "Immigration Law Center" in Montgomery, Alabama are more than eager to help with leaflets and flyers.[121]

The benefits include:

- ✓ Food Stamps
- ✓ Supplemental Security Income
- ✓ Temporary Assistance for Needy Families (TANF)
- ✓ State Children's Health Insurance Program (SCHIP)

As America bears the load and the landscape of her culture is forever changed for the worse, her enemies are making money from taxpayers in the process...a great deal of it.

In the midst of a brutal, ongoing recession, the federal government nevertheless welcomed 74,654 refugees in 2009. The White House announced in October of 2010 that refugee admissions for fiscal year (FY) 2011 would be 80,000, the same as for the current year. There are now five to six unemployed people competing for each available job, but elite humanitarians don't care how difficult it is for today's refugees to get a foothold through employment. Local papers continue to publish sad stories of refugees who are running out of benefits as they hopelessly try to find employment in a tough jobs depression. Some are so desperate that they consider returning to their home country (which apparently cannot be so bad as originally characterized). ...

The ugly truth is there is a lot of money to be had through the Refugee Industrial Complex. Catholic Charities has a big collection plate permanently stationed in Washington for its supposed good works, which might raise eyebrows about the separation of church and state. The Conference of Catholic Bishops 2009 Migration and Refugee Services report shows $58,025,605 in government grants and contracts going to that organization. Other religious groups stand foursquare at the taxpayer trough also, like the Lutheran Immigration and Refugee Services, which got $29,907,000 in 2009. ~ Brenda Walker, Social Contract Press[122]

An antagonistic government calls these enclaves "seed programs"[123] and when local citizens become active in resisting, they are labeled as "pockets of resistance".[124]

Do these sound like warfare terms to you? They are meant to be.

It may seem unfair to claim Rome as the root of this conspiracy, but it is rightly deserved and little discussed.

> *The Catholic Church—through the U.S. Conference of Catholic Bishops' Committee on Migration—both paved the road for Barack Hussein Obama's ultimate takeover of Free West society and continues to actively enable the Fundamental Transformation of America by sinking the US in a tsunami of illegal aliens.*
>
> *In coming to Obama's aid in erasing forever America's borders, the bishops sold the USA out, including its Catholics, for the proverbial 30 pieces of silver.*
>
> *In biblical terms, Obama and the Catholic bishops—who both birthed his progress to the seat of power and back him on his Fundamental Transformation mission—are in league with the devil. The certain-to-come protestations of the bishops should fall on the same deaf ears they use to shun all pleas of mercy from Americans overwhelmed by invaders in their home towns and cities.* ~ Judi McLeod, Canada Free Press [125]

Secret Subversives

In 1928, the two men on the ballot for president were the Democrat Governor of New York, Alfred E. Smith and the Republican Secretary of Commerce Herbert Hoover. The issue of Smith's Catholic religion came up in an exchange between himself and lawyer Charles Marshall via editorials printed in *Atlantic Monthly* magazine.

Marshall warned that when torn between the best interests of America and the best interests of the Church, devout Catholics were always at risk of choosing Rome over the Land of the Free.

> *The deduction is inevitable that, as all power over human affairs not given to the State by God, is given by God to the Roman*

Catholic Church, no other churches or religious or ethical societies have in theory any direct power from God and are without direct divine sanction, and therefore without natural right to function on the same basis as the Roman Catholic Church in the religious and moral affairs of the State. The result is that that Church, if true to her basic political doctrine, is hopelessly committed to that intolerance that has disfigured so much of her history. This is frankly admitted by Roman Catholic authorities. ...

Furthermore, the doctrine of the Two Powers, in effect and theory, inevitably makes the Roman Catholic Church at times sovereign and paramount over the State. ...

We quote Pope Leo in his encyclical letter on The Christian Constitution of States: *"Over the mighty multitude of mankind, God has set rulers with power to govern, and He has willed that, one of them (the Pope) should be the head of all." We quote Pope Leo in his encyclical letter on* The Reunion of Christendom: *"We who hold upon this earth the place of God Almighty."* ~ Charles C. Marshall, Atlantic Monthly[126]

Smith lost the election but was soon immortalized in an annual dinner hosted by the Church that requires the two American finalists for the presidency to appear before one of the most powerful Papal emissaries in the world—the Cardinal of the Archdiocese of New York—and make him laugh.

Today's dinners are presided over by the aristocratic descendent of the NY Governor, Alfred E. Smith IV.

The dinners continue even in off election years where luminaries from all walks show homage to Rome, from the director of the FBI, to the Chairman of the Joint Chiefs of Staff, to the Secretary of State.

During the 2008 dinner, soon-to-be President Barack Obama may have taken a swipe at his benefactors in what appeared on the surface to be a self-deprecating joke.

"It is often said that I share the politics of Alfred E Smith and the ears of Alfred E. Neuman." ~ Michael Cooper and Jeff Zeleny, NY Times[127]

Just who "Alfred E. Neuman" was patterned after for Mad Magazine by artist Harvey Kurtzman remains a mystery but, Governor Alfred E. Smith was certainly known to Kurtzman as they were contemporaries.

If a President isn't careful, that's the kind of joke that will put a knife-wielding man in the East Room[128] or an armed felon in your elevator.[129]

Endnotes

[1] *IRS Lost Lois Lerner's Emails In Tea Party Probe*, CBS/AP, 13 June 2014, CBS News
http://www.cbsnews.com/news/irs-lost-lois-lerners-emails-in-tea-party-probe/

[2] *IRS Says It Has Lost Emails From 5 More Employees*, Stephen Ohlemacher, AP, 5 September 2014, Yahoo!News
http://news.yahoo.com/competing-views-irs-treatment-tea-party-173818981—politics.html

[3] *IRS Canceled E-Mail Back-Up Service – Weeks After Lerner Hard Drive Crash*, Ed Morrissey, 23 June 2014, HotAir
http://hotair.com/archives/2014/06/23/irs-canceled-e-mail-back-up-service-weeks-after-lerner-hard-drive-crash/

[4] *IRS Finds More Key Hard-Drive Crashes, Claims No Evidence of Tampering*, Josh Hicks, 8 September 2014, Washington Post
http://www.washingtonpost.com/blogs/federal-eye/wp/2014/09/08/irs-finds-more-key-hard-drive-crashes-claims-no-evidence-tampering/

[5] *ADAMS: Inside the Black Panther Case*, J. Christian Adams, 25 June 2010, The Washington Times
http://www.washingtontimes.com/news/2010/jun/25/inside-the-black-panther-case-anger-ignorance-and-/#!

[6] *U.S. Government Used Taxpayer Funds to Buy, Sell Weapons During "Fast and Furious," Documents Show*, unattributed, 26 September 2011, FoxNews
http://www.foxnews.com/politics/2011/09/26/us-government-bought-and-sold-weapons-during-fast-and-furious-documents-show/

[7] *ATF's Mysterious Grenade Smuggler Case: New Photos, Documents Turned Over to Congress*, Sharyl Attkisson, 25 April 2012, CBS News
http://www.cbsnews.com/news/atfs-mysterious-grenade-smuggler-case-new-photos-documents-turned-over-to-congress/

[8] *Operation Fast & Furious...Rocket Launchers?* Moe Lane, 17 September 2011, Red State.com
http://www.redstate.com/diary/Moe_Lane/2011/09/17/operation-fast-furious-rocket-launchers/

[9] *Full Coverage: ATF's Fast and Furious Scandal*, series of articles on the "scandal" posted by the LA Times on 20 June 2012
http://www.latimes.com/nation/atf-fast-furious-sg-storygallery.html

[10] *Fast and Furious Guns at Mexican Beauty Queen's Murder Scene*, Jack Phillips, 19 December 2012, Epoch Times
http://www.theepochtimes.com/n3/4153-fast-and-furious-guns-at-mexican-beauty-queen-s-murder-scene/

[11] *Another Murder Linked to US Gunwalker Case*, Sharyl Attkisson, 24 June 2011, CBS News
http://www.cbsnews.com/news/another-murder-linked-to-us-gunwalker-case/
 This was the kind of reporting that got Sharyl Attkisson *removed* from the Catholic Broadcasting Service.

[12] *Knights Templar Attack Federal Police Helicopter in Michoacan*, Ovemex, 25 May 2011, Borderland Beat

http://www.borderlandbeat.com/2011/05/knights-templar-attack-federal-police.html

[13] *The Hysteria In Mexico Caused By Fast & Furious*, Mary Chastain, 5 August 2012, Breitbart.com
http://www.breitbart.com/Big-Government/2012/08/04/The-Hysteria-In-Mexico-Caused-By-Fast-Furious

[14] *Police Chief Killed with Rifle Lost in ATF Gun-Tracking Program*, Richard Serrano, 5 July 2013, LA Times
http://articles.latimes.com/2013/jul/05/nation/la-na-nn-atf-fast-furious-20130705

[15] *FBI Criminal Informant Complicit in Brian Terry's Death*, Bob Owens, 1 December 2011, PJ Media
http://pjmedia.com/blog/fbi-criminal-informant-complicit-in-brian-terrys-death-pjm-exclusive/

[16] *ICE Agent's Family Files Wrongful Death Claim Against Justice Dept.*, Sharyl Attkisson, 20 June 2012, CBS News
http://www.cbsnews.com/news/ice-agents-family-files-wrongful-death-claim-against-justice-dept/

[17] *CONFIRMED: The DEA Struck A Deal With Mexico's Most Notorious Drug Cartel*, Michael Kelley, 13 January 2014, Business Insider
http://www.businessinsider.com/the-us-government-and-the-sinaloa-cartel-2014-1

[18] *Documents: ATF Used "Fast and Furious" To Make The Case For Gun Regulations*, Sharyl Attkisson, 7 December 2011, CBS News
http://www.cbsnews.com/news/documents-atf-used-fast-and-furious-to-make-the-case-for-gun-regulations/

[19] *Friday October 24, 2014 – Sharyl Attkisson & Jody Hice*, interview with Rick Wiles of TruNews
https://www.trunews.com/friday-october-24-2014-sharyl-attkisson-jody-hice/

[20] *Ex-CBS Reporter's Book Reveals How Liberal Media Protects Obama*, Kyle Smith, 25 October 2014, the New York Post
http://nypost.com/2014/10/25/former-cbs-reporter-explains-how-the-liberal-media-protects-obama/

[21] *Sharyl Attkisson's Computer Intrusions: "Worse Than Anything Nixon Ever Did"*, Erik Wemple, 27 October 2014, the Washington Post
http://www.washingtonpost.com/blogs/erik-wemple/wp/2014/10/27/sharyl-attkissons-computer-intrusions-worse-than-anything-nixon-ever-did/

[22] *Sharyl Attkisson Resigns From CBS News*, Dylan Byers, 10 March 2014, POLITICO
http://www.politico.com/blogs/media/2014/03/sharyl-attkisson-to-leave-cbs-news-184836.html

[23] *Calderón Calls for Restoring Assault Weapons Ban*, Brian Knowlton, 20 May 2010, the NY Times
http://thecaucus.blogs.nytimes.com/2010/05/20/calderon-calls-for-restoring-assault-weapons-ban/?_php=true&_type=blogs&_php=true&_type=blogs&_php=true&_type=blogs&partner=rss&emc=rss&_r=2

[24] *Darrell Issa: Eric Holder "Owns" Fast & Furious*, Tim Mak, 10 October 2010, Politico
http://www.politico.com/news/stories/1011/65556.html

[25] *Darrell Issa Not Joining Calls for Eric Holder to Quit Over "Fast and Furious"*, Jerry Markon, 2 December 2011, Washington Post

http://www.washingtonpost.com/politics/darrell-issa-not-joining-calls-for-eric-holder-to-quit-over-fast-and-furious/2011/12/02/gIQAHsSSMO_story.html
[26] *Supervisors in ATF Gun Operation Are Promoted*, Richard Serrano, 16 August 2011, LA Times
http://www.nationaljournal.com/white-house/remember-the-irs-tea-party-scandal-get-ready-for-round-two-20140205
[27] *IRS Official Who Oversaw Unit Targeting Tea Party Now Heads ObamaCare Office*, unattributed, 17 May 2013, FoxNews
http://www.foxnews.com/politics/2013/05/17/second-irs-official-to-leave-amid-tea-party-scandal/
[28] *Wars of Reason, Wars of Principle - Setting the Record Straight*, Barack Obama, September 2004, The Network Journal (for "black professionals")
http://www.tnj.com/archives/2004/september2004/final_word.php
[29] *Obama's Failed Promise to Close Gitmo: A Timeline*, David Wagner, 28 January 2013, The Wire
http://www.thewire.com/global/2013/01/obama-closing-guantanamo-timeline/61509/
[30] *Chronology of Libya's Disarmament and Relations with the United States*, The Arms Control Association
https://www.armscontrol.org/factsheets/LibyaChronology
[31] *How Libya Got Off the List*, Eben Kaplan, 16 October 2007, the Council on Foreign Relations
http://www.cfr.org/libya/libya-got-off-list/p10855
[32] *Lockerbie Bomber Freed From Jail*, unattributed, 20 August 2009, BBC News
http://news.bbc.co.uk/2/hi/uk_news/scotland/south_of_scotland/8197370.stm
[33] *$4 Million Stash Linked to Lockerbie Bomber*, Joseph Farah, 24 December 2009, WorldNetDaily
http://www.wnd.com/2009/12/119880/
[34] *Abu Hamza "Secretly Worked for MI5" to "Keep Streets of London Safe"*, Philip Sherwell, 7 May 2014, the Telegraph
http://www.telegraph.co.uk/news/worldnews/northamerica/usa/10814816/Abu-Hamza-secretly-worked-for-MI5-to-keep-streets-of-London-safe.html
[35] *Libyan Islamic Fighting Group joins al Qaeda*, Bill Roggio, 3 November 2007, the Long War Journal
http://www.longwarjournal.org/archives/2007/11/libyan_islamic_fight.php
[36] *Former Al-Qaeda Leader Says that the CIA Runs Al-Nusra, Al-Qaeda*, interview posted via "GlobalResearchTV" on YouTube
https://www.youtube.com/watch?v=3yfTwsJtUvw

If the interview has been taken down, conduct an internet query with similar words of the title to include the names "Nabil Na'eem Abul Fattah" and "Ayman Al-Zawahiri".
[37] *"The West Is To Be Forgotten. We Will Not Give Them Our Oil"*, unattributed, 17 May 2011, Russia Today
http://rt.com/news/libya-oil-gaddafi-arab/
[38] *Saka: Africans Will Remember Gaddafi For One Important Achievement*, Saka, 15 December 2012, Mathaba.net
http://www.mathaba.net/news/?x=632109

[39] *Libya's Qaddafi Taps "Fossil Water" to Irrigate Desert Farms*, Sarah A. Topol, 23 August 2010, the Christian Science Monitor
http://www.csmonitor.com/World/Africa/2010/0823/Libya-s-Qaddafi-taps-fossil-water-to-irrigate-desert-farms

[40] *Who Shot Gaddafi? New video shows blood pouring from dictator immediately before death but mystery surrounds coup de grace.* David Williams, 21 October 2011, the Daily Mail
http://www.dailymail.co.uk/news/article-2051361/GADDAFI-DEAD-VIDEO-Dictator-begs-life-summary-execution.html

[41] *NATO Bombs the Great Man-Made River*, 27 July 2011, Human Rights Investigations.org
http://humanrightsinvestigations.org/2011/07/27/great-man-made-river-nato-bombs/

[42] *Judge Dismisses Congressmen's Lawsuit Over Obama Administration's Libya Intervention*, Steven Nelson, 20 October 2011, the Daily Caller
http://dailycaller.com/2011/10/20/judge-tosses-congressional-lawsuit-against-libya-intervention-kucinich-and-jones-hint-at-an-appeal/

[43] *Ron Paul Believes Libya Intervention an "Impeachable" Offense*, Steven Nelson, 22 March 2011, the Daily Caller
http://dailycaller.com/2011/03/22/ron-paul-believes-libya-intervention-an-impeachable-offense/

[44] Expunged from the internet. Find one example from my blog, here:
http://johnnycirucci.com/wp/wp-content/uploads/2014/08/jesuit-bitches-in-libya-rubio-mccain-kirk-graham.png

[45] *Gunmen Go Door-to-Door to Find and Execute Christians in Libya*, Morgan Lee, 25 February 2014, the Christian Post
http://www.christianpost.com/news/gunmen-go-door-to-door-to-find-and-execute-christians-in-libya-115136/#!

[46] *Hillary Clinton: Reptilian Sociopath*, Johnny Cirucci, YouTube
https://www.youtube.com/watch?&v=DFJR1Lv49L8

[47] *We Came, We Saw, He Died: What Hillary Clinton Told News Reporter Moments After Hearing of Gaddafi's Death*, unattributed, 21 October 2011, the Daily Mail
http://www.dailymail.co.uk/news/article-2051826/We-came-saw-died-What-Hillary-Clinton-told-news-reporter-moments-hearing-Gaddafis-death.html

[48] *Clinton Scandal Is Tough To End Regardless Of Evidence, Or Lack Of It, Some Want To "Believe The Worst"*, Jonathan Weisman, 22 November 1998, the Baltimore Sun (p. 2)
http://articles.baltimoresun.com/1998-11-22/news/1998326038_1_scandal-committee-republican-hillary-clinton/2

[49] *Weiner's In-Laws and the SECRET Muslim Brotherhood Connections REVEALED*, Walid Shoebat and Ben Barrack, no date, Shoebat.com
http://www.shoebat.com/documents/secretConnections.htm

[50] *The Promise of a Pro-American Libya*, John McCain, Lindsey Graham, Mark Kirk And Marco Rubio, 7 October 2011, the Wall Street Journal
http://online.wsj.com/news/articles/SB10001424052970203388804576613293623346516

[51] *Libya Imposes Sharia Laws*, Ekaterina Ryzhkova, 12 December 2013, New Eastern Outlook
http://journal-neo.org/2013/12/12/rus-liviya-vvodit-shariat/

[52] *Military Timeline From Night of Benghazi Attack Begs More Questions*, Jennifer Griffin and Adam Housley, 11 November 2012, FoxNews
http://www.foxnews.com/politics/2012/11/11/military-timeline-from-night-benghazi-attack-begs-more-questions/
[53] *Ambassador Rice: Benghazi Attack Began Spontaneously*, NBC News staff and wire services, 16 September 2012, NBC News
http://usnews.nbcnews.com/_news/2012/09/16/13896494-ambassador-rice-benghazi-attack-began-spontaneously?lite
[54] *EXPLOSIVE: Filmmaker "Behind The Benghazi Attack" Found To Be A CONFIRMED MUSLIM Agent Who Worked With U.S. Government*, Walid Shoebat and Ben Barrack, 10 June 2014, Shoebat.com
http://shoebat.com/2014/06/10/filmmaker-behind-benghazi-attack-found-confirmed-muslim-agent-worked-us-government/
[55] *SHOCKING: Company that Created Obamacare Website LINKED to Benghazi Video*, Walid Shoebat, Ben Barrack and Keith Davies, 17 June 2014, Shoebat.com
http://shoebat.com/2014/06/17/company-botched-obamacare-website-tied-benghazi-video/
[56] *Broadwell: Petraeus Knew of Benghazi Plea for Help*, Gil Ronen, 11 November 2012, Arutz Sheva
http://www.israelnationalnews.com/News/News.aspx/161964#.UKB2bWchx8F
[57] *The Red Line and the Rat Line*, Seymour Hersh, 17 April 2014, the London Review of Books
http://www.lrb.co.uk/v36/n08/seymour-m-hersh/the-red-line-and-the-rat-line
[58] Whistleblower Attorney: Benghazi Attack Was About 400 SAM Missiles Stolen by Some "Very Ugly People", 13 August 2013, originally from the Washington Free Beacon, taken down but reposted by Free Republic
http://www.freerepublic.com/focus/news/3054244/posts
[59] *BREAKING NEWS: Two Sources in Chicago Diplomatic Circles Identify Ambassador Chris Stevens as Gay*, Kevin DuJan, 14 September 2012, HillBuzz
http://hillbuzz.org/breaking-news-two-sources-in-chicago-diplomatic-circles-identify-ambassador-chris-stevens-as-gay-meaning-state-department-sent-gay-man-to-be-ambassador-to-libya-64291
[60] *Claim: Obama Hid "Gay Life" to Become President*, Jerome Corsi, 11 September 2012, WorldNetDaily
http://www.wnd.com/2012/09/claim-obama-hid-gay-life-to-become-president/#!
[61] *Exclusive: Did Turkey Play a Role in Benghazi Attack?* Clair Lopez, 31 October 2012, The Clarion Project
http://www.clarionproject.org/analysis/riorg-exclusive-did-turkey-play-role-benghazi-attack
[62] *The Many Questions Surrounding the Bengazi* [sic] *Scandle* [sic], Rick Wiles, 1 November 2012, TruNews (archived at Free Republic—how is this taken down so quickly?!)
http://www.freerepublic.com/focus/f-news/2953423/posts
[63] *Hillary Clinton's State Department Cut Security in Libya Before Deadly Terror Attacks, Sen. Ron Johnson Says*, PoltiFact review of Representative Ron Johnson's allegations: TRUE

http://www.politifact.com/wisconsin/statements/2014/may/19/ron-johnson/hillary-clintons-state-department-reduced-security/

[64] *House: U.S. Embassy in Libya Asked for Extra Security, Request Denied*, Joel Gehrke, 12 October 2012, the Washington Examiner
http://washingtonexaminer.com/house-u.s.-embassy-in-libya-asked-for-extra-security-request-denied/article/2509580#!

[65] *Congressman: Benghazi Attackers Knew Location Of Ambassador's Safe Room*, Catherine Herridge, 15 November 2013, FoxNews
http://www.foxnews.com/politics/2013/11/15/benghazi-attackers-reportedly-knew-location-ambassador-safe-room/

[66] *Al Qaeda, ex-Gitmo Detainee Involved In Consulate Attack, Intelligence Sources Say*, unattributed, 20 September 2012, FoxNews
http://www.foxnews.com/politics/2012/09/19/top-administration-official-says-strike-in-libya-was-terror-attack/

[67] *Behind Benghazi Attack Trained in the U.S.*, Western Journalism, YouTube on the Johnny Cirucci channel
https://www.youtube.com/watch?v=l_N0aTx0SWA&

[68] *Libyan President Tells NBC: "Foreigners" Involved in U.S. Consulate Attack*, unattributed, 15 September 2012, NBC News
http://worldnews.nbcnews.com/_news/2012/09/15/13885782-libyan-president-tells-nbc-foreigners-involved-in-us-consulate-attack?lite

[69] *Fox News Reporting: 13 Hours in Benghazi*, Bret Baier, 5 September 2014, FoxNews
http://www.foxnews.com/on-air/fox-news-reporting/transcript/fox-news-reporting-13-hours-benghazi

[70] This is common sense so I'm not worried about this source. "Doug" from San Antonio called the Rush Limbaugh radio show in October of 2012. He claimed to be a retired Lieutenant Colonel and 15 year Special Operations planner veteran. He sounds legit in the call and simply confirms what we know to *clearly* be the case in any nation bigger than Freedonia: communications regarding sensitive personnel and locations are near-instantaneous.

The call can be heard and seen on the "Right Scoop" YouTube channel with the title of *Rush Military Caller Says That Obama Ordered No Response to Benghazi Attack*
https://www.youtube.com/watch?v=IljKmmZyCiw

What this also proves is how much political theater the Republican Party is responsible for. No serious, informed politician buys the Obama line that help couldn't get there because there just wasn't enough time or warning.

[71] *Could U.S. Military Have Helped During Libya Attack?* Sharyl Attkisson, 20 October 2012, CBS News
http://www.cbsnews.com/news/could-us-military-have-helped-during-libya-attack/

[72] *EXCLUSIVE: CIA Operators Were Denied Request For Help During Benghazi Attack, Sources Say*, Jennifer Griffin, 26 October 2012, FoxNews
http://www.foxnews.com/politics/2012/10/26/cia-operators-were-denied-request-for-help-during-benghazi-attack-sources-say/

[73] *Ambassador Stephens Death and the Coming Military Coup*, Dave Hodges, 3 November 2012, The Common Sense Show
http://www.thecommonsenseshow.com/2012/11/03/ambassador-stephens-death-and-the-coming-military-coup/

[74] *General Blames "Night Stalker" for Military Purge*, Michael Maloof, 5 November 2013, WorldNetDaily
http://www.wnd.com/2013/11/general-blames-night-stalker-for-military-purge/
[75] *"Earpiece Envy": White House Colleagues Skeptical About Why Valerie Jarrett Has Detail*, Alex Pappas, 25 August 2013, the Daily Caller
http://dailycaller.com/2013/08/25/earpiece-envy-white-house-colleagues-skeptical-why-valerie-jarrett-has-detail/
[76] *Former Navy SEALs Died After Coming To The Aid Of Others*, Fran Townsend, 23 September 2012, CNN
http://www.cnn.com/2012/09/21/world/africa/libya-consulate-attack/
[77] *Eleanor Clift: Ambassador Stevens Wasn't Murdered; He Died From "Smoke Inhalation"*, Cheryl Chumley, 12 May 2014, Washington Times
http://www.washingtontimes.com/news/2014/may/12/eleanor-clift-ambassador-stevens-wasnt-murdered-di/#!
[78] *"He Is Still Alive!": Video shows the moment ambassador's body is pulled from embassy ... as witness says he was breathing*. Daily Mail and AP, 17 September 2012, the Daily Mail
http://www.dailymail.co.uk/news/article-2204626/Chris-Stevens-death-Video-shows-ambassadors-body-pulled-embassy.html
[79] *They All Lied About How Ambassador Christopher Stevens Died in Benghazi*, Diane Sori, 1 July 2013, the Tea Party Tribune
http://www.teapartytribune.com/2013/07/01/they-all-lied-about-how-ambassador-christopher-stevens-died-in-benghazi/
[80] *May It Please Trey Gowdy*, David Weigel, 8 May 2014, Slate.com
http://www.slate.com/articles/news_and_politics/politics/2014/05/trey_gowdy_leads_the_benghazi_select_committee_the_south_carolina_republican.html
[81] *Benghazi Investigation Results: Republican Controlled House Committee Finds Obama Admin Innocent of Wrongdoing*, Dean Garrison, 24 November 2014, Freedom Outpost
http://freedomoutpost.com/2014/11/benghazi-investigation-results-republican-controlled-house-committee-finds-obama-admin-innocent-wrongdoing/
[82] *House Panel: No Administration Wrongdoing in Benghazi Attack*, Carolyn Lochhead, 1 August 2014
http://www.sfgate.com/politics/article/House-panel-No-administration-wrongdoing-in-5663509.php?cmpid=twitter
[83] *Oh Look, Rep. Mike Rogers Wife Stands To Benefit Greatly From CISPA Passing*, Mike Masnick, 18 April 2013, Techdirt
https://www.techdirt.com/articles/20130417/16253022748/oh-look-rep-mike-rogers-wife-stands-to-benefit-greatly-cispa-passing.shtml
[84] *Looks Like Ross Perot Was Right About The "Giant Sucking Sound"*, unattributed, 11 February 2011, Business Insider
http://www.businessinsider.com/looks-like-ross-perot-was-right-about-the-giant-sucking-sound-2011-2
[85] *Clinton Dispenses NAFTA Pact to Skeptical AFL-CIO*, Martin Kasindorf, 5 October 1993, Newsday, reposted at MIT
http://tech.mit.edu/V113/N47/nafta.47w.html
[86] *Despite Opposition, Obama Verges on Trade Deal Disaster*, John Nichols, 13 October 2011, the Nation

http://www.thenation.com/blog/163958/obama-wrong-wrong-wrong-about-free-trade

[87] *Plea For Help From Chinese Labor Camp Worker Paid $1.61 per MONTH Found Stuffed In Oregon Woman's Halloween Decorations From Kmart*, Helen Pow, 26 December 2012, the Daily Mail
http://www.dailymail.co.uk/news/article-2253572/Julie-Keith-letter-Plea-help-Chinese-labor-camp-worker-stuffed-Oregon-womans-Halloween-decorations.html

[88] *Heartbreaking Pictures Of The Chinese Toddlers Tied Up All Day Because Their Parents Can't Afford Child Care*, Foreign Service, 22 April 2010, the Daily Mail
http://www.dailymail.co.uk/news/article-1267794/Tethered-safe-Chinese-workers-forced-tie-youngsters-work-afford-child-care.html

[89] *"Forced To Stand For 24 Hours, Suicide Nets, Toxin Exposure And Explosions": Inside The Chinese Factories Making iPads for Apple*, Mark Duell, 27 January 2012, the Daily Mail
http://www.dailymail.co.uk/news/article-2092277/Apple-Poor-working-conditions-inside-Chinese-factories-making-iPads.html

[90] *$250,000 Roadster: "Proof" of Steve Jobs' Genius*, Toby Hagon, 9 January 2012, Drive.com
http://www.drive.com.au/motor-news/250000-roadster-proof-of-steve-jobs-genius-20120109-1pr4x.html

[91] *The Story Behind Steve Jobs' Mercedez Benz And Its Missing License Plate*, 27 October 2011, the Edible Apple blog
http://www.edibleapple.com/2011/10/27/the-story-behind-steve-jobs-mercedez-benz-and-its-missing-license-plate/

[92] *Jobs the Jerk*, Farhad Manjoo, 25 October 2011, Slate.com
http://www.slate.com/articles/technology/technology/2011/10/steve_jobs_biography_the_new_book_doesn_t_explain_what_made_the_.html

[93] *"Stop Invasion!" Thousands Protest At Anti-Immigration Rally In Italy*, Russia Today, 19 October 2014, YouTube
https://www.youtube.com/watch?v=d8jpC9CuqJQ&

[94] *UK: 1,400 non-Muslim Children Exploited By Muslim Rape Gangs, Authorities Did Nothing "For Fear Of Being Thought As Racist"*, Robert Spencer, 26 August 2014, Jihad Watch
http://www.jihadwatch.org/2014/08/uk-1400-non-muslim-children-exploited-by-muslim-rape-gangs-authorities-did-nothing-for-fear-of-being-thought-as-racist

[95] *No Way, Jose`! DUI Illegals Treated As "Special"*, Chelsea Schilling, 22 May 2008, WorldNetDaily
http://www.wnd.com/2008/05/64918/

[96] *Feds Say Sacramento Shooting Suspect Was Deported Twice, Had Drug Conviction*, Sam Stanton, Andy Furillo, Cynthia Hubert, Richard Chang and Marissa Lang, 25 October 2014, the Sacramento Bee
http://www.sacbee.com/news/local/crime/article3368389.html

[97] *TARGETED! This Veteran Was Terrorized and Disarmed by His Own Police*, Johnny Cirucci, 15 June 2013, the Patriot Press
http://johnnycirucci.com/wp/johnnys-latest-columns/targeted/

[98] *Black-Clad Einsatzgruppen Confiscate Guns in California*, William Norman Grigg, 18 November 2013, Lew Rockwell.com

http://www.lewrockwell.com/lrc-blog/black-clad-einsatzgruppen-confiscate-guns-in-california/
[99] *BREAKING: America's Worst Gun Control Bill (CA AB 1014) Passes Committee*, Robert Farago, 1 July 2014, The Truth About Guns
http://www.thetruthaboutguns.com/2014/07/robert-farago/breaking-americas-worst-gun-control-bill-ca-ab-1014-passes-committee/
[100] *CA Governor Signs AB 1014: Gun Confiscation By Accusation*, 30 September 2014, The Philosophy Behind The Trigger blog
http://notonemoregunlaw.blogspot.com/2014/09/ca-governor-signs-ab-1014-gun.html
[101] *Obamacare Provision: "Forced" Home Inspections*, Joshua Cook, 13 August 2013, Ben Swann.com
http://benswann.com/obamacare-provision-forced-home-inspections/
[102] *San Bernardino County May Sue San Francisco Over "Dumping" Of Illegal Immigrant Convicts*, unattributed, 4 July 2008, the LA Times
http://latimesblogs.latimes.com/laplaza/2008/07/san-bernardino.html
[103] *Fading Into Irrelevance*, unattributed, 30 June 2012, the Economist
http://www.economist.com/node/21557757
[104] *NY Democrats Seek Citizen Rights For Illegal Immigrants*, Carl Campanile, 15 September 2014, the NY Post
http://nypost.com/2014/09/15/democratic-pols-seek-amnesty-rights-under-ny-state-law-for-illegal-immigrants/
[105] *Live Updates: Obama Announces Executive Amnesty for Illegals*, unattributed, 20 November 2014, Breitbart
http://www.breitbart.com/Big-Government/2014/11/20/Live-Updates-Obama-Exec-Amnesty-Speech
[106] *Horowitz: Forget Amnesty, Congress Voted to Give Welfare to Illegal Immigrants*, Daniel Horowitz, 12 June 2014, Breitbart.com
http://www.breitbart.com/Big-Government/2014/06/12/Congress-Votes-To-Give-Welfare-To-Illegal-Aliens
[107] *Archbishop Joins Immigrant Rights Rally*, unattributed, 24 April 2006, AP News Archive
http://www.apnewsarchive.com/2006/Archbishop-Joins-Immigrant-Rights-Rally/id-134c5129e04902ea93b841a137b3335d
[108] *Tancredo Slams Pope On Immigration*, 17 April, 2008, Anne C. Mulkern, the Denver Post
http://www.denverpost.com/ci_8960784?source=rss
[109] *Pope Francis Calls on U.S. to Welcome Illegal Immigrants*, Robert Wilde, 16 July 2014, Breitbart.com
http://www.breitbart.com/Big-Government/2014/07/15/Pope-Welcome-Them
[110] *EXCLUSIVE: TSA Allowing Illegals to Fly Without Verifiable ID, Says Border Patrol Union*, Brandon Darby, 11 July 2014, Breitbart.com
http://www.breitbart.com/Breitbart-Texas/2014/07/11/Exclusive-TSA-Allowing-Illegals-to-Fly-Without-Verifiable-ID-Says-Border-Patrol-Union
[111] *Lawmaker Denied Ft. Sill Entry After Reports of Displacing Soldiers to Accommodate Illegal Aliens*, unattributed, 2 July 2014, Judicial Watch
http://www.judicialwatch.org/blog/2014/07/lawmaker-denied-ft-still-entry-reports-displacing-soldiers-accommodate-illegal-aliens/

[112] *Obama to Push Immigration Bill as One Priority*, Julia Preston, 8 April 2009, NY Times http://www.nytimes.com/2009/04/09/us/politics/09immig.html?_r=0
[113] *Church Raising Money For Illegals*, Leo Hohmann, 11 July 2014, WorldNetDaily http://www.wnd.com/2014/07/church-raising-money-for-illegals/
[114] *Religious "Charities" Profit From Open Borders*, Leo Hohmann, 16 July 2014, WorldNetDaily
http://www.wnd.com/2014/07/religious-charities-profit-from-open-borders/
[115] *Gene Robinson, First Openly Gay Episcopal Bishop, Announces His Divorce*, Sarah Bailey, 3 May 2014, Religion News Service
http://www.religionnews.com/2014/05/03/gene-robinson-first-openly-gay-episcopal-bishop-divorce/
[116] *Episcopal Presiding Bishop: Individual Salvation Is "Heresy, Idolatry"*, David Virtue, 16 July 2009, Catholic Online
http://www.catholic.org/news/national/story.php?id=34091
[117] *Diversity, Not Jesus, Saves Says Presiding Bishop*, George Conger, 20 May 2013, Anglican Ink
http://anglicanink.com/article/diversity-not-jesus-saves-says-presiding-bishop
[118] *Washington National Cathedral*, Wikipedia
https://en.wikipedia.org/wiki/Washington_National_Cathedral
[119] *Christian Woman Praying to Christ Ejected from MUSLIM Prayers at National Cathedral*, Pamela Geller, 14 November 2014, Pam Geller.com
http://pamelageller.com/2014/11/christian-woman-praying-to-christ-ejected-from-muslim-prayers-at-national-cathedral.html/
[120] *Refugees in U.S. State Drawn To Welfare, Jihad*, Leo Hohmann, 5 September 2014, WorldNetDaily
http://www.wnd.com/2014/09/refugees-in-u-s-state-drawn-to-welfare-jihad/
[121] *Refugees Eligibile* [sic—lawyers!] *For Federal Public Benefits*, Edited by Boyd F. Campbell, Attorney at Law and Civil Law Notary, Immigration Law Center, L.L.C., Montgomery, Alabama, Telephone: (334) 832-9090, E-mail: usvisa@visaus.com
http://www.visaus.com/benefits.html
  Feel free to reach out to these vermin and let them know how you feel.
[122] *Refugee Resettlement Is a Racket ... and Somalis Prove It*, Brenda Walker, Social Contract Press, Volume 21, Number 1 (Fall 2010)
http://www.thesocialcontract.com/artman2/publish/tsc_21_1/tsc_21_1_walker_refugee.shtml
[123] *U.S. Government "Breeding Terrorists" – in Minnesota*, Leo Hohmann, 2 September 2014, WorldNetDaily
http://www.wnd.com/2014/09/u-s-government-breeding-terrorists-in-minnesota/
[124] *EEEK! "Pockets Of Resistance" To Refugee Resettlement Have Developed; ORR Hires "Welcoming America" To Head Off More*, Ann Corcoran, 15 July 2013, Refugee Resettlement Watch
http://refugeeresettlementwatch.wordpress.com/2013/06/15/eeek-pockets-of-resistance-to-refugee-resettlement-have-developed-orr-hires-welcoming-america-to-head-off-more/
[125] *The Road to Hell Obama Is Taking The World Down Created By U.S. Catholic Bishops*, Judi McLeod, 28 July 2014, Canada Free Press

http://canadafreepress.com/index.php/article/the-road-to-hell-obama-is-taking-the-world-down-created-by-u.s.-catholic-bi

[126] *An Open Letter to the Honorable Alfred E. Smith*, Charles C. Marshall, 1 April 1927, the Atlantic
http://www.theatlantic.com/magazine/archive/1927/04/an-open-letter-to-the-honorable-alfred-e-smith/306523/?single_page=true

[127] *McCain and Obama Palling Around? Must Be the Al Smith Dinner*, Michael Cooper and Jeff Zeleny, 16 October 2008, NY Times
http://thecaucus.blogs.nytimes.com/2008/10/16/mccain-and-obama-palling-around-must-be-the-al-smith-dinner/

[128] *Armed Intruder at White House Got to East Room*, Michael Shear and Michael Schmidt, 29 September 2014, NY Times
http://www.nytimes.com/2014/09/30/us/white-house-intruder-got-farther-than-first-reported-official-says.html

[129] *Obama Rode in Elevator With an Armed Felon, Congressman Says*, Reid Epstein, 30 September 2014, the Wall Street Journal
http://online.wsj.com/articles/obama-rode-in-elevator-with-armed-convicted-felon-1412114785

Chapter 2

The Manchurian Messiah of Mystery

The man in charge on September 11th, 2012 was Barack Hussein Obama.

Obama has a background obscured in mystery and intrigue. He is openly hostile to America and what made her great and he has steered her into almost unavoidable destruction.

While on the campaign trail in Columbia, Missouri on October 30th, 2008, Obama proclaimed "We are 5 days away from fundamentally transforming the United States!"[130]

But he wasn't going to start from scratch. He was building on the work of previous administrations across both of America's perennial political parties.

What he *did* do was take that agenda and put it into overdrive.

In December of 2013, a press release told Americans that the "Affordable Healthcare Act" (a.k.a. "Obamacare") was working flawlessly and Obama, himself, had signed himself up for the "Bronze Plan". This would later turn out to be untrue. In a short, unrepeated story, Fox News' Ed Henry stated that Obama hadn't enrolled himself per se, his staff did it for him. However, "Healthcare.gov" was unable to identify who he was.[131]

Barack Obama has at least 2 aliases and perhaps more.

The first alias is one most of us have heard, "Barry Soetoro". This name derives from Stanley Ann Dunham's remarriage to Indonesian citizen Lolo Soetoro. Dunham is Obama's legal mother and she is listed as having died in 1995 of uterine cancer.

We will examine the Dunham family's CIA roots in a later chapter but it is instructive to notice that a man who would name his daughter after himself has questionable motives. It has been corroborated and confirmed that the elder Dunham was the authority that gave Barack Obama to pornographer and pedophile, radical black Communist Frank Marshall Davis for a "black influence". Davis may well have been Obama's biological father as well as sexual abuser.[132]

Stanley Ann Dunham is said to have died just four months after the release of Obama's autobiography, *Dreams From My Father*[133]. The timing of these key events seemed to be a type of unveiling before his meteoric rise. It makes the cremation of Dunham's body somewhat of a concern.

> *She died in November 1995, as Mr. Obama was starting his first campaign for public office. After a memorial service at the University of Hawaii, one friend said, a small group of friends drove to the South Shore in Oahu. With the wind whipping the waves onto the rocks, Mr. Obama and Ms. Soetoro-Ng placed their mother's ashes in the Pacific, sending them off in the direction of Indonesia.* ~ Janny Scott, New York Times[134]

As Obama took over the White House in 2008, his grandmother died. She, too, would be cremated and her ashes scattered over her daughter's.[135]

With prophetic intuition, Obama would pen an autobiography while he was nothing more than a "community organizer" for the Left-wing activist group "Acorn" in Chicago.

Author and journalist Jack Cashill would stun his readers by making the well-researched claim that domestic terrorist William Ayers secretly wrote Obama's autobiography[136]. Ayers, himself, would say as much more than once[137]. Obama's half-brother Ndesandjo would draw fire for stating several of the family claims in the book were inaccurate.[138]

It was almost as if a past was being fabricated for Obama by a powerful entity behind him. It is the same entity that has the ability to inundate American education with radical Leftists, Communists and terrorists and that is exactly where William Ayers ended up; teaching America's impressionable youth.

> *William Ayers, Distinguished Professor of Education and Senior University Scholar at the University of Illinois at Chicago (retired), member of the executive committee of the Faculty Senate and founder of both the Small Schools Workshop and the Center for Youth and Society, taught courses in interpretive and qualitative research, oral history, creative non-fiction, urban school change, and teaching and the modern predicament.* ~ BillAyers.org[139]

Barry Soetoro

Investigative reporter Aaron Klein noted about Obama's use of the name "Barry Soetoro":

> *A 2007 Associated Press photograph taken by Tatan Syuflana, an Indonesian AP reporter and photographer, surfaced last week on*

> *the Daylife.com photographic website showing an image of Obama's registration card at Indonesia's Fransiskus Assisi school, a Catholic institution.*
>
> *In the picture, Obama is registered under the name Barry Soetoro by his stepfather, Lolo Soetoro. The school card lists Barry Soetoro as a Indonesian citizen born Aug. 4, 1961, in Honolulu, Hawaii. His religion is listed as Muslim.* ~ Klein[140]

In this admonition we begin to see exactly who the power is behind Barack Hussein Obama and his ongoing agenda to destroy America from within. It is an ancient hatred that began in mankind's first rebellion against God in Babylon. It was scattered at Babel, but reconstituted in Egypt and was spread by Greece into Rome where it metamorphosized into something far more powerful than just a single empire. It has become the heart and brains of a worldwide Machine that wields the banks of London, the slave labor of Beijing and the military might of Washington, DC. At its center is an amalgamation of all esoteric, gnostic, mystical-arts paganism with the trappings of Christianity and it wears the robes of "Christ's Vicar on Earth": the Roman Catholic Pope.

The enforcement arm of this Machine is Satan's Special Forces: the Society of Jesus, more commonly known as the Jesuits.

Those who think Barack Obama is *just* a Communist or *just* an Islamic Agent of the Muslim Brotherhood or of Saudi Arabia have no answer to the question: where are all the judges, generals and Republican politicians? How does Obama's agenda not have a single, powerful public enemy?

The Man of Many Names

Barack Obama's second known alias stems from his Social Security Number.

In an effort to find out why Obama's SSN traces back to a state he's never lived in, Jack Cashill contacted registered paralegal Susan Daniels and she told him something startling:

> *Barack Obama had been using a Social Security number issued in Connecticut between 1977 and 1979, a state in which he never lived or even visited at that time in his life. ...*
>
> *"All I can say," says Daniels of 042-68-4425, "is that it's phony and [Obama] has been using it, with it first appearing on his Selective Service document in 1980."* ~ Cashill[141]

The name associated with this Social Security Number isn't "Barack Obama" or "Barry Soetoro" but "Harrison J. Bounel".[142]

Obama's education is just as mysterious. One Philadelphia school teacher noted:

> *While preparing a research assignment on our country's first African American president, I was startled to find much of Barack Obama's records are missing or sealed from the public.*
>
> *President Obama attended Punahou School in Honolulu, one of Hawaii's top private institutions. However, Obama has refused to release his high school transcripts and SAT scores to the public, despite numerous requests by citizens and journalists.*
>
> *Obama's financial records at the Punahou School and Occidental College have not been released. ...*
>
> *In 1981, at age 20, Obama transferred from Occidental College to Columbia University. His transcripts at Columbia also remain sealed. ...*
>
> *In 1981, at age 20, Obama transferred from Occidental College to Columbia University. His transcripts at Columbia also remain sealed. ...*
>
> *His thesis on "Soviet Nuclear Disarmament" also remains unavailable.*
>
> *Obama's Harvard Law School Records are sealed. So are his LSAT scores.*
>
> *Obama lectured at the University of Chicago Law School from 1992 until 2004. Reporters have been unable to find any scholarly articles authored by him.*
>
> *It is customary for presidents running for office to disclose their medical records. Obama's medical records have yet to be released.*
>
> *Obama's fully visible passport has not been released (in 2010, the White House posted a partially blurred version on their website).* ~ Chalktalk[143]

Chelsea Schilling of WorldNetDaily corroborates the teacher's conundrum and says the missing/lost/sealed records go back even further to Obama's kindergarten class.[144]

A man who had "illegal" access[b] to Obama's passport was later found dead. Not surprisingly, local law enforcement was tight-lipped about the details.

> *A key witness in a federal probe into passport information stolen from the State Department was fatally shot in front of a District church, the Metropolitan Police Department said yesterday.*
>
> *Lt. [sic] Quarles Harris Jr., 24, who had been cooperating with a federal investigators, was found late Thursday night slumped dead inside a car, in front of the Judah House Praise Baptist Church in Northeast, said Cmdr. Michael Anzallo, head of the department's Criminal Investigations Division. ...*
>
> *The Washington Times reported April 5 that contractors for the State Department had improperly accessed passport information for presidential candidates Sens. Hillary Rodham Clinton, Barack Obama and John McCain[c], which resulted in a series of firings that reached into the agency's top ranks.* ~ The Washington Times[145]

Wikipedia describes Wayne Allyn Root as *an American politician, entrepreneur, television and radio personality, TV producer, political commentator and national best-selling author*[146]. Root noted about his supposed Columbia University classmate:

> *I called Obama "the Ghost of Columbia University." I pointed out (as I've said in the media for many years now) that Obama may have been registered at Columbia, may have graduated from Columbia, but he was rarely (if ever) seen for the two years in-between. It's a strange, mysterious and frightening story.*
>
> *Is he the real-life "Manchurian Candidate?" What explains Obama having just enough skeletal proof that he was there (one photo, one roommate, one professor, one friend)...but never seen in a class, never on anyone's radar screen, almost invisible. A total 2-year blackout. It's like a story straight out of a novel about the CIA or KGB. He graduated Columbia, but it's almost as if he never went there.* ~ Wayne Allen Root, The Blaze[147]

Allow me to re-emphasize that we are talking about the man guiding the most powerful nation in the world, today. The Republican Party, FBI, CIA, Federal judges, the United States military, mainstream media,

---

[b] "Illegal" access to a document that is evidence of illegal activities is, in actuality, legal.
[c] "Hillary Rodham Clinton" and John McCain are key figures in the Jesuit/CIA menagerie.

"Conservative" pundits...all remain loyally quiet about Barack Obama's mysterious past.

Where's the Birth Certificate?

Perhaps the best Obama identity "controversy" is his birth certificate.

Article II, Section 1, paragraph 5 of the United States Constitution mandates:

> *No Person except a natural born Citizen, or a Citizen of the United States, at the time of the Adoption of this Constitution, shall be eligible to the Office of President...*

The purpose for this clause is to mitigate the risk that a foreign-born insurgent with few ties to America would gain the highest office and much more easily destroy her from within.

It's safe to say, that is exactly what has happened.

The issue of Obama's place of origin is a forbidden topic and those who break the taboo disappear—like CNN news commentator Lou Dobbs who left CNN and was picked up by Fox News until his inappropriate questions relegated him to the graveyard of true Fox journalists: "Fox Business".[148]

On May 18th, 2012, Dobbs told the CEO of the Republican polling corporation Adam Geller that he has been mystified[149] by the failure of candidates like former Massachusetts governor Willard Mitt Romney to discuss Obama's Constitutional eligibility. At the time, it was all over the Drudge Report that Obama's literary agent had printed a bio stating that he was born in Kenya.[150]

In 2011, NY Democrat Congressman Edolphous Towns introduced the "Presidential Records Act of Amendments of 2011" which attempted to permanently seal off Obama's records.[151]

Democrat Congressmen are expected to cover for a Democrat administration. But it is support for Obama from the "mainstream" *Right* that has American Patriots desperate to understand why.

Arizona Republican Senator John McCain approached his race against Obama in 2008 as a man wanting to lose. While the Republican base was clamoring for real opposition to the clear-and-present danger in Obama's candidacy, McCain was actively rebuking them.

When Cincinnati radio host Bill Cunningham warmed up the crowd before a McCain fundraiser by emphasizing Barack Obama's middle name—"Hussein"—McCain excoriated him.

> *ABC News' John Berman reports: Senator John McCain apologized profusely today for comments made by radio host Bill Cunningham who was introducing him at an event in Cincinnati. Cunningham referred to the Illinois Senator three times as "Barack Hussein Obama."* ~ Jennifer Parker, ABC News[152]

"Hussein" is one of the most popular names amongst muslims worldwide. Husayn ibn Ali was the favored grandson of the prophet Muhammad and he died at the Battle of Karbala in 680 AD, in the same way so many Christians are dying across Africa and the Middle East today—he was beheaded.[153]

In the discussion of Obama's origins, any who question the accepted narrative are immediately slandered as "birthers"—kooks...people who wear tinfoil hats.

The biggest names in "Conservative" talk—Rush Limbaugh, Bill O'Reilly, Mark Levin, etc.—actively avoid the issue. When watchers or listeners bring it up, they are mocked.

When Fox News' Sean Hannity brought the issue up with supposed Right-wing bomb-thrower Ann Coulter, she handled it as if she were Eleanor Clift or Katie Couric.[154]

If it were proven that Barack Obama was, indeed, ineligible to hold the office of President of the United States, every appointment he's ever made, every piece of legislation he's ever signed (including the "Affordable Healthcare Act", a.k.a. "Obamacare"), every Executive Order he's ever dictated—all become nullified.

The issue is the third rail of his administration and, at the very least, "Conservatives" who believe it's a non-issue should simply state "I need to look further into it," or "I have no opinion at this time."

Glenn Beck called concern over Obama's Constitutional ineligibility "The dumbest thing I've ever heard."[155]

In spite of this hedge of protection that has been set up around Obama, Americans still began to ask questions, and it forced the administration to respond.

On April 27th of 2011, White House.gov released Barack Obama's official long-form birth certificate.[156]

Four days later, the media cycle came to a screeching halt and careened off into a new direction when the Obama administration announced, "We got bin Laden!" It was if the event were a trump card just waiting to be played.

Rather than journalists staying calm and maintaining the issue, they chastened anyone not caught up in the Patriotic euphoria (something that looked forced and surreal coming from the hard-Left of the political spectrum):

> *Last Wednesday, President Obama concluded his remarks about the release of his birth certificate by chiding his critics — and the press — with words that now seem far more ominous after the United States raid that killed Osama bin Laden.*
>
> *"We do not have time for this kind of silliness," Mr. Obama said. "We've got better stuff to do. I've got better stuff to do. We've got big problems to solve. And I'm confident we can solve them, but we're going to have to focus on them — not on this."* ~ Michael Shear, the New York Times[157]

Independent journalists soon found more than a few reasons to be concerned about the announcement.

In 2007 former Pakistani Prime Minister Benazir Bhutto told David Frost on his program *Frost Around the World*, that bin Laden was already dead[158]. Russia's state news agency *Pravda* was incredulous that Frost obliviously rolled over the announcement without follow-up.[159]

Bhutto, herself, quickly fell victim to assassination after attending an event for the Pakistani Peoples Party in late December of that same year.

Another Russian source—Russia Today—interviewed former NSA Analyst-turned-independent-journalist Wayne Madsen who asserted that Bhutto's death was a hit initiated by the CIA.[160]

The SEAL Team that conducted the raid to get bin Laden executed him on sight, although he was surrounded only by his wife—depending upon which official story you read.[161]

Americans were first told that the SEALs fought their way through withering fire from al Qaeda to get to where bin Laden was hiding. This was later retracted. It turned out that there was no firefight.[162]

The body of whomever it was that the SEALs shot on sight was brought back to the USS Carl Vinson where it was dumped into the ocean without a single sailor witnessing the event.[163]

In 2012, Navy SEAL Matt Bissonnette claimed in his book *No Easy Day* that he shot bin Laden. Two years later, Navy SEAL Rob O'Neill would claim *he* shot bin Laden[164]. O'Neill now says his life is in danger.[165]

Is America being betrayed and misinformed by even her Special Forces operators?

The supposed mastermind behind the 9/11 attacks, Khalid Sheik Mohammed, was waterboarded no fewer than 183 times to "break" him[166]. He was Osama bin Laden's lieutenant.

Bin Laden, himself, can rightly be called the greatest intelligence asset of the entire "War on Terror" yet he was shot on sight and dumped in the ocean.

Photos released which purportedly showed the dead terrorist had to be retracted when it was proven that they were faked[167]. A Freedom of Information request demanding to see the real photos was denied by a Federal Judge.[168]

The sensational White House Situation Room photo featuring National Security Advisor, now Director of the CIA John Brennan, Barack Obama, then Secretary of Defense Robert Gates (a Bush appointee), Chairman of the Joint Chiefs of Staff Admiral Mike Mullins and Vice President Joe Biden along with an aghast Hillary Clinton was also admitted to be staged[169]. The media proclaimed this suspenseful photo depicted America's leaders watching every step the SEALs made but it was later disclosed there was no "live feed" of the raid.[170]

A Closer Look

The Obama long-form birth certificate released by the White House has, itself, proven to be less than authentic.

- a smiley face in an official signature
- a stamp spelling error
- identical typewriter splats proving digital replication
- multiple layers that peel away from the pdf

It is a document that appears to have been fabricated by an amateur[171]. Again, this is critical identification concerning the man sitting in the White House.

The birth certificate was legally declared a forgery by one of the most famous jurisdictions in the country—Maricopa County, Arizona Sheriff Joe Arpaio[172]—yet, to date, no action has been taken. Ted Cruz, Rand Paul, Sarah Palin, Allen West—not a single key Republican figure will even broach the subject.

Even more disturbing than his birth certificate is what you find when you peel back the layers of Barack Obama's life.

But to do that, we need some more background.

Barack Obama's Mystery Religion

Most Americans don't know that Barack Obama is actually quite popular amongst Catholics. Although many American Catholics lean to the Right on the political spectrum, Roman Catholicism is a worldwide religion with 1.2 billion adherents[173]. Most of *them* lean quite decidedly to the Left.

Does Church policy follow popular sentiment, or lead it?

In 2008, American Catholics helped put Barack Obama in office, and many in the Catholic Conservative minority like author, speaker and founder of the Eagle Forum, Phyllis Schlafly, were not pleased. Catholics have been giving overwhelmingly to Leftist and even Communist organizations like ACORN and the Campaign for Human Development. Many have been duped into believing they're "helping the poor".[174]

The more important question is, why is Catholic leadership behind such a subversive, hard-Left agenda?

Barack Obama's rhetoric has been pricking the ears of "Liberal" Catholics; some of whom are saying, "He sounds just like I do!"[175]

Many will be surprised to know that Obama's Communist roots have Catholic origins.

As Andrew Higgins of the Washington Post noted[176], while much a due is made of Obama's 1 year at a muslim madrasa, the rest of his time in Indonesia was spent under Catholic tutelage.

Former NSA analyst-turned-whistleblower and investigative journalist Wayne Madsen has pieced together extensive clues that run from Barack Obama through his (apparent) mother and beyond his grandparents. At every step of the way, they are intertwined with the Communist Party. Madsen considered this "infiltration" by CIA assets but Obama is clearly a hard Left ideologue. It is the *United States* which has suffered at his hands, not any Communist insurgency he has belonged to.

How can the CIA work so well with Communists?

Obama's own work in 1983 for Business International Corporation, a CIA front that conducted seminars with the world's most powerful leaders and used journalists as agents abroad, dovetails with CIA espionage activities conducted by his mother, Stanley Ann Dunham in 1960s post-coup Indonesia on behalf of a number of CIA front operations, including the East-West Center at the University of Hawaii, the U.S. Agency for International Development (USAID), and the Ford Foundation. Dunham met and married Lolo Soetoro, Obama's stepfather, at the East-West Center in 1965. Soetoro was recalled to Indonesia in 1965 to serve as a senior army officer and assist General Suharto and the CIA in the bloody overthrow of President Sukarno.

Barack Obama, Sr., who met Dunham in 1959 in a Russian language class at the University of Hawaii, had been part of what was described as an airlift of 280 East African students to the United States to attend various colleges...

Lolo Soetoro, who Dunham married in March 1965, departed Hawaii for Indonesia on July 20, 1965, some three months prior to the CIA's coup against [Indonesian President] Sukarno [many Javanese have only 1 name]. Soetoro, who served [General] Suharto [also only 1 name] as an Army colonel, was clearly called back from the CIA-connected East-West Center to assist in the coup against Sukarno, one that would eventually cost the lives of some one million Indonesian citizens....

In 1967, after arriving in Indonesia with Obama, Jr., Dunham began teaching English at the American embassy in Jakarta, which also housed one of the largest CIA stations in Asia and had significant satellite stations in Surabaya in eastern Java and Medan on Sumatra. ...

In fact, Obama's mother was teaching English for the U.S. Agency for International Development (USAID), which was a major cover for CIA activities in Indonesia and throughout Southeast Asia, especially in Laos, South Vietnam, and Thailand. ~ The Madsen Report[177]

Madsen went on in his exposé to remark how Obama's mother Stanley Ann Dunham was helpful to both the Soviet Union and the One-World Agenda Ford Foundation.[178]

Obama's grandmother, Madelyn Dunham, was connected to the CIA as first female vice president at the Bank of Hawaii in Honolulu—a facility much used by the Central Intelligence Agency.[179]

Madelyn Dunham died just before Obama was elected president, in early November 2008.[180]

William Blum, writing for the blog of FBI whistleblower Sibel Edmonds, also noted Obama's connection to the CIA through "Business International".[181]

Questions arise regarding Stanley Ann Dunham and the supposed timeline of her giving birth to Obama. A discrepancy exists due to her being in Seattle, Washington attending the University there and not in Honolulu, Hawaii in August of 1961.[182]

Michael Shrimpton, a British barrister with Intelligence credentials, is claiming that the CIA has both photographic and DNA proof that Stanley Ann Dunham isn't Barack Obama's biological mother.[183]

But even if Dunham is Obama's biological mother, there's an excellent chance his real father was Communist pedophile pornographer Frank Marshall Davis.

Documentary filmmaker Joel Gilbert thinks he has the evidence, to include sordid pictures of young Ann posing nude and in dominatrix-style outfits for Davis.[184]

Barry's Catholic Mentor

Jimmy Carter's National Security Advisor was Zbigniew Brzezinski. Both Brzezinski[185] and his son Mark[186] are close Obama advisors. Daughter Mika has an equally high-profile job working as a host at the hard-Left media outlet MSNBC.[187]

Brzezinski was teaching at Columbia when Obama was supposedly attending.[188]

Brzezinski is literally the man behind America's foremost Islamic enemy, al Qaeda and its former front man, Osama bin Laden.[189]

Brzezinski is a Catholic Pole of strong passions; he hates Russia[190] almost as much as he adores Rome.

Although Brzezinski received his higher education at McGill and Harvard, the Jesuits had him first, through Loyola High School in Montreal.[191]

First Lady Rosalynn Carter and Zbigniew Brzezinski meet with Cardinal Stefan Wyszynski, National Archives/Public Domain – Wikimedia Commons

A connection that is much more likely is that Obama was working with Brzezinski and future CIA Director John Brennan on jihad and opium while visiting Pakistan in the 1980's.[192]

Brzezinski had (I'm sure still has) a direct line to the Vatican. Karol Józef Wojtyła—Pope John Paul II—was a personal friend.

> ***Aleksandra Ziólkowska-Boehm:*** *From my recollections of a conversation I had with your father and the commentary in your own book "Power and Principle", I know of your close and warm contacts with Pope John Paul II. How would you define the role of the Pope in Catholicism, in the world, after over 10 years of his pontificate?*
>
> ***Brzezinski:*** *To me, Pope John Paul II is the first true spiritual and religious leader on a global scale in the history of mankind. Up*

until now, all religious leaders appealed to a limited audience both theologically and geographically. John Paul II overcomes these limitations not only by effectively and skillfully using the mass media, but also by the power of his personality and his deep spirituality.

At the same time, as far as the Catholic faith is concerned, the Pope strives to strengthen and rebuild the Church which has gone somewhat astray after the post Vatican II reformatory zeal. The way I see it, the Pope wants to ensure that the Church remains the guardian of faith, while preventing ecumenism from degenerating into indifference. ~ A Conversation With Zbigniew Brzezinski, The Roots Are Polish[193]

John Paul II didn't always see eye-to-eye with the Society of Jesus. But things smoothed out after they tried repeatedly to kill him.

Endnotes

[130] *"Fundamentally Transforming the United States of America"*, David Weigel, 18 October 2011, Slate.com
http://www.slate.com/blogs/weigel/2011/10/18/_fundamentally_transforming_the_united_states_of_america_.html

[131] *Healthcare.gov Can't Verify Barack Obama's Identity*, Tim Brown 24 December 2013, Freedom Outpost.com
http://freedomoutpost.com/2013/12/healthcare-gov-cant-identify-barack-obama-staff-attempts-sign-obamacare/
Actual video report can be viewed on my YouTube channel, here:
https://www.youtube.com/watch?v=RsAo7_zPbqE&

[132] *Obama's Red Mentor Was a Pervert*, Cliff Kincaid, 24 August 2008, Accuracy in Media
http://www.aim.org/aim-column/obamas-red-mentor-was-a-pervert/
    Cliff Kincaid is, himself, almost certainly on the CIA payroll—he expends endless effort trying to discredit alternative media—but maybe that's how he got this information.

[133] *The 44th President Was His Mother's Son*, David Maraniss, 11 May 2012, the Washington Post
http://www.washingtonpost.com/opinions/the-44th-president-was-his-mothers-son/2012/05/11/gIQA6NV1IU_story.html
    As a sycophant of both Clinton and Obama, could this Post editor shove his head any further up their assess?
    —And this is who brings us our "news".

[134] *A Free-Spirited Wanderer Who Set Obama's Path*, Janny Scott, 14 March 2008, New York Times
http://www.nytimes.com/2008/03/14/us/politics/14obama.html?pagewanted=all&_r=0
    aw, "Stanley" was a "free spirited wanderer" who lived all over the world to follow her "spirit"...or to go where the CIA sent her.

[135] *Obama Attends Memorial for His Grandmother*, Dan Nakaso, 24 December 2008 (Merry Christmas, America—I had to surf for the date on this useless piece, too), USA Today via ABC News—and both aren't worth wiping your ass with.
http://abcnews.go.com/Politics/story?id=6522475&page=1&singlePage=true

[136] *Science Points to Ayers Authorship of Obama's "Dreams"*, Jack Cashill, 29 October 2008, Cashill.com
http://www.cashill.com/intellect_fraud/science_points.htm

[137] *Bill Ayers Admits For Second Time He Wrote Obama's "Dreams From My Father"*, Noel Sheppard, 27 March 2011, Newsbusters
http://newsbusters.org/blogs/noel-sheppard/2011/03/27/bill-ayers-admits-second-time-he-wrote-obamas-dreams-my-father

[138] *Obama Brother Disputes "Dreams" Autobiography*, Jerome Corsi, 20 December 2013, WorldNetDaily
http://www.wnd.com/2013/12/obama-brother-disputes-dreams-autobiography/#!

[139] *Biography*, Bill Ayers.org
http://billayers.org/biographyhistory/

you communist piece of shit...you couldn't even get your own ".com" domain. Burn in Hell, Venkman.

[140] *Was Young Obama Indonesian Citizen?* Aaron Klein, 17 August 2008, WorldNetDaily.com
http://www.wnd.com/2008/08/72656/

[141] *Another Look At Obama's Social Security Number*, Jack Cashill, 17 March 2011, WorldNetDaily.com
http://www.wnd.com/2011/03/275861/

[142] *Barack Hussein Obama and Harrison J. Bounel*, Jason Kissner, 17 April 2014, American Thinker.com
http://www.americanthinker.com/2014/04/_barack_hussein_obama_and_harrison_j_bounel.html

[143] *Obama's Missing Records Make Research Assignments Difficult*, Christopher Paslay, 3 July 2012, Chalk & Talk
http://chalkandtalk.wordpress.com/2012/07/03/obamas-missing-records-make-research-assignments-difficult/

[144] *Obama: Where Have All His Records Gone?*, Chelsea Schilling, 9 June 2009, WorldNetDaily.com
http://www.wnd.com/2009/06/100613/

[145] *Key Witness In Passport Fraud Case Fatally Shot*, unattributed, 19 April 2008, The Washington Times
http://www.washingtontimes.com/news/2008/apr/19/key-witness-in-passport-fraud-case-fatally-shot/#!

[146] *Wayne Allyn Root* Wikipedia.org
http://en.wikipedia.org/wiki/Wayne_Allyn_Root

[147] *Ghost of Columbia – Part II: Legendary Columbia Professor Never Heard of Obama*, Wayne Allyn Root, 7 June 2013, TheBlaze.com
http://www.theblaze.com/contributions/ghost-of-columbia-part-ii-legendary-columbia-professor-never-heard-of-obama/

[148] *Fox Business Network Cancels Judge Andrew Napolitano's Freedom Watch*, Matt Welch, 9 February 2012, Reason.com
http://reason.com/blog/2012/02/09/fox-business-networks-cancels-judge-andr

[149] *Lou Dobbs Mystified by Apparent "Taboo" on Barack Obama's "Kenyan Birth"*, American Power blog
http://americanpowerblog.blogspot.com/2012/05/lou-dobbs-mystified-by-apparent-taboo.html

[150] *The Vetting – Exclusive – Obama's Literary Agent in 1991 Booklet: "Born in Kenya and raised in Indonesia and Hawaii"*, Joel B. Pollak, 17 May 2012, Breitbart.com
http://www.breitbart.com/Big-Government/2012/05/17/The-Vetting-Barack-Obama-Literary-Agent-1991-Born-in-Kenya-Raised-Indonesia-Hawaii

It absolutely proves my point that "Conservative" Breitbart.com should list this disclaimer with this story!
Note from Senior Management:
Andrew Breitbart was never a "Birther," and Breitbart News is a site that has never advocated the narrative of "Birtherism." In fact, Andrew believed, as we do, that President Barack Obama was born in Honolulu, Hawaii, on August 4, 1961.

[151] *Dems Want Law To Keep Obama Records Secret*, Judicial Watch, unattributed, 04 October 2011
http://www.judicialwatch.org/blog/2011/10/dems-want-law-to-keep-obama-records-secret/

[152] *McCain Apologizes Profusely for "Hussein Obama"*, Jennifer Parker, 26 February 2008, ABC News
http://abcnews.go.com/blogs/politics/2008/02/mccain-apologiz/

[153] *Death of Husayn ibn Ali 680*, username RozeneRozene, 17 February 2014, Religions of the World
http://religionwiki.mvcsnow.org/death-of-husayn-ibn-ali-680/

[154] *Ann Coulter To Trump, Birthers: Drop The Issue*, Real Clear Politics, 11 April 2011
http://www.realclearpolitics.com/video/2011/04/11/ann_coulter_to_trump_birthers_drop_the_issue.html

[155] *Glenn Beck On Birther Issue: "Dumbest Thing I've Ever Heard"*, Drew Zahn, 4 January 2010, WorldNetDaily.com
http://www.wnd.com/2010/01/120992/

[156] *President Obama's Long Form Birth Certificate*, Dan Pfeiffer, 27 April 2011, the White House Blog
http://www.whitehouse.gov/blog/2011/04/27/president-obamas-long-form-birth-certificate

[157] *Obama's Remarks on Birth Certificate Take on New Meaning*, Michael D. Shear, 2 May 2011, NY Times
http://thecaucus.blogs.nytimes.com/2011/05/02/obamas-remarks-on-birth-certificate-controversy-take-on-new-meaning/?_php=true&_type=blogs&_php=true&_type=blogs&_r=1

[158] *Benazir Bhutto tells David Frost in 2007 Osama Bin Laden Has Been Murdered*, Johnny Cirucci, YouTube
https://www.youtube.com/watch?v=hLir_wRRPO4&

[159] *Benazir Bhutto Named Osama bin Laden's Killer Before Her Death*, Pravda, 15 January 2008
http://english.pravda.ru/world/asia/15-01-2008/103426-benazir_bhutto_osama-0/

[160] *CIA Linked to Benazir Bhutto's Assassination?* unattributed, Russia Today, 26 December 2009
http://rt.com/usa/cia-linked-to-benazir-bhutto-s-assassination/

[161] *The Killing Of Osama bin Laden: How The White House Changed Its Story*, Robert Booth, 4 May 2011, The Guardian
http://www.theguardian.com/world/2011/may/04/osama-bin-laden-killing-us-story-change

[162] *The Killing Of Osama bin Laden: How The White House Changed Its Story*, Robert Booth, 4 May 2011, the Guardian
http://www.theguardian.com/world/2011/may/04/osama-bin-laden-killing-us-story-change

[163] *Revealed: Military emails Show That NO U.S. Sailors Witnessed Osama bin Laden's Secret Burial At Sea*, Daily Mail Reporter, 21 November 2012, Daily Mail
http://www.dailymail.co.uk/news/article-2236617/Revealed-Military-emails-NO-U-S-sailors-witnessed-Osama-bin-Ladens-secret-burial-sea.html

[164] *Who Shot Bin Laden? A Tale of Two SEALs*, Matthew Cole, 6 November 2014, NBC News
http://www.nbcnews.com/news/investigations/who-shot-bin-laden-tale-two-seals-n241241
[165] *The Navy SEAL Who Shot Bin Laden Thinks His Life Is In Danger*, Hunter Walker and Amanda Macias, 12 November 2014, Business Insider
http://www.businessinsider.com/seal-who-says-he-shot-osama-thinks-his-life-is-in-danger-2014-11
[166] *How We Broke KSM*, Gary Buiso, 6 May 2012, the New York Post
http://nypost.com/2012/05/06/how-we-broke-ksm/
[167] *AP Retracts Photo Purporting To Show Osama bin Laden's Dead Body*, unattributed, 01 May 2011, Pasadena Star-News
http://www.pasadenastarnews.com/20110502/updated-1233-am-ap-retracts-photo-purporting-to-show-osama-bin-ladens-dead-body
[168] *Judge Denies Freedom Of Information Request To Release bin Laden Photos*, Associated Press, 26 April 2012, Fox News.com
http://www.foxnews.com/world/2012/04/26/judge-denies-freedom-information-request-to-release-bin-laden-photos/
[169] *Deception: Situation Room Photo Staged*, Don Irvine, 6 May 2011, Accuracy in Media
http://www.aim.org/don-irvine-blog/deception-situation-room-photo-staged-2/
[170] *Osama bin Laden Dead: Blackout During Raid On bin Laden Compound*, Steven Swinford, 4 May 2011, the Telegraph
http://www.telegraph.co.uk/news/worldnews/al-qaeda/8493391/Osama-bin-Laden-dead-Blackout-during-raid-on-bin-Laden-compound.html?sms_ss=email&at_xt=4dc1ce3920772825%2C0
[171] Obama Birth Certificate: Confirmed Forgery According To Top Experts, Michael Thomas, 15 December 2013, Storyleak.com
http://www.storyleak.com/obama-birth-certificate-confirmed-forgery-according-top-experts/
[172] *Arpaio: Obama Birth Record "Definitely Fraudulent"*, Associated Press, 17 July 2012, Yahoo! News
http://news.yahoo.com/arpaio-obama-birth-record-definitely-fraudulent-010211250.html
[173] *How Many Roman Catholics Are There In The World?* 14 March 2013, the BBC
http://www.bbc.com/news/world-21443313
[174] *The Catholic Connection to Barack Obama*, Phyllis Schlafly, 2008, Creators Syndicate
http://www.creators.com/conservative/phyllis-schlafly/the-catholic-connection-to-barack-obama.html
[175] *President Obama's Catholic Sensibility*, Michele Dillon, 18 May 2009, The Immanent Frame
http://blogs.ssrc.org/tif/2009/05/18/president-obamas-catholic-sensibility/
[176] *Catholic School In Indonesia Seeks Recognition For Its Role In Obama's Life*, Andrew Higgins, 9 April 2010, Washington Post
http://www.washingtonpost.com/wp-dyn/content/article/2010/04/08/AR2010040805858.html

We're so grateful for Andrew showing us how foolish we were to fear Barack Obama's upbringing—for that is the tone of this idiot's puff-piece.

[177] *The Story of Obama: All in The Company*, Wayne Madsen, 18 August 2010, the Wayne Madsen Report, reposted at InfoWars
http://www.infowars.com/bombshell-barack-obama-conclusively-outed-as-cia-creation/
[178] *ibid*
[179] *ibid*
[180] *Obama's Grandmother Dies*, Jeff Zeleny, 3 November 2008, NY Times
http://thecaucus.blogs.nytimes.com/2008/11/03/obamas-grandmother-dies/?_php=true&_type=blogs&_r=0
[181] *Barack Obama, His Mother, and the CIA*, William Blum, 5 July 2012, Boiling Frogs Post
http://www.boilingfrogspost.com/2012/07/05/barack-obama-his-mother-and-the-cia/
[182] *How Could Stanley Ann Dunham Have Delivered Barack Hussein Obama Jr. In August Of 1961 In Honolulu, When Official University Of Washington Records Show Her 2680 Miles Away In Seattle Attending Classes That Same Month?* Pamela Geller, January 2009, Atlas Shrugs
http://pamelageller.com/2008/10/how-could-stanl.html
[183] *British Intelligence Adviser: Stanley Ann Dunham is not Barack Obama's Real Mother*, Dean Garrison, 17 April 2014, Freedom Outpost
http://freedomoutpost.com/2014/04/evidence-stanley-ann-dunham-barack-obamas-real-mother/
[184] *Was Communist Mentor Intimate With Obama's Mother?* Jerome Corsi, 14 June 2012, WorldNetDaily
http://www.wnd.com/2012/06/was-communist-mentor-intimate-with-obamas-mother/
[185] *Obama Adviser Leads Delegation to Damascus*, Eli Lake, 12 February 2008, the NY Sun
http://www.nysun.com/foreign/obama-adviser-leads-delegation-to-damascus/71123/
   Here he is, spearheading the downfall of Syria for his Luciferian masters.
[186] *Brzezinski Family Business – Cold War*, Daniel Zubov, 28 August 2014, Sputnik News
http://sputniknews.com/columnists/20140828/192431312.html
[187] *MSNBC's Mika Brzezinski Brings Dose of Sexism to Secret Service Debate*, Erik Wemple, 1 October 2014, the Washington Post
http://www.washingtonpost.com/blogs/erik-wemple/wp/2014/10/01/msnbcs-mika-brzezinski-brings-dose-of-sexism-to-secret-service-debate/
   Read the story for some good laughs at the expense of BOTH the Post and PMS NBC.
[188] *Is Obama Hiding Something From His College Days?* Aaron Klein, 29 September 2008, WND
http://www.wnd.com/2008/09/76504/#!
[189] *Sleeping With the Devil: How U.S. and Saudi Backing of Al Qaeda Led to 9/11*, 5 September 2012, Washington's Blog
http://www.washingtonsblog.com/2012/09/sleeping-with-the-devil-how-u-s-and-saudi-backing-of-al-qaeda-led-to-911.html
   Pretty good links. The supposed interview of Brzezinski by CNN lists no details and the questions are posed by "INTERVIEWER" but the root web address goes back to George Washington University so hopefully it's not just a bunch kids making shit up. If it were, I doubt that would be the venue!
   Regardless, the assertion that Brzezinski is the man behind al Qaeda is quite solid.

[190] *Barack Obama and Zbigniew Brzezinski - Obama's Real Motives*, archive.org
https://archive.org/details/BarackObamaAndZbigniewBrzezhinski-ObamasRealMotives
This is a video copy of the audio interview between Red Pill Libtard Webster Griffin Tarpley and rabid anti-Semite Jeff "the Hair" Rense.

It's worth listening to because Tarpley is an historian with good facts.

I honestly have no idea how Libtards can take the Red Pill and not be converted but, in Tarpley's case, he could very well be another controlled opposition coadjutor as he received his doctorate from "Catholic University".
http://tarpley.net/biography/

[191] *Zbigniew Brzezinski: National Strategy and US Education*, Leonard Liggio, 23 January 2012, Smart Economy
http://smarteconomy.typepad.com/smart_economy/2012/01/zbigniew-brzezinski-national-strategy-and-us-education.html

[192] *John Brennan – The CIA -Zbigniew Brzezinski – Columbia University and Obama*, 10 January 2013, Conservative Treehouse
http://theconservativetreehouse.com/2013/01/10/john-brennan-the-cia-zibgnew-brezinski-columbia-university-and-obama/

[193] *A Conversation With Zbigniew Brzezinski*, Aleksandra Ziólkowska-Boehm, The Roots Are Polish
http://freepages.genealogy.rootsweb.ancestry.com/~atpc/heritage/articles/aleksandra/roots-brzezinski.html

Chapter 3

"Vatican Assassins"[d]

Assassination is reputed to be the forté of the Company of Loyola: the Jesuits.

Interestingly, the same is said of the CIA. We will examine the connection at length but, for now, it's important to point out that "the Company" is a euphemism for both the Jesuit Order[194] and the Central Intelligence Agency.[195]

Researchers and critics claim that Jesuit priests are "made" by secret black rituals and oaths taken similar to Masons or the Mafia. A "leak" of this special oath can be found in Appendix A of this book and it contains the following vow:

> *I do further promise and declare that I will, when opportunity presents, make and wage relentless war, secretly and openly, against all heretics, Protestants and Masons, as I am directed to do, to extirpate them from the face of the whole earth; and that I will spare neither age, sex nor condition, and that will hang, burn, waste, boil, flay, strangle, and bury alive these infamous heretics; rip up the stomachs and wombs of their women, and crush their infants' heads against the walls in order to annihilate their execrable race. That when the same cannot be done openly I will secretly use the poisonous cup, the strangulation cord, the steel of the poniard, or the leaden bullet, regardless of the honour, rank, dignity or authority of the persons, whatever may be their condition in life, either public or private, as I at any time may be directed so to do by any agents of the Pope or Superior of the Brotherhood of the Holy Father of the Society of Jesus.*

By deductive reasoning we can assume that forms of killing invisible to detection would be highly prized by such an organization—an organization that also prizes the accumulation of wealth by donations to the Catholic Church generally and to the Company in specific, as well as less reputable means.

---

[d] Eric Jon Phelps has a fascinating book by this title. He is a controversial figure due to his self-avowed racism. Some have questioned whether he is purposefully maligning his information on the Jesuits or manipulatively so.

As a result, deaths may have been recorded in history that have never been attributed to "foul play" yet whose circumstances are, at best, quizzical.

In a 365-day year, the probability of two men dying on the same day are 1 in 133,225. If you choose a specific day that is significant, that number goes up even higher.

On July 4th, 1826, Founding Father John Adams died within 5 hours of his friend, Founding Father Thomas Jefferson.[196]

Were they murdered?

The Jesuit order has been subversive from its inception and its machinations have gotten it thrown out of nearly every country its emissaries have found residence in.

Even the Vatican, itself, has attempted to disband these rogues. On July 21st, 1773, Pope Clement XIV commanded the order disband (we will look more at this later). A mere 41 years later they would be restored by intrigue. On August 7th, 1814, Pope Pius VII ordered Jesuit restoration, while under coercion in prison.

When the order was given, it was not received well by many around the world, including John Adams and Thomas Jefferson.

> *Not all the American leadership class was happy about the Jesuits' return. John Adams and Thomas Jefferson, intellectuals as they were, were interested in everything; and in a correspondence which sealed the friendship of former rivals until their deaths within hours of one another, they often wrote about what they were reading; but they sometimes wrote about religion and Jesuits. On May 6, 1916, Adams wrote:*
>
>> *I do not like the late Resurrection of the Jesuits. They have a General, now in Russia, in correspondence with the Jesuits in the U.S. who are more numerous than every body knows. Shall we not have Swarms of them here? In as many shapes and guises as ever the king of the Gypsies ... assumed? In the shape of Printers, Editors, Writers School masters, etc. I have lately read Pascalls Letters over again, and four Volumes of the History of the Jesuits. If ever any Congregation of Men could merit eternal Perdition on Earth and in Hell, According to these Historians though like Pascal true Catholicks, it is the Company of Loiola. Our System however of Religious*

> *Liberty must afford them an Asylum. But if they do not put the Purity of our Elections to a sever Tryal, it will be a Wonder.*

On August 1, 1816, Jefferson replied:

> *I dislike, with you, their restoration; because it marks a retrograde step from light to darkness. We shall have our follies without doubt. Some one or more of them will always be afloat. But ours will be the follies of enthusiasm, not bigotry, not Jesuitism. Bigotry is a disease of ignorance, of morbid minds; enthusiasm of the free and buoyant. Education and free discussion are the antidotes of both. We are destined to be a barrier against the returns of ignorance and barbarism. Old Europe will have to lean on our shoulders, and to hobble along at our side, under the monkish trammels of priests and kings, as she can.*

> *Without intending to do so, the founders were laying out a formula by which Jesuit education might succeed.* ~ The American Jesuits: A History, Raymond Schroth[197]

By adopting the relativistic egalitarianism of "the Enlightenment", did these two men seal their own doom?

It is important to note that the author of the above citation is, himself, a Jesuit. Raymond A. Schroth is a Jesuit priest, journalist and professor.[198]

Ignatius Loyola's "little company of friends" would appear to have a "little black book" and a long memory.

It's a book with a *lot* of names crossed out.

The "War Between the States"

The Jesuits in education are as invisible as they have made much of history to be. It would be a great shock for many Americans to find out that the Company of Loyola and the Vatican were considered the chief suspects behind both the chaos of the Civil War and the murder of America's Civil War President.

> *President Abraham Lincoln actually laid the chaos of the Civil War at the feet of the Black Pope* [the Jesuit Superior General, known as the "Black Pope" for his average priest cassock yet wielding the power of a Pontiff]. *In seeing and proclaiming the Unseen Hand, Lincoln knew he was ripe for the "poison cup" or "the leaden*

bullet":

"This war would never have been possible without the sinister influence of the Jesuits. We owe it to Popery that we now see our land reddened with the blood of her noblest sons. ..."

"The Protestants of both the North and South would surely unite to exterminate the priests and the Jesuits, if they could learn how the priests, the nuns, and the monks, which daily land on our shores, under the pretext of preaching their religion ... are nothing else but the emissaries of the Pope, of Napoleon III, and the other despots of Europe, to undermine our institutions, alienate the hearts of our people from our constitution, and our laws, destroy our schools, and prepare a reign of anarchy here as they have done in Ireland, in Mexico, in Spain, and wherever there are any people who want to be free. ..."

"'New projects of assassination are detected almost every day, accompanied with such savage circumstances, that they bring to my memory the massacre of St. Bartholomew and the Gunpowder Plot. We feel, at their investigation, that they come from the same masters in the art of murder, the Jesuits ...'"

"'So many plots have already been made against my life, that it is a real miracle that they have all failed, when we consider that the great majority of them were in the hands of skilful Roman Catholic murderers, evidently trained by the Jesuits.'"

"I know that Jesuits never forget nor forsake. But man must not care how and where he dies, provided he dies at the post of honour and duty." ~ Fifty Years in the Church of Rome, Reverend Charles Chiniquy[199]

The evidence of a vast Roman Conspiracy was so overwhelming that a military tribunal was convened rather than a civil court.[200]

The assassination conspirators were harbored at the boarding house of staunch Catholic Mary Surratt, at whose trial no fewer than *five* Catholic priests attested to her "impeccable character".[201]

She may very well have had one. It was her son John, who had been studying to become a Catholic priest[202], that had brought co-conspirator John Wilkes Booth to her boarding house to plot the assassination of Abraham Lincoln.[203]

After Lincoln was murdered, Surratt left the country and ended up in Rome.[204]

He was eventually found in Egypt[e] where he was arrested and extradited.

Like Surratt, Booth was also quietly associated with Roman Catholicism. It would have been unusual to have commiserated with a family of passionate Catholics and not have that common thread in the conspiracy.

> *The Booth family had traditionally been Episcopalian. Clergyman Charles Chiniquy, however, stated that John Wilkes Booth was really a Roman Catholic convert, later in life. A historian, Constance Head, also declared that Booth was of this religion. Head, who wrote the 1982 paper "Insights on John Wilkes Booth from His Sister Asia's Correspondence," published in the Lincoln Herald, quoted from a letter of Booth's sister, Asia Booth Clarke, in which she wrote that her brother was a Roman Catholic. Booth Clarke's memoir was published after her death. Terry Alford, a college history professor and a leading authority on the life of John Wilkes Booth,[24] has stated, "Asia Booth Clarke's memoir of her brother John Wilkes Booth has been recognized as the single most important document available for understanding the personality of the assassin of President Abraham Lincoln", and "no outsider could give such insights into the turbulent Booth's childhood or share such unique personal knowledge of the gifted actor". Testimony given at the trial of John Surratt showed that at his death, Booth had a Catholic medal on his person. Court evidence showed his attending a Roman Catholic church service on at least two occasions. Like his sister Asia, he received education at a school established by an official of the Catholic Church.* ~ Wikipedia[205]

Civil War physician and Union General Thomas Maley Harris was convinced of Jesuit collusion behind the assassination of Abraham Lincoln.

> *The organization of the Hierarchy is a complete military despotism, of which the Pope is the ostensible head; but of which, the Black Pope, is the real head. The Black Pope is the head of the order of the Jesuits, and is called a General. He not only has the absolute command of his own order, but directs and controls the general policy of the church ...*

---

[e] Rome has almost as much in common with Egypt as America now does with Rome.

It would seem that the Jesuits had had it in mind, from the beginning of the war, to find an occasion for the taking off of Mr. Lincoln. ... ~ Rome's Responsibility for the Assassination of Abraham Lincoln, General Thomas M. Harris[206]

The Ku Klux Klan is reputed to have been founded by "unknown Confederate Army veterans".

The first Klan was founded in 1865 in Pulaski, Tennessee, by six veterans of the Confederate Army.[14] The name is probably derived from the Greek word kuklos (κύκλος) *which means circle, suggesting a circle or band of brothers.[15]* ~ Wikipedia[207]

Author and activist Anton Chaitkin claims that it was Confederate General and "Grand Master" of Scottish Rite Freemasonry Albert Pike—whose statue adorns our nation's capital—that actually created the KKK. Pike was also instrumental in an elite Masonic sub-organization known as the "Knights of the Golden Circle"[208]. The esoteric use of the circle is shared by both organizations.

Wikimedia Commons: dbking

Although Roman Catholicism has the reputation as being staunch foes of Free Masonry, there are many powerful Catholics who have found to have also been practitioners of "the Craft".

John Wilkes Booth was just such a man. He was a member of Albert Pike's "Knights of the Golden Circle" and it is entirely possible that *he escaped death.*

Lincoln's assassin, John Wilkes Booth, was a member of Pike's Knights of the Golden Circle. He was in New Orleans during the winter of 1863-64 and conspired with Pike, Benjamin, Slidell and Admiral G.W. Baird to assassinate Lincoln. Baird later identified the body of Captain James William Boyd as Booth's. (Boyd was in fact a Confederate spy who resembled Booth and was used as a patsy. His body was dumped into an Arsenal Prison sinkhole used to dump dead horses.) ~ Dr. Henry Makow[209]

In 1872, Finis Bates was so convinced that he had met with and spoken to Booth long after his supposed hanging that Bates began an obsessed quest to track him down and put it all to paper.

Bates wasn't just using anecdotal hearsay, he conducted an evidence-based manhunt that built an impressive case.

John Wilkes Booth
Member of the Unseen Hand

This story I could not accept as a fact without investigation, believing, as the world believed, that John Wilkes Booth had been killed at the Garret home in Virginia on or about the 26th day of April, 1865, by one Boston Corbett, connected with the Federal troops in pursuit of him, after he (Booth) had been passed through the Federal military lines which formed a complete cordon surrounding the City of Washington, D. C., on the night of and after the assassination of President Lincoln.

But after many years of painstaking and exhaustive investigation, I am now unwillingly, and yet unanswerably, convinced that it is a fact that Booth was not killed, but made good his escape by the assistance of some of the officers of the Federal Army and government of the United States, located at Washington traitors to President Lincoln, in whose keeping was his life co-operating with Capt. Jett and Lieuts. Ruggles and Bainbridge, of the Confederate troops, belonging to the command of Col. J. S. Mosby, encamped at Bowling Green, Virginia. ... ~ The Escape And Suicide of John Wilkes Booth, Finis Langdon Bates[210]

Bates then gives pain-staking details about Booth's deformed thumb on his right hand and scarred brow as proof of his identity.

Several witnesses recognized Booth when presented with his photograph and one alleged witness knew him before and after the hanging. That was none other than Scottish Rite Grand Master, General Albert Pike of the Confederate Army.

Bates recounted the story as was told to him by Col. M. W. Connolly, a leading newspaper editor.

"One night I was in the Pickwick Hotel barroom talking to Gen. Albert Pike, who had come down from Washington on legal business. ... It was in 1884 or 1885..."

"I was about to leave, was waiting for a pause in order to excuse myself; Gen. Pike was explaining how he had been credited with the authorship of 'The Old Canoe,' which he said was written by some woman; just then my Village Mills friend came in accompanied by some one, I think Long Scurlock, who used to edit the Chronicle at Cleburne, Texas. ... I was watching Gen. Pike closely (trying to get away), when suddenly he threw up his hands, his face white as his hair and beard, and exclaimed:

"'My God! John Wilkes Booth!' He was much excited, trembled like an aspen, and at my suggestion went to his room. He seemed weakened by the shock, the occasion of which I could not realize at the moment. I saw him climb the stairs to his room and turned to look for my Village Mills acquaintance, but could not find him." ~ Bates[211]

The Precedent For Injustice

America's first Freemasonic whistleblower was a man named William Morgan, an officer who served with distinction in the War of 1812.

Although some have doubted whether Morgan served, an online register of officers from the war from the Commonwealth of Pennsylvania does list a "Morgan, William, Capt."[212] Morgan was born in Virginia and moved to New York so the association is possible.

An official U.S. government archive has an enlisted William Morgan shown as having been discharged from Capt. Lewis B. Willis's Co., 12th Infantry, Legion of the United States.[213]

The rolls of military service for the War of 1812 are, at best, sketchy but it is also possible (if not probable) that questions surrounding Morgan's service were fabricated to discredit him.

When Morgan struck at the Masons, they struck back.

Morgan belonged to the Masonic lodge in Rochester. When he attempted to join the Batavia lodge he was denied admission.[6] Angered by the rejection, Morgan announced that he was going to publish a book entitled Illustrations of Masonry,[7] critical of the Freemasons and describing their secret degree work in great detail.

...

> *A group of individuals, some allegedly Freemasons, gathered at Morgan's house claiming that he owed them money. On September 11, 1826, Morgan was arrested for a loan which a creditor claimed he had not repaid ... according to the law, he could be held in debtors' prison until the debt was paid, making it more difficult to publish his book. He was jailed in Canandaigua. ...*
>
> *There are conflicting accounts about what followed. The most common version is that Morgan was taken in a boat to the middle of the Niagara River and drowned, as he was never seen again.[8] In 1848 Henry L. Valance allegedly confessed to his part in the murder on his deathbed, a story recounted in chapter two of Reverend C. G. Finney's book* The Character, Claims, and Practical Workings of Freemasonry *(1869).[9] ~ Wikipedia*[214]

The local sheriff claimed that Morgan went with his captors freely and the subsequent trial gave out no serious punishments of indicted Batavia Lodge Masons.[215]

Americans the nation over were so outraged that an anti-Masonic movement arose which became the country's 1st third party. The minutes from a meeting of this third party in Massachusetts are a fascinating read and a sad statement on how far that state has slidden.

> *"When in the course of human events," the accustomed safeguards of society are destroyed, the usual guarantees for the secure enjoyment and protection of life, liberty, character, and the pursuits of happiness are impaired, and an appeal to the laws of the land administered by the constituted authorities, for the protection and defence of injured innocence is fruitless and unavailing. When the crimes of murder, arson, kidnapping, perjury and violence go unpunished, and the guilty go free, when the temple of justice is profaned by perjury, and the ermine of the judge menaced by contemptuous and mute witnesses, when the legal administration of public justice is paralyzed and all confidence in its protection is gone, when the temple of justice may well be represented by the virgin weeping and leaning on its broken columns and pouring forth her lamentations in vain over its ruins. ...*
>
> *... We shall proceed to give our views of the cause of these alarming evils and threatening dangers, and the only remedy that will dry up the fountain of these bitter waters, and give security and stability to our republican Institutions, and confidence in the secure, equal and*

impartial administration of justice, and render the laws of equal operation, over every description of persons, high or low, rich or poor, powerful or weak, and * *"'a terror to evil doers, and a praise to those that do well.'"*[f] ~ the Antimasonic State Convention of Massachusetts, Antimasonic Party (Mass.)[216]

Did you know that the Lincoln conspirators all wore hoods on the gallows?

Wild Knight In Malta

The founder of the Office of Strategic Services (precursor to the CIA) and the "father of Central Intelligence" was Roman Catholic Knight of Malta William Joseph "Wild Bill" Donovan. He was also an influential Wall Street attorney.[217]

The Knights of Malta are a front group for temporal Catholic power—*political* power amongst nation states.

The Independent (a British newspaper) tried to make light of the pull the Knights of Malta have but were forced to acknowledge this:

> *Leaked lists of their supposed membership read like a Who's Who of the global establishment: the first President George Bush; Rupert Murdoch; the head of the CIA; Tony Blair; Michael Bloomberg. All, apparently, signed-up representatives of the Sovereign Military Hospitaller Order of Saint John of Jerusalem of Rhodes and of Malta.*
>
> *"The Knights are your CIA, your politicians, your lobbyist, your previous, present and future presidents," Google tells us. "They are the most powerful group known to man. They are the agents of the dark lord."*[218]

In a similar tone, Josh Keating of *Foreign Policy* magazine noted that, like the Vatican, the "Hospitallers" are a completely sovereign and independent political entity:

> *In a speech in Doha on Monday, veteran New Yorker journalist Seymour Hersh ... alleged that former JSOC head Gen. Stanley McChrystal — later U.S. commander in Afghanistan — and his*

---

[f] This is a *brilliant* reference to Romans 13! When so many of today's cowardly Christians use that passage to excuse their inaction in the face of evil, these proud citizens used it as a clarion call for action when faced with that same over-arching conspiracy!

> *successor, Vice Adm. William McRaven, as well as many other senior leaders of the command, are "are all members of, or at least supporters of, Knights of Malta." ...*
>
> *The Sovereign Military Hospitaller Order of Saint John of Jerusalem of Rhodes and of Malta is a Roman Catholic organization based in Rome with around 13,000 members worldwide. ...*
>
> *The leader of the order, referred to as the prince and grand master, is elected for life in a secret conclave and must be approved by the pope. ...*
>
> *Despite having no fixed territory besides its headquarters building in Rome, the order is considered a sovereign entity under international law. It prints its own postage stamps and coins — though these are mostly for novelty value — and enjoys observer status at the United Nations, which classifies it as a nonstate entity ... The Knights maintain diplomatic relations with 104 countries. The order does not have official relations with the United States, though it has offices in New York, for the United Nations delegation, and Washington, for its representation at the Inter-American Development Bank.*
>
> *...Alleged members have included former CIA Directors William Casey and John McCone, Chrysler Chairman Lee Iacocca, and GOP fixture Pat Buchanan...*[219]

They have the power to assassinate at will, and they have.

General Stanley McChrystal helped cover-up[220] the assassination of Pat Tillman.[221]

In June of 2002, Tillman left it all to join the United States Army because, as President George W. Bush stated, "You're either with us, or you're with the terrorists."[222]

Tillman used his intense focus and top physical conditioning to make it into the Army's elite 75th Ranger Battalion but when he arrived in Afghanistan he quickly became disillusioned[223]. Rather than killing terrorists, many in the military were guarding Afghan poppy fields.[224,225]

Tillman had been corresponding with radical Leftist agitator Noam Chomsky regarding how he and so many other American young men had been duped.[226]

Soon, his Chain of Command became aware of his disposition. He had become a liability. Tillman became a victim of "friendly fire": he was executed by a 3-round burst of NATO 5.56mm to his face.[227]

Like the bin Laden raid, the official account of Pat Tillman's death changed several times.[228]

Although he wears a "Special Forces" tab, Stanley McChrystal is no George Patton. He's a "big supporter" of Barack Obama[229] and banned the Fox News Channel[230] from his Operations Center. He wants "serious action" taken on curtailing the right of Americans to own firearms[231] and he's a staunch proponent of "gay rights".[232]

Seventh Day Adventist Pastor Bill Hughes wrote this of Lee Iacocca in his book *The Secret Terrorists*:

> *Lee Iacocca was the man in charge of the Dearborn Division of the Ford Motor Company, who dispatched Carl Renas to go to Washington D.C. to get the car that JFK was in when he was assassinated. Iacocca was the head of the Dearborn Division until he became President of Ford Motor Company in 1970. Iacocca was part of the cover-up because he suppressed evidence concerning JFK's assassination.*
>
> *What connection does he have with the Catholic Church? In Iacocca's autobiography he says,*
>
>> *It took me a number of years to fully understand why I had to make a good confession to a priest before I went to Holy Communion, but in my teens I began to appreciate the importance of this most misunderstood right of the Catholic Church. In later years, I found myself completely refreshed after confession. I even began to attend weekend retreats where the Jesuits in face-to-face examinations of conscience made me come to grips with how I was conducting my life. — Iacocca: An Autobiography, Bantam Books, p. 8.*
>
> *Roman Catholic Lee Iacocca, head of the Dearborn division of the Ford Motor Co. was the one who dispatched Carl Renas to get the limousine that had the evidence of multiple bullets that were shot from multiple guns that killed John F. Kennedy. Isn't it amazing that many years later as President of Chrysler, Lee Iacocca went to Congress and asked for financial help? Since Catholic Iacocca had been such an obedient servant to his Jesuit masters, another*

obedient Catholic by the name of Thomas "Tip" O'Neill used his power as Speaker of the House to get Lee Iacocca all the money he needed.[233]

Character Assassination

It seems that at every turn, the most die-hard "anti-Communists" in the CIA and FBI were sexual deviants.

FBI Director J. Edgar Hoover's perversions are legendary, from his reputed cross-dressing[234] to his secret lover, Deputy Director Clyde Tolson.[235]

This is even more disturbing when one looks at the cabal behind the assassination of President John F. Kennedy—an assassination that honest alternative researchers resoundingly pin on the CIA.

Slandered by media as a "crackpot", Leroy Fletcher Prouty was a military professional who worked at the Pentagon as an Air Force Lieutenant Colonel in Intelligence during the Kennedy assassination.

> *It is appropriate that Fletcher Prouty, who has died of organ failure following stomach surgery at the age of 84, will best be remembered as the model for the mysterious Colonel X, played by Donald Sutherland, in Oliver Stone's film JFK.*
>
> *Prouty, who believed the assassination of President John F Kennedy was a coup d'état perpetrated by elements of the United States military and intelligence communities, was a career military man who spent a decade liaising between the Pentagon and the CIA. After*

Feeding the Hand that Kills You

According to E. Howard Hunt, the man Lyndon Baines Johnson put in charge of murdering the sitting president was Cord Meyer.

That meant the job was as good as done, because Meyer's wife was one of Jack Kennedy's revolving mistresses.

Mary Pinchot Meyer would, herself, be terminated with extreme prejudice in broad daylight on the grounds of Jesuit-run Georgetown University by a man who claimed he was a professor there.

As much as John F. Kennedy infuriated every possible Luciferian power center on Earth, was it his own immorality that sealed his doom?

leaving the US Air Force (USAF), he became an outspoken critic of the intelligence establishment, although by the time JFK was filmed, he had been relegated to the fringes along with countless other conspiracy crackpots. ~ Michael Carlson, Guardian[236]

Not only is Prouty a Kennedy assassination whistleblower, he believes the conspiracy goes far beyond just the CIA.

> SOURCES:
>
> Mary Pinchot Meyer, JFK Mistress, Assassinated By CIA, New Book Says, Christina Wilkie, 19 April 2012 (see "This Day In History"), Huffington Post http://www.huffingtonpost.com/2012/04/19/mary-pinchot-meyer-jfk-mistress-assassinated_n_1434191.html
>
> CIA Operative E. Howard Hunt Confession on the JFK Assassination, Johnny Cirucci YouTube https://www.youtube.com/watch?v=wIAQdtzp-jI&

The assassination of President John F. Kennedy ... has demonstrated that most of the major events of world significance are masterfully planned and orchestrated by an elite coterie of enormously powerful people who are not of one nation, one ethnic grouping, or one overridingly important business group. They are a power unto themselves for whom those others work. Neither is this power elite of recent origin. Its roots go deep into the past.

Kennedy's assassination has been used as an example of their methodology. Most thinking people of this country, and of the world believe that he was not killed by a lone gunman. Despite that view, the cover story created and thrust upon us by the spokesmen of this High Cabal has existed for three decades. It has come from the lips of every subsequent President and from the top media representatives and their spokesmen. They are experienced, intelligent people who are aware of the facts. Consider the pressure it must take to require all of them, without exception, to quote the words of that contrived cover story over and over again for nearly three decades.

This is the evidence we have of the significance of the Kennedy assassination. But it is only one example. Other major events, such as the development and escalation of the Vietnam War, have been manipulated in a similar manner. ...

As a result [of holding these views], *I am aware I may be attacked in the same fashion as Oliver Stone even before his movie JFK appeared in the theaters. The attack consists of words like conspiracy and paranoia similar to the verbal accusations during the Inquisition. ~ JFK: The CIA, Vietnam, and the Plot to Assassinate John F. Kennedy*, L. Fletcher Prouty[237]

Interesting choice of words.

Calling All Deviants

David Ferrie was as odd as he was useful to the CIA, whether in flying mafia thugs around[238] or agitating against Communists in New Orleans, the would-be Catholic priest was a reliable asset.

Ferrie started his Jesuit education first at St. Ignatius High School in Cleveland Ohio[239] and then on to Jesuit John Carroll University.[240]

Ferrie suffered from a rare skin condition known as *alopecia areata*, and lost his body hair which he would compensate for by wearing gaudy red-haired wigs and drawing his eyebrows across his forehead.

Ferrie was supposedly[g] defrocked from being a Catholic priest due to homosexual lust. Jim Garrison would describe Ferrie as "a helluva pilot, also a hypnotist, a defrocked priest, and a fag...."[241]

District Attorney of Orleans Parish Earling Carothers "Jim" Garrison suspected both David Ferrie and New Orleans businessman Clay Shaw of being conspirators in the assassination of President John F. Kennedy. He also disclosed that Ferrie, Shaw and even Jack "Pinky" Ruby were homosexuals and their deviancy played a role in their crimes. He found that Lee Harvey Oswald fit in with them as a "switch-hitter who couldn't satisfy his wife."[242]

Garrison—the only public figure who actively investigated the assassination of America's sitting President as a *conspiracy*—had Shaw arrested. Garrison's key witness, Perry Russo, linked Shaw to Ferrie and Oswald. Russo would claim overhearing them all discussing how to kill Kennedy. Russo was discredited because his original confession came as a result of hypnosis and the use of sodium pentathol ("truth serum"). The supposed risk of a hypnotist planting a suggestion in Russo's mind was

---

[g] Author Peter Levenda's *Sinister Forces* trilogy has been cited for his belief that Ferrie remained a priest in a secret Catholic sect—one that included excessive sexual perversion.
Principia Discordia » Principia Discordia » Techmology and Scientism » High Weirdness » Sinister Forces
http://www.principiadiscordia.com/forum/index.php?topic=34787.0

enough to get Shaw acquitted.[243]

But, as John Simkin of Spartacus Educational notes:

> *Attorney General Ramsay Clark, stated that the FBI had already investigated and cleared Shaw "in November and December of 1963" of "any part in the assassination". As Garrison has pointed out: "The statement that Shaw, whose name appears nowhere in the 26 volumes of the Warren Commission, had been investigated by the federal government was intriguing. If Shaw had no connection to the assassination, I wondered, why had he been investigated?"*[244]

After U.S. Attorney General Robert Kennedy had mafia gambling gangster Carlos Marcello deported to Guatemala, he quietly returned in an aircraft piloted by Ferrie[245]. Marcello was an important ally in CIA dealings in Cuba[246], especially after Castro put a stop to all illicit gambling trades.[247]

Another key figure in the Kennedy conspiracy was Guy Banister.

In October of 1967, after getting constantly eviscerated by the mainstream press, Garrison gave an interview to Eric Norden of Playboy in the hopes of getting his side of the story out.

> **Garrison:** *At the time Oswald started his so-called Fair Play for Cuba Committee, two men — Hugh Ward and Guy Banister — operated a private investigative agency at 544 Camp Street in downtown New Orleans. ...*
>
> *Guy Banister was one of the most militant right-wing anti-Communists in New Orleans. He was a former FBI official and his headquarters at 544 Camp Street was a clearinghouse for Cuban exile and paramilitary right-wing activities. ...*
>
> *In the Ramparts article you mentioned earlier, ex-FBI agent Bill Turner revealed that both Banister and Ward were listed in secret Minutemen files as members of the Minutemen and operatives of a group called the Anti-Communism League of the Caribbean, which was allegedly used by the CIA in the overthrow of the Guatemalan government in 1954. ...*
>
> **Norden:** *Were any of the other figures in the alleged conspiracy connected with Banister?*
>
> **Garrison:** *Yes, David Ferrie was a paid investigator for Banister, and the two men knew each other very well. During 1962 and 1963, Ferrie spent a good deal of time at 544 Camp Street and he made a*

> *series of mysterious long–distance phone calls to Central America from Banister's office. We have a record of those calls.*
>
> **Norden:** *Where are Banister and Ward now?*
>
> **Garrison:** *Both have died since the assassination — Banister of a heart attack in 1964 and Ward when the plane he was piloting for New Orleans Mayor De Lesseps Morrison crashed in Mexico in 1964. De Lesseps Morrison, as it happened, had introduced Clay Shaw to President Kennedy on an airplane flight in 1963.*[248]

Clay Shaw's Army Intelligence roots ran all the way back to an interesting country: Italy.

> *Jim Garrison clearly proved the CIA was involved in the assassination through Clay L. Shaw. He writes:*
>
>> *"... we discovered Shaw's extensive international role as an employee of the CIA. Shaw's secret life as an Agency man in Rome trying to bring Fascism back to Italy was exposed in articles in the Italian press ... To me among the most significant revelations were ... the confirmation by both Victor Marchetti and Richard Helms that Clay Shaw had been an agent of the Central Intelligence Agency." {16}*
>
> *Shaw [was] booked in the Jesuit stronghold of New Orleans for conspiracy to kill President Kennedy. Aided by the CIA's Italian Roman Catholic lawyer, Salvatore Panzeca, he was acquitted, although ... [Hollywood Director] Oliver Stone was told years later by presiding Judge Edward Haggerty, an Irish Roman Catholic and Papal Knight, who in keeping the Order's trial on track refused to admit Shaw's alias into the record, that he "did not believe a word of Shaw's testimony." Years later Richard Helms, one of "Wild Bill" Donovan's OSS case officers who became President Richard M. Nixon's Director of the CIA, admitted that Shaw had been a contract agent for the CIA, called "the Company" like the Jesuit Order. ~ Vatican Assassins, Eric Phelps*[249]

David Ferrie would also die before he could give testimony of a surprise cerebral hemorrhage.[250]

Jim Garrison paid for his dedication with his marriage[251]. He lived to see himself immortalized in the Oliver Stone movie *JFK* (1991) and then died less than a year later of cancer at 70.[252h]

Federal Bureau of Obfuscation

With good reason was the FBI a willing partner in the public slaughter of President John F. Kennedy. Like the CIA, they don't work for the American people and never did.

The Federal Bureau of Investigation was created by Charles Joseph Bonaparte, a distant relation to French Emperor Napoleon Bonaparte.[253]

Bonaparte was from Lord Baltimore's Catholic colony of Mary-land, from the very namesake city of her benefactor. The Jesuits were in the business of gathering *intelligence* on their enemies and the FBI would do that in spades. They readily admit the origins of their creator from their own "about us", though with only a short phrase amongst his "accomplishments".

> *As a Catholic* [Bonaparte] *was never absent from his pew in Baltimore Cathedral on Sunday mornings...*[254]

But soon, the FBI would metastasize into far worse than just an intelligence-gathering operation and graduate into actually facilitating disasters and helping to cover them up once they occurred.

In his review of the book *Pretty Boy Floyd*[255], NY Times critic Sidney Zion reminds us of how the FBI quietly chose to ignore the big criminal interests that were destroying America and focus on the sensationalized banditos robbing a single bank here and there—even to the extreme of telling the American public, "There's no such thing as 'organized crime'."

> *...after his G-men cut down John Dillinger outside the Biograph movie house in Chicago, J. Edgar Hoover elevated Charles Arthur (Pretty Boy) Floyd to Dillinger's exalted position as Public Enemy No. 1, catapulting him over such bank-robbing peers as Baby Face Nelson, Machine Gun Kelly and Ma Barker and her sons.*
>
> *In the summer of 1934, the following candidates failed to make Mr. Hoover's F.B.I. hit parade: Meyer Lansky, Lucky Luciano, Bugsy*

---

[h] I will mention later how weaponized cancer was being experimented with by the CIA in New Orleans and it is a story that involves key players in the Kennedy assassination.

To date, the author has no proof that Judge Garrison was murdered by the Company but he was most certainly a target, especially after being immortalized by *JFK*.

> *Siegel, Frank Costello, Owney Madden, Lepke Buchalter, Gurrah Shapiro, Dutch Schultz, Albert Anastasia, Tommy Lucchese, Joe Profaci, Moe Dalitz—to name just a few of the lads who ran organized crime in the United States.*
>
> *It was Hoover's genius to play up the hick bandits who roamed the sticks, living off pathetically unsecured banks, while ignoring the men who ran America's rackets. Intent on setting himself up as the Godfather of law enforcement, Hoover understood that to tangle with the mob was a prescription for failure, for it inevitably meant taking on the big-city political bosses and the labor unions, those bedrocks of the New Deal. During the Depression, nobody but the mobsters seemed to have the cash so badly needed by the pols.*[256]

Zion explains this away as a practical necessity for the FBI—the United States government was *afraid* to do its job and go after the Mafia.

The reality is that the FBI was doing the bidding of a higher authority.

Italian blogger Piazza del Popolo points us towards a helpful source.

> *According to Maria Antoinetta Calabro' in her book "Le Mani Della Mafia" (The Hands of the Mafia), for decades the Sicilian Mafia and its American counterparts used the Vatican bank, known as IOR (Institute for Religious Works) to launder its money.*[257]

Missing Evidence

Whenever there has been a tragedy of political significance, the FBI immediately shows up, not to investigate, but to cover up any wrongdoing that traces back to traitors in the United States government.

> *We reported that Jayna Davis, who investigated the Murrah Building bombing as a reporter for the NBC TV station in Oklahoma City, told us that the FBI confiscated 23 surveillance tapes from cameras trained on the Murrah Bldg. and the nearby area. Those tapes have not been made public.* ~ Reed Irvine and Cliff Kincaid, Accuracy in Media[258]
>
> *Surveillance footage from the Sandy Hook Elementary School massacre was released Friday.*
>
> *The video comes over a year after the Newtown mass shooting that left 20 children and six educators dead. However, much of the content is redacted.* ~ Brent McCluskey, Guns.com[259]

The FBI is withholding at least another 84 surveillance tapes that were seized in the immediate aftermath of the attack on the Pentagon. ~ Steve Watson, Infowars[260]

The 9/11 Research blog has a detailed record of the efforts from institutions like Judicial Watch that have filed Freedom of Information Act requests to divulge suppressed evidence such as surveillance video from September 11th. It is an extensive list.[261]

In 2013, Epix films produced what could be the premier documentary[262] on the destruction of TWA Flight 800 in 1996. Written, produced and directed by Kristina Borjesson, it showcased the men and women who were there, from bereaved families to eye witnesses to on-site experts. These experts, like Flight Operations and Chief Safety Investigator Robert Young, Explosive Ordinance Disposal technician Bob Heckman and Senior Accident Investigator Hank Hughes all recounted a shocking and treasonous allegation: FBI personnel came on the scene, took over the investigation and blatantly tampered with the evidence.

Qui Bono? "Who Benefits?"

Why was John F. Kennedy killed?

The Kennedys were outsiders, empowered by Joseph Kennedy's illicit gains in banking and booze. In 1960, the Kennedy Machine found the votes needed in Chicago and Lyndon Johnson gave the Democrats Texas, resulting in a squeaky win over Richard Nixon.[263]

Jack Kennedy was a serial philanderer[264] who wasn't expected to have an agenda of his own.

Jackie's Faustian Bargain

11 March 1962: Did Jackie Kennedy arrange for her husband's death as a result of his serial philandering?

En route to India and Pakistan for a "good will tour", First Lady Jacqueline Kennedy had the perfect opportunity (or cover?) for a "long" private audience with Pope John XXIII.

She was traditionally dressed head-to-toe in black to include a black mantilla.

If true, as with any "deal with the devil", she lived to regret it.

Perhaps the meeting was far from her mind over a year and a half later when on November 22nd 1963, her husband's brains were blown out as she rode next to him in Dallas.

SOURCES: *Mrs. Kennedy Visits Pope, Has Long, Private Audience – Spokesman-Review* http://johnnycirucci.com/wp/?attachment_id=3024

But he did.

When Kennedy got into office, he intended to either finish the Communists or make peace with them—not perpetuate a draining Cold War.[265]

Kennedy saw the CIA as a threat to national security (which it was and is) and vowed to splinter into a thousand pieces and scatter them to the wind.[266]

Kennedy attempted to compete with the Federal Reserve by ordering Congress to obey its Constitutional responsibility and print real silver certificates.[267]

And, in 1961, Kennedy made an appeal to the press to more faithfully guard state secrets while vowing, himself, to guard against the undue influence of "secret societies" that he claimed had a dangerous agenda[268]. Although he was talking about Communism, many have wondered if he had something else in mind.

> *I want to talk about our common responsibilities in the face of a common danger. ...*
>
> *The very word "secrecy" is repugnant in a free and open society; and we are as a people inherently and historically opposed to secret societies, to secret oaths and to secret proceedings. We decided long ago that the dangers of excessive and unwarranted concealment of pertinent facts far outweighed the dangers which are cited to justify it. Even today, there is little value in opposing the threat of a closed society by imitating its arbitrary restrictions. Even today, there is little value in insuring the survival of our nation if our traditions do not survive with it. And there is very grave danger that an announced need for increased security will be seized upon by those anxious to expand its meaning to the very limits of official censorship and concealment. That I do not intend to permit to the extent that it is in my control. And no official of my Administration, whether his rank is high or low, civilian or military, should interpret my words here tonight as an excuse to censor the news, to stifle dissent, to cover up our mistakes or to withhold from the press and the public the facts they deserve to know.*[269]

Who benefited from Jack Kennedy's death?

—everyone in power.

Dr. Mary's Monkey

During the 50's and 60's, while conducting research on a vaccine for polio, a viral form of cancer was discovered. The polio cultures were grown on monkey organs that eventually transported a viral strain of cancer to the host. This polyoma virus behaved very much like Simian Virus #40 ("SV40") yet had not been seen in humans.

The CIA (and the Jesuits behind them) immediately saw the assassination applications from this knowledge and took the research over. A bodyguard for key scientist Dr. Mary Sherman was none other than CIA asset Lee Harvey Oswald. His involvement was almost certainly instrumental in his being targeted as fall-guy for the Kennedy assassination.

Dr. Mary Sherman died in a freak accident related to her research. The story is well-told in the excellent book *Dr. Mary's Monkey* by Edward T. Haslam (Trine Day, 2007).

The lead doctor on the polio vaccine project was Alton Ochsner who was working with the ground-breaking data initiated by Dr. Jonas Salk.

Salk found that injecting dead forms of the virus allowed the human host to create antibodies that would fight future infections.

It was these polio vaccines grown on monkey organs that doomed many children to die of cancer. Insidiously, many more would die later as the dormant virus was activated by some quirk of biological circumstance.

Although Haslam, himself, attributes the contraction of cancer by kids injected with the polio vaccine as a true accident, the dangers and outcomes were completely covered up by the United States government.

The 1950's in America was an era of polio hysteria—especially after the disease claimed the life of Franklin Roosevelt. Physicians and politicians wanted results *now*. Like war profiteers, pharmaceutical monopolies had much to gain from the panic.

Alton Ochsner rushed to bring results and would later pay for his efforts with the life of his grandson.

In order to assuage American fears that the vaccines were untested and liable to cause more harm than good, Ochsner injected his grandson—Eugene "Davey" Davis—with a vaccine provided by Cutter Laboratories in Berkeley, California.

Davey died a short time later.[270]

How to Keep a Secret

Apparently, when the Luciferian Elite install a sexual deviant, only *they* are allowed to disclose the perversion. If you think about it, this is an important side of their blackmail, "Why should I toe *your* line when anyone else can do to me what you have threatened?"

After officiating a homosexual "wedding", Joan Rivers was interviewed on the run by the Sunday Times whose reporter asked hopefully, "Will we see the first gay president?" Rivers shot back, "We already have that with Obama." While walking away she also stated, "You know Michelle is a tranny."[271,272]

She may have sealed her fate by refusing to apologize or back down.[273]

Two months later she was dead.

The cause of her death? During a non-invasive (no cutting of the skin), non-life-threatening medical procedure, something went "terribly wrong". So wrong, in fact, that at least one doctor is asking if there was malpractice involved.[274]

It is interesting to note that, of only 3 people that she banned from her funeral, Michelle Obama was one of them.[275]

Assassination Central

As far as assassination goes, the OSS's "Wild Bill" Donovan was the mastermind behind one of the most infamous assassinations in United States history; the murder of General George S. Patton.

An astonishing book by Robert K. Wilcox, *Target Patton*[276], lays out the conspiracy that holds Donovan at the front and Dwight D. Eisenhower along with Omar Bradley at the top.

Cox states that Donovan used OSS

Was Joan Rivers An "Illuminati Sacrifice"?

Joan Rivers was 81 at the time of her death and she was born in 1933.

The pop tart "Beyoncé" was born on the date of Rivers' "terrible accident" in 1981 and she is 33.

Now, before you scoff, understand that numerology, astrology and dates are critical to the Luciferian Elite.

My opinion? After Rivers marked herself for destruction, the satanists quickly found the numbers they wanted and made it happen.

[hat/tip Johnny's wife]

assassin Douglas Bazata[277] to utilize an unorthodox pneumatic gun that could shoot untraceable debris as projectiles at close range to wound Patton while being driven through Heidelberg, Germany in December of 1945.

To everyone's surprise, despite terrible wounds, Patton started to recover in the hospital. His location and status was leaked to the Soviet spy agency, the NKVD (precursor to the KGB), and they finished him.

Such co-operation between "enemies" to kill a prominent, patriotic American is a Jesuit calling-card.

Patton had seen the Soviet scourge first-hand, how the Red Army had raped, murdered, pillaged and looted its way through Eastern Europe and half of Germany. He had also seen the shocking complicity between Washington and Moscow.

Patton's anti-Communist sentiments were making his superiors increasingly uncomfortable as there had been much secret collusion between them.

The prolonging of World War II and the empowering of the Communist Soviet Union played right into Jesuit hands—both the birthplace of the Reformation (Germany) and its most fertile growing fields (the U.S. and the U.K.) would continue to be punished.

> *Patton, who distrusted the Russians, believed Eisenhower wrongly prevented him closing the so-called Falaise Gap in the autumn of 1944, allowing hundreds of thousands of German troops to escape to fight again. This led to the deaths of thousands of Americans during their winter counter-offensive that became known as the Battle of the Bulge.*
>
> *In order to placate Stalin, the 3rd Army was also ordered to a halt as it reached the German border and was prevented from seizing either Berlin or Prague, moves that could have prevented Soviet domination of Eastern Europe after the war.* ~ Tim Shipman, the Telegraph[278]

George Patton had seen it all from within the leadership inner circle.

According to Wilcox, it was the threat from Patton that he would out America's leaders as traitors as well as his towering character as a proven wartime leader that earned him a death sentence.

What American would possibly be part of murdering our greatest battlefield general? —One who owed his allegiance to Rome, and not

Washington.

For repeatedly subverting American interests for Papal priorities, William Donovan was lavishly rewarded, even before the end of the 2nd World War.

> ...in July 1944 Pope Pius XII awarded Donovan the "Grand Cross of the Order of St. Sylvester", the oldest and most prestigious of papal knighthoods, and the highest Catholic award ever received by an American. Less than one hundred men have received this award throughout history. ~ Knights of Malta, bibliotecapleyades.net[279]
>
> ***Order of St. Sylvester > Notable Members***
>
> *In July 1944, Pope Pius XII created Major General William Joseph Donovan, father of the CIA, Knight Grand Cross of the Order.* ~ Wikipedia[280]
>
> ***Order of St. Sylvester...***
>
> *This was the Order of the Golden Militia under a new name. Prior to the year 1841 it was known as the Militia of the Golden Spur or Golden Militia ... it undoubtedly is the oldest and, at one time, was one of the most prized of the papal orders.* ~ Pontifical Decorations, Catholic Encyclopedia[281]

The garrote around the neck of America is the international banks lead by the United States "central bank", the so-called "Federal Reserve" which is managed by the accountants of Rome, the Rothschilds.

But the knives in America's back are her intelligence organizations from the FBI to the NSA to the CIA.

They are all clearly driven by a malignant authority that wishes to greatly harm the United States. [italics suspended]

> ...the Catholic Church ... is the most divisive force in America. The March 19, 1984, issue of *U.S. News and World Report* examined two secret Catholic elite religious societies in this country: the Knights of Malta with one thousand U.S. members who are prominent in government, business, or professional life and Opus Dei with three thousand members of widely varied backgrounds. The Knights of Malta organization dates back to the time of the Crusades; its members include some of our nation's most prominent Catholics: CIA Director William Casey; William Wilson; Vernon Walters; Senators Denton and Domenici; Alexander Haig; William

Sloan; and William F. Buckley, creator and leader of Young Americans for Freedom, from which a large proportion of the Reagan administration team were drawn. Because many Knights and recipients of the Order's honors have worked in or around the CIA, critics sometimes suggest a link between the two. **The CIA has been dominated by the Catholic hierarchy.** [emphasis mine]

According to members, the order serves "as an international defender of the Church."[1] In June of each year a ceremony is held in Rome for Knights of Malta which includes the "swearing of allegiance to the defense of the Holy Mother Church."[8] ... Knights are committed to defending the Church. Only the most devout and obedient are invited to join the Knights and Opus Dei (which its detractors have compared to mind-controlling cults).[8] ... It is inevitable that the best interests of the Vatican and those of the United States are not always going to be the same. For this reason, no one can possibly swear complete allegiance to both and mean it. The acts and attitudes of the Knights of Malta in the Reagan administration seem to reflect this complete allegiance to the Catholic Church rather than to our country. ...

Consider the intensity of the commitment of these secret society members as "international defenders of the Church." It is hardly a secret that one of the most important American advances in "defending the Church" by Catholic elitists was the creation of the Central Intelligence Agency (CIA). The activities of the CIA go far beyond intelligence gathering of an international nature.[10] The CIA serves as an agency through which secret "assistance" to the Holy Mother Church can be provided by secret American society members acting as her defenders:

> During the CIA's formative years, Protestants predominated. ... Somehow, however, Catholics wrested control of the ClA's coven-action section. It was no coincidence that some of the agency's more grandiose operations were in Catholic countries of Latin America and the Catholic regime of South Vietnam.[11]

For creating the Office of Strategic Services (OSS), the wartime predecessor to the CIA, and this special arrangement with the Vatican,

> General William "Wild Bill" Donovan was decorated in July 1944 by Pope Pius XII with the Grand Cross of the Order of Saint Sylvester, the oldest and most prestigious of

papal knighthoods. This award has been given to only one hundred other men in history, who, "by feat of arms or writings or outstanding deeds have spread the faith and have safeguarded and championed the Church.[11,12]

Donovan did more to safeguard and champion the Church than any other American, and he was rewarded for his services with the highest Catholic award ever received by an American. No doubt, thousands of others have striven with their deeds for similar recognition. ~ *American Democracy & the Vatican*, Stephen D. Mumford[282]

Endnotes

[194] *Ten Things You Didn't Know (About the Jesuits)*, Paul Brian Campbell SJ, 16 August 2010, People for Others reposted at Free Republic
http://www.freerepublic.com/focus/religion/2571797/posts
     The point is to reference the Jesuits magazine—*Company*.

[195] *The Company (Central Intelligence Agency or CIA nickname)*, Barry Popik.com
http://www.barrypopik.com/index.php/new_york_city/entry/the_company_central_intelligence_agency_or_cia_nickname

[196] *This Day in History—July 4, 1826: Thomas Jefferson and John Adams Die*, History.com
http://www.history.com/this-day-in-history/thomas-jefferson-and-john-adams-die

[197] *The American Jesuits: A History*, Raymond A. Schroth, New York University Press (2007), p. 57

[198] *The American Jesuits: A History*, "What's New", Books, Fordham magazine, Winter '08, p. 34
http://www.fordham.edu/images/whats_new/magazine/winter08/books.pdf

[199] *Fifty Years in the Church of Rome*, Charles Chiniquy, Adam Craig (1889) pp. 388, 472, 493, 499, 501 and 506

[200] *The Historian's Lincoln: Pseudohistory, Psychohistory, and History*, Gabor Boritt and Norman Forness, University of Illinois Press (1996), p. 351

[201] *The Hanging Of Mary Surratt*, Mike Scruggs, undated, The Tribune Papers
http://www.ashevilletribune.com/asheville/heritage/Surratt%203.htm

[202] *Images of John Surratt, Famous American Trials: Trial of the Lincoln Assassination Conspirators 1865*, University of Missouri-Kansas City, Law
http://law2.umkc.edu/faculty/projects/ftrials/lincolnconspiracy/surrattj.html

[203] *The Family Plot to Kill Lincoln*, David Stewart, 28 August 2013, the Smithsonian
http://www.smithsonianmag.com/history/the-family-plot-to-kill-lincoln-2093807/?no-ist

[204] *John Harrison Surratt, Jr*, Find A Grave.com
http://www.findagrave.com/cgi-bin/fg.cgi?page=gr&GRid=6139

[205] *John Wilkes Booth > Background and Early Life*, Wikipedia
http://en.wikipedia.org/wiki/John_Wilkes_Booth#Background_and_early_life
     Again, can't see how anyone would disdain this kind of scholarship. This is *infinitely* more trustworthy than any blog.

[206] *Rome's Responsibility for the Assassination of Abraham Lincoln*, General Thomas M. Harris, Williams Pub. Co. (1897), pp. 48-49, 64-65

[207] *Ku Klux Klan > First KKK*, Wikipedia
http://en.wikipedia.org/wiki/Ku_Klux_Klan#First_KKK

[208] *The Scottish Rite's KKK Project*, Anton Chaitkin, undated, unsourced
http://www.theforbiddenknowledge.com/hardtruth/scottishriteproject.htm
     Unable to check the veracity of this but the introduction seems straight—
...the edited text of the speech delivered by Mr. Chaitkin to the Labor Day weekend conference of the Schiller Institute in suburban Washington, D.C.
     —and Chaitkin is a LaRouche "Truther".

[209] *Illuminati Murdered at least Two More Presidents*, Henry Makow, 16 May 2007, HenryMakow.com
http://www.henrymakow.com/002009.html

[210] *The Escape And Suicide of John Wilkes Booth: Or, The First True Account Of Lincoln's Assassination, Containing A Complete Confession By Booth*, Finis Langdon Bates, J. L. Nichols (~1907), PREFACE, pp. 5-6

[211] *ibid*, pp. 222-225

[212] *PA Officers in the war of 1812: Company Officers of Pennsylvania*, Ancestry.com http://www.rootsweb.ancestry.com/~GENHOME/ofc1812.htm

[213] *War of 1812 Discharge Certificates Appendix IV: List of Soldiers by Unit*, Archive.gov http://www.archives.gov/research/military/war-of-1812/1812-discharge-certificates/soldiers-by-unit.html

[214] *William Morgan (anti-Mason) > Book on Freemasonry* and *Disappearance*, Wikipedia http://en.wikipedia.org/wiki/William_Morgan_(anti-Mason)#Book_on_Freemasonry

[215] *The Morgan Affair*, David Barrett, Pietre-Stones Review of Freemasonry http://www.freemasons-freemasonry.com/freemasonry_morgan_affair.html

[216] *An Abstract of the Proceedings of the Antimasonic State Convention of Massachusetts*, Antimasonic Party (Mass.). State Convention, the Boston Press (1831), pp. 52-53

[217] *Wild Bill Donovan – COI*, Karen Holt, 26 January 2012, the Examiner http://www.examiner.com/article/wild-bill-donovan-coi

[218] *Caped Crusaders: What Really Goes On at the Knights of Malta's Secretive Headquarters?* Evgeny Lebedev, 29 March 2014, the Independent http://www.independent.co.uk/news/world/europe/caped-crusaders-what-really-goes-on-at-the-knights-of-maltas-secretive-headquarters-9217469.html

[219] *Who Are the Knights of Malta—and What Do They Want?* Joshua Keating, 19 January 2011, Foreign Policy http://www.foreignpolicy.com/articles/2011/01/19/who_are_the_knights_of_malta_and_what_do_they_want

[220] *In the Name of Pat Tillman: Good Riddance to Stanley McChrystal*, Dave Zirin, 25 June 2010, The Nation http://www.thenation.com/article/mcchrystals-pat-tillman-connection

[221] *AP: New Details on Tillman's Death*, Martha Mendoza, Associated Press, 27 July 2007, the Washington Post http://www.washingtonpost.com/wp-dyn/content/article/2007/07/26/AR2007072602025.html

[222] *"You Are Either With Us Or Against Us"*, 6 November 2001, CNN http://edition.cnn.com/2001/US/11/06/gen.attack.on.terror/

[223] *New Book Describes Pat Tillman As Increasingly Disillusioned With Iraq War*, Chris McGreal, 15 September 2009, the Guardian http://www.theguardian.com/world/2009/sep/15/pat-tillman-iraq-book

[224] *U.S. Troops Patrolling Poppy Fields In Afghanistan*, 18 October 2012, Washington's Blog http://www.washingtonsblog.com/2012/10/14066.html

[225] *Production of Opium by Afghans Is Up Again*, Rod Nordland, 15 April 2013, New York Times http://www.nytimes.com/2013/04/16/world/asia/afghanistan-opium-production-increases-for-3rd-year.html

[226] *Noam Chomsky on Pat Tillman's Death*, Johnny Cirucci YouTube https://www.youtube.com/watch?v=NtNdloJ4aKo&

[227] *Was The Pin-Up Boy Of Bush's War On Terror Assassinated?* Charles Laurence, 3 August 2007, the Daily Mail
http://www.dailymail.co.uk/news/article-473037/Was-pin-boy-Bushs-War-Terror-assassinated.html
[228] *FAMILY DEMANDS THE TRUTH / New Inquiry May Expose Events That Led to Pat Tillman's Death*, Robert Collier, 25 September 2005, the San Francisco Chronicle
http://www.sfgate.com/news/article/FAMILY-DEMANDS-THE-TRUTH-New-inquiry-may-expose-2567400.php
[229] *McChrystal "A Great Supporter" of Obama*, David Jackson, 20 March 2012, USA Today
http://content.usatoday.com/communities/theoval/post/2012/03/mcchrystal-a-great-supporter-of-obama/1#.VBhgv1d37k8
[230] *McChrystal Banned Fox News From Headquarters: Marc Ambinder*, unattributed, 24 June 2010, Huffington Post
http://www.huffingtonpost.com/2010/06/24/mcchrystal-banned-fox-new_n_623884.html
[231] *McChrystal Says "Serious Action" Needed On Gun Control*, Claudine Zap, 8 January 2013, Yahoo! News
http://news.yahoo.com/blogs/the-lookout/mcchrystal-says-serious-action-needed-gun-control-174328785.html
[232] *McChrystal's Social Liberalism and the Integration of Gays in the Military*, Marc Ambinder, 24 June 2010, the Atlantic
http://www.theatlantic.com/politics/archive/2010/06/mcchrystals-social-liberalism-and-the-integration-of-gays-in-the-military/58663/
[233] *The Secret Terrorists*, Bill Hughes, Truth Triumphant Ministries (2002), p. 67
[234] *J. Edgar Hoover > Personal Life*, New World Encyclopedia
http://www.newworldencyclopedia.org/entry/J._Edgar_Hoover#Personal_life
[235] *J. Edgar Hoover: Gay or Just a Man Who Has Sex With Men?* Susan James, 16 November 2011, ABC News
http://abcnews.go.com/Health/edgar-hoover-sex-men-homosexual/story?id=14948447
[236] *L Fletcher Prouty*, Michael Carlson, 21 June 2001, the Guardian
http://www.theguardian.com/news/2001/jun/22/guardianobituaries
[237] *JFK: The CIA, Vietnam, and the Plot to Assassinate John F. Kennedy*, L. Fletcher Prouty, Skyhorse Publishing (2011). Bullshit digital copy has no page numbers. These are the first two pages of Chapter 21.
[238] *David Ferrie*, House Select Committee on Assassinations – Appendix to Hearings, Volume 10, 12, p. 106.
http://www.aarclibrary.org/publib/jfk/hsca/reportvols/vol10/html/HSCA_Vol10_0055b.htm
[239] *Saint Ignatius High School (Cleveland, Ohio) Alumni*, a Wiki series book published by Wiki LLC
[240] *The Carroll News*- Vol. 16, No. 14, 20 May 1936, John Carroll University
http://collected.jcu.edu/cgi/viewcontent.cgi?article=1055&context=carrollnews
[241] *Richard Billings' New Orleans Journal*, Dick Billings's personal notes on consultations and interviews with Garrison
http://www.jfk-online.com/billings2.html

[242] *Case Closed: Lee Harvey Oswald and the Assassination of JFK* Gerald Pozner, Open Road Media (2013), a useless e-book without page numbers and I'm not counting them

The only thing "closed" was asshole author Gerald Pozner's mind. His "e-book" was nothing more than a clear attempt to cover the conspiracy and discredit American heroes like Jim Garrison who was so overwhelmed with the predominant sexual perversion of his suspects he thought it was the very motivation for why they wanted to see Kennedy dead.

He was later shocked to see a much bigger picture, thanks to information he received from L. Fletcher Prouty.

The original information comes from an interview Garrison gave to James Phelan of the Saturday Evening Post. The way Poser uses it, my guess is that Phelan was a Leftist moron, as well but if I can get the original interview I will.

[243] *JFK Assassination Conspiracy: Perry Russo Fingered Clay Shaw—While Hypnotized*, John Pope, 15 November 2013, the New Orleans Times-Picayune
http://www.nola.com/politics/index.ssf/2013/11/jfk_assassination_conspiracy_p.html

[244] *American History > The Assassination of JFK > Clay Shaw*, John Simkin, undated, Spartacus Educational
http://spartacus-educational.com/JFKshaw.htm

[245] *Carlos Marcello and the Assassination of President Kennedy*, Don Fulsom, 3 October 2009, Crime Magazine
http://www.crimemagazine.com/carlos-marcello-and-assassination-president-kennedy

[246] *Carlos Marcello: The Man Behind the JFK Assassination*, Stefano Vaccara, Enigma Books (2013), p. 94

[247] *Outgoing Obama "Car Czar" Makes Yet Another Communist Reference*, Tiffany Gabbay, 17 August 2011, the Blaze
http://www.theblaze.com/stories/2011/08/17/outgoing-obama-car-czar-makes-yet-another-communist-reference/

[248] *Jim Garrison: Interview with Playboy 5: Oswald and Banister in New Orleans*, originally published October 1967 with unknown centerfold (don't look it up, you pervert), reposted here:
http://22november1963.org.uk/jim-garrison-oswald-banister-new-orleans

[249] *Vatican Assassins: "Wounded In the House of My Friends"*, Eric Jon Phelps, self-published (2001), pp. 601, 608

[250] *Jim Garrison: Interview with Playboy 12: David Ferrie*, October 1967, reposted here:
http://22november1963.org.uk/jim-garrison-david-ferrie

[251] *Woman vs. Man vs. Patriarchy in JFK*, Jennifer Kesler, 16 March 2008, the Hathor Legacy
http://thehathorlegacy.com/woman-vs-man-vs-patriarchy-in-jfk/

This feminist drivel is the only source I could find on Garrison and wife Elizabeth getting a divorce in 1978 and it references Machine hatchet-job *False Witness* by Patricia Lambert. It is my assessment that Lambert was contracted to exploit Garrison's tumultuous marriage for the Luciferians.

[252] *Jim Garrison, 70, Theorist on Kennedy Death, Dies*, Bruce Lambert, 22 October 1992, New York Times
http://www.nytimes.com/1992/10/22/obituaries/jim-garrison-70-theorist-on-kennedy-death-dies.html

[253] *Charles Joseph Bonaparte: His Life and Public Services*, Joseph Bishop, C. Scribner's sons (1922), pp. 6-9
[254] *Bonaparte Founded G-Men*, Don Bloch, 18 August 1935, the Washington Star, reposted on the FBI's government website
http://www.fbi.gov/about-us/history/brief-history/docs_star1935
[255] *Pretty Boy Floyd*, Larry McMurtry and Diana Ossana, Simon & Schuster (2010)
[256] *A Legend in J. Edgar Hoover's Time*, Sidney Zion, 16 October 1994, New York Times
http://www.nytimes.com/books/99/01/10/specials/mcmurtry-floyd.html
[257] *The Catholic Church and the Mafia*, 23 March 2014, Piazza del Popolo via her *Mozzarella Mama* blog
http://www.mozzarellamama.com/2014/the-catholic-church-and-the-mafia/
[258] *FBI Withheld Vital Evidence*, Reed Irvine and Cliff Kincaid, 7 June 2001, Accuracy in Media
http://www.aim.org/media-monitor/fbi-withheld-vital-evidence/
  One of the rare times Cliff Kincaid and "Accuracy in Media" are helpful—only because they are frothing up Conservitards to look at jihadis and not their own government.
[259] *Heavily Redacted Sandy Hook Surveillance Video Released*, Brent McCluskey, 28 December 2013, Guns.com
http://www.guns.com/2013/12/28/heavily-redacted-sandy-hook-surveillance-video-released-video/
[260] *FBI Withholding 84 More Tapes of Pentagon on 9/11*, Steve Watson, 17 May 2006, InfoWars
http://infowars.net/articles/may2006/170506Pentagon_videos.htm
[261] *Pentagon Attack Footage*, 9-11 Research
http://911research.wtc7.net/pentagon/evidence/footage.html
[262] *TWA Flight 800*, an Epix original documentary
http://www.epixhd.com/twa-flight-800/
  As of this writing Netflix is carrying this film and I highly recommend watching it wherever you can find it.
[263] *Did JFK Steal The 1960 Election?* Roger Stone, 7 December 2010, the Stone Zone
http://stonezone.com/article.php?id=391
[264] *All The President's Women*, Sara Stewart, 10 November 2013, NY Post
http://nypost.com/2013/11/10/all-the-presidents-women-3/
[265] *Cuban Communism*, Irving Louis Horowitz, Transaction Publishers (1967), p. 68
[266] *The Brothers: John Foster Dulles, Allen Dulles, and Their Secret World War*, Stephen Kinzer, Macmillan (2013), p. 303
  If Allen [Dulles] had not yet confronted the implications of the Bay of Pigs disaster, Kennedy had. In private he cursed "CIA bastards" for luring him into it, and wished he could "splinter the CIA into a thousand pieces and scatter it into the winds."
[267] *Executive Order 11110 - Amendment of Executive Order No. 10289 as Amended, Relating to the Performance of Certain Functions Affecting the Department of the Treasury*, June 4, 1963, Gerhard Peters, The American Presidency Project
http://www.presidency.ucsb.edu/ws/?pid=59049
[268] *President John F. Kennedy Addresses The Secret Society Conspiracy*, Johnny Cirucci YouTube
https://www.youtube.com/watch?v=hkqMTmXmrEA&

[269] *The President and the Press: Address before the American Newspaper Publishers Association*, 27 April 1961
http://www.jfklibrary.org/Research/Research-Aids/JFK-Speeches/American-Newspaper-Publishers-Association_19610427.aspx
[270] *The Cutter Incident: How America's First Polio Vaccine Led to the Growing Vaccine Crisis*, Paul A. Offit, Yale University Press (2007), p. 80
[271] *Joan Rivers to the Sunday Times: Obama is "gay"...Michelle is a "tranny"*. Johnny Cirucci YouTube
https://www.youtube.com/watch?v=xaTvurvaWc8&
[272] I had intended to reference our first homosexual president calling his wife "Michael" but it's clear that when he was speaking to the Joint Ass-Kissers, he was talking about Admiral Ass-Kisser "Michael" Mullen. *Obama Refers to His Wife as "Michael"*, ShockDoctrin, YouTube
https://www.youtube.com/watch?&v=8cgk732vfGQ
[273] *Joan Rivers jokes Obama Is Gay, First Lady Is Transgender*, Lisa France, 7 July 2014, CNN
http://www.cnn.com/2014/07/04/showbiz/celebrity-news-gossip/joan-rivers-michelle-obama-gay-transgender/
[274] *Joan Rivers Vocal Problems—Was There Malpractice During Her Endoscopy?* Dr. Lillian Glass, 29 August 2014
http://drlillianglassbodylanguageblog.wordpress.com/2014/08/29/joan-rivers-vocal-problems-was-there-malpractice-during-her-endoscopy/
[275] *The Celebs Joan Rivers "Banned" From Her Funeral*, unattributed, 9 September 2014, the Sydney Morning Herald
http://www.smh.com.au/lifestyle/celebrity/the-celebs-joan-rivers-banned-from-her-funeral-20140909-10eik6.html

The other two were talk show host Chelsea Handler and pop slut "Adele". Never heard of "Chelsea Handler" but Rivers was spot on with the other two!!!

[276] *Target Patton*, Robert K. Wilcox, Regnery 2008
[277] *Douglas DeWitt Bazata, Artist And O.S.S. Officer, Dies at 88*, Eric Pace, 22 August 1999, NY Times
http://www.nytimes.com/1999/08/22/world/douglas-dewitt-bazata-artist-and-oss-officer-dies-at-88.html
[278] *General George S. Patton Was Assassinated To Silence His Criticism Of Allied War Leaders Claims New Book*, Tim Shipman, 20 December 2008, the Telegraph
http://www.telegraph.co.uk/news/worldnews/northamerica/usa/3869117/General-George-S.-Patton-was-assassinated-to-silence-his-criticism-of-allied-war-leaders-claims-new-book.html
[279] *Knights of Malta*, NewWorldOrder, reposted at bibliotecapleyades.net
http://www.bibliotecapleyades.net/sociopolitica/esp_sociopol_malta01.htm

Normally, I would not even think of using a completely anonymous and uncited blog *but* my next citation corroborates Donovan receiving the "Order of St. Sylvester" and I have a third that I am working on.

[280] *Order of St. Sylvester > Notable Members*, Wikipedia
https://en.wikipedia.org/wiki/Order_of_St._Sylvester#Notable_members
[281] *Pontifical Decorations*, Catholic Encyclopedia
http://www.newadvent.org/cathen/04667a.htm

[282] *American Democracy & the Vatican: Population Growth & National Security*, Stephen D. Mumford, Amer Humanist Association (1984), pp. 171-173

Mumford is a flaming Communist absolutely bent on mass genocide to fix the lie of "out of control population growth" and he laughably considers Rome as the enemy of both Communism and genocide!!! But as the Luciferians have shown themselves to be too smart by half in attempting to control both sides of the Hegelian conflict, we will exploit "Professor" Mumford's research to our advantage.

Chapter 4

War: What Is It Good For?

Bond: *I need a passport and matching credit cards.*

Mathis: *Why? MI6 run out of plastic?*

Bond: *Well, oddly, right now, you're the only person I think I can trust.*

Mathis: *That is odd.*
But I guess when one is young, it seems very easy to distinguish between right and wrong.
As one gets older, it becomes more difficult.
The villains and the heroes get all mixed up.

~ Quantum of Solace (2008)

Modern warfare between nation states is an enterprise wholly manufactured by the Luciferian Elite for three general purposes:

I. To make obscene amounts of money.

II. To slaughter the commoners and cull the "useless eaters[283]".

III. To punish the enemies of Rome.

Enemies have been created and crises have been contrived in order to motivate populations to give up rights and make drastic sacrifices for the Elite that they would not normally make.

Good Americans thank a soldier with no legs for endless deployments in the "War on Terror" to "protect our freedoms" as they hold their hands up in surrender to be humiliated by a naked body scanner at the airport.

—And it's all by design.

The Best Enemies Money Can Buy

How would it be possible for a man's company to be seized by the government for violating the *Trading with the Enemy Act*, having been caught sending goods directly to Nazi Germany during World War II as well as having been implicated in a military coup attempt against Franklin

Roosevelt, and yet have nothing happen to him?

We have just described Yale Skull and Bones alum, Connecticut Senator Prescott Bush, father of former CIA Director and Yale Skull and Bones alum George Herbert Walker Bush (also America's 41st President) and grandfather of Yale Skull and Bones alum George Walker Bush (America's 43rd President). Prescott Bush was directly implicated in empowering the 3rd Reich.[284]

With good reason does the CIA regularly recruit from Yale.[285,286]

Another prominent member of Yale's Skull and Bones Society is John Forbes Kerry.[287]

In 2007, while on the campaign trail, Kerry was asked a question at the University of Florida, Gainesville, that precipitated a violent response from school security. Video of the incident would go viral as the young man who asked Kerry the question would cry out to campus security during his manhandling, "Don't taze me, bro!"

Although many Americans are familiar with what happened to student Andrew William Meyer, very few know what it was that caused him to be immediately subdued.

—Meyer had asked Kerry about his involvement in Skull and Bones.[288]

In the 2004 Presidential election, America was given the electoral choice between John Forbes Kerry, Yale Skull and Bones '66, and George Walker Bush, Yale Skull and Bones '68.

Enough heads were being turned that CBS News risked a report on the subject. Correspondent Rebecca Leung interviewed Alexandra Robbins, author of *Secrets of the Tomb*[289], who remarked;

> *"Skull and Bones is so tiny. That's what makes this staggering," says Robbins. "There are only 15 people* [who get "tapped"] *a year, which means there are about 800 living members at any one time."*
>
> *But a lot of Bonesmen have gone on to positions of great power, which Robbins says is the main purpose of this secret society: to get as many members as possible into positions of power.*
>
> *"They do have many individuals in influential positions," says Robbins. "And that's why this is something that we need to know about."*

> *President Bush has tapped five fellow Bonesmen to join his administration. Most recently, he selected William Donaldson, Skull and Bones 1953, [to be] the head of the Securities and Exchange Commission. Like the President, he's taken the Bones oath of silence.*[290]

During that campaign, NBC journalist Tim Russert asked both candidates at different appearances on his *Meet the Press* about the affiliation which they both quickly dodged.

Russert died 4 years later at the young age of 58, of a heart attack, although his physician, Dr. Michael Newman, stated Russert's coronary artery disease was well under control via medication and exercise.[291]

Those exact words were used to describe Andrew Breitbart's physical condition before his heart attack.[292]

Breitbart was only 43 years old and on the verge of announcing very damaging information regarding Barack Obama's past.[293]

Shortly after the autopsy, Breitbart's coroner, Michael Cormier, died of arsenic poisoning.[294][i]

Follow the Money

War is business, and wherever the United States military has been sent, Elites within the "Super Class" have made astonishing, if despicable profits.

The German chemical company *Interessen-Gemeinschaft Farbenindustrie* ("IG Farben") was a powerful entity before and during WWII. Farben was the maker of "Zyklon B", the gas that slaughtered many Concentration Camp victims, Jews, Christians, homosexuals and gypsies.

It was also an organization that invested heavily in the Third Reich.[295]

Bayer and BASF are names many Americans recognize today. Those companies enabled the 3rd Reich and Adolf Hitler utilized their help in attaining critical synthetic forms of rubber and oil.[296]

As well as contributing several hundred thousand reichsmarks to the Nazi Party, IG Farben was a key player behind the Holocaust.

---

[i] We'll examine the use and roles of secret societies like the Skull and Bones more closely in Chapter 16, "Ancient Hate".

> *After a contract was initiated by a March 2, 1942 contract with "IG Farbenindustrie AG Auschwitz", the synthetic rubber and oil plant at Dwory (near Auschwitz III-Monowitz, which provided forced labor) was under construction in November 1943). The Buna Chemical Plant) produced synthetic oil and rubber (from coal) was the beginning of SS activity and camps in this location during the Holocaust. At its peak in 1944, this factory made use of 83,000 slave laborers. The pesticide Zyklon B, for which IG Farben held the patent, was manufactured by Degesch (Deutsche Gesellschaft für Schädlingsbekämpfung), which IG Farben owned 42.2 percent of (in shares) and which had IG Farben managers in its Managing Committee. Today, the plant operates as "Dwory S.A." ... ~ Holocaust Research.org[297]*

You would intuitively expect Farben to have been severely punished by the Allies after the war but that did not happen.

> *After the defeat of the Third Reich at the International Military Tribunal held in Nuremberg, the United States, as the occupying power, conducted trials against the top officials of three major industrial concerns—Krupp, Flick, and I. G. Farben. ...*
>
> *All the defendants were acquitted of the first count, nine were found guilty of the second. Krauch, Fritzter Meer – the board member responsible for the entire Buna production – Ambros, Butefisch and Durrfeld were found guilty of the third. ...*
>
> *The IGF plants located in the Soviet zone of occupation were nationalised, however, in the zones occupied by the Western powers no change of ownership took place.*
>
> *Basically the conglomerate was broken up into its original three major component parts – Bayer, BASF, and Hoechst – whose balance sheet by the end of the 1950's already exceeded that of the original IGF. ~ Holocaust Research.org[298]*

A former I.G. Farben salesman would later rise to be one of the most powerful men in the world, perhaps not by coincidence.

> *In the early 1940s, the I.G. Farben Chemical Company employed a Polish salesman who sold cyanide to the Nazis for use in Auschwitz. The same salesman also worked as a chemist in the manufacture of the poison gas. ... After the war the salesman, fearing for his life, joined the Catholic Church and was ordained a priest in 1946. One of his closest friends was Dr. Wolf Szmuness, the mastermind*

behind the November/78 to October/79 and March/80 to October/81 experimental hepatitis B vaccine trials conducted by the Center for Disease Control in New York, San Francisco and four other American cities that loosed the plague of AIDS upon the American people. The salesman was ordained Poland's youngest bishop in 1958. After a 30-day reign his predecessor was assassinated and our ex-cyanide gas salesman assumed the papacy as Pope John Paul II.

1990 is the right time with the right leaders: ex-chief of the Soviet secret police Mikhail Gorbachev, ex-chief of the CIA George Bush, ex-Nazi cyanide gas salesman Pope John Paul II, all bound by an unholy alliance to ring in the New World Order. ~ Behold A Pale Horse, Milton William Cooper[299]

Hoechst AG is another dark company and their latest invention is abortion in a bottle[300]—a pill that will kill an unborn child before there is need to go to a Planned Parenthood clinic. However, what is less well publicized are the terrible after-effects like a woman being unable to pass the body of her dead child and life-threatening infections resulting or serious internal bleeding occuring.[301]

Truly sick minds are responsible for this drug's name: 'R "U" 4 "86".

We Have Met the Enemy and He Works on Wall Street

Economist, historian, writer and Hoover Institute Fellow, Dr. Antony C. Sutton (1925-2002) found that the American I.G. Board of Directors held some interesting "interlocks" with other powerful companies.

Carl Bosch: Ford Motor Co. A-G

Edsel B. Ford: Ford Motor Co. Detroit

H.A. Metz: Director of I.G. Farben, Germany and Bank of Manhattan (U.S.)

C.E. Mitchell: Director of Federal Reserve Bank of N.Y. and National City Bank

Walter Teagle: U.S. Director Federal Reserve Bank of New York and Standard Oil of New Jersey[302]

Dr. Sutton noted that Walter Teagle and Standard Oil helped keep the German war effort afloat almost single-handedly.[303]

Standard Oil was founded by John David Rockefeller.[304]

Skull & Boned

The Bush family have been Elite power-players in American politics for generations and they have been vetted by the Yale Skull and Bones secret society.

Secret societies are gateways to power for the Elite, initiating them into a literal Luciferian agenda and blackmailing them with sexual, sadistic and satanic rituals.

> *The Bushes' ties to John D. Rockefeller and Standard Oil go back 100 years, when Rockefeller made Buckeye Steel Castings wildly successful by convincing railroads that carried their oil to buy heavy equipment from Buckeye. George H. Walker helped refurbish the Soviet oil industry in the 1920s, and Prescott Bush acquired experience in the international oil business as a 22-year director of Dresser Industries. George H.W. Bush, in turn, worked for Dresser and ran his own offshore oil-drilling business, Zapata Offshore. George W. Bush mostly raised money from investors for oil businesses that failed. Currently, the family's oil focus is principally in the Middle East.* ~ Kevin Philips, the LA Times[305]

Attached to Elite families like the Bushes are perennial apparatchiks that roam the halls of power regardless of who the figurehead is. Two such men are Donald Rumsfeld and Dick Cheney; chief architects behind the "War on Terror".

By 2011, the "War on Terror" killed 225,000 human beings with 365,000 wounded to include 6,000 of America's sons as well as a $5,000,000,000,000 debt. That breaks down to each American owing $16,000.[306]

Today, the military/industrial complex has direct access into the veins of Lady Liberty.

> *The Halliburton Company, the Dallas oil services company bedeviled lately by an array of accounting and business issues, is benefiting very directly from the United States efforts to combat terrorism.*
>
> *From building cells for detainees at Guantánamo Bay in Cuba to feeding American troops in Uzbekistan, the Pentagon is increasingly relying on a unit of Halliburton called KBR, sometimes*

referred to as Kellogg Brown & Root.

Although the unit has been building projects all over the world for the federal government for decades, the attacks of Sept. 11 have led to significant additional business. ...

The government business has been well timed for Halliburton, whose stock price has tumbled almost two-thirds in the last year because of concerns about its asbestos liabilities, sagging profits in its energy business and an investigation by the Securities and Exchange Commission into its accounting practices back when Vice President Dick Cheney ran the company. ~ Jeff Gerth and Don Van Natta, NY Times[307]

Gerald Ford (who spied on the Warren Commission as a member and fed intelligence back to Lyndon Baines Johnson and J. Edgar Hoover[308]) stands with his Chief of Staff Donald Rumsfeld and Assistant Chief of Staff Dick Cheney on 28 April 1975.

Antony Sutton wrote exhaustively on how secret societies conspired with Wall Street to empower America's greatest enemies.

In the introduction to his work *America's Secret Establishment*, Dr. Sutton named names.

We trace the extraordinary Skull and Bones influence in a major Hegelian conflict: Naziism vs. Communism. Skull and Bones members were in the dominant decision-making positions—Bush, Harriman, Stimson, Lovett, and so on—all Bonesmen, and instrumental in guiding the conflict through use of "right" and "left." They financed and encouraged the growths of both philosophies and controlled the outcome to a significant extent. This was aided by the "reductionist" division in science, the opposite of historical "wholeness." By dividing science and learning into narrower and narrower segments, it became easier to control the whole through the parts.[309]

Not only did Prescott Bush get away with high treason, repeatedly, but two successive generations of the Bushes ruled over America from the White House with more on the way.

To those who rule on behalf of their benefactors to harm and enslave America, it's all a big game. The names change each round but they still stay the same.

Prescott Sheldon Bush and his protégé Richard Milhous Nixon

Never mind the potential for name fatigue.
Former U.S. President George W. Bush likes the idea of a 2016 presidential matchup between his Republican brother Jeb Bush and Democrat Hillary Clinton.

In an interview as part of the rollout of a book he has written about his father, former President George H.W. Bush, Bush said he is urging Jeb to try to make it three Bush presidents. ~ Steve Holland, Reuters[310]

The propaganda they receive from eager sycophants in the media is indescribable.

Why Hillary vs. Jeb Would Be Great for America

They're both qualified, respectful of each other (shocker!), and represent the vast majority of middle America. So what's not to like about another Clinton/Bush race for 2016?

When you mention the prospect of Clinton vs. Bush 2016 a funny thing happens.

First, there is the reflexive response: "Oh no, not again. We don't need more dynastic politics in this country."

But upon further reflection, you realize Jeb Bush vs. Hillary Clinton would be a great race and actually good for the country. ~ Mark McKinnon, the Daily Beast[311]

The Bushes and Clintons "represent Middle America" the way Louis XIV and Marie Antoinette "represented" the French peasantry. They would be "good for the country" the way Jack Kevorkian was good for his patients.

When we catch them cavorting and having fun with each other on the golf course[312] (after all the harm they've done), we are supposed to be surprised.

George W. Bush Says Bill Clinton Is His "Brother From Another Mother"

An unlikely bromance

Former Presidents George W. Bush and Bill Clinton broadcast their unlikely bromance on social media Tuesday when Clinton posted a picture of himself reading Bush's new book.

Clinton's #HowAreYouStillNotOnTwitter hashtag is a reference to his President's Day tweet this year, which ribbed the younger Bush for not having an account. This time, Bush responded. He posted Clinton's tweet on Instagram with the caption, "Thanks, 42! Hope you like the book about your pal, #41. #HowAreYouSTILLNotOnInstagram #PresidentialGrammers #BrotherFromAnotherMother".

This is not the first public display of affection between the two former presidents. Clinton often refers to himself as the "black sheep son" of the Bush family, and Bush challenged Clinton to the ALS Ice Bucket Challenge earlier this year. Their bipartisan friendship is all the more remarkable given that Clinton beat Bush's father, President George H. W. Bush, in the 1992 election, ousting Bush Sr. after only one term in office. ~ Tessa Berenson, Time[313]

It was the CIA who built an empire for the Bushes and Clintons on a mountain of cocaine.

This could only be possible if a malignant international agency were at work pulling the strings.

The Fourth Reich

The worst political plagues of modernity—from Nazism to Communism—were birthed by the Society of Jesus.

> [Wherever] *a totalitarian movement erupts, whether Communist or Nazi, a Jesuit can be found in the role of "adviser" or leader... ~ The Federal Reserve Conspiracy & Rockefellers*, Emanuel Josephson[314]

Adolf Hitler's *"tour de force"*, *Mein Kampf* was so heavily edited by a vehemently anti-Semitic Jesuit priest it was practically ghost-written by him.

Otto Strasser was a key figure in the Nazi Party of the 1930's. During Adolf Hitler's brief stint in prison, Strasser's brother Gregor shared rulership of the party with Gottfried Feder. It was an unhappy partnership with the Strasser brothers emphasizing the *socialist* part of the National Socialist Party inasmuch as they pushed for urbanization of the commoners and state control of land[315]. They were true Luciferian visionaries and their efforts would later be renewed under United Nations "Agenda 21".

Strasser would write an exposé on his time with Adolf Hitler titled *Hitler and I*.[316]

In it, he made the astounding statement that *Mein Kampf* was a chaotic mess of rants that was completely reorganized by a Jesuit priest.

> *In its original form Mein Kampf was a veritable hotch-potch of commonplaces, schoolboy reminiscences, personal opinions, expressions of personal animosity. ...*
>
> *The whole was written in the style of a fifth-form schoolboy, and a not very intelligent one at that. Only a single chapter, if I am to believe Father Staempfle, who twice revised the entire manuscript, was really original. This was the chapter on propaganda.*
>
> *Good Father Staempfle, a priest of great learning, editor of a paper at Miessbach, spent months rewriting and editing Mein Kampf. He eliminated the more flagrant inaccuracies and the excessively childish platitudes. Hitler never forgave Father Staempfle for getting to know his weaknesses so well. He had him murdered by a "special death squad" on the night of June 30, 1934.*[317]

Wikipedia *Deutsch* confirms this.

Bernhardt Staempfle S.J.

Fr. Bernhard Rudolf Staempfle (17 April 1882 in Munich – 1 July 1934 in the Dachau concentration camp near Munich) (Pseudonyms: Redivivus;) Spectator Germaniae) was a German religious, theologian and publicist. He was especially known as the editor of the anti-Semitic newspaper Miesbacher Anzeiger. The research part, accepted that he was an important employee of Adolf Hitler's book Mein Kampf.[318]

The existence of the anti-Semitic magazine *Miesbacher Anzeiger* is confirmed via the *Essays of German Jewish Studies*.[319]

In his book *Hitler Speaks*, reformed Nazi Hermann Rauschning stated that Hitler drew his inspiration for order and regime from both the Jesuits and the Vatican.[j]

> — *"...I have learned especially from the Jesuit Order. Moreover, as far as I remember, Lenin did the same...there has never been anything more grandiose on the earth than the hierarchical organization of the Catholic Church. Directly I carried much of this organization into my own party..."*

> — *"You took the Church's hierarchical organization, and Freemasonry designing an Order, with his vow of obedience, discretion and with its esoteric doctrine that manifests itself in the gradual initiation. ... But what have you taken in the 'Protocols of the Elders of Zion'?" I asked.*[320]

The Jesuits would have much to do with the "Protocols of Zion" as well.

This was a mutually-aggrandizing arrangement and the Nazi Party was empowered on the back of the Catholic Church.

> *...Hitler came to power on the back of Catholic support. Catholic leaders never supported the Weimar experiment with democracy, which they saw as a legacy of the Enlightenment and the* Kulturkampf. *The "Enabling Act," which was the legal instrument giving Hitler the power to rule by decree, passed by the Reichstag*

---

[j] Please forgive the choppy translation from French to English.

> *on March 24, 1933, was able to squeak through only after it was endorsed by Monsignor Ludwig Kaas, the leader of the Center Party. Kaas acted in coordination with the German bishops. Four days later, on March 28, the German Bishops rescinded their ban on Nazi party membership. On April 1, Cardinal Adolf Bertram of Breslau addressed German Catholics in a letter, warning them "to reject as a matter of principle all illegal or subversive activities." ~ Pope Benedict XVI: A Biography of Joseph Ratzinger*, John Allen[321]

In a series of policies enacted between 1871 to 1878 known as Kulturkampf ("cultural struggle"), Otto von Bismarck expelled the Jesuits from Prussia and Germany and did all he could to mitigate interference in German affairs by the Vatican.

> *In Germany, partly in response to the "divisive" dogma of* [Vatican I's Papal] *infallibility, Bismarck began his* Kulturkampf *("culture struggle"), a policy of persecution against Catholicism. Religious instruction came under state control and religious orders were forbidden to teach; the Jesuits were banished; seminaries were subjected to state interference; Church property came under the control of lay committees; civil marriage was introduced in Prussia. Bishops and clergy resisting* Kulturkampf *legislation were fined, imprisoned, exiled. ~ Hitler's Pope*, John Cornwell[322]

These slights put Germany in the crosshairs of the most dangerous people on Earth: the Jesuits.

The 3rd Reich was cunningly created by the Company and then aimed at one of Rome's most hated enemies—the Jews. Their "chastisement" was prolonged by Papal puppets like 33° Freemason Franklin Roosevelt who returned fleeing Jewish refugees back to Europe and kept rail lines sending Jews to their deaths free from bombardment.[323]

As with any movement, it required the will of the people to function. Because Fascism masked its totalitarian designs by appealing to nationalist identity amongst the citizenry, it has been purposefully mislabeled as a "Right-wing" ideology. This couldn't be further from the truth.

The key word in defining what "Nazism" was/is, is *"socialism"*.

> *National Socialism, German* Nationalsozialismus, *also called Nazism or Naziism, totalitarian movement led by Adolf Hitler as head of the Nazi Party in Germany. In its intense nationalism, mass appeal, and dictatorial rule, National Socialism shared many elements with Italian fascism.* ~ Encyclopædia Britannica[324]

It was as convenient as it was powerful in the hands of the Holy See.

> *Remember that Hitler and Mussolini remained Catholics to the end and were never excommunicated from the Church. So did thousands of the worst Nazi war criminals, whom the Vatican smuggled out of Europe into safe havens in South America. Such archcriminals are honored with Catholic funerals and, like Mafia members, die with the assurance that their Church will continue to say Masses in order to get them out of purgatory and eventually into heaven.* ~ *A Woman Rides The Beast*, Dave Hunt [325]

The foundational component of Fascism is the co-opting of major industries, manufacturing, banking and private wealth.

But Fascism is profoundly Luciferian and shares all of the same agenda of the original humanistic rebellion from Babylon through Communism to the death and rebirth of the muslim Caliphate—all manipulated by Superclass families[k], Rome and, ultimately, satan.

> *In place of Christianity, [Fascism] offered a new religion of the divinized state and the nation as an organic community.*
>
> *...it is simply a fact that in the 1920s fascism and fascistic ideas were very popular on the American left.*
>
> *[Roosevelt]'s defenders openly admitted their admiration of fascism. Rexford Guy Tugwell, an influential member of [Roosevelt]'s Brain Trust, said of Italian Fascism, "It's the cleanest, neatest most efficiently operating piece of social machinery I've ever seen. It makes me envious." "We are trying out the economics of Fascism without having suffered all its social or political ravages," proclaimed the New Republic's editor George Soule, an enthusiastic supporter of the [Roosevelt] administration.*[12]
>
> *Fascism, like Progressivism and Communism, is expansionist because it sees no natural boundary to its ambitions. For violent variants, like so-called Islamofascism, this is transparently obvious. But Progressivism, too, envisions a New World Order.* ~ *Liberal Fascism*, Jonah Goldberg[326]

When the people rise up and defeat the (pseudo) right hand of Fascism, the Elite raise up the Left hand.

---

[k] "Superclass" is a term coined by former Kissinger Associates managing director David Rothkopf in his 2008 book of the same name to describe the 6,000 some-odd individuals who have the wealth to immediately effect the political policies of nation states.

Former UK Minister of Parliament and Cabinet Member Charles Higham was shocked by the depth of collusion from Western monied interests to create the Nazi threat and subsequently fuel the post-war rise of Communism. He wrote in his book *Trading With The Enemy*:

> *A presidential edict, issued six days after December 7, 1941, actually set up the legislation whereby licensing arrangements for trading with the enemy could officially be granted. Often during the years after Pearl Harbor the government permitted such trading. ...*
>
> *As for Roosevelt, the Sphinx still keeps his secrets. That supreme politician held all of the forces of collusion and betrayal in balance, publicly praising those executives whom he knew to be questionable. Before Pearl Harbor, he allowed such egregious executives as James D. Mooney of General Motors and William Rhodes Davis of the Davis Oil Company to enjoy pleasant tête-à-têtes with Hitler and Göring, while maintaining a careful record of what they were doing. During the war, J. Edgar Hoover, Adolf A. Berle, Henry Morgenthau, and Harold Ickes kept the President fully advised of all internal and external transgressions. ...*
>
> *Why did even the loyal figures of the American government allow these transactions to continue after Pearl Harbor?*[327]

Minister Higham was as perplexed in 1983 as Americans are today. How can such poisonous policies promoted by puppets and politicians not be proscribed and prosecuted by Patriots?

—because they're promulgated by the Papacy.

Interlocked

One of the men who funded both the Nazi and Soviet threats to the West was Henry Ford.

> *A post-war Congressional subcommittee investigating American support for the Nazi military effort described the manner in which the Nazis succeeded in obtaining U.S. technical and financial assistance as "quite fantastic".*[tt] ...
>
> *At the outbreak of the war Ford-Werke placed itself at the disposal of the* Wehrmacht *for armament production. ... ~ Wall Street and the Rise of Hitler*, Antony C. Sutton[328]

Ford-Werke's American holders were a lifeline that kept the industrial legs of the cooperative effort alive.

It was working so well, Ford extended help to Germany's old ally, Soviet Russia.

> *A U.S. Air Force bombing intelligence report written in 1943 noted that,*
>
>> *Principal wartime activities [of the Ford plant] are probably manufacture of light trucks and of spare parts for all the Ford trucks and cars in service in Axis Europe (including captured Russian Molotovs).*[16]
>
> *The Russian Molotovs were of course manufactured by the Ford-built works at Gorki, Russia. In France during the war, passenger automobile production was entirely replaced by military vehicles and for this purpose three large additional buildings were added to the Poissy factory. The main building contained about 500 machine tools, "all imported from the United States and including a fair sprinkling of the more complex types, such as Gleason gear cutters, Bullard automatics and Ingersoll borers.*[17] ~ Sutton [329]

Investigations into criminal activities of high treason were made impossible as America's law enforcement bodies were as equally co-opted as her political ones.

Ratlines

At the conclusion of WWII, Nazis leaders were given safe passage to South America by the power of the Vatican.

> *Germany is fighting to keep sealed the Adolf Eichmann files detailing the years the Holocaust chief logistical organiser spent on the run before he was captured by Mossad agents.*
>
> *Those hoping to have a 50-year secrecy order overturned believe the government is embarrassed by details within that may prove German and Vatican officials colluded in his escape and freedom.*
>
> *Indeed, the Church's practise of protecting its own perpetrators of vicious crimes has already been well established with the tragic revelations of thousands of victims of child sex abuse by cleric paedophiles.*
>
> *For the current papacy under the German pope, Benedict XVI, the 4,500 page Eichmann dossier could be the "smoking gun" that would shoot down his plans to canonize Pope Pius XII (1939-58), aka "Hitler's Pope."* ~ Julian Kossoff, the Daily Telegraph[330]

Joseph Ratzinger (Pope Benedict XVI) was, himself, a member of the Nazi Youth. This is usually spun to focus on how the Ratzinger family suffered while resisting the Nazis.[331]

Upon his ascension to Holy See, Cardinal Ratzinger's Nazi past did cause some discomfort. Not surprisingly, Leftist Jews were still eager to recognize him[332] in the best interest of "interfaith dialogue".[333]

In fact, former Israeli President Shimon Peres recently beseeched the current Jesuit Pope, Jorge Mario Bergoglio, to create an ecumenical "United Nations of Religions" under his authority[334]. Skeptics are concerned that Peres was put up to the idea by Papal insiders for cover.

From Rome to Rio

Horst Wagner was a Nazi that had the blood of at least 350,000 Jews on his hands.

In her book *Beloved Criminal*[335], Gisela Heidenreich writes of the monster who, at one time, wooed her mother.

> *After escaping from a Nuremberg jail in 1948, he later explained to Heidenreich's mother how he was aided on his way to South America on the so-called Kloster Line, being given sanctuary in a number of convents and holy orders in Austria before heading to Rome.*
>
> *There the German bishop Alois Hudal, priest-confessor to the German Catholic community in the city, arranged for him to get a Red Cross passport in 1951. ...*
>
> *Hudal also arranged the paperwork for Franz Stangl, the commandent of the extermination camps of Sobibor and Treblinka, to flee to Brazil on a Red Cross passport using Vatican funds. ...*
>
> *Wagner settled in Bariloche, 1,000 miles south of Buenos Aires on the edge of Patagonia, and celebrated weekly in Bavarian-style houses with old S.S. comrades, drinking beer and singing the marching songs of the lost regime.*[336]

Pope Pius XII has been ruefully nicknamed "Hitler's Pope" and it does little to heal old wounds when Catholic leaders continually petition for him to be canonized. Even recently, Pope Francis has stated that he's considering it.[337]

Further proof of war being used to punish the enemies of Rome resides in a 1999 lawsuit.

Nazi war criminals helped ease the way for their expatriation with gold they stole from their victims. Surviving members of a forgotten holocaust in Croatia attempted to get justice from the Catholic Church.

> ... the "hidden Holocaust" which, though well-known to scholars, is rarely, mentioned elsewhere, presumably because of the active involvement of the Catholic Church, which used the terror to win an estimated 200,000 to 300,000 new converts.[4] The current lawsuit is on behalf of three groups of victims in the Croatian Holocaust: the Serbs, who were obliged to wear blue armbands marked with a "P" for Orthodox (Pravoslavac), the Jews, who had to wear the Star of David, and the Roma (whose extermination by the Nazis is called the Porajmos). ...no serious historian disputes the claimants' account of the origin of the "victim gold":
>
>> Serbians, Jews, and the Roma were slaughtered in their villages after unspeakable tortures or burned alive in their churches. Those that were not murdered were expelled to Serbia proper after being despoiled of all their property or forcibly converted to the Roman Catholic faith by Franciscan and Roman Catholic clergy. Many were used as slave labourers. The remaining people were taken to concentration camps where the majority perished.[5]
>
> ~ Lawsuit: Nazi Gold Funded Vatican Ratlines, Concordat Watch[338]

A United States Federal Appeals court has dismissed the case claiming that the Vatican bank is "immune" from such prosecution.[339]

Rome does, indeed, have a long arm.

Free Reign

In 1933, Prescott Bush co-ordinated with several large Wall Street firms and attempted a military coup against the Leftist Freemason Franklin Roosevelt.[340,341] It was lose/lose for America; Fascists if they win, Communists if they lose. Unfortunately for the conspirators, they chose the wrong man for the job.

Major General Smedley D. Butler was the only Marine Corps officer to be awarded not one, but *two* Congressional Medals of Honor. He had seen more than his fair share of bloodshed in the Banana Wars where Wall Street fruit interests used Marines to strong-arm themselves massive profits in

Central and South America. Butler wrote a blistering indictment of the profiteering which he delivered as a speech and later a 51-page pamphlet published by Round Table Press titled appropriately *War Is A Racket* in 1935. His sentiments then easily read as if spoken by veterans today, broken and disenfranchised by the never-ending "War on Terror"—but only if you multiply Butler's figures by several times.

> *The normal profits of a business concern in the United States are six, eight, ten, and sometimes twelve percent. But war-time profits — ah! that is another matter — twenty, sixty, one hundred, three hundred, and even eighteen hundred per cent — the sky is the limit.*
> ...
>
> *Take our friends the du Ponts, the powder people... They were a patriotic corporation.*
>
> *...let's look at their average yearly profit during the war years, 1914 to 1918. Fifty-eight million dollars a year profit we find! ... An increase in profits of more than 950 per cent. ...*
>
> *How many of these war millionaires shouldered a rifle? How many of them dug a trench? How many of them knew what it meant to go hungry in a rat-infested dug-out? ...*

But Major General Butler refused to be the front man for the coup against Roosevelt and in 1933 he turned informant on Prescott Bush and co-conspirators like Ambassador to the Soviet Union Averell Harriman (Skull and Bones class of 1913) who's Guarantee Trust made profits off of both the Nazis and the Communists.

No action was taken.

Dull-es a Knife in the Back

Playing the game of shuffling dictators in South America for wealthy interests was really Rome's forté.

Everette Howard Hunt, Jr. was the CIA's key agent for a host of important assignments in the 60's from assassinating a sitting President[342] to framing another President in the Watergate burglary.[343]

He also had a hand in overthrowing the government of Guatemala in 1954.

Then-President Jacobo Arbenz had opened elections to all parties and had even gone so far as to take back some of the land stolen by wealthy international interests. At that time, 3% of Guatemalan landowners held 70% of the land so Arbenz nationalized over 1.5 million acres—including land belonging to his own family—and redistributed it to *peóns* (peasants) and *campesinos* (farmers).[344]

The problem for President Arbenz was that much of that land belonged to the United Fruit Company who quickly called in some favors from the Dulles brothers.[345]

Everything you need to know about Dwight Eisenhower's Secretary of State John Foster Dulles or his Director of the CIA Allen Dulles can be found in John Dulles' son, (Allen's nephew)—Avery Dulles.

Avery was a Jesuit priest and a Laurence J. McGinley Professor of Religion and Society at Fordham University[346]. He would eventually become a Cardinal in a move even the press was shocked by.

> *When Pope John Paul II designated dozens of new cardinals in early 2001, there were three from the United States. Archbishops Edward M. Egan of New York and Theodore E. McCarrick of Washington were unsurprising choices; it is common for heads of archdioceses to be given red hats. But the selection of Father Dulles was extraordinary. Although his was an influential voice in American Catholicism, he was not even a bishop, let alone an archbishop.*
>
> *The appointment was widely seen as a reward for his loyalty to the pope, but also an acknowledgment of his work in keeping lines of communication open between the Vatican and Catholic dissenters in America.* ~ the New York Times[347]

Avery Dulles had lines of communication that were critical to Rome.

The Dulles brothers were powerful friends for anyone on Wall Street to have and it spelled the end of the Arbenz Administration in 1954.

As E. Howard Hunt explained, the *real* authority behind "regime change" was the Catholic Church.

> *We had gotten the "OK" from Cardinal Spellman* [in New York] *to go ahead with this and I wouldn't presume to trace the lines of authority within the Catholic Church—how they get their information that they do. We've always said, in an admiring way, that the Jesuits form the greatest intelligence service in the world. Always have.* ~ *A Coup Made in America*[348]

Certainly, if one were interested in intelligence, there would be no better organization behind the enterprise than the Vatican.

> *The Vatican's constituency of 980 million followers is at least three times the number of citizens in any Western democracy and is exceeded only by the population of China. Even more important, these 980 million people are scattered throughout the world, many of them holding high political, military, and commercial positions in non-Catholic countries. Moreover, the pope has thousands of secret agents worldwide. They include Jesuits, the Knights of Columbus, Knights of Malta, Opus Dei, and others. The Vatican's Intelligence Service and its field resources are second to none. ~ A Woman Rides The Beast*, Dave Hunt[349]

Francis Cardinal Spellman had been carefully situated to oversee the United States strategies for World War II.

> *New York's Cardinal Francis Spellman, the most powerful cleric in U.S. history, maintained control of the U.S. Catholic war effort during World War II. He was named head of the U.S. military chaplains and was deeply involved in post-war measures against the Soviets. Spellman was also instrumental in selection of South Vietnamese president and devout Catholic, Ngo Dinh Diem. ~ The Neo-Catholics*, Betty Clermont[350]

He would later be responsible for America's premier dead-end, self-imposed bloodletting; the Vietnam War.

Cardinal Spellman's War

If ever there was proof of a malignant entity running and ruining America from afar, it is Vietnam.

The Vietnam war was a veritable meatgrinder that destroyed the finances and lives of both Middle Class America and all but the Catholic Elite of Vietnam.

> *The Defense Department reported that the overall cost of the Vietnam war was $173 billion (equivalent to $770 billion in 2003 dollars). Veteran's benefits and interest would add another $250 billion ($1 Trillion in 2003 dollars).*
>
> *But the real cost of the war was its impact on the economy, including agriculture. ~ The Vietnam War*, Living History Farm.org[351]

Total Number of Deaths in the Vietnam War

Estimates of the number of casualties vary, with the Vietnamese government suggesting as many as 3.1 million violent war deaths, Vietnamese and foreigners, soldiers included.[1][2] A detailed demographic study calculated 791,000–1,141,000 war-related Vietnamese deaths, both soldiers and civilians, for all of Vietnam from 1965 to 1975. The study came up with a most likely Vietnamese death toll of 882,000, which included 655,000 adult males (above 15 years of age), 143,000 adult females, and 84,000 children.[3] ~ Wikipedia[352]

For Rome, punishing heretic Vietnamese and Protestant Americans for almost 20 years was a master stroke and the man who wielded that stroke for the Holy See was Francis Cardinal Spellman.

FRANCIS CARDINAL SPELLMAN, who was Archbishop of New York from 1939 until his death in 1967, was a major figure in American political life and the history of the Roman Catholic Church. In both the political and the ecclesiastical arenas, he sought power avidly and used it aggressively. He was the confidant, adviser and sometime agent of Presidents from Franklin D. Roosevelt to Lyndon B. Johnson. And he was influential in New York politics. As the Catholic military vicar to the American armed forces—a

---

Francis Cardinal Spellman

The office of "Cardinal" was created by the Vatican based upon senior priests who voted on who would be the next Pope—*cardo* being Latin for "principle axis."

But Rome wanted to emphasize the *temporal* or Earthly authority of such a caste and presented them as a European would present a member of the knighthood—"Alfred **Lord** Tenyson"... "Edward **Cardinal** Egan."

This practice was de-emphasized after Vatican II but the tradition still exists when the point needs to be made.

SOURCES:

Cardinal (Catholicism), Wikipedia.org
http://en.wikipedia.org/wiki/Cardinal_(Catholicism)

Cardinal Sins, Merrill Perlman, 21 February 2012, Columbia Journalism Review
http://www.cjr.org/language_corner/cardinal_sins.php

post separate from but complementary to his position as Archbishop—he supervised chaplains around the world and was a familiar visitor to battlefields during World War II and the wars in Korea and Vietnam. ~ the New York Times[353]

Media analyst and author Avro Manhattan (1914–1990) was a staunch critic of Papal manipulation in world affairs.[354]

Manhattan disclosed the shocking evidence that Rome used assassination and clandestine agents to facilitate the Vietnam War in an agenda to embroil Orthodox Russia and Protestant America in a Rome revenge scheme.

Although Manhattan believed that the Vatican and her emissaries truly wanted to stamp out Communism, this is proven to be completely false as the war policy *guaranteed* no clear victory, only ongoing bloodshed.

Why would the Holy See want to vanquish the most successful method of population control and enslavement (Communism) it had created? [italics suspended]

> In 1947, the Cold War began. Hatred against Communist Russia was promoted, headed by the Vatican which sent a statue of our Lady of Fatima, with her "message" on a "pilgrimage" around the world. She was sent from country to country to arouse anti-Russian odium. Whole governments welcomed her.
>
> ...The Fatima cult is derived from the alleged appearance of the Virgin Mary to three sickly children at Fatima, Portugal, in 1917. With the appearance of Bolshevik Russia and world communism, the cult soon was transformed into an ideological crusade. It was used extensively in the anti-Russian ideological war carried out by Pius XII, Cardinal Spellman and John Foster Dulles. ...
>
> The new Catholic Secretary of the U.S. Navy [Francis Matthews], strangely enough, soon afterwards began unusually active contacts with other prominent American Catholics. Among these, Father Walsh, Jesuit Vice-President of Georgetown University[1]; Cardinal Spellman, the head of the American Legion; the leaders of the Catholic War Veterans and with Senator McCarthy, the arch-criminal senator, who upon the advice of a Catholic priest, was just beginning his infamous campaign which was to half paralyze the U.S. for some years to come. ...

---

[1] You'll see a lot more on Georgetown.

Jesuit Father Walsh, the foremost Catholic authority in the U.S. and a former Vatican Agent in Russia (1925), told the American people that "President Truman would be morally justified to take defensive measures proportionate to the danger." Which, of course, meant the use of the atom bomb.[7] When the U.S. went ahead with the manufacture of the hydrogen bomb, even the Chairman of the Atomic Commission, Senator Brian MacMahon, shrank in horror at the prospect of the sure massacre of fifty million people with such a monster weapon.[8]

...the U.S. Secretary of State, John Foster Dulles ... was the center of powerful anti-Communist groups and anti-Russian lobbies, whose chief objective was in total harmony with that of the Vatican. These groups were disproportionally influenced by the Catholic elements and with few notable exceptions, were supported by the Catholic Church in the U.S.

When therefore, the Vietnam problem came increasingly to the fore both the Vatican and the U.S. focused their joint activities toward that country. The chief formulators of the strategy were Secretary of State John Foster Dulles in the diplomatic field, and Cardinal Spellman in the ecclesiastical. The importance of the latter was paramount, since Cardinal Spellman was the linchpin between Washington and the Vatican. This was so because Spellman had the ear not only of powerful politicians and military men in the U.S. but equally that of the Pope, a personal friend of his. ~ *Vietnam: Why Did We Go?* Avro Manhattan[355]

Commiserating Catholic Communists In Castro's Cuba

How could America suffer nearly two decades of bloodletting, stalemate and war profiteering at the hands of tiny Vietnam?

—Because the Jesuit "Father General" wanted it that way.

How could Fidel Castro, still alive at this writing, survive the anti-Communist wrath of the Central Intelligence Agency who had slaughtered a sitting President in broad daylight? This is the same organization that had weaponized cancer and heart-attack guns[356] at their disposal since the early 60's.

—Because Castro was *created* by the Society of Jesus and they run the CIA. [italics suspended]

History confirms that Fidel Castro is an undercover Jesuit. ... The fidelity of this man is to serve the will of the General of the Jesuits (Society of Jesus), based in The Vatican. ...

Fidel Castro attended three Jesuit institutions [to include the] *Colegio Lasalle* and *Colegio Dolores*.

He attended a Jesuit university in "preparatory studies" — ... what we might call a program of "General Studies" — at Bethlehem College. "General Studies" because, after enrollment there, he went to law school.

After graduating from law school [he joined the] Orthodox Christian Democratic Party ... [which] is the Roman Catholic party. ...

Castro was obviously working full for Jesuits when he joined the Christian Democratic Party as a young lawyer. By the time of the Cuban revolution in 1958-59, the Jesuits in Latin America were Marxist-Leninist ideology...

... in 1963, the Jesuits became fanatical far-left Communists, led by Pedro Arrupe, a Marxist and a great supporter of Fidel Castro. [Fr. Malachi] Martin documented in his book "The Jesuits and the Betrayal of the Roman Catholic Church" ... how Jesuits proceeded to foment Communist revolutions throughout Latin America and Africa with the help of Castro. ~ *Fidel Castro – Perfil de un Jesuita Clandestino*, Espada del Espíritu[357]

Once Castro was thoroughly trained, his Spanish Jesuit handler Armando Llorente was "exiled" from Cuba although this was for show as Castro never truly fell out of favor with Rome. Llorente (who died in 2007 at 91) would tell Spanish media that he waited in exile for Fidel to repent.[358]

As further theater, Pope John XXIII "excommunicated" Castro in 1962 but the official announcement was made by Dino Staffa, the "Secretary of the Congregation for Seminaries"[359]. Staffa was not the official representative of Vatican authority from one sovereign state to another.

The show began to wane by 1998 when Pope John Paul II visited the tiny nation[360]. After Castro retired and left Cuba to the care of his brother Raul, the mask came off entirely. Benedict XVI openly met with the Communist dictator and "slammed [the] U.S. embargo."[361]

The Jesuits and 9/11

On September 11th, 2001, two planes made architectural engineering history by causing three massive buildings to pancake into their own footprint; World Trade Center 1, 2 and 7.[362]

That morning, Vice President Dick Cheney (former Chairman and CEO of Halliburton) gave orders that at least one underling felt obliged to question, according to the Congressional testimony of Transportation Secretary Norman Mineta who was in the room at the time. Mineta assumed these were orders to stand down from shooting the jetliner that supposedly hit the Pentagon.[363]

On September 10th, 2001, Defense Secretary Donald Rumsfeld made the shocking announcement that he had "lost" $2,300,000,000,000.[364]

Rumsfeld was attending Law School at Georgetown in 1956[365] when he was "inspired" to jump into politics

When something struck the Pentagon on September 11th, the location of the damage was Budget and Accounting[366]. There is no video footage of an aircraft hitting the Pentagon and the flightpath presented to the American public for Flight 77 (a number significant to mystics) by government sources suggests a near inhuman accomplishment by a highly-trained, expert multi-engine pilot.[367,368]

The majority of the 9/11's Islamist hijackers were from Saudi Arabia with at least 5 having received flight training directly from U.S. military installations.[369]

Rather than focus on the involvement of supposed ally Saudi Arabia in the worst terror event on American soil, the Bush/Cheney/Rumsfeld administration sent the United States military to Afghanistan to guard opium fields[370] and oversee a massive increase in crop yield.[371,372]

Over a decade later, Congress finally addressed 28 pages of the "9/11 Commission" report that had been "classified" due to how badly they implicated Saudi Arabia[373]. Critics saw this as a bait & switch distraction. Increasing numbers of American were beginning to question the official 9/11 narrative. American insiders implicated in the conspiracy were willing to sell out lesser international players, especially if there was little risk to them being ousted or prosecuted.

"Something Far Worse"

Right after 9/11, thirteen members of the bin Laden family were secretly escorted back to Saudi Arabia on one of America's Presidential aircraft.[374]

Former Vice President, Dick Cheney, recently promised something far worse than 9/11 was on the horizon for the United States.[375]

In September of 2013, nuclear weapons were transferred from military facilities in Texas to South Carolina "off the record".

Shortly after that, South Carolina Republican Senator (and reputed closet homosexual[376]) Lindsey Graham spoke to media about how America was under the threat of nuclear terrorism from Syria. He specifically mentioned New York City or Charleston as targets.[377]

This may have been the kindling for the most devastating false flag in human history except military insiders turned whistleblower and gave independent media the story.[378]

Since then there have been repeated purges of leadership guarding America's nukes.[379,380] It seems a nuclear false flag attack is high on the agenda of those in control of the United States.

The plan for a nuclear false flag attack on America was recently confirmed by world-renown hacker Marcel-Lehel "Guccifer" Lazar—the Romanian who broke into the personal e-mail accounts of Colin Powell, George W. Bush and several government agencies. Lazar claimed the targets he saw were Chicago and an unnamed city in Pennsylvania.

Not surprisingly, he's in prison.[381]

Such devastation would not have bothered Barack Obama as he's already stated America could easily "absorb another 9/11".[382]

This is who has been chosen as America's leadership.

Commissioned

The 9/11 Commission seemed to have the same agenda as the Warren Commission—obfuscate the truth to hide high treason conducted by the CIA (and the authority behind them, Rome).

The only thing compelling conspirators to give information up publicly was partisan finger-pointing. Under harsh cross-examination, Bush

Attorney General John Ashcroft made a shocking accusation.[383]

During the summer of 1995, the then-Deputy Attorney General wrote a memorandum that forbade the sharing of intelligence regarding international terror plots between agencies in the United States government[384]. This memo was pivotal in covering the tracks of agents plotting 9/11—many of them were operating in the American government, itself.

Ashcroft's accusation was that the author of that memo was Clinton appointee Jamie Gorelick, a *member* of the 9/11 Commission.

When asked by journalists if they intended to question Gorelick on her culpability for over 3,000 American dead, the Republican Chairman of the Commission, former NJ Governor Thomas Kean retorted, "People ought to stay out of our business."[385]

Gorelick is a consummate career treason gate-keeper having previously covered up the shooting down of TWA flight 800.[386]

She was handsomely rewarded with millions from the Fannie Mae/Freddie Mac housing corruption bubble[387] and later went on to apply her expertise with British Petroleum[388] for the environmental terrorism they conducted on April 20th, 2010 in the Gulf of Mexico; the Deepwater Horizon oil platform explosion.

BP chief executive Tony Hayward avoided crushing losses to his investment portfolio by selling the bulk of his shares in company stock just a few weeks before the disaster.[389]

Not Very Intelligent

In the "War on Terror[m]" it would seem that "intelligence-gathering" only works one way in the United States—whatever harms the American people the most.

Prior to 9/11, a listening operation known as *Able Danger* kept tabs on Osama bin Laden and anything he had plans for. Georgetown's own George Tenet, then Director of the CIA, was perfectly positioned to keep that intelligence buried.[390]

As the 9/11 Commission was continuing its sophistry, Bill Clinton's

---

[m] By giving a conflict the name "War on Terror" the Luciferian Elite have insured no end to the profiteering and bloodletting imposed upon the American people. When will "Terror" finally be conquered?

National Security Advisor, Samuel "Sandy" Berger used his clearance to enter the National Security Archives and stuff wads of highly-classified documents pertaining to terrorist plots down his pants and into his socks to later be destroyed. He claimed he was trying to "help the Commission[391]" and the funny thing is, he wasn't lying—they both had the same agenda.

When held to account by officials for obfuscating an ongoing investigation into the most deadly terror attack on United States soil, Berger had his security clearance revoked for three years by the Bush administration.[392]

I ask again: how is such bold treason spanning both well-kept political parties possible?

—It is being promulgated by powerful Papists.

9/11 was thoroughly enabled and co-ordinated by traitors within the United States. Sheepherders and Islamists living in caves had nothing to do with that level of sophistication.

> *Three of the men identified as the hijackers in the attacks on Tuesday have the same names as alumni of American military schools, the authorities said today. The men were identified as Mohamed Atta, Abdulaziz al-Omari and Saeed al-Ghamdi.*
>
> *The Defense Department said Mr. Atta had gone to the International Officers School at Maxwell Air Force Base in Alabama; Mr. al-Omari to the Aerospace Medical School at Brooks Air Force Base in Texas; and Mr. al-Ghamdi to the Defense Language Institute at the Presidio in Monterey, Calif.* ~ *"Missed Cues"*, the New York Times[393]

Former San Francisco Mayor Willie Brown was warned to cancel his planned trip to NYC on September 11th, 2001[394,395] and George W. Bush's Secretary of State Condoleezza Rice was implicated[396]. What is the connection between those two political figures other than their race?

The unspeakable treason of 9/11 was overseen by Jesuit-educated Director of the CIA George Tenet who received his Georgetown "Bachelor of Science in Foreign Service" in 1976.[397]

9 days after 9/11, President George W. Bush mocked the American people in an address to Congress:

> *Americans are asking "Why do they hate us?"*
>
> *They hate what they see right here in this chamber: a democratically elected government. Their leaders are self-appointed. They hate our freedoms: our freedom of religion, our freedom of speech, our freedom to vote and assemble and disagree with each other.*
>
> *They want to overthrow existing governments in many Muslim countries such as Egypt, Saudi Arabia and Jordan.*[398]

The real terrorists were the ones giving Bush his marching orders and, if there were ever any "freedom of religion", "freedom of speech" or "freedom to vote" before 9/11 they died in the onslaught of anti-terror legislation that followed.

"Freedom of Religion"?

It was George Bush's Attorney General John Ashcroft who helped seize the Indianapolis Baptist Temple on tax evasion after a decision rendered by Federal Judge Sarah Evens-Barker.[399,n]

Many in the Bush family have been vetted by the Luciferian Elite via Yale's Skull and Bones secret society while Ashcroft would accomplish the same process via the parallel secret society, also at Yale, of "Saint Elmo".[400]

"Freedom of Speech"?

In response to the staged false flag shooting that resulted in the death of Federal Judge John Roll and wounding of Congresswoman Gabrielle Giffords in Tucson, Arizona (see *Down the Rabbit Hole*, p. 347), the Republican House handed Barack Obama the *Federal Restricted Buildings and Grounds Improvement Act of 2011*, which he quickly signed into law. The bill creates purposefully-misnamed "free speech zones" that quell the right of protest around America's Elite political class. Essentially, wherever the United States Secret Service is deployed, citizens are stripped of their First Amendment rights.[401]

One would assume that such a clear violation of the Bill of Rights would quickly be nullified in a court of law. To date, no such ruling has

---

[n] The Indianapolis Baptist Temple was seized in January of 2001 but I include it as an example because George Bush has the false reputation of being a friend to Christendom.

It also bears out my virulent criticism of career Leftist women with multiple last names being wholly unqualified for critical authority positions such as Federal Judge.

"Freedom to Vote"?

In 2010 the Tea Party Revolution in response to the election of Barack Obama and the surly passage of the "Affordable Healthcare Act" (written behind closed doors) was crushed by the Republican leadership in the House of Representatives. The handful of upstarts who were elected that year were completely marginalized and the Republican Party actively sought out existing fiscal hawks for punitive action, insuring that the financial destruction of the United States would continue unabated.[402]

Pre-Planned

On August 2nd, 1990, Saddam Hussein invaded Kuwait.

Iraq had been suffering heavily from war with Iran. In a surprising move of betrayal, several Middle East neighbors were worsening the cost by taking a loss in their oil output through over-production to hammer Hussein. Saddam was mystified as to why Arab brothers would subvert their own self-interests to help crush the Iraqi economy.

> *During the Arab League Summit, held in Baghdad, in late May 1990, the Iraqi President ... demanded $27 billion from Kuwait, while blaming Kuwaiti and Saudi greed for oil, and equating them with an act of war against Iraq. Kuwait, Saudi Arabia and United Arab Emirates (UAE) responded that they would lower their oil output, but – in essence – all the corresponding Iraqi demands were in vain: Arab countries continued producing more oil than assigned to them by the OPEC, thus lowering the price. The result was that the Iraqi economy experienced increasing problems while attempting to recover from the long war with Iran. ~ Iraqi Invasion of Kuwait; 1990*, Tom Cooper and Brig.Gen. Ahmad Sadik (IrAF)[403]

This same tactic is being used today to focus on another target of the One-World Elite; Russia.[404]

Kuwait was further provoking her neighbor by illegally tapping in to Iraqi deposits via slant-drilling and border disputes.[405]

In July of 1990, the United States ambassador to Iraq was told to assure Saddam Hussein that the United States would keep "hands off" as the Iraqis did what they needed to keep afloat.

The record of the meeting on 27 July 1990 between Saddam Hussein and U.S. Ambassador to Iraq April Glaspie is now available. Saddam initiated the meeting, at which Glaspie thought she was going to see Iraqi Foreign Minister Tariq Aziz. Still Glaspie gave Saddam something he had not expected. She told him, in clear terms, that America did not object to raising the dollar price of oil to a figure in the mind-twenties and described the Kuwaiti-Iraqi border dispute as an inter-Arab affair in which America did not wish to interfere.

The Saddam-Glaspie meeting was followed by considerable inter-Arab activity which culminated in a meeting in Riyadh between Kuwait, Iraq and Saudi Arabia on 31 July 1990. Iraq, emboldened by Glaspie's green light and friendly letter of 27 July 1990 from George Bush to Saddam, made much of the fact that it was being bled to death economically. ~ The Rise, Corruption and Coming Fall of the House of Saud, Saïd Aburish[406]

Many considered George H.W. Bush sending a woman as an ambassador to a conservative Middle Eastern nation as inept at best and self-destructive at worst. In hindsight, however, Glaspie's gender may have made it much easier for her to be marginalized if the wrong questions were asked.

When April C. Glaspie was named U.S. ambassador to Iraq in 1987, she was, it seemed, a rising diplomatic star. Only 45, and one of a handful of U.S. experts on the Arab world, she was the first woman to head an American embassy in the Middle East.

*Today, Glaspie is a bureaucratic non-person. Although the State Department maintains that she is handling important special assignments, Glaspie is effectively being held incommunicado—forbidden to talk either to the press **or to Congress**.*

The ambassador's dramatic slide began last July 27 when, according to an Iraqi transcript that leaked out later, she told Iraqi President Saddam Hussein that the United States would not take a position in the growing border dispute between Iraq and Kuwait. ~ Norman Kempster, LA Times [emphasis mine][407]

Within a month of the Hussein/Glaspie meeting, Iraq would invade Kuwait.

Citizens in all nations were distraught over the chaos. Americans were concerned that the battle would precipitate a world war.

Before a joint session of Congress, George H.W. Bush struck a discordant tone, speaking as if the turmoil was of no concern because an outcome was already determined—and world leaders from East to West were all onboard.

> *We stand today at a unique and extraordinary moment. The crisis in the Persian Gulf, as grave as it is, also offers a rare opportunity to move toward an historic period of cooperation. Out of these troubled times, our fifth objective—a new world order—can emerge: a new era—freer from the threat of terror, stronger in the pursuit of justice, and more secure in the quest for peace. An era in which the nations of the world, East and West, North and South, can prosper and live in harmony. A hundred generations have searched for this elusive path to peace, while a thousand wars raged across the span of human endeavor. Today that new world is struggling to be born, a world quite different from the one we've known. ... A world in which nations recognize the shared responsibility for freedom and justice. ... This is the vision that I shared with President Gorbachev in Helsinki. He and other leaders from Europe, the Gulf, and around the world understand that how we manage this crisis today could shape the future for generations to come.*[408]

The date was September 11th, 1990.

As President George Bush #41 was speaking to Congress, military men at the Pentagon were putting the finishing touches on a plan already worked out to invade Iraq. The facilities there were working flawlessly as proof of how well-designed the notorious 5-sided structure was. It's foundation was precipitously laid just a few months before America was dragged into World War II; on September 11th, 1941.[409]

Why 9/11?

Why has the date of September 11th been repeatedly chosen by Luciferians for advancing the One-World Order? Scholar-in-Residence at Faithlife Corporation, Dr. Michael S. Heiser has an answer.

Heiser is no armchair blogger. He earned his M.A. and Ph.D. in Hebrew Bible and Semitic Languages.

Revelation 12 speaks of a "great sign" in heaven.

> *A great sign appeared in heaven: a woman clothed with the sun, and the moon under her feet, and on her head a crown of twelve*

stars; and she was with child; and she cried out, being in labor and in pain to give birth.

Then another sign appeared in heaven: and behold, a great red dragon having seven heads and ten horns, and on his heads were seven diadems. And his tail swept away a third of the stars of heaven and threw them to the Earth. And the Dragon stood before the woman who was about to give birth, so that when she gave birth he might devour her child.

And she gave birth to a son, a male child, who is to rule all the nations with a rod of iron; and her Child was caught up to God and to His Throne. ~ Revelation 12:1-5, NASB (some capitalization added)

Heiser has taken this information and applied it literally.

Some scholars contend that the Gospel Message was passed on as far back as Adam to his children and they to theirs, via the stars.[410]

The heavens declare the Glory of God; and the firmament sheweth His Handywork. ~ Psalm 19:1, KJV (some capitalization added)

Job 38 may have spoken to this practice.

As YHWH chastens Job regarding His Divine Plan and Wisdom, He asks;

Canst thou bind the chains of the Pleiades, or loose the bands of Orion?

Canst thou lead forth the Mazzaroth in their season? ~ Job 38:31-32, Mechon Mamre

This is the only place in Scripture where the Mazzaroth is mentioned. Its actual definition is in dispute but experts believe it was an astrological discipline that utilized stellar constellations as aids in teaching YHWH's Message. "Astrology" has been subsequently perverted by paganism much as other Messianic truths have been.

It is interesting to note that, of the major constellations, only Orion and the Pleiades are gravitationally-linked[411]. Other constellations are illusions of perspective.

Applying Revelation 12 to the constellations results in surprising specificity.

Most scholars agree that "the woman" is Israel and the "Child" is the foretold Messiah; Yeshua ha Nazareth.

There is only one female constellation, Virgo, the virgin, who's chief star is Spica.

For 20 days each year, Virgo is literally "clothed with the sun". Our sun passes in front of, or "through" Virgo. Depending on when, the sun appears to be in the middle of the constellation, Virgo's "abdomen".

Sometimes, while the sun is passing "through" Virgo, the moon is at her "feet".

Norton's Star Atlas places 12 stars visible to the naked eye around the Virgin's "head".[412]

Above the Virgin's head can sometimes be found a conjunction between Regulus and Jupiter and the constellation of Leo. Regulus is the "king's star" as Jupiter is the "king's planet". This alignment was highly prized in presaging a royal birth.

Leo is Hebraic symbology of Messiah; the "Lion of the Tribe of Judah". [Genesis 49:9, Revelation 5:5]

At other times, two more constellations can be seen below the Virgin; Scorpio and Libra. In ancient days they were considered to be a single constellation[413]. It is a collection of stars with many associations, not just of the Latin *Scorpius* (creature with the burning sting), to include that of a dragon.[414]

All of these events occur simultaneously on a very specific day in history for a tiny span of 80 minutes°: September 11th, 3 BC—what Heiser believes to be the true birthday of Jesus Christ.[415]

It appears to be a date the Luciferians are eager to appropriate with their own blood sacrifice.

° Was this the duration of Miriam's labor?

Endnotes

[283] *The Last Word on Overpopulation*, James Corbett, 15 February 2011, The Corbett Report
http://www.corbettreport.com/the-last-word-on-overpopulation/
    "Useless Eaters" is a Luciferian phrase most clearly connected with one of their prized theologians, Thomas Malthus.
[284] *How Bush's Grandfather Helped Hitler's Rise To Power*, Ben Aris in Berlin and Duncan Campbell in Washington, 25 September 2004, the Guardian
http://www.theguardian.com/world/2004/sep/25/usa.secondworldwar
[285] *CIA Comes to Yale in Search of New Recruits*, Janeen Hayat, 2 November 2001, Yale Daily News
http://yaledailynews.com/blog/2001/11/02/cia-comes-to-yale-in-search-of-new-recruits/
[286] *It's No Secret: Yale Likes CIA*, Randall Beach, 4 November 2001, the New Haven Register, re-posted on Free Republic.com
http://www.freerepublic.com/focus/f-news/563526/posts
[287] *The 15 Most Powerful Members Of "Skull And Bones"*, Thornton McEnery, 20 February 2011, Business Insider
http://www.businessinsider.com/skull-and-bones-alumni-2011-2?op=1
[288] *Student Tasered, Arrested At Kerry Forum*, Associated Press, 18 September 2007, NBC News.com
http://www.nbcnews.com/id/20835952/ns/us_news-crime_and_courts/t/student-tasered-arrested-kerry-forum/
[289] *Secrets of the Tomb: Skull and Bones, the Ivy League, and the Hidden Paths of Power*, Alexandra Robbins, Back Bay Books, 2002
[290] *Skull And Bones: Secret Yale Society Includes America's Power Elite*, Rebecca Leung, 2 October 2003, "60 Minutes", CBS News
http://www.cbsnews.com/news/skull-and-bones/
[291] *Tim Russert's Death: Questions, Answers*, Miranda Hitti, 16 June 2008, WebMD Health News
http://www.webmd.com/heart-disease/news/20080616/tim-russerts-death-questions-answers
[292] *Breitbart's Editor in Chief Says His Boss "the Picture of Health"*, Carol Felsenthal, 6 March 2012, The Hill
http://thehill.com/blogs/pundits-blog/media/214309-breitbarts-editor-in-chief-says-his-boss-the-picture-of-health
[293] *Andrew Breitbart Announced Release of Damning Obama Video Before His Death*, Jim Hoft, 1 March 2012, Gateway Pundit
http://www.thegatewaypundit.com/2012/03/breitbart-announced-release-of-damning-obama-video-before-his-death/
[294] *What a Coincidence! Breitbart's Coroner Dead From Arsenic Poisoning?* unattributed, 2 May 2012, Russia Today
http://rt.com/usa/coroner-arsenic-death-breitbart-456/
[295] *I.G. Farben I.G. Farbenindustrie AG German Industry and the Holocaust*, Chris Webb, 2010, Holocaust Education & Archive Research Team, Holocaust Research Project.org
http://www.holocaustresearchproject.org/economics/igfarben.html

[296] *ibid*
[297] *ibid*
[298] *ibid*
[299] *Behold A Pale Horse*, Milton William Cooper, Light Technology Publishing (1991), pp. 89-90
[300] *Company That Made Zyklon B for Nazi Holocaust Made RU 486 for Abortions*, Carole Novielli, 23 February 2014, LifeNews
http://www.lifenews.com/2014/02/23/company-that-made-zyklon-b-for-nazi-holocaust-made-ru-486-for-abortions/
[301] *Quick Facts About RU-486*, National Right to Life
http://www.nrlc.org/abortion/ru486/
[302] *Wall Street and the Rise of Hitler*, Antony Sutton, Arlington House (1976), p. 27
[303] *A People's History of the United States*, The Thistle, Volume 13, Number 2: Dec., 2000/Jan., 2001., Massachusetts Institute of Technology
http://web.mit.edu/thistle/www/v13/3/oil.html
[304] *John D. Rockefeller*, History.com
http://www.history.com/topics/john-d-rockefeller
[305] *Bush Family Values: War, Wealth, Oil*, Kevin Phillips, 8 February 2004, the LA Times
http://articles.latimes.com/2004/feb/08/opinion/op-phillips8
[306] *The $5 Trillion War on Terror*, Mark Thompson, 29 June 2011, Time
http://nation.time.com/2011/06/29/the-5-trillion-war-on-terror/
[307] *In Tough Times, a Company Finds Profits in Terror War*, Jeff Gerth and Don Van Natta Jr., 13 July 2002, NY Times
http://www.nytimes.com/2002/07/13/business/in-tough-times-a-company-finds-profits-in-terror-war.html
[308] *9 Things You May Not Know About Gerald Ford*, Sarah Pruitt, 12 July 2013, History.com
http://www.history.com/news/9-things-you-may-not-know-about-gerald-ford
[309] *America's Secret Establishment: An Introduction To The Order of Skull & Bones*, Antony C. Sutton Trine Day
Updated Reprint 2002, p. 14
[310] *George W. Bush Likes Idea of Jeb Bush vs Hillary Clinton in 2016*, Steve Holland, 10 November 2014, Reuters
http://www.reuters.com/article/2014/11/10/us-usa-georgewbush-idUSKCN0IU1KC20141110
[311] *Why Hillary vs. Jeb Would Be Great for America*, Mark McKinnon, 13 April 2014, the Daily Beast
http://www.thedailybeast.com/articles/2014/04/13/why-hillary-v-jeb-would-be-great-for-america.html#
[312] *Ex-Presidents Bush, Clinton Play Golf in Maine*, Associated Press, 28 June 2005, USA Today
http://usatoday30.usatoday.com/news/nation/2005-06-28-golf_x.htm
[313] *George W. Bush Says Bill Clinton Is His "Brother From Another Mother"*, Tessa Berenson, 13 November 2014
http://time.com/3584031/george-bush-bill-clinton/#3584031/george-bush-bill-clinton/
[314] *The Federal Reserve Conspiracy & Rockefellers: Their Gold Corner*, Emanuel M. Josephson, Chedney Press (1968), p. 73

[315] *Otto Strasser*, History Learning Site
http://www.historylearningsite.co.uk/otto_strasser.htm
[316] *Hitler and I*, Otto Strasser, Houghton Mifflin (1940)
[317] *Hitler and I*, Otto Strasser, Houghton Mifflin (1940), pp. 56-57
[318] *Pater Bernhard Rudolf Stempfle*, Wikipedia (Deutsch)
http://de.wikipedia.org/wiki/Bernhard_Stempfle
[319] *Essays in German Jewish Studies*, Volume 1, edited by William Collins Donahue, Martha B. Helfer, Camden House (2011), p. 117
[320] *"Hitler M'a dit"*, Hermann Rauschning, Coopération Paris (1939), p. 122-123
[321] *Pope Benedict XVI: A Biography of Joseph Ratzinger*, John Allen, A&C Black (2001), p. 27
[322] *Hitler's Pope: The Secret History of Pius XII*, John Cornwell, Penguin Books (1999), p. 14
[323] *The Man who Would Be God*, Burt Prelutsky, 22 June 2009, Townhall
http://townhall.com/columnists/burtprelutsky/2009/06/22/the_man_who_would_be_god#!
[324] *National Socialism*, Encyclopædia Britannica
http://www.britannica.com/EBchecked/topic/405414/National-Socialism
[325] *A Woman Rides The Beast*, Dave Hunt, Harvest House (1994), pp. 90-91
[326] *Liberal Fascism: The Secret History of the American Left, From Mussolini to the Politics of Meaning*, Jonah Goldberg, Doubleday (2008), pp. 7-8, 9, 11, 21
[327] *TRADING WITH THE ENEMY: An Exposé of The Nazi-American Money Plot 1933-1949*, Charles Higham, Delacorte Press (1983) pp. 8-9
[328] *Wall Street and the Rise of Hitler*, Antony C. Sutton, G S G & Associates Pub (1976), p. 64
[329] *ibid*, p. 65
[330] *The Pope, Eichmann and the Nazi "Ratlines"*, Julian Kossoff, 17 March 2010, Telegraph
http://blogs.telegraph.co.uk/news/juliankossoff/100030163/the-pope-eichmann-and-the-nazi-ratlines/
[331] *Don't Mention the Pope's Hitler Youth Past, Says the Vatican*, Nick Squires and Tim Butcher, 12 May 2009, the Telegraph
http://www.telegraph.co.uk/news/worldnews/europe/vaticancityandholysee/5314338/Dont-mention-the-Popes-Hitler-Youth-past-says-the-Vatican.html
[332] Pope Dogged by Hitler Youth Past, Susan James, 12 February 2013, Yahoo! News
http://news.yahoo.com/hitler-youth-past-dogged-pope-benedict-despite-jewish-215603378—abc-news-topstories.html
[333] *What Joseph Ratzinger Did During the War*, unattributed, April 2005, BeliefNet
http://www.beliefnet.com/Faiths/2005/04/What-Joseph-Ratzinger-Did-During-The-War.aspx
[334] *Pope Francis And Shimon Peres Discuss The Establishment Of A "United Nations Of Religions"*, Michael Snyder, 8 September 2014, End of the American Dream
http://endoftheamericandream.com/archives/pope-francis-and-shimon-peres-discuss-the-establishment-of-a-united-nations-of-religions

This is a blog but it has several mainstream citations. Not as many as a typical Johnny Cirucci column but worth a visit. :)

[335] Gisela Heidenreich is, indeed, a prolific author yet I can find no record of the book, *Beloved Criminal: A Diplomat In The Service Of The Final Solution*. The historical facts are accurate and the UK Daily Mail is a good source that vets its "news". Perhaps I missed the original German title or the book has not been published yet. Regardless, Horst Wagner was a Nazi war criminal who was secreted out of Europe and away from punishment by Rome.

[336] *How Top Nazi Used "Ratline" Escape Route To Flee To South America After The War, By Daughter Of Woman He Seduced*, Allan Hall, 10 February 2012, the Daily Mail http://www.dailymail.co.uk/news/article-2099282/How-Nazi-used-ratline-escape-route-flee-South-America-war-daughter-woman-seduced.html

[337] *St. Pius XII? Pope Francis Mulling It Over, Says Vatican Source*, Andrea Gagliarducci, 1 August 2013, the National Catholic Register http://www.ncregister.com/daily-news/st.-pius-xii-pope-francis-mulling-it-over-says-vatican-source

[338] *Lawsuit Charges That Nazi Gold Funded Vatican Ratlines*, Concordat Watch.eu http://www.concordatwatch.eu/topic-6151.834

[339] *Court: Vatican Bank Can't Be Tried In U.S. For Storing Nazi Loot*, unattributed, 30 December 2009, Associated Press via Haaretz http://www.haaretz.com/news/court-vatican-bank-can-t-be-tried-in-u-s-for-storing-nazi-loot-1.1099

[340] *The Whitehouse Coup*, BBC Radio 4, 23 July 2007 http://www.bbc.co.uk/radio4/history/document/document_20070723.shtml

[341] *In Search of History: The Plot to Overthrow FDR*, History Channel documentary http://shop.history.com/in-search-of-history-the-plot-to-overthrow-fdr-dvd/detail.php?p=68850

[342] *CIA Operative E. Howard Hunt Confession on the JFK Assassination*, confession was taken by Howard Hunt's son, St. John Hunt, Johnny Cirucci YouTube https://www.youtube.com/watch?v=wlAQdtzp-jl&

[343] *Watergate Figure E. Howard Hunt Dies*, unattributed, 24 January 2007, USA Today http://usatoday30.usatoday.com/news/washington/2007-01-23-hunt-obit_x.htm?csp=24

[344] *The CIA's 1954 Guatemala Coup on Behalf of United Fruit Company*, Johnny Cirucci YouTube https://www.youtube.com/watch?v=ukGp9kxIF5Y&

[345] *Ghosts of Guatemala's Past*, Stephen Schlesinger, 3 June 2011, New York Times http://www.nytimes.com/2011/06/04/opinion/04schlesinger.html

[346] *Biographical Information, Avery Cardinal Dulles, S.J.*, Fordham University http://www.fordham.edu/dulles/Bio.shtml

[347] *Cardinal Avery Dulles, Theologian, Is Dead at 90*, Robert McFadden, 12 December 2008 http://www.nytimes.com/2008/12/13/us/13dulles.html?pagewanted=all

[348] *A Coup Made in America*, written and directed by Nadine Pequeneza and Alan Mendelsohn, Hit Play Productions http://hitplayproductions.ca/project/a-coup-made-in-america/

[349] *A Woman Rides The Beast*, Dave Hunt, Harvest House (1994), [digital] p. 57

[350] *The Neo-Catholics: Implementing Christian Nationalism In America*, Betty Clermont, SCB Distributors (2011)

Digital copy from near-useless Google; the official search engine of the Luciferian One World Order.
[351] *The Vietnam War*, Bill Ganzel, 2007, Living History Farm.org
http://www.livinghistoryfarm.org/farminginthe50s/life_08.html
[352] *Vietnam War Casualties > Total Number of Deaths in the Vietnam War*, Wikipedia
https://en.wikipedia.org/wiki/Vietnam_War_casualties#Total_Number_of_Deaths_in_the_Vietnam_War
[353] *Guileless And Machiavellian*, William Shannon, 28 October 1984, the New York Times
http://www.nytimes.com/1984/10/28/books/guileless-and-machiavellian.html
[354] *Avro Manhattan > Life*, Wikipedia
https://en.wikipedia.org/wiki/Avro_Manhattan#Life
[355] *Vietnam: Why Did We Go?* Avro Manhattan, Chick Publishing (1984), pp. 20, 24, 25, 26, 27, 38
[356] *Church Committee Hearings: the CIA "Heart Attack Gun" (1975)*, Johnny Cirucci YouTube
https://www.youtube.com/watch?v=vzDSnTv6A8o&
[357] *Fidel Castro – Perfil de un Jesuita Clandestino*, Espada del Espíritu
http://espadadelespiritu.foroactivo.com/t1521-fidel-castro-perfil-de-un-jesuita-clandestino
[358] *Jesuita que fue profesor de Castro espera que pida perdón por sus pecados*, 07/06/2007, Cuba Encuentro
http://www.cubaencuentro.com/cuba/noticias/jesuita-que-fue-profesor-de-castro-espera-que-pida-perdon-por-sus-pecados-36971
[359] *The Mystery of Fidel Castro's Excommunication*, Andrea Tornielli, 3 February 2012, the Vatican Insider
http://vaticaninsider.lastampa.it/en/the-vatican/detail/articolo/cuba-fidel-castro-papa-el-papa-pope-vaticano-vatican-12303/
[360] *Pope John Paul II Visits Cuba*, unattributed, 25 January 1998, American Catholic.org
http://www.americancatholic.org/features/cuba/
[361] *Pope Meets Cuba's Fidel Castro, Slams U.S. Embargo*, Philip Pullella and Jeff Franks, 28 March 2012, Reuters
http://www.reuters.com/article/2012/03/29/us-cuba-pope-idUSBRE82Q18W20120329
[362] *World Trade Center 7 ... What Do Your Eyes Tell You?* –unattributed, 16 September 2012, Washington's Blog
http://www.washingtonsblog.com/2012/09/world-trade-center-7-what-do-your-eyes-tell-you.html
[363] *911 Commission: Trans. Sec. Testifies Cheney Gave Secret Orders*, Johnny Cirucci, YouTube
https://www.youtube.com/watch?v=m6Z8ssKfcgA&
[364] *The Day Before 9/11 Rumsfeld Admits Pentagon Missing Astounding $2.3 Trillion*, Johnny Cirucci, YouTube
https://www.youtube.com/watch?v=NmnOf4yShyA&
[365] Did he "drop out"? The *Encyclopedia of American History* lists his entry into Georgetown as "1956"
http://www.fofweb.com/History/MainPrintPage.asp?iPin=EAHrX239&DataType=AmericanHistory&WinType=Free
Aleksi Tzatzev of *Business Insider* cites Bradley Graham's *By His Own Rules: The*

Ambitions, Successes, and Ultimate Failures of Donald Rumsfeld, pages 44-5 with a date of "1960"...4 years apart.
http://www.businessinsider.com/famous-law-school-dropouts-2012-10?op=1
[366] *Pentagon 9/11*, Defense Studies Series, Alfred Goldberg, Sarandis Papadopoulos, Diane Putney, Nancy Berlage, Rebecca Welch, Historical Office of the Secretary of Defense, Navy Department Library
http://www.history.navy.mil/library/online/pentagon_9-11.htm
[367] *The 9/11 Hijackers: Amateur Aviators Who Became Super-Pilots on September 11*, Shoestring, 12 July 2012, 911Blogger
http://911blogger.com/news/2011-07-12/911-hijackers-amateur-aviators-who-became-super-pilots-september-11
    Excellent post with 40 footnotes.
[368] Testimony of veteran airline pilot Glen Stanish, founder of Pilots for 9/11 Truth. *More proof a plane did not hit PENTAGON*, William Finley YouTube
https://www.youtube.com/watch?v=JTJehfQkuyE
[369] *Alleged Hijackers May Have Trained At U.S. Bases*, John Barry, 14 September 2001, The Daily Beast, Newsweek
http://www.newsweek.com/alleged-hijackers-may-have-trained-us-bases-152495
[370] *U.S. Occupation Leads to All-Time High Afghan Opium Production*, 13 November 2013, Washington's Blog
http://www.washingtonsblog.com/2013/11/us-drug-afgahnistan-opium.html
    Please note embedded YouTube of Geraldo Rivera interviewing Marine Corps BN CDR for FoxNews regarding his mission to guard Afghan opium fields.
[371] *Record Opium Yield in Afghanistan in 2014*, Agencia EFE, 12 November 2014, Vida Latina San Diego
http://www.vidalatinasd.com/news/2014/nov/12/record-opium-yield-in-afghanistan-in-2014/
[372] *Russia Says U.S. Should Eradicate Afghan Opium*, Jonathon Burch, 28 March 2010, Reuters
http://www.reuters.com/article/2010/03/28/us-afghanistan-russia-opium-idUSTRE62R0QH20100328
[373] *Inside the Saudi 9/11 Coverup*, Paul Sperry, 15 December 2013, the New York Post
http://nypost.com/2013/12/15/inside-the-saudi-911-coverup/
[374] *U.S. Senate Committee on Environment & Public Works*, Hearing Statements, 23 July 2004, Senate.gov
http://www.epw.senate.gov/hearing_statements.cfm?id=254256
[375] *Cheney: Next Attack On U.S. Will Be "Something Far More Deadlier" Than 9/11*, 14 October 2014, RT
http://rt.com/usa/195956-cheney-kristol-interview-terror-torture/
[376] *Lindsey Graham Gay? Conservative Group ALIPAC Demands Senator "Admit Homosexuality"*, 20 June 2010, the near-useless Huffington Post
http://www.huffingtonpost.com/2010/04/20/lindsey-graham-gay-conser_n_544554.html
[377] *Lindsey Graham to Charleston: Support War in Syria or Be Nuked!* Joshua Cook, 6 September 2013, Ben Swann.com
http://benswann.com/lindsey-graham-to-charleston-support-war-in-syria-or-be-nuked/

[378] *Senator Warns of Nuke Strike on S. Carolina After Missing Nuke Report*, Anthony Gucciardi, 5 September 2013, StoryLeak.com
http://www.storyleak.com/senator-warns-nuke-attack-s-carolina/
[379] *Air Force General Michael Carey Fired for Epic Drunken Bender in Moscow*, Stephen Rex Brown, 20 December 2013, New York Daily News
http://www.nydailynews.com/news/national/air-force-general-michael-carey-fired-epic-drunken-bender-moscow-article-1.1554042

Key signs that these are political purges are how deep they have to dig for excuses; "drunkenness", "gambling", "sexual harassment"...it's interesting that the general was in Moscow. Did he see a nuclear false flag coming that so devastated him he reached out to the only nation in the world standing against the New World Order? I would have.

[380] *U.S. Air Force Fires Two More Nuclear Commanders Amid Leadership Crisis*, Associated de-Press-ed, 3 November 2014, via the Guardian
http://www.theguardian.com/world/2014/nov/04/us-air-force-fires-two-more-nuclear-commanders-amid-leadership-crisis
[381] *For Guccifer, Hacking Was Easy. Prison Is Hard.* Andrew Higgins, 10 November 2014, NY Times
http://www.nytimes.com/2014/11/11/world/europe/for-guccifer-hacking-was-easy-prison-is-hard-.html?_r=0

Lazar had a much more thorough statement that the Times very conveniently redacted and instead labeled him to be a conspiracy kook...after he saw the most intimate correspondences from the top world leaders.

[382] *United States Could "Absorb" Another Terror Attack, Obama Says in Woodward Book*, 22 September 2010, FoxNews
http://www.foxnews.com/politics/2010/09/22/obama-divided-afghan-war-woodward-book/
[383] *How Chinagate Led to 9/11*, Jean Pearce, 25 May 2004, FrontPage Magazine
http://archive.frontpagemag.com/readArticle.aspx?ARTID=12894
[384] *GORELICK MEMO + SUPPLEMENTARY MATERIAL*, the Antechamber.net
http://www.theantechamber.net/UsHistDoc/Gorelick/GmPsIndex.htm
[385] *"People Ought to Stay Out of Our Business"*, Kathryn Jean Lopez, 14 April 2004, National Review
http://www.nationalreview.com/corner/78355/people-ought-stay-out-our-business-kathryn-jean-lopez
[386] *Oklahoma City, TWA Flight 800, and the Gorelick Connection*, Jack Cashill, 16 May 2004, WorldNetDaily
http://www.wnd.com/2004/04/24209/
[387] *Fannie Mae and the Vast Bipartisan Conspiracy*, Jack Shafer, September 2008, Slate.com
http://www.slate.com/articles/news_and_politics/press_box/2008/09/fannie_mae_and_the_vast_bipartisan_conspiracy.html
[388] *Gorelick to Head BP Congressional Team*, Ryan Reilly, 2 June 2010, Main Justice.com
http://www.mainjustice.com/2010/06/02/gorelick-to-head-bp-legal-team/
[389] *BP Chief Tony Hayward Sold Shares Weeks Before Oil Spill*, Jon Swaine and Robert Winnett, 5 June 2010, the Telegraph

http://www.telegraph.co.uk/finance/newsbysector/energy/oilandgas/7804922/BP-chief-Tony-Hayward-sold-shares-weeks-before-oil-spill.html

[390] *Ex-Army Officer Accuses CIA of Obstructing Pre-9/11*, Paul Church and Ray Nowosielski, 20 January 2013, TruthOut.org
http://truth-out.org/news/item/14008-ex-army-officer-accuses-cia-of-obstructing-pre-9-11-intelligence-gathering

[391] *Feds Probe Clinton Aide Over Missing Papers*, unattributed, 21 July 2004, CNN
http://www.cnn.com/2004/ALLPOLITICS/07/20/berger.probe/

[392] *Berger Will Plead Guilty To Taking Classified Paper*, John Harris and Allan Lengel, 1 April 2005, Washington Post
http://www.washingtonpost.com/wp-dyn/articles/A16706-2005Mar31.html

[393] *AFTER THE ATTACKS: MISSED CUES; Saudi May Have Been Suspected in Error, Officials Say*, Kevin Sack, 16 September 2001
http://www.nytimes.com/2001/09/16/us/after-attacks-missed-cues-saudi-may-have-been-suspected-error-officials-say.html

[394] *Willie Brown Got Low-Key Early Warning About Air Travel*, Phillip Matier and Andrew Ross, 12 September 2001, the San Francisco Chronicle, posted at SFGate.com
http://www.sfgate.com/bayarea/matier-ross/article/Willie-Brown-got-low-key-early-warning-about-air-3314754.php

[395] *9/11 Widows React to Rice's Testimony*, transcript from the PMS NBC show "Screwball" with former Jimmy Carter speechwriter Chris "You'll Need A Spittle Guard To Watch Me" Matthews, 8 April 2004, NBC News
http://www.nbcnews.com/id/4696092/ns/msnbc-hardball_with_chris_matthews/t/widows-react-rices-testimony/

It's always fun to get a little punchy when you've got hundreds of endnotes. Did you catch this one...?

[396] If the reader finds better links, feel free to send them to me: johnny@johnnycirucci.com

Prison Planet had an original link but it now goes nowhere:
http://www.prisonplanet.com/911/warned.htm

There is this from the blog IndyMedia; *White House Link To 9-11 Plot Found*, 11 August 2003
http://la.indymedia.org/news/2003/08/76853_comment.php

[397] *George Tenet Fast Facts*, a very special Christmas posting by our friends at the Catholic News Network
http://www.cnn.com/2013/08/06/us/george-tenet-fast-facts/

[398] *Text: President Bush Addresses the Nation*, President Bush's address to a joint session of Congress and the nation, 20 September 2001, the Washington Post
http://www.washingtonpost.com/wp-srv/nation/specials/attacked/transcripts/bushaddress_092001.html

[399] *Supreme Court Meeting on Baptist Temple*, Julie Foster, 12 January 2001, WorldNetDaily
http://www.wnd.com/2001/01/7802/

[400] *Connecticut Journal: Inside Yale's Secret Societies*, Jerry Guo, 29 May 2008, Gadling
http://gadling.com/2008/05/29/connecticut-journal-inside-yales-secret-societies/

[401] Two sources for this, one from the Right and one from the Left—the fascists in your captured government still got away with it: *Criminalizing Free Speech: Is This What*

Democracy Looks Like? John Whitehead, 6 March 2012, Huffington Post
http://www.huffingtonpost.com/john-w-whitehead/tresspass-bill_b_1321224.html
 Obama Signs "End To Free Speech", Bob Unruh, 12 March 2012, WorldNetDaily
http://www.wnd.com/2012/03/obama-signs-end-to-free-speech/
[402] *GOP Steering Committee Shuffles Conservatives*, Jonathan Strong, 3 December 2012, Roll Call
http://www.rollcall.com/news/gop_steering_committee_shuffles_conservatives-219601-1.html
[403] *Iraqi Invasion of Kuwait; 1990*, Tom Cooper and Brig.Gen. Ahmad Sadik (IrAF), 16 September 2003, Arabian Peninsula & Persian Gulf Database
http://www.acig.org/artman/publish/article_213.shtml
[404] *Why OPEC Has Declared an Oil War on Russia*, Dr. Kent Moors, 17 October 2014, Oil and Energy Investor
http://oilandenergyinvestor.com/2014/10/opec-declared-oil-war-russia/
[405] *It's Time to Think Straight About Saddam*, John K. Cooley, 23 December 1997, New York Times
http://www.nytimes.com/1997/12/23/opinion/23iht-edcool.t.html
[406] *The Rise, Corruption and Coming Fall of the House of Saud*, Saïd Aburish, A&C Black (2005), p. 175
[407] *Insider : U.S. Ambassador to Iraq Muzzled by Washington : April Glaspie met with Saddam Hussein shortly before his army invaded Kuwait. Now she is a bureaucratic non-person, and--some fear--a scapegoat as the Administration's prewar policy is debated.* Norman Kempster, 5 February 1991, the LA Times
http://articles.latimes.com/1991-02-05/news/wr-840_1_april-glaspie
[408] *Address Before a Joint Session of Congress (September 11, 1990)*, George H. W. Bush, the Miller Center, University of Virginia
http://millercenter.org/president/bush/speeches/speech-3425
[409] *September 11, 1941: Pentagon Construction Begins*, Steve Melito, 11 September 2006, HIS GlobalSpec CR4, Civil Engineering
http://cr4.globalspec.com/thread/2343/September-11-1941-Pentagon-Construction-Begins
[410] *Signs in the Heavens*, Dr. Chuck Missler, Koinonia House
http://www.khouse.org/articles/2014/1193/
[411] *Is the Astronomy in the Book of Job Scientifically Consistent?* J. Warner Wallace, 20 November ?, Cold-Case Christianity
http://coldcasechristianity.com/2013/is-the-astronomy-in-the-book-of-job-scientifically-consistent/
[412] *The Heavens Declare*, J. Preston Eby, 26 April 1999, Philologos
http://philologos.org/bpr/files/c006.htm
[413] *Libra Constellation*, Constellation Guide
http://www.constellation-guide.com/constellation-list/libra-constellation/
[414] *Scorpius Constellation: Facts About the Scorpion*, Kim Ann Zimmermann, 6 August 2012, Space.com
http://www.space.com/16947-scorpius-constellation.html
[415] *Dr. Michael Heiser: Revelation 12 and Astral Prophecy Place the Birth of Christ on 9/11*, Johnny Cirucci YouTube
https://www.youtube.com/watch?v=KQt9pBSYY5Y

Chapter 5

A Sovereign Unto Itself

Most people have no idea that the geographic location of Catholic power—the Vatican—is literally a sovereign city-state just like ancient Athens or Babylon. Even the word "Vatican" shows its true origins in pagan rebellion, not dedication to Jesus Christ or YHWH.

The Vatican is literally a city of the dead, built upon the graves of Rome's ancestors, the Etruscans. On those same slopes were grown vineyards to fuel pagan festivals.

> **Vatika** *has several other related meanings in ancient Etruscan. It was the name of a bitter grape that grew wild on the slope, which the peasants made into what became infamous as one of the worst, cheapest wines in the ancient world. The name of this wine, which also referred to the slope where it was produced, was Vatika. It was also the name of a strange weed that grew on the graveyard slope. When chewed, it produced wild hallucinations, much like the effect of peyote mushrooms; thus,* vatika *represented what we would call today a cheap high. In this way, the word passed into Latin as a synonym for "prophetic vision."*
>
> *Much later, the slope became the circus, or stadium, of the mad emperor Nero. It was here, according to Church tradition, that Saint Peter was executed, crucified upside down, and then buried nearby. This became the destination of so many pilgrims that the emperor Constantine, upon becoming half-Christian, founded a shrine on the spot, which the Romans continued to call the Vatican Slope. A century after Constantine, the popes started building the papal palace there. ~ The Sistine Secrets: Michelangelo's Forbidden Messages in the Heart of the Vatican*, Benjamin Blech and Roy Doliner[416]

In 751 AD, Pope Zachary settled the dispute of who should rule the empire of the Franks by crowning Pepin the Younger. Pepin responded by crushing the Lombards and donating the *Exarchate of Ravenna*, about half of modern Italy, to Rome. His son, Charlemagne, would later expand this territory and Pope Leo III crowned him "Emperor".

French troops remained as mercenaries, guarding the Papal States until the mid-19th century.

But after the outbreak of the Franco-Prussian War (for which Prussia would be severely punished by Rome), Napoleon III recalled his garrison and Italian nationalists quickly took advantage. The "Kingdom of Italy" annexed the Papal States in 1870 and left Pope Pius IX with no sovereign territories. He locked himself within his remaining estate and declared that he was "Prisoner in the Vatican".

Pius IX (Giovanni Mastai-Ferretti) was also the first Pope to declare himself "infallible" at the First Vatican Council.[417]

This standoff between the Vatican and Italy continued until February of 1929 when a compromise was reached: the Catholic Church would give up her remaining title to land within Italy but have a new city-state created for her uncontested use to include the massive luxury fortress complex of *Castel Gandolfo*.

Pius XI (two Pius' later[p]) signed on behalf of the Catholic Church and Italian Premier Benito Mussolini signed on behalf of King Victor Emmanuel of Italy.[418]

As a result of the Lateran Treaty, "Vatican City" mints its own coins and controls the flow of mail by creating its own stamps—stamps that other nations recognize.[419]

Just as the United States government has appropriated the top-level internet domain code of ".gov", Vatican City has done for the top-level domain ".va"[420]. The Catholic Church has subsequently reserved the ".catholic" domain as well.[421]

The Papal City-State has its own Royal Coat of Arms. In it are two keys: a gold key symbolizing the Pope's authority "in the heavens" and a silver key representing his authority among men[422]...or, perhaps more accurately, *over* men.

Vatican City has its own Praetorian Guard, the *Guardia Svizzera* (or "Swiss Guard").

The *Guardia Svizzera* are only depicted in the media as Renaissance-era costumed men holding pikes for an honor guard.

Nothing could be further from reality.

---

[p] Readers should note the convention of Popes choosing special names from which to ascend to the office of Holy See is exactly the same as any other world Royal; by such a name they claim the Divine Rite of rulership over their fellow man.

> *The guards, who are independent of the Swiss armed forces, are employed by the Roman Catholic Church under the leadership of the pope, to whom they swear fealty in a ceremony at Belvedere Court. As is common with any elite military corps, competition is intense for inclusion in the Swiss Guards. New recruits must be unmarried Roman Catholic males with Swiss citizenship, between 19 and 30 years of age, and at least 5 feet 8 inches (1.74 metres) tall; they must have a professional diploma or high school degree and must complete basic training with the Swiss military. (Historically, new recruits also had to prove they were free of physical deformities, and commanding officers were traditionally of noble lineage.)* ~ Encyclopedia Britannica[423]

When Pope Benedict's former butler, Paolo Gabriele, attempted to expose incidents of corruption amongst Church leadership, he was quickly found and arrested by these "Vatican Police" and promptly thrown into "Vatican Jail".[424]

Mirroring disturbing disclosures from the Catholic Church, unmarried Guardians have their own homosexual secret society.

This has mostly been kept quiet except for a 1998 double homicide of a "gay" Guardian's commander and wife (suspected of being his bisexual lover).

However, in January of 2014 a heterosexual Guard broke to the Swiss newspaper *Schweiz om Sonntag* that he was distressed over the constant propositioning he was enduring at the hands of priests who accosted him while on duty.[425]

Within the Swiss Guard is the Catholic Secret Police, known as the "Vigilance Office". It handles security for anyone seeking an audience with the Vicar of Christ, which is kept extremely tight.

> *The police forces of Italy or any other secular state are not allowed into the Vatican except for group audiences with the Pope. Only the papal staff is permitted to carry out security tasks behind the walls of the pontifical enclave in Rome.* ~ the New York Times [426]

Like the Secret Service, the *Guardia Svizzera*, is only as efficient as they are allowed to be.

"We Run The Pope"

> *I had the opportunity to study intensive Spanish in Mexico. On the last day of the course, my young instructor surprised me, he spoke*

> *English. I had no idea. He asked me about my Christian faith and then focused his questions on my beliefs about the Bible. Since I had barely been a repentant Christian a year, I had only read through the Bible once by that time. But having taken a couple of courses in my first semester at Pacific Christian college, I summarized Bible history the best I could.*
>
> *He proceeded to tell me my history was all wrong. The he said something so outlandish about his view of Bible history, that it didn't even stick in my memory from that day to this. But it was what he said next that astounded me. "I am a Jesuit priest," he said, as we started out of the classroom for the last time. Then, having gotten my attention, he said to me, "We are not **under** the Pope, we **run** the Pope. What the Pope pronounces is only what the broad consensus of people agrees to. Then we tell the Pope what to say, and the Pope pronounces it as doctrine." ~ Why They Changed The Bible*, David Daniels[427]

Russian occultist and mystic Helena Petrovna Blavatsky (1831–1891) considered herself a conduit of ancient wisdom and secret esoteric knowledge. She helped found a research and publishing institute named the "Theosophical Society" and her crowning publication was *Isis Unveiled*. In it, she addressed how the Catholic Church was the tool of a pagan black-magic group that calls itself "the Society of Jesus".

> *The Church is henceforth an inert tool, and the Pope a poor weak instrument in the hands of this Order. But for how long? Until the end comes... ~ Isis Unveiled*, H.P. Blavatsky[428]

Blavatsky accused the Jesuits of steering the entire Church when they claimed fealty unto death for the Pope.[429]

Another enlightening source on the inner circles of the Elite is Edith Starr Miller; the Lady Queenborough (1887-1933).

> *Edith Starr Miller ... was a British blue blood on par with Princess Diana. She understood occult religions and secret societies as she experienced them first hand—her husband was the 1st Baron of Queenborough, treasurer of the League of Nations and member of British Union of Fascists who helped secure oil monopolies for John D. Rockefeller. ~* archive.org[430]

In 1933, she published *Occult Theocracy* and showed her readers the Luciferian leanings of whom they thought they "elected" to serve them.

Not surprisingly, Lady Queenborough died shortly after her book was released. She was in the process of getting a divorce from her husband, Almeric High Paget, 72, 1st Baron of Queenborough, on grounds of "cruelty".

> ...she died suddenly in Paris Jan. 16th, 1933 at the age of 45. She had been in good health. Even the Grand Lodge of Canada records that she died "under suspicious circumstances". All records have been lost.
>
> No newspaper article or obituary was published; no record of a coroner's report remains. Details of her life have been expunged, save for a New York Times clipping announcing her wedding in 1921. ... ~ Edith Starr Miller—Murdered for Exposing Conspiracy, Richard Evans[431]

Lady Queensborough noted that the Jesuits are so powerful they could "break" with Rome or simply control the White Pope, which appears is what they have been doing for generations.[432]

The Jesuits are disturbingly comfortable with absorbing popular paganism: in the 17th and 18th centuries, while conducting "missionary work" in China, the Jesuits amalgamated Confucianism with their already-syncretised Christian/pagan beliefs.[433]

Not being dedicated Christians, they were only interested in raw power.

In an effort to reign in the Jesuits, Clement XI sent his legate Charles-Thomas Maillard De Tournon to China. Emperor Kangxi ("Kang-Hi") imprisoned de Tournon at Macao where he later perished.[434]

According to Lady Queenborough, the Emperor had a Jesuit in his ear that was directly responsible for the Papal emissary's death. De Tournon had just been ordained a Cardinal.[435]

This war between the Black and White Popes proves that they obey the Holy See "as a corpse" with "no opinion or will" of their "own or any mental reservation whatever" only when it suits them.[436]

In 1981, when Karol Józef Wojtyła (Pope John Paul II) attempted to wrest control from the Jesuits by replacing their Superior General Pedro Arrupe with his own appointment, he started a clock ticking.

In a few short weeks, an attempt on his life was made.

It is extremely interesting to see corporate media blame John Paul for "alienating" his own Marines.

> *John Paul alienated the people he needed to have on his side in his grand project of a "second evangelisation". The Jesuits, with 23,000 members still the world's biggest male religious order, were the first to feel the lash. When their leader, the much-loved Father Pedro Arrupe, was felled by a stroke in August 1981, John Paul suspended constitutional procedures and imposed a "personal delegate of the Holy Father". An 80-year old Jesuit, Paolo Dezza, was named and, by astute footwork, enabled the tension to subside. Two years later, the Jesuits calmly elected a new general, Peter-Hans Kolvenbach.*
>
> *The attempt to redirect the Jesuits failed...* ~ Peter & Margaret Hebblethwaite and Peter Stanford, the Guardian [437]

Father Malachi Martin (1921-1999) was one of the most prominent men in the Catholic Church. Author, famed demon exorcist and personal friend of Pope Paul VI, Martin was amongst the rare few who were granted leave of his association with the Company of Loyola. He later became one of their harshest critics.

In his book *The Jesuits*[438], Martin gave us insight free of media whitewashing.

In the Spring of 1981, John Paul II had a secret meeting in regards to firing the Black Pope.

> *On May 13, 1981, within three weeks of that private papal conference (to fire Arrupe), John Paul II was struck by two bullets from the Browning semiautomatic pistol of paid hitman Mehmet Ali Agca. By mistake, as it was later explained, the Pontiff was rushed to the Roman hospital of Gemelli rather than to the special hospital unit organized solely for papal use. He was given blood from the public blood bank; the private supply kept in readiness was never used.*
>
> *In rapid succession, Pope John Paul underwent two major operations and suffered the consequences of the transfusion of impure blood; he contracted a severe case of hepatitis. At the height of the Pontiff's crisis, on May 28, Cardinal Wyszynski of Warsaw died. Wyszynski was John Paul's closest friend, and had made his career.* ~ *The Jesuits*, Malachi Martin[439]

Father Malachi apparently died of a brain hemorrhage after falling down the stairs in his apartment in 1999.[440]

There are many, however, who feel that Martin was murdered.[441]

Was Martin getting too close to the truth?

> *At his death, Father Martin was at work on what he said would be his most controversial and important book entitled Primacy: How the Institutional Roman Catholic Church Became a Creature of the New World Order, it was to deal with power and the papacy, and analyzed the revolutionary shift in the ancient dogma of primacy that lies at the heart of what many now see as the first breakdown of papal power in two millennia. It was to be a book about the Vatican's political landscape as we approach a new pontificate, and as a book of predictions about papal power and the world in the first decades of the new millennium.* ~ Father Charles Fiore[442]

This unpublished work was to be Martin's "most explosive yet" from the man who had uncovered actual Catholic satanic rituals designed to enthrone the devil in the Vatican.

> *...he had become increasingly outspoken about pedophilic Satanism at the heart of the Vatican throughout the College of Cardinals and all the way down to local parishes, which he said were in league with a secret Masonic diabolicus that began following the "enthronement of the fallen Archangel Lucifer" in the Roman Catholic Citadel on June 29, 1963. This horrid ritual, as Martin had called it, had two primary objectives: 1) to enthrone Lucifer as the real Prince over Rome; and 2) to assure the sorcerous inception and embodiment in flesh of that immaterial spirit that would fill the pope also known as Petrus Romanus.*
>
> *In* The Keys of This Blood: The Struggle of World Dominion, *Martin had written:*
>
>> *Most frighteningly for John Paul, he had come up against the irremovable presence of a malign strength in his own Vatican and in certain bishops' chanceries. It was what knowledgeable Churchmen called the "superforce." Rumors, always difficult to verify, tied its installation to the beginning of Pope Paul VI's reign in 1963. Indeed Paul had alluded somberly to "the smoke of Satan which has entered the Sanctuary"...an oblique reference to an enthronement ceremony by Satanists in the Vatican.*[145]

~ Tom Horn and Cris Putnam [443]

Reformed

The Protestant Reformation was the most important event for Christendom post the Resurrection of Jesus Christ.

"Religion" can be defined as the rituals, systems and human hierarchies prescribed in the quest for spiritual fulfillment.

Both Protestant Christians and Jews believe that there was only one "religion" given by YHWH to Moses. However, the Old Testament is rife with examples of the failure of the Israelites to have the ritual direct their hearts towards true worship and not insincere rote. [Jeremiah 4:4]

Even the Mosaic system of animal sacrifice—critical to the forgiveness of sins [Hebrews 9:22]—was found to be detestable in the Eyes of YHWH because of Israel's hardened, unloving hearts. [Isaiah 1:13, Hosea 6:6]

Because of this, Jesus of Nazareth told His disciples, "Do as the Pharisees say, not as they do!" [paraphrased—see Matthew 23:3]

It was the power that came with religion which was most threatened by the upstart Rabbi. The high priest of Jesus' day—Caiaphas—lead the conspiracy to have Him killed by Rome.

This was the beginning of the Luciferian Conspiracy between Rome and apostate Jews (a *balanced* look at Judaism and Israel will be portrayed in Chapter 17). These should not be equated with good and sincere Jewish leaders of Christ's time like Nicodemus and Joseph of Arimathea.

Dr. Chuck Missler aggregated the astounding legal travesties that were committed in no fewer than 6 trials Jesus endured.[444]

Jesus broke the bonds of religion as surely as a serpent is trod underfoot [Genesis 3:15].

This ideal of personal freedom over institutional oppression is why Protestants were able to have so much success in helping to form the "American Experiment". Passionate self-determination was declared at Golgotha!

Early Christians gathered in their homes and continued the Jewish traditions of studying Scripture but now their hearts were filled with wonder at seeing so many passages fulfilled.

Yet they were not left in peace.

Soon persecution arose from all who were threatened by this new "Gospel" message of individual freedom—both Jew and Roman.

This new Faith spread like wildfire throughout the Empire and beyond.

In response, Rome began to persecute and slaughter those who walked in "The Way".

One of the first recorded "false flags[q]" occurred in 64 AD. The Great Fire of Rome burned for 6 days and most historians credit Nero with its kindling yet he blamed the catastrophe on the followers of Christ.

Christians were tortured, enslaved, imprisoned, burned alive and fed to wild animals for sport, yet still they increased in number.

In the Sign of the Cross Shall You Conquer

Within 200 years, Rome became a splintered realm with factions rallying around two men, Maxentius and Constantine.

At the Battle of Milvian Bridge, General Flavius Valerius Constantinus claimed to have had a vision—the God of the Christians, Jesus Christ, told him "In this Sign [the Cross], shall you conquer."

Church historian Eusebius claimed the vision was shared by Constantine's men as well[445]. The Sign of the Cross would shield them against the pagan magic of Maxentius.

Flavius Valerius took this literally and ordered his men to paint crosses on their shields.

At the conclusion of the battle, Maxentius had drowned in the Tiber and his army was completely routed.

Constantine later vanquished his remaining rival, Licinius, and soon reigned supreme as the 57th Emperor of Rome.

Though a great many scholars dispute the authenticity of Constantine's vision, few dispute the reforms he instituted upon his ascension to World Ruler.[446]

---

[q] A "false flag" can be defined as an event staged by an authority in its own domain that brings harm to its people and is used as an excuse for action against that authority's enemies. See Chapters 9 and 10.

Emperor Constantine stopped pagan sacrifice (particularly infanticide), outlawed the abuse of slaves, stopped execution by crucifixion, set the precedent of the free exercise of religion and gave special privileges to Christians, in particular.

Whether intended, or not, it was a brilliant political move. Jesus Christ, Himself, had said "Whoever is not against us, is for us." [Luke 9:50]

Constantine reigned an astounding 31 years over an Empire that would frequently devour its rulers in less than 31 months, sometimes within 31 days.

42 years and nearly 10 Emperors later, Theodosius I would create the "Holy Roman Empire" by making Christianity the state religion of Rome. Generations of pagans that traced their mystery-religion worship through Greece back to Babylon were suddenly "Christians". They blended their beliefs with Christian doctrine in a syncretism that became *Roman Catholicism*.

Early Christians knew nothing of centralized authority.

For 300 years after the Advent of Jesus Christ, Christians gathered in their homes, broke bread with each other, celebrated their Savior and studied how He fulfilled the Hebrew Scriptures. When there was dissent or heresy, knowledgeable circuit-riders like the Apostle Paul visited or sent letters of instruction.

The Bible lauds those who uphold the ideals of Martin Luther and America's Founders—those who were/are *self determinate* in what was important for their spiritual destiny do best. Not even the Apostle Paul was to be taken without question. [Acts 17:10-12]

Rome undid it all.

Take Heart, A Solution Has Arisen!

A new movement is throwing off the chains of centralized Church authority.

Called the house-church movement, it is the inspiration of Beresford Job and it advocates a return to Christians meeting in their homes, sharing fellowship and worship of Christ and deciding their *own* spiritual destinies rather than relying on Church clergy to give it to them.

Around the world, from China to Sudan, persecuted Christians are already following this pattern.

As persecution increases in America, Christ has set in motion how it can be used for good.

Learn more at http://www.house-church.org

A priesthood was reinstituted in direct abrogation of Scripture [I Timothy 2:5]. It required celibacy, guaranteeing sexual perversion amongst its adherents for *centuries*.

It amassed great wealth and power through "indulgences"—supposed spiritual concessions granted by Church authorities in return for gifts payable to Rome.

Most of all, it gave "absolution" of sin to lords and kings who confessed their misdeeds to their "holy fathers". This would be perfected under the Jesuits.

In 1835, the Library of Congress received exhibit BX3705, book A2M65; *Secreta Monita Societatis Jesu; The Secret Councels of the Society of Jesus.*[447]

The editor/translator of the work, Robert Breckinridge, was convinced that it was the same book found in the British Museum circa 1596, at the Jesuit College at Paderborn, in Westphalia circa 1658, in London via the collection of a "Dr. Compton" circa 1669, in Amsterdam circa 1717, the Library of British Prime Minister Sir Robert Walpole circa 1722, in Cologne, France circa 1727 and making its way to Princeton, NJ in 1831.

It was his contention that the original author spoke Spanish before he learned Latin[448]. It is interesting to note that the founder of the Society, Ignatius Loyola, and his original cohort were Spaniards, although we may never know who actually wrote *Secreta Monita*.

However, if authentic, it is an astounding find.

It is also a terrible proof of the excesses of "religion".

> *Let confessors not neglect to interrogate their penitents, (but cautiously) about their name, family relations, parents, friends, estates, and then to examine their expectancies, state, intentions and resolutions, which ought to be moulded favorably to the society, if not so already.* ~ Secreta Monita[449]

Jesuits are instructed that, if someone is sick or on their deathbed, their guilt and confessions are to be exploited for both intelligence and wealth.[450]

If a wife is heartbroken over an adulterous husband, Jesuits are to exploit it to their advantage.[451]

But when it came to intelligence gathering, even the Jesuits spied upon Jesuits. As Lady Queenborough noted, not only is there a strict system of reporting based upon a military "chain of command", but the spies have spies who watch *them* as well.

> *"...an elaborate system of espionage and delation forms part of the recognized order of every house, and, in direct contrast to the ancient indictment and confession of faults in open conventual chapter, every inmate of a house is liable to secret accusation to its superior, while the superior himself may be similarly delated to the provincial or the general."*

> *"Nor is the general himself exempt from control on the part of the society, lest by any possible error he be unfaithful to its interests. A consultative council is imposed on him by the general congregation, consisting of six persons, whom he may neither select nor remove..."* ~ Miller[452]

Endnotes

[416] *The Sistine Secrets: Michelangelo's Forbidden Messages in the Heart of the Vatican*, Benjamin Blech and Roy Doliner, HarperCollins (2008). Another page-less digital copy. This excerpt is taken from the first few pages of Chapter 1.

[417] *"The Prisoner of the Vatican": Pope Pius IX and the 19th Century*, Pat McNamara, 7 December 2010, patheos: Catholic
http://www.patheos.com/Resources/Additional-Resources/The-Prisoner-of-the-Vatican.html

[418] *Pope Becomes Ruler Of A State Again*, Arnaldo Cortesi, 7 June 1929, NY Times posted via "On This Day"
http://www.nytimes.com/learning/general/onthisday/big/0607.html#article

[419] *Coins and Stamps*, Vatican City-State
http://www.vaticanstate.va/content/vaticanstate/en/stato-e-governo/note-generali/monete-e-francobolli.html

[420] *Delegation Record for .VA*, Internet Corporation for Assigned Names and Numbers (ICANN)
http://www.iana.org/domains/root/db/va.html

[421] *The Vatican Sets Rules For New Internet Domain: Sorry, Catholic Bloggers*, Eric Lyman, 8 November 2013, Religion News Service
http://www.religionnews.com/2013/11/08/vatican-sets-rules-new-internet-domain-sorry-catholic-bloggers/

[422] *STATE OF VATICAN CITY Flag, Coat of Arms and Seal*, Holy See Press Office, 9 June 2013
http://www.vatican.va/news_services/press/documentazione/documents/sp_ss_scv/insigne/sp_ss_scv_stemma-bandiera-sigillo_en.html

[423] *Guardia Svizzera*, Encyclopædia Britannica, 21 May 2013
http://www.britannica.com/EBchecked/topic/577173/Swiss-Guards

[424] *Pope's Butler Arrested Over Vatican Letters Allegedly Exposing Corruption*, Tom Kington, 25 May 2012, the Guardian
http://www.theguardian.com/world/2012/may/25/pope-butler-arrest-vatican-letters

[425] *Vatican's Pope-Protecting Swiss Guards Accused Of Secret Gay Lobby*, Barbie Nadeau, 24 January 2014, Daily Beast
http://www.thedailybeast.com/articles/2014/01/24/vatican-s-pope-protecting-swiss-guards-accused-of-secret-gay-lobby.html#

[426] *Besides Swiss Guard, New Force Now Protects Pope*, 14 May 1981, New York Times
http://www.nytimes.com/1981/05/14/world/besides-swiss-guard-new-force-now-protects-pope.html

[427] *Why They Changed The Bible*, David Daniels, Chick Publications (2014), pp. 96-97
    Hat/tip to Christian J. Pinto for this great citation.

[428] *Isis Unveiled: A Master-Key to the Mysteries of Ancient and Modern Science and Theology, Volume II – Theology*, H. P. Blavatsky, Theosophical University Press (1877), p. 332

[429] *Isis Unveiled: A Master-Key to the Mysteries of Ancient and Modern Science and Theology, Volume II – Theology*, H. P. Blavatsky, Theosophical University Press (1877), p. 330

[430] This is a *knowledgable* user-offered review found on the Archive.org listing of Lady Queenborough's book by "PhilInNYC" on 26 January 2012. I don't usually cite such things but a quick look at other sources bears this out and it was concise and powerful. Thanks Phil!
https://archive.org/details/OccultTheocracy

[431] *Edith Starr Miller—Murdered for Exposing Conspiracy*, Richard Evans, 25 January 2012, Henry Makow.com
http://www.henrymakow.com/unsung_heroine_--_illuminati_d.html

[432] *Occult Theocracy*, Edith Starr Miller; Lady Queenborough, Imprimerie F. Paillart (1933), p. 311

[433] *Chinese Rites Controversy*, Wikipedia
https://en.wikipedia.org/wiki/Chinese_Rites_controversy

[434] *Charles-Thomas Maillard De Tournon*, Catholic Encyclopedia
http://www.newadvent.org/cathen/15001a.htm

[435] *Occult Theocracy*, Edith Starr Miller; Lady Queenborough, Imprimerie F. Paillart (1933), p. 312

[436] *ibid*, p. 312

[437] *Obituary: Pope John Paul II*, Peter & Margaret Hebblethwaite and Peter Stanford, 2 April 2005, the Guardian
http://www.theguardian.com/world/2005/apr/02/guardianobituaries.catholicism

[438] *The Jesuits*, Malachi Martin, Simon & Schuster (2013)

[439] *The Jesuits*, Malachi Martin, Simon & Schuster (2013), pp. 79-80, 94

[440] *Malachi Martin; Death*, Wikipedia.org
http://en.wikipedia.org/wiki/Malachi_Martin#Death

[441] *Fr. Malachi Martin: Hero or Fraud?* Traditional Catholic Remnant blog
http://traditionalcatholicremnant.wordpress.com/2012/11/02/fr-malachi-martin-hero-or-fraud/

This was actually a quote within the cite but I felt the need to edit the "IT'S THE JEWS!" stupidity—either true moronic prejudice or Jesuit-inspired provocateuring, it matters not.

[442] *Father Malachi Martin Dead at 78*, Father Charles Fiore, 28 July 1999, the Fatima News Network
http://www.fatima.org/news/newsviews/malachi.asp

[443] *Petrus Romanus: The False Prophet And The Antichrist Are Here*, Thomas Horn and Cris Putnam, Defender (2012), p. 80

[444] *The Day We Were Freed: The Ultimate Injustice*, Dr. Chuck Missler, April 2000, Personal Update, K-House Ministries
http://www.khouse.org/articles/2000/217/

[445] *The Life of the Blessed Emperor Constantine by Eusebius Pamphilus*, edited by Dan Graves, Christian History.org
https://www.christianhistoryinstitute.org/study/module/constantine/

[446] *Constantine The Great*, Larry L. Ping, Department Secretary, Southern Utah University Social Sciences
http://www.suu.edu/faculty/ping/documents/CONSTANTINETHEGREAT.doc

[447] *Secret Counsels of the Society of Jesus*, Robert Breckinridge, Baltimore: Edward J. Cole & Co. 1835
found at the internet archive.org

https://archive.org/details/secretamonitasoc00brec
Library of Congress entry:
http://lccn.loc.gov/2007567148

[448] *Secret Counsels of the Society of Jesus*, pp. 7-8
[449] *ibid*, p. 62
[450] *ibid*, p. 68
[451] *ibid*, p. 70
[452] *Occult Theocrasy*, Edith Starr Miller; Lady Queenborough, Imprimerie F. Paillart (1933), p. 310

Chapter 6

From Christ to Cromwell: The Battle Against Tyranny

"Us" Verses "Them"

In discussing conspiracies that entail an "us" verses a "them", it's important to define who the two sides are.

In general, "us" are the common people who live hand-to-mouth, who stress over bills, and who live their lives one day to the next. "Them" are those whose wealth allows them to possess anything their undisciplined hearts' desire. The vast majority of "them" know nothing of toil and, worse, they use their wealth to bleed those of "us" who *do* produce so that they might steal even *more*.

Although "they" have the advantage of "us", "they" *fear* "us" because "we" far outnumber "them" and, when stripped down, *mano a mano*, "we" are far superior to "them" in the ways that matter; compassion, courage, intestinal fortitude and integrity (on average or under duress).

As a result of this, "they" have devised schemes that keep "us" divided and weak. Thanks to human nature, it's easy: race, lust, sloth, gender, lust (it's worth a second mention). Add distractions like entertainment, sports and completely co-opted media who keep the people from being informed and you've got an entire planet of slaves.

But humans are made in the Image of the Divine, and it is a spark that is indomitable when empowered by righteousness and communion with our Creator. Even small pockets of informed resistance can be extremely dangerous.

In fact, there are rams and sheepdogs that live amongst the sheep. They live off of personal discipline, self control and *sacrifice* born of love.

In the top 10 of everyone's classic movie list should be *The Magnificent Seven* (1960).

Based upon the brilliant Akira Kurosawa black and white film *Seven Samurai* (1954), it was directed by John Sturges and starred the Russian actor Yuli Borisovich Bryner ("Yul Brynner"), Steve McQueen, Charles Bronson, James Coburn, Robert Vaughn and the best Jewish Mexican of all time; Eli Wallach.

A small village of farmers south of the border has been raided year after year by bandits. Forced to hide their women, they are left with barely enough food to survive until the next raid. They take it upon themselves to travel north and find mercenaries to help them. They gather up everything of value they have to buy guns with.

In Texas they come across a gunfighter named "Chris" (Brynner) and their hardship story endears them to him.

Times are hard for cowboys, too, and Chris puts together a team of 7 willing soldiers to give the village a good defense.

While they train, Bronson's character "Bernardo O'Reilly" is adopted by three boys who see the man who had a Mexican mother as one of them. When their fathers fall short against the banditos, one of the boys tells Bernardo that their fathers are cowards. Bronson takes the boy over his knee and spanks him and delivers one of the best monologues in movie history.

> *Don't ever say that again about your fathers. They are not cowards! You think I am brave because I carry a gun? Your fathers are much braver because they carry **responsibility**. —For you, your brothers, your sisters and your mothers. This responsibility is like a big rock that weighs a ton. It bends and it twists them until finally it buries them into the ground. Nobody says they have to do it. They do it because they love you and because they want to. I have **never** had this kind of courage. Running a farm, working like a mule, with no guarantee what will become of it—this is "bravery". That's why I never even started anything like that. That's why I never will.*

America is *filled* with brave men.

Most of them have been conditioned by a Christian upbringing that has taught them;

> *By the sweat of your brow shall you eat bread.* ~ Genesis 3:19

—And again in the New Testament;

> *For even when we were with you, this we commanded you—If any will not work, neither let him eat.* ~ II Thessalonians 3:10

For these men, failure to provide for their wives and children is not an option.

Personal discipline was always important to Godly folk but it wasn't until the Great Experiment—the United States of America—that it was seen as a truly *individual* endeavor.

A phrase coined by Max Weber in his book *The Protestant Ethic and the Spirit of Capitalism*[453] became synonymous with Bible-belt American citizenry; the Protestant Work Ethic. Wikipedia smartly contrasts this ideal with Catholic dedication to Rome's hegemony[454]:

> *The Protestant work ethic (or the Puritan work ethic) is a concept in theology, sociology, economics and history which emphasizes hard work, frugality and diligence as a constant display of a person's salvation in the Christian faith, in contrast to the focus upon religious attendance, confession, and ceremonial sacrament in the Catholic tradition.*

Religion: the Chains that Bind

From the 4th century onward the Catholic Church grew in power and abuse to a crescendo we know today as "the Inquisition". The "Synod of Toulouse" (the "Council of Toulouse") set the governing canon for the Inquisitors. Regulation 14 states[455]:

> *Lay people are not permitted to possess the books of the Old and New Testament, only the Psalter, Breviary, or the Little Office of the Blessed Virgin, and these books not in the vernacular language.*

Rome was about *control* and that is *exactly* what "religion" provides those in power.

One of the most oft-quoted phrases in human history is done by most who have no idea it was Jesus Christ who said it; *You shall know the Truth and the Truth shall make you free.* [John 8:32].

Christians believe that Jesus is *the Way, the Truth and the Life* [John 14:6] yet it is the agenda of the Luciferian Ruling Elite to obfuscate and hide "Truth". As a result, those who do not actively seek it for themselves are destroyed by their lack of knowledge [Hosea 4:6].

This was the prison Christendom and the entire world was living in—ruled by Rome—until a renegade priest named Martin Luther nailed 95 theses to All Saints Cathedral in Wittenberg, Germany.

The Protestant Reformation was the spark that lit the fire of Divine Conviction in the hearts of common men.

Previous to it, revolutions against tyranny ultimately failed because they were man-centered outbursts.

The slave/gladiator revolt of the Third Servile War against Rome in the 1st Century BC pitted Crixus, Oenomaus and Spartacus against the finest army in the world. Starting with a revolt at the gladiator training camp near Capua, the rebels repeatedly defeated Roman attempts to stop them. These successes combined with unclear goals allowed the Romans time to martial Crassus and his legions to corner the slave army in southern Italy. The former slaves made themselves vulnerable because they looted the countryside instead of striking the capital or dispersing across the Alps.[456]

Ever-so-slowly, mankind matured and recovered from the curse of making men king. [I Samuel 8:1-18] The Divine model given the Jews was for YHWH to be the governing Authority with decentralized judges to administer order and justice.

But Luciferians seek *control* over their fellow man.

In large nations, a feudal system was developed to oppress the people with a tiny Elite at the top, insulated by a pampered aristocracy around them, protected by a Praetorian class of knights/samurai/soldiers who enforced the plundering of the peasantry.

Yet even the aristocracy rebelled, and the lords of England attempted an unheard-of thing in 1215; they forced the monarch of their time—King John—to limit his power by a document.

The Magna Carta ushered in the "rule of law" (but only for the aristocracy) creating a "due process" for criminal charges, representation for taxation or impressment into military service and punishment commensurate with the crime—which had to be proven to have been committed—as well as several other important precedents.

Few know that one of the most powerful enemies of the Magna Carta was the Vatican.

> *The Vatican has consistently fought every democratic advance from absolute monarchies toward government by the people, beginning with England's Magna Carta (June 15, 1215), "the mother of European Constitutions." That vital document was denounced immediately by Pope Innocent III (1198-1216), who "pronounced it null and void and excommunicated the English barons who obtained it"[2] and absolved the king of his oath to the barons.[3] Encouraged by the pope, King John brought in foreign mercenaries to fight the barons, bringing great destruction upon the country.*

> *Subsequent popes did all in their power to help John's successor, Henry III, overturn the Magna Carta, impoverishing the country with papal taxes (salaries to the numerous imported Italian priests were three times the crown's annual revenue). Nevertheless, the barons finally prevailed. ~ A Woman Rides The Beast*, Dave Hunt[457]

One of the most renown accounts of Christian martyrdom is Foxe's *Book of Martyrs* and it is entirely focused on how the Catholic Church viciously and brutally attempted to maintain complete control of Christendom and the Bible.

William Tyndale

An English contemporary of Martin Luther, William Tyndale was a leading figure in the Protestant Reformation. He, too, utilized Gutenberg's movable-type press to profligate his English translation of the New Testament[458]. In response to a Vatican apologist who said that the people were better off having the Pope's laws than God's, he is quoted as having said:

> *I defie the Pope and all his lawes. If God spare my life, ere many yeares I wyl cause a boy that driveth the plough to know more of the Scripture, than he doust.*[459]

Having worked hard on the New Testament, Tyndale weathered harsh Counter-Reformation critics who hounded him incessantly. He was forced by persecution to flee London and ended up in the heartland of Luther's Germany, stopping first in Hamburg and later in Cologne. There, he continued to work on an English translation of the Old Testament.[460]

As the Protestant firebrand continued to translate under cover, he was located by a British agent of Rome who befriended him under false pretense. The BBC tells the end of William Tyndale's story.

> *Soon afterwards Tyndale was betrayed by his friend Henry Phillips. He was arrested for heresy by imperial authorities and imprisoned for over 500 days in Vilvoorde Castle. On 6 October 1536, Tyndale was tried and convicted of heresy and treason and put to death by being strangled and burned at the stake. By this time several thousand copies of his New Testament had been printed.*
>
> *It was reported that Tyndale's last words before his death were "Lord, open the king of England's eyes." Just three years later Henry VIII published his English "Great Bible" based on Tyndale's work. Even though Tyndale's translation of the Old Testament*

remained unfinished at his death, his work formed the basis of all subsequent English translations of the Bible, including the "King James" version of 1611.[461]

It was lenient for the Inquisitors to strangle Tyndale before burning him. Many other victims didn't fare as well, from Hugh Latimer to Joan of Arc. They were burned alive.

Vicious, Vindictive Vatican

When Rome couldn't arrest a "heretic" in time, as was the case with great reformer John Wycliffe, they pulled his body out of the grave, *then* burned him.

Wycliffe was truly a man ahead of his age.

Before Martin Luther nailed his Theses to the door of the All Saints Chapel, John Wycliffe was speaking passionately against Catholic doctrines in England.

He was a visionary of the 14th century.

> *Noting that the Bible said the gospel was to be given freely, Wycliffe attacked the money-grabbing and impoverishing practices of the medieval church. He criticized such unscriptural practices as prayers to saints, pilgrimages and the selling of indulgences. He also condemned confessions, images and celibacy. Decrying the feudal power of the church, he held that each person was directly responsible to God. ...*
>
> *In 1376 Wycliffe wrote* On Civil Dominion, *in which he said, "England belongs to no pope. The pope is but a man, subject to sin; but Christ is the Lord of lords, and this kingdom is held directly and solely of Christ alone."* ~ Visionary Media[462]

Lacking the linguistic skills to translate Greek, Hebrew and Aramaic from early Canon manuscripts, Wycliffe was the inspiration and leadership behind an effort to translate the Latin Vulgate into common English.

Not surprisingly, the Reformer was well-loved by peasants and commoners and this kept both Royal and Papal authorities at bay, though he was under constant threat of prosecution by them.[463]

Wycliffe suffered not one, but two strokes in 1384[464]. Although some sources report his death as the 28th of December and some the 30th, a modern Bible publisher has this breakdown of the dates:

> *While Wycliffe was in the parish church on Holy Innocents' Day, Dec. 28, 1384, he again suffered a stroke, and was carried out the side-door of his church, in his chair. John Wycliffe died on the last day of the year, three days later.*[465]

Are the significant dates tell-tale signs of John Wycliffe's assassination?

It's surprisingly easy to induce a stroke. Anything from hydrogen peroxide[466] to insulin[467] to cocaine[468] can constrict the flow of blood to the brain sufficient to cause one.

Are there ancient secrets of assassination kept by the Vatican and later given to the Company of Loyola for targets like John Wycliffe?

Perhaps we are stretching credulity with these questions but there can be no doubting the shocking vehemence with which Rome attacks her enemies.

> *Much of the wealth of the Roman Catholic Church was acquired through the confiscation of the property of the pitiful victims of the Inquisitions. Even the dead were exhumed to face trial and property was taken from their heirs by the Church. One historian writes:*
>
>> *The punishments of the Inquisition did not cease when the victim was burned to ashes, or immured for life in the Inquisition dungeons. His relatives were reduced to beggary by the law that all his possessions were forfeited. The system offered unlimited opportunities for loot....*
>>
>> *This source of gain largely accounts for the revolting practice of what has been called "corpse-trials."... That the practice of confiscating the property of condemned heretics was productive of many acts of extortion, rapacity and corruption will be doubted by no one who has any knowledge either of human nature or of the historical documents.... no man was safe whose wealth might arouse cupidity, or whose independence might provoke revenge.*[11]
>
> ~ *A Woman Rides The Beast*, Dave Hunt [469]

Even so, Britannia.com had this inspiring conclusion to John Wycliffe's story:

The effect of Wycliffe's teaching extended far beyond the British Isles. King Richard II's first wife, Anne of Bohemia, was daughter of the Holy Roman Empower, Charles IV. When she died prematurely in 1394, her attendants carried Wycliffe's ideas to the very Imperial Court in Prague. There they were taken up by theologians at Charles' University, such as Jan Hus.

At the same time it ordered Hus to be burned at the stake outside of the city, the Council of Constance, in 1415, decreed that Wycliffe's remains in England should be dug up, his bones burned and the ashes scattered on the water. His incorporeal remains, however, were like raindrops which fell over all of England, producing fertile soil for William Tyndale, Thomas Cranmer and later English Reformers.[470]

Still Saving

In yet another incident of school violence, a Florida State alum named Myron May opened fire on campus in November of 2014. He was a poster child for whom the burgeoning American Police State considers an "enemy". Police claim he had "anti-government documents" in his possession and media have reported that his Facebook page had Bible verses and conspiracy theories posted.[471]

Even though guns are outlawed on nearly every school campus in America, making FSU a "gun-free" kill zone, the incident is being used as a propaganda tool to call for more "gun control".

We will never know the story from Myron May's point of view. Police claimed he failed to yield to them and killed him at the scene.

Jason Derfuss was one of the students shot that day. He was hit in the back as he ran. When he got to cover, he pulled off his backpack to find the bullet lodged in a book he had just checked out—it had miraculously saved his life.

The book was *Great Medieval Thinkers: John Wyclif.*[472][r]

Brother Against Brother

The crowning achievement of English Protestants was the Geneva

---

[r] The motto of the media outlet Russia Today is "Question More". Was the FSU shooting completely fabricated with a little sugar-coating of this story to make it go down more easily? Who is the target audience here? Who is most likely to rebel against gun control measures as a result of this shooting?

Bible, yet it was outlawed by "Protestant" King Charles I.

> *The Geneva Bible was the first full-length Bible to be published in the English language. Its original compilers and publishers produced 144 separate editions between 1560 and 1644 AD, beyond which time King Charles I and Archbishop William Laud forbade its printing in England. The Geneva Bible virtually disappeared until modern times. The Geneva Bible is now available in a hardcover edition published in 2006 by Tolle Lege Press.*[1]

> *It was the Geneva Bible (rather than the King James Bible) that was preferred by the Puritans who colonized New England, and the Pilgrims probably brought the Geneva Bible with them on the Mayflower. One reason the Puritans preferred the Geneva Bible was due to its thorough annotations.* ~ Conservapedia[473]

Although born and raised Anglican, Charles had many questioning if he was a secret puppet of Rome. He and his father James I arranged for him to marry Catholic "Infanta" (heiress to a Spanish or Portugese throne) Maria Anna.[474]

The Spaniards were too suspicious, however, and the engagement was broken off. Instead, James and Charles arranged to marry a different Catholic royal, Henrietta Maria of France, daughter of Marie de' Medici— one of the most powerful families in the world then *and* now.

As with all Elites, Charles lavishly spent the people's wealth on wars to expand his power, but when he ascended to the thrown in 1625 there was a Parliament representing the will of the citizenry. Sharing power is not something kings do well.

A tax called "Ship Money" had been levied on coastal counties during time of war to maintain the Royal Navy. Charles began collecting it, without Parliament's consent, on the entire nation, year round.[475]

But it was the King's betrayal of Protestantism that lit the fuse of the English Civil War.

> *In October the native Irish, largely Catholics, claimed Charles I's authority for their attacks against the Protestant English and Scottish settlers who had taken their lands. This was seen by many as yet more evidence of Charles I's part in a Catholic conspiracy to destroy Protestantism. This became just one part of what was termed the Grand Remonstrance to the King, drafted by John Pym and his circle, which detailed Charles I's abuses ... since 1625. ...*

Charles I moved for the impeachment of Pym and four of his followers. On 4 January 1642 the King entered the Commons chamber with an armed guard to effect the arrest himself of the MPs. The Speaker, William Lenthall, refused to tell him where they were...

Charles left the capital five days after this humiliation, and in his absence John Pym and his allies pushed through in March 1642 the Militia Ordinance (an Ordinance and not an Act because it never received the Royal Assent). This placed the command of each county's armed forces in the hands of their supporters.

At the same time Charles I issued his own commissions of array assigning his followers to organise their own armed forces in the counties. ~ Parliament.uk[476]

Rightly can the accusation be made that Rome was behind *both* American and British Civil Wars.

Lord Protector

Out of the Protestant Reformation grew hearty sects like the Puritans. They were hard-working, disciplined souls who did their best to live Christian virtue.

Such a man was Oliver Cromwell.

When war broke out, Cromwell's disciplined, religious mind made him a natural leader and excellent field tactician much as it did Pennsylvania Quaker Dick Winters in WWII, whose exploits were immortalized in the HBO series "Band of Brothers".[477]

Amgueddfa Cymru, National Museum Wales

It was Cromwell's leadership that thwarted the Roman insurgency.

At the battles of Naseby and Langport in June and July 1645, the first showing of the Parliamentarian New Model Army under Thomas Fairfax and Oliver Cromwell, the Royalists suffered major losses.

Charles I's surrender in May 1646 concluded the first phase of the civil war, though he rejected all proposals intended to bring a peace. However, he did reach a secret agreement with the Scots regarding Presbyterianism in England, which incensed the English

Parliament.

The Civil War reached the end of its next phase with Charles's trial and execution in January 1649. ... ~ The British Library Board[478]

Edith Starr Miller, the Lady Queenborough, also credits Cromwell with putting the Jesuits into dire straits.

The Jesuit power, much weakened in England by ... the advent of Cromwell, persisted nevertheless in its efforts to recapture its former status in that land. During the reign of James II, it schemed and intrigued incessantly through its representatives Father St. Germain[2] and his successor Father Columbière.[3] After the enactment of the limitation of the English throne to Protestant succession the Jesuit diplomatists were hard put. ~ Miller[479]

On January 20th, 1649, Charles I was executed for treason.

A series of feckless Parliaments were raised and dissolved and Oliver Cromwell was the only man with strength to rule yet the restraint not become an autocrat. Cromwell held the title of "Lord Protector" and when he was offered the crown in 1657 he refused in fury. Why had they cut the head off of one king only to raise up another?

While Cromwell reigned, England was free.

But less than a decade from the death of England's traitor sovereign, Oliver Cromwell's daughter, Elizabeth, fell ill. A doctor was sent to her but she died despite his care.

Shortly thereafter, Cromwell started to suffer from what some have called "malaria" and the same doctor attended him. He died on September 3rd, 1658 at only 59 years old, the anniversary of his two greatest victories at Dunbar and Worcester.

Accounts of his death have caused experts to now question if he was poisoned.[480]

In an entry for the *Journal of the Royal College of Physicians of London*, Dr. Leonard Jan Bruce-Chwatt, an expert in malaria[481], uncovered Cromwell's healer as his killer—George Bate, physician to secret Catholic Charles I and a Royalist.[482]

Shortly after Cromwell's death, Charles II was rushed back from exile in Scotland and reinstituted as the monarch of England. On his deathbed, he converted to Roman Catholicism.[483]

Endnotes

[453] *The Protestant Ethic and the Spirit of Capitalism*, Max Weber, Allen & Unwin (1930)
[454] *Protestant Work Ethic*, Wikipedia.org, in English
http://en.wikipedia.org/wiki/Protestant_work_ethic
[455] *Regulations Of The Synod Of Toulouse Concerning The Inquisition, (1229)*, Scroll Publishing.com
http://www.scrollpublishing.com/store/Inquisition.html
[456] *The Civil Wars*, Book I, Appian, edited by Horace White, Perseus Digital Library
http://www.chlt.org/sandbox/perseus/appian.cw_eng/page.14.a.php
[457] *A Woman Rides The Beast*, Dave Hunt, Harvest House (1994), p. 54
[458] *English Bible History: William Tyndale*, GreatSite.com
http://www.greatsite.com/timeline-english-bible-history/william-tyndale.html
[459] *Sermon Given at Matins on Sunday 27 November 2011*, The Reverend Andrew Tremlett, Canon in Residence, Westminster Abbey
http://www.westminster-abbey.org/worship/sermons/2011/november/sermon-given-at-matins-on-sunday-27-november-2011
[460] *Translator William Tyndale Strangled and Burned*, Church History Timeline, Christianity.com
http://www.christianity.com/church/church-history/timeline/1501-1600/translator-william-tyndale-strangled-and-burned-11629961.html
[461] *More Information About: William Tyndale*, History, BBC
http://www.bbc.co.uk/history/people/william_tyndale
[462] *John Wycliffe: Setting the Stage for Reform*, Visionary Media, Winter 2004 Issue
http://www.vision.org/visionmedia/biography-john-wycliffe/613.aspx
[463] *John Wycliffe on His Death Bed*, Diana Severance, Ph.D., Christianity.com
http://www.christianity.com/church/church-history/timeline/1201-1500/john-wycliffe-on-his-death-bed-11629868.html
[464] *John Wycliffe, The Rev. John Stacey*, 8 May 2013, Encyclopædia Britannica
http://www.britannica.com/EBchecked/topic/650168/John-Wycliffe/8039/Wycliffes-attack-on-the-church
[465] English Bible History: John Wycliffe, GreatSite.com
http://www.greatsite.com/timeline-english-bible-history/john-wycliffe.html
[466] *Hydrogen peroxide-induced stroke: elucidation of the mechanism in vivo.* J Neurosurg, January 2009
http://www.ncbi.nlm.nih.gov/pubmed/18928358
[467] *Hyperglycemia, Insulin, and Acute Ischemic Stroke*, Rajesh Garg, MD; Ajay Chaudhuri, MD; Frederick Munschauer, MD; Paresh Dandona, MD, PhD, American Heart Association Journal
http://stroke.ahajournals.org/content/37/1/267.full
[468] *Cocaine-Induced Stroke Often Deadly*, Todd Neale, 7 February 2013, MedPage Today
http://www.medpagetoday.com/MeetingCoverage/ISC/37237
[469] *A Woman Rides The Beast*, Dave Hunt, Harvest House (1994), pp. 74-75
[470] *John Wycliffe (1324-1384)*, Britannia.com
http://www.britannia.com/bios/jwycliffe.html

[471] *Police Identify Shooter in Florida State Tragedy*, Sean Rossman, Karl Etters and John Bacon, 20 November 2014, USA Today
http://www.usatoday.com/story/news/nation/2014/11/20/fsu-guman/19310741/
[472] *Books Likely Saved Apopka Student's Life In Florida State Shooting*, Amanda McKenzie, 20 November 2014, News 13
http://www.mynews13.com/content/news/cfnews13/news/article.html/content/news/articles/cfn/2014/11/20/fsu_shooting_books.html
[473] *Geneva Bible*, Conservapedia
http://www.conservapedia.com/Geneva_Bible
[474] *King Charles I (1600-1649)*, Luminarium: Encyclopedia Project
http://www.luminarium.org/encyclopedia/kingcharles.htm
[475] *The Making of the United Kingdom*, Nigel Kelly, Jane Shuter and Rosemary Rees, Heinemann (1998), p. 52
[476] *The Civil War > The Breakdown of 1641-2*, Parliament.uk
http://www.parliament.uk/about/living-heritage/evolutionofparliament/parliamentaryauthority/civilwar/overview/the-breakdown/
[477] *The Making of the United Kingdom*, Nigel Kelly, Jane Shuter and Rosemary Rees, Heinemann (1998), p. 56
    This is a simplistic school text for "youngers" but it's general summaries are helpful in telling a complex story quickly.
[478] *Charles I's Death Warrant*, The British Library Board
http://www.bl.uk/onlinegallery/takingliberties/staritems/51charlesdeathwarrant.html
[479] *Occult Theocrasy*, Edith Starr Miller; Lady Queenborough, Imprimerie F. Paillart (1933), pp. 312-313
[480] *Cromwell "Was Murdered"*, unattributed, 4 April 2000, BBC News
http://news.bbc.co.uk/2/hi/uk_news/701207.stm
[481] *Leonard Jan Bruce-Chwatt*, Royal College of Physicians, Munk's Roll: Volume IX
http://munksroll.rcplondon.ac.uk/Biography/Details/625
[482] *George Bate—Cromwell's Devious Physician*, L.J. Bruce-Chwatt, MD, FRCP, posted at Reformation.org
http://www.reformation.org/dr-george-bate.html
[483] *Rear Window: The Merry Protestant Who Died A Catholic: A Royal Conversion*, Brian Cathcart, 16 January 1994, The Independent
http://www.independent.co.uk/voices/letters/rear-window-the-merry-protestant-who-died-a-catholic-a-royal-conversion-1407235.html

Chapter 7

The Company

With Their First Pope, Jesuits Are Making a Comeback,
Newsweek

Is the Pope a Catholic? Of course. But Francis is a Jesuit, too: a member of the elite worldwide Society of Jesus (SJ) founded in 1540 by St Ignatius of Loyola, its organisation [sic] and discipline reflecting his military background. Soldiers for Christ or God's awkward squad, self-regarding or selfless – depending on the point of view – for the first time in history this Catholic order has its own man as pontiff. ...

August marked the 200th anniversary of the Jesuit "Restoration" (after a 50-year row with the Vatican, when they survived only in Catherine the Great's Russia). Since January 3rd, when the pontiff kicked off celebrations with a special mass in Rome, there have been worldwide events to mark it. Later this month, Belvedere College in Dublin will host a major conference and, of course, Jesuit teachers like the poet Gerard Manley Hopkins and pupils like the author James Joyce will be remembered. But chatter will inevitably revolve around the contemporary order's most famous son, and the question on all lips: has the Society finally taken over the church; or has the church finally embraced the Society?[484]

As we've seen with nearly every mainstream media story about the Company of Loyola, Newsweek mentions the "Restoration" of the Jesuits but neglects to recount any of the reasons for their dissolution. —Nations, governments and sovereigns around the world were demanding it.

Íñigo López de Loyola was born to Spanish aristocrats in 1491, in the Basque region of Spain. While fighting the French in the battle of Navarre, the young knight was struck by a cannon ball wounding one leg and breaking another. Cut down in his prime, he was denied the glory of battle that was his due. He spent some time recuperating and immersed himself in spiritual literature.

This began his redirection of martial zeal...somewhat. He was still a very focused soldier.

When he was able, Loyola set off to visit the Benedictine Monks at

Montserrat and their shrine for the "Blessed Virgin". While there, he claimed to have had a vision of the Queen of Heaven and her Child. The vision encouraged him to purge himself and that is what he did in a cave outside of Manresa. For 10 months, the soldier lived a spartan life in prayer, fasting and flagellation. He was ordained a priest and his zeal attracted followers. They decided to form a community to stamp out the fledgling Reformation. He was given an audience with Pope Paul III who made it official.

The year was 1540 AD, just 23 years after Luther made his Protest.

Was this all Loyola's idea, based upon visions and a conversion, or was this a savvy move by Catholic Elites to create dependable foot-soldiers for the Counter-Reformation?

Secreta Monita has a section that instructs the methods for recruiting young men from wealthy families that fits Loyola's experience perfectly. Was this method created by Loyola and subsequent Jesuits or simply perfected by them?

> *As the greatest difficulty exists, in alluring the children of the great, noble, and powerful, whilst they are with their parents, who are training them to succeed to the situations they themselves occupy, —they should be persuaded by our friends, rather than our members, to place them in other provinces, at remote universities, in which we teach, previous instructions being given to the professors of the quality and condition of the youths, —and so, we may readily and certainly conciliate their good will towards the society. ~ Secreta Monita*[485]

Loyola named his community "the Society of Jesus" but the foundation of their movement was fanatical dedication to Christ's "Vicar on Earth", the Pope.

The order is highly secretive and it has been alleged the secrecy is due to its focus; subversion, assassination, acquiring wealth, power and position, all leading to toppling of governments whenever deemed fit.

Similar to the Freemasons (who, themselves, may have been subverted or even created by the Jesuits), there are levels of trust and secrecy culminating at a mystic pinnacle where a terrible oath is administered.

At present, there are few sources for this supposed oath. One is a work of French fiction called *Rome Souterraine* ("Subterranean Rome") by Charles Didier[486], and verified as accurate by former Jesuit priest Alberto

Rivera.

Rivera is legendary amongst those critical of the Company though there is not much in print regarding him. Perhaps *Secreta Monita* and its English translator Robert Breckinridge explain why; their very lives were at stake.

> ... *an expelled Jesuit is, I apprehend, a rarer being, even than a candid one. They know little of priests, little of Rome, nothing of the spirit of the Society of Jesus, as they profanely call themselves, who can for one moment suppose, that the high and trusty dignitaries of the order, (and none else knew their secrets,) — would escape with expulsion, and the power to reveal them.*
>
> *The cord, the bowl, the dagger, are instruments not perfectly unknown to this fraternity; and none ever knew better, that the dead speak not.*
>
> *...it is the plain interest of the society, that the dismissed, and still more deserters, should be wholly crushed.*
>
>> *VIII. The misfortunes and disastrous events which befall them, ought to be immediately published, but at the same time solicit for them the prayers of the righteous, lest we should be suspected of malevolence; but, amongst ourselves, in every way exaggerate them, thus to retain others.*
>
> ~ *Secreta Monita*[487]

Any ex-Jesuits who survived were to be discredited.[488]

Anyone of import that was swayed by what they said were to be *unswayed*.

> ... *such noblemen or prelates as the dismissed may have begun to obtain any influence or credit with, should be drawn and bound to the society by every kind of benefit; it should be urged upon them, that the common good of an order, whose fame equals its utility to the church, ought to predominate over the private advantage of any individual; but if their regard for the dismissed should continue, it will be profitable, besides urging the real causes of their dismission* [sic], *to add other things, which although not certain, may be made to appear probable.* ~ *Secreta Monita*[489]

It was a publisher of Evangelical tracts—Jack Chick—who immortalized Rivera in a series of comic books titled after its first issue,

"Alberto".[490]

Covert Catholic Convert

"Conservative" / "Liberal", "Tory" / "Labour", "Republican" / "Democrat"—Western world leaders all seem to have the same agenda regardless of their packaging.

How did Labour Leftist Tony Blair walk in such harmony with "Conservative" Republican George Bush on war in Iraq and Afghanistan, even in light of false intelligence about "weapons of mass destruction"?

It was little-reported that, before the war, both Blair and Bush contrived a secret scheme to overcome popular hesitation about invading Iraq by painting a U.S. military aircraft to resemble a civilian United Nations plane and get it shot down. Later, the same scenario would play out perfectly in Ukraine via Malaysian flight MH-17.[491]

Originally, it was an operation envisioned by General Hugh Shelton[492], chairman of the Joint Chiefs of Staff during the Clinton Administration. Shelton was kept at his post when "Republican" George Bush took over from "Democrat" Bill Clinton.

False flags are the ultimate crime of a nation's leaders upon their own citizens. Instead of honoring their sacred trust to protect the lives and rights of the governed, they betray and murder them for advances in enslavement policies and war profiteering on the backs of their children.

Not only is this agenda real in the West, it's common. Today, false flags are occurring in the United States and the West (Ottawa, Sydney and Paris) at nearly one a week.

How can such high treason occur again and again without any resistance from other leaders or institutions?

Back to Tony Blair for a clue.

After he had left office, Blair channeled King Charles II and converted to Roman Catholicism. Critics suspected that Blair had always been an agent of Rome and he waited until it was politically-expedient to make the association public. The great Irish Protestant orator Reverend Ian Paisley called him "a fool".[493]

Since his conversion, Blair has gone on to chair a foundation dedicated to stream-lining the way for a "globalization of faith"[494]. He has even taught a course to "future leaders" at Yale on the subject.[495]

Blair's foundation was partially bankrolled by Jewish Ukrainian steel magnate Victor Pinchuk[496], a good friend of Jesuit-educated Bill Clinton[497]. Clinton was on-hand to help launch Blair's foundation.[498]

While Blair has risen, Paisley has fallen.

Even as I write, I have been alerted to the sad news that the Reverend Ian Paisley has gone to be with the Lord[499]. His death was announced by his wife, Eileen, on the 12th of September[500] which leads one to question, "Did Ian Paisley die on 9/11?"

To date, I have no evidence of foul play but Paisley was surely a thorn in the Vatican's side. Certainly, assassinating someone elderly is easy enough.

Still, questions regarding the authenticity of the Paisley / Didier / Rivera Jesuit Blood Oath are fair.

Perhaps those questions are best answered by *Secreta Monita*'s editor, Robert Breckinridge, who's insight transcends the fact that he was writing from the early 19th century.

> *There is in this case one peculiar circumstance which gives to the authenticity of the* Secreta Monita, *the seal of absolute certainty, while it casts the darkest shade over the society.*
>
> *Why have the Jesuits any secret rules or instructions, or principles of conduct or objects of effort? Why this secrecy?*
>
> *And how, at so early a period of their history, as the end of the sixteenth century, was the author of this work, supposing him to have been no Jesuit, to have known with such certainty, the existence and the nature of such secrets?* ~ Robert Breckinridge[501]

What is this "secret Jesuit oath"?

According to Reverend Paisley, (who cited a Congressional Library source document[502]), it is a shocking narrative of assassination, subversion and satanism. I have included it, in its entirety in Appendix A.

Are there Jesuit subversives who really topple governments and kill sovereigns for their "Superior General"?

Napoleon Bonaparte's companion in exile and executor of his papers, General Charles Tristan, the Comte de Montholon, had this to say regarding the emperor's dealings with the Catholic Church—authorities who too often mixed "spiritual" power with "temporal" authority:

> *But there is a religious society, the tendency of which is highly dangerous, and which should never have been admitted into the territories of the empire — viz., the Society of Jesus. Its doctrines are subversive of all monarchical principles. The General of the Jesuits desires to be sovereign master, the sovereign of sovereigns. Everywhere that the Jesuits are tolerated, they strive for power, at any price. Their society is by nature fond of ruling, and nourishes, therefore, an irreconcilable hatred of all existing power. Any action, any crime, however atrocious it may be, is meritorious, if committed- for the interest of the society, or by the orders of its General. The Jesuits are all men of talent and learning. They are the best existing missionaries, and would be, were it not for their ambition of ruling, the best instructing body, for the propagation of civilisation and the development of its progress. ~ History of the Captivity of Napoleon at St. Helena*[503]

Why would Montholon have such revulsion towards the Jesuits?

France was a key battleground for the Company and they rode the French Revolution right into Napoleon's reign of blood.

> *III. Kings and princes ought to be impressed with the truth that under present circumstances, the Catholic faith cannot exist without politism—but this demands great discretion; for which purpose our members must have rendered themselves acceptable to the great, and acquainted with their most secret purposes.*
>
> *IV. They should have the advantage of the most recent, important, and certain information, from every quarter.*
>
> *V. It would be advantageous, if we could cautiously and secretly foment dissentions amongst nobles and princes, even to the mutual wasting of their strength; but if they seem likely to be reconciled, the society should immediately endeavor to pacify them, lest it should be effected by some other intervention. ...*
>
> *IX. In fine, let the society, by acquiring the favors and authority of princes, endeavor at least to effect this, —that all shall fear, who will not love us. ~ Secreta Monita*[504]

Even if the reader finds this incredulous, the multiplicity of Jesuit expulsions shows that governments around the world took the threat quite seriously.

> *Between 1555 and 1931 the Society of Jesus was expelled from at least 83 countries, city-states and cities, for engaging in political intrigue and subversive plots against the welfare of the State, according to the records of a Jesuit priest of repute* [Thomas J. Campbell]. ... *Practically every instance of expulsion was for political intrigue, political infiltration, political subversion, and inciting to political insurrection.* ~ The Babington Plot, J.E.C. Shepherd[505]

Those nations that were truly sovereign had a quick and easy solution: kick the Jesuits out.

But those countries that were ruled by Vatican agents had a more difficult problem: how to rid themselves of Loyola's infiltrators without offending the Mother Church?

> *By the 18th century, Jesuits had become so influential, powerful and elitist that European courts panicked and started expelling the order from their territories. They were accused of fomenting social revolts, being agents of the Pope and moulding impressionable young minds. In 1767, Pope Clement XIV signed an act ordering the Suppression of the Society of Jesus, which was enforced in Catholic countries such as France, Spain and Portugal.* ~ Gianluca Mezzofiore, International Business Times[506]

Clement XIV's predecessor was going to dissolve the Jesuits but the very night before he signed the order, he died.

> *In fact, the Jesuits, the great defenders of the Catholic faith have actually exercised their power to undermine the authority of the church and bring it to its knees. The reason the Jesuits retaliated against the Catholic church was that the Jesuits were at one time dissolved as a Catholic order because of their subversive conduct. The subversion of the European nations by the Jesuits became so great that an immense amount of military and political pressure was brought against the pope by the European nations. Finally, Pope Clement XIII decided on the 3rd of February 1769 to dissolve the Jesuits. While Jesuits are under an oath of allegiance to the pope, that oath is secondary to their extreme oath of allegiance to the Jesuit General:*
>
>> *I do further promise and declare, that I will have no opinion or will of my own, or any mental reservation whatever, even as a corpse or cadaver [*perinde ac cadaver*] but unhesitatingly, obey each and every command that I*

> *may receive from my superiors in the Militia of the Pope and Jesus Christ.*[125]
>
> *The night before Pope Clement XIII was to execute the dissolution, however, he suddenly fell ill and died. Prior to his death he cried out "I am dying ... It is a very dangerous thing to attack the Jesuits."*[124] *~ Solving the Mystery of Babylon the Great*, Edward Hendrie[507]

After Carlo della Torre di Rezzonico (Clement XIII) died, his successor, Giovanni Vincenzo Antonio Ganganelli, chose the name Clement XIV. He showed that he had the will do follow up on di Rezzonico's design to dissolve the Company and did so, though reluctantly, with his bull *Dominus ac Redemptor*.

Not only did the Jesuits poison Clement, they did it in such a way that actually caused his body to start decomposing before he died in a long, agonizing manner. To this day, what they murdered Clement XIV with is unknown. [italics suspended]

> ... the Pontiff gradually lost his voice while ... his tongue and throat became so inflamed that he was driven to keep his mouth perpetually agape in an attempt to obtain, through the freshness of the air, some relief from his sufferings. He, who had been so strong and untiring, became as weak as an infant; his limbs betrayed him and he could scarcely drag himself from chair to couch. Alternately he would be a prey to insomnia or fall into a stupor from which he could not be roused. His martyrdom was indescribable. He made heroic efforts to conceal his condition, fighting the complaint inch by inch with all the energy he could muster in his debilitated state. His gaiety flickered out; he became morose, irascible and suspicious; the virus after devastating his body attacked his mind. For hours this Pontiff, so wise and so diligent, would sit at his window pathetically intent on dazzling the passers-by with the reverberation of the sun's rays on a hand mirror. In his moments of lucidity he would express feelings of the most admirable fortitude and resignation. The physical and mental tortures he endured drew tears of compassion from those who served him.
>
> "I knew", he is reported to have said, "that I would pay with my life for what I did; but I never anticipated such a long-drawn-out agony and such refinement of cruelty!"
>
> There has been much controversy over the mysterious cause of Clement's death, which occurred on September 28th, 1774, but

nothing has been definitely proved as to its nature. The autopsy would have been a difficult one at any period, as decomposition had actually preceded death, and in those days it was wellnigh impossible to cope with such conditions. The Pontiff himself was obviously obsessed with the conviction that he had been poisoned and it was the popular belief amongst his contemporaries. The details of his laying-out are horrifying. His remains had to be encased in plaster, and Cardinal Marefoschi, who according to the ceremonial should have placed a cloth over the dead Pope's face, feigned illness so as to escape the ordeal, the major-domo who had to take his place being so overcome that he closed his eyes and threw the veil in the direction of the bed without approaching it. ~ *The Triple Crown: An Account of the Papal Conclaves*, Valérie Pirie[508]

Doubt not that the Company has a long, institutional memory.

Francis told journalists at a special audience for the media that after his election on Wednesday night, some cardinals had jokingly suggested he should name himself Pope Clement XV.

"That way you can take revenge on Clement XIV for suppressing the Society of Jesus," Francis quoted one cardinal as joking with him shortly after he was elected.

The journalists roared with laughter. ~ Reuters[509]

Laughter? Those attending to Clement XIV's body couldn't even put him in state, he was so disfigured.

Perhaps the only thing worth laughing over is the stock of modern "journalism". The horrible assassination of Clement XIV is nowhere to be found in any "mainstream" account regarding Rome's new Jesuit Pope.

It is no coincidence that the name "Clement" has not been taken since 1774.

Reuters goes on to report that Jorge Mario Bergoglio took the name "Francis", for the first time in Vatican history, to honor the founder of the *Franciscan* order.

But there is another Francis that holds a special place in the annals of the Counter-Reformation.

Francis de Sale was the 16th century Bishop of Geneva for the Catholic Church and he is venerated as the man who re-converted 72,000 Protestants fresh off the Reformation[510]. Countering the Reformation of 1517 is the very reason the Jesuit Order was founded, 17 years later.

De Sale was educated at the prestigious *Lycée Louis-le-Grand*, then known as the *Collège de Clermont*; a Jesuit institution.[511]

> *Louis-le-Grand, founded in 1563, is located in the heart of the Quartier Latin, the traditional student's area of Paris. Rich in history, architecture, culture, this area is home to some of the oldest and most prestigious educational establishments in France including the Sorbonne and the Collège de France.*
>
> *Louis-le-Grand plays an important role in the education of French elites. Many of its former pupils have become statesmen, diplomats, prelates, marshals of France, members of the* Académie française, *and men and women of letters. "The Jesuit College of Paris", wrote Élie de Beaumont in 1862, "has for a long time been a state nursery, the most fertile in great men". Indeed Molière, Voltaire, and Victor Hugo are former students who became famous writers, and Georges Pompidou, Valéry Giscard d'Estaing, and Jacques Chirac, all presidents of the French Fifth Republic, spent time on the benches of Louis-le-Grand. Renowned foreign students of the Lycée include King Nicholas I of Montenegro and Léopold Sédar Senghor, the first president of Senegal.*
>
> *During World War II, student Jacques Lusseyran founded the resistance group* Volontaires de la Liberté.[1] ~ Wikipedia[512]

But the plot of revenge didn't end there. *All* of those heretic nations would have to be punished.

Writer and speaker Darryl Eberhart put together a list of Jesuit expulsions (he believes it isn't comprehensive, either):

> ➤ *1579, 1581, 1586, and 1602 – Elizabeth I, Queen of England*
> ➤ *1604 – James I, King of England [This was the 5th expulsion of the Jesuits from England!]*
> ➤ *1614 – Japan*
> ➤ *1618 – the Kingdom of Bohemia*
> ➤ *1716, 1783 – China*
> ➤ *1719 – Peter the Great of Russia*

- 1759 – King Joseph I of Portugal [He believed the Jesuits attempted to assassinate him in 1758.]
- 1764 – King Louis XV of France
- 1816 – Russian Czar Alexander I [He expelled the Jesuits from Moscow and St. Petersburg.]
- 1820 – Russian Czar Alexander I [He expelled the Jesuits from all of Russia.]
- 1820, 1835, 1868 – Spain
- 1834 – Portugal [2nd expulsion of the Jesuits from Portugal]
- 1848 – Switzerland
- 1848, 1859 – Italy
- 1872 – Guatemala
- 1872 – German-Prussian Empire
- 1873 – Mexico
- 1874 – Brazil
- 1875 – Ecuador and Columbia
- 1880, 1901 – France [2nd and 3rd expulsions of the Jesuits from France]
- 1884 – Costa Rica
- 1901 – Portugal [3rd expulsion of the Jesuits from Portugal]

NOTE: The Jesuits were expelled from England five times! The Jesuits were also expelled three times from predominantly Roman Catholic Spain, three times from predominantly Roman Catholic Portugal, and three times from predominantly Roman Catholic France! The Jesuits were also expelled numerous times from various predominantly Roman Catholic countries in South and Central America.[513]

A Dish Best Served Cold

Few schemes of revenge are more deft or more deniable than when carried out by another nation's army.

Enter Napoléon Bonaparte.

Or, more precisely, "enter the man *behind* Napoléon Bonaparte", Emmanuel-Joseph Sieyès.

> *He ... played a major role in organizing the coup d'état that brought Napoleon Bonaparte to power (1799).*

> *The son of a notary of Fréjus, Sieyès was educated for an ecclesiastical career at the Sorbonne and rose in the church to become vicar-general (1780) and chancellor (1788) of the diocese*

of Chartres. ... ~ Encyclopædia Britannica[514]

"Abbé Sieyès" was Jesuit-educated. As we will see in the next and subsequent chapters, this is a process for both selecting and indoctrinating agents of the Company.

> *Born at Fréjus on May 3, 1748, Emmanuel Joseph Sieyès got his primary education from the Jesuits in his hometown and continued into advanced study in theology. Appointment as a canon in the cathedral chapter of Tréguier (1775) brought him the appellation of Abbé (used in France not only for abbots but also for churchmen without a parish), and by the eve of the French Revolution he had been promoted to vicar general of the bishop of Chartres.* ~ Your Dictionary.com[515]

In 1804, Pius VI was "invited" by Bonaparte to crown him emperor which the Pope did on November 2nd of that same year.[516]

Many believe that Bonaparte was acting on behalf of the Company and this appears to be borne out by how Pius VI (Count Giovanni Angelo Braschi) was imprisoned shortly thereafter. He died 6 weeks later.[517]

Because Napoléon Bonaparte had invaded Italy and scattered the Cardinals from Rome, they gathered in Vienna to elect Barnaba Niccolò Maria Luigi Chiaramonti, Pope. He took the name Pius VII and was imprisoned by Bonaparte as his predecessor was.[518]

Only one act would stop Emperor Bonaparte from imprisoning each Vicar of Christ.

> *Pius VII had resolved to restore the Society during his captivity in France; and after his return to Rome he did so with little delay; 7 August, 1814, by the Bull "Solicitudo omnium ecclesiarum," and therewith, the general in Russia, Thaddeus Brzozowski, acquired universal jurisdiction.* ~ the Catholic Encyclopedia[519]

Once the Jesuits were restored, their wrath was aimed at France's burgeoning Protestant population, represented mainly by John Calvin's Huguenots.

The Huguenots had suffered for 250 years under Catholic persecution. This was continued under repeated Catholic French Royals.

> *By law the regency should have passed to Antoine de Bourbon, the leader of the Huguenots. But the mother of the boy kings* [Francis II, Charles IX and Henry III], *Catherine de Medici, called in the*

Catholic Guises and assumed the regency herself. She was an ardent Catholic at the time of the Counter Reformation, and though she wanted peace, she also, with the help of the Pope and the King of Spain, wanted to rid France of "the contagious disease of Protestantism." ~ ReformationSA.org[520]

De Medici's reign of Catholic terror ushered in the French Wars of Religion which culminated in the Saint Bartholomew's Day Massacre.

The St. Bartholomew's Day massacre (Massacre de la Saint-Barthélemy in French) in 1572 was a targeted group of assassinations, followed by a wave of Catholic mob violence, both directed against the Huguenots (French Calvinist Protestants), during the French Wars of Religion. Traditionally believed to have been instigated by Catherine de' Medici, the mother of King Charles IX, the massacre took place five days after the wedding of the king's sister Margaret to the Protestant Henry III of Navarre (the future Henry IV of France). This marriage was an occasion for which many of the most wealthy and prominent Huguenots had gathered in largely Catholic Paris.

The massacre began in the night of 23-24 August 1572 (the eve of the feast of Bartholomew the Apostle), two days after the attempted assassination of Admiral Gaspard de Coligny, the military and political leader of the Huguenots. The king ordered the killing of a group of Huguenot leaders, including Coligny, and the slaughter spread throughout Paris. Lasting several weeks, the massacre expanded outward to other urban centres and the countryside. Modern estimates for the number of dead across France vary widely, from 5,000 to 30,000.

The massacre also marked a turning point in the French Wars of Religion. The Huguenot political movement was crippled by the loss of many of its prominent aristocratic leaders, as well as many re-conversions by the rank and file, and those who remained were increasingly radicalized. Though by no means unique, it "was the worst of the century's religious massacres."[2] Throughout Europe, it "printed on Protestant minds the indelible conviction that Catholicism was a bloody and treacherous religion".[3] ~ Wikipedia[521]

Persecution of the Huguenots continued in France through the 17th and 18th centuries with Protestant families being forcibly displaced, sent to the galleys as slaves and imprisoned. All were ordered to convert to Catholicism or die. Protestant preachers were summarily executed.[522]

By the time of Napoleon, they were so oppressed he brokered them a respite by allowing their return to France if they would turn their churches over to be run by the state[523]. Even that didn't last and, today, the French Calvinist Huguenots no-longer exist.

Some have considered Napoleon Bonaparte's downfall to have occurred as a result of arrogance but is it possible that such a skilled commander would suddenly lose his vision?

Perhaps, having accomplished all Jesuit missions, he was ordered to have his men fall upon their swords.

> *During the summer an armistice was agreed to. Napoleon met with Austria's foreign minister, Count Clemens von Metternich, and the discussions did not go well. Napoleon told Metternich that he would give him nothing because Austria had not defeated him and that he would beat Austria again. Metternich described Napoleon's troops as boys and old men and told Napoleon that he was lost. In a rage, Napoleon told Metternich that he knew of nothing of what goes on in a soldier's mind, that he, Napoleon, grew up on the battlefield and cared little for the lives of a million men. Metternich replied that he wished all of Europe could hear what he had just said. Metternich accused him of having sacrificed French soldiers for his own ambitions. Napoleon boasted of having spared French soldiers by sacrificing Poles and Germans, which outraged Metternich – a German.*
>
> *Napoleon's diplomacy not having gone well, in October he faced four powers in what was to be known as the Battle of the Nations, Russia, Prussia, Austria and Sweden, near the Saxon city of Leipzig. It was a three-day war in which Napoleon was outnumbered and suffered heavily from his enemy's 1,400 artillery pieces. Napoleon's army had 38,000 casualties and lost 30,000 as prisoners. Napoleon's total losses for the year were around 400,000. It sent Napoleon retreating back toward France, Napoleon crossing westward over the Rhine River on November 2, 1813.* ~ Macrohistory[524]

But the real immolation came when Bonaparte extended his army into Russia for what he called "the Second Polish War" to help shore up Catholic Poland and punish Czar Alexander I. By 1820, the Czar would have his fill of the Jesuits. [italics suspended]

> The court of Russia, quiet, and apparently indifferent, suffered them to proceed in the work of universal monarchy which they were

anxious to found; numbers of Jesuits already swarmed on the coasts of the Baltic, on the banks of the Dwina, and in the neighbourhood of Siberia; one missionary had even reached Astracan; and the morality of the Jesuits was nearly becoming triumphant, when the boldness of Father Pholop [Dutch Jesuit Jan Philipp Roothaan who would succeed Tadeusz Brzozowski as Superior General] in the court of Russia dissolved all their projects, and frustrated their fairest hopes.

Among the courtiers at St. Petersburg was a young prince, the son of one of Alexander's most powerful ministers; the Jesuits thought that he might afford them considerable support if they could attach him to themselves; they laid their snares, flattered his ambition, promised him high honours and unlimited power, gave him to understand that even the crown of Russia was a trifle in comparison with that which they were disposed to bestow on him; in short, by alluring and urging the young prince, they caused him to abjure his religion and secured his fidelity to the new faith by the most solemn oaths.

This conversion, though effected in secret, was very soon discovered; and, indeed, the young prince himself avowed that he was a Roman Catholic.

His father had recourse to entreaties, caresses, menaces, and allurements: the youth's resolution was not to be shaken; he would die for the faith he had adopted.

The irritated minister complained to the emperor, requesting that his majesty would either avenge him, or allow him to retire from court.

The Jesuits, still more powerful, exerted all their strength, and employed all their intrigues; they sent away Fathers Pholop and De Grivel from Russia; raised alarms in the court and in the capital; accused the minister who persecuted them of falsehood and calumny; and would have caused his removal, had not the minister at the time detected their manœuvres, and obtained certain proofs of a conspiracy concerted in Poland, in which the Jesuits had undertaken to place the crown of that country on the head of a kin descended from the Poniatowskis.

Astounded at these mighty projects, and terrified at the audacity of these religious conquerors, Alexander ordained that his states should be totally purged of the Jesuits; he sent troops to take possession of their houses and lands, in order that their numerous serfs might be prevented from revolting.

He was no longer overawed by the presence of [Polish Superior General Tadeusz] Brosossoski [who had taken residence in Russia after Pope Clement XIV ordered their suppression in 1773]; that general was just dead; and, if we may believe the Jesuits, his death, far from being natural, must have been brought on by secret poison. ~ *The Literary Gazette*, 1827 [paragraphs added to ease reading][525]

The good people of Russia had no idea how terrible a cost would be exacted from them by the Jesuits for this "affront".

Jesuitical

No one weaves deception better than the Jesuits. They are Rome's chief defenders of Babylonian paganism vice true Christian theology. If rank-and-file Catholics knew this, the Jesuits would be burned at the stake as *they* used to burn Protestants.

But their technique is flawless.

> *Like anyone trying to promote a falsehood, Rome poses with many masquerades and diversionary tactics to confuse and deceive the world. Her most effective pageantry, we will name "Double Face", unfolds something like this: A personage of great influence within the Catholic Church or Jesuit Order emerges on the public scene, vigorously giving support to some liberal and off-shoot radical teaching. Wide and tremendous public exposure is generated as the controversial issues are declared on one side—while the Church and pope condemning and excommunicating adherents on the other side. Interestingly though, the advocate, who after many years of work, often a life-time, spreading and planting his controversial seeds, who has been publicly denounced and excommunicated as one who opposes the pure doctrines of the Church—is, just before death, reconciled, forgiven, and warmly received back into the Church of Rome. Years later, the "radical" teachings now become incorporated as the "pure" doctrines of Rome. Bishop of Ypres, Cornelis Jansen, and his "Jansenists", Andrew Rarnsay, Jesuit Adam Weishaupt's Illuminati, Cagliostro, Jesuit George Tyrrell, the Modernist model, and French Jesuit mystic, Teilhard de Chardion [sic], whose brilliant and fascinating theories and speculations while living, launched, after his death, the controversial Liberation Theology—are men whose rumblings are prime examples of Rome's "Other" Face as she moves ever steadily toward "change" into her true Babylonian Religious role.* ~ *The Grand Design Exposed*, John

Daniel[526]

Pierre Teilhard de Chardin (1881-1950) was a French philosopher, paleontologist, geologist and Jesuit priest and he was the foremost advocate for Darwinian evolution under the guise of Christianity. He further espoused a very Eastern vision of all sentient beings forming a final collective in who he claimed was Jesus Christ.

> *Pope Emeritus Benedict XVI, for example, who as a young theologian named Joseph Ratzinger criticized Teilhard's views, a few years ago praised Teilhard's "great vision" of the cosmos as a "living host."*
>
> *Benedict's successor, Pope Francis, has also invoked Teilhard-sounding concepts about the ongoing development of human consciousness, and Vatican observers say it would not be surprising if Teilhard made an appearance in an encyclical on the environment that Francis is currently writing.*
>
> *Teilhard "is definitely being quoted or invoked in ways we haven't seen in decades, and really never before by the Roman magisterium," said the Rev. Paul Crowley, a Jesuit at Santa Clara University who has studied Teilhard. ...*
>
> *At the same time, scholars such as David Grummett and Sister Elizabeth Johnson have been honing and deploying Teilhard's often arcane ideas, and the American Teilhard Association has an agenda busy with conferences and publications. It is "the emergence of Teilhard de Chardin," as John Haught titled a 2009 essay in Commonweal magazine.*
>
> *There's even a major documentary on Teilhard in the works, with a blurb from NPR's Cokie Roberts: "Bringing Teilhard de Chardin alive to another generation could not come at a more opportune time." ...*
>
> *He was as much mystic as scientist, and his concepts could be so idiosyncratic and esoteric that they fed right into the ecology-and-spirituality movement that blossomed in the 1970s and beyond. Teilhard tends to be quoted by the left...* ~ David Gibson, Religion News Service[527]

De Chardin's teachings would pave the way for the Jesuits to one day introduce mankind to their creator: ET. We'll look more into that in Chapter 20.

Consequently to his agenda to overwhelmingly support Darwinian Evolution, de Chardin needed to encourage a changed view about Original Sin and the ultimate destiny of mankind.

> *PIERRE TEILHARD DE CHARDIN was a Jesuit priest and well-known paleontologist who tried to reconcile and unify science with religion. His philosophy has kindled unusual provocation in the literary world. Although he desired that his book* The Phenomenon of Man *not be read as a meta-physical or theological essay, but as a scientific treatise, libraries generally classify it under philosophy and religion.*
>
> *De Chardin's beliefs are a synthesis of religion and science, resulting in a theory somewhat resembling Christian Science. ...*
>
> *The ideas of Teilhard de Chardin are in harmony with the Jesuit conception of original sin and its transmission from Adam. Individual responsibility is lost as finally the mind of each individual becomes assimilated into the universal mind of Christ. The Catholic doctrine of original sin, through inheritance, has as its corollary the universal grace of Christ, and the book presents this grace as the consciousness of evolution, which finally draws all mind and matter into the universal mind of Christ. It outlines an attempt to synthesize the evolutionary theory with Catholic doctrine and offers a probable future of such a unity. Universal sin and the universal grace of Christ absorb all individuality into a pantheistic complex of mind and matter, which culminates in the Omega point.*
> ~ Henry G. Hadley, Ministry magazine[528]

For turn-of-the-century evolutionists, the "missing link" between apes and humans was all that was left to prove the reliability of Darwin's theory. They soon found it, or so they thought.

> *In 1912 Piltdown Man hit the headlines. Evidence of the evolutionary 'missing link' between apes and humans had been found, in England. For the next 40 years this momentous discovery influenced research into human evolution.*
>
> *Then in 1953 Piltdown hit the headlines again, this time revealed as a hoax, a scientific fraud of shocking proportions.* ~ the Natural History Museum of London[529]

How did they do it?

> *... bone fragments were presented as the fossilised remains of a previously unknown early human. These fragments consisted of parts of a skull and jawbone, said to have been collected in 1912 from a gravel pit at Piltdown, East Sussex, England. The Latin name* Eoanthropus dawsoni *("Dawson's dawn-man", after the collector Charles Dawson) was given to the specimen. The significance of the specimen remained the subject of controversy until it was exposed in 1953 as a forgery, consisting of the lower jawbone of an orangutan deliberately combined with the cranium of a fully developed modern human.* ~ Wikipedia[530]

Later, it was discovered that Charles Dawson had someone standing behind him, orchestrating the hoax: Pierre Teilhard de Chardin.

Harvard Paleontologist Stephen Jay Gould wrote extensively on Piltdown.

> *Of the original trio* [of possible conspirators]—*Dawson, Teilhard, and* [keeper of paleontology at the British Museum Arthur] *Smith Woodward—only Teilhard was still living when Kenneth*[206] *Oakley, J. S. Weiner, and W. E. le Gros Clark proved that the Piltdown bones had been chemically stained to mimic great age, the teeth artificially filed to simulate human wear, the associated mamal remains all brought in from elsewhere, and the flint "implements" recently carved. The critics had been right all along, more right than they had dared to imagine. The skull bones did belong to a modern human, the jaw to an orangutan. As the shock of revelation gave way to the fascination of whodunit, suspicion quickly passed from two members of the trio. Smith Woodward had been too dedicated and too gullible; moreover, he knew nothing of the site before Dawson brought him the original bones in 1912. (I have no doubt whatsoever of Smith Woodward's total innocence.) Teilhard was too famous and too present for any but the most discreet probing. He was dismissed as a* [naïve] *young student who, forty years before, had been duped and used by the crafty Dawson. Dawson acting alone became the official theory; professional science was embarrassed, but absolved.* ~ Clark University[531]

Although both science and news media worked to keep de Chardin out of the spotlight, Gould uncovered the smoking gun of his guilt.

> [In a letter to Kenneth Oakley] *Teilhard then goes on to discuss Piltdown* [site] *2 and, in trying to exonerate Dawson, makes his fatal error. He writes:*

> *He [Dawson] just brought me to the site of Locality 2 and explained me [sic] that he had found the isolated molar and the small pieces of skull in the heaps of rubble and pebbles raked at the surface of the field.*
>
> *But this cannot be. Teilhard did visit the second site with Dawson in 1913, but they did not find anything. Dawson "discovered" the skull bones at Piltdown 2 in January 1915, and the tooth not until July 1915. And now, the key point: Teilhard was mustered into the French army in December 1914 and was shipped immediately to the front, where he remained until the war ended. He could not have seen the remains of Piltdown 2 with Dawson, unless they had manufactured them together before he left (Dawson died in 1916).*[532]

Perhaps there is something to the accusation that the Jesuits pull the world and the Church where they do not want to go by taking two steps forward and only one step back.

Although de Chardin was mildly disciplined for his doctrines, by the time of Pope Benedict XVI, he was heralded as a man of "great vision".

> *...our address to God becomes an address to ourselves: God invites us to join with him, to leave behind the ocean of evil, of hatred, violence, and selfishness and to make ourselves known, to enter into the river of his love.*
>
> *This is precisely the content of the first part of the prayer that follows: "Let Your Church offer herself to You as a living and holy sacrifice". This request, addressed to God, is made also to ourselves. It is a reference to two passages from the Letter to the Romans. We ourselves, with our whole being, must be adoration and sacrifice, and by transforming our world, give it back to God. The role of the priesthood is to consecrate the world so that it may become a living host, a liturgy: so that the liturgy may not be something alongside the reality of the world, but that the world itself shall become a living host, a liturgy. This is also the great vision of Teilhard de Chardin: in the end we shall achieve **a true cosmic liturgy**, where the cosmos becomes a living host. And let us pray the Lord to help us become priests in this sense, to aid in the transformation of the world, in adoration of God, beginning with ourselves. That our lives may speak of God, that our lives may be a true liturgy, an announcement of God, a door through which the distant God may become the present God, and a true giving of ourselves to God. ~ Homily of His Holiness Benedict XVI,*

Vatican.va [emphasis in the original][533]

Banged Up

The biggest hole in Darwinian evolution has been explaining the origination of all matter. Here, too, the Jesuits would come to the rescue of secular "science".

> *According to the Big Bang theory, the expansion of the observable universe began with the explosion of a single particle at a definite point in time. This startling idea first appeared in scientific form in 1931, in a paper by Georges Lemaître, a Belgian cosmologist and Catholic priest.* ~ the American Museum of Natural History[534]

Lemaître was educated by Jesuits[535] then trained to be a Jesuit priest[536] but, like Adam Weishaupt, is only rarely listed as one.[537]

We certainly are grateful to the Company of Loyola for the brilliance that can be summarized by "First there was nothing, then it exploded."

But secular science ate it up as it was just the validation that was needed to keep God out of the picture.

Once again, in picking sides between the All-Seeing Eye of Lucifer the Watcher and the Almighty Creator of the Universe, the Jesuits choose the Adversary.

> *Are the Bible and the big bang theory in agreement? No. And informed persons, on both sides of the issue are aware of this fact. Paul Steidl, an astronomer, has noted:*
>
>> *[N]o astronomers would ever think of the big bang as the creation event of Genesis. The big bang was invented specifically for the purpose of doing away with the creation event. An astronomer would laugh at the naivety of anyone who chose to equate the two events (1979, p. 197).*
>
> ~ Wayne Jackson, the Christian Courier[538]

Just the Facts, Ma'am

Creationism is the literal interpretation of the Genesis account but Genesis is not written for Western minds and it can be a tough sell to non-Christians and even Christians (but it is possible).

A much easier battle to win is "Intelligent Design"; the idea that there is a Designer behind the Creation. Of course the follow-on to that debate is the question "Who?" It may very well be the foundation of what Christians fear will be "the Great Deception".

There are a myriad of excellent resources to defend Intelligent Design. If you like documentaries, as I do, Ben Stein's *Expelled: No Intelligence Allowed* is outstanding. An older documentary (currently available on YouTube) is *Darwin's Deadly Legacy* from Corral Ridge Ministries on the utility of Evolution for genocide. But if you want real science, get Illustra Media's documentaries such as *Unlocking the Mystery of Life* or *The Privileged Planet*.

For some quick facts on Intelligent Design and proof of who the real close-minded religious druids are, turn to Appendix C.

Vatican II

Catholics may be surprised to know that a future Pope and a Jesuit were behind Vatican II—both of them were Leftist Germans.

Joseph Cardinal Ratzinger and his mentor, "Progressive" Jesuit (read: "Communist") theologian Karl Rahner, were two of the chief theologians who steered Vatican II.[539]

One important pronouncement to come from that synod was *extra ecclesiam nulla salus*: "Outside the Church there is no salvation."

This idea strikes at the heart of the Protestant Reformation.

Christians who derive their theology from the Bible are clear: the Gospel Message is completely "intolerant". Salvation of the soul can only come through the Son of God, Jesus Christ, *alone*. No institution may insinuate themselves between the sinner and the Savior for their aggrandizement. [Acts 4:7-12]

Catholic clergy may attempt to assuage concerns by claiming that *extra ecclesiam nulla salus* means the Catholic Church *represents* Christ[540] but the word is *ecclesiam* not *Christus*.

Benedict would later soften this agenda for a more important one that also came from Vatican II: ecumenism—the gathering of all religions under Roman authority. This would be done in the guise of being "more inclusive".[541]

Fresh off of Vatican II, Rome reached out to the "World Council of Churches" and in 1965, a "Joint Working Group" was established to find commonality amongst the irreparably uncommon.

JWG with the Roman Catholic Church

Among those churches which are not members of the WCC, the most notable is the Roman Catholic Church (RCC). Since 1965 a Joint Working Group (JWG), co-sponsored by the WCC and the RCC, has met regularly to discuss issues of common interest and promote cooperation. Plenary meetings are held annually; an executive group meets twice in between. The JWG's two co-secretaries from the Pontifical Council for Promoting Christian Unity (PCPCU) and the WCC help to coordinate contact between the WCC and the departments (or dicasteries) of the Vatican. ~ World Council of Churches[542]

Today, Pope Francis is preaching a sermon the WCC likes to hear: "Christian unity" and "social justice" (a phrase *invented* by the Jesuits).

WCC General Secretary Shares with Pope Aspirations for Unity, Justice and Peace

In an audience with Pope Francis in the Vatican, the World Council of Churches (WCC) general secretary Rev. Dr Olav Fykse Tveit stressed the significance of Christian unity. He also expressed appreciation for Pope Francis's call to pray for peace in Syria and his call for churches to remember the poor, encouraging Christians to work for economic justice.

The WCC general secretary, who represents a fellowship of 345 member churches in more than 110 countries, expressed these views on 7 March during his visit to Rome hosted by the Pontifical Council for Promoting Christian Unity of the Roman Catholic Church. ~ World Council of Churches[543]

The doctrinal help of Jesuit Karl Rahner was indispensable to Benedict XVI, even if Rahner did have his weaknesses. The chaste priest was notorious in keeping a girlfriend[544] but with sexual perversions so prevalent in the Church far worse than this, it is easily overlooked by the media.

The Fourth Beast

"Thus he said: 'The fourth beast will be a fourth kingdom on the Earth, which will be different from all the other kingdoms and will devour the whole Earth and tread it down and crush it. As for the ten horns, out of this kingdom ten kings will arise; and another will arise after them, and he will be different from the previous ones and

> *will subdue three kings. He will speak out against the Most High and wear down the saints of the Highest One, and he will intend to make alterations in times and in law..."* ~ Daniel 7:23-25, NASB

As Protestants look to a future Beast to change their calendars, a Jesuit has already done so.

> *Semiramis became known as the fertility goddess Ishtar. She took on many names in different cultures including Isis, Diana, Astarte, Ishtar, Aphrodite, Venus, and Easter. She was even identified with Mary as Mary was falsely deified and took on the titles "Mother of God" and "Queen of Heaven". Her son Tammuz took on many names as well such as Horus, Apollo, Sol, Krishna, Hercules, Mithra, and finally Jesus.* ~ Mystery Babylon the Religion of the Beast, Rav Sha'ul[545]

Being dedicated to this pagan goddess, Rome employed the Company to align the celebration of Ishtar and the Spring Equinox with Passover and our celebration of Christ's death and resurrection. [italics suspended]

> Papal, Catholic, pagan Rome adopted the pagan sungod calendar of her predecessor and mentor, Caesar's Imperial Rome. Julius Caesar got his calendar from the pagan religions of both the Eastern and Western sun worshiping religions of his ancestors. Roman Catholicism viciously attacked all who kept the Scriptural calendar and slaughtered millions of Jews and true Christians who followed Yahweh's ancient ways. She insisted on controlling the calendar and ordered all to adopt her corrupt computations. The results were predictable. By the year 1582 the Julian calendar was off by 11 days and began to be embarrassing to the "fisherman, lord god, the pope". Pope Gregory XIII then called on his own church version of the "Gestapo", the Jesuits for a fix. They then provided a Jesuit, Christopher Clavius, S.J[546], who became the architect of the Gregorian calendar! This heathen was a German Jesuit mathematician and "pseudo astronomer" and became the main engine of the modern Gregorian calendar used by Christianity today. With this Jesuit calendar, came also the Jesuit astronomy or, as is known today, the "heliocentric universe". With his introduction of the new Catholic calendar, Pope Gregory XIII demonstrated to the world that the changing of "times and seasons" is centered in Rome, and not on Scripture and certainly not centered on the Holy One of Israel. This was an interesting "trick" and was probably related to countering the Protestant reformation, which was going on in Europe at the time. The protestors failed to protest or counter this change and the Christian Church remains ignorant of

it to this present day! ...

The Gregorian calendar was accepted in England and her colonies by an act of Parliament in 1752! Russia would not accept this Roman calendar until the Communist revolution in the early 20th century. ~ Messianic Rabbi James Talbott[547]

Ruptured

Some of the most pernicious teachings in Protestant Christianity have Jesuits at the root of them.

Communism and socialism were Jesuit heresies that succeeded because they found a niche in human laziness. Proponents are invited to ignore the Divine Requirement to eat bread "by the sweat of your brow" because a governmental authority will take "from the rich" and provide for you.

The same is true of Dispensationalism and the "Pre-Tribulation Rapture" which teaches Christians that they don't need to prepare for hard times, nor fight injustice because they will be whisked away "at any moment".

The two men most responsible for Dispensationalism, the Pre-Tribulation Rapture and Christian Zionism are John Nelson Darby and Cyrus Ingerson Scofield.

The political prosperity of the nation of Israel is not in the same class as Dispensationalism and the Pre-Tribulation Rapture, and can simply be considered "misguided" in Christian doctrine. If the Prodigal Son prospered in his raucous living, he would have no need to return to his father. We will discuss how Jacob's children are played by the Elite in Chapter 17.

Anne Chamberlain of the *Idaho Observer* wrote a phenomenal column showing the twisted history of Dispensationalism and the Pre-Tribulation Rapture. Scofield's involvement in "questionable financial transactions"[548], jail time[549] and abandonment of his Catholic wife and children[550,551] have been corroborated by the author. [italics suspended]

> In 1767, a Chilean-born Catholic Priest, Manuel de Lacunza y Diaz came to Imola, Italy, when the Jesuits were expelled from Spain because of their brutality. There he claimed to be a converted Jew named Rabbi Juan Jushafat Ben-Ezra. Under that alias, he wrote a 900 page book titled, *The Coming of Messiah in Glory and Majesty*. Lacunza theorized that the Church would be taken to be with the Lord to escape the reign of Antichrist in the last 3-1/2 years of the age, some 45 days before Jesus' final return to Earth. During that

45 days (while the Church was in heaven), God would pour out His wrath upon the wicked remaining on Earth.

In 1828, "Glory and Majesty" was translated into English by a radical cultist London preacher named Edward Irving. Lacunza's views could have died there, for most in England saw Irving as a heretic.

At the same time Margaret MacDonald from Port Glasgow, Scotland, claimed she received divine revelations from God about a rapture. According to MacPherson, Miss Margaret had occultic ties, including a friendship with a girl who was into psychic powers and automatic writing. She sent her vision in a letter to Irving and, shortly thereafter, her revelation showed up in print. In September, 1830, *The Morning Watch*, a periodical put out by Irving's church, published, "Commentary on the Epistles to the Seven Churches in the Apocalypse."[1] ...

About the same time as Margaret Macdonald's vision, John Nelson Darby was playing with the dispensationalist idea of dividing history into ages or "dispensations." Many prophecy teachers of today credit John Darby with the origin of these teachings because he was a well-educated man who authored many books. In fact, Darby went to see Margaret and her family shortly after she gained notoriety for her vision, and in later years, claimed them as his own. ...

On at least one occasion Darby went to Saint Louis and met with Presbyterian minister James H. Brookes (1830-1897), Scofield's mentor and a key leader in the Niagara Bible Conferences. The conferences were held annually from 1876 to 1897, initially in different resort locations around the U.S. and, as of 1883 at Niagara-on-the-Lake, Ontario—the Queen's Royal Hotel. It was there that the fundamentalist movement was born and solidified. It then began to shape the Christian landscape in the United States and laid the foundation for "Premillennialism," the foundation for Christian Zionists. ...

At the outbreak of the American Civil War, Cyrus I. Scofield (1843-1921), a Michigan native, lied about his age in order to enlist in the Confederate Army in 1861, where he served in the 7th Tennessee infantry for a year.

In 1866 he married a Roman Catholic girl named Leontine Cerre. They had two girls, Abigail and Helene.

According to sweetliberty.org[3], as a young con-artist in Kansas after the Civil War, Scofield met up with John J. Ingalls, an aging Jewish lawyer/senator. Pulling strings both in Kansas and with his compatriots back east, Ingalls assisted Scofield in gaining admission to the Bar and procured his appointment as the federal attorney for Kansas. Scofield committed perjury when he took his oath, stating that he had never voluntarily borne arms against the United States. He was forced to resign after six months because of questionable financial transactions.

By 1877, Scofield was making a living on swindles and schemes and writing bogus checks. Ingalls and Scofield became partners in a railroad scam which led to Scofield serving time for criminal forgery.

In 1879, while he was in prison, a group of Christian women who had a jail ministry witnessed to Scofield and he made a profession of faith in Christ. He then began to study the writings of John Darby and embraced Darby's theology about the rapture and the need for Jews to resettle the land of Israel...

In 1877, Scofield had deserted his first wife and his two daughters and left them destitute. According Wikipedia, this was "perhaps because of alcoholism," but Joseph Canfield[3] asserts: "The very sudden quashing of the criminal charges without proper adjudication suggests that Scofield's career was in the hands of someone who had clout never available to either Ingalls, Pomeroy, or anyone of the Choteau Clan. But, the career was to be of such a nature that Leontine, the Catholic wife, had to go."

Scofield then took as his mistress a young girl from the St. Louis Flower Mission. He later abandoned her for Hettie Hall von Wartz whom he married in 1884. Leontine filed for divorce in 1881, finalized in 1883, listing "abandonment" as a reason. ~ Anne Wilder Chamberlain, the Idaho Observer[552]

Scofield craftily changed the Islamic invader of Israel—Magog (Ezekiel 38 & 39)—into Russia. Although the Scythians, identified by Josephus as their descendents, eventually migrated to Ukraine and the Steppes of Russia[s] this was only one stop in their historical heritage and they now live everywhere in the world. Their original home, however, is modern

---

[s] Using onomatopoeia (a word is defined by what it sounds like) to link the people of "Rosh" to "Russia" is on the same level of scholarship that says stinkweed comes from skunks and the moon is made of cheese.

Turkey.[553,554]

Jesuit priest Manuel Lacunza, a.k.a. "Juan Josafat Ben-Ezra" was, indeed, a principle theologian behind changing Protestant perceptions of the End Times and pulling Rome out of the spotlight and pushing Israel into it.

His Wikipedia entry is too charitable by half.

> *Manuel Diaz Lacunza S.J. (born Santiago, Chile, 1731; died Imola, Italy around June 18, 1801) was a Jesuit priest who used the penname Juan Josafat Ben-Ezra for his main work on the interpretation of the prophecies of the Bible. ...*
>
> *Lacunza believed [read "espoused"] that he had made some "new discoveries, real, solid, undeniable, and of the greatest importance" for the discipline of theology.*
>
> *The first of these "new discoveries" was that the end of the world would not be an instantaneous destruction of God's creation. He denied "that the world—that is, the material bodies or celestial globes that God has created (among which is the one on which we live)—has to have an end or return to chaos or nothingness ... This idea is not found often in Scripture before the opposite idea is stated and I agree with the best interpreters."*
>
> *Secondly, Lacunza concluded that the Biblical expressions "end of the age" and "end of the world" refer to two different times. He understood the "end of the age" or "day of the Lord" as merely the end of a phase of human history that would be closed by the coming of Christ and the beginning of His kingdom on Earth. At this time the living would be judged and the Jews converted, after which a new society would be established for a thousand-year reign of justice and peace.* ~ Wikipedia[555]

With Rome so clearly depicted as the 4th and final Beast of both Daniel and Revelation, Jesuits needed to disconnect Christians from that interpretation and they used Preterism and Futurism to do it.

Preterism is the idea that most of prophecy has already taken place. It was concocted by a Jesuit.

> *Preterism was first advanced in 1604 by Jesuit Luis de Alcasar to destroy the Reformed Protestant teaching that the papacy was Mystery Babylon, the Great Whore and the historical Antichrist.*

What Scholars Had To Say About Preterism

Henry Alford (an Anglican Greek scholar)

> *"The praeterist view found no favour and was hardly so much as thought of in the time of primitive Christianity. Those who lived near the date of the book of Revelation itself had no idea that its groups of imagery were intended merely to describe things then passing, and to be in a few years completed. This view is said to have been first promulgated in anything like completeness by the Jesuit Alcasar, in his "Vestigatio Arcani Sensus in Apocalypsi" (1604). Very nearly, the same plan was adopted by Grotius. The next great name among this school of interpreters is that of Bossuet the great antagonist of Protestantism."*

Charles Hodge

Also dismissing the Jesuit-Romanist Preterist approach, Charles Hodge noted that the preterists of his time for the most part were German Rationalists.

> *"[they] were German interpreters who, denying any real prediction of the future, confine the views of Daniel and John to their contemporary history".*

He lists some of the liberal scholars such as Ewald, DeWette and Lucke, who not only denied the predictive element in Scripture but also denied the inspiration and authority of the Word of God. ~ Bulletin for Biblical Christianity Today, Dr. Ronald Cooke[556]

Preterism wasn't accepted by large groups of Protestants and an alternative interpretation of the End Times was put forth.

Futurism is more appealing in that it acknowledges that much of prophecy is yet future but it distracts from the 4th Beast and paints the anti-Christ as a man who suddenly appears just before the Tribulation and who stands alone, apart from any organization or system.

It, too, was fabricated by a Jesuit.

Francisco Ribera (1537-1591) of Salamanca, Spain, published a 500 page commentary on the grand points of Babylon and Antichrist, the object being to set aside the Protestant teaching that the Papacy is the Antichrist. In his commentary, he assigned the first chapters of Revelation to the first century. The rest he restricted to a literal three and a half years a the end of time. He taught that the Jewish temple would be rebuilt by a single individual antichrist who would abolish the Christian religion, deny Christ, pretend to be God, and conquer the world.[8]

According to Schaff:

> *The events of the Apocolypse from ch. 4 to the close lie beyond the second advent of Christ. ... [he was joined by] Lacunza ... another Jesuit, who wrote under the name of Ben-Ezra "On the coming of the Messiah in glory and majesty," and taught premillennial advent...*

*Ribera's commentary laid the foundation for the greta structure of **Futurism**, which would be built upon and expanded by those who followed. Ribera's teaching was further popularized by Robert Bellarmine (1544-0621), an Italian cardinal and the most renowned of all Jesuit controversialists.[10]*

*After accepting the Jesuits' **Futurist System** (and the **Preterist System**...) millenarian Protestants no longer saw Rome as a present but only a distant future threat.[11] We should also mention Irving's system saw no hope of victory over the present forces of evil except "by the brightness of his coming" in the second advent. With no hope, why try to conquer all things for Christ? ~ Death of the Church Victorious, Ovid Need[557]*

There will be a "catching up" as is stated in I Thessalonians 4:16-17 but even the very word "rapture" is derived from the Latin Vulgate[558]. The Latin *raptura* actually has a military conquest application.

> ***Etymology:*** *"Rapture" is derived from Middle French rapture, via the Medieval Latin raptura ("seizure, rape, kidnapping"), which derives from the Latin raptus ("a carrying off").[17]* ~ Wikipedia[559]

In Matthew 24, Jesus, Himself, clearly stated; *first* comes the Tribulation, *then* the gathering/rapture.

> *"But immediately after the Tribulation of those days the sun will be darkened, and the moon will not give its light, and the stars will fall from the sky, and the powers of the heavens will be shaken. And then the Sign of the Son of Man will appear in the sky, and then all the tribes of the earth will mourn, and they will see the Son of Man coming on the clouds of the sky with power and great glory. And*

He will send forth His angels with a great trumpet and they will gather together His Elect from the four winds, from one end of the sky to the other." ~ Matthew 24:29-31 NASB (some capitalization added, including the word "tribulation" because, clearly, Jesus is talking about *the* Tribulation)

This same, clear timeline is paralleled in the Gospel of Mark.

"But in those days, after that Tribulation, THE SUN WILL BE DARKENED AND THE MOON WILL NOT GIVE ITS LIGHT, AND THE STARS WILL BE FALLING from Heaven, and the powers that are in the heavens will be shaken. Then they will see THE SON OF MAN RETURNING IN CLOUDS with great power and glory! And then He will send forth the angels, and will gather together His Elect from the four winds, from the farthest end of the Earth to the farthest end of Heaven!" ~ Mark 13:24-27 NASB (some capitalization added)

A "Pre-Tribulation Rapture" was unheard of before John Nelson Darby created it in 1827. In order to reconcile the Scriptural contradictions that he caused, Darby was forced to dream up two separate returns of Christ.

If one accepted Darby's view of the secret rapture... Benjamin Wills Newton pointed out, then many Gospel passages must be "renounced as not properly ours." ...this is precisely what Darby was prepared to do.

Too traditional to admit that biblical authors might have contradicted each other, and too rationalist to admit that the prophetic maze defied penetration, Darby attempted a resolution of his exegetical dilemma by distinguishing between Scripture intended for the Church and Scripture intended for Israel...

The task of the expositor of the Bible was, in a phrase that became the hallmark of dispensationalism, "rightly dividing the word of truth". ~ *The Roots of Fundamentalism*, Ernest Sandeen[560]

Hal Lindsey and David Jeremiah are two of the most well-known expositors who passionately promulgate a pre-Tribulation Rapture. A name much less well-known is Carol C. Carlson, a woman who ghost-wrote books for both of them including Lindsey's watershed work *The Late Great Planet Earth* in 1970[561]. Is Carlson a secret emissary of Rome?

Lindsey is a man whose background is steeped in mystery. In 1977, *People* reported that his conversion to Evangelical Christianity "broke up" his first marriage[562]. More recent sources claim he has been divorced twice more and on his fourth wife.[563,564]

It has been reputed that Lindsey's two daughters, Robin and Jenny, have attended Jesuit Gonzaga University[565,566]. LinkedIn lists a "Jenny Lindsey-Patrick" having attended Gonzaga from 1982 to 1985.[567]

"Take Up Your Cross And Follow Me"

While Christians all over the world receive Tribulation persecution, pampered Westerners emotionally hunker down and put their hope in Jesuit falsehoods claiming that I Thessalonians 5:9-11 protects them from "wrath".

The Anti-Christ, war, famine, death, persecution; Christians will endure the first 5 Seals of the Scroll of Revelation as the 5th Seal is a revealing of Christians beheaded by the Beast. The Wrath of God is not kindled until the breaking of the 6th Seal and the Return of Jesus Christ. [Revelation 6]

Turmoil and tribulation are not "wrath". They are the guaranteed result of a good Christian Witness. Only those who endure tribulation and overcome it will be Saved.

> *"Behold, I send you out as sheep in the midst of wolves; so be shrewd as serpents and innocent as doves."*
>
> *"But beware of men, for they will hand you over to the courts and scourge you in their synagogues; and you will even be brought before governors and kings for My Sake, as a Testimony to them and to the Gentiles."*
>
> *"But when they hand you over, do not worry about how or what you are to say; for it will be given you in that hour what you are to say. For it is not you who speak, but it is the Spirit of your Father who speaks in you."*
>
> *"Brother will betray brother to death, and a father his child; and children will rise up against parents and cause them to be put to death. You will be hated by all because of My Name, but it is the one who has endured to the end who will be saved."* ~ Matthew 10:16-22, NASB (some capitalization added)

Endnotes

[484] *With Their First Pope, Jesuits Are Making a Comeback*, Tim Willis, 5 September 2014, Newsweek
http://www.newsweek.com/their-first-pope-jesuits-are-making-comeback-267930

[485] *Secret Counsels of the Society of Jesus*, Robert Breckinridge, Baltimore: Edward J. Cole & Co. (1835), p. 87

[486] *Rome Souterraine*, Charles Didier, Paulin Press 1848, pp. 349-351, digital versions available from the Internet Archive, American Libraries;
https://archive.org/details/romesouterraine01didigoog

[487] *Secret Counsels of the Society of Jesus*, Breckinridge, pp. 5, 80

[488] *ibid*, p. 77

[489] *ibid*, p. 78

[490] *Alberto* series, Chick Publications
http://www.chick.com/catalog/assortments/0931.asp

[491] *Bush "Plotted To Lure Saddam Into War With Fake UN Plane"*, Andy McSmith, 03 February 2006, the Independent
http://www.independent.co.uk/news/world/americas/bush-plotted-to-lure-saddam-into-war-with-fake-un-plane-465436.html

[492] *Clinton Aide's Idea: Let Iraq Shoot Down U.S. Plane*, Justin Elliott, 15 October 2010, Salon.com

[493] *"You're A Fool!": How Protestant Rev Ian Paisley Reacted To Tony Blair's Revelation He Was Converting To Catholicism*, Matt Chorley, 20 January 2014, the Daily Mail
http://www.dailymail.co.uk/news/article-2542541/Youre-fool-How-protestant-Rev-Ian-Paisley-reacted-Tony-Blairs-revelation-converting-Catholicism.html

[494] *Faith & Globalisation* [sic], the Tony Blair Faith Foundation.org, "We provide leaders with the knowledge, analysis and skills to navigate the complexity of religions impact in the world."
http://tonyblairfaithfoundation.org/projects/supporting-leaders

[495] *Faith and Globalization: Tony Blair Teaches at Yale*, Dan Colman, 5 January 2010, Open Culture.org
http://www.openculture.com/2010/01/faith_and_globalization_tony_blair_teaches_at_yale.html

[496] *Revealed: Tony Blair and the Oligarch Bankrolling His Charity*, Robert Mendick and Edward Malnick, 10 February 2013, the Telegraph
http://www.telegraph.co.uk/news/politics/tony-blair/9859780/Revealed-Tony-Blair-and-the-oligarch-bankrolling-his-charity.html

[497] *As Pro-European Protests Seize Ukraine, Jewish Oligarch Victor Pinchuk Is a Bridge to the West*, Maria Danilova, 13 December 2013, Tablet Magazine
http://www.tabletmag.com/jewish-news-and-politics/155976/ukraines-western-face

[498] *The Profitable Delusion Shared by Bill Clinton and Tony Blair*, Alexander Chancellor, 5 July 2014, the Spectator
http://www.spectator.co.uk/life/long-life/9253321/dont-worry-what-blair-and-clinton-have-gained-in-wealth-they-have-lost-in-stature-heres-why/

[499] *Protestant Firebrand Ian Paisley Dies at 88*, Shawn Pogatchnik, AP posted by Time magazine

http://time.com/3339097/protestant-firebrand-ian-paisley-dies-aged-88/#3339097/protestant-firebrand-ian-paisley-dies-aged-88/

[500] *Ian Paisley, Death of a Political Behemoth: Cameron, Blair and Robinson Lead Tributes*, John Mulgrew, 12 September 2014, the Belfast Telegraph
http://www.belfasttelegraph.co.uk/news/local-national/northern-ireland/ian-paisley-death-of-a-political-behemoth-cameron-blair-and-robinson-lead-tributes-30582232.html

[501] *Secret Counsels of the Society of Jesus*, Breckinridge, p. 13

[502] *The Jesuit Oath Exposed*, Professor Arthur Noble, 5 April 2000, the European Institute of Protestant Studies
http://www.ianpaisley.org/article.asp?ArtKey=jesuit

[503] *History Of The Captivity Of Napoleon At St. Helena, by General Count Montholon, The Emperor's Companion In Exile, And Testamentary Executor*, London, Henry Colburn, Great Marlborough Street, 1846, Vol II, p. 388
Internet Archive, California Digital Library,
https://archive.org/details/historyofcaptivivol1and2montiala

Charles Chiniquy cites this same source for a great parallel quote from Napoleon, himself; *The Jesuits are a military organization, not a religious order. Their chief is a general of an army, not the mere father abbot of a monastery. And the aim of this organization is power—power in its most despotic exercise —absolute power, universal power, power to control the world by the volition of a single man* [i.e., the Superior General of the Jesuits]. *Jesuitism is the most absolute of despotisms—and at the same time the greatest and most enormous of abuses...* I've gone through the work, repeatedly. It's not there, I'm afraid.

[504] *Secret Counsels of the Society of Jesus*, Breckinridge, pp. 100, 103

[505] *The Babington Plot*, J.E.C. Shepherd, Wittenburg Publications (1987), p. 12

[506] *Pope Francis: The Jesuit History of Suppression and Theology of Liberation*, Gianluca Mezzofiore, 14 March 2013, International Business Times
http://www.ibtimes.co.uk/pope-francis-jesuit-bergoglio-446121

[507] *Solving the Mystery of Babylon the Great*, Edward Hendrie, Great Mountain Publishing (2013), p. 53

[508] *The Triple Crown: An Account of the Papal Conclaves*, Valérie Pirie, Clement XIV (Ganganelli) 1769—1774, Pickle Publishing
http://www.pickle-publishing.com/papers/triple-crown-clement-xiv.htm

[509] *Pope Francis Resisted Revenge Over 18th Century Clement XIV*, unattributed 16 March 2013, Reuters
http://www.reuters.com/article/2013/03/16/us-pope-jesuits-idUSBRE92F09620130316

[510] *The Catholic Controversy: A Defense of the Faith*, Francis de Sales, Burns and Oates, London (1886)

[511] *St. Francis de Sales—Patron Saint of Writers and Journalists*, Psyche Orsburn, 2013, Pen Central.com
http://www.thepencentral.com/view/articles/st-francis-de-sales-patron-saint-of-writers-and-journalists-488

[512] *Lycée Louis-le-Grand*, Wikipedia

http://en.wikipedia.org/wiki/Coll%C3%A8ge_de_Clermont
[513] *The Jesuit Order – The Society of Jesus*, Darryl Eberhart, Tackling the Tough Topics, 18 December 2009, posted here:
http://www.toughissues.org/the%20jesuit%20oder.htm
[514] *Emmanuel-Joseph Sieyès*, 18 July 2014, Encyclopædia Britannica
http://www.britannica.com/EBchecked/topic/543510/Emmanuel-Joseph-Sieyes
[515] *Comte Emmanuel Joseph Sieyès Facts*, Biography, Your Dictionary.com
http://biography.yourdictionary.com/comte-emmanuel-joseph-sieyes
[516] *Italy in the Age of the Risorgimento 1790 - 1870*, Harry Hearder, Routledge (2014), p. 100
[517] *Pius VI*, Encyclopædia Britannica
http://www.britannica.com/EBchecked/topic/462354/Pius-VI
[518] *The Pope Who Outlasted a Tyrant*, Matthew Bunson, undated, Catholic Answers.com
http://www.catholic.com/magazine/articles/the-pope-who-outlasted-a-tyrant
 Perhaps a better title would've been, "The Tyrant Who Was The Tool of the Company"...idiot. Just LOVE the Catholic apologists.
[519] *The Jesuits After the Restoration (1814-1912)*, the Catholic Encyclopedia
http://www.newadvent.org/cathen/14100a.htm
[520] *The Huguenots - Their Faith, History, and Impact*, ReformationSA.org
http://reformationsa.org/index.php/reformation/121-the-huguenots-their-faith-history-and-impact
[521] *St. Bartholomew's Day Massacre*, Wikipedia.org
http://en.wikipedia.org/wiki/St._Bartholomew's_Day_massacre
[522] *The Persecution of Huguenots and French Economic Development, 1680-1720*, Warren Candler Scoville, University of California Press (1960)
[523] *A Rescuer's Story: Pastor Pierre-Charles Toureille in Vichy France*, Tela Zasloff, University of Wisconsin Press (2003), p. 20, however the entire Chapter 2, *To Be a Huguenot*, pp. 9-33 is well worth reading.
[524] *Napoleon's Wars, Mistakes and Fall*, Macrohistory and World Timeline
http://www.fsmitha.com/h3/h34-np4e.html
[525] *The Literary Gazette, Journal of the Belle Letters*, published by H. Colburn (1827), p. 663
[526] *The Grand Design Exposed*, John Daniel, CHJ Publishing (1999), pp. 122-123
[527] *U.S. Nuns Haunted by Dead Jesuit: the Ghost of Pierre Teilhard de Chardin*, David Gibson, 22 May 2014, Religion News Service
http://www.religionnews.com/2014/05/22/nuns-jesuit-vatican-teilhard-de-chardin/
[528] *The Philosophy of Pierre Teilhard De Chardin*, Henry G. Hadley, March 1967, Ministry magazine
https://www.ministrymagazine.org/archive/1967/03/the-philosophy-of-pierre-teilhard-de-chardin
[529] *Piltdown Man - the Greatest Hoax in the History of Science?* the Natural History Museum of London
http://www.nhm.ac.uk/nature-online/science-of-natural-history/the-scientific-process/piltdown-man-hoax/
[530] *Piltdown Man*, Wikipedia
http://en.wikipedia.org/wiki/Piltdown_Man
[531] *The Piltdown Conspiracy*, Stephen Jay Gould, 1983, Clark University

http://www.clarku.edu/~piltdown/map_prim_suspects/Teilhard_de_Chardin/Chardin_Prosecution/piltdownconsiracy.html
[532] *ibid*
[533] *Homily of His Holiness Benedict XVI*, Cathedral of Aosta, 24 July 2009, Vatican.va
http://www.vatican.va/holy_father/benedict_xvi/homilies/2009/documents/hf_ben-xvi_hom_20090724_vespri-aosta_en.html
[534] *Georges Lemaître, Father of the Big Bang, Cosmic Horizons: Astronomy At The Cutting Edge*, Steven Soter and Neil deGrasse Tyson, 2000, the American Museum of Natural History
http://www.amnh.org/education/resources/rfl/web/essaybooks/cosmic/p_lemaitre.html
[535] *The Faith and Reason of Father George Lemaître*, Joseph R. Laracy, Catholic Culture.org
http://www.catholicculture.org/culture/library/view.cfm?recnum=8847
[536] *How a Catholic Priest Gave Us the Big Bang Theory*, Alex Higgins, 29 December 2007, the American Chronicle
http://www.freerepublic.com/focus/religion/1945606/posts
[537] *Lemaitre the Jesuit: Father of Big Bang Theory*, QuantumPork
http://www.quantumpork.com/index.php?option=com_content&view=article&id=103:lemaitre-the-jesuit-father-of-big-bang-theory&catid=30:qp-cosmology&Itemid=13
[538] *The Big Bang Theory vs. God's Word*, Wayne Jackson, the Christian Courier
https://www.christiancourier.com/articles/133-the-big-bang-theory-vs-gods-word
[539] *Benedict XVI: "Let Me Tell You the Story of My Council"*, Giacomo Galeazzi, 10 October 2012, the Vatican Insider
http://vaticaninsider.lastampa.it/en/the-vatican/detail/articolo/concilio-18806/
[540] *Without the Church There Is No Salvation*, Philip C. L. Gray, 1999, Catholic Education Resource Center
http://catholiceducation.org/articles/apologetics/ap0043.html
[541] *Ratzinger Denies The Dogma "Extra Ecclesiam Nulla Salus"*, Tradition in Action.org
http://www.traditioninaction.org/ProgressivistDoc/A_006_RatzingerSalvation.htm
[542] *JWG with the Roman Catholic Church*, World Council of Churches
http://www.oikoumene.org/en/what-we-do/jwg-with-roman-catholic-church
[543] *WCC General Secretary Shares with Pope Aspirations for Unity, Justice and Peace*, World Council of Churches
http://www.oikoumene.org/en/press-centre/news/wcc-general-secretary-shares-with-pope-aspirations-for-unity-justice-and-peace
[544] *Karl Rahner's Girlfriend*, John Vennari, 28 April 2004, Catholic Family News, reposted at Free Republic
http://www.freerepublic.com/focus/religion/1126324/posts
[545] *Mystery Babylon the Religion of the Beast*, Rav Sha'ul, self-published, no date, p. 53

By the citation this would appear to be a shady source but this work comes from what appears to be a ministry that is hard-core Messianic Jew, recognizing the Truth of the Gospel but only through "Yashua" and not "Jesus" and the auther seems to be quite knowledgable. Like so many other questionable sources, I use it because it seems to confirm what we already know and be corroborated by others that we recognize as being of good repute.

In case you want to look further they can be found at The Sabbath Covenant.com

http://www.sabbathcovenant.com/index.htm
   Be careful of legalism but understand you will never know the real Jesus until you know His Hebrew heritage...and ours.
[546] *Christopher Clavius*, Wikipedia
https://en.wikipedia.org/wiki/Christopher_Clavius
[547] *The Gregorian Calendar vs Gods Holy Calendar*, Rav James Talbott, 17 October 2013, NavigatingThroughProphecy.com
http://navigatingthroughprophecy.com/2013/10/17/the-gregorian-calendar-vs-gods-holy-calendar/
[548] *C.I. Scofield > Biography*, Wikipedia
http://en.wikipedia.org/wiki/C._I._Scofield#Biography
   Please note Wikipedia's citations. I do *not* believe that reports of Scofield being imprisoned were fabricated.
[549] *C. I. Scofield - The Rest of the Story*, Thomas Williamson, March 2012, the Northern Landmark Missionary Baptist Newsletter, Baptist Pillar.com
http://www.baptistpillar.com/article_780c.html
[550] *Scofield: The Man Behind The Myth*, Homestead.com
http://poweredbychrist.homestead.com/files/cyrus/scofield.htm
[551] *Divorced Pastor Cyrus Ingerson Scofield – Author of the Scofield Reference Bible*, Truth with Snares.org
http://truthwithsnares.org/no-one-will-be-left-behind-but-you-will-be-separated/divorced-pastor-cyrus-ingerson-scofield-author-of-the-scofield-reference-bible/
   Better copy of the Atchison County, Kansas divorce decree.
[552] *A Little History: Cyrus I Scofield and the Tribulation*, Anne Wilder Chamberlain, May 2009, the Idaho Observer
http://proliberty.com/observer/20090507.htm
[553] *Joel Richardson Debunks Russian Invasion of Israel*, Johnny Cirucci, YouTube
https://www.youtube.com/watch?v=XHczzdPXGbg
[554] *Joel Richardson Identifies Magog As Turkey, Not Russia*, Johnny Cirucci, YouTube
https://www.youtube.com/watch?v=dCVI_DfEyfU
[555] *Manuel Lacunza*, Wikipedia
http://en.wikipedia.org/wiki/Manuel_Lacunza#Lacunza.27s_Ideas
[556] *Bulletin for Biblical Christianity Today*, Dr. Ronald Cooke, via the European Institute of Protestant Studies, posted 3 August 2001
http://www.ianpaisley.org/article.asp?ArtKey=twaddle
[557] *Death of the Church Victorious*, Ovid Need, Sovereign Grace Publishers (2002), pp. 43-45
[558] *Rapture*, the ABC's of Prophecy, Rapture Ready
https://www.raptureready.com/abc/rapture.html
   Good luck with that, sleepy.
[559] *Rapture > Etymology*, Wikipedia
https://en.wikipedia.org/wiki/Rapture
[560] *The Roots of Fundamentalism: British and American Millenarianism 1800-1930*, Ernest R. Sandeen, University of Chicago Press (1970), pp. 65-67
[561] *Books by Carole C. Carlson*, goodreads.com
https://www.goodreads.com/author/list/16629.Carole_C_Carlson

[562] *Hal Lindsey Says the Wave of the Future Is Armageddon, and 14 Million Buy It*, Lucretia Marmon, 4 July 1977, People
http://www.people.com/people/archive/article/0,,20068235,00.html
[563] *Hal Lindsey*, Notable Names Database
http://www.nndb.com/people/157/000117803/
[564] *Hal Lindsey's on wife #4*, Sermon Index
http://www.sermonindex.net/modules/newbb/viewtopic.php?topic_id=53766&forum=48
[565] *Left Behind By The Jesuits*, Reformation.org
http://www.reformation.org/left-behind-by-jesuits.html
[566] *Pre-Trib Hypocrisy*, Dave MacPherson, Tribulational Central.com
http://tribulationcentral.com/guest/mc-hypocrisy.html
[567] *Jenny Lindsey-Patrick*, LinkedIn
https://www.linkedin.com/pub/jenny-lindsey-patrick/b/794/639

Chapter 8

A Good Jesuit Education

Two of the most important human endeavors today are medicine and law—they are also two of the most lucrative. Both doctors and lawyers take their wealth and usually move into politics with it.

They guard their industries with a foreign language that insulates them from the common people, isolates their insider knowledge and allows them to charge exorbitant rates for their services.

That language is Latin: the tongue of the Roman Empire.

Society of Spies

The phrase "Jesuit-educated" is not as inoffensive as it might first appear. Although thousands upon thousands of students pass through Jesuit institutions with no exposure to a secret Luciferian agenda, as professors, administrators and officials, Jesuits can scout for promising young talent to be molded in their image.

The number of those that have gone through that process to attain high office is shocking.

Again we reference *Secreta Monita*—college officials weren't running schools as much as they were gathering intelligence on the local community (and abusing the confessional to do so).

> *Let the rectors of colleges endeavor to obtain intelligence of the houses, gardens, farms, villages, and other estates which may be owned by the first nobility, merchants or citizens, and if it can be done, the taxes and rents by which they may be burthened; but cautiously, for it can be done most effectually by confession, companionship and private conversations, wherefore when a confessor obtains a rich penitent, let him immediately inform the rector, and try to cherish him by every method. ~ Secreta Monita*[568]

Taking over the education of future generations became an immediate top priority for the Company.

They quickly created whole institutions of their own and infiltrated secular ones. Their exacting discipline was seen as highly prized and attracted the youth of the Elite. This was promoted by propaganda as nothing less than "heroic".

> *It was the world's finest school system... It was serving customers who were essential to the company's top-down strategic approach.*
>
> *...heroic leadership, though, has something to do with pulling off what seems impossible to everyone else. The Jesuits built a school system that was impossible for any European to have conceived at the time.*
>
> *...heroic leadership involves bold imagination and the desire to take bold chances. Jesuits freed themselves from the European mindset in order to see the world through a very different lens. And so, heroes in India and Paraguay ventured far out on limbs, not pausing to worry whether those limbs would support them. How could they not take the chance? They were involved in the "greatest enterprise in the world today." And those limbs held while Paraguay Jesuits pushed a progressive agenda ... that few of their contemporaries would dare imagine, much less approve or attempt. ~ Heroic Leadership: Best Practices from a 450-Year-Old Company That Changed the World*, Chris Lowney[569]

Jesuit instructors are expert in scouting future talent and, once found, they will bend their subjects to their agenda, either willingly...or unwillingly.[570]

Get Fluked

Many news junkies will remember the college student, Sandra Fluke, who made headlines helping the Obamacare agenda of taxpayer-funded "contraception"—society must pay for licentious lifestyles and the illusion of sex without consequences.

Franklin Roosevelt is credited with having said;

> *Nothing in politics ever happens by accident. If it happens, you can bet it was planned that way.*

The quote is hotly contested with no known sources but, regardless if it originated with America's 33° Shriner Freemason 32nd President, it's absolutely true.

What many Americans didn't know was that Sandra Fluke was no common college co-ed but a radical activist.[571]

Fluke testified before Jesuit-trained Nancy Pelosi and an audience of sympathetic Democrats.

How did she get that kind of clout? —She's a Georgetown Law student.

For good reason is Georgetown in the heart of Washington DC; it is the command center from which the Company directs the affairs of America.

> *Congress is in recess this week, but that didn't stop House Democrats from holding a hearing to take testimony from a Georgetown law student who was barred from testifying in last week's hearing about President Obama's policy on contraceptives, health insurance and religiously affiliated organizations.*
>
> *That hearing drew fire from supporters of the administration's approach for featuring an all-male panel to start, followed in the afternoon by a second panel that included two women opposed to mandatory coverage of contraceptives by insurers.*
>
> *Somewhat ironically, Sandra Fluke, who has become the poster child for the Democrats since she was not permitted to appear before the House Oversight and Government Reform Committee hearing, would likely not be affected by the policy as a member of a student, rather than an employer-provided health insurance plan.*
>
> *Even more ironic: Georgetown already offers contraceptive coverage as part of its employee health plans.* ~ Julie Rovner, NPR[572]

How does a Catholic college cover "contraceptives"? Is there one agenda promoted publically and an entirely separate agenda promoted privately?

Barack Obama called Sandra Fluke *personally* to thank her for her bravery[573] in fostering her radical Leftist agenda of personal promiscuity; the agenda of Georgetown's Jesuits.

Obama is a completely manufactured weapon of mass destruction who has been monitored his entire life, via his CIA family (ultimately run by the Jesuits), the Communist community (created by the Jesuits), and overseen in Indonesia by Catholic priests (many of whom were trained by Jesuits and secretly ordained as Jesuits).

The Teleprompter In Chief

Although Americans have no idea who Barack Obama is, it is clear that he is heavily controlled by powers beyond him.

Obama is so controlled, he is required to speak from a teleprompter even when he is before a classroom of 6th grade children, as was the case in Falls Church, VA in January of 2010.

Even Left-wing comic Jonathan Leibowitz (more popularly known as "Jon Stewart") couldn't pass up the opportunity to lampoon this event[574], but the idea that Obama is handled from a higher power just as, if not more malignant towards America than he is, is no laughing matter.

Who is telling Obama what to say?

—Jesuits are...through their agents like Jon Favreau.

Favreau started his political career via an internship with Skull and Bones alum John Kerry while attending Jesuit Holy Cross.

From there, his Leftist ideology passed the test for the Society of Jesus and he was given to Barack Obama, as this propaganda puff piece from the Boston Globe states:

> *He got his start in Washington in Kerry's press-office during a Holy Cross internship, when he helped ghostwrite op-ed pieces for the Bay State senator. He so impressed David Wade, Kerry's chief of staff, that Wade hired him as one of the first recruits to Kerry's presidential campaign. Watching Favreau's talents emerge was like "a scene in 'Good Will Hunting,'" said Wade, marveling at Favreau's journey.*
>
> *"To paraphrase Forrest Gump, interns are like a box of chocolates; you never know what you're going to get. Some treat Washington internships like cameo appearances on the "West Wing." Jon ended up in the real West Wing because he had the opposite approach," Wade said. "He had a soul. He cared about Massachusetts and progressive ideals in keeping with the best of Jesuit education."*
>
> *During the 2004 Democratic National Convention, Favreau was famously dispatched by Kerry's team to tell Obama, who was delivering the keynote address, to remove a line in his speech that was too similar to what Kerry was going to say. A year later Obama hired him and Favreau became the second youngest head*

speechwriter in presidential history.[575]

It's fascinating that Favreau required the dogma of the Leftist politicians he served to marry up with what the Jesuits taught him.

Favreau is now off to Hollywood where the Company also has many friends.

John Kerry was a poignant choice for vetting the speech-writer. Not only is he an overt, practicing Catholic[576], he recently proclaimed that he was traveling to Rome as "the first Catholic Secretary of State in 33 years," to meet Rome's first Jesuit Pope.[577]

A few months later, Kerry would show his deft international negotiating prowess by speaking with Russian Foreign Minister Sergei Lavrov about the burgeoning new Cold War between the U.S. and Russia as well as Israel's Prime Minister Benjamin Netanyahu about Mideast Peace.

Where did they all go for these critical talks? To Rome!

> *With Israel in the middle of an election campaign and European leaders pressing for a UN Security Council resolution on a negotiating deadline that Israel opposes, Secretary of State John Kerry traveled to Rome on Sunday to seek a compromise.*
>
> *Kerry will spend the next few days meeting Israeli and Palestinian leaders, the new European foreign policy chief, and the foreign ministers of Russia, France, Britain, and Germany in an effort to find a compromise that Washington can accept.*
>
> *In Rome, Kerry met with Foreign Minister Sergey Lavrov of Russia on Sunday. In addition to the Israeli-Palestinian issue, the two men were expected to discuss disagreements over Syria and Ukraine. Washington has harshly condemned Russia's annexation of Crimea and Russian military intervention in eastern Ukraine, which Moscow continues to deny.*
>
> *Kerry will hold talks with Prime Minister Benjamin Netanyahu of Israel in Rome on Monday, and then fly to Paris to consult with European colleagues before traveling to London to meet Palestinian and Arab League officials on Tuesday.* ~ Steven Erlanger, New York Times[578]

London is the financial hub for Rome so he basically won't be leaving.

Nowhere in media coverage is there a report that Kerry met with his

Jesuit Pope. His visit to the Pope's back yard was purely coincidental.

Who was the Catholic Secretary of State previous to John Kerry, Skull and Bones '66? —Georgetown alum[579] General Alexander Haig[580]: the man quick to take the reins[581] after a Bush family friend[582] tried to assassinate Ronald Reagan in 1981.

Haig was an excellent provocateur, one who appeared to be a Patriot on the outside but who's agenda was world destabilization and constant conflict for the United States.

> *Former Secretary of State Alexander Haig is now posthumously being recast as the quintessential soldier-patriot. The truth is, he had a dark side: wiretapping for Richard Nixon, facilitating the operations of a military spy ring that stole classified documents from the White House, sabotaging peace negotiations over Vietnam and détente with the USSR, and unduly hastening Nixon's exit from office. Haig is most lauded as the man who, according to conventional wisdom, held the presidency together during the depths of Watergate. But that evaluation obscures Haig's true role in the Nixon White House.*
>
> *He began to come to prominence in 1968 when Fritz Kraemer, who had helped Haig rise within the Pentagon, recommended him to another protégé, Henry Kissinger, as Kissinger's military advisor on the Nixon National Security Council. ...*
>
> *In 1981, when President Reagan was shot, Haig told the Cabinet and the press, "As of now, I am in control here in the White House," and by this obvious mis-stating of the correct chain of succession forever disqualified himself from further high office. In retrospect he claimed his outburst had been no more than a "poor choice of words;" rather, the statement was symptomatic of Haig's lifelong attitude toward democratically elected public officials and presidential power.*
>
> *...When Haig was 10, his father died of cancer, and his Irish American mother raised her children in the Catholic church.[6] He attended Saint Joseph's Preparatory School in Philadelphia and graduated from Lower Merion High School in Ardmore, Pennsylvania. He then studied at the University of Notre Dame for two years, before transferring to the United States Military Academy, where he graduated in 1947. Haig earned a master's degree in business administration from Columbia Business School in 1955, and a master's degree in international relations from*

Georgetown University in 1961. His thesis was on the role of military officers in making national policy. ~ Tom Shachtman, author of *The Forty Years War*[583]

Three Ways To Sunset

If you're looking to know where Jesuits teach, there are 28 overtly Jesuit-run Universities in the United States—many of them have surprisingly secular-sounding names:

Boston College	Marquette University
Canisius College	Regis University
College of the Holy Cross	Rockhurst University
Creighton University	Saint Joseph's University
Fairfield University	Saint Louis University
Fordham University	Saint Peter's University
Georgetown University	Santa Clara University
Gonzaga University	Seattle University
John Carroll University	Spring Hill College
Le Moyne College	University of Detroit Mercy
Loyola Marymount University	University of San Francisco
Loyola University Chicago	University of Scranton
Loyola University Maryland	Wheeling Jesuit University
Loyola University New Orleans	Xavier University

There are twice as many Jesuit-run secondary schools.[584]

Then there are the quiet associations with secular schools like Campion Hall at Oxford or Campion College at the University of Regina in Saskatchewan[585]. At one time, the Yale Divinity school was considering a merger.[586]

Secret Secular Jesuits: Campions of the Catholic World Order

With the unprecedented success of Puritan Protestant Oliver Cromwell to give the English common man his destiny back, manipulators from Rome needed to go underground—or, more precisely, "undergraduate".

Given how powerfully the Company of Loyola has used the usurpation of education, it perks a researcher's eyes when he sees evidence of other secret organizations doing the same.

Franciscan-educated New Ager Robert Bauval (who claims the Bible is full of "myths") wants to pull the curtain back just enough for you to see the secret "Rosicrucians" but not any further. This tactic has worked for the Jesuits for millennia.

Knowingly or unknowingly, this is what Bauval does regarding how the Luciferian Elite reacted to the English Civil War.

> *Open parliamentary rebellion finally came in 1642. After a failed attempt to arrest five members of Parliament, Charles I and his Royalist supporters quit London and set up court-in-exile at Oxford, that traditional hub of elitist intellectuals and scholars. Ti was there, in the following years, that a strange fraternity of literati bean to meet, calling themselves—evocatively—the "Invisible Collage". The earliest surviving written reference to this mysterious Invisible College comes from the celebrated physicist, Robert Boyle (1627-1691), in a letter he wrote to his tutor in France in 1646. In this letter Boyle states that he is now diligently applying himself to "natural philosophy" based on the principles of "our new philosophical college" and requests certain books from his tutor that "will make you extremely welcome to our Invisible College". A few months later, in 1647, Boyle again mentions the Invisible College in a letter to a friend...*
>
> *The term "Invisible College", as well as the description of its activities and concerns given above, immediately brings to mind, of course, the Invisible College of the Rosicrucian brotherhood. ...*
>
> *It turns out that Boyle had spent some time in Paris in his youth, during an educational tour of France and Geneva, and it is not impossible that he could have heard of the Rosicrucian Invisible College through his tutors or other acquaintances. Frances Yates observes that there is, on face value, an uncanny similarity in the terminology used by Boyle in this letters to his tutor and the terminology used by Francis Bacon in New Atlantis.*[587]

100 years previous, Ignatius Loyola was also in Paris creating his own secret society.[588]

In 1560, a man named Edmund Campion was getting his Bachelor of Arts at Oxford. He took the required Anglican "Oath of Supremacy" but, inward, he was a devout Catholic. He was eventually discovered and forced to leave Oxford for Ireland. From Ireland, Campion made his way to the English university of Douai in France and, eventually, to Rome where he became a Jesuit in 1573. In 1580 he was sent back to England to help reclaim her for the Pope[589]. In 1581, a secret anti-Protestant pamphlet titled

Decem Rationes ("Ten Reasons") appeared on the Oxford campus. Campion was found to be the author. He was arrested for subversion, tried and convicted of treason. Campion was hung in December of 1581. Rome beatified him in 1886 and canonized him in 1970.[590]

Neophyte Catholic and former British Prime Minister Tony Blair went to Oxford. Perhaps he secretly spent some time in the private academic community on campus run by the Jesuits there.

It's called "Campion Hall".[591]

We will discuss Jesuit use of proxy secret societies like the Rosicrucians in Chapter 16.

Priests Without Collars

By name...by association...and the third way Jesuits have effected education is by covert subversion—no cassocks, no crucifixes; all undercover.

Seventh Day Adventists have been the rare minority voice amongst Protestant sects who doggedly pursue the wrongs of Rome in general and of the Jesuits in specific.

SDA scholar Dr. B. G. Wilkerson wrote in his book *Truth Triumphant*:

As the Jesuits were already in control of Spain and Portugal, they accompanied the conquerors principally for the purpose of converting the St. Thomas Christians. It was the unhappy lot of India to experience the crushing weight of these haughty monks. These men were skilled in sublimated treachery and trained for years in the art of rapid debate in which they could trap an opponent by the cunning use of ambiguous terms; consequently, the simple, trusting St. Thomas Christians were no match for them. The Jesuits proposed to dominate all schools and colleges.

This they sought to accomplish in non-Catholic schools by occupying the pulpits and the professorial chairs, not as Jesuits, but as professed adherents of the Protestant churches to which these schools belonged. As an example of their success by 1582, only forty-eight years after the order was founded, they controlled two hundred eighty-seven colleges and universities in Europe, some of which were of their own founding.

It was their studied aim to gain entrance, under the guise of friendship, into services of the state and to climb up as advisers to the highest officers, where they could so influence affairs as to bring them into the orbit of Rome. They were past masters of the ways of deception. They were adept in the policy of secretly bringing on a public disaster, simultaneously providing for salvation from the last terrors of that disaster; thus they would be credited with salvation from the extremity of the calamity, while others were blamed for its cause.[592]

According to Edith Starr Miller, Lady Queenborough, not only have the Jesuits infiltrated schools, governments and other religions—they've even infiltrated other orders within the Catholic Church.

"The question has long been hotly debated whether, in addition to these six avowed grades, there be not a seventh, answering in some degree to the Tertiaries of the Franciscan and Dominican orders, secretly affiliated to the society, and acting as its unsuspected emissaries in various lay positions. This class is styled in France 'Jesuits of the short robe', and some evidence in support of its actual existence was alleged during the lawsuits against the company under Louis XV. The Jesuits themselves deny the existence of any such body, and are able to adduce the negative disproof that no provision for it is to be found in their constitutions. On the other hand, there are clauses therein which make the creation of such a class perfectly feasible if thought expedient. One is the power given to the general to receive candidates secretly, and to conceal their admission, for which there is a remarkable precedent in the case of Francis Borgia, duke of Gandia, afterwards himself general of the society; the other is an even more singular clause, providing for the admission of candidates to the company by persons who are not themselves members of it. ..." ~ Miller[593]

Was Robert Bauval educated by a Franciscan or a Jesuit? Although we may never know, a tree is known by its fruit. [Matthew 12:33]

Jesuit Agent Resurrected

When Leon Panetta was chosen by Barack Obama to be the Director of the CIA, many observers were shocked. Panetta was a Bill Clinton bureaucrat who hadn't been in public office since 1997.

What made Panetta important was his experience in a broad range of endeavors...and his Jesuit education at Santa Clara University— "the Jesuit University of the Silicon Valley".[594]

Panetta had been a Congressman for 16 years as a Democrat

Representative from California and left a key office, chairing the House Committee on Budget, to become Clinton's 1993-94 Director of the Office of Management and Budget.

From there, he became Bill Clinton's Chief of Staff from 1994 through 1997. He was resurrected from anonymity to become Barack Obama's CIA Director from 2009 to 2011 and then became the Secretary of Defense.

How could Leon Panetta go from crunching numbers in the 90's to leading the most dreaded intelligence agency and military in the world 10 years later? —He could be trusted to betray them all for a higher authority.

Panetta was the Secretary of Defense on September 11th, 2012 when the United States military stood down to see 4 Americans tortured and killed after a 13 hour battle at the CIA waystation in Benghazi, Libya.

Man-portable air-defense missiles taken from Benghazi quickly went to Syria, where they were used to take pot-shots at a Russian passenger airliner.[595]

Obama needed the best man he could find to replace Jesuit-educated Leon Panetta at the Department of Defense. Many were surprised to see him nominate a former Republican Senator from Nebraska, Charles Timothy "Chuck" Hagel. Why choose a Republican Episcopalian Cornhusker to be the Secretary of Defense for such a radical Leftist administration?

Perhaps because he's a *Jesuit-approved* Episcopalian. Hagel was a

---

The Amazonian Myth

Having women treated like men in the military is a win/win for those who wish to see America destroyed. Not only does it obliterate unit cohesion (especially when women are given command over men) but it adds to the number thrown into the meatgrinder of war.

The reality that women are not warriors has been repeatedly buried along with more than a few bodies.

One of the first casualties was Kara Hultgreen. In 1994, she was headlining everywhere as the first "Naval fighter pilot" until she crashed her F-14 during a routine carrier landing. Hultgreen was killed on impact.

Later it was disclosed that she was given preferential treatment in flight school when male counterparts would've "washed out".

Private Jessica Lynch was just a truck driver. She was never supposed to see combat. But in Iraq (as in *all* modern war) there were no front lines. When her

professor at the "Edmund A. Walsh School of Foreign Service" at Georgetown when he got the call[596]. He was so unqualified his own party filibustered the nomination[597] but what the Jesuits want, the Jesuits get.

Hagel, however, has been short-lived and tendered his resignation after a year and a half. Perhaps he was made privy to something that so shook him, he didn't want to be around when it happened.

Obama chose physicist Ashton Carter to replace him.

How does a doctorate in physics make Ashton Carter qualified to lead America's military? Carter received his degree while at an adjunct college under Oxford. The name of that college is "St. John's".[598]

St. John's was founded with a very specific agenda in mind.

> *St John's College is a constituent college of the University of Oxford. It was founded in 1555 by the merchant Sir Thomas White, intended to provide a source of educated Roman Catholic clerics to support the Counter-Reformation under Queen Mary. St John's is the wealthiest college in Oxford, with a financial endowment of £340 million as of 2012...* ~ Wikipedia[599]

Now where would a "Counter-Reformation" adjunct college get such powerful backing?

For a hard-Left Communist/muslim sympathizer, Barack Obama sure has a

---

convoy took a wrong turn, they were quickly surrounded and captured.

The other soldiers in the unit were killed or executed.

Lynch was brutally raped and sodomized—as would be expected when treasonous, spineless Pentagon generals like Martin Dempsey throw a young girl into a uniform and then onto a battlefield with barbaric foes.

The truth was immediately covered up and a yarn was spun about Lynch fighting like an Amazon until all of her ammo was exhausted.

The War Machine needed the myth to continue so more young women would sign up.

SOURCES:

Gender-Norming Update, Walter E. Williams, 4 April 1997, George Mason University
http://econfaculty.gmu.edu/wew/articles/97/gendernorming.htm

Lynch Kept Firing Until She Ran Out Of Ammo, Susan Schmidt and Vernon Loeb, 3 April 2003, Pittsburgh Post-Gazette

penchant for Catholic-educated apparatchiks.

Top Man at the Pentagon

The top officer in the United States Military is the Chairman of the Joint Chiefs of Staff. Currently (late 2014), that man is Martin Dempsey.

Dempsey wears his heritage as an "Irish Catholic" on his sleeve[600]. Before entering West Point, Dempsey attended John S. Burke Catholic High School[601] in Goshen, NY.

> http://old.post-gazette.com/nation/20030403rescuenatp3.asp
>
> *Jessica Lynch: I Was Raped—POW Claims Military Manipulated Her Story*, Diana Lynne, 6 November 2003, WorldNetDaily
> http://www.wnd.com/2003/11/21645/

Dempsey is quite comfortable serving under the likes of Barack Obama. Is it because he shares Obama's agenda?

While speaking to the premier Catholic University, Notre Dame, Dempsey seemed keenly aware of current and projected world population growth[602] (those tracking world population are usually intent on *lowering* world population, often by scurrilous means).

Dempsey is fully on-board with the push to destroy the cohesion and effectiveness of the United States military by the forced infusion of women at all levels as well as open homosexuals. Dempsey is so supportive, he is even pushing full benefits for homosexual couples in uniform.[603]

In 2013, Dempsey made the assertion that putting women in combat roles "strengthens" military effectiveness.[604]

Taking reality and inverting it, especially in a way that causes duress or harm, has been colloquialized as "Gaslighting" after the 1938 British play Gas Light ("Angel Street" in the U.S.).

An excellent example of "Gaslighting" is Californian Democrat Congresswoman Nancy Pelosi making the statement that creating a socialized healthcare system that brings in an extra 30 million Americans will actually lower the self-imploding $18 trillion national debt.[605]

The more ignorant or unaware a populace, the more effective this tactic is.

Speaking in Unison

When the current Speaker of the House, John Boehner (R, OH) took the gavel from Nancy Pelosi (D, CA)[†], he gave her a kiss.

Boehner is the "Opposition Party watchdog" presiding over the most lawless, treasonous Democrat administration in America's history yet he has firmly vowed Barack Obama will *not* face impeachment.[606]

That lawlessness has given the Democrat Party their greatest electoral defeat in decades. November 2014 has seen the Republican House get even stronger and the Senate turned over to them as well.

Before all the votes were counted, the new Senate Majority Leader, Mitch McConnell vowed to work with Barack Obama and that he has no intention of threatening the "Affordable Healthcare Act", a.k.a. "Obamacare".[607]

An exposé by *The Nation* gave insight into how McConnell got where he is (as well as how he is controlled). A vessel in the shipping fleet belonging to his father-in-law, James Chao, was found by Columbian law enforcement to be smuggling cocaine.[608]

John Boehner has certified that Barack Obama is a lawful president: "natural-born" and a Christian[609], in spite of Obama, himself, claiming the United States is no-longer a Christian nation.[610]

The Crying Speaker[611] attended Moeller Catholic High School in Cincinnati where he shed even more tears during a commencement address in 2011.[612]

Boehner then went on to Jesuit-run Xavier University and graduated in 1977.[613]

When Boehner's predecessor Nancy Pelosi was sworn in back in 2007, she brought her mentor with her—Stephen A. Privett of the Society of Jesus. She then made Privett the first Jesuit in American history to give the invocation for Congress.[614]

Pelosi's House Chaplain was Catholic priest Daniel P. Coughlin—the first Catholic priest to hold the office (a shocking milestone). After an 11 year reign, Coughlin sat down and was honored by new Speaker John

---

[†] Nancy Pelosi was born in the Catholic stronghold of Baltimore, Mary-land. Like so many other poisonous California politicians, she was planted there, not native-born.

Boehner[615] who saw to his replacement—Patrick J. Conroy of the Society of Jesus.[616]

In March of 2014, Boehner and Pelosi reached across the "impassable gulf" of their supposed differences to invited Pope Francis to address Congress.[617]

He's a Jesuit, too.

The Catholic Intelligence Agency

Like George W. Bush's Director of the CIA, George Tenet, the current Director has been especially selected.

John Brennan graduated from "The Jesuit University of New York"—Fordham—in 1977.[618]

He started his career off as Director with an ominous and treasonous swearing in, by another Leftist Papal agent, Vice President Joe Biden. They did so on a Constitution minus the Bill of Rights.[619]

It is fascinating to note that, as much control as the Luciferian Elite have, they still fear both the Rule of Law and oaths bound by the God of the Bible.

In 2009, Catholic Supreme Court Chief Justice John Roberts flubbed the word "faithfully" when administering the Presidential oath to Barack Obama, "I will *faithfully* execute the Office of the President of the United States."[620]

They later repaired to the "quite setting" of the White House Map Room where the oath was given again.

> *The president said he did not have his Bible with him, but that the oath was binding anyway.* ~ AP[621]

Sure it was. Just as surely as Barack Obama has a treasured, personal Christian Bible.

Joe Biden is the man who gloated over Obama's shoulder before he signed the "Affordable Healthcare Act" (a.k.a. "Obamacare") into law, "This is a big f*#king deal!"[622]. Although Obamacare was an Orwellian monstrosity constructed behind closed doors with the Republicans on the outside[623], House Speaker John Boehner has promised to leave it completely intact.[624]

As the new Jesuit Pope came under fire for some surprisingly Left-leaning public comments, Joe Biden rushed to his defense.

> *Vice President Biden went out of his way at a speech to the United Auto Workers union Wednesday to take on one of Pope Francis' strongest critics.*
>
> *"A couple weeks ago Ken Langone, who I don't know, a billionaire founder of Home Depot, predicted that the pope — Pope Francis' critique of income inequity will be, quote, 'a 'hurdle' for very wealthy Catholic donors, who seem to think hurt feelings trump the teachings of the Bible," Biden said, referring to a December interview with the Home Depot founder.*
>
> *Langone claimed to CNBC that one potential major donor to a cathedral restoration project was concerned about Pope Francis' economic rhetoric about capitalist economies.*
>
> *"I've told the cardinal, 'Your Eminence, this is one more hurdle I hope we don't have to deal with. You want to be careful about generalities. Rich people in one country don't act the same as rich people in another country,'" Langone said he told Cardinal Timothy Dolan of the donor.*
>
> *Biden appeared amazed by the comments as a Democrat pushing the Obama administration's income equality message. As the most prominent Catholic on the president's team, Biden seemed to be personally offended by the comments.* ~ Evan Santoro, Buzzfeed[625]

But John Brennan swearing in on a Constitution minus the Bill of Rights can more easily be understood in light of Barack Obama's "kill list" that included American citizens deemed execution-worthy based upon government's unchecked assessment of danger...to the United States government.

> *A stunning report in the New York Times depicted President Obama poring over the equivalent of terrorist baseball cards, deciding who on a "kill list" would be targeted for elimination by drone attack. The revelations — as well as those in Daniel Klaidman's recent book — sparked public outrage and calls for congressional inquiry.*
>
> *Yet bizarrely, the fury is targeted at the messengers, not the message. Sen. John McCain (R-Ariz.) expressed dismay that presidential aides were leaking national security information to bolster the president's foreign policy credentials.* ~ Katrina vanden

Heuvel, the Washington Post[626]

Civil libertarians have been warning that yesterday's "Islamist" terrorists are today's average American.

The United States Army is now briefing soldiers that Evangelical Christians and Tea Party activists are a terror threat.[627]

The FBI considers tax protestors and fiscal conservatives distraught over American currency going off the gold standard as an "extremist" security risk.[628]

If you are an abortion protestor, Homeland Security is watching you.[629]

In fact, if you think government is out-of-control, you're in the Militia, as far as DHS is concerned.

> *A recently published "lexicon" distributed to thousands of federal, state, and local law enforcement agencies by the Department of Homeland Security (DHS) targets citizens concerned about their Second Amendment rights and the steady encroachment of the federal government, categorizing such as "militia extremists."*
>
> *The "lexicon," marked Unclassified/For Official Use Only (FOUO), is dated November 10, 2011, and was sent out by email to law enforcement and homeland security agencies on November 14 by LaJuan E. Washington of the DHS Office of Intelligence and Analysis. ...*
>
> *Its definition of "militia extremists" states:*
>
>> *Groups or individuals who facilitate or engage in acts of violence directed at federal, state, or local government officials or infrastructure in response to their belief that the government deliberately is stripping Americans of their freedoms and is attempting to establish a totalitarian regime. These individuals consequently oppose many federal and state authorities' laws and regulations, (particularly those related to firearms ownership), and often belong to armed paramilitary groups. They often conduct paramilitary training designed to violently resist perceived government oppression or to violently overthrow the US Government.*
>
> ~ Patrick Poole, PJ Media[630]

On the basis of nothing more than an official memorandum[631], Barack Obama can execute you.

It is eerie that the NY Times would called CIA Director John Brennan Obama's "priest whose blessing has become indispensable to Mr. Obama[632]," when picking drone strike execution targets. With a sense of dread, we can look back upon reports that government census-takers were gathering precise GPS data on where certain citizens live.[633]

Brennan had already proved the Elite could depend on him when he sanitized Barack Obama's passport in 2008[634]. This was important because Obama, when trying to one-up Hillary Clinton and John McCain on his international acumen, let it out that he had been traveling to Pakistan during the 80's when it was illegal for Americans to do so.

As with every important bit of information we get from him, he was spurred by his ego to go off-teleprompter.

The write-up from the NY Times is fascinating if you've learned to read between the lines.

> *"Experience in Washington is not knowledge of the world,"* [Obama] *continued, provoking laughter among those present. "This I know. When Senator Clinton brags, 'I've met leaders from 80 countries,' I know what those trips are like. I've been on them. You go from the airport to the embassy. There's a group of children who do a native dance. You meet with the C.I.A. station chief and the embassy and they give you a briefing. You go take a tour of plant that"* with *"the assistance of USAID has started something. And then, you go."*
>
> *During the speech, Mr. Obama also spoke about having traveled to Pakistan in the early 1980s. Because of that trip, which he did not mention in either of his autobiographical books "I knew what Sunni and Shia was before I joined the Senate Foreign Relations Committee," he said.*[635]

From his homosexual Pakistani roommate (and lover?) in college to his admitted drug use[636], it's not a leap to suggest that "Barry" was a drug mule for the CIA.

Brennan has made himself indispensible as a purveyor of Islamist terror. He has a direct line to Jihadi Central: the Royal House of Saud.

While he was the CIA Station Chief in Saudi Arabia, Brennan

converted to Islam and has even been on the Hajj to Mecca[637]. Given his staunch Roman Catholic background this is a chilling sign of just how dedicated an agent of Rome Brennan is.

Behind the All-Seeing Eye

The attacks of September 11th ushered in the Orwellian Police State for America, and the foundation of that Police State was the treasonously misnamed "Patriot Act". If a citizen ever has a question about what a piece of legislation does, simply invert its name in best Gaslighting fashion.

The "Patriot Act" was written by Vietnamese Catholic Professor Viet D. Dinh.[638]

Professor Dinh teaches at Georgetown.

He shares time teaching young American law students with comrades like Louis Michael Seidman. In December of 2012, Seidman wrote an op-ed for the New York Times titled *Let's Give Up on the Constitution* where he called America's founding document "archaic, idiosyncratic and downright evil."[639]

The only cabal of Communists to whom the United States Constitution is "evil" are the Counter-Reformation Luciferians of Rome, and their minions, because it was a truly revolutionary charter.

From the explosion of the Reformation came minds like Charles-Louis de Secondat, Baron de Montesquieu, Royal Society Fellow John Locke and preeminent jurist Sir William Blackstone. These were the men that fed the minds of America's Founding generation. They *shattered* the feudalism of human history and gave self determination and self preservation to the common man. Nowhere else in the human endeavor were peasants allowed to own property and arms with which to defend it. By the sweat of their brows they tilled the land. Many died and some prospered.

The Reformation was the acorn, America became the oak tree. It was a nation dominated by a new class of people—the "Middle Class"; strong, independent, moral.

Rome is not interested in sharing authority over humanity and the American Experiment is her greatest enemy. [italics suspended]

> John Paul II denounce[d] Protestants and the idea that men ought to be free.... The oppression, persecution, and even martyrdom of those who refused allegiance to Rome has been her consistent policy. For example, the Concordat between Pius IX and Ecuador

of September 26, 1862, established Roman Catholicism as the state religion and forbade other religions. All education was to be "strictly controlled by the Church." A later law declared that "only Catholics might be regarded as citizens of Ecuador."[4] ...

John Paul II is not being honest with us. Historic evidence (and not only from the distant past) is abundant in testifying that Roman Catholicism suppresses basic freedom whenever, wherever, and however she can. The claim of papal infallibility becomes the justification for such tyranny, a tyranny which Roman pontiffs have repeatedly expressed and enforced in Christ's name and as His alleged vicars. As von Dollinger, himself a devout Catholic, has pointed out:

> The whole life of such a man [the pope], from the moment when he is placed on the altar to receive the first homage by the kissing of his feet, will be an unbroken chain of adulations.
>
> Everything is expressly calculated for strengthening him in the belief that between himself and other mortals there is an impassable gulf, and when involved in the cloud and fumes of a perpetual incense, the firmest character must yield at last to a temptation beyond human strength to resist.[6]

Pope Gregory XVI's (1831-46) The Triumph of the Holy See and the Church over the Attacks of the Innovators is one example among many. Its major thesis was that popes had to be infallible in order to fulfill the office of a true monarch. As absolute monarch over Church and state, Gregory rejected freedom of conscience, not only within the Church but in society as a whole, as "a false and absurd concept." Freedom of the press was equal madness.

Gregory's successor was Pius IX, convener of Vatican I. He was of the same mind with regard to the most elementary human freedoms. Popes had openly declared Rome's opposition to the United States and its freedom-granting constitution from the moment of that nation's birth. Pius IX did the same. The Catholic World frankly expressed the Roman Catholic view of the U.S. form of government:

> ... we do not accept it, or hold it to be any government at all. ... If the American Republic is to be sustained and preserved, it must be by the rejection of the principle of the Reformation, and the acceptance of the Catholic

principle...[7]

~ *A Woman Rides The Beast*, Dave Hunt[640]

Good Ole Georgetown

Meryl Chertoff also teaches law at Georgetown[641]. She's the wife of our 2nd Secretary of "Homeland Security", Michael Chertoff. Chertoff, along with billionaire and former Nazi collaborator[642] George Soros have found terrorism and "security" particularly lucrative. Both have reaped rewards from the sale of "naked body scanners" to airports.[643]

The cultural training that has evolved from airport "security" would be an appalling revelation to America's Founders. Citizens strip off clothing, hold their arms up in surrender, are scanned by possibly carcinogenic radiation and have virtual naked pictures taken of them and stored[644]. Children are traumatized, the elderly are bullied and the attractive are mauled.

This is what the George W. Bush administration created: "Homeland Security".

The German news site *Zeiten Schrift* claims that East Germany's former head of the "Ministry for State Security"—the Stasi—Markus Johannes "Mischa" Wolf, along with former KGB chief Yevgeny Primakov (1991-96) helped build the new bureaucracy.[645]

Who in the United States can or would pull Communist Secret Police expertise from East Germany and the Soviet Union? What level of treachery would even think of such a thing? Where are the rest of America's leaders while this is happening?

The Bush clan is controlled indirectly through affiliations with literal Nazis, the CIA and secret societies like Skull and Bones but also directly via Papal agents in each and every administration.

> *Shortly after Pope Benedict XVI's election in 2005, President Bush met with a small circle of advisers in the Oval Office. As some mentioned their own religious backgrounds, the president remarked that he had read one of the new pontiff's books about faith and culture in Western Europe.*
>
> *Save for one other soul, Bush was the only non-Catholic in the room. But his interest in the pope's writings was no surprise to those around him. As the White House prepares to welcome*

Benedict on Tuesday, many in Bush's inner circle expect the pontiff to find a kindred spirit in the president. Because if Bill Clinton can be called America's first black

president, some say, then George W. Bush could well be the nation's first Catholic president.

This isn't as strange a notion as it sounds. Yes, there was John F. Kennedy. But where Kennedy sought to divorce his religion from his office, Bush has welcomed Roman

Catholic doctrine and teachings into the White House and based many important domestic policy decisions on them.

"I don't think there's any question about it," says Rick Santorum, former U.S. senator from Pennsylvania and a devout Catholic, who was the first to give Bush the "Catholic president" label. "He's certainly much more Catholic than Kennedy." ~ Daniel Burke, the Washington Post[646]

The same is true regardless of Party affiliation. Left or supposed Right, Republican or Democrat, all are safely controlled by Rome.

Recently, Barack Obama's Treasury Secretary, former NY Federal Reserve Chairman Timothy Geithner, (ironically, a tax cheat[647]), has been replaced by Jack Lew, a Georgetown Law graduate.[648]

Barack Obama's current Chief of Staff is Denis McDonough, Masters from the Georgetown School of Foreign Service, class of '96. McDonough was one of the men in the Situation Room photo depicted as having occurred while America's top officials watched the "killing of Osama bin Laden".[649]

The current President of the European Commission (the "European Union") is José Manuel Durão Barroso, former Prime Minister of Portugal. Barroso took courses and internships at Georgetown[650] and eventually taught classes at the Georgetown School for Foreign Service.[651]

The President of the European *Council* (plans European policy) is Herman Van Rompuy, staunch Dutch Roman Catholic, raised from his youth at Jesuit *Sint-Jan Berchmanscollege* (Grammar School) in Brussels and *Katholieke Universiteit Leuven* (Catholic University of Leuven)[652]. He has taught at Lessius Hogeschool[653] (once openly Jesuit, now merged with several other schools[654]).

At every level, the men and women guiding world policy were trained by, and *chosen* by the Society of Jesus.

Perhaps one of their most faithful students was William Jefferson Clinton.

Endnotes

[568] *Secret Counsels of the Society of Jesus*, Robert Breckinridge, Baltimore: Edward J. Cole & Co. (1835), p. 64

[569] *Heroic Leadership: Best Practices from a 450-Year-Old Company That Changed the World*, Chris Lowney, Loyola Press (2010), p. 228

[570] There is a clip floating around YouTube of a Bill Clinton makeup session before an address where he is just *gone*. He is *not* in his body at that moment. There is another of Clinton in a child-like state that some have likened to hypnosis. As of this writing, they can both be found at *A Hypnotised* [sic] *Bill Clinton* on the YouTube channel of "kyle NewsAndSheeit":
https://www.youtube.com/watch?v=OANCHSvscxQ

[571] *Sandra Fluke's Appearance Is No Fluke*, Just a Grunt, 2 March 2012, Jammie Wearing Fools
http://www.jammiewf.com/2012/sandra-flukes-appearance-is-no-fluke/

[572] *Law Student Makes Case For Contraceptive Coverage*, Julie Rovner, 23 February 2012, NPR
http://www.npr.org/blogs/health/2012/02/23/147299323/law-student-makes-case-for-contraceptive-coverage

[573] *Obama Backs Student in Furor With Limbaugh on Birth Control*, Jonathan Weisman, 2 March 2012, the NY Times
http://thecaucus.blogs.nytimes.com/2012/03/02/boehner-condemns-limbaughs-comments/?_r=0

[574] *Obama Speaks to a Sixth-Grade Classroom*, The Daily Show with Jon Stewart
http://thedailyshow.cc.com/videos/1b43o1/obama-speaks-to-a-sixth-grade-classroom

[575] *Leaving West Wing to Pursue Hollywood Dream*, Tracy Jan, 3 March 2013, the Boston Globe
http://www.bostonglobe.com/metro/2013/03/03/obama-speechwriter-jon-favreau-leaves-west-wing-for-screenwriting/Evt7Rtg5ax9dwbnVjFfOgJ/story.html

[576] *John Kerry on His Catholic Faith in 2004 Third Presidential Debate*, Berkley Center For Religion, Peace & World Affairs at Georgetown University, 13 October 2004
http://berkleycenter.georgetown.edu/quotes/john-kerry-on-his-catholic-faith-in-2004-third-presidential-debate

[577] Working With the Vatican Against Modern Slavery, John Kerry, Secretary of State, 20 April 2014, State.gov
http://www.state.gov/secretary/remarks/2014/04/224999.htm

[578] *Kerry Tries to Ease Conflict Over Palestinian Statehood Bid*, Steven Erlanger, 15 December 2014, New York Times
http://www.bostonglobe.com/news/world/2014/12/15/kerry-tries-ease-conflict-over-palestinian-statehood-bid/MJr00gV1D8oraVb08F4tIK/story.html

[579] *Alexander Haig*, Biography.com
http://www.biography.com/#!/people/alexander-haig-9325072

[580] *Hundreds Attend Funeral Mass for Alexander Haig, Former U.S. Secretary of State*, Richard Szczepanowski, 3 March 2010, the Catholic Standard
http://cathstan.org/main.asp?SectionID=2&SubSectionID=2&ArticleID=3565&TM=37871.11

[581] *When Reagan Was Shot, Who Was "In Control" at the White House?* Richard Allen, 25 March 2011, the Washington Post
http://www.washingtonpost.com/opinions/when-reagan-was-shot-who-was-in-control-at-the-white-house/2011/03/23/AFJlrfYB_story.html

[582] *Hinckley's Kin Slated to Dine With Bush's Son*, UPI, 31 March 1981, Oregon Bulletin
http://www.scribd.com/doc/187990634/Hinckley-s-Kin-Slated-to-Dine-With-Bush-s-Son

[583] *Alexander Haig's Dark Side - Roman Catholic War Criminal*, Tom Shachtman, 22 February 2010, u2r2h blog
http://u2r2h.blogspot.com/2010/02/alexander-haigs-dark-side-roman.html

[584] Listing of Jesuit Secondary Schools by The Jesuit Secondary Education Association (JSEA)
http://www.jsea.org/schools

[585] Associate Member Institution, Association of Jesuit Colleges & Universities
http://ajcunet.edu/institutions?Page=DTN-20140916030634

[586] *Jesuit College Plans To Merge with Yale*, unattributed, 21 July 1967, the Harvard Crimson
http://www.thecrimson.com/article/1967/7/21/jesuit-college-plans-to-merge-with/

[587] *The Master Game: Unmasking the Secret Rulers of the World*, Graham Hancock and Robert Bauval, Red Wheel Weiser (2011), p. 334

[588] *Saint Ignatius of Loyola*, Rev. Edward A. Ryan, S.J., last updated 7 July 2013, Encyclopædia Britannica
http://www.britannica.com/EBchecked/topic/350127/Saint-Ignatius-of-Loyola/4328/Period-of-study

[589] *Edmund Campion : biography*, FamPeople.com
http://www.fampeople.com/cat-edmund-campion

[590] *Campion, Saint Edmund*, The Columbia Encyclopedia, 6th ed. (2014)
http://www.encyclopedia.com/topic/Saint_Edmund_Campion.aspx

[591] *Welcome to Campion Hall*, University of Oxford
http://www.campion.ox.ac.uk/

[592] *Truth Triumphant*, Benjamin George Wilkinson, Hartland Publications (1997), pp. 307-308

[593] *Occult Theocrasy*, Edith Starr Miller; Lady Queenborough, Imprimerie F. Paillart (1933), p. 309

[594] *Leon Panetta, Former U.S. Defense Secretary and CIA Director, to Speak at Santa Clara University Commencement June 15*, Santa Clara University Today
http://www.scu.edu/news/releases/release.cfm?c=15928

[595] I tried to get the best sources for you on this but both "Sky News" and Haaretz ridiculously show pictures of massive platform-launched SAMs that are used by standing militaries, not "rebel" insurgencies.

The Haaretz headline also calls the projectiles "rockets" as if idiots on the ground shot unguided RPGs at a relatively fast moving target. It's pretty unusual for a jetliner to avoid getting hit by not one, but two guided missiles but there a countless variables in this story from jihadi retards possibly not knowing how to shoot the damn things to those wily Russians possibly outfitting their passenger liners with surface-to-air missile counter-measures. A smart move for anything flying into or out of Damascus.

"Sky News" put their headline in quotes as if the facts are in dispute!

"Missiles Fired At Passenger Jet Over Syria", unattributed, 29 April 2013, Sky News
http://news.sky.com/story/1084647/missiles-fired-at-passenger-jet-over-syria
    Report: *Two Rockets Fired At Russian Passenger Plane Flying Over Syria, No Injuries*, unattributed, 29 April 2013, Haaretz
http://www.haaretz.com/news/middle-east/report-two-rockets-fired-at-russian-passenger-plane-flying-over-syria-no-injuries-1.518249

[596] *Georgetown's Chuck Hagel Nominated for Defense Secretary*, School of Foreign Service, Georgetown University
http://sfs.georgetown.edu/georgetown-chuck-hagel-nominated-secretary-defense

[597] *Why Republicans Are Filibustering Chuck Hagel*, Chris Cillizza, 14 February 2013, the Washington Post
http://www.washingtonpost.com/blogs/the-fix/wp/2013/02/14/why-republicans-are-filibustering-chuck-hagel/

[598] *Ashton Carter*, St. John's College, Oxford
http://www.sjc.ox.ac.uk/167-7652/Ashton-Carter.html

[599] *St. John's College, Oxford*, Wikipedia
http://en.wikipedia.org/wiki/St._John%27s_College,_Oxford

[600] *Irish Catholic Kid from New Jersey New Chairman, Joint Chiefs of Staff*, Tom Gallagher, 31 May 2011, the National Catholic Reporter
http://ncronline.org/blogs/ncr-today/irish-catholic-kid-new-jersey-new-chairman-joint-chiefs-staff

[601] *Gen. Dempsey's Remarks at the John S. Burke Catholic High School Commencement Ceremony*, JCS.mil
http://www.jcs.mil/Media/Speeches/tabid/3890/Article/7848/gen-dempseys-remarks-at-the-john-s-burke-catholic-high-school-commencement-cere.aspx
    Dempsey delivered the 2012 commencement at his alma matter.

[602] *General Dempsey's Remarks at a Notre Dame*, Questions and Answers, JCS.mil
http://www.jcs.mil/Media/Speeches/tabid/3890/Article/11087/general-dempseys-remarks-at-a-notre-dame-questions-and-answers.aspx

[603] *Martin Dempsey Committed To Equality For Married Gay Couples In The Military*, Carlos Santoscoy, 8 July 2013 On Top magazine
http://www.ontopmag.com/article.aspx?id=15768&MediaType=1&Category=26
    I guess if you take it in the ass this is the magazine for the butch one.

[604] *Dempsey: Allowing Women in Combat Strengthens Joint Force*, Cheryl Pellerin, 24 January 2013, American Forces Press Service
http://www.defense.gov/news/newsarticle.aspx?id=119100

[605] *Joel Hay: Obamacare a Deficit Fighter?* Joel W. Hay, 15 January 2013, the Ocean County Register
http://www.ocregister.com/articles/health-383520-billion-obamacare.html

[606] *John Boehner Says He Disagrees With Calls To Impeach Obama*, Sabrina Siddiqui, 9 July 2014, Huffington Post
http://www.huffingtonpost.com/2014/07/09/john-boehner-obama-impeachment_n_5570677.html

[607] *"Trust But Verify": Mitch McConnell Says He Won't Shut Down The Government Or Abolish All Of Obamacare But Dares President To Cooperate With New Republican Majority*, David Martosko, 5 November 2014, Daily Mail

http://www.dailymail.co.uk/news/article-2822293/Moderate-Mitch-McConnell-says-won-t-shut-government-abolish-Obamacare-clues-Republican-Senate-leader-s-plan-emerge.html
 As happens so often, the Daily Mail was ordered to soften the original story who's headline was even more strong regarding McConnell's commitment to not touching MessiahCare. Sorry I didn't think to screenshot it at the time.

[608] *Mitch McConnell's Freighted Ties to a Shadowy Shipping Company*, Lee Fang, 30 October 2014, The Nation
http://www.thenation.com/article/186689/mitch-mcconnells-freighted-ties-shadowy-shipping-company

[609] *From Obama and Boehner, Duck-and-Cover Politics*, Ruth Marcus, 16 February 2011, the Washington Post
http://www.washingtonpost.com/wp-dyn/content/article/2011/02/15/AR2011021506091.html

[610] *Obama: America Not a Christian Nation*, John Eidsmoe, 15 April 2009, New American magazine
http://www.thenewamerican.com/usnews/politics/item/2576-obama-america-not-a-christian-nation

[611] *Weeper of the House: Why Does John Boehner Cry So Much?* Dr. Steven Berglas, 2 December 2013, POLITICO
http://www.politico.com/magazine/story/2013/12/weeper-of-the-house-john-boehner-cries-100557.html

[612] *At Moeller, John Boehner ('68) Chokes Up*, Howard Wilkinson, 26 April 2011, Cincinatti.com
http://www.moeller.org/document.doc?id=2152

[613] *John Boehner, Class of '77, Is Featured On The Cover Of This Week's Issue Of Time Magazine*, 8 November 2010, Xavier News & Events
http://www.xavier.edu/news/John-Boehner-Class-of-77-is-featured-on-the-cover-of-this-weeks-issue-of-Time-magazine.cfm?grp_id=1

[614] *USF President Delivers Prayer at Opening of Congress*, USFmagazine, the University of San Francisco
http://usf.usfca.edu/usfmagazine/spring07/n4_privcongress.html

[615] *Speaker Boehner Thanks Father Coughlin For 11 Years of Service as House Chaplain*, Michael Ricci, 14 April 2011, Speaker of the House John Boehner
http://www.speaker.gov/general/speaker-boehner-thanks-father-coughlin-11-years-service-house-chaplain

[616] *Jesuit Father Pat Conroy Confirmed as U.S. House Chaplain*, Kaitlyn Schnieders, 13 June 2011, National Jesuit News
http://www.jesuit.org/blog/index.php/tag/jesuit-father-patrick-conroy/page/2/

[617] *Boehner and Pelosi Invite Pope Francis to Congress*, Elizabeth Dias, 13 March 2014, Time
http://time.com/23805/pope-francis-john-boehner-nancy-pelosi-congress/#23805/pope-francis-john-boehner-nancy-pelosi-congress/

[618] *John Brennan, FCRH '77, Confirmed to Head CIA*, Patrick Verel, no date, Fordham University
http://www.fordham.edu/Campus_Resources/enewsroom/topstories_2658.asp

[619] *John Brennan Sworn In On First Draft Of Constitution – Without The Bill Of Rights*, Tom McCarthy, 8 March 2013, the Guardian
http://www.theguardian.com/world/us-news-blog/2013/mar/08/john-brennan-constitution-bill-of-rights

Gotta love the subheading on this piece—written either by Machine shills or criminally stupid slaves:
Early version of the constitution used to swear-in new CIA director lacks the part about due process before the law. Oops

"Oops" my ass.

[620] *Obama Retakes Oath Of Office After Roberts' Mistake*, 22 January 2009, CNN
http://www.cnn.com/2009/POLITICS/01/21/obama.oath/index.html?eref

[621] *Obama Retakes Oath Of Office After Flub*, AP, 22 January 2009, NBC News
http://www.nbcnews.com/id/28780417/ns/politics-white_house/t/obama-retakes-oath-office-after-flub/

[622] *Joe Biden: "This Is A Big Fucking Deal"*, Richard Adams, 23 March 2010, the Guardian
http://www.theguardian.com/world/richard-adams-blog/2010/mar/23/joe-biden-obama-big-fucking-deal-overheard

[623] *Democrats Reid, Pelosi Ponder Crafting Obama's Final Healthcare Bill Behind Closed Doors*, Andrew Malcolm, 5 January 2010, the LA Times
http://latimesblogs.latimes.com/washington/2010/01/healthcare-senate-house-democrats-obama.html?utm_source=feedburner&utm_medium=feed&utm_campaign=Feed%3A+topoftheticket+(Top+of+the+Ticket)

[624] *Boehner: Too Late to Just Repeal Obamacare*, Matt Fuller, 24 April 2014, RollCall
http://blogs.rollcall.com/218/boehner-too-late-to-just-repeal-obamacare-says-gop-should-tackle-immigration/

[625] *Joe Biden Defends Pope Francis On Economics "As A Practicing Catholic"*, Evan Santoro, 5 February 2014, Buzzfeed
http://www.buzzfeed.com/evanmcsan/joe-biden-defends-pope-francis-on-economics-as-a-practicing#1v3wzwo

[626] *Obama's "Kill List" Is Unchecked Presidential Power*, Katrina vanden Heuvel, 12 June 2012, the Washington Post
http://www.washingtonpost.com/opinions/obamas-kill-list-is-unchecked-presidential-power/2012/06/11/gJQAHw05WV_story.html

[627] *Does Army Consider Christians, Tea Party, a Terror Threat?* Todd Starnes, 23 October 2013, FoxNews
http://www.foxnews.com/opinion/2013/10/23/does-army-consider-christians-tea-party-terror-threat/

[628] *FBI Warns Of Threat From Anti-Government Extremists*, Patrick Temple-West, 6 February 2012, Reuters
http://www.reuters.com/article/2012/02/07/us-usa-fbi-extremists-idUSTRE81600V20120207

[629] *Homeland Security Targets Anti-Abortion Activists as Domestic Terrorists*, Paul Joseph Watson, 2 April 2012, InfoWars
http://www.infowars.com/homeland-security-targets-anti-abortion-activists-as-domestic-terrorists/

[630] *Homeland Security: You're All "Militia Extremists" Now*, Patrick Poole, 5 February 2012, PJ Media
http://pjmedia.com/blog/homeland-security-lexicon-youre-all-militia-extremists-now/
[631] *Chilling Legal Memo from Obama DOJ Justifies Assassination of U.S. Citizens*, Glenn Greenwald, 5 February 2013, the Guardian
http://www.theguardian.com/commentisfree/2013/feb/05/obama-kill-list-doj-memo
[632] *Secret "Kill List" Proves a Test of Obama's Principles and Will*, Jo Becker and Scott Shane, 29 May 2012, New York Times
http://www.nytimes.com/2012/05/29/world/obamas-leadership-in-war-on-al-qaeda.html?pagewanted=all&_r=0
[633] *Census GPS-Tagging Your Home's Front Door*, Bob Unruh, 5 May 2009, WorldNetDaily
http://www.wnd.com/2009/05/97208/
[634] *Did CIA Pick Sanitize Obama's Passport Records?* Jerome Corsi, 8 January 2013, WorldNetDaily
http://www.wnd.com/2013/01/did-cia-pick-sanitize-obamas-passport-records/
[635] *Obama Says Real-Life Experience Trumps Rivals' Foreign Policy Credits*, Larry Rohter, 10 April 2008, NY Times
http://www.nytimes.com/2008/04/10/us/politics/10obama.html?pagewanted=print&_r=0
[636] *Almost Everything Barack Obama's Ever Said About Marijuana Over The Years*, Andrew Kaczynski, 21 January 2014, BuzzFeed
http://www.buzzfeed.com/andrewkaczynski/barack-obama-weed#1de3sof
[637] *John Brennan: From Mecca to Washington*, Daniel Greenfield, 18 February 2013, FrontPage Magazine
http://www.frontpagemag.com/2013/dgreenfield/john-brennan-from-mecca-to-washington/
[638] Profile on Viet D. Dinh, Bankroft PLLC
http://www.bancroftpllc.com/professionals/viet-d-dinh/
[639] *Let's Give Up on the Constitution*, Louis Michael Seidman, 30 December 2012, New York Times
http://www.nytimes.com/2012/12/31/opinion/lets-give-up-on-the-constitution.html?pagewanted=all&_r=0
[640] *A Woman Rides The Beast*, Dave Hunt, Harvest House (1994), pp. 123-124
[641] *Meryl Chertoff*, Our Faculty, Georgetown Law
http://www.law.georgetown.edu/faculty/chertoff-meryl-j.cfm
[642] *The Guilt-Free Record Of George Soros*, Extension of Remarks by the Honorable Mark Souder (R, IN), 29 September 2006, Congressional Record of the 109th Congress (2005-2006)
http://thomas.loc.gov/cgi-bin/query/z?r109:E29SE6-0050:
Special thanks to Representative Souder as this 60 interview has been *expunged* from the internet.
[643] *Getting Rich from the TSA Naked-Body Scanners*, Raven Clabough, 18 November 2010, the New American
http://www.thenewamerican.com/economy/commentary/item/3938-getting-rich-from-the-tsa-naked-body-scanners

[644] *Dear America, I Saw You Naked And Yes, We Were Laughing. Confessions of an ex-TSA Agent.* Jason Harrington, 30 January 2014, POLITICO
http://www.politico.com/magazine/story/2014/01/tsa-screener-confession-102912.html?hp=f1#.UuvYwHddV6Q

[645] *Markus Wolff von US-Homeland Security eingestellt*, Zeiten Schrift, January-February 2005, volume 2
http://www.zeitenschrift.com/news/markus-wolff-von-us-homeland-security-eingestellt

[646] *A Catholic Wind in the White House*, Daniel Burke, 13 April 2009, the Washington Post
http://www.washingtonpost.com/wp-dyn/content/article/2008/04/11/AR2008041103327_pf.html

[647] *Timothy Geithner Says He Regrets Tax Mistakes*, Barbara Hagenbaugh and Sue Kirchhoff, USA Today, no date, ABC News
http://abcnews.go.com/Business/story?id=6704526

[648] *Georgetown Law Alumnus Jacob "Jack" Lew (L'83) Nominated as Treasury Secretary*, Georgetown Law, 10 January 2013
http://www.law.georgetown.edu/news/georgetown-law-alumnus-nominated-as-treasury-secretary.cfm

[649] *Denis McDonough (MSFS'96) Will Be President Obama's Next Chief of Staff*, Georgetown School of Foreign Service
http://sfs.georgetown.edu/denis-mcdonough-msfs-next-obama-chief-staff

[650] *José Manuel Barroso*, bio from the European Commission, pdf available from the Internet Archive
http://web.archive.org/web/20090521074402/http://ec.europa.eu/commission_barroso/president/pdf/cv_2009_president_en.pdf

[651] *President of the European Commission Speaks at International Event*, Georgetown Law, 22 May 2014
http://www.law.georgetown.edu/news/web-stories/president-of-the-european-commission-speaks-at-international-georgetown-law-event.cfm

[652] *Herman Van Rompuy*, European Council.Europa.eu
http://www.european-council.europa.eu/the-president/biography

[653] *Herman Van Rompuy > Early Life, Career and Family*, Wikipedia
https://en.wikipedia.org/wiki/Herman_Van_Rompuy#Early_life.2C_career_and_family

[654] *Lessius Hogeschool*, Wikipedia (Dutch)
https://nl.wikipedia.org/wiki/Lessius_Hogeschool

Chapter 9

The Clinton Years: When The False Flag Was Perfected

In 1975, a university professor by the name of Carroll Quigley published an unusual 1300-page treatise on the agenda of the Ruling Elite entitled *Tragedy and Hope*. It would later be read by some of the most powerful people in the world.

On the Power of the Banking Family Cartels:

> *The names of some of these banking families are familiar to all of us and should be more so. They include Baring, Lazard, Erlanger, Warburg, Schroder, the Speyers, Mirabuad, Fould, and above all Rothschild and Morgan. Even after these banking families became fully involved in domestic industry by the emergence of financial capitalism, they remained different from ordinary bankers...they were almost equally devoted to secrecy and the secret use of financial influence in political life. These bankers came to be called "international bankers" and, more particularly, were known as "merchant bankers" in England, "private bankers" in France, and "investment bankers" in the United States...*

> *One of their less obvious characteristics was that they remained as private unincorporated firms, usually partnerships, until relatively recently, offering no shares, no reports, and usually no advertising to the public. ... This persistence as private firms continued because it ensured the maximum of anonymity and secrecy to persons of tremendous public power who dreaded public knowledge of their activities...*[655]

On the Secret Control of Nations by Central Banks:

> *...the powers of financial capitalism had another far-reaching aim, nothing less than to create a world system of financial control in private hands able to dominate the political system of each country and the economy of the world as a whole. This system was to be controlled in a feudalist fashion by the central banks of the world acting in concert, by secret agreements arrived at in frequent private meetings and conferences. The apex of the system was to be the Bank for the International Settlements in Basle, Switzerland, a private bank owned and controlled by the world's central banks, which were themselves private corporations. Each central bank, in*

> *the hands of men like Montagu Norman of the Bank of England, Benjamin Strong of the New York Federal Reserve Bank, Charles Rist of the Bank of France, and Hjalmar Schact of the Reichsbank, sought to dominate its government by its ability to control Treasury loans, to manipulate foreign exchanges, to influence the level of economic activity in the country, and to influence cooperative politicians by subsequent economic rewards in the business world.*
>
> *In each country the power of the central bank reseted largely on its control of credit and money supply.*[656]

On the Existence of Secret Societies Which Subvert Democracy

> *There does exist and has existed for a generation, an international Anglophile network which operates, to some extent, in the way the radical Right believes the Communists act. In fact, this network, which we may identify as the Round Table Groups, has no aversion to cooperating with the Communists, or any other groups, and frequently does so. I know of the operations of this network because I have studied it for twenty years and was permitted for two years in the early 1960's, to examine its papers and secret records. I have no aversion to it or to most of its aims and have, for much of my life, been close to it and to many of its instruments.*[657]

On Political "Choice"

> *The chief problem of American political life for a long time has been how to make the two Congressional parties more national and international. The argument that the two parties should represent opposed ideals and policies, one, perhaps, of the Right and the other of the Left, is a foolish idea acceptable only to the doctrinaire and academic thinkers. Instead, the two parties should be almost identical...*[658]

On page 968, Quigley mentions a connection of finance from London to New York that "penetrated deeply into university life, the press and the practice of foreign policy."

If there is any secret organization that has its hands "deeply into university life" extending out to "foreign policy" it is the Company of Loyola.

This "line" would coalesce to become a triumvirate;

1. slave labor and goods from Communist China
2. London as the hub of finance
3. Washington DC the coercive military force behind the agenda

The head of this triumvirate appears to be Rome.

In 1992, Bill Clinton would thank Carroll Quigley in his speech of acceptance to run for the Presidency of the United States.

> *As a teenager, I heard John Kennedy's summons to citizenship. And then, as a student at Georgetown, I heard that call clarified by a professor named Carol* [sic] *Quigley...*[659]

Clinton was chosen early and brought before then-President Kennedy via the American Legion's *Boys Nation* program.[660]

It was as a student at Georgetown that Clinton learned from professor Caroll Quigley.

The Jesuit institution is proud of them both.

> *Clinton has often noted as major influences his professors at Georgetown, particularly the late Carroll Quigley and Rev. Joseph Sebes, S.J., as well as Rev. Otto Hentz, S.J., who still teaches at Georgetown.*
>
> *Hentz asked the young Clinton, a Baptist, if he had considered becoming a Jesuit. The professor has said he believes the curriculum and the Catholic and Jesuit influence at Georgetown had a profound influence on the future president. ~ The Clinton Lectures*, Georgetown University [661]

There is a direct line of empowering from George Bush to Bill Clinton to George Bush as Presidents of the United States and it is composed of a powdery white substance.

Kill the Messenger

Gary Webb was a reporter for the *San Jose Mercury News* and he was unique in his field: he was a real reporter.

Webb originally started to make the front page by covering the story of a convicted drug trafficker who began racking up lawsuit wins based upon the idea that being imprisoned *and* having property confiscated was judicial "double jeopardy".

As Gary, himself, would later note;

> *Faced with the prospect of setting thousands of dopers free or returning billions in seized property, the U.S. Supreme Court would later overturn two of its own rulings in order to kill off the inmate's suit. ...*
>
> *Two years earlier, I'd written a series for the Mercury called "The Forfeiture Racket," about the police in California busting into private homes and taking furniture, televisions, Nintendo games, belt buckles, welfare checks, snow tires, and loose change under the guise of cracking down on drug traffickers. Many times they'd never file charges, or the charges would be dropped once the victims signed over the loot. ~ Dark Alliance[662]*

A woman got in touch with Webb, after reading his work, to see if he would help her imprisoned boyfriend. He, too, had been thrown in jail and had his property confiscated.

But there was a new twist: he had information that the organization behind the trafficking was the Central Intelligence Agency. In fact, they brought a CIA trafficker to court to help convict the man.

> *The CIA. He used to work for them or something. He's a Nicaraguan too. Rafael knows him, he can tell you. He told me the guy had admitted bringing four tons of cocaine into the country. Four tons! And if that's what he's admitted to, you can imagine how much it really was. And now he's back working for the government again. ~ Dark Alliance[663]*

The star government witness turned out to be Oscar Danilo Blandón, a Nicaraguan drug pimp who was covering Los Angeles in cocaine. This sounded incredulous so Webb did his homework.

> *Now there were two separate sources saying—in court—that Blandón was involved with the Contras and had been selling large amounts of cocaine in Los Angeles. And when the government finally had a chance to put him away forever, it had opened up the cell doors and let him walk. ~ Dark Alliance[664]*

Few Americans know that cocaine smuggling was the grease that moved the cogs within the Iran-Contra scandal. Getting weapons secretly to Nicaraguan Contras was the purview of retired Marine Corps Lieutenant Colonel Oliver North.

North would work arm-in-arm with CIA Director George H.W. Bush on "READINESS EXERCISE: 1984" (REX 84) along with Jesuit Boston College alum Louis Giuffrida[665] of FEMA as a plan for complete suspension of Constitutional rights during an "emergency situation" in the United States.[666]

Uncovering cocaine trafficking by the CIA launched Gary Webb into a 3-part series of columns that were an instant success despite his being constantly attacked by both the government and his media peers.[667]

Webb would later be found dead and ruled a "suicide" by the corner[u] despite there being *two* bullet wounds to his head.[668]

It has been revealed that media attacks on Webb were co-ordinated by the CIA to destroy Webb's reputation.[669]

> *Nine years after investigative reporter Gary Webb committed suicide, Jesse Katz, a former Los Angeles Times reporter who played a leading role in ruining the controversial journalist's career, has publicly apologized — just weeks before shooting begins in Atlanta on* Kill the Messenger, *a film expected to reinstate Webb's reputation as an award-winning journalist dragged through the mud by disdainful, competing media outlets.* ~ Nick Schou, LA Weekly[670]

Nearly 20 years later, Gary Webb's story is starting to gain traction. It should be noted, however, that all political figures involved are well out of office.

A movie starring Jeremy Renner was released in 2014 about Webb's story titled *Kill the Messenger*.

His Fate Was Sealed

Smuggling cocaine into the United States required skilled pilots with superior technological aids for radio transmissions and deception.

One of the men conducting that mission was Adler Berriman Seal.

During the 1990's, Barry Seal was using advanced radar and communication gear the CIA had given him to fly drugs and weapons in and out of a little airport in Mena, Arkansas. There were some original difficulties with the local authorities but the governor was quickly brought in

---

[u] Perhaps this was a coroner who was comfortable logging "accidental" mob deaths with the explanation, "He fell on a knife 14 times."

on the operation and began to enjoy large amounts of cash and coke for himself, his family and his administration.

That Governor was William Jefferson Clinton.

One of the pilots that helped Barry Seal was also training Nicaraguans to fly supplies in and out of their country from that same base of operations in Mena.

Terry K. Reed started his government service as an Air Force intelligence analyst in Vietnam. He would go on to write a scathing exposé based upon his experiences titled *Compromised*[671] and the story started with his own "deal with the devil".

While conducting bombing damage assessments, Reed was brought in on the secret that the North Vietnamese were lining their supply routes with American Prisoners of War and POW camps. The military targeted them all, anyway.

Reed was told by his commanding officer, "Help plan the missions or we'll ship you out in disgrace and bring in someone who will." He helped with the bombings and never forgave himself. This experience propelled Reed to turn whistleblower after his experiences with the CIA in Mena and beyond.

> *I can attest to something that I, like others, had often wondered about: does the CIA sponsor candidates to the office of U.S. president?*
>
> *The answer is yes.*
>
> **I witnessed the creation of a counterfeit president.** ~ *Compromised* [emphasis his][672]

After Reed published his tell-all book he was disappointed to see the media cover up the story or attack it whenever it was referenced. He considered it "Liberal bias" and, for the bulk of media organizations that may have been true, but controlling information is easy when only 6 mega-corporations decide what "news" is.[673]

The CIA conducting operations on U.S. soil is illegal but it was and is done, anyway. Recall that the current Director was sworn in on a Constitution minus the Bill of Rights.

Not only was the CIA running guns out and cocaine in from the U.S. to Nicaragua, but they were stealing assault weapons from the Army and

National Guard[674] to do it as well as making illegal weapons in Arkansas.[675]

This is in stark contrast to the strict restrictions on Americans trying to exercise their 2nd Amendment rights.

The right to "keep and bear arms" was never intended to be anything less than a citizen check on government tyranny. Every proponent of "gun control" knows this, from Charles Schumer (D, NY) to Diane Feinstein (D, CA) to Barack Obama. Their arguments for "safety" and "common sense" ring hollow in light of the frightening advances in government power, intrusion and enforcement. Nearly every single Federal Agency has its own SWAT team and armored vehicles.

One Founding Father who has been erased from history knew quite well the purpose of the 2nd Amendment.

Tench Coxe was a merchant who had been accused of doing business with the British but, upon seeing their heavy-handed disarming of Americans wherever they went, became an outspoken Patriot. He served as a delegate of Pennsylvania to the Constitutional Convention and was a member of the Madison and Jefferson administrations. Coxe had this to say about "gun control":

> *What Is An "Assault Weapon"?*
>
> A *true* "assault weapon" is a shoulder-fired firearm capable of shooting calibers larger than normally found in a handgun and either has a selector control (lever or button) to alternate between "semi" and automatic fire or simply shoots fully automatic.
>
> The Firearm Owners Protection Act of 1986 (remember to invert the name of a piece of legislation to understand what it does) which Ronald Reagan signed into law, made these weapons exorbitantly expensive and now, only the wealthy Elite have the ability to own one.

> *As civil rulers, not having their duty to the people before them, may attempt to tyrannize, and as the military forces which must be occasionally raised to defend our country, might pervert their power to the injury of their fellow citizens, the people are confirmed by the article in their right to keep and bear their private arms. ...*

> *Who are the militia? Are they not ourselves? Is it feared, then, that we shall turn our arms each man 'gainst his own bosom. Congress have no power to disarm the militia. Their swords, and every other terrible implement of the soldier, are the birthright of an American. ... the unlimited power of the sword is not in the hands of either the federal or state governments, but, where I trust in God it will ever*

remain, in the hands of the people. ~ The James Madison Research Library and Information Center[676]

Disarming the Middle Class is a key component of the Counter-Reformation. In this effort, one of the Vatican's most valuable allies has been the Catholic Connecticut Dodd family.

> *Chris Dodd grew up in a large Irish Catholic family listening to his father's tales of crusading for justice. Thomas Dodd had chased the Dillinger gang as an FBI agent, and prosecuted Nazi war criminals and the Ku Klux Klan as a government lawyer. As a U.S. senator from Connecticut in the 1950s and '60s he was a protégé of [Lyndon Johnson] and was seriously considered as his running mate in 1964. But in June 1967, Dodd was censured by his Senate colleagues, in a 92–5 vote, for allegedly diverting more than $100,000 of his campaign funds for personal use.* ~ Newsweek[677]

Thomas Dodd was promoted as a vehement FBI Nazi-fighter, yet as a United States Senator he would use the 1938 Nazi Gun Control Act as the basis for his 1968 Gun Control legislation[678], forced into law with the help of the CIA assassination of John F. Kennedy.

Dodd had originally offered the bill shortly after Kennedy's killing in 1964 but it did not get through committee. Like so many other bad pieces of legislation, Dodd would continue to bring the bill back until weak opposition from the National Rifle Association allowed it to pass in 1968.[679]

Chris Dodd would pick up where his father Thomas Dodd left off, helping to engineer a staggering housing bubble[680] that burst all over the American taxpayer.

Instead of being prosecuted, he was rewarded. The top 3 names that received political contributions from Fannie Mae and Freddie Mac were in this order: Dodd, Obama, Kerry.[681]

Combined, the Dodd family has been ruling Americans for Rome for 60 years.

In 2011, Chris Dodd would finally leave Congress for one of the few endeavors even more lucrative: Hollywood. Dodd is now Chairman and CEO of the Motion Picture Association of America.[682]

It is a foregone conclusion that he is still working for the same masters.

Little Rock Candy

The Clinton administration was finding that cooperating with the CIA had its perks. They had negotiated to take a dime off every coke dollar and Barry Seal was literally kicking dufflebags loaded with cash out of his Piper Seneca into the waiting arms of Clinton fund-raiser, Dan Lasater.[683]

Although Lasater would later be thrown to the wolves (as so many inconsequential figures have been for the illusion of "justice") and convicted of drug trafficking, Bill Clinton would quickly pardon him because he needed his 2nd Amendment rights "to go hunting". Unimportant issues like Lasater drugging and deflowering a teenage girl[684] were quickly swept aside.

It pays to be on the ruling team.

As Terry Reed got more deeply involved in the Mena operation, he began to have some doubts, which he brought to his Japanese-national CIA handler, Aki Sawahata.

> *"Aki, is this all legal? Sounds like we're going to great lengths to avoid detection by other Feds. Who do we consider our enemy here?"*

> *"Terry-san, we are CIA! We are not law enforcement. We are not Justice Department. We are not Treasury Department. We are CIA! We answer to director, who answers to president. You are dealing with very top level. These other agencies are not in loop. They not cleared for major foreign policy decisions. CIA has to work this way all over world. We are not breaking law. We are above law."*[685]

They're All In It Together

Working hand-in-hand with the Democrats in Arkansas during the 1980's were the Republicans in DC—specifically, the Bush family.

In George Herbert Walker Bush's hip pocket was deadly Cuban hitman Félix Ismael Rodríguez.

Rodríguez worked closely with E. Howard Hunt on Operation 40—the failed invasion of Cuba—as well as being sent on several high-profile missions including a failed attempt to assassinate Fidel Castro[v]. He is suspected of also having been involved in John F. Kennedy's

---

[v] The CIA was unstoppable except when it came to Jesuit-trained Catholic Communist Fidel Castro; then they were hapless and incompetent.

assassination.[686]

When the CIA caught up with Ernesto "Che" Guevara, Felix Rodriguez was there to interrogate him before he was executed[687]. As Guevara bled out, Rodriguez took the Rolex watch off his wrist[688] and proudly displayed it to anyone who was interested for the rest of his life.

Rodriguez was also in Mena, helping Terry Reed train Nicaraguan rebels.[689]

Why would a bunch of hard-Left Democrats (who had masqueraded as Southern "blue-dog" Democrats to get to the Governor's Mansion in Arkansas) work with silver-spoon Republican Elites to run guns and drugs to Nicaragua to oust a Leftist government?

The more Terry Reed worked with them all, the more he sensed that his world paradigm was terribly flawed. The media...presidential elections...even elections for key Legislators...it was all a farce—a rigged game. [italics suspended]

> Here was what seemed a strange alliance. A state run by Democrats in bed with a Republican administration in Washington, and both conspiring to evade Congress's prohibiting against aiding or abetting the Contras. It was so steeped with hypocrisy.
>
> Was the CIA the invisible force that had the power to *compromise* these political pillars of the nation?
>
> Were these same invisible forces operating only in Arkansas or throughout the nation? He wondered. But why limit it to the nation? Perhaps the world functioned under one control. Could that control be the CIA? Was there a secret alliance of agents worldwide who operated as they pleased?
>
> Religion, he had come to realize, was a form of social control. Was politics as well? Was it just a game like professional sports, simply to divert public attention from what was really happening? Was it all just a placebo?
>
> While driving back to OSI [CIA logistical front company "Overseas International"] Terry was strangely quiet and withdrawn. He was feeling manipulated by the social order he had been raised to obey and now he had doubts about his previous motivations in life.
>
> "You're very quiet, Terry-san," [Reed's CIA handler Aki] Sawahata said after a few minutes.

"Aki, I've got to ask you a question. It's funny I've never asked, considering all the time we've spent together. Are you a Republican or a Democrat?"

"I am a political atheist. I work for the CIA."

"What does that mean?"

"That means Agency is politics. Agency is the government. Everything else is just puppets, a big game, Terry-san. You did not know that?"

If Terry Reed was not a liability before, he certainly was now. Those who see behind the curtain are always a threat. ...

But those who feared him would not pull the trigger themselves. They would not resort to such dirty, Mob-style methods. They would use a much more clean, convenient and safe way to "terminate" him. Simply manufacture a criminal profile, construct a crime, and let the "system" do the rest. Reed would find that when irritated, the United States government could simply use its internal resources to eliminate an asset. ~ *Compromised*[690]

While working in the machine tool industry in Oklahoma, Reed was brought in by the local FBI office to help investigate the shady dealings of Soviet citizen Joseph Bona. Bona was a Hungarian KGB agent who spoke 7 languages and, according to Special Agent Wayne "Buzz" Barlow, was responsible for the deaths of at least 3 international spies. Bona was helping export critical technology through his KGB front company "Technoimpex" and an affiliated American Company, "Northwest Industries" (NWI). Reed noted:

> *The Soviets didn't have to steal the technology they desperately needed and couldn't produce. They simply had to come to America and buy it. [And t]he Japanese were more than willing to do business, even if they didn't own what they were selling. ...what the Japanese couldn't provide them, the KGB was apparently going to "procure" through legitimate business ties they were establishing in North America. ~ Compromised*[691]

In 1987, it was discovered that Toshiba had sold important submarine stealth technology (specifically the ability to precision-machine submarine propellers to reduce cavitation) to the Soviet Union. It produced some great political theater as legislators hit Toshiba radios with sledgehammers for the unwitting American public[692]. Less than a year later, not only were all modest penalties against Toshiba erased, the skids for foreign trading had gotten thoroughly greased.

> *It was only last July that eight sledgehammer-wielding members of Congress smashed a Toshiba radio-cassette recorder on the Capitol grounds to protest the company's illegal sale of submarine technology to the Soviet Union.*
>
> *The Senate, acting on its version of an omnibus trade bill, quickly voted to ban the Japanese manufacturing giant from its lucrative $2.5-billion-a-year U.S. market, and one House member said Toshiba deserved a Benedict Arnold traitor's award.*
>
> *But now the burst of anger has dissipated under the impact of one of the most pervasive and sophisticated lobbying efforts in Washington in many years. The version of the trade bill that cleared the Senate last week and the House the week before nearly obliterates the punishment for Toshiba by limiting the ban to its annual $200 million in sales to the U.S. government.* ~ Robert Rosenblatt, LA Times[693]

Terry Reed would also find that Joseph Bona weathered his FBI "investigation" without a hitch. In fact, the United States government was excited to hear Reed say he wanted to co-operate with the KGB agent on manufacturing illicit weapons in Mexico.[694]

High-level officials in the United States government were enabling the Soviet Union to overcome the stifling chains of Communism and keep strategic parity with America and the very intelligence agencies that were supposed to protect from espionage were helping get the job done.

> *Emery West, the president of NWI* [Northwest International] *and a former Hungarian refugee, was deeply involved with the CIA, FBI and KGB.* ~ Stolen Honor, David Taus[695]

Soon, Reed was having dinner with Bona and the arrangement was making him have that queer feeling of being manipulated again.

> *A myriad of thoughts raced through Terry's head. Here he was, dining with someone he was sure was a communist agent. A man he liked, to be sure, but a communist agent nonetheless. And Terry was fronting for the CIA. Another strange alliance? He had looked behind the curtain in Arkansas and seen that American politics was a charade. Was geopolitics a charade, too, he wondered?* ~ Compromised[696]

A conspiracy this big implies leadership within all organizations were dancing to a tune played by an outside, malignant musician: Rome.

The Making of a President

Barry Seal had told his CIA daredevil pilot partner Terry Reed that he had a blackmail insurance policy to keep him wealthy and alive. He had caught the sons of the President doing and selling drugs.

> *"Barry, are you telling me George Bush's kids are in the drug business?"*
>
> *"Yup, that's what I'm tellin' ya. A guy in Florida who flipped for the DEA has got the goods on the Bush boys. Now I heard this earlier from a reliable source in Colombia, but I just sat on it then, waitin' to use it as a trump card, even got some tape recordin's. [expletive], I even got surveillance videos catchin' the Bush boys red-handed. I consider this stuff my insurance policy. It makes me and my mole on the inside that's feedin' the stuff to me invincible. Now this is real sensitive shit inside of U.S. Customs and DEA, and those guys are pretty much under control." ~ Compromised*[697]

What Barry Seal didn't take into account was how easily the players he thought he was pitting against each other could reconcile. They all answered to a higher authority who kept them in line and out of trouble.

This was obvious as the CIA repeatedly colluded with their supposed arch-nemesis, the KGB.[698]

Barry Seal could not possibly have imagined that, between the Clinton and Bush camps was a voice they all obeyed.

Because of this, not only was it easy to tie up the loose ends, it was a combined effort.

In 1985, Seal gave testimony to the Presidential Commission on Organized Crime. His testimony was then used against him and the Internal Revenue Service slapped a $29 million jeopardy tax assessment on him, stripping him of all his property.

District Court Judge Frank Palozola sentenced Seal to evening confinement at the Baton Rouge, Louisiana Salvation Army halfway house. The only thing the judge didn't do was paint a bullseye on Seal's back. He was perfectly anchored to the same public place every evening until morning and that's exactly where a Medellín hit team riddled him with bullets on February 19th, 1986.[699,700]

Flagged

> **False flag** *(or **black flag**) describes covert military or paramilitary operations designed to deceive in such a way that the operations appear as though they are being carried out by entities, groups, or nations other than those who actually planned and executed them. Operations carried out during peace-time by civilian organizations, as well as covert government agencies, may by extension be called false flag operations if they seek to hide the real organization behind an operation. Geraint Hughes uses the term to refer to those acts carried out by "military or security force personnel, which are then blamed on terrorists."[1]* ~ Wikipedia[701]

In 64 AD, Rome suffered a terrible fire that burned for nearly a week and destroyed 75% of the city. Citizens suspected that emperor Nero had started it but instead, he scapegoated the troublesome and burgeoning population of new Christians.[702]

At the turn of the century, Cuba was an allure to American business for trade in sugar and iron. The Elite were eager to rid the hemisphere of Spanish influence, and the sinking of the U.S.S. Maine (and loss of her 266 sailors) was the catalyst for war. However, controversy swirls around the grave of the warship to this day and the original government explanation of a Spanish mine no-longer holds water.[703]

In May of 1915, a German U-boat sank the ocean liner RMS Lusitania and she lost an astounding 1,195 passengers to the icy waters of the Atlantic. It was an outrage that was called to mind repeatedly by politicians and media alike until America joined WWI less than 2 years later. What was discovered well afterward was that it was the American and British governments that put those passengers at risk by loading the Lusitanian with arms for the war.[704]

In 1932, Germany's political landscape was strewn with schisms caused by competing parties and interests. In January of the following year, German President Paul von Hindenburg appointed the powerful Nazi Party's Adolph Hitler, Chancellor. Hitler was extremely ambitious but had learned from his failed strong-arm coup[705] of a decade earlier. Less than two months after becoming Chancellor, Germany's building of parliament—the Reichstag—burned to the ground. German communists were blamed and the furor was a wave of emotion that Hitler rode into becoming *Führer*. Few now dispute that Nazis started the blaze.[706]

Success breeds success and 6 years later *der Führer* had his eyes on Poland. In late August of 1939, the German Secret Police (Gestapo) located an isolated radio outpost along the Silesian border near the town of Gleiwitz. The three operators were subdued by "Poles" and the radio station was taken over and began broadcasting a message of Polish resistance that likely no one heard because it was only a relay station. Later, a Polish sympathizer was dragged by the Gestapo in a drugged state to the location where he was executed as "proof" of the "aggression"[707]. A few days after that, in September, Germany invaded Poland.

"Remember the Maine!" In 1962, members of the United States military recommended[708] to President John F. Kennedy that innocent Americans be murdered[709] and Communist Cubans could be blamed as provocation for war with Cuba. In the most perverse sense of irony Operation: NORTHWOODS even offered to blow up a U.S. warship in Guantanamo Bay, creating a new take on Spanish philosopher Jorge Santayana's famous phrase[710], "Those who are oblivious to history are doomed to repeat it." Some have pondered whether Kennedy's refusal contributed to his assassination.

In 1964, American aid to South Vietnam was only in the form of "advisors" and Special Operations units. After a series of attacks on the Navy destroyer U.S.S. Maddox in the Gulf of Tonkin, Congress gave Lyndon Johnson carte blanche to send tens of thousands of young men to be maimed and killed for a massive new "military/industrial complex"[711]. Later it was found, no such attacks ever occurred.[712]

In 1967, Johnson would again be implicated in the Israeli attack on the U.S.S. Liberty. We'll take a detailed look at that incident in Chapter 17.

A well-cited column from Washington's Blog lists these further examples.

> *Soviet leader Nikita Khrushchev admitted in writing that the Soviet Union's Red Army shelled the Russian village of Mainila in 1939, and declared that the fire originated from Finland as a basis launching the Winter War four days later*
>
> *The CIA admits that it hired Iranians in the 1950's to pose as Communists and stage bombings in Iran in order to turn the country against its democratically-elected prime minister*
>
> *The former Italian Prime Minister, an Italian judge, and the former head of Italian counterintelligence admit that NATO, with the help of the Pentagon and CIA, carried out terror bombings in Italy and other European countries in the 1950s and blamed the communists, in order to rally people's support for their governments in Europe in their fight*

against communism. As one participant in this formerly-secret program stated: "You had to attack civilians, people, women, children, innocent people, unknown people far removed from any political game. The reason was quite simple. They were supposed to force these people, the Italian public, to turn to the state to ask for greater security" (and see this)(Italy and other European countries subject to the terror campaign had joined NATO before the bombings occurred). And watch this BBC special...

A U.S. Congressional committee admitted that – as part of its "Cointelpro" campaign – the FBI had used many provocateurs in the 1950s through 1970s to carry out violent acts and falsely blame them on political activists

An Algerian diplomat and several officers in the Algerian army admit that, in the 1990s, the Algerian army frequently massacred Algerian civilians and then blamed Islamic militants for the killings (and see this video; and Agence France-Presse, 9/27/2002, French Court Dismisses Algerian Defamation Suit Against Author)[713]

In 2005 a group of contractors from the Zapata Corporation fired at a United States Marine Corps outpost in Fallujah, Iraq. This odd occurrence was chalked up to the "fog of war"[714]. "Zapata Corporation" is a CIA front company founded by former CIA Director George H.W. Bush[715]. The apparent motive being, the more Marines get shot at and hurt in Iraq, the more contracts are delivered to Zapata and other mercenary organizations. War is business.

Allies shooting at allies may come as an awful shock, but a very high-profile example cropped up later that same year when two British operatives were apprehended by Iraqi police for shooting up the police station in Basra[716]. The two commandos were dressed as Iraqi civilians and at least one Iraqi minister accused them of fomenting sectarian violence in the Shiite-dominated southern province that bears the same name[717]. Basra police suddenly were portrayed as crazed "militia"[718] requiring an astounding force of tanks and helicopters to quickly rescue the two offenders[719]. This was in sharp contrast to the 15 sailors and Marines captured by the Iranian navy two years later, whom British Elites felt were of no high priority.[720]

Previous to modern times, empires and governments conducted false flags where their own citizens were killed to aggrandize the power of that empire. Today, Western administrations kill or pretend to kill their own citizens but use the political capital to further enslave them, as if *they* are the enemy.

This, too, speaks of a malignant outside control.

The Clinton Administration would take the use of false flags against American citizens to shocking levels (only to be surpassed by the Bush and Obama administrations).

August 21-31, 1992: Ruby Ridge

Randy and Vicki Weaver were conspiracy theorists.

They believed that their government was growing tyrannical and out-of-control. To them, it was only a matter of time before the freedoms they'd loved so well were all but memories. They decided to relocate to the mountains of Idaho and live "off grid". Once there, they became friendly with another separatist group, the Aryan Nations. As the name suggests, the group was profoundly racist, believing that super-wealthy Elites like the Rothschilds were part of a Jewish cabal pushing the New World Order.[w]

They made excellent targets for the Clinton administration. Both the ATF and FBI were sent to create problems where they didn't exist, looking to infiltrate and entrap their victims as they've done countless times before and since.

> *The FBI has received substantial criticism over the past decade — much of it valid — but nobody can deny its record of excellence in thwarting its own Terrorist plots. Time and again, the FBI concocts a Terrorist attack, infiltrates ... communities in order to find recruits, persuades them to perpetrate the attack, supplies them with the money, weapons and know-how they need to carry it out — only to heroically jump in at the last moment, arrest the would-be perpetrators whom the FBI converted, and save a grateful nation from the plot manufactured by the FBI.* ~ Glenn Greenwald, Salon[721]
>
> *We've talked multiple times about how the FBI seems to spend an awful lot of time stopping its own terrorist plots, and it appears to have done so yet again. iamtheky points us to the story of a "terrorist plot" to blow up the capitol averted... thanks to the fact that the whole thing was planned by the FBI, so it was pretty easy to stop the one dupe who thought it was real. Now, as some people*

---

[w] This distraction amongst the "Truth" or "Freedom" movement was fostered by the Company and works as powerfully today as it did then. See *Chapter 17: It's the Jews!*

always point out, these kinds of operations do seem to get people off the street who wouldn't mind causing harm to Americans, but it's unclear if any of them would ever actually have the means to do so in reality. What's telling is that these seem to be basically the only terrorist plots we hear about the FBI stopping these days—which makes you wonder if they just have too much free time to manufacture plots to stop. ~ TechDirt[722]

Defense lawyers in the trial of seven Michigan militia members want a mistrial, claiming they should have been given details about the past work of an FBI agent who infiltrated the group.

Attorneys found out only this week that agent Steve Haug was the handler for a New Jersey man who was paid by the FBI to collect information on white supremacists and hate groups, starting in 2003. The informant was a right-wing radio host and blogger who made threats against critics and public officials while on the FBI payroll.

Attorney William Swor told a judge Wednesday that prosecutors had an obligation to turn over material that could aid the defense. The government says there was no violation.

Militia members are accused of conspiring to commit rebellion. ~ Associated Press[723]

The ATF sent a snitch to Randy Weaver disguised as a fellow freedom fighter. At first he asked for Weaver to get him an automatic weapon but Weaver said he couldn't do that. Then they prodded him to saw down some shotguns which was easy enough for Weaver to do. That was the hook they needed to extort Randy Weaver to become an informant on his Aryan friends.

Or so it was thought.

When the ATF put the squeeze on Weaver, he reacted in a way they didn't expect. He told them he didn't care what they had on him, he wasn't going to turn.

As a result, the ATF swore out a warrant for Weaver's arrest for altering shotguns below the legal barrel length…like they had asked him to do.

Weaver decided to stay on his property and hunker down to make the government come to him.

And come they did.

They staked out the residence with surveillance cameras and snipers but it wasn't long before Weaver sniffed them out—or rather, the family dog did. 14 year old Sammy Weaver was out with the dog when he rooted out a Federal agent. They all tore off down the mountain until, suddenly, the Feds opened fire grievously wounding Weaver's dog. At that, Sammy tried to return fire and the military-grade weapons the agents were using nearly sawed Sammy's arm off. In shock, he turned and ran up the access road but Federal agents riddled his back with bullets, killing him.

The rest of the family scurried towards the house in response to the gunfire, not knowing what was going on. In the ensuing firefight, U.S. Marshall Bill Degan was killed, Randy Weaver was wounded and family friend Kevin Harris was also shot and wounded.

Randy's wife, Vicki, ran to the door with 10 month old Elisheba in her arms. FBI sniper Lon Horiuchi shot her in the face, splattering the infant with her mother's flesh. No doubt remained regarding what Horiuchi had carefully targeted with his state-of-the-art optics—a woman holding an infant. Vicki died, slumped over her baby.

Soon, the Idaho National Guard was called in with M113 armored personnel carriers, destroying all the family property outside the house and running over and killing another family dog, according to the testimony of Rachel Weaver.[724]

As the siege wore on, government agents mocked Weaver's grief from their savagery over loudspeakers, "Good morning Mrs. Weaver – we're having pancakes, what are you having for breakfast?"[725]

Eventually, sympathetic civilian negotiators intervened on the Weavers' behalf and were able to talk the survivors down[726]. Randy Weaver was acquitted of all charges.[727]

Not a single Federal agent was fired, demoted, pursued or prosecuted for the blood they spilled that day.

The First World Trade Center Bombing

The 1993 World Trade Center bombing was the efforts of Ramzi Yousef and Omar Abdel-Rahman, a.k.a. "the Blind Sheik". Rahman was repeatedly granted freedom of movement to travel from Sudan to the U.S. to Egypt and back to America. This was touted by government and media reports as "admitted errors".[728]

The FBI had a man on the inside the whole time. He thought he was there to stop them, but, in fact, he was there to monitor their progress and facilitate the plot.

There was a brilliant 2011 movie called *The Veteran* that depicted this sophistry perfectly[729]. Directed and written by Matthew Hope and starring Toby Kebbell, a young British "para" (airborne) soldier is recruited by the Secret Service to (unbeknownst to him) insure that the terrorists welcomed into Britain have all the drugs and guns they need to destabilize the UK. The answer to the resulting terror plots was to be more taxpayer investments into the military/industrial complex and the Police State.

It's a *real* agenda that's working like a charm in Great Britain.

> *The UK has more CCTV cameras per capita than any European country, yet figures released in July 2009 by the European Commission and United Nations showed Britain's recorded rate of violent crime surpassed any other country in Europe.* ~ Wired[730]

Emad Salem was an exceptionally-accomplished Egyptian intelligence operative who had penetrated the jihadist cell planning to bomb the WTC. He worked to painstakingly ingratiate himself with "the Blind Sheik" and the FBI was in touch with him regularly.

The plot continued to mature until Rahman began to pressure Salem to build the bomb for the conspirators. Salem told his FBI handler he was in a bind. What should he do? The response came, *"Build the bomb."*

Salem was so shocked by the this that he thought he was being set up and immediately began recording his conversations with the FBI.[731]

Salem built the bomb for Rahman, Yousef and the FBI and then, suddenly, the FBI "lost track" of the lot of them[732], just as the DoJ and ATF "lost track" of the machine guns, sniper rifles and hand grenades they had given to the Sinaloa drug cartel.

The resulting detonation in WTC1 resulted in 6 deaths but no appreciable damage to the building.

For those within the United States government treasonously planning to kill Americans with as much shock as possible for political use, it was clear that more preparation was needed. The next time an event was planned, they would have to spend extensive effort towards more thorough and exotic forms of demolition and keep the truck bombs as cover for the public.

Controlled Opposition

Fox News is one the most popular mainstream news outlets in America. It is strongly contrasted by the overt Left-wing bias of the other news agencies. Featuring supposed Right-wing ideologues like Irish Catholics Sean Hannity and Bill O'Reilly, what Fox News has become is the creation of Australian billionaire Rupert Murdoch.

Amongst Murdoch's lesser-known accolades are that he is a Knight of Malta[733] and a Papal Knight of Saint Gregory.[734]

A frequent guest of Hannity and O'Reilly is NY prosecutor Andrew McCarthy. McCarthy had prosecuted the Blind Sheik for the 1993 WTC bombing and later wrote a book on the event titled *Willful Blindness*.[735]

The book was red meat to the Fox News audience: political correctness had enabled an Islamist threat to outwit a hamstrung but dutiful FBI.

In his book, McCarthy admitted that he had seen firsthand the repeated "missteps" and "mistakes" the FBI had made, yet failed to accuse FBI leadership with anything more than "willful blindness".

Perhaps a cursory look at NY prosecutor Andrew C. McCarthy will explain his lack of vision.

- a graduate of Cardinal Hayes Catholic High School in Bronx, NY[736]
- a graduate of Jesuit Fordham University Law School[737]
- —and an outspoken proponent of destroying the Bill of Rights in favor of fighting the so-called "War on Terror"[738]

April 19th, 1993: Waco

As Randy Weaver was going to trial for refusing to help the government fabricate a terror threat, the FBI and ATF were already on their next assignment: the take-down of more apocalyptic Christians, this time, in Waco, Texas.

The Branch Davidians were an off-shoot of Seventh Day Adventists who considered the United States government to be the Whore of Babylon. As one Davidian blog stated:

> *In Revelation Chapter 17, it states that a figurative woman (that represents the USA's capital/leadership) is figuratively drunk with confusion/Babylon in her forehead (referring to her way of thinking/mind/forehead) on her own wine (referring to her*

ideals/visions).[739]

Seventh Day Adventists are some of the most outspoken critics of the Catholic Church and the Jesuit order via their best teachers such as Walter Veith, Doug Batchelor and Bill Hughes.

In 1929, strict Adventist and Bulgarian immigrant Victor Tasho Houteff presented SDA leadership with his vision of the 144,000 remnant listed in the Book of Revelation titled *The Shepherd's Rod.*[740] Adventist leadership shunned Houteff's vision and he was disenrolled. He subsequently began the Branch Davidian movement based upon his teachings.

It's likely that the Davidians of Texas were outside of the mainstream enough as to elicit their being targeted by Bill Clinton and his Attorney General Janet Reno. It is no coincidence that Seventh Day Adventists are high on Rome's hit list. The conspirators felt that Waco Davidians were separated enough from other sects of Christianity that, when they were persecuted, no other Christians would come to their aid.

They were absolutely right.

The Davidians had retreated to a compound in Waco and were awaiting the final judgment before Christ's Return. They were living "off grid" and that was a problem for the United States government.

Just as they did at Ruby Ridge, the ATF used the imprimatur of "firearms violations" to conduct an armed SWAT raid but the Davidians were better prepared than the Weaver family.

Only two days after the WTC bombing, Federal agents stormed the compound but the Davidians resisted. Two hours later, 6 Davidians were dead but so were 4 black-clad, assault weapon-wielding Federal agents.[741]

All evidence of the thoroughly-filmed raid was locked away or "lost".[742]

Three men who were outside the Davidian compound during the initial raid later attempted to return to their families after the shooting started. Two were arrested. A third didn't fare as well.

> *SUNDAY, FEBRUARY 28, 1993: Michael Schroeder, a Branch Davidian, is killed while he tries to return to the main building. Texas Rangers begin an investigation but are barred by the FBI from continuing.* ~ PBS Frontline[743]

Michael's bullet-ridden unarmed body was left to lay in a ravine for days after he was executed[744]. This was done to send a message, just like the body of "suicidal jumper" JP Morgan technology chief Gabriel Magee was left on the adjacent rooftop 30 stories below for hours after police arrived for any other would-be banker whistleblowers to see.[745]

When news media showed up at the Waco conflagration, the armor-clad soldiers of the FBI and ATF were livid that they were being filmed and brutally pushed back journalists under the premise that they had moral authority because they had taken casualties in their aggression.[746]

It became clear that the lid was off and no further assaults could be made so the government laid siege to the Mount Carmel compound.

Again, the Branch Davidians showed that they were prepared and, after 2 months, little had changed.

They were now surrounded by tanks and armored fighting vehicles, just as they believed they would be.

An apocalyptic end to their existence? They had no idea how right they were.

On April 19th, 1993 (a date carefully chosen), a specially configured tank rammed the Davidian compound, setting the building on fire[747]. A short time later, the entire facility was engulfed in flames. 76 men, women and children succumbed to that inferno.

To validate the raid, the few surviving Branch Davidians were charged

---

This Day In History

Numbers are important to the Luciferian World Elite. Significant dates are used to curry favor with interdimensional agencies as well as communicate the presence of their "Unseen Hand".

The span of 18, 19 and 20 April throughout history have always been important to them. When significant events are being planned, this range of dates is a favorite.

For the Jesuits, it begins with April 19th, 1541; the day Ignatius Loyola became the first "Superior General".

21 April 753 BC: close enough to our span of dates, Rome is considered to be founded on this festival of the shepherd-god of *Pales*.

20 April 571 AD: held by many to be the birth date of the prophet Muhammad.

20 April 1889: Adolf Hitler is born.

19 April 1775: first shot of the Revolutionary War is fired at Lexington.

with "murder" and "conspiracy". They were acquitted.[748]

Now, citizen rights are far more curtailed and the Davidians would certainly be convicted in a "court of law". In today's America, lifting your hands to protect your face during a law enforcement gang-beating constitutes "resisting arrest".[749,750,751,752]

The total count of American dead (not including government agents) was at least 83, that we know of. One of the Federal snipers shooting women and children from afar during that siege was none other than FBI agent Lon Horiuchi.

> *Was the FBI really at Waco to contain a siege or were trigger-happy agents purposely brought to the Davidian church to finish off the job the Bureau of Alcohol, Tobacco and Firearms botched?*
>
> *Yesterday, the Fort Worth Star-Telegram reported that FBI agent Charles Riley said all the way back in June 1993 that he heard shots fired from a sniper post occupied by agent Lon Horiuchi, according to court documents filed by Branch Davidians and relatives as part of a wrongful-death suit scheduled to go to trial next month.*
>
> *...Horiuchi was the paid assassin the FBI used Aug. 22, 1992 — eight months earlier — to plug a fatal hole in the head of Vickie Weaver, an unarmed mother clutching her 10-month-old baby during a similar siege at Ruby Ridge, Idaho. It seems Lon*

---

19 April 1933: Franklin Roosevelt takes America off the gold standard.

17-19 April 1961: failed Bay of Pigs invasion of Cuba.

19 April 1982: NASA declares Sally Ride is an "astronaut", not because she is qualified, but because she is a woman.

19 April 1989: 16" turret No. 2 explodes on the USS Iowa killing 45 sailors.

19 April 1993: FBI/ATF slaughter 83 men women and children in Waco, TX.

19 April 1995: 168 die, many of them children, when the Alfred P. Murrah Building in Oklahoma City is bombed.

19 April 2005: Cardinal Joseph Ratzinger becomes "Pope Benedict XVI".

20 April 2010: British Petroleum's oceanic drilling rig *Deepwater Horizon* explodes killing 11 men and *tens of thousands* of animals in the Gulf of Mexico.

SOURCES:

Saint Ignatius Of Loyola, Fr Myron Pereira SJ, Campion Calls.com

> *Horiuchi is something of a specialist — the FBI's go-to guy when it's open season on women and children.*
>
> *...Horiuchi was indicted for manslaughter by Idaho authorities for the shooting, but the charges were thrown out. ... And now we have reason to believe that eight months after the incident at Ruby Ridge, one that ultimately cost U.S. taxpayers $3.1 million in a civil settlement with Randy Weaver, Horiuchi was assigned to another volatile siege with civilians — including women and children.* ~ Joseph Farah, WorldNetDaily[753]

> http://www.campion-calls.com/pages/jesuitignatius.htm
>
> FDR Library exhibit, Action to Action The Concise of Encyclopedia of Economics, Great Depression, Robert J. Samuelson
> http://www.nps.gov/hofr/upload/April%2019-2.pdf
>
> The Exact Date Of The Prophet's Birth, Hijra Calendar.com
> http://www.hijracalendar.com/article1.htm

In an interview with Rick Martin of *The SPECTRUM*, author Eric Jon Phelps, implicated both Horiuchi and the FBI in a Papal plot to punish American Patriots.

> **Martin:** *Let me just back-up here for a minute. What comes to mind is Louis Freeh, head of the FBI.*
>
> **Phelps:** *Roman Catholic, good altar boy. Probably a Knight of Columbus; I can't prove it. But anybody with that kind of power has got to be a Knight of Columbus.*
>
> *And the Knights of Columbus implement Jesuit politics. And Louis Freeh was the one behind the Waco atrocity and the Oklahoma City bombing atrocity. And his top sniper was a Japanese Roman Catholic named Lon Horiuchi.*
>
> *So, it's Roman Catholics in control, Knights in control of the FBI, who carried out all of this killing. And those two men, Louis Freeh and Lon Horiuchi are personally accountable to Cardinal O'Connor of New York. And Cardinal O'Connor of New York is the most powerful Cardinal in the country. He is the military vicar. ... Cardinal O'Connor is the King of the American Empire. And he rules his Empire from that Palace, St. Patrick's Cathedral, "the little Vatican".*[754]

Oklahoma City

On **April 19th, 1995**, 168 people—including 19 children—were killed in a bomb attack on the Alfred P. Murrah Federal building in Oklahoma City.

The iconic images of dead children helped dramatically increase the power of the Federal government as well as rocketed Bill Clinton into a 2nd term.

Since that terrible event, the accusation of "Timothy McVeigh!" has silenced many a Christian, Libertarian, Constitutionalist or Pro-Life activist and has started an avalanche of ever-more restrictive legislation like the Antiterrorism and Effective Death Penalty Act of 1996.

> *The Antiterrorism and Effective Death Penalty Act of 1996 is the product of legislative efforts stretching back well over a decade and stimulated to passage in part by the tragedies in Oklahoma City and the World Trade Center.*
>
> *Title I of the Act substantially amends federal habeas corpus law as it applies to both state and federal prisoners whether on death row or imprisoned for a term of years by providing: a bar on federal habeas reconsideration of legal and factual issues ruled upon by state courts in most instances; creation of a general 1 year statute of limitations; creation of a 6 month statute of limitation in death penalty cases; encouragement for states to appoint counsel for indigent state death row inmates during state habeas or unitary appellate proceedings; and a requirement of appellate court approval for repetitious habeas petitions.* ~ Charles Doyle, Federation of American Scientists[755]

The truck bomb that blew up inside the parking garage of World Trade Center 1 in 1993 was instructive to America's enemies (her own government). Although it was strategically parked next to support structures, little damage was done and only 6 Americans lost their lives. A lot more damage would need to be done for true political success. The apparent lesson learned there was, "*pre wire*" and engineers and eye witnesses would claim that is exactly what they did in Oklahoma City two years later.[756]

Not a Truck Bomb

In April of 2014, the false flag that was the Boston Marathon bombing was so evident to unbiased journalists and researchers[757] that another serious event occurred as an apparent distraction.

A fertilizer plant just outside of Waco, Texas went up in an earth-shattering explosion. As amateur video began to emerge, it became clear that an airborne munition snaked its way through smoke plume of the fire that was already raging to obliterate the entire building[758,759,760]. The sound of inbound ordinance is distinctive and unmistakable.[761]

Was this the first instance of a drone strike on American soil?

Residents were evacuated for considerable distances due the danger of toxic fumes[762]. These fumes were not present in Oklahoma City 18 years before.

Evidence of pre-wiring, particularly of demolition infrastructure directly beneath the day room (that produced such mortifying propaganda of dead and bloody children) may have been what got bombing first responder OKCPD officer Terrance Yeakey tortured and killed.

Sergeant Terry Yeakey was one of the first emergency personnel on the scene after the bomb(s) went off and he immediately began saving lives and pulling people out of the debris—a feat that should've been impossible in the wake of an ammonium nitrate truck bomb.

Yeakey would later be found dead and pronounced to have committed suicide.

The only reliable information regarding Terry and what happened to him came from his own family. A letter Terry wrote to bombing survivor Ramona McDonald clearly implied there were dangerous "secrets" Terry knew about the bombing. It is now in the possession of Yeakey's mother, Loudella.[763]

McDonald had received an anonymous call telling her to stop looking into what happened because it was part of an important government anti-terrorist operation.

> *Ramona McDonald, who formed a group called Heroes of the Heart to bring a negligence suit against the Federal Government, was told that McVeigh was set up by an anonymous caller asking her to drop the case. The caller stated that the bombing was a failed sting operation where John Doe 2, also a federal agent, was supposed to defuse the bomb at the last second. It was a matter of national security and we have no idea how many other bombs have been defused or attacks subverted due to these types of operations he*

pleaded. Of course no one would have believed this story if she hadn't recorded the entire conversation.[149] ...

The government has also told the public that an honest policeman named Sgt. Terrance Yeakey committed suicide due to his guilt about not being able to help more at the bombing or because of his failed marriage. What we are not told is that he investigated the crime despite being told to "cease and desist," was taking video photos of the crime scene and that he was cooperating with and had written a letter to Ramona McDonald. We are also not told that he feared for his life so he took out an insurance policy and told his former wife that they needed to get married so that the policy would be in effect should he be killed. (By the way an insurance policy doesn't pay for suicide). Other issues we weren't told included that there was no police investigation, no autopsy, and no attempt to lift finger-prints from the suicide despite being a standard procedure in the case of an officer's death. He was receiving death threats and the investigation has remained sealed to everyone, including his family members. His family had [their] phone tapped and was under police surveillance after the suicide. His sister requested his video camera and any film that the officer would have had and the police department wouldn't give it to her. When they finally decided to give it to her...all the film was missing, later explaining that [it] was all pornography... There were also break-ins and thinly veiled threats against family members. And finally, just to add insult to injury, the police department wouldn't even pay for the funeral.[151] ...

On May 8, 1996 Sgt. Yeakey tried to cut himself in the wrists, neck and throat, then, after losing approximately two pints of blood, got out of his car, walked a mile and-a-half over rough terrain, crawled under a barbed-wire fence, waded through a culvert, then laid down in a ditch and shot himself in the head. It was ruled a suicide on the spot and required no further investigation.[153] ~ Phoenix Rising: The Rise and Fall of the American Republic, Donald Lett, Jr[764]

The New York Times would give an account of Sergeant Yeakey's death. Noticeably absent from it were the details that pointed away from suicide and toward torture and murder.

A police sergeant who rescued at least four people at the site of the Oklahoma City bombing committed suicide this week but left no note, prompting friends and co-workers to speculate that he was driven by guilt at not being able to have saved more lives and by despondency over a troubled family life, the police said.

The sergeant, Terrance Yeakey, 30, was found on Wednesday in a field near his hometown, El Reno, about 30 miles west of Oklahoma City. Sergeant Yeakey had apparently tried to slit his wrists, then shot himself to death, three days before he was to receive the department's medal of valor, the police said. ~ AP, New York Times[765]

According to Loudella Yeakey[766], Ramona McDonald later suffered a broken marriage, financial hardship and eventual commitment to a mental facility. Such an internment can be an extremely effective way of silencing dangerous witnesses.

Loose Ends

After the Oklahoma City bombing, there were reports of a "John Doe #2". These were very damaging to the official "lone gunman" explanation.

Enter Salt Lake City attorney Jesse Trentadue.

Jesse's brother, Kenneth Michael Trentadue, was a typical "bad boy" with a good heart. Frequently in trouble with the law, it didn't shock his brother when he was told Kenny was again placed in jail in June of 1995 for violating his parole.

In August of '95, Ken was transferred to the Department of Justice's Federal Transfer Center in Oklahoma City.

Three days later, he was dead of an apparent "suicide".

The Chief Medical Examiner for the State of Oklahoma at the time, Dr. Fred Jordan, felt otherwise.

In a statement to local Fox 25 News[767], Jordan told reporter Phyllis Williams he felt Trentadue was brutally tortured and murdered by federal agents.

> *I think it's very likely he* [Kenneth Trentadue] *was murdered. I'm not able to prove it. I have temporarily classified the death as undetermined. You see a body covered with blood, removed from the room as Mr. Trentadue was, soaked in blood, covered with bruises, and you try to gain access to the scene and the government of the United States says no, you can't.*
>
> *They* [the Federal government] *continued to prohibit us from having access to the scene of his death, which is unheard of, until about five months later. When we went in [the cell] and luminoled, it lit*

up like a candle because blood was still present on the walls of the room after four or five months. But at that point we have no crime scene, so there are still questions about the death of Kenneth Trentadue that will never be answered because of the actions of the U.S. government.[768]

Why would Federal agents torture and kill an obscure convict? —It all had to do with "John Doe No. 2".

The official story about the Oklahoma City bombing has always been, "Lone, homicidal Christian militia Constitutionalist Timothy McVeigh targeted the Alfred P. Murrah building with an ammonium nitrate truck bomb."

Ken Trentadue was mistakenly ID'd as a possible "John Doe #2", Richard Lee Guthrie[769]. If the government's "lone gunman" explanation was going to be kept alive, Ken would have to be dead—unbelievably, at the hands of the FBI.[770]

It was Jesse Trentadue's Freedom of Information Act crusade that began opening the floodgates which would later include implications that, not only were there more than one "perpetrator", but that the team was trained by our own government.

Thanks to evidence from the prison infirmary and coroner, it became quite apparent that "lawmen" from the FBI had *tortured* and *murdered* Ken Trentadue.

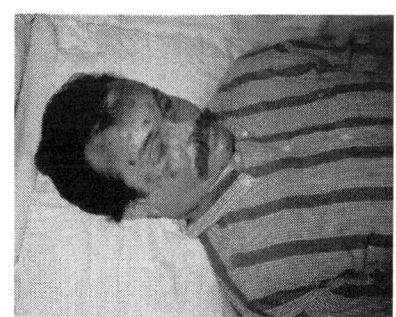

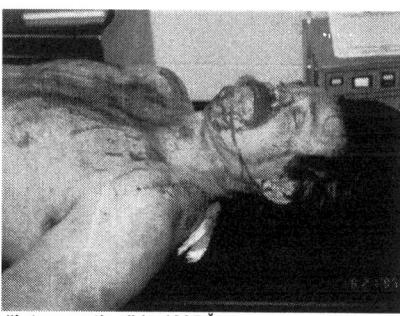

Ken Tretadue after FBI "interrogation" in 1995.[x]

Just like similar so-called "miscues", this wasn't an "interrogation gone wrong". It was Standard Operating Procedure right from the pages of the Nazi SS or Soviet KGB; *terminate loose ends*. The exact same scenario

---

[x] Special thanks to attorney Jesse Tretadue. Please visit Ken's page: www.kennethtrentadue.com

would play itself out when the FBI went to "question" Ibragim Todashev, a friend of Boston bombing suspect Tamerlan Tsarnaev.

Todashev was shot 6 times in the torso and once in the back of the head...execution style.[771]

Perhaps the best document Jesse Trentadue freed from government files was the sworn statement of bombing "co-conspirator" Terry Nichols where he implicated high-placed government officials and agencies at every level of the bombing plot.

> *I cannot possibly discuss in this Declaration all the information I have concerning the Oklahoma City bombing and others involved. But crucial parts of this terrorist act remain hidden from the American people—especially the identities of "Others Unknown," who collaborated with McVeigh in the bombing. ...*
>
> *One was acting as a government provocateur. The other was a high-ranking federal government official. I believe both men are now being protected by the federal government in a cover up to escape its responsibility for the loss of life in Oklahoma. ...*
>
> *In December of 1992, Timothy McVeigh told me that while he was serving in the U.S. Army, he had been recruited to carry out undercover missions. McVeigh did not say who recruited him, or specify the nature of his mission. McVeigh did say, however, that he was to begin making contacts with a "network" of people after the first of the year and that he was to take no action in furtherance of this mission until called upon. McVeigh said he would soon be making his first contact down south."*
>
> *McVeigh's first contact came one month later, in Florida. It was with Roger Moore: a gun dealer who lived in Royal, Arkansas...*[772]

Not only does this bring us back to the President who didn't inhale[773], but it ties a thread of treason and deceit that leads all the way forward to the Obama Justice Department and Eric Holder.

> *At the time of the bombing, our current United States Attorney General, Eric Holder, was managing FBI sting operations as U.S. attorney for the District of Columbia —and sitting in line to take over as deputy attorney general, which he did in 1997. One of Holder's first jobs was to cover up the FBI's role in the bombing.* ~ Pat Shannan, American Free Press[774]

The Jesuit Communist Powers that Molded Bill Clinton

James William Fulbright was one of the most powerful men in the Senate. He was also a Communist and a vehement racist.

In 1956, Fulbright signed the so-called Southern Manifesto denouncing school desegregation with then-Democrat and 33rd Degree Scotish-Rite Freemason[775] Strom Thurmond. Thurmond was protected at his Senate seat for an astounding 47 years and was replaced by a man of equally questionable loyalties, Lindsey Graham.

Fulbright, who held office for 31 years, also helped filibuster the Civil Rights Bill of 1964 and then refused to sign it[776] after his friend Lyndon Johnson talked him in to allowing cloture.[777]

Fulbright was a Communist collaborator who repeatedly attempted to warm the American people to thoughts of life under shared property and wealth. [italics suspended]

> In their dealings with the communist world, Fulbright declared, Americans must abandon old myths and adapt themselves to new realities. The character of Soviet-American relations had changed. ... In this new era of "peaceful coexistence" it was imperative that Americans adopt a more flexible, sophisticated approach to [Communism]. "We must dare to think unthinkable things..." ...
>
> It was quite possible for freedom and democracy to exist in a socialist or communist country, the Arkansan pointed out. ...
>
> The United States was going to have to come to grips with the fact that Castro and Castroism were not going to disappear in a season. Efforts to bring Cuba down through a policy of political and economic boycott had failed. ...
>
> Although the Senate was virtually empty when Fulbright delivered old myths and new realities [title of his filibuster speech], the wire services reported it verbatim on the twenty sixth, and the national press gave it extensive and immediate coverage. By the end of the week, virtually every press pundit of note had written at least on column on the speech. "Fulbright Shows His Skill Again," proclaimed Drew Pearson in "The Washington Merry-go-Round." "The significant thing about the recent Fulbright full-dress speech...is that its author has an almost perfect score on foreign affairs," Pearson proclaimed. ...

> ...Pravda called Fulbright's speech a "light which has lit up a new realistic tendency in Washington's political thinking." Izvestia, the official newspaper of the Soviet government, devoted nearly three columns to a glowing appraisal.[19] Cuba's unofficial minister in charge of revolution, Che Guevara, thanked Fulbright for recognizing "Cuba is here to stay."[20] ~ *J. William Fulbright, Vietnam, and the Search for a Cold War Foreign Policy*, Randall Bennett Woods[778]

During the heyday of Communism in the 1960's, it was the agenda of the Luciferians to simply merge the U.S. with the U.S.S.R.

When bank examiner Norman Dodd investigated tax-exempt foundations on behalf of Congressman B. Carroll Reece, he was shocked to be exposed to this agenda. In an interview with G. Edward Griffin, Dodd implicated both billionaires and intelligence agencies: mankind's foremost enemies.

> *Rowan Gaither was, at that time, President of the Ford Foundation. Mr. Gaither had sent for me, when I found it convenient to be in New York. He asked me to call upon him at his office, which I did.*
>
> *Upon arrival, after a few amenities, Mr. Gaither said, "Mr. Dodd, we have asked you to come up here today, because we thought that, possibly, off the record, you would tell us why the Congress is interested in the activities of foundations such as ourselves."*
>
> *And, before I could think of how I would reply to that statement, Mr. Gaither then went on, and voluntarily stated, "Mr. Dodd, all of us who have a hand in the making of policies here, have had experience either with the OSS during the war, or with European economic administration after the war. We have had experience operating under directives. The directives emanate, and did emanate, from the White House. Now, we still operate under just such directives. Would you like to know what the substance of these directives is?"*
>
> *I said, "Yes, Mr. Gaither, I would like very much to know." Whereupon, he made this statement to me, "Mr. Dodd, we are here to operate in response to similar directives, the substance of which is that we shall use our grant-making power so to alter life in the United States, that it can be comfortably merged with the Soviet Union."*[779]

Un-American in the House

Syndicated newspaper columnist Andrew Russell "Drew" Pearson was called on the carpet by Senator Joseph McCarthy for being a Communist sympathizer (which he clearly was[780]) but was defended by the only man who didn't vote for funding Un-American Activities investigations—J. William Fulbright.[781]

McCarthy's whole career was marked by playing dirty[782]. This made him an appealing figure for controlled opposition.

America had become so rife with blatant Communists from government to education to entertainment to media that a little outrageous grand-standing and persecution was needed to give them all cover and sympathy.

It was all organized by the Jesuits.

> *On the day that McCarthyism was born, and unseasonably warm spell was broken in Washington, D.C. It was January 7, 1950, and record-breaking temperatures—on the 6th it had reached 72 degrees—gave way to a return of winter cold. Winds announcing the cold front blew through the city at 40 mph, causing minor damage to a couple trees and a storefront window.*
>
> *That night, a meeting took place at the Colony restaurant, a four-star establishment in downtown Washington. Attending were four men: Georgetown University politics professor Charles Kraus, attorney William A. Roberts, Fr. Edmund A. Walsh, a Jesuit and the head of Georgetown's School of Foreign Service, and Wisconsin Senator Joseph McCarthy. ...*
>
> *On February 9, 1950, a little more than a month later, McCarthy made his infamous speech in Wheeling, West Virginia, announcing he had a list of the names of 205 communists in the State Department. Many in the media, even the Catholic media, had no doubt that Walsh had been the spur that propelled McCarthy. The Catholic magazine the Churchman wrote in 1951 that McCarthy "only fires the guns that are made for him by Father Edmund Walsh, SJ." The Christian Century referred to Walsh as McCarthy's advisor. In 1953 leftist journalist I.F. Stone claimed that McCarthy "has had the guidance of Father Walsh." In* McCarthy: The Man, the Senator, the Ism, *published in 1952, Washington insiders Jack Anderson and Ronald W. May endorsed Pearson's account.* ~ Mark Judge, the American Spectator[783]

When it came time to put Joe McCarthy out to pasture, it was Irish Catholic *Eugene* McCarthy, Democrat from Minnesota, that helped get the job done along with Fulbright by "Gene's" side.[784]

Fulbright was institutional in herding America towards loss of sovereignty and answering to a centralized world authority.

> *His most notable achievement in the House was the 1943 Fulbright Resolution, putting the House on record as favouring U.S. participation in a postwar international organization. This organization at its founding in 1945 was named the United Nations.*
> ~ Encyclopædia Britannica[785]

What he also did was carefully rear young William Jefferson Clinton in the ways of Communism.

Bill Clinton got the special Soviet World Tour. He was just like any other typical American student—helping Marxists in London tone down their anti-Vietnam war rhetoric to appear more publicly acceptable.

> *Stepping up his campaigning against the war, Clinton joined meetings with Group 68, Americans backed by the pro-Soviet British Peace Council. Tariq Ali, the former radical student leader, described Group 68 as being on the soft wing of his hardline coalition.*
>
> *In the autumn, Clinton helped organise demonstrations outside the American embassy in Grosvenor Square. In the evening, protesters held a candlelit vigil attended by Jessica Mitford, the writer, and Paul Jones, the pop singer. ...*
>
> *A month later, Clinton took part in a weekend of demonstrations near Grosvenor Square. On the first day, protesters led by Vanessa Redgrave dropped cards with the names of war victims into a black coffin. ...*
>
> *On the second day, Clinton organised a church service to provide Americans with an alternative to more radical protests by British Marxists. He asked an American priest, Richard McSorley, to read a prayer at the service in St Mark's American church near the embassy.* ~ "Fedora" of FReeper Research[y][786]

---

[y] A shady attribution, to be sure, but a *phenomenal* piece showing detailed insider knowledge—and perhaps that's why there's no clear credit. They don't want to end up "Arkansided".

Father Richard McSorely was a Jesuit priest "committed to pacifism"[787]. The Company was holding Bill Clinton's hand all around the world and giving him big-name support for his Communist activities.

From there, it was off to the Soviet Bloc for immersion in Communist culture. [italics suspended]

> One influential Johns Hopkins Asian specialist linked to IPR was Chinese Communist apologist Owen Lattimore, accused by Joseph McCarthy in 1950 of being "Moscow's top spy" and "one of the principal architects of our Far Eastern policy". Declassified files available today indicate that while McCarthy was exaggerating by calling Lattimore Moscow's top spy, Lattimore had been flagged by the FBI as a suspected Communist and potential security risk as early as May 1941, when he was being considered for a position as the Roosevelt administration's political advisor to Chinese Nationalist leader Chiang Kai-shek. ...
>
> That December McSorley would again encounter Clinton in Oslo, Norway. Clinton, who had recently spent Thanksgiving vacation in Ireland with his fellow Moratorium protestor Tom Williamson, was now on his way to the Soviet Union, following in the footsteps of his new roommate Strobe Talbott.
>
> Talbott was a Russian affairs scholar and intern journalist for TIME. He had begun visiting Moscow in 1968 and had developed contacts in the USSR. ...
>
> In late 1969, after staying with Richard Stearns for a couple weeks in October, Clinton began rooming with Talbott and their friend Frank Aller. Aller, a draft dodger and China scholar, was doing academic work similar to Talbott's, making trips to Switzerland to receive the unpublished notes of Edgar Snow, an academic advocate of the Chinese Communists who was linked to the old Institute of Pacific Relations network. ... Clinton's autobiography recalls how he often made Talbott and Aller breakfast while they were doing their work...
>
> Clinton stayed in Moscow about five days. Several accounts say he left via the Soviet airline Aeroflot, but Clinton says "Nikki and her Haitian friend Helene put me on the train".
>
> In either case, Clinton's next stop was Prague, Czechoslovakia, where he arrived on January 6, 1970. There he looked up the family of his Oxford friend Jan Kopold. Kopold's family was well-

connected in Czech Communist circles. Clinton received a guided tour of Prague from Marie Svermova, the widow of Czech Communist Party hero Jan Sverma, who was Jan Kopold's grandfather. ~ "Fedora"[788]

Bill Clinton was made from the ground up by the Company of Loyola to be a Weapon of Mass Destruction aimed at the heart of the American people. They would later do much worse with a puppet President who has been so completely manufactured, some seriously question if he was conceived in a test-tube.

Endnotes

[655] *Tragedy & Hope: A History of the World in Our Time*, Carroll Quigley, Macmillan (1966), p. 67
[656] *ibid*, p. 339
[657] *ibid*, p. 950
[658] *ibid*, p. 1262
[659] *William J. Clinton; Address Accepting the Presidential Nomination at the Democratic National Convention in New York*, 16 July 1992, The American Presidency Project http://www.presidency.ucsb.edu/ws/?pid=25958
[660] *Five Decades Ago, Bill Clinton Meets JFK*, unattributed, 24 July 2013, NBC News http://www.nbcnews.com/news/other/five-decades-ago-bill-clinton-meets-jfk-f6C10736784
[661] *The Clinton Lectures*, Georgetown University http://www.georgetown.edu/clinton-lectures.html
[662] *Dark Alliance: The CIA, the Contras, and the Crack Cocaine Explosion*, Gary Webb, Seven Stories Press (1998), pp. 22, 24
[663] *ibid*, p. 25
[664] *ibid*, p. 38
[665] *Nomination of Louis O. Giuffrida To Be Director of the Federal Emergency Management Agency*, February 24, 1981, The American Presidency Project http://www.presidency.ucsb.edu/ws/?pid=43453
[666] *Oliver North & George Bush Created "READINESS EXERCISE: 1984" FEMA Martial Law Plan*, Johnny Cirucci YouTube
https://www.youtube.com/watch?v=chWH0n-EGLo&
This is a great snippet from an unknown documentary I highjacked from YouTube that includes testimony from the Iran/Contra hearings that was squashed by chairman Daniel In-No-Way, Demo-rat Senator from Hawaii.
[667] *Investigative Reporter Gary Webb on C.I.A. Drug-Trafficking*, Johnny Cirucci, YouTube https://www.youtube.com/watch?v=6aXANxeFZt0&
[668] *Reporter's Suicide Confirmed By Coroner*, Sam Stanton, 15 December 2004, the Sacramento Bee
http://web.archive.org/web/20080507054818/http://dwb.sacbee.com/content/news/story/11772749p-12657577c.html
[669] *Managing a Nightmare: How the CIA Watched Over the Destruction of Gary Webb*, Ryan Devereaux, 25 September 2014, the Intercept
https://firstlook.org/theintercept/2014/09/25/managing-nightmare-cia-media-destruction-gary-webb/
[670] *Ex-L.A. Times Writer Apologizes for "Tawdry" Attacks*, Nick Schou, 30 May 2013 http://www.laweekly.com/2013-05-30/news/gary-webb-jess-katz-crack/
[671] *Compromised*, Terry Reed and John Cummings, Clandestine Publishing (1995)
[672] *ibid*, p. xi
[673] *These 6 Corporations Control 90% Of The Media In America*, Ashley Lutz, 14 June 2012, Business Insider
http://www.businessinsider.com/these-6-corporations-control-90-of-the-media-in-america-2012-6
[674] *Compromised*, p. 115

[675] *Compromised*, pp. 62-63
[676] *Tench Coxe: Representative to the Continental Congress*, The James Madison Research Library and Information Center
http://www.madisonbrigade.com/t_coxe.htm
[677] *Chris Dodd Fights for His Reputation*, Mark Hosenball, 29 May 2009, Newsweek
http://www.newsweek.com/chris-dodd-fights-his-reputation-80237
[678] *"Gun Control's" Nazi Connection*, an unattributed, undated column that originally appeared in *Guns & Ammo* magazine in May 1993 and has been re-posted by Jews for the Preservation of Firearms Ownership—an *outstanding* organization.
http://jpfo.org/filegen-a-m/GCA_68.htm
[679] *The Gun Control Act Of 1968*, William Vizzard, undated, the Second Amendment Foundation, reposted by Jews for the Preservation of Firearms Ownership
http://jpfo.org/articles-assd02/gca68-nra4.htm
[680] *Federal Government Was Culprit in Housing and Economic Crisis, Says Congressional Report*, Fred Lucas, 8 July 2009, CNS News
http://cnsnews.com/news/article/federal-government-was-culprit-housing-and-economic-crisis-says-congressional-report
[681] *Update: Fannie Mae and Freddie Mac Invest in Lawmakers*, Lindsay Mayer, 11 September 2008, Open Secrets.org
http://www.opensecrets.org/news/2008/09/update-fannie-mae-and-freddie/
[682] *Chris Dodd's Leading Role*, unattributed, 2 March 2011, Washington Post—this piece of shit walked right out of Congress and right onto the plane to the People's Republic of Mexipornia. No job-surfing for bloodsuckers like him!
http://www.washingtonpost.com/wp-dyn/content/article/2011/03/01/AR2011030106474.html
[683] *Compromised*, pp. 148, 150
[684] *Double Standards on Pedophilia*, Quin Hillyer, 5 October 2006, the American Spectator
http://spectator.org/articles/46365/double-standards-pedophilia
[685] *Compromised*, pp. 158-159
[686] *Felix Rodriguez*, Spartacus Educational
http://spartacus-educational.com/JFKroderiguez.htm
[687] *On Anniversary of Che Killing, CIA's Felix Rodriguez Remembers*, Andrea Billups and Kathleen Walter, 10 October 2013, Newsmax
http://www.newsmax.com/Newsfront/che-guevara-cia-cuba-killing/2013/10/08/id/529906/
[688] *Che Guevara, Félix Rodríguez and the Rolex GMT*, A.Morgan, 22 August 2011, watchfinder
http://thewatch.watchfinder.co.uk/timeless/che-guevara-felix-rodriguez-and-the-rolex-gmt
[689] *Compromised*, p. 176
[690] *Compromised*, Terry Reed and John Cummings, Clandestine Publishing (1995), pp. 182-183
[691] *Compromised*, p. 26
[692] *Congress Seeks Ban Against Toshiba Products For Transfer Of Submarine Technology To Russia*, archived video, 1 July 1987, NBC News
http://www.nbcuniversalarchives.com/nbcuni/clip/5112639334_s12.do

[693] *Intense Lobbying Cools U.S. Anger at Toshiba*, Robert Rosenblatt, 1 May 1988, LA Times
http://articles.latimes.com/1988-05-01/business/fi-3406_1_toshiba-america
[694] *Compromised*, p. 216
[695] *To Be A Hero, Stolen Honor: Inside the FBI, CIA and the Mob*, David Richard Taus, First Edition Design Pub (2014), another stupid "e-book" that isn't listed with page numbers. Trust me it's there. I'm not counting them. Look for the subheading "Hungarian Connection to SAT" —CIA logistics front company "Southern Air Transport" based in Miami, Florida. So much for that "not allowed to operate domestically" bullshit.
[696] *Compromised*, p. 224
[697] *ibid*, p. 252
[698] *ibid*, p. 258
[699] *ibid*, p. 261
[700] *Barry Seal > Death*, Wikipedia
http://en.wikipedia.org/wiki/Barry_Seal#Death
[701] *False Flag*, Wikipedia
https://en.wikipedia.org/wiki/False_flag

I wanted to change things up with a different encyclopedic source but the internet didn't have any at first blush.
[702] *Nero Persecutes The Christians, 64 A.D.*, EyeWitness to History.com
http://www.eyewitnesstohistory.com/christians.htm
[703] *The Destruction of USS Maine*, Department of the Navy—Naval History And Heritage Command, history.navy.mil
http://www.history.navy.mil/faqs/faq71-1.htm
[704] *Secret of the Lusitania: Arms Find Challenges Allied Claims It Was Solely a Passenger Ship*, Sam Greenhill, 19 December 2008, the Mail
http://www.dailymail.co.uk/news/article-1098904/Secret-Lusitania-Arms-challenges-Allied-claims-solely-passenger-ship.html
[705] *Hitler's Beer Hall Putsch*, Jennifer Rosenberg, undated, about.com
http://history1900s.about.com/cs/thirdreich/a/beerhallputsch.htm
[706] *Historians Find "Proof" That Nazis Burnt Reichstag*, Tony Paterson, 15 Apr 2001, the Telegraph
http://www.telegraph.co.uk/news/worldnews/europe/germany/1310995/Historians-find-proof-that-Nazis-burnt-Reichstag.html

April of 2001. 5 months later, America's *biggest* false flag brought a war without end.
[707] *The Gleiwitz Incident: the "First Man to Die" in the War*, World War II Today
http://ww2today.com/the-gleiwitz-incident-and-the-first-man-to-die-in-world-war-ii
[708] MEMORANDUM FOR THE SECRETARY OF DEFENSE, Justification for US Military Intervention in Cuba, 13 March 1962, L.L. Lemnitzer, Chairman, Joint Chiefs of Staff
http://johnnycirucci.com/wp/?attachment_id=3026
[709] *U.S. Military Wanted to Provoke War With Cuba*, David Ruppe, 1 May 2001, ABC News
http://abcnews.go.com/US/story?id=92662&page=1

May of 2001. 4 months later, America's *biggest* false flag brought a war without end.

[710] *George Santayana*, Wikiquote
http://en.wikiquote.org/wiki/George_Santayana#Vol._I.2C_Reason_in_Common_Sense
[711] *Eisenhower Farewell Address (Full)*, someoddstuff, President Dwight Eisenhower's Farewell Address to the nation January 17, 1961, YouTube
https://www.youtube.com/watch?v=CWilYW_fBfY
[712] *The Gulf of Tonkin Events: 50 Years Later*, John White, 12 March 2014, New American magazine
http://www.thenewamerican.com/culture/history/item/17820-the-gulf-of-tonkin-events-50-years-later
[713] *Americans Are Finally Learning About False Flag Terror*, 24 November 2013, Washington's Blog
http://www.washingtonsblog.com/2013/11/false-flag.html
[714] *Marines Jail Contractors in Iraq*, David Phinney, 7 June 2005, CorpWatch
http://www.corpwatch.org/article.php?id=12349
[715] Harbinger Group Inc. (NYSE:HRG), formerly Zapata Corporation, is a holding company based in Rochester, New York, and originating from an oil company started by a group including the former United States president George H. W. Bush. Various writers have alleged links between the company and the United States Central Intelligence Agency. In 2009, it was renamed the Harbinger Group Inc.
Harbinger Group, Wikipedia, as of 23 September 2014
http://en.wikipedia.org/wiki/Zapata_Corporation
[716] *Iraqi Police Detain Two British Soldiers in Basra*, China View, 19 September 2005, Xinhuanet
http://news.xinhuanet.com/english/2005-09/19/content_3514065.htm
[717] *Iraqi MP Accuses British Forces in Basra of "Terrorism"*, al Jazeera, 20 September 2005, reposted via uruknet.info
http://www.uruknet.info/?p=15978
[718] *UK Soldiers "Freed From Militia"*, unattributed, 20 September 2005, BBC News
http://news.bbc.co.uk/2/hi/middle_east/4262336.stm
[719] *British Smash Into Iraqi Jail To Free 2 Detained Soldiers*, Ellen Knickmeyer and Jonathan Finer, 20 September 2005, the Washington Post
http://www.washingtonpost.com/wp-dyn/content/article/2005/09/19/AR2005091900572.html?nav=rss_world
[720] *British Expect Iran to Begin Release of 15 Captive Sailors, Marines "Within Hours"*, unattributed, 4 April 2007, FoxNews
http://www.foxnews.com/story/2007/04/04/british-expect-iran-to-begin-release-15-captive-sailors-marines-within-hours/
[721] *The FBI Again Thwarts Its Own Terror Plot*, Glenn Greenwald, 29 September 2011, Salon
http://www.salon.com/2011/09/29/fbi_terror/
[722] *FBI Saves Us From Another Of Its Own Terrorist Plots*, unattributed, 20 February 2012, TechDirt
https://www.techdirt.com/articles/20120217/13271317794/fbi-saves-us-another-its-own-terrorist-plots.shtml
[723] *Defense In Militia Case: Feds Withheld Key Info*, Associated Press, 21 March 2012, the Sandusky Register
http://www.sanduskyregister.com/article/1675626

[724] *The Legend of Ruby Ridge*, Secret Rulers of the World, Trio, hosted by G. Edward Griffith, currently found on the YouTube channel of Jew-hating retard "WesternVoices"
https://www.youtube.com/watch?v=-a0rg6Nn4T8
[725] *Weaver Awarded $3.1 Million from US Government*, Gary Shade, no date, Shade's Landing
http://www.firearmsandliberty.com/ruby2.html
[726] *Ruby Ridge: The Truth and Tragedy of the Randy Weaver Family*, Jess Walter, Harper (1995), pp. 352-353
[727] *Idaho's Tragedy at Ruby Ridge*, Syd Albright, 14 September 2014, Coeur d'Alene Press
http://www.cdapress.com/columns/syd_albright/article_44130b08-6a05-582f-b64d-839d98c45aa8.html
[728] *THE TWIN TOWERS; Rahman Errors Admitted*, Douglas Jehl, 7 March 1993, New York Times
http://www.nytimes.com/1993/03/07/nyregion/the-twin-towers-rahman-errors-admitted.html
[729] *The Veteran (2011): Shocking Truth From The Silver Screen*, Johnny Cirucci, 20 October 2013, The Patriot Press
http://johnnycirucci.com/wp/entertainment-reviews/the-veteran/
[730] *Investigation: A Sharp Focus on CCTV*, Heather Brooke, 1 April 2010, Wired
http://www.wired.co.uk/magazine/archive/2010/05/start/investigation-a-sharp-focus-on-cctv
[731] *Tapes Depict Proposal to Thwart Bomb Used in Trade Center Blast*, Ralph Blumenthal, 28 October 1993, New York Times
http://www.nytimes.com/1993/10/28/nyregion/tapes-depict-proposal-to-thwart-bomb-used-in-trade-center-blast.html
[732] *CBS News: FBI Fully Aware of 1993 World Trade Center Bomb Plot*, a report from CBS' Dan Rather-biased aired in October of 1993 and reposted on my YouTube
https://www.youtube.com/watch?&v=Bvqrj869ie8
[733] *Caped Crusaders: What Really Goes On at the Knights of Malta's Secretive Headquarters?* Evgeny Lebedev, 29 March 2014, the Independent
http://www.independent.co.uk/news/world/europe/caped-crusaders-what-really-goes-on-at-the-knights-of-maltas-secretive-headquarters-9217469.html
[734] *Should Rupert Murdoch's Papal Knighthood Be Rescinded?* 8 July 2011, The Catholic Herald
http://www.catholicherald.co.uk/commentandblogs/2011/07/08/debate-should-rupert-murdochs-papal-knighthood-be-rescinded/
[735] *Willful Blindness*, Andrew C. McCarthy, Encounter Books (2008)
[736] *Andrew C. McCarthy*, bio, the Library Thing
http://www.librarything.com/author/mccarthyandrewc
Note, no mention of his time at Jesuit Fordham!!!
[737] *Andrew C. McCarthy*, bio, the American Freedom Law Center
http://www.americanfreedomlawcenter.org/about/advisory-board/andrew-c-mccarthy/
[738] *Top Terror Prosecutor Is a Critic of Civilian Trials*, Benjamin Weiser, 19 February 2010, New York Times
http://www.nytimes.com/2010/02/20/nyregion/20prosecutor.html?_r=0

[739] When I originally wrote on this topic for a column in May of 2014, this site I referenced was up and running (though it didn't look very professional): http://branchdavidian.com/
    Currently, it shows up with just a white screen, which is interesting. Hell, maybe it's me. Wouldn't be the first time I've been hacked.
[740] *The Shepherd's Rod*, V.T. Houteff, 1930
http://www.the-branch.org/Shepherds_Rod_Volume_1_Houteff
[741] *The Standoff in Waco*, Alex Hannaford, 18 April 2013, the Texas Observer
http://www.texasobserver.org/the-standoff-in-waco/
[742] This is a snippet from an excellent documentary by MGA Films titled "Waco: A New Revelation" (1999,), posted on my YouTube under the title Gov't "Loses" Surveillance Records From the 1993 Waco Raid;
https://www.youtube.com/watch?&v=TDFQe5C2H8M
    The film can currently be found on YouTube if you query its title.
[743] *Waco: the Inside Story*, unattributed and undated, PBS Frontline's chronology of events at Waco
http://www.pbs.org/wgbh/pages/frontline/waco/timeline.html
[744] Michael Dean Schroeder's family memorial blog
http://www.wizardsofaz.com/waco/mike1.html
[745] *JP Morgan Bankers Hold Minute's Silence For Technology Chief Gabriel Magee Who Plunged To His Death From Canary Wharf Headquarters*, Martin Robinson, 28 January 2014, the Daily Mail
http://www.dailymail.co.uk/news/article-2547275/BREAKING-NEWS-Man-30s-dies-plunge-JP-Morgan-headquarters-Canary-Wharf.html
[746] *ATF Not Happy To See Media Arrive At Waco*, Johnny Cirucci YouTube
https://www.youtube.com/watch?&v=KjjvJf591qk
    I believe this is a snippet that I took from the documentary, *Waco: The Rules of Engagement* (1997) by William Gazecki, Dan Gifford & Michael McNulty.
[747] *Specially Designed Gov't Tanks Set Fire To The Waco Compound*, Johnny Cirucci YouTube
https://www.youtube.com/watch?&v=yNmZOyHia7k
    I don't recall the documentary source but you can see flame projecting from the armored vehicle as it pulls away from ramming the compound building.
    This is the description I put below the video:
The M728 Combat Engineer Vehicle was based upon the M60 main battle tank. Although an apparatus for projecting flame was not standard, it was easily adapted to the vehicle.
[748] *11 in Texas Sect Are Acquitted Of Key Charges*, Sam Verhovek, 27 February 1994, New York Times
http://www.nytimes.com/1994/02/27/us/11-in-texas-sect-are-acquitted-of-key-charges.html
[749] *The Horror Every Day: Police Brutality In Houston Goes Unpunished*, Emily DePrang, 4 September 2013, the Texas Observer
http://www.texasobserver.org/horror-every-day-police-brutality-houston-goes-unpunished/
    I'm not about badmouthing cops but today's atmosphere is fast approaching the Third Reich.

[750] *Dashcam Nails Cops Who Beat Man While Shouting "Stop Resisting Arrest"*, Cory Doctorow, 28 August 2014, BoingBoing
http://boingboing.net/2014/08/28/dashcam-nails-cops-who-beat-ma.html
[751] *Stop Resisting Execution: Cold-Blooded Arizona Cops Assassinate Suspect with His Hands in the Air*, Kimberly Paxton, 3 February 2014, the D.C. Clothesline
http://www.dcclothesline.com/2014/02/03/stop-resisting-execution-cold-blooded-arizona-cops-assassinate-suspect-hands-air/
[752] *Resisting Arrest Charge Is Turning Our Country Into A Police State*, Georgia Sand, 16 June 2010, CopBlock.org
http://www.copblock.org/323/resisting-arrest-charge-is-turning-our-country-into-a-police-state/
[753] *The FBI's Favorite Hitman*, Joseph Farah, 14 September 1999, WorldNetDaily
http://www.wnd.com/1999/09/1440/
[754] *The Most Powerful Man In The World?* Rick Martin, 15 April 2000, Forbidden Knowledge.com
http://www.theforbiddenknowledge.com/hardtruth/blackpope.htm
[755] *Antiterrorism and Effective Death Penalty Act of 1996*, summary by Charles Doyle, 3 June 1996, Federation of American Scientists, American Law Division
http://fas.org/irp/crs/96-499.htm
[756] *Eyewitnesses & Experts Claim Gov't Insiders Pre-Wired the Alfred P. Murrah Building*, Johnny Cirucci YouTube
https://www.youtube.com/watch?&v=1yIFPIvcWQI

This is a snippet from the definitive work on the Oklahoma City bombing, *A Noble Lie: Oklahoma City 1995* (2011) by Holland Vandennieuwenhof and James Lane. http://www.anoblelie.com/

As is *so* true with *so* many people in the public arena, both men have been total assholes to me to date. The journalistic integrity of the film is peerless—experts and witnesses who were *there* tell the story. Just don't try to communicate with the producers unless you're very important.

[757] *From Boston to the New World Order*, Johnny Cirucci, 15 May 2013, The Patriot Press
http://johnnycirucci.com/wp/johnnys-latest-columns/from-boston-to-the-new-world-order/
[758] photograph of light source in the smoke at The Patriot Press
http://johnnycirucci.com/wp/?attachment_id=3027
[759] same photograph with helpful illustration
http://johnnycirucci.com/wp/?attachment_id=3028
[760] explosion pattern indicative of an ordinance strike
http://johnnycirucci.com/wp/?attachment_id=3029
[761] Yeah...I figured you'd want to see/hear *this*; *West Texas Fertilizer Plant Explosion collage*, Johnny Cirucci, YouTube
https://www.youtube.com/watch?v=asep5c64wRo
[762] *Texas Explosion: Firefighters Battle Toxic Cloud Of Noxious Ammonium Nitrate*, Michael Zennie and Anna Edwards, 18 April 2013, Daily Mail, taken down, interestingly enough, but archived at 24tanzania.com
https://24tanzania.com/texas-explosion-firefighters-battle-toxic-cloud-of-noxious-ammonium-nitrate/

[763] *Sergeant Terry Yeakey's Mom Reads His Letter to Ramona McDonald*, Johnny Cirucci YouTube
https://www.youtube.com/watch?&v=OOeVu5oxeQU
[764] *Phoenix Rising: The Rise and Fall of the American Republic*, Donald Lett, Jr., AuthorHouse (2008), pp. 342-343
[765] *A Policeman Who Rescued 4 in Bombing Kills Himself*, AP, 11 May 1996, New York Times
http://www.nytimes.com/1996/05/11/us/a-policeman-who-rescued-4-in-bombing-kills-himself.html
[766] *William Wagener Interviews Loudella Yeakey on the Death of Her Son, Terry*, Johnny Cirucci YouTube
https://www.youtube.com/watch?v=PJDfLUGBYkk&
[767] I'm deeply grateful to "hillbillyjihad32" for uploading this critical piece of local news footage that he snagged from his VCR. Unfortunately for us, it appears that hillbillyjihad32 had no idea how to operate the frigging thing nor what the control marked "TRACKING" does. I was going to upload it to my own channel but it's so poor, I'll just hang on to it for safekeeping and link to hillbillyjihad32's channel for you (who also, apparently, types with his CAPSLOCK on): *OKLAHOMA STATE MEDICAL EXAMINER SPEAKING OUT AGAINST CLINTON-RENO JUSTICE DEPARTMENT*, hillbillyjihad32 YouTube
https://www.youtube.com/watch?v=86hZhcjZHE8
[768] *A Coverup That Won't Stay Covered*, Paul Craig Roberts, 3 December 2003, LewRockwell.com
http://www.lewrockwell.com/2003/12/paul-craig-roberts/a-coverup-that-wont-stay-covered/
[769] *Attorney: Sealed Documents Indicate OKC Inside Job*, Paul Joseph Watson & Alex Jones, 23 February 2007, Prison Planet, reposted at the Patriot Press
http://johnnycirucci.com/wp/blog/2015/01/13/docs-indicate-okc-inside-job/
[770] *Kenneth Michael Trentadue, Connection to the Oklahoma City Bombing*, Wikipedia.org, as of 24 September 2014
http://en.wikipedia.org/wiki/Kenneth_Michael_Trentadue#Connection_to_the_Oklahoma_City_bombing
[771] *Rachel Maddow Admits the FBI Made a "Mess" Executing Ibragim Todashev*, JohnnyCirucci YouTube
https://www.youtube.com/watch?v=ZIBO8E2Uock
[772] *Declaration of Terry Lynn Nichols Regarding Gov't Involvement in the OKC Bombing*, Johnny Cirucci, Scribd
http://www.scribd.com/doc/221913581/Declaration-of-Terry-Lynn-Nichols-Regarding-Gov-t-Involvement-in-the-OKC-Bombing
[773] CBS interview with Willie Clinton, 29 March 1992, posted at the pothead YouTube channel of Medical Marijuana – MarijuanaSafe titled, *Marijauna Quotes: Bill Clinton - I didnt inhale*
https://www.youtube.com/watch?v=CeXGnSpjgNM
[774] *Did Eric Holder Cover Up FBI's Role In '95 OKC Bomb Plot?* Pat Shannan, 31 December 2011, American Free Press
https://americanfreepress.net/?p=2086
[775] The South Carolina Spartansburg Herald-Journal proudly declares Thurmond's accomplishment...on a tiny blurb in the middle of page 14, October 24th, 1969.

http://johnnycirucci.com/wp/?attachment_id=3031
[776] *TWO TRAGIC Flaws kept Arkansas Sen. J. William Fulbright...*, Theo Lippman, 16 February 1995, the Baltimore Sun
http://articles.baltimoresun.com/1995-02-16/news/1995047036_1_orval-faubus-fulbright-state-senators
[777] *J. William Fulbright, Vietnam, and the Search for a Cold War Foreign Policy*, Randall Bennett Woods, Cambridge University Press (1998), p. 58
[778] *ibid*, pp. 59-61
[779] *"Transcript of Norman Dodd Interview"*, 1982 A.D., with G. Edward Griffin
http://www.supremelaw.org/authors/dodd/interview.htm
[780] *Drew Pearson*, Spartacus Educational
http://spartacus-educational.com/USApearsonD.htm
[781] *Blocking a Gazan's Path to San Diego*, Fidaa Abed, 15 August 2008, U-T San Diego
http://www.utsandiego.com/uniontrib/20080815/news_mz1e15abed.html
    What a great citation this is!!! Poor Fidaa Abed had a Fulbright Commie scholarship—delivered to him by "Condoleeza" Rice, and yet he still suffered persecution because he was a muslim so-called "Palestinian".
    But he sure knows his American Commie personality history, doesn't he.
[782] *Joseph McCarthy*, Spartacus Educational
http://spartacus-educational.com/USAmccarthy.htm
[783] *Joe McCarthy's Jesuit*, Mark Judge 21 July 2005, the American Spectator
http://spectator.org/articles/48284/joe-mccarthys-jesuit
[784] *Joseph McCarthy: Reexamining the Life and Legacy of America's Most Hated Senator by Arthur L. Herman*, an unattributed, undated book review from the NY Times
http://www.nytimes.com/books/first/h/herman-mccarthy.html
[785] *J. William Fulbright*, Encyclopædia Britannica, 21 July 2004
http://www.britannica.com/EBchecked/topic/221757/J-William-Fulbright
[786] *Road to Moscow: Bill Clinton's Early Activism from Fulbright to Moscow*, Fedora, 22 August 2007, FReeper Research, posted via Free Republic.com
http://www.freerepublic.com/focus/f-news/1884984/posts
[787] *Richard McSorley, 88; Jesuit Priest Committed to Pacifism*, Washington Post, 22 October 2002, the LA Times
http://articles.latimes.com/2002/oct/22/local/me-mcsorley22
[788] *Road to Moscow: Bill Clinton's Early Activism from Fulbright to Moscow*, Fedora, 22 August 2007, FReeper Research, posted via Free Republic.com
http://www.freerepublic.com/focus/f-news/1884984/posts

Chapter 10

Flagged

Doctor Hall: I'd like to start with some simple word associations. Just tell me the first word that pops into your head. For example, I say, "Day" and you might say...
James Bond: Wasted.

Hall: alright... —Gun.
Bond: Shot.

Hall: Agent.
Bond: Provocateur.

Hall: Woman?
Bond: Provocatrix.

Hall: Heart.
Bond: Target.

Hall: Murder.
Bond: Employment.

Hall: Country.
Bond: England.

Hall: Skyfall.

...

Hall: Skyfall.

...

Bond: Done.

~ *Skyfall* (2012)[789]

Day of Infamy

As researchers examine the anomalies and treasonous acts behind 9/11, they are drawn to similarities to another terrible event in America's recent past: Pearl Harbor.

Franklin Roosevelt has been enshrined in the American Psyche by his initials, although the amount of damage the Shriner Freemason did may be incalculable.

One of the worst moments in United States history was the interning of Japanese Americans during WWII.

It was all done via Roosevelt Executive Order 9066[790]. An entire population of citizens, imprisoned for their ethnicity by nothing more than the command of one man.

It gives insight into the real villain behind Pearl Harbor.

In 1989, the BBC produced a documentary titled "Sacrifice at Pearl Harbor"[791] cataloguing many of the facts that proved Franklin Delano Roosevelt and all who served him were high traitors.

> *...Roosevelt ... provoked the attack, knew about it in advance and covered up his failure to warn the Hawaiian commanders.*
>
> *... [He] blinded the commanders at Pearl Harbor and set them up by—*
>
> *1. denying intelligence to Hawaii (HI)*
> *2. on Nov 27, misleading the commanders into thinking negotiations with Japan were continuing to prevent them from realizing the war was on*
> *3. having false information sent to HI about the location of the Japanese carrier fleet.*
>
> ~ *What Really Happened*[792]

The Purple, J-19, Coral Machine Cipher/JNA-20 and JN-25 codes were all broken and United States Intelligence was reading coded Japanese messages regularly by the Fall of 1941.

Truly, Pearl Harbor was a "Day of Infamy" but not in a way Americans know.

Hooked

In December of 2012, building on the success of previous false flags, traitors inside the United States government upped the ante with an entire Elementary School attacked by an assault weapon-wielding lone gunman.

The agenda was increased measures against the 2nd Amendment and feeding the mass-surveillance monster; another terrible battle in the war on

America's independent Middle Class.

With a precision unrivaled by the world's greatest assassins, Adam Lanza burst into Sandy Hook Elementary and killed 20 children and 6 adults with no survivors.

> *According to [medical examiner] Dr. [H. Wayne] Carver and State Police, Lanza shot each victim between 3 and 11 times during a 5 to 7 minute span. If one is to average this out to 7 bullets per individual—excluding misses—Lanza shot 182 times, or once every two seconds. Yet according to the official story Lanza was the sole assassin and armed with only one weapon. Thus if misses and changing the gun's 30-shot magazine at least 6 times are added to the equation Lanza must have been averaging about one shot per second—extremely skilled use of a single firearm for a young man with absolutely no military training and who was on the verge of being institutionalized. Still, an accurate rendering of the event is even more difficult to arrive at because the chief medical examiner admittedly has no idea exactly how the children were shot or whether a struggle ensued.* ~ Professor James Tracy, Global Research[793]

It was reported that the school had recently installed a top-of-the-line surveillance and security system, yet no video of the shooting or Lanza on the premises was released.[794]

As if waiting on cue, California Democrat Senator Diane Feinstein immediately revisited her sunsetted 1994 "Assault Weapons Ban". Surprisingly, it failed to find the votes for passage.

A few short months later, the Senate threw out a more cunning attack on the 2nd Amendment. This time, the focus was on "common sense background checks" and the salesmen were "moderates" like Republican Pat Toomey of Pennsylvania and Democrat Joe Manchin of West Virginia. Both humiliated their constituents with this effort, particularly Manchin who had previously been given an "A" rating by the NRA.[795]

What Americans didn't know was that the brains behind the effort was radical gun-grabber Charles Schumer (D, NY), and that it was a Trojan Horse of gun confiscation via the medical industry[796]. Under the guise of "mental instability", citizens could have their firearms confiscated with no real due process.[797]

Although there were no substantive gains at the national level, states used the incident with shocking success.

Connecticut already had some of the most confiscatory gun laws in the nation[798] (not to mention the fact that having a firearm within 1000 feet of a school was already illegal[799]) but the Democrat-controlled state piled on with banning magazines and so-called "assault weapons" and adding even more Orwellian privacy violations for prospective gun purchasers.[800]

Colorado enacted laws so outrageous and onerous to her population that two key Democrats were ousted from their seats[801] in recalls and a third promptly resigned once she was targeted as a key proponent.[802]

It was worse in the first Catholic colony of Maryland.

Last week, Maryland Governor Martin O'Malley (D) signed into law sweeping gun control legislation, Senate Bill 281. ...

[the] *new law will ban 45 specific types of commonly owned semiautomatic firearms, require future purchasers of handguns to obtain a license to do so, mandate reporting of lost or stolen firearms within an arbitrary time period, and institute a ban on the sale, manufacture, purchase or transfer of magazines capable of holding more than ten rounds of ammunition. ~ Ammoland*[803]

But the worst of these was New York where the restrictions were so heavy-handed that Governor Andrew Cuomo, son of former NY Governor Mario Cuomo, had to railroad them through by suspending a state Constitutional requirement to allow 3 days for both legislators and citizens to familiarize themselves with any proposed bill[804]. New Yorkers who were already restricted to handgun magazines of 10 rounds were suddenly whittled down to only 7 and, since then, police have started making arrests.[805]

The fallout after Sandy Hook wasn't just in the passing of draconian gun control legislation in states all over the nation. 2nd Amendment advocates with no staying power folded everywhere.

The controversial firm Cerberus[806] immediately put up for sale "Freedom Group" which included AR-15 manufacturer Bushmaster.[807]

Walmart pulled Bushmaster rifles from their web site[808] and Dicks went even further pulling all "modern sports rifles".[809]

The Discovery Channel axed their very popular program "American Guns" from their lineup.[810]

The Weinstein Company of Hollywood cancelled promotional events for "Jack Reacher" and "Django Unchained" (it just wasn't the right time to race-bait with guns).[811]

After showcasing billionaire gun-grabber Michael Bloomberg, *Meet the Press*' David Gregory opined that no pro-gun Senators would come defend the 2nd Amendment on his program.[812]

The sketchy details of Adam Lanza that emerged had trouble connecting him to the crime—or to reality, in general.

> *Sandy Hook has been the most misreported story in recent memory, but a few facts may have emerged. To date, authorities have not located any confirmed diagnosis for Adam Lanza. Relatives and former classmates say he had Asperger's syndrome, but this mild form of autism has no correlation with violence. The boy is described as anything but menacing – rather, as withdrawn, antisocial, even "meek", according to an official at his high school, who explained that Adam was only assigned a psychologist because a scrawny, cringing loner might be tormented by peers.* ~ Lionel Shriver, the Guardian[813]

The NY Daily News reported one "family friend" as saying Lanza was "like a ghost".[814]

Several of Lanza's neighbors told Inside Edition no one knew him, he was a "mystery".[815]

The Wall Street Journal called into question whether Lanza's mother Nancy had any connection to Sandy Hook Elementary as was originally reported.[816]

> *A former school board official in Newtown called into question earlier reports that Nancy Lanza had been connected to Sandy Hook Elementary School, possibly as part of the teaching staff.*
>
> *"No one has heard of her,"* said Lillian Bittman, who served on the local school board until 2011. *"Teachers don't know her."* ~ Wall Street Journal[817]

When questioned whether or not Nancy Lanza had a connection to Sandy Hook, Connecticut State Trooper Lieutenant Paul Vance stared for a moment as if dumbstruck, then began to give a long monologue about how thoroughly they examined the crime scene.[818]

Vance would later make a veiled threat toward "conspiracy theorists" whom he lumped in with supposed Lanza impersonators and warned that he was working very closely with "Federal authorities" to prosecute those who posted opinions on the internet deemed as "misinformation".[819]

Shortly after the attacks of 9/11, George W. Bush said this before the U.N.—

> *"Let us never tolerate outrageous conspiracy theories concerning the attacks of September the 11th; malicious lies that attempt to shift the blame away from the terrorists, themselves, away from the guilty. To inflame ethnic hatred is to advance the cause of terror..."*
> ~ the Washington Post[820]

More recently, the Prime Minister of England, "Conservative" David Cameron also spoke before the U.N. about "conspiracy theorists" lumping them in with anti-Semites and the ultimate Orwellian catch-all; "extremists". He used the Western Intelligence-created threat of ISIS as the reason why world governments should crack down on civil rights.

> *"We must be clear: to defeat the ideology of extremism we need to deal with all forms of extremism – not just violent extremism. ..."*
>
> *"The peddling of lies: that 9/11 was a Jewish plot and the 7/7 London attacks were staged. ..."*
>
> *"For governments, there are some obvious ways we can do this. We must ban preachers of hate from coming to our countries. We must proscribe organisations that incite terrorism against people at home and abroad. We must work together to take down illegal online material like the recent videos of ISIL murdering hostages. And we must stop the so called non-violent extremists from inciting hatred and intolerance in our schools, our universities and yes, even our prisons."*
>
> *"Of course there are some who will argue that this is not compatible with free speech and intellectual inquiry."*
>
> *"But I say: would we sit back and allow right-wing extremists, Nazis or Klu Klux Klansmen to recruit on our university campuses? No."*
>
> *"So we shouldn't stand by and just allow any form of non-violent extremism."*[821]

Cameron would also adjure internet providers and social networking to take down so-called "extremist material"[822]. Perhaps the kind of "extremism" he has in mind is from those who ask too many questions.

It should be particularly troubling to citizens in both the U.S. and the U.K. that these heads of state are making such statements before a body completely unaccountable to the people Bush and Cameron supposedly represent.

Corporate media took original reports of multiple shooters and distilled them down to one "lone crazed gunman".

> *One of the most important red flags of a staged shooting is a second gunman, indicating the shooting was coordinated and planned. There are often mind control elements at work in many of these shootings. The Aurora "Batman" shooter James Holmes, for example, was a graduate student actually working on mind control technologies funded by the U.S. government. There were also chemical mind control elements linked to Jared Lee Loughner, the shooter of Congresswomen Giffords in Arizona in 2011.*
>
> *According to multiple eyewitness reports from Aurora, Colorado, including at least one caught on camera by mainstream media news reports in Colorado, James Holmes did not operate alone. There was a second shooter involved. But the media quickly eliminated any mention of a second shooter from its coverage, resorting to the typical cover story of a "lone gunman."*
>
> *Today, the exact same thing is happening with the Newton, CT school shooting.* ~ Mike Adams, Natural News[823]

Local CBS Channel 2 interviewed an eye witness who said that police escorted a man in camouflage pants from the woods surrounding Sandy Hook Elementary to one of their squad cars.[824]

WICC AM 600 reported that "two shooters" were found at Sandy Hook, one was dead and the second was in custody.[825]

Immediately after the event, many media sources linked Adam's brother Ryan to the shooting and the older Lanza was even arrested at one point.[826]

But the picture that emerged was an extremely murky understanding of Adam that melds into Ryan. Did Ryan somehow help create the Adam Lanza the media has given us? Were pictures of Ryan manipulated and creeped out to become the wide-eyed "Adam Lanza"?

> *Perhaps most astonishingly, this suspect arrested in the woods was named in an Associated Press report as 24-year-old Ryan Lanza. The original report has long since vanished of course, but you can see it referenced here. This was despite the fact that Ryan had already been named as the deceased suspect inside the school, lying next to two handguns.*
>
> *Ryan Lanza was actually at work in Hoboken, New Jersey, that morning when his name and photo began circulating in the media. And so, for most of Friday, the 'lone shooter' was erroneously reported as "Ryan Lanza, confirmed dead." At the same time, we were being told that Ryan's girlfriend and a room-mate were reported missing, also from Hoboken, New Jersey.*
>
> *So this isn't just a case of mistaken identity, as later claimed when it was suggested that Adam had a piece of identification belonging to his brother on his person. Not one, but BOTH Lanza brothers were being placed by "law enforcement officials" at the scene of the shooting. It could be that Ryan's quick reflexes to leave his workplace to get on a bus to go back to his apartment while protesting innocence via his Facebook page may have saved his life.*
> ~ Niall Bradley, Veteran's Today[827]

Just two weeks before the shooting, Attorney General Eric Holder made a special visit to Connecticut to talk gun control with Democrat governor Dannel Malloy.[828]

Holder was there to push "Project Longevity".

> *The initiative, known as Project Longevity, will send new federal grant money to Connecticut and involve agents, academics and social workers working for or with the FBI and the U.S. Bureau of Alcohol, Tobacco, Firearms and Explosives.* ~ Reuters[829]

Eric Holder's entire career has been built around disarming the American people[830] which has suited those who created his special brand of black Communism in Rome quite well.

The behavior of the attending coroner, D. Wayne Carver II, during one press conference was nothing short of bizarre.

He had no details on the number of wounds, or genders of the victims, got the murder weapon wrong and at times seemed intoxicated or inebriated.[831]

The AR-15 Lanza is reported to have used has been at the top of the political hit list for some time.

> *The gunman who killed 20 first-graders and six adults at a Connecticut elementary school, shooting many multiple times, used a military-style rifle rigged to quickly reload, the state's chief medical examiner said Saturday.*
>
> *Dr. H. Wayne Carver II, the medical examiner, said the victims at Sandy Hook Elementary School in Newtown died Friday morning from "a very devastating set of injuries."*
>
> *Carver said of the seven autopsies he personally performed, the victims had "three to 11 wounds apiece" and were shot in the head, extremities and torso — two of them at close range.*
>
> *"I believe everybody was hit more than once," he said.*
>
> *Carver said the shooter was able to reload so quickly because he had taped two magazines together.* ~ NY Newsday[832]

Sadly, the media couldn't get on the same gun-control page and NBC reported that Lanza used *four* handguns and left the AR-15 in the car.[833]

The causal link between powerful hallucinogenic pharmaceuticals and aberrant, homicidal and suicidal behaviors grows more sure following both research and evidence in the past of suspects like Adam Lanza.[834]

Connecticut Assistant Attorney General Patrick B. Kwanashie gave astounding testimony at a Freedom of Information hearing regarding why the state continues to refuse the release of Adam Lanza's medical records.[835]

Corporate media have reported that there were no alcoholic or narcotic traces in Adam Lanza's body[836], but the actual toxicology report from Medical Examiner Wayne Carver remains undisclosed.[837]

Connecticut law enforcement withheld the 911 recordings for over a year.

> *The same day the FBI released video showing Aaron Alexis hunting down people in the halls of the Washington Navy Yard, Connecticut law enforcement officials were defending their refusal to make public 911 recordings from December's Sandy Hook Elementary School massacre.*
>
> *The Connecticut officials lost; the state's Freedom of Information*

Commission on Wednesday ordered the state's attorney in Danbury, Stephen Sedensky III, to release the recordings. But Sedensky plans to appeal, promising to extend a legal battle that has raised the question of when the public's right to know supersedes the need for sensitivity toward victims' families — especially when the victims were young children gunned down in their classrooms. ~ the LA Times[838]

And even the Times noted the strange sensitivity of Attorney Sedensky.

The secrecy is striking in light of the quick release of information — from 911 recordings to pictures and video — in other notorious crimes.[839]

Of the handful of witnesses at Sandy Hook perhaps the one who embodies the controversy best is Gene Rosen.

Gene is the owner/operator of "Gene's Trusty Pet Service, LLC". On his "About" page he admits experience in acting.

In the past, Gene has been involved in community theater and Public Access Television where he hosted a program that reported on the local theater scene.[840]

A video clip has appeared on YouTube of Gene practicing Sandy Hook shooting interviews.[841]

It's a good thing Gene practiced because he was quite popular with the media.[842]

Possibly the most shocking aspect of the Newton shooting was the decision to raze to the ground the entire Sandy Hook Elementary school.

Workers Demolishing Sandy Hook Elementary School Required To Sign Confidentiality Agreements

Contractors demolishing Sandy Hook Elementary School are being required to sign confidentiality agreements forbidding public discussion of the site, photographs or disclosure of any information about the building where 26 people were fatally shot last December.

Selectman Will Rodgers said officials want to protect the Newtown school where the 20 children and six educators were killed...

Project manager Consigli Construction has barricaded the property and intends to screen the perimeter to prevent onlookers from taking photographs. Full-time security guards will ensure the site is not disturbed. ...

Jim Juliano, a member of the Public Building and Site Commission, said he initially considered whether the heightened precautions might be excessive. But he believes extra vigilance is needed to shield Sandy Hook families and the community from exploitation. ~ Fox News[843]

But most of all is the pay-off. Sandy Hook has been as successful for the destruction of America's self-defending Middle Class today has the OKC bombing was in the 90's (and is still a powerful tool of anti-Tea Party reproach).

Recognizing that Congress has zero interest in passing more gun control, Obama used his weekly radio address to reflect on the heinous crime at Sandy Hook Elementary and encourage communities and community-level gun control activists to rally behind the cause.

In a transcript carried by UPI, Obama mentioned the sadness that engulfed Americans following Sandy Hook. He said this sadness brought "a sense of resolve...[that] we must change."

This means gun control... ~ Breitbart[844]

The Land of Make-Believe

The evening of the mass shooting in Aurora, Colorado[845] at the Century Theater (which prohibits firearms on the premises[846]), the movie *Batman: Dark Knight Rising* was being shown.

One of the previews played before the feature began was of the James Bond movie *Skyfall*. During that preview, a large neon sign with the word "AURORA" was shown[847]. Experts in mind manipulation believe this could have been a behavioral trigger.

The trailer, itself, has an astounding sequence where Bond is being debriefed by a psychoanalyst with a verbal Rorschach test and the associations paint a picture of a mind-controlled assassin.

The Dark Knight Rises had a very interesting prop that was used. A map of "Gotham City" maintained by the Gotham PD in multiple movies had an important island renamed. The sports stadium that was destroyed by the villain Bane with spectacular special effects was located on the island of

"South Hinkley".[848]

The prop master for Dark Knight Rises was Scott Getzinger, a man with an impressive resumé and copious experience in make-believe[849]. 8 months before the Sandy Hook shooting, Getzinger died in a car accident just outside of his home—Newton, Connecticut.[850]

A troubling media account calls into question the kind of care Getzinger received.

> *State police initially characterized his injuries as non-life threatening.* ~ The Stamford Advocate[851]

At a public hearing for "Gun Violence Prevention & Children's Safety", Getzinger's wife—Susan McGuinness Getzinger—made an astounding statement in support of the 2nd Amendment and gave an ominous warning of systemic corruption before Connecticut Governor Dannel Malloy.[852]

Another odd coincidence is that the author behind the dystopic New World Order hit *The Hunger Games*, Suzanne Collins, also lives in Newton, Connecticut.[853]

> *The hit movie "The Hunger Games" takes place in a dystopian future where the poor and wretched masses live under the high tech tyranny of a wealthy elite. Is the movie depicting the kind of society the elite is trying to establish for the New World Order?* ~ Vigilant Citizen[854]

Radio talk show host Alex Jones interviewed a Black Op State Department insider named Steve Pieczenik (more on them both in Chapter 12) and Pieczenik stated unequivocally that Sandy Hook was a false flag.

> *A woman who lives in Sandy Hook who's worth $600,000,000...named Suzanne Collins, she's written all [of] the Hunger Game...books and, literally, it comes out of her script—the assassination of children in schools, the assassination of children in a dystopic society, the fact that she had "no comment"...and secondly you had a whole group of actors—Gene Rosen, who came out of the Crisis Actors group—I always refer my readers to IS-42, Social Media [in] Emergency Management, the official course launched in summer by [the] Emergency Management Institute— which you and I pay for—it's a whole school on how to create disasters.*

Gene Rosen was not only not a psychologist he was a FEMA advisor and also in Texas plus you have kids who were in various acting schools... ~ The Alex Jones Show[855]

Connecticut "Department of Emergency Management and Homeland Security" held a FEMA course entitled *FEMA L-366 Planning for the Needs of Children in Disasters* [856] on the day of the shooting[857] less than 20 miles away.

The Catholic Connection

The more you look at the Newton incident, the more you get a surreal sense that the entire town was in on a plot to deceive America for the furtherance of her destruction.

An early report from the Canadian Broadcasting Corporation stated that Adam Lanza was dressed in black "as clergy" and that he was able to enter the school with a "Bushwacker" assault rifle[z] only because he was mistaken for clergy.[858]

That makes little sense for secular, public Sandy Hook Elementary, but it makes much more sense if the call came in from St. Rose of Lima parochial school less than 8 miles away.

Some of the first footage CNN aired as "chaos" from Sandy Hook turned out to be a drill at St. Rose.[859]

A vigil for the "victims" of the shooting was held—not in the vicinity of the school grounds—but by Parish Monsignor Robert Weiss at St. Rose.[860]

Monsignor Weiss has been in high demand since the shooting and was one of the first to be interviewed for his reaction.[861]

Monsignor Weiss is speaking frequently in diverse places about the tragedy and often mentions Newtown's unusual residents such as Suzanne Collins.[862]

Two days after the "massacre", St. Rose church received a "bomb threat" and was evacuated.[863]

St. Rose parishioner Mike Coppola shared his photograph of a "cross in the clouds" on day of the bomb scare with Monsignor Weiss[864]. Weiss

---

[z] There is no such thing, but there is a "Bushmaster" .223 semiautomatic rifle.

stated that listening to a "visionary from Medjugorje" (a reported Marian apparition in Croatia) uncovered for him that it was proof he must "witness the faith".[865]

While speaking to the Chief Administrators of Catholic Education in 2013, Monsignor Weiss admitted that drills for the St. Rose compound had not only been conducted, but that they had been projected and planned via computer simulation. That's quite sophisticated for such a small town.[866]

Another key player in the Sandy Hook menagerie is the President and CEO of Newtown Savings, John F. Trentacosta.

Florida Atlantic University Professor Dr. James Tracey noted this about Trentacosta:

> ...*John Trentacosta ... owns the property next to the Lanzas' 36 Yogananda Street residence* [supposedly where Adam Lanza murdered his mother], *at 34 Yogananda, is President and CEO of Newtown Savings Bank and serves in an advisory capacity to the Federal Reserve Bank of New York.*
>
> *Newtown Savings' Chief Financial Officer, William McCarthy, owns 12 Crestwood Drive, directly behind Sandy Hook Elementary.*
>
> *William Lavery, Trentacosta, and McCarthy serve together on the C. H. Booth Library's Board of Trustees, although Lavery presently occupies an emeritus post.*
>
> *In his capacity at Newtown Savings, Trentacosta collaborated with the United Way of Western Connecticut to establish the Sandy Hook School Support Fund. Logged and dated web posts suggest the Fund's announced founding predated the event by three days. Much like the subsequent rapid establishment of "One Fund Boston," a single day after the Sandy Hook massacre, on Saturday, December 15, 2012, Trentacosta speedily announced the Sandy Hook Fund on his Newtown Savings blog.* ~ the Memory Hole blog[867]

Trentacosta is a graduate of both Manhattan College and Iona College[868]. Both schools are run by the Institute of the Brothers of the Christian Schools—a Catholic society that has an identical mission to the Jesuits. They share identical "spirit" and "zeal".[869]

The Jesuits even have a university named after their mutual patron saint.[870]

Down the Rabbit Hole

The mass shooting in Tucson, AZ, on January 8th, 2011 is worth a quick look for the anomalies and quirks, alone.

Congresswoman Gabrielle Giffords was subscribed to supposed shooter Jared Lee Loughner's YouTube channel.[871]

A 9 year old girl listed as one of the victims who also died that day, Christina-Taylor Green, was born on September 11th, 2001.[872]

Christina-Taylor Green's mother trademarked Christina-Taylor Green products on 9/11/07. Roxanna Green now sells Christina-Taylor Green products for the Christina-Taylor Green Memorial Foundation. Most revolve around butterflies [a symbol oft-used in mind-control] *and 9/11 – We must "never forget".* ~ Stephanie Sledge, the Government Rag[873]

Loughner remains the invisible perpetrator whom no one has seen either in person or even video footage of[874]. This is in spite of the media report that the FBI has surveillance video of the "rampage"...unreleased, of course.[875]

Giffords is never in public without her husband/handler who always has a hand on her in some fashion. She repeats the same jokes and phrases. Are these the effects of her injuries or something more sinister?[876]

Loughner received "community organizer" training from a Bill Ayers program.[877]

As a teen, Loughner was briefly interned into the Pima County Juvenile Detention Center for petty offenses and even hospitalized at Sonora Behavioral Center when he appeared to lose his senses at school.[878]

The Pima County Juvenile Detention Center participates in the Juvenile Detention Alternative programs sponsored by the W. Haywood Burns Institute.

The life partner of domestic terrorist William Ayers, Bernadine Dohrn (also a Weather Underground terrorist) is on the W. Haywood Burns Institute Board of Directors.[879]

Gabrielle Giffords is a household personality yet a Federal judge died in the shooting whom no one has heard of; John Roll.[880]

Loughner supposedly used hallucinogenic drugs that either turned him into a homicidal maniac or perhaps were part of a course of treatments for mind control.[881]

Best of all was the experimental suspended animation technology from NASA and DARPA used on Giffords.[882]

Giffords' husband Mark Kelly has an identical twin brother, Scott. *Both* are NASA astronauts. In light of the high strangeness surrounding all three people it must be asked: has cloning technology been used by NASA scientists to bring any of these figures to life...or *back* to life?

You've Got Anthrax Mail

A week after September 11th, 2001, anthrax-laden letters were sent to ABC News, NBC News, the New York Post and the National Enquirer. Later, they were sent to the offices of Democrat Senators Tom Daschle and Patrick Leahy. 17 were made ill and 5 eventually died.

Originally thought to have been the second punch to the jihadist attacks on 9/11, evidence began to force the FBI to come up with new suspects.

Biological weapons expert Steven Hatfill was the first man placed in their sights. He vehemently defended himself in a court of law and the American taxpayer gave him $5.8 million for the Bush Administration's malfeasance.

The FBI applied extreme pressure on Hatfill in an effort to make him crack psychologically and perhaps even kill himself. [italics suspended]

> In 2001, the immediate assumption was that the anthrax attacks were orchestrated by al-Qaida. Amid intense media attention, investigators attempted to determine the source of the letters. ...
>
> The man falsely accused by the FBI of sending letters laced with deadly anthrax spores has received a big settlement from the government, but never an apology for destroying his life.
>
> What's more, Dr. Steven J. Hatfill told TODAY's Matt Lauer during his first interview since the September 2001 attacks, neither the Justice Department nor the FBI has been held accountable for breaking the law and lying in their pursuit of him.
>
> "I love my country," Hatfill, 56, told Lauer. But, he added, "I learned a couple things. The government can do to you whatever they want. They can break the laws, federal laws, as they see fit ... You can't turn laws on and off as you deem fit. And the Privacy

Act laws were put in place specifically to stop what happened to me. Whether we're at war or have been attacked, the foundation of society is that you hold to the laws in place. I used to be somebody that trusted the government. Now I really don't trust anything." ...

In July 2002, then-Attorney General John Ashcroft named Hatfill a "person of interest" in the anthrax mailings.

As Hatfill found himself vilified in the media, his anger grew. He told Lauer he blamed the media for the false reports about him, not understanding that the media was reporting false information that came from anonymous government sources.

"I didn't know this at the time. I just thought it was the press sensationalizing things. It wasn't till much, much later we learned that it was actually intentionally done by the Justice Department," Hatfill said.

Hatfill said he survived only because he had faithful friends who refused to abandon him, even when ordered to by the FBI.

"I was fortunate that I had a band of brothers and they never left my side. I still work with them to this day. Patriots, soldiers, highly decorated men. And that gives you the strength, just to be in their company, to carry on."

He is angry that the government feels that it can tell people to abandon their friends.

"I don't know of any law that permits the FBI to go by your closest friends and say, 'You're not to associate with Dr. Hatfill.' What they're trying to do is socially isolate you as part of the stress." ~ Mike Celizic, TODAY[883]

Their next suspect was much more susceptible to the tactic.

In 2008, the FBI formally declared Army biologist Bruce Ivins to be the *new* "lone gunman" behind the anthrax attacks[884]. Ivins just previously helped the Federal Bureau of Instigation in their original "investigation". He, apparently, fit the patsy profile they were looking for.

> *Months after the anthrax mailings that terrorized the nation in 2001, and long before he became the prime suspect, Army biologist Bruce Ivins sent his superiors an email offering to help scientists trace the killer.*

Already, an FBI science consultant had concluded that the attack powder was made with a rare strain of anthrax known as Ames that's used in research laboratories worldwide.

In his email, Ivins volunteered to help take things further. He said he had several variants of the Ames strain that could be tested in "ongoing genetic studies" aimed at tracing the origins of the powder that had killed five people. He mentioned several cultures by name, including a batch made mostly of Ames anthrax that had been grown for him at an Army base in Dugway, Utah.

Seven years later, as federal investigators prepared to charge him with the same crimes he'd offered to help solve, Ivins, who was 62, committed suicide. At a news conference, prosecutors voiced confidence that Ivins would have been found guilty. They said years of cutting-edge DNA analysis had borne fruit, proving that his spores were "effectively the murder weapon."

To many of Ivins' former colleagues at the germ research center in Fort Detrick, Md., where they worked, his invitation to test the Dugway material and other spores in his inventory is among numerous indications that the FBI got the wrong man.

What kind of murderer, they wonder, would ask the cops to test his own gun for ballistics? ~ Stephen Engelberg, Greg Gordon, Jim Gilmore and Mike Wiser, Pro Publica[885]

Whether he was killed or truly did commit suicide, the bottom line was that Ivins was dead in July[886] and promptly named as the suspect in August. The FBI never had to bring their case into a courtroom.

Ivins was a specialist in vaccines at the U.S. Army Medical Research Institute of Infectious Diseases at Fort Detrick, Maryland and it was later found that the anthrax that was used was not only highly weaponized but that Ivins had neither the opportunity nor the means to create the powder.

Like the Warren Commission and the 9/11 Commission, the intelligence apparatus that was treasonously killing Americans for an international master attempted to put real investigators off the scent by submitting thousands of pages of investigatory subterfuge. [italics suspended]

Buried in FBI laboratory reports about the anthrax mail attacks that killed five people in 2001 is data suggesting that a chemical may have been added to try to heighten the powder's potency, a move that some experts say exceeded the expertise of the presumed killer.

The lab data, contained in more than 9,000 pages of files that emerged a year after the Justice Department closed its inquiry and condemned the late Army microbiologist Bruce Ivins as the perpetrator, shows unusual levels of silicon and tin in anthrax powder from two of the five letters.

...the FBI lab reports released in late February give no hint that bureau agents tried to find the buyers of additives such as tin-catalyzed silicone polymers.

The apparent failure of the FBI to pursue this avenue of investigation raises the ominous possibility that the killer is still on the loose.

A McClatchy analysis of the records also shows that other key scientific questions were left unresolved and conflicting data wasn't sorted out when the FBI declared Ivins the killer shortly after his July 29, 2008, suicide.

One chemist at a national laboratory told McClatchy that the tin-silicone findings and the contradictory data should prompt a new round of testing on the anthrax powder. ...

An FBI spokesman declined to comment on the presence of tin or to answer other questions about the silicon-tin connection. ...

"There's no way that an individual scientist can invent a new way of making anthrax using silicon and tin," said Stuart Jacobsen, a Texas-based analytical chemist for an electronics company who's closely studied the FBI lab results. "It requires an institutional effort to do this, such as at a military lab." ...

FBI officials say it's all a moot point, because they're positive they got the right man...

However, the FBI never found hard evidence that Ivins produced the anthrax or that he scrawled threatening letters seemingly meant to resemble those of Islamic terrorists. Or that he secretly took late-night drives to Princeton, N.J., to mail them.

The FBI declared Ivins the killer soon after paying $5.8 million to settle a suit filed by another former USAMRIID researcher, Steven Hatfill, whom the agency mistakenly had targeted earlier in its investigation. ~ Greg Gordon, McClatchy[887]

The FBI was so sloppy in their cover-up that even politicians started clamoring for an investigation of their investigation[888]. Not surprisingly, however, they did not press the issue.

As a result of the Anthrax letter attacks, two staunch Democrats who had dragged their feet on the so-called "Patriot Act" chose to move forward. Both Tom Daschle and Patrick Leahy changed their positions and began to support the Orwellian monstrosity.[889]

Patriot's Day

Within a decade, the exact same scenario would be played again with only slightly different props.

It was April, 2013. Tax Day, "Patriot's Day" and the Boston Marathon all coincided.

After the bomb went off in Boston, "Constitutionalist Christians" like patsy Timothy McVeigh were foremost on the minds of the corporate media. Salon.com ran with the title, "Let's Hope The Boston Marathon Bomber Is A White American".[890]

Columnist David Sirota lamented how "white male privilege" kept "lone gunmen" from being castigated for whichever group they represented.

MSNBC's Chris Matthews was quick to get on the bandwagon and relate the bombing to "Tax Day".[891]

Matthews is one of the most well-known vitriolic Leftists in mainstream media.

What isn't as well known is that he had a special Catholic education starting with Jesuit La Salle College High School and then on to Jesuit Holy Cross. He has an honorary degree from Jesuit Fordham, as well.[892]

He was cultivated by the premier Catholic Leftist of his day, Thomas P. "Tip" O'Neill. Matthews was his top aide. O'Neill held his protected seat in Congress for thirty four years—ten of those as Speaker of the House of Representatives.

O'Neill was a graduate of Jesuit-run Boston College.[893]

As Jesuit-trained Jon Favreau would tell Barack Obama what to say in his speeches, Chris Matthews would do the same for President Jimmy Carter.[894]

Obama senior advisor David Axelrod, also immediately suggested that the bombing was related to a "Tax Day" protest of blood.[895]

It is interesting to note that each time a "Constitutionalist" is blamed for lashing out, their attack does maximum damage to their own cause and never puts "New World Order" authors in the slightest harm. Are they truly that inept, or are they not what we have been told?

Unfortunately for the media, their "militia" narrative started to fall apart, and the new suspects were much more palatable (eliciting fewer questions from the general public): Chechen Islamists.

Shortly after the headlines hit, pictures began to surface of Boston teeming with military contractors from "Craft International". They all wore the same khaki trousers, black jackets and ball caps with the skull logo from a comic book character.

A past president of "Craft International" was the since-murdered former Navy SEAL Chris Kyle.[896]

"The Craft" is also an insider name for Freemasonry.[897]

But what was most interesting about the contractors was that they were all wearing black backpacks, just like what housed the "pressure-cooker bomb" that was reported to have been used by the terrorists.

Soon, Boston was literally invaded by SWAT and soldiers on the lookout for the same "Chechen terrorist" that Russian Intelligence had told U.S. authorities about months before.

When suspects Dzhokhar and Tamerlan Tsarnaev were located by police they were immediately engaged with gunfire in spite of being, themselves, unarmed and yelling, "Don't Shoot! It wasn't us!"[898]

Dead patsies tell no tales.

Soon, police had a man in custody that they had stripped naked—presumably as a result of him being a bombing suspect. The suspect had a striking resemblance to Tamerlan Tsarnaev.[899]

However, Tamerlan later turned up dead, both run over and shot[900]. Law enforcement claimed that his own brother ran him over to escape police[901]. Why Dzhokhar also shot his brother was not immediately disclosed.

Bostonians were pulled from their homes by "Police Officers" outfitted like soldiers in an all-out effort to find the remaining unarmed teenager. It was clear that Martial Law lockdown was being beta-tested in the Leftist haven.

Dzhokhar Tsarnaev was eventually found hidden in a boat and another "shootout" ensued. Despite the hail of gunfire[902], Tsarnaev got out of the boat unscathed[903]. Later it was revealed that Tsarnaev had somehow received a terrible wound to his throat—one that conveniently kept the boy from talking[904]. Authorities would claim that the young Tsarnaev had tried to shoot himself rather than surrendering[905]...the only problem was, he wasn't armed[906] (so much for the "shootout").

After public sympathy was garnered for the young patsy via a trendy Rolling Stone cover[907], the Massachusetts State Police released an overtly-fabricated counter photo of a youth who failed to resemble Tsarnaev emerging from the boat with a single Robocop laser tracer on his forehead[908]. It was accepted by media without question.

Ricin Shine

As the official narrative explaining the Boston marathon bombing began to attract loud critics, two more events occurred, almost as if they were staged distractions.

The first you've already read of; just outside of Waco, a fire at the West Fertilizer Company storage and distribution facility turned into an earth-shattering explosion and conflagration on April 17th 2013. Audio from witness camera-phones gives evidence of an incoming munition with some video stills showing a light source in the fire's plume of smoke separate from the actual flames just before the explosion.[909] It is possible, if not probable, that an aircraft of some kind (helicopter, drone, etc.) outside of the field of view was used to deliver a munition (such as a remotely or internally-guided missile) masked by the large cone of smoke already rising from the plant. It could very well have been America's first domestic drone strike.

On April 16th, 2013, a letter laced with the deadly poison ricin was "intercepted" by the government mail sorting facility in Washington, DC. It was addressed to Mississippi Republican Senator Roger Wicker.

The next day, another ricin-laced letter was intercepted, this one was addressed to Barack Obama.

Mississippi resident Paul Kevin Curtis was arrested in connection with the letters which were signed with his signature phrase, "I am KC and I approved this message."

After obtaining legal representation, Curtis was quietly released (much more quietly than when he was apprehended).[910]

Those who attempted to examine the story found media describing Curtis as a janitor who moonlighted as an Elvis impersonator. Most readers immediately wrote Curtis off as a "nut" and moved on.

However, Curtis was at the center of a shocking story. While cleaning at the North Mississippi Medical Center, he claimed to have stumbled upon freezers full of human body parts which he took as evidence of a ghoulish organ trade and attempted to alert local political representatives. However, no action was taken in response. [italics suspended]

> A man who identified himself as "Kevin Curtis of Booneville" claimed online that he had a cleaning contract with Northeast Mississippi Medical Center before being fired.
>
> In fact, Curtis claims to have a longstanding feud with the medical center, his employer he claims from 1998 through 2000. On his website, Curtis wrote that during his employment at the Tupelo hospital he stumbled upon a "refrigerator full of dismembered body parts and organs wrapped in plastic in the morgue."
>
> Curtis claimed the discovery was part of a mafia-related human body parts trafficking ring on his Facebook site.
>
> He also posted criticisms of Sen. Roger Wicker, claimed that he ran into Wicker several times and that "he seemed very nervous speaking to me and would make a fast exit to the door" after talking about his case against the hospital.
>
> He said he had personally sent out more than a million emails in one year, "detailing what happened to me."
>
> In August 2000 he filed a federal equal employment opportunity lawsuit against his former employer.
>
> Curtis was dismissed by the hospital via a termination letter dated March 14, 2000. The termination was signed by Mike Davis, the then-director of environmental services. ~ Dustin Barnes and Jerry Mitchell, the Clarion-Ledger[911]

Cutting out the organs of victims and prisoners for big money is the calling card of the Luciferian Elite.

In Communist China, a mobile execution van is used to maximize the profit from the organs of condemned prisoners.[912]

In the Jesuit war on Christian Russia, the tactic was used in Serbia and is being used in Ukraine (which we'll discuss in the next chapter).

In Western nations where public scrutiny is greater, it is a trade that relies heavily on so-called "organ donors". Each year, the medical industry gives itself more leeway in redefining nefarious phrases like "brain dead" or "mental vegetable".

> *...there have been persistent questions about whether patients with massive brain injury, apnea, and loss of brain-stem reflexes are really dead. ...*
>
> *The arguments about why these patients should be considered dead have never been fully convincing. The definition of brain death requires the complete absence of all functions of the entire brain, yet many of these patients retain essential neurologic function, such as the regulated secretion of hypothalamic hormones.[2] Some have argued that these patients are dead because they are permanently unconscious (which is true), but if this is the justification, then patients in a permanent vegetative state, who breathe spontaneously, should also be diagnosed as dead, a characterization that most regard as implausible. Others have claimed that "brain-dead" patients are dead because their brain damage has led to the "permanent cessation of functioning of the organism as a whole."[3] Yet evidence shows that if these patients are supported beyond the acute phase of their illness (which is rarely done), they can survive for many years.[4] The uncomfortable conclusion to be drawn from this literature is that although it may be perfectly ethical to remove vital organs for transplantation from patients who satisfy the diagnostic criteria of brain death, the reason it is ethical cannot be that we are convinced they are really dead.* ~ Robert D. Truog, M.D., and Franklin G. Miller, Ph.D., the New England Journal of Medicine[913]

This farce is enforced and encouraged by the United States Federal government.

> *Surgeons retrieving organs to be transplanted just after a patient's heart has stopped beating will no longer have to wait to make sure it doesn't start up again if new proposals are adopted.*
>
> *At present when doctors are retrieving organs they have to wait at*

least two minutes to ensure it doesn't spontaneously start again.

Critics now fear seriously ill patients could be viewed more like tissue banks than sick people if the plans to change rules about organ donation go ahead.

There is currently a ban on considering anyone to be a potential donor before doctors and family members have independently decided to stop trying to save them.

That is poised to be eliminated if the plans by the group that co-ordinates organ allocation in the United States are adopted.

The proposed changes by the United Network for Organ Sharing, the Richmond nonprofit organization that coordinates organ donation under a contract with the federal government, are part of the first major overhaul of the 2007 guidelines governing "donation after cardiac death," or DCD, which accounted for 6% of the 28,000 organs transplanted in 2010. ~ the Daily Mail[914]

More and more frequently, patients are recovering from a medical emergency to see "doctors" preparing to hack their vital organs out and quickly put them up for sale.[915,916]

Organ transplanting is a process not even fully understood by modern medicine and can sometimes end in bizarre tragedy.

A heart transplant recipient who married the former wife of the heart donor, has committed suicide in the same way as the donor did.

Twelve years ago, Sonny Graham's heart was failing and he was on the verge of death, until he received a call from doctors, saying a donor heart had just become available.

That heart belonged to Terry Cottle, 33, who had committed suicide by shooting himself in the head.

The operation was a success and soon after, Mr Graham, 69, contacted the organ donor agency, saying he wanted to thank Mr Cottle's family. ...

In a newspaper article published in 2006, Mr Graham said he felt an instant and unusual attachment when he met his donor's widow.

"I felt like I had known her for years," Mr Graham said. "I

couldn't keep my eyes off her. I just stared."

But now, 12 years after the operation, Mrs Graham's life has been rocked by another tragedy.

Mr Graham killed himself with a shotgun, in circumstances similar to those which claimed Mr Cottle's life.

His friends said he had shown no signs of being depressed and were at a loss to explain his sudden death.

According to scientists, there are more than 70 documented cases of transplant patients taking on some of the personality traits of the organ donors. ~ the Telegraph[917]

"Affordable Healthcare Act" (Obamacare) deathpanels are giving the *appearance* of slowing the trade but that is only because organs are now being denied to those enrolled[918]. There are still many wealthy recipients waiting for theirs.

With each passing year, it is becoming more and more unhealthy for the American Middle Class to live under their own government.

I am Johnny Cirucci and I approved this message.

Endnotes

[789] The nuanced acting in this scene is absolutely masterful. Daniel Craig exudes cynicism and sarcasm until the end of the take.

If one doesn't know the plot, it looks as if a mind-controlled assassin is being debriefed.

In the movie, "Skyfall" is the Bond family property in Scotland and the deduction I make is that it was being suggested through his testing that Bond should retire.

Overall, the movie was not as good as the previous two Daniel Craig James Bond films because it was a forced anniversary with needless connections to the silly Bond extravagance of the past but Craig is just such a believable toughguy it's still worth watching.

Skyfall Word Test Scene "Day Wasted", HenriDesrochers YouTube
https://www.youtube.com/watch?v=pgi487sRy6c

[790] *Obama's Martial Law Executive Order: Tightening the Noose Around the Necks of Americans*, Johnny Cirucci, 19 March 2012, Johnny Cirucci.com
http://www.johnnycirucci.com/_mgxroot/page_news_obamas_martial_law_executive_order.html

[791] *Sacrifice at Pearl Harbor, BBC (1989)*, Johnny Cirucci YouTube
https://www.youtube.com/watch?v=N_olaNrP2SM&

[792] *ibid*

[793] *The Sandy Hook School Massacre: Unanswered Questions and Missing Information*, Prof. James F. Tracy, 26 September 2014, Global Research
http://www.globalresearch.ca/the-sandy-hook-school-massacre-unanswered-questions-and-missing-information-2/5404355

[794] *The Reason Why Sandy Hook Surveillance Tapes & 911 Calls Were Sealed*, HistoricalRecordsVLT YouTube
https://www.youtube.com/watch?&v=WKVMUsfnGDY

[795] *NRA Targets Manchin, A-Rated Once, Gun Debate Grows Personal*, Julie Bykowicz, 13 June 2013, Bloomberg
http://go.bloomberg.com/political-capital/2013-06-13/nra-targets-manchin-a-rated-nra-member-as-gun-debate-grows-personal/

[796] *Schumer-Toomey-Manchin Gun Control Bill: Cuts HIPAA Privacy for Mental Health Records*, David S. Addington, 12 April 2013, the Daily Signal
http://dailysignal.com/2013/04/12/schumer-toomey-manchin-gun-control-bill-cuts-hipaa-privacy-for-mental-health-records/

[797] *DSM5: The Secret Weapon That Will Usher In The Police State*, Johnny Cirucci, 18 June 2013, the Patriot Press
http://johnnycirucci.com/wp/johnnys-latest-columns/dsm5/

[798] *Connecticut Gun Laws Among Most Strict in U.S.*, Ryan Beckwith, 15 December 2012, Monterey County Herald
http://www.montereyherald.com/20121215/connecticut-gun-laws-among-most-strict-in-us

[799] *Where Angels Tread: Gun-Free School Zone Laws and an Individual Right to Bear Arms*, Amy Hetzner, 2011, Marquette University
http://scholarship.law.marquette.edu/mulr/vol95/iss1/1/

[800] *Wayne LaPierre Rips New Connecticut Gun Laws*, Breanna Edwards, 4 April 2013, POLITICO
http://www.politico.com/story/2013/04/connecticut-gun-laws-nra-wayne-lapierre-89641.html
[801] *Colorado Lawmakers Ousted in Recall Vote Over Gun Law*, Jack Healy, 11 September 2013, NY Times
http://www.nytimes.com/2013/09/11/us/colorado-lawmaker-concedes-defeat-in-recall-over-gun-law.html?_r=1&
[802] *Democratic Colorado State Senator Resigns To Avoid Recall Over Gun Law*, 27 November 2013, FoxNews
http://www.foxnews.com/politics/2013/11/27/democratic-colorado-state-senator-resigns-to-avoid-recall-over-gun-law/
[803] *Maryland: Governor Signs Sweeping Anti Gun Rights Bill into Law*, 20 May 2013, Ammoland
http://www.ammoland.com/2013/05/maryland-governor-signs-sweeping-anti-gun-rights-bill-into-law/#axzz2jbUYHPKm
[804] *NYS SAFE Act: Andrew Cuomo Signs Law Imposing Burdensome Gun Regulations*, Michael Br [that's what it says], 16 January 2013, Policy Mic
http://mic.com/articles/23393/nys-safe-act-andrew-cuomo-signs-law-imposing-burdensome-gun-regulations
[805] *Lockport Police Catch Flak for SAFE Act Arrest*, Nancy Fischer, 16 October 2013, the Buffalo News
http://www.buffalonews.com/city-region/lockport/lockport-police-catch-flak-for-safe-act-arrest-20131016
[806] *Major Gunmakers Gobbled Up by Cerberus*, Frank Whalen, 16 December 2011, American Free Press
http://americanfreepress.net/?p=1892
[807] *Cerberus to Sell Gunmaker After Massacre*, Mark Thompson, 18 December 2012, CNN
http://money.cnn.com/2012/12/18/news/cerberus-bushmaster/
[808] *Walmart Removes Bushmaster Rifle From Website After Sandy Hook Shootings*, Cheryl Phillips, 18 December 2012, the Examiner
http://www.examiner.com/article/walmart-removes-bushmaster-rifle-from-website-after-sandy-hook-shootings

Holy SHIT that f__king site is filled with spam. The name sounds professional but that's about it. They are the WORST spam whores.

[809] *Dick's Sporting Goods Pulls "Modern Sports Rifles" From All Stores*, 18 December 2012, NBC
http://www.nbcbayarea.com/news/national-international/NATL-Dicks-Sporting-Goods-Pulls-Modern-Sports-Rifles-From-All-Stores-183968971.html
[810] *Discovery Channel Pulls The Plug On American Guns After Sandy Hook Shooting*, 18 December 2012, Perez the flamer Hilton
http://perezhilton.com/2012-12-18-american-guns-cancelled-discovery-sandy-hook-related
[811] *"Django," "Jack Reacher" Events Cancelled Following Sandy Hook*, Jon Crow, 18 December 2012, Yahoo!
https://www.yahoo.com/movies/bp/django-jack-reacher-events-cancelled-following-sandy-hook-190910735.html

[812] *David Gregory: No Pro-Gun Rights Senators Would Go On Meet The Press*, 16 December 2012, Breitbart via news inc
http://landing.newsinc.com/shared/video.html?freewheel=69016&sitesection=breitbartprivate&VID=23997621
[813] *The Scapegoating of Nancy Lanza*, Lionel Shriver, 23 December 2012, the Guardian
http://www.theguardian.com/commentisfree/2012/dec/23/no-tears-nancy-lanza-newtown-mother
[814] *EXCLUSIVE: Inside the Mind of Newtown Killer Adam Lanza; He "Was Like A Ghost"*, Matthew Lysiak, 19 December 2012, NY Daily News
http://www.nydailynews.com/news/national/exclusive-mind-newtown-killer-article-1.1223612
[815] *Adam Lanza's Neighbors Discuss His Disposition (no one knew the Lanzas) - Inside Edition*, Johnny Cirucci YouTube
https://www.youtube.com/watch?&v=4UmMhVK8OP8
 I had to hunt hard for this as it was taken down.
[816] *Nation Reels After Gunman Massacres 20 Children at School in Connecticut*, James Barron, 14 December 2012, the NY Times
http://www.nytimes.com/2012/12/15/nyregion/shooting-reported-at-connecticut-elementary-school.html?hp&_r=2&
[817] *Details Emerge About Family of Suspected Gunman*, Tammy Audi, Heather Haddon, Erica E. Phillips and Tamer El-Ghobashy, 14 December 2012, the Wall Street Journal
http://blogs.wsj.com/metropolis/2012/12/14/details-emerge-about-family-of-suspected-newtown-school-gunman/?KEYWORDS=TAMER+EL-GHOBASHY
[818] *Bizarre Glitch During Q&A At The 8am Press Conference (12/15) :Newtown Connecticut School Shooting*, HistoricalRecordsVLT
https://www.youtube.com/watch?&v=qid9sE51d1k
 You mealy-mouthed piece of shit. The American people will know who is protecting them and who has betrayed their trust.
[819] *CT State Trooper Paul Vance Threatens Sandy Hook Conspiracy Theorists*, Johnny Cirucci YouTube
https://www.youtube.com/watch?&v=Y5UXUHoUKN4
[820] *Text: President Bush Addresses the U.N.*, 10 November 2001, the Washington Post
http://www.washingtonpost.com/wp-srv/nation/specials/attacked/transcripts/bushtext_111001.html
[821] *David Cameron gave his closing speech at the 69th session of the United Nations General Assembly (UNGA)*. gov.uk
https://www.gov.uk/government/speeches/pm-speech-at-the-un-general-assembly-2014
[822] *David Cameron: Google, Facebook and Twitter Have Duty To Take Down Extremist Material*, Steven Swinford, 14 Nov 2014, the Telegraph
http://www.telegraph.co.uk/news/politics/david-cameron/11230325/David-Cameron-Google-Facebook-and-Twitter-have-duty-to-take-down-extremist-material.html
[823] *Newtown School Shooting Story Already Being Changed By The Media*, Mike Adams, 16 December 2012, Natural News taken down and reposted by InfoWars
http://www.infowars.com/newtown-school-shooting-story-already-being-changed-by-the-media-to-eliminate-eyewitness-reports-of-a-second-shooter/

I don't know why this was taken down but I'm still comfortable with the clip I have.

[824] *Second Man "In Camo Pants And Dark Jacket" Arrested At Scene Of Connecticut School Shooting*, Niall Bradley, YouTube
https://www.youtube.com/watch?&v=apwTd-B_MP8

[825] *Second Shooter Arrested Near Sandy Hook Elementary School*, Niall Bradley YouTube
https://www.youtube.com/watch?v=8qEoYxqmyAM&

[826] *"It Was My Brother. I Think My Mother Is Dead. Oh My God": Moment Accountant Sibling Of School Shooter Saw Himself Named As Killer On TV In Case Of Mistaken Identity*, Lydia Warren and Beth Stebner, 14 December 2012 the Daily Mail
http://www.dailymail.co.uk/news/article-2248327/Ryan-Lanza-Moment-brother-Adam-Lanza-saw-CNN-mistakenly-report-Sandy-Hook-shooter.html

Someone needs to tell these Limeys how to write a frigging headline that isn't a paragraph long. Plenty of tits & ass in the sidebar, though. So much for that erudite English education.

[827] *Sandy Hook Massacre: Official Story Spins Out Of Control*, Niall Bradley, 20 December 2012, Veterans Today
http://www.veteranstoday.com/2012/12/20/sandy-hook-massacre-official-story-spins-out-of-control/

[828] *Holder Announces Bid to Cut Connecticut Gun Violence*, John Christoffersen, 28 November 2012, ABC Eyewitness News 7
http://7online.com/archive/8899319/

[829] *US Officials to Target Gun Violence in Connecticut*, David Ingram, 27 November 2012, Reuters
http://www.reuters.com/article/2012/11/27/usa-guns-idUSL1E8MQ9BZ20121127

[830] *The Vetting - Holder 1995: We Must "Brainwash" People on Guns*, Joel B. Pollak, 18 March 2012, Breitbart
http://www.breitbart.com/Big-Government/2012/03/18/Holder-Fight-Guns-Like-Cigarettes

[831] *Sandy Hook School shootings- Dr. H. Wayne Carver, Chief Medical Examiner- Full Press Conference*, Billy Moschella, Jr. YouTube
https://www.youtube.com/watch?&v=DVLCSqoZYqY

[832] *Connecticut Chief Medical Examiner: School Massacre Perpetrators Used Military-Style Rifles That Were Rigged To Reload Quickly; Sandy Hook Autopsies "Worst I've Seen"*, Matthew Chayes and Kevin Deutsch, 16 December 2012, Newsday but surprisingly taken down...fortunately reposted at SOTT.net
http://www.sott.net/article/254797-Connecticut-Chief-Medical-Examiner-School-massacre-perpetrators-used-military-style-rifles-that-were-rigged-to-reload-quickly-Sandy-Hook-autopsies-worst-I-ve-seen

[833] *Sandy Hook shooting - AR-15 Rifle was left in the car! - NaturalNews TV*, mcvayja YouTube
https://www.youtube.com/watch?&v=xqrWzpFZAns

[834] *Gun control? We need medication control! Newton elementary school shooter Adam Lanza likely on meds; labeled as having "personality disorder"*, Mike Adams, 16 December 2012, Natural News
http://www.naturalnews.com/038353_gun_control_psychiatric_drugs_adam_lanza.html

[835] *Sandy Hook Shootings—Call to Release Lanza's psychiatric drug history*, Able Child YouTube
https://www.youtube.com/watch?&v=ruMLt_PpU28
[836] *Adam Lanza Toxicology Test Shows No Drugs, Alcohol, Prescription Meds In Shooter's Body: Officials*, Dave Collins, 21 May 2013, Huffington Blows
http://www.huffingtonpost.com/2013/05/21/adam-lanza-drugs-alcohol_n_3313088.html
[837] *Release the Criminal Report and Lanza's Medical Records*, Don Pesci, 5 July 2013, Connecticut Commentary
http://donpesci.blogspot.com/2013/07/release-criminal-report-and-lanzas.html#more
[838] *Sandy Hook 911 Debate Pits Privacy Against Public's Right To Know*, Tina Susman, 30 September 2013, the LA Times
http://www.latimes.com/nation/nationnow/la-na-nn-newtown-tapes-20130930-story.html#page=1
[839] *ibid*
[840] *Gene's Background*, Gene's Trusty Pet Service, LLC
http://genespetservice.com/about
[841] *Gene Rosen Caught Rehearsing His Lines On Camera! A Must See!!!* RandomShotsVideos YouTube
https://www.youtube.com/watch?&v=igfczc6m5M4
[842] *Gene Rosen Witness of Sandy Hook Shooting Caught Lying! Part One*, RandomShots174 YouTube
https://www.youtube.com/watch?v=NxSUGGIAwiU&bpctr=1417477733
I'm surprised this is still up as it has an "offensive content" warning label on it. Let me know if it gets taken down, I've got it backed up.
[843] *Workers Demolishing Sandy Hook Elementary School Required To Sign Confidentiality Agreements*, AP, 15 October 2013, Fox News
http://www.foxnews.com/us/2013/10/15/workers-demolishing-sandy-hook-elementary-school-required-to-sign/
[844] *Obama Marks Sandy Hook Anniversary With Call for More Gun Control*, AWR Hawkins, 14 December 2013, Breitbart
http://www.breitbart.com/Big-Government/2013/12/14/Obama-Marks-Sandy-Hook-Anniversary-With-Calls-For-More-Gun-Control
[845] *The Aurora Massacre: Cry for More Gun Control or Requiem Requiring Restraint and Re-education?* Johnny Cirucci, 23 July 2012, the Patriot Press
http://johnnycirucci.com/wp/johnnys-latest-columns/the-aurora-massacre/
[846] *Did Colorado Shooter Single Out Cinemark Theater Because It Banned Guns?* Dr. John R. Lott Jr., 10 September 2012, Fox News
http://www.foxnews.com/opinion/2012/09/10/did-colorado-shooter-single-out-cinemark-theater/
A rare, outstanding column from Knight of Malta Murdoch's FauxNews.
[847] *Aurora Again: Skyfall Anew*, Loren Coleman, 8 November 2012, CopycatEffect
http://copycateffect.blogspot.com/2012/11/skyfall.html
[848] *CONFIRMED: Section of Gotham Renamed "Sandy Hook" in Latest "Dark Knight" Release*, 20 December 2012, InfoWars
http://www.infowars.com/confirmed-section-of-gotham-renamed-sandy-hook-in-latest-dark-knight-release/

[849] *Scott Getzinger(1965–2012)*, IMDb
http://www.imdb.com/name/nm0004050/
[850] *R.I.P. Scott Getzinger*, 9 April 2012, Deadline
http://deadline.com/2012/04/scott-getzinger-obituary-prop-master-254411/#
[851] *Newtown Man Dies In Stamford Accident*, 7 April 2012, the Stamford Advocate
http://www.stamfordadvocate.com/news/article/Newtown-man-dies-in-Stamford-accident-3465225.php
[852] *CT Gov. Malloy tells Susan McGuinness Getzinger he will look into school corruption*. Susan McGuinness YouTube
https://www.youtube.com/watch?v=XOneii4VFas
[853] *"Hunger Games" Not Mentioned In Sandy Hook Elementary School Shooting*, Jon Holley, 14 December 2012, the Examiner
http://www.examiner.com/article/hunger-games-not-mentioned-sandy-hook-elementary-school-shooting
[854] *"The Hunger Games": A Glimpse at the Future?* 5 April 2012, Vigilant Citizen
http://vigilantcitizen.com/moviesandtv/the-hunger-games-a-glimpse-at-the-new-world-order/
[855] *Crisis Actors Used at Sandy Hook! Special Report*, TheAlexJonesChannel YouTube
https://www.youtube.com/watch?&v=shQSVhS0hLw
[856] FEMA L-366 Planning for the Needs of Children in Disasters course description screen shot
http://johnnycirucci.com/wp/wp-content/uploads/2013/12/CT-DEMHS-planning-needs-of-children-in-disasters-14DEC2012-details.jpg
[857] Department of Emergency Services & Public Protection, Emergency Management & Homeland Security, State of Connecticut, schedule for December 2012
http://www.ct.gov/demhs/ical/calendar.asp?date=12%2F14%2F2012&calendar_ID=0
  Can't believe this is still up! I've got a screen shot just in case.
[858] *Canadian Broadcasting Corporation: Adam Lanza Was Dressed As Clergy*, Johnny Cirucci YouTube
https://www.youtube.com/watch?v=bddgfHXnRVY&
[859] *CNN Airs Footage of St Rose of Lima Drill, Claims It's Sandy Hook*, Johnny Cirucci YouTube
https://www.youtube.com/watch?v=A3AamQyMvLs&
[860] *Hundreds Attend Packed Vigil for Connecticut School Shooting Victims*, Kerry Wills and Christina Boyle, 15 December 2012, the New York Daily News
http://www.nydailynews.com/new-york/hundreds-attend-packed-vigil-conne-school-shooting-victims-article-1.1220797
[861] *Monsignor Robert Weiss Describes Scene at Sandy Hook Elementary After Massacre*, 15 December 2012, the Star-Ledger
http://videos.nj.com/star-ledger/2012/12/video_monsignor_robert_weiss_d.html
[862] *Monsignor Robert Weiss at CACE* [Chief Administrators of Catholic Education] *October 2013*, Rock Mason YouTube
https://www.youtube.com/watch?v=qutiT6JT7dI
[863] *Newtown, Connecticut Church Bomb Threat: St. Rose Of Lima Evacuated*, 16 December 2012, Huffington Libtard
http://www.huffingtonpost.com/2012/12/16/bomb-threat-newtown-church_n_2311882.html

[864] *Newtown: One Year Later*, The CatholicTV Network YouTube
https://www.youtube.com/watch?v=1IRajF8nCZg
[865] *ibid*
[866] *The St. Rose of Lima - Sandy Hook Deception*, The Paulstal Service YouTube
https://www.youtube.com/watch?v=aP_Os00ZkgY&
   Great video. Let me know if it was taken down, I've backed it up.
[867] *Influential Figures Surround Sandy Hook Crime Scenes*, Namesnot Mary and James Tracy 30 June 2014, Memory Hole blog
http://memoryholeblog.com/2014/06/30/influential-figures-surround-sandy-hook-crime-scenes/
[868] *John Trentacosta*, LinkedIn as of 01 December 2014
https://www.linkedin.com/in/johntrentacosta
   Let me know if this is down. I have a screenshot.
[869] *Institute of the Brothers of the Christian Schools*, Catholic Encyclopedia
http://www.newadvent.org/cathen/08056a.htm
[870] *La Salle University Mission Statement*, La Salle.edu
http://www.lasalle.edu/la-salle-university-mission-and-goals/
[871] *Did Giffords Subscribe To Assassin's YouTube?* Jerome Corsi, 9 January 2011, WorldNetDaily
http://www.wnd.com/2011/01/249381/
[872] *Seeking Answers in the Wake of the Tucson Massacre*, Andrew W. Griffin, 20 May 2011, the Red Dirt Report
http://www.reddirtreport.com/general/seeking-answers-wake-tucson-massacre
[873] *So Long Loughner: A Life Sentence For A Framed Patsy*, Stephanie Sledge, 6 November 2012, the Government Rag
http://www.thegovernmentrag.com/so-long-loughner-a-life-sentence-for-a-framed-patsy.html
[874] *Jared Lee Loughner Takes Plea – Game Over! Real Faqs Suppressed*, Stephanie Sledge, 8 August 2012, the Government Rag
http://thegovernmentrag.wordpress.com/2012/08/08/jared-lee-loughner-takes-plea-game-over/
[875] *Jared Loughner's Alleged Rampage Caught on Tape: FBI Reviews Surveillance Video*, Pierre Thomas, 19 January 2011, CBS News
http://abcnews.go.com/US/jared-loughners-alleged-rampage-caught-tape-fbi-reviews/story?id=12644306
[876] *Gabby Giffords Hoax - Exact Same Speech and "Yogurt Joke" Used Over and Over*, The Paulstal Service, YouTube
https://www.youtube.com/watch?v=Po0ugnMFRFo
[877] *Bill Ayers, Communist Provided Arizona Shooter's Curriculum?* Aaron Klein, 10 January 2011, WND
http://www.wnd.com/2011/01/249429/#!
[878] *Jared Lee Loughner Takes Plea – Game Over! Real Faqs Suppressed*, Stephanie Sledge, 8 August 2012, the Government Rag
http://thegovernmentrag.wordpress.com/2012/08/08/jared-lee-loughner-takes-plea-game-over/
[879] *ibid*

[880] *Gabrielle Giffords Was Not The Target ~ It Was U.S. Federal Judge John Roll: The Sheriff's Judge Who Upheld The Constitution And Reversed Congress's Brady Bill!* 22 August 2012, Political Vel Craft
http://politicalvelcraft.org/2012/08/22/u-s-federal-judge-john-roll-murdered-the-sheriffs-judge-who-upheld-the-constitution-and-reversed-congress/
[881] *Jared Loughner Used Legal Hallucinogen Salvia*, International Business Times, 18 January 2011
http://www.ibtimes.com/jared-loughner-used-legal-hallucinogen-salvia-256267
[882] *An Evil Plot Begins to Unfold to Take Control of the Mind...* Stephanie Sledge, 12 October 2012, the Government Rag
https://thegovernmentrag.wordpress.com/2012/10/12/update-12oct2012-an-evil-plot-begins-to-unfold-to-take-control-of-the-mind/
[883] *Exonerated Anthrax Suspect: FBI Harassed Me*, Mike Celizic, 16 April 2010, TODAY
http://www.today.com/id/36565308/ns/today-today_news/t/exonerated-anthrax-suspect-fbi-harassed-me/
[884] *U.S. Officials Declare Researcher Is Anthrax Killer*, unattributed, 6 August 2008, CNN
http://www.cnn.com/2008/CRIME/08/06/anthrax.case/index.html
[885] *New Evidence Adds Doubt to FBI's Case Against Anthrax Suspect*, Stephen Engelberg, Greg Gordon, Jim Gilmore and Mike Wiser, 10 October 2011, Pro Publica
http://www.propublica.org/article/new-evidence-disputes-case-against-bruce-e-ivins
[886] *Apparent Suicide In Anthrax Case*, David Willman, 1 August 2008
http://articles.latimes.com/2008/aug/01/nation/na-anthrax1
[887] *FBI Lab Reports On Anthrax Attacks Suggest Another Miscue*, Greg Gordon, 19 May 2011, McClatchy
http://www.mcclatchydc.com/2011/05/19/114467_fbi-lab-reports-on-anthrax-attacks.html?rh=1

Yeah... "miscue" ... like falling on a knife fourteen times.
[888] *Inquiry Sought Into Anthrax Probe*, Josh Meyer, 8 August 2008, the LA Times
http://articles.latimes.com/2008/aug/08/nation/na-anthrax8
[889] *Dr. Graeme MacQueen : The 2001 Anthrax Deception - The Case for a Domestic Conspiracy*, The Mind Renewed, YouTube
https://www.youtube.com/watch?v=9a0i91-npyE

Fantastic program hosted by Christian cerebralist Julian Charles...can't say enough good things about either.
[890] *Let's Hope The Boston Marathon Bomber Is A White American*, David Sirota, 16 April 2013, Salon
http://www.salon.com/2013/04/16/lets_hope_the_boston_marathon_bomber_is_a_white_american/
[891] *Chris Matthews: Bombing Might Be Domestic Attack In Response To Tax Day*, Charlie Spiering, 15 April 2013, the Washington Examiner
http://www.washingtonexaminer.com/chris-matthews-bombing-might-be-domestic-attack-in-response-to-tax-day/article/2527265#!
[892] *La Salle University to Present Honorary Degree to MSNBC's Chris Matthews*, University Marketing and Communication, 24 September 2014, La Salle University
http://www.lasalle.edu/blog/2014/09/24/la-salle-university-to-present-honorary-degree-to-msnbcs-chris-matthews/

[893] *Boston College Celebrates Tip O'Neill Despite Troubling Abortion Record*, Matthew Archbold, 23 October 2012, the Cardinal Newman Society
http://www.cardinalnewmansociety.org/CatholicEducationDaily/DetailsPage/tabid/102/ArticleID/1632/Boston-College-Celebrates-Tip-O%e2%80%99Neill-Despite-Troubling-Abortion-Record.aspx
[894] *Chris Matthews*, Discover the Networks
http://www.discoverthenetworks.org/individualProfile.asp?indid=1759
[895] *Axelrod: Obama Thinks Boston Bombings Could Be Related to "Tax Day"*, Daniel Halper, 16 April 2014, the Weekly Standard
http://www.weeklystandard.com/blogs/axelrod-obama-thinks-boston-bombings-could-be-related-tax-day_717924.html#!
[896] *"Remembering Chris Kyle"*, Press Release, Craft International, 3 February 2013
http://www.thecraft.com/Remembering_Chris_Kyle.html
[897] *"Craft"*, the Masonic Dictionary
http://www.masonicdictionary.com/craft.html
[898] *Attempted Execution of the Tsarnaev Brothers in Watertown, MA*, Johnny Cirucci, YouTube
https://www.youtube.com/watch?v=_9wpKZB_TM4&

Now here's the real creepy thing...there's another video put out by the local news station "WCVB, ABC 8" with a *completely different* audio, one that implies a "shootout" like the bimbo "Meredith Dake" put in her video title.

WCVB -- WATCH: Shootout Between Suspects, Officers in Boston, Meredith Dake, YouTube
https://www.youtube.com/watch?v=5h1mLTR4UYk
[899] *VIDEO: Bomber Suspect Tamerlan Tsarnaev Appears To Be Alive, Naked And Handcuffed*, unattributed, 20 April 2013, 21st Century Wire
http://21stcenturywire.com/2013/04/20/video-was-tamerlan-tsarnaev-murdered-suspect-seen-alive-naked-and-handcuffed/
[900] *Boston Bombings: Tamerlan Tsarnaev Was Shot By Police And Run Over And Dragged By A Vehicle*, unattributed, 21 October 2014, InSerbia News
http://inserbia.info/today/2013/05/boston-bombings-tamerlan-tsarnaev-was-shot-by-police-and-run-over-and-dragged-by-a-vehicle/
[901] *Younger Bomb Suspect DID Kill His Own Brother By Running Him Over, Says Boston Police Chief*, Snejana Farberov and Paul Thompson, 21 April 2013, the Daily Mail
http://www.dailymail.co.uk/news/article-2312643/Boston-bomb-suspect-Commissioner-Ed-Davis-says-Dzhokhar-Tsarnaev-killed-brother.html
[902] *Boat Where Dzhokhar Tsarnaev Hid "Looked Like Swiss Cheese" After Shootout*, Adam Gabbatt, 20 April 2013, the Guardian
http://www.theguardian.com/world/2013/apr/20/boat-watertown-dzhokhar-tsarnaev-swiss-cheese
[903] CBS photo uploaded to the Patriot Press
http://johnnycirucci.com/wp/wp-content/uploads/2013/05/Dzhokhar-Tsarnaev-emerges-from-his-hide-on-his-own.jpg
[904] *Bombing Suspect Throat Injury Prevents Questioning Dzhokhar Tsarnaev For Now*, Brad Knickerbocker, 21 April 2013, the Christian Science Monitor
http://www.csmonitor.com/USA/2013/0421/Bombing-suspect-throat-injury-prevents-questioning-Dzhokhar-Tsarnaev-for-now-video

[905] *Investigators Probe Whether Boston Bomb Suspect Dzhokhar Tsarnaev Tried To Kill Himself*, Erik Ortiz, 21 April 2013, NY Daily News
http://www.nydailynews.com/news/crime/bomb-suspect-dzhokhar-tsarnaev-throat-injury-self-inflicted-article-1.1323323
 Yeah...holding my breath on *that* "investigation".
The 19-year-old was captured Friday with unspecified throat injuries. According to CBS News, a bullet wound to the back of the neck could have been a failed suicide bid as cops closed in.
[906] *Dzhokhar Tsarnaev Was Unarmed During the Boat Shootout With Police*, Margaret Hartmann, 25 April 2013, the Daily Intelligencer, NY Magazine
http://nymag.com/daily/intelligencer/2013/04/tsarnaev-was-unarmed-during-the-boat-shootout.html
[907] *Jahar's World*, Janet Reitman, 17 July 2013, Rolling Stone
http://www.rollingstone.com/culture/news/jahars-world-20130717
[908] *Dzhokhar Tsarnaev's Capture in Watertown; A Massachusetts State Police Sergeant was outraged by Rolling Stone's decision to put Dzhokhar Tsarnaev on its cover and in reaction, released dramatic photos of his capture.* WWLP 22 News
http://interactives.wwlp.com/photomojo/gallery/8338/162766/dzhokhar-tsarnaevs-capture-in-watertown/tsarnaev-emerges-from-boat/
 If you need more because this joke was taken down, search the information from the caption:
In this photo, taken by Massachusetts State Police Sgt. Sean Murphy and obtained by Boston Magazine, a sniper trains his bead on Boston bombing suspect Dzhokhar Tsarnaev as a massive manhunt comes to an end on April 19, 2013.
 Murphy released the images, telling the magazine he was outraged by Rolling Stone's decision to put Dzhokhar Tsarnaev on its cover.
[909] *West Texas Fertilizer Plant Explosion collage*, Johnny Cirucci, YouTube
https://www.youtube.com/watch?v=asep5c64wRo&
[910] *Charges Dropped Against Mississippi Man In Ricin Case*, Eyder Peralta and Bill Chappell, 23 April 2013, NPR
http://www.npr.org/blogs/thetwo-way/2013/04/23/178622842/suspect-in-ricin-letters-is-released-on-bond
[911] *Ricin Letters Suspect Paul Kevin Curtis Sued Hospital Over Firing*, Dustin Barnes and Jerry Mitchell, 17 April 2013, the Clarion-Ledger
http://www.clarionledger.com/article/20130417/NEWS/130417029/
[912] *China's Hi-Tech "Death Van" Where Criminals Are Executed And Then Their Organs Are Sold On Black Market*, Andrew Malone, 27 March 2009, the Daily Mail
http://www.dailymail.co.uk/news/article-1165416/Chinas-hi-tech-death-van-criminals-executed-organs-sold-black-market.html
[913] *The Dead Donor Rule and Organ Transplantation*, Robert D. Truog, M.D., and Franklin G. Miller, Ph.D., 14 August 2008, the New England Journal of Medicine
http://www.nejm.org/doi/full/10.1056/NEJMp0804474?query=TOC&
[914] *Surgeons Won't Have To Wait To Make Sure A Heart Has Stopped Beating Before Harvesting Organs Under New Guidelines*, 20 September 2011, the Daily Mail
http://www.dailymail.co.uk/news/article-2039656/New-organ-donation-rules-Surgeons-wont-wait-make-sure-heart-stopped.html

[915] *Patient Wakes Up as Doctors Get Ready to Remove Organs*, Sydney Lupkin, 9 July 2013, ABC News
http://abcnews.go.com/Health/patient-wakes-doctors-remove-organs/story?id=19609438
[916] *Doctors Wanted to Harvest Patient's Organs, But He Woke Up*, Sarah Zagorski, 17 September, LifeNews
http://www.lifenews.com/2014/09/17/doctors-wanted-to-harvest-this-comatose-patients-organs-but-then-he-woke-up/
[917] *Heart Transplant Man Dies Like Suicide Donor*, 7 April 2008, the Telegraph
http://www.telegraph.co.uk/news/worldnews/1584248/Heart-transplant-man-dies-like-suicide-donor.html
[918] *Implications of the Affordable Care Act for Kidney Transplantation*, Christine S. Rizk, JD, and Sanjiv N. Singh, MD, JD, March 2012, Virtual Mentor
http://virtualmentor.ama-assn.org/2012/03/pfor3-1203.html

Chapter 11

The Fall And Rise of Saint George, The Dragon-Slayer

In 1980 a redux of the 1936 serial *Flash Gordon* hit theaters. In it, Flash becomes a folk hero amongst the realms oppressed by "Ming the Merciless". Ming eventually catches up to Flash and corners him on the doomed floating city of the hawkmen. Before he knocks down the city, Ming offers Flash a deal.

> ***Emperor Ming:*** *You want to destroy me.*
> ***Flash Gordon:*** *It's the only way to save Earth.*
> ***Emperor Ming:*** *What if I granted you a kingdom?*
> ***Flash Gordon:*** *If you what?*
> ***Emperor Ming:*** *Ming the Merciless, ruler of the universe, offers Flash Gordon of Earth a kingdom of Mongo, to rule over as his own.*
> ***Flash Gordon:*** *You're crazy. Why would you do that?*
> ***Emperor Ming:*** *Because I've never before met your like. You're a hero, don't you see that? Who better to rule a kingdom? Your moon is very close now. Earth's end might come within hours.*
> ***Flash Gordon:*** *You'd call off the attack?*
> ***Emperor Ming:*** *I could.*
> ***Flash Gordon:*** *Everyone would be saved?*
> ***Emperor Ming:*** *Yes... and no. After the earthquakes and tidal waves, they won't be the same human beings. They'll be more docile. Tractable. Easier for you to rule, in the name of Ming.*
> ***Flash Gordon:*** *You mean they'd be slaves.*
> ***Emperor Ming:*** *Let's just say they'll be satisfied with less.*

Forcing common men to be "satisfied with less" has been a Luciferian agenda since Babylon but it wasn't until Communism that such a goal was attainable.

From its inception to the most powerful Marxist states around the world, Communism has been the tool of the Jesuits.

One of the most renown minds of the Catholic Church was Thomas Aquinas (1225-1274). What most don't know about Aquinas is that his writing is the foundation of Communism—so much so that his work *Doctor Communis* (Theologian for All) might more appropriately be rendered Doctor Communist.

His best-known writing, *Summa Theologica*, is a massive treatise with some surprising thoughts on property and goods.

> ... *the aggregation of goods has no place in God...* ~ Question 26 of the Divine Beatitude

> ... *joyous possession of good requires partnership...* ~ Question 32 the Knowledge of the Divine Persons

> *Isidore says (Etym. 5:4) that "the possession of all things in common, and universal freedom, are matters of natural law."* ~ Whether the Natural Law Can Be Changed?

> *It would seem unlawful for a man to possess a thing as his own. For whatever is contrary to the natural law is unlawful. Now according to the natural law all things are common property: and the possession of property is contrary to this community of goods. Therefore it is unlawful for any man to appropriate any external thing to himself.* ~ of Theft and Robbery

In the 2014 Kevin Costner movie *3 Days to Kill*, Costner plays a retired CIA field agent brought back into service with a deal he can't refuse: he has been given brain cancer and will be allowed to die unless he kills the target he has been given—then he will receive the "antidote" for his cancer.

Such bioengineering of cancer and cancer cures is highly likely. Did emissaries of the Elite weave this into the plot? Were they alerting their audiences or simply conditioning them?

In the movie, Costner's character "Ethan Renner" returns to a Paris apartment he uses from time to time and finds that an entire troop of Africans has broken into it and taken residence there.

The tough-as-nails assassin doesn't take matters into his own hands, but goes to the police who tell him he will take care of the family of Africans until after winter. Forced to endure their presence, Costner warms to them and they all bond...but only he pays the rent.

Eternal Enemies

The American Experiment is powered by Reformation ideals. As a result the core leadership at the Vatican and in Rome will forever be America's mortal enemies.

A South American advisor to Jesuit Pope Francis heartily agrees with his criticisms of "capitalism" and says these ideals are "incompatible" with the Church.

> *Taking direct aim at libertarian policies promoted by many American conservatives, the Honduran cardinal who is one of Pope Francis' top advisers said Tuesday (June 3) that today's free market system is "a new idol" that is increasing inequality and excluding the poor.*
>
> *"This economy kills," said Cardinal Oscar Rodriguez Maradiaga, quoting Francis frequently in a speech delivered at a conference on Catholicism and libertarianism held a few blocks from the U.S. Capitol.*
>
> *The pope, Maradiaga said, grew up in Argentina and "has a profound knowledge of the life of the poor." That is why, he said, Francis continues to insist that "the elimination of the structural causes for poverty is a matter of urgency that can no longer be postponed."* ~ David Gibson, Religion News Service[919]

It is critical to note that the majority of capitalist woes and excesses occur when Elites *subvert* the very nature of capitalism by monopolizing resources and gouging patrons. The most wealthy "capitalists" turn out to be nothing of the sort.

> *Later, in justifying his establishment of one of the most ruthless monopolies mankind has been forced to witness, John* [D. Rockefeller] *said simply, "Competition is a sin."* ~ *David*, William Hoffman[920]

A featured writer at the National Catholic Reporter lays this all out quite well. [italics suspended]

> One thing to note about libertarianism is that it is first and foremost liberal, in the sense of classical Enlightenment liberals like John Locke. Liberalism arose as a political philosophy at a time when hostility to the Catholic church was well received, and many assumptions that contradict truths held obvious and foundational by the Catholic church remain tied up in liberal, and therefore libertarian, reasoning. Chief among them is the philosophical preference for the primacy of private property rights over all other institutions or conditions, including the common good. ...
>
> In the Catholic tradition, this is reversed. The guarantee of private property ownership, and the good of it, can only be premised on the common good, and must be formulated in relation to the needs of

the vulnerable. As John Chrysostom writes:

> Therefore ... those who have something more than necessity demands and spend it on themselves instead of distributing it to their needy fellows and servants, they will be meted out terrible punishments. For what they possess is not personal property; it belongs to their fellow servants.

This Patristic formulation echoes similarly through Ambrose and Augustine, all the way down to medieval heritors like Aquinas, who writes that private property is a good insofar as it leads to a better dispensation of things which can then contribute to the common good, and like his predecessors believes that "on this respect man ought to possess external things, not as his own, but as common, so that, to wit, he is ready to communicate them to others in their need." ...

Taken together, this current of tradition tracks well with Pope Francis' words on property in *Evangelii Gaudium*: "The social function of property and the universal destination of goods are realities which come before private property. The private ownership of goods is justified by the need to protect and increase them, so that they can better serve the common good."

So libertarianism mis-imagines two fundamental poles of its consideration, at least by Catholic lights: both the human person and property. By imagining the right of property to precede the common good of humankind, libertarian philosophy departs sharply from the Catholic imagination, which sees in all things the goodness and generosity of God, and in his people a right to the use of things that provide for the material necessities of life. For this reason, libertarian philosophy and politics cannot be brought into harmony with a Catholic socio-political imagination. ~ *Catholicism and Libertarianism Clash Over Property and the Common Good*, Elizabeth Stoker-Bruenig[921]

Bruening is no blogger. She is an accomplished Leftist, prized and featured in several well-known publications.[922]

In his 1923 encyclical *Studiorum Ducem,* Pope Pius XI (born "Ambrogio Damiano Achille Ratti") commemorated Thomas Aquinas in ways that are unusual, to say the least.

> *In a recent apostolic letter confirming the statutes of Canon Law, We declared that the guide to be followed in the higher studies by*

young men training for the priesthood was Thomas Aquinas. The approaching anniversary of the day when he was duly enrolled, six hundred years ago, in the calendar of the Saints, offers Us an admirable opportunity of inculcating this more and more firmly in the minds of Our students and explaining to them what advantage they may most usefully derive from the teaching of so illustrious a Doctor. ...

Such a combination of doctrine and piety, of erudition and virtue, of truth and charity, is to be found in an eminent degree in the angelic Doctor and it is not without reason that he has been given the sun for a device; for he both brings the light of learning into the minds of men and fires their hearts and wills with the virtues. ~ Studiorum Ducem[923]

If you're curious as to why the Pope should speak in capitalized, plural pronouns, that's because in *ex cathedra* ("from the chair"), he is God.[924]

Reduced

Containing undesirables from Indian reservations to Nazi concentration camps to Soviet gulags to Franklin Roosevelt's Japanese/American internment, all have the common ancestor of Jesuit "reductions" in South America.

In a presentation for the internet-based "Humanities and Social Sciences Network"[925], Professor Robert H. Jackson—Boston University, UC Berkley and the Rockefeller Foundation[926]—gave a general overview of the Reductions.

> *Beginning in 1609, the Jesuits established an extensive chain of missions in the borderlands of Paraguay, Argentina, and Brazil.*
>
> *The Jesuit missions, also known as reducciones, were by all accounts the most successful group of missions established on the fringes of Spanish America, and at their height in the early 1730s had a population of as many as 140,000 Guarani. The so-called Jesuit republics were the subject of contemporary literature (Candide), as well as modern literature and film (The Mission).*[927]

The Mission (1986) is a Jesuit propaganda film with gun control advocate Liam Neeson[928], Jeremy Irons and reputed Knight of Malta Robert De Niro[929] (also a gun control advocate[930]). De Niro plays a wounded and demoralized soldier who is given new life and new purpose by the Jesuits, just like their founder.

Like so many on the Left, Professor Jackson either unwittingly or knowingly mischaracterizes these Jesuit prison camps as "Christian utopias." He goes on to mention the Jesuit "militia" and how useful it was to the Spanish royals.

> *In the 1620s and 1630s, slave raiders from Sao Paulo (bandeirantes), forced the Jesuits to relocate a number of missions, until they organized a Guarani militia and defeated the raiders in 1641.*
>
> *The Guarani militia became a useful tool to the Spanish government in the region, but was also a source of tension with the local settlers. In 1750, Spain and Portugal signed the Treaty of Madrid to establish the boundaries between Spanish and Portuguese territory in South America.*
>
> *Portugal was to receive the seven missions located east of the Uruguay River, and the Guarani were to relocate.*
>
> *Instead they revolted, leading to the socalled* [sic] *Guarani War.*[931]

Also like many on the Left, Jackson has a callous disregard for the sanctity of life and uses emotionally-disassociated terms to describe mass death within the "Reduction" populations.

> *The Guarani population in the Jesuit missions was a high fertility and high mortality population. Guarani women bore children, but mortality rates were also high and the population experienced low to moderate rates of growth. Periodic epidemics culled the populations, but there generally was a rebound or recovery following the epidemic outbreaks.*[932]

The militarist intent of these communes was betrayed by their strategic locations for the Spanish empire. They were all colonial in nature.[933]

The Reductions also brought the Jesuits and their Royal backers great wealth; a somewhat incongruous enterprise for "Christian evangelists".

> *Starting in the 1600s, the Jesuits created a communist regime in Paraguay that eventually brought* [their] *demise in the 1700s.*
>
> > *The Jesuits, as is well known, held very large regions of Paraguay under missionary control from 1650 to 1750. More than a quarter million natives worked under their direction, and no payment was made directly to them. ... They were educated, trained, housed, clothed, fed and, to*

> *some extent, amused, but what became of the surplus profits of their labours, and of the extensive trading that was carried on? Over two thousand boats are said to have been engaged in carrying merchandise and goods on the Parana River; and the economic value of the Reductions was beyond doubt very great: so great in deed as to have awakened the envy of Spanish and Portuguese traders. Robertson [contemporary historian] estimated that the reductions represented at least $25,000,000 capital for the Society. – Boyd Barrett,* The Jesuit Enigma, *New York: Boni & Liveright, p. 211.*

The Reductions were communist communes set up as manufacturing facilities using the Guarani Indians as slave laborers. The products they produced were sold in Europe and greatly enriched the Jesuit order. ~ The Enemy Unmasked, Bill Hughes[934]

Before the days of *Avtomat Kalashnikov* rifles and *Schmeisser* submachine guns, large groups of prisoners were hard to handle with just a few Jesuit priests. The Company needed to use brains over brawn. Later, they would be able to appropriate the "brawn" of whole nations.

The appeal of wealth redistribution is that recipients can live a somewhat easier life, though it is a utopia that has always disappointed.

In South America, "social justice" would become the cry for taking from "the rich" and giving to "the poor". What usually happens, however, is that the super-rich exploit the poor to bleed the few real producers in the Middle Class.

If this seems like the perfect weapon to be used in the Counter-Reformation, it's not by coincidence.

The phrase "social justice" was coined by the Jesuit theologian and mentor to Pope Leo XIII, Father Luigi Taparelli D'Azeglio.

> *Pope Leo XIII's social encyclical* Rerum Novarum, *published in 1891, drew on insights from his former teacher, Taparelli. ~ Real Social Justice*, Ryan Messmore[935]

The utility of Communism was immediately seized upon by the Vatican.

> *Taparelli's influence on Leo XIII is evident in the encyclical Aeterni Patris (1879) on restoring Thomistic philosophy and in the Magna Charta of Catholic social thought, Rerum Novarum (1891),*[4] *the last*

draft of which was written by Taparelli protégé Matteo Liberatore. The Jesuit Nell-Breuning employed Taparelli's principles of sociality (or solidarism, as rephrased by Heinrich Pesch, SJ) and subsidiarity in the drafting of Pius XI's Quadragesimo Anno. Indeed, Pius XI believed that Taparelli's writings could "never be studied enough" (Divini illius magistri, 1939) and ranked him in importance for Catholic thought right after Saint Thomas. ~ Thomas C. Behr, University of Houston[936]

Professor Behr betrays his ideological blindness by comparing *Rerum Novarum* to the Magna Carta as they couldn't be more diametrically opposed in their intent.

In the interests of full disclosure, Vincenzo Gioacchino Raffaele Luigi Pecci (Pope Leo XIII) published *Rerum Novarum* on May 15th, 1891 when the industrialist Robber Barons were strip-mining humanity in their unbridled lust. Nor did Leo XIII endorse the full confiscation of property nor the complete redistribution of wealth and goods.

However, he most certainly did channel his Communist Jesuit mentor, Taparelli with terms like "proletarian" and phrases like "...the spirit of revolutionary change...".

> *The elements of the conflict now raging are unmistakable, in the vast expansion of industrial pursuits and the marvellous* [sic]*discoveries of science; in the changed relations between masters and workmen; in the enormous fortunes of some few individuals, and the utter poverty of the masses; the increased self reliance and closer mutual combination of the working classes...*
>
> *We approach the subject with confidence, and in the exercise of the rights which manifestly appertain to Us, for no practical solution of this question will be found apart from the intervention of religion and of the Church. It is We who are the chief guardian of religion and the chief dispenser of what pertains to the Church...*
>
> *"It is lawful," says St. Thomas Aquinas, "for a man to hold private property; and it is also necessary for the carrying on of human existence." But if the question be asked: How must one's possessions be used? —the Church replies without hesitation in the words of the same holy Doctor: "Man should not consider his material possessions as his own, but as common to all, so as to share them without hesitation when others are in need."* ...
>
> *As regards the State, the interests of all, whether high or low, are*

> *equal. The members of the working classes are citizens by nature and by the same right as the rich; they are real parts, living the life which makes up, through the family, the body of the commonwealth; and it need hardly be said that they are in every city very largely in the majority. It would be irrational to neglect one portion of the citizens and favor another, and therefore the public administration must duly and solicitously provide for the welfare and the comfort of the working classes; otherwise, that law of justice will be violated which ordains that each man shall have his due. To cite the wise words of St. Thomas Aquinas: "As the part and the whole are in a certain sense identical, so that which belongs to the whole in a sense belongs to the part."*$^{(27)}$ *Among the many and grave duties of rulers who would do their best for the people, the first and chief is to act with strict justice—with that justice which is called distributive—toward each and every class alike. ~ Rerum Novarum,* Pope Leo XIII[937]

These doctrines would metastasize into a literal "weapon of mass destruction" when further refined by Jesuit students like Karl Marx. The Czars had curtailed the actions of the Company further and further in Russia until they were expelled completely. There was much to be atoned for and the Society of Jesus is long on memory and short on mercy.

Saint George and the Dragon

Karl Peter Ulrich was the Prussian monarch who took over ruling Russia in 1762. He renamed himself "Peter III" and married a Prussian woman named Sophie Friederike Auguste von Anhalt-Zerbst-Dornburg.

He couldn't even speak Russian.

Ulrich managed to alienate everyone around him from his wife to his personal guard. His ouster was only a matter of time.

Within 6 months of his ascension, he was forced to abdicate. He was removed to Ropsha, outside of St. Petersburg where he died—most likely by assassination.[938]

Sophie Friederike dawned the moniker "Catherine II" and took over rule of Russia. Many believe she was the driving force behind her husband's death.

Catherine was an admirer of Peter the Great and continued to institute reforms for Russian modernization, though Russia's serfs had a long way to go to be released from their near slave-like status.

Catherine was also a friend of the American Revolution. Although she was not at odds with the English, she considered their aristocracy to be foppish and incompetent (true then and today). She refused to grant their request for Russian soldiers to fight against the Americans and single-handedly negotiated peace between the protagonists—a very important endeavor given that both France and Spain had chosen to aid the Americans in an effort to weaken the United Kingdom. The British attempted to bribe Catherine with the island of Minorca if she would use her influence to cause France to leave the rebels without aid and the Empress leaked the information to Louis XVI, much to the humiliation of Britain.[939]

As a result, both London and Rome started to hatch plots that would last for centuries needlessly pitting Russia and America against each other.

> *...one has to first set the (historical) record straight before understanding why the anti-Russian policies were devised in the West. It all started more than two centuries ago... Unknowingly, perhaps, the Russians may be suffering today because of their former monarch's sympathies for George Washington and the American revolutionaries...*
>
> *... "Peter the Great" (as the Western historians have fondly dubbed him) was, in fact, merely Peter I. He was not "Great," anymore than Mikhail Gorbachev was "Great." As an (American) Orthodox Christian priest once told me, "Peter I opened Russia's window to the West, but forgot to put up a screen."*
>
> *For, everything BAD that has happened to Russia in the last two centuries has come from the West – as an apparent revenge for Catherine the Great's support of the American revolutionaries. Thus, the Russian Czars attracted the wrath of the British royalty and the London bankers who bemoaned the loss of a rich colony (America – now regained under the auspices of the NWO [New World Order]).*
>
> *In light of the above, ... the NWO also brainwashed the (predominantly Christian) America into believing that the (predominantly Christian) Russia was supposedly our main foe. After some eight decades of the "NWO speak" in the Western media, the terms "Soviet" and "Russian" are being used interchangeably as if they were synonyms. They are not. ...*
>
> *From its outset in 1917, to its death in 1991, the "Soviet" system has been inherently "anti-Russian!" Tens of millions of Russian victims of the Soviets, along with thousands of destroyed or*

desecrated Orthodox Christian churches, are a tragic reminder of this. ~ Bob Djurdjevic, Washington Times[940]

Catherine the Great was very much a child of the Enlightenment and, as a result, believed in "religious tolerance".

It would be the undoing of both her and her nation.

Company Playground

Although a good (perhaps "great") leader, Catherine the Great was quite human in her lusts and failings.

After the suppression of the Jesuits by Pope Clement XIV in 1773, she allowed the Company of Loyola to repair to Russia.[941]

It was this "tolerance" that would set the stage for Russia's darkest hours.

The Jesuits neither forgot nor forgave Alexander I for their expulsion in 1820 and he died 5 years later of "mysterious" circumstances.[942]

He was succeeded by his brother, Nicholas I, who reigned until 1855. He also perished under questionable circumstances. Known to have an iron physique and nearly as little compassion, Nicholas I died in Crimea, supposedly of double pneumonia. Experts, however, have seen evidence of poisoning and the rumor has been spread that the Iron Czar poisoned *himself*[943] after the Crimean War had gone badly for him.

A Constitution is a document that delineates the scope of, and puts restrictions upon, government. This is a philosophy that sprang from the Reformation—the idea that the individual is responsible before God for their well-being and that there are "rule of law" limitations upon Earthly authorities.

The aspirations of America's Protestant Rebellion were quite contagious.

After freeing Russian serfs in 1861 and instituting a Russian Constitution, the successor of Nicholas I—Alexander II (his son)—was assassinated in March of 1881 when "separatists" threw bombs at his carriage. They missed their target and wounded Cossacks that were guarding the Czar. He insisted upon attending them and when he emerged from his carriage more bombs were thrown and they eventually found their mark.

The Czars were typical of the Ruling Class, however, and made it easy for their enemies to foment hatred and subversion. Alexander II was as bold in his reforms for Russia as he was his own depravity, installing his mistress in the same mansion that housed his legal wife and family. It was in caring for orphans of the Crimean War that Alexander II chose from among them, his concubine—Catherine Dolgorukaya. They had several illicit children.[944]

Russia, at this time, was still very much a feudal society with well-defined class strata. Although Russia was not dominated by the Vatican, the nation was steered by the second leg of the Roman Empire; Orthodoxy[aa]. The Reformation ideals of self-determination and fierce independence that marked America's beginning had not yet taken root.

Pyotr Alexeyevich Romanov ("Peter the Great"), who ruled Russia from 1682 to 1725 pulled her into modernization and used the bodies of his own people to do it. The foundation of Russia's imperial capital—Saint Petersburg (interestingly named after Romanov's namesake patron saint, the Apostle Peter), were the bodies of 100,000 dead serfs.[945]

Soon, popular discontent became organized.

> *Union of Liberation, Russian Soyuz Osvobozhdeniya: first major liberal political group in Russia. The Union was founded in St. Petersburg in January 1904 to be a covert organization working to replace absolutism with a constitutional monarchy. Originally the creation of liberal nobility, it soon was dominated by middle-class, professional people, who gave the union a new militance.* ~ Encyclopædia Britannica[946]

The Jesuits took their experiences with the South American *reducciones* and fed them to a German Jewish aristocrat who had never held a "proletariat" working-class job in his life—Karl Heinrich Marx.

> *Marx was an average student. He was educated at home until he was 12 and spent five years, from 1830 to 1835, at the Jesuit high school in Trier, at that time known as the Friedrich-Wilhelm Gymnasium. The school's principal, a friend of Marx's father, was a liberal and a Kantian and was respected by the people of Rhineland but suspect to authorities. The school was under*

[aa] The Byzantine Empire survived temporal Rome for 1,000 years after her fall. Byzantium and her capital of Constantinople remained the seat of the Roman Empire until conquered by the Ottoman Turk Caliphate (the Scimitar of Muhammad) in 1453. Like the Roman Empire, the Byzantine Empire has morphed into a religious one, though she does not have a Company of assassins to see her will done.

surveillance and was raided in 1832. ~ Karl Marx, Biography.com[947]

The timing was unmistakable.

Marx and Engels fleshed out their "science of socialism" during the same time frame as Luigi Taparelli D'Azeglio's "social justice." This leads to an interesting speculation: Did lines of influence exist between the Jesuit and Marx?

The Communist Manifesto was published the same year that the Society of Fraternal Democrats called for social justice. Under Communism, wealth redistribution was to be used for social ends. In this structure, private property for personal gain was viewed as the cornerstone of the class system, and was seen as the cause of social injustices and strife. Wealth redistribution, therefore, was aimed at producing a society where all people were economically equal. Hence, the abolition of bourgeois property (that of the capitalist class) was the key to Communism. ~ Social Justice: Theft to All, Carl Teichrib[948]

It was no coincidence that Marx hailed from a Catholic bastion within the heart of the Reformation.

Marx was a bourgeois Jew [his father was a wealthy, upper-middle class lawyer, not working middle class] *from a predominantly Catholic city within a country whose official religion was evangelical Protestantism.* ~ Karl Marx: A Life, Francis Wheen[949]

Now the weapon was pointed at Russia's weakest point—ruled by arrogant Elites, the poor underclass was desperate for "justice" of any kind. This was where the Union of Liberation came in.

The Union of Liberation (Russian: Союз Освобождения, *English transliteration:* Soyuz Osvobozhdeniya) *was a liberal political group founded in St. Petersburg, Russia in January 1904 under the influence of Peter Struve, a former Marxist. Its goal was originally the replacement of the absolutism of the Tsar with a constitutional monarchy. Its other goals included an equal, secret and direct vote for all Russian citizens and the self-determination of different nationalities (such as the Poles) that lived in the Russian State. The origins of the Union of Liberation can be traced back to 1901 when Russian liberal exiles created a periodical called Liberation which included ideas such as a constitutional monarchy.* ~ Wikipedia[950]

Not surprisingly, it was an extremely secretive organization. Critics and researchers have wondered if the secrecy was to hide a foreign hand.

> *Despite its obvious importance in the history of the Russian Revolution, very little is known about the structure and operations of the Union. All writing about the Union in these respects has had to rely almost exclusively on the brief, semi-autobiographical account by one of its most active organizers, Prince Dmitirii Ivanovich Shakhovskoy,[1] and on bits of information scattered among the memoirs of a few other ex-members.[2]* ~ Terence Emmons, Russian Review[951]

Shakhovskoy would go on to become a key figure in the "Bolshevik Revolution" and later serve in the First State Duma (Soviet Legislature) until he was executed by the NKVD.

> *In an ironic twist of fate, many of the same NKVD staff who worked at the site* [where Shakhovskoy was shot and dumped] *were later targeted by purges and found themselves executed at the same shooting range — they now lie with their erstwhile victims in mass graves, and their remains are now indistinguishable.* ~ Alexander Annin, the Moscow Times[952]

Note that the Union's original goal was to replace the Czar with a constitutional monarchy—an Elite bounded by the Rule of Law.

That is most assuredly *not* a Marxist ideal and the Union's founder, Pyotr Berngardovich Struve, emerged as a true Russian Patriot who turned his back on Jesuitical Marxism.

> *Peter (or Pyotr or Petr) Berngardovich Struve (Russian: Пётр Бернга́рдович Стру́ве; ... January 26, 1870, Perm – February 22, 1944, Paris) was a Russian political economist, philosopher and editor. He started out as a Marxist, later became a liberal and after the Bolshevik revolution joined the White movement. From 1920 he lived in exile in Paris, where he was a prominent critic of Russian Communism.* ~ Wikipedia[953]

Although the "White" movement was not allowed to survive, this seems to be where Russian Orthodox Father Georgi Gapon drew his inspiration from.

In 1905, Father Gapon lead a peaceful protest at the Winter Palace in St. Petersburg to speak against the conditions for peasant workers from both wealthy industrialists and the government of Czar Nicholas II. It was reported that Nicholas told his Cossack Guards to "treat them like rebels" and 200 were killed with 800 wounded.[954]

This incompetence helped light the flame of the Jesuit-hatched "October Revolution".

> *The instruments of this new alliance between the Soviets and the Vatican were to be the Jesuits, described as the hereditary enemies of the Orthodox Church. Reportedly, there were large numbers of representatives of the Jesuit Order in Moscow during the Revolution.* ~ Descent Into Darkness, James Zatko[955]

But to *truly* punish a people, you need a puppet with few connections to them.

Herod, who would think nothing of slaughtering all the boys in Bethlehem from 2 years old to newborn, wasn't a Jew, he was an Edomite.[956]

Napoleon Bonaparte wasn't French, he was from Corsica.[957]

Adolf Hitler wasn't Teutonic, he was Austrian.[958]

With good reason has Barack Hussein Obama failed to produce a valid birth certificate.

And to *really* hurt Russia, you need a Georgian-born[959] Jesuit priest, named Ioseb Besarionis Dze Jugashvili—later repackaged as "Joseph Stalin" (or, as his Free Mason admirer Franklin Roosevelt used to call him, "Uncle Joe"[960], the kindly mass-murderer). [italics suspended]

> Josef Vissarionovich Dzhugashvili, Ioseb Besarionis Dze Jughashvili; Russian: Ио́сиф Виссарио́нович Джугашви́ли Iosif Vissarionovich Dzhugashvili) (December 18 1878 – March 5, 1953), better known by his adopted name, Joseph Stalin (Иосиф Сталин, Iosif Stalin; *stalin* meaning "made of steel".
>
> Josef was born to influential Catholic parents Vissarion "Beso" Dzhugashvili and Ekaterina "Keke" Geladze. His father Beso was a successful and relatively wealthy local businessman. However, in later biographies, he is variously described as poor, dirt poor and a violent alcoholic.
>
> Whatever the real truth, Josef was accepted into the Catholic Cappuchin run school at Gori. He graduated in 1892 first in his class and at the age of 14 he was accepted to enter the "Orthodox"

Seminary of Tiflis (Tbilisi, Georgia), a Jesuit institution to be trained as a Jesuit priest.

In spite of contrary history written about the Jesuit run Seminary, the Jesuits remained in Russian territory after the order was banned by Alexander I in 1820, maintaining control of several institutions, including the Seminary of Tiflis.

Stalin himself openly admitted the Jesuit control of the institution in his famous interview with Jewish Journalist Emil Ludwig (Cohen):

Ludwig: *What impelled you to become an oppositionist? Was it, perhaps, bad treatment by your parents?*

Stalin: *No. My parents were uneducated, but they did not treat me badly by any means. But it was a different matter at the Orthodox theological seminary which I was then attending. In protest against the outrageous regime and the Jesuitical methods prevalent at the seminary, I was ready to become, and actually did become, a revolutionary, a believer in Marxism as a really revolutionary teaching.*

Ludwig: *But do you not admit that the Jesuits have good points?*

Stalin: *Yes, they are systematic and persevering in working to achieve sordid ends. But their principal method is spying, prying, worming their way into people's souls and outraging their feelings. What good can there be in that? For instance, the spying in the hostel. At nine o'clock the bell rings for morning tea, we go to the dining-room, and when we return to our rooms we find that meantime a search has been made and all our chests have been ransacked. ... What good point can there be in that?*

While accounts of his time at Tiflis have been changed many times, it is universally accepted that Stalin was the star pupil of the Seminary. As a result, the events of 1899 remain shrouded in mystery.

In the final week of his studies, having completed seven (7) years as the star pupil of the Jesuits, Stalin is variously claimed to have quit or been expelled. Neither account, adequately explains how a seminary student of seven years, suddenly appeared influential and active in coordinating the Georgian Social-Democratic movement less than 12 months later—an achievement that could not possibly have happened without substantial support.

The more credible and controversial conclusion is that Stalin did graduate from the Jesuit Seminary as a proper Jesuit priest, with his first assignment being to infiltrate and manage the Georgian underground against the Russian Tsarist Government.

Again, the fact that Stalin was awarded an academic position at the Tiflis Observatory gives credence to his Jesuit credentials and completed study. His double life as a secret leader of the May day uprising of 1901 less than 2 years from graduating from the Jesuit seminary attests to his skill as a key Jesuit agent. ~ *Joseph Stalin, One-Evil.org*[961]

It is critical to note that, although Russia is considered an "Orthodox" nation, her most important institutions were infiltrated and even run by Jesuits.

And Stalin did very much punish Russia.

History texts have been rewritten to hide the demonic brutality of Communism behind the sensationalized evil of Nazism. The rare school child who has heard of Adolf Hitler knows nothing of Mao tse Dung or Joseph Stalin. Yet they far outstripped the Austrian corporal in mass slaughter.

Stalin's extremely brutal 30-year rule as absolute ruler of the Soviet Union featured so many atrocities, including purges, expulsions, forced displacements, imprisonment in labor camps, manufactured famines, torture and good old-fashioned acts of mass murder and massacres (not to mention World War II) that the complete toll of bloodshed will likely never be known.

An amoral psychopath and paranoid with a gangster's mentality, Stalin eliminated anyone and everyone who was a threat to his power – including (and especially) former allies. He had absolutely no regard for the sanctity of human life.

But how many people is he responsible for killing?

In February 1989, two years before the fall of the Soviet Union, a research paper by Georgian historian Roy Aleksandrovich Medvedev published in the weekly tabloid Argumenti i Fakti estimated that the death toll directly attributable to Stalin's rule amounted to some 20 million lives (on top of the estimated 20 million Soviet troops and civilians who perished in the Second World War), for a total tally of 40 million. ~ Palash Ghosh[962]

"Chairman Mao"

As impossible as it would seem, Mao tse Dung's hands are even bloodier than Joseph Stalin's.

Mao tse Dung may be the most brutal, vicious killer in the history of mankind. He slaughtered so many of his own people, an accurate accounting is impossible as bodies and mass graves are still being found. Estimates range from 70 to 100 million human beings[963]. One source has him slaughtering 60,000,000 Chinese in 5 years by starvation[964]. Stalin would punish Ukraine with 7,000,000 dead by starvation, as well.[965]

Since then, China remains the last major Communist power.

—And it was all made possible by traitors in the American government starting with Harry S. Truman and George C. Marshall.

> *President Truman's amazing desertion of Nationalist China, so friendly to us throughout the years following the Boxer Rebellion (1900), has been thus summarized (NBC Network, April 13, 1951), by Congressman Joe Martin:*
>
>> *President Truman, on the advice of Dean Acheson, announced to the world on December 15, 1925, that unless communists were admitted to the established government of China, aid from America would no longer be forthcoming. At the same time, Mr. Truman dispatched General Marshall to China with orders to stop the mopping up of communist forces which was being carried to a successful conclusion by the established government of China.*
>
> *Our new Ambassador to China, General of the Army George C. Marshall, conformed under White House directive (see his testimony before the Combined Armed Services and Foreign Relations Committees of the Senate, May, 1951)to the dicta of Relations Combined Armed Services and Foreign Relations Committees of the Senate, May, 1951) to the dicta of the State Department's Communist-inclined camarilla, and made further efforts to force Chiang to admit Communists to his Government in the "effective" numbers, no doubt, which Mr. Truman had demanded in his "statement" of December 15. The great Chinese general, however, would not be bribed by promised "loans" and thus avoided the trap with which our State Department snared for Communism the states of Eastern Europe. He was accordingly paid*

> *off by the mishandling of supplies already en route, so that guns and ammunition for those guns did not make proper connection, as well as by the eventual complete withdrawal of American support as threatened by Mr. Truman. ...*
>
> *Thus President Truman, Ambassador Marshall, and the State Department prepared the way for the fall of China to Soviet control. They sacrificed Chiang, who represented the Westernized and Christian element in China, and they destroyed a friendly government, which was potentially our strongest ally in the world— stronger even than the home island of maritime Britain in this age of air and guided missiles. ~ The Iron Curtain Over America*, John Beaty[966]

The Chinese were heretics that had thrown the Jesuits out in 1724[967]. They needed to be punished.

—And Communism was the perfect Jesuit-created weapon to do it with.

"The Perestroika Deception"

The hand of Communism has been so heavy upon the United States that some have wondered, "Did the Soviet Union really collapse?" Is there a secret agenda to turn the USA into the USSR?

Thanks to "KGB defector" Anatoliy Golitsyn, many on the Right think this is exactly the case.

> *Golitsyn is an ex-KGB officer who defected to the West back in 1961, in his own words to "warn the American Government about the adoption of the current grand strategy for Communism and the political role of the KGB and the use of disinformation and controlled political opposition which the strategy entailed, and...help the West neutralise KGB penetration of their governments."*
>
> *Golitsyn's overarching thesis, the so-called "grand strategy," is laid out in painstaking detail over two books: "New Lies for Old" (1984) and "The Perestroika Deception" (1985), which can be summarized as follows:*
>
> *The Soviets developed a long-range strategy to defeat the West back in the late 1950s based on a Leninist strategy of strategic deception and subterfuge, replete with a planned collapse — including*

potentially tearing down the Berlin Wall (which Golitsyn first detailed in a 1978 memorandum embedded at the end of this post) – in combination with perestroika and glasnost, words whose true definitions were far different than those the West ascribed to them.

These moves according to Golitsyn were designed to invite the West's capital, technology and most of all gullibility/trust to Russia, which it could then use to build itself up, and, while the West moved leftward and intertwined itself inextricably with Russia and other socialist states, "converge" and dominate the West under a world government headed by none other than the Russians and Chinese. ~ Benjamin Weingarten, The Blaze[968]

Both Golitsyn and another KGB defector—Lt. Col. Yuri Ivanovich Nosenko—would be highly scrutinized with a shocking conclusion that the chief intelligence services of the U.S.S.R., the U.K. and the U.S. were all colluding.[969]

It was impossible for Golitsyn to publish a book that wasn't first thoroughly vetted by the CIA. A higher power was in control.

Father Malachi Martin made the astounding assertion that the Soviet Union was *ordered* to collapse.

In an interview with John McManus for New American magazine in June of 1997, Malachi Martin said this:

McManus: *What do you mean by the "capstone"?*

Martin: *The underlying force I have written about in Windswept House is structured very much like a pyramid. It is wide at the bottom where many individuals work for its goals and hope to be elevated to a higher place. There are fewer and fewer inhabitants in each of the ascending steps in the structure. Only a very few form its ultimate directorate, the capstone of the pyramid. These individuals have no loyalty to the nations they came from; they are a new type of human being, an internationalist who seeks to control mankind. Each is a godless and, collectively, they intend to use religion, governments, and anything they find useful to impose their will.*

It is my opinion, for instance, that the USSR didn't disintegrate naturally but was ordered to collapse. Gorbachev was told to vacate his power base, and also to inform other leaders of the Soviet bloc nations to do likewise. Those orders came from the capstone. ~ John McManus, the New American[970]

Mikhail Gorbachev oversaw the destruction of the USSR which critically weakened Russia. Gorbachev ran to a surprising source for safe haven: George H.W. Bush. Bush turned over the military base at the Presidio in California to the former Communist and it became a base of operations for Gorbachev's continued subversive efforts under the guise of "environmentalism".

It is a place of special significance to Rome.

> *San Francisco history remained devoid of Europeans until 1775, when the Spanish, long having a stronghold in Southern California, ventured north on a "Sacred Expedition" led by Gaspar de Portola. In 1776, the Spanish founded the Presidio Army Base and the Catholic Church commenced capturing and enslaving the San Francisco Ohlone population. Later, ranchers grazed San Francisco's green hills with cattle and continued until an upstart nation to the east, the United Stated of America, set her sights westward to the Pacific's shining seas.* ~ San Francisco.com[971]

The Presidio has been the reward of other Congressional Catholic Communist faithful like Pennsylvania Democrat Congressman John Murtha (ensconced in power until carried out in a pine box[972]) and former House Speaker Nancy Pelosi.

> *"Among the unpublicized facts about Nancy Pelosi was that she was an investor in a real estate investment entity called PRESIDIO PARTNERS, which set up shortly after the Nixon Administration's first closure of federal military bases around the US,".*

> *"Among the choicest real estate properties were (a) San Francisco's Presidio Fort then the headquarters for the Sixth US Army (b) Treasure Island and Yreba Buena Island, the US Navy's parcels in San Francisco Bay (c) The Hunter's Point Naval Base, then biggest US Navy base between Seattle Washington Long Beach and San Diego California."*

> *Pelosi's involvement in the disposal of federal military surplus land is matched only by Gorbachev, who as founder of Green Cross International (GCI) devised a mechanism for converting American military bases to civilian uses converting the bases over to "global centers for sustainability". Gorbachev's mission of converting American military bases to global centers for sustainability came just two years after he resigned as president of the Soviet Union on*

December 25, 1991. ~ Judi McLeod, Canada Free Press[973]

A Convenient Distraction of Death

But the bloodletting wasn't finished.

When you're an enemy of the Company, you remain *forever* on their hit-list.

This is what the good Russian Orthodox people of Yugoslavia found out near the turn of the century.

In December of 1998, Congress began impeachment proceedings against William Jefferson Clinton.

In January of 1999, Clinton committed the American military to a 500 year old religious conflict between Bosnian muslims and Serbian Christians in the former Yugoslavia…aiding the Islamists against their Orthodox foes.

The action was sold to the American people as necessary due to inhuman atrocities created by Serbian "ethnic cleansing", but a decade later it emerged that Albanian muslims self-inflicted "cleansing" on innocent locals.

> *Eve-Ann Prentice, a British journalist who covered the Kosovo war for the Guardian and the London Times, testified during Slobodan Milosevic's trial in the Hague. He said that rather than being driven out by the Serbs, "The KLA [Kosovo Liberation Army] told ethnic Albanian civilians that it was their patriotic duty to leave because the world was watching. This was their one big opportunity to make Kosovo part of Albania eventually, that NATO was there, ready to come in, and that anybody who failed to join the exodus was not supporting the Albanian cause."* ~ Andy Wilcoxson, World Net Daily[974]

Even the "atrocities" were hotly contested at the time as nothing more than contrived provocations for war.

> *…in Belgrade, Gen. Wesley K. Clark, the NATO commander, and Gen. Klaus Naumann, chairman of the NATO military council, were sitting with President Slobodan Milosevic of Yugoslavia. They came brandishing a plastic portfolio of color photographs documenting a massacre of Albanians three days earlier by Serbian security forces in the Kosovo town of Racak.*
>
> *They also came with threats of NATO air strikes.*

> *This was far from their first encounter with the Serbian leader, but this time, they recalled, they found a newly hardened man with a bunker mentality.*
>
> *"This was not a massacre," Milosevic shouted. "This was staged. These people are terrorists."*
>
> *When General Clark warned him that NATO would "start telling me to move aircraft," Milosevic appeared infuriated by the prospect of bombings. He called the general a war criminal.* ~ Elaine Sciolino and Ethan Bronner, New York Times[975]

There were, however, atrocities found to have been committed upon the Christian Serbs—nothing less than slavery, rape, torture and "organ harvesting".

> *On Tuesday, Clint Williamson — an American diplomat appointed EU prosecutor in 2011 to investigate crimes against humanity in Kosovo — released a scathing statement that accused the Kosovo Liberation Army (KLA) of murdering a handful of people and then trafficking their kidneys, livers, and other body parts. KLA leaders now run the tiny Balkan country's government.*
>
> *"If even one person was subjected to such a horrific practice, and we believe a small number were, that is a terrible tragedy and the fact that it occurred on a limited scale does not diminish the savagery of such a crime," Williamson said in the statement.*
>
> *Williamson determined that KLA fighters tortured and killed around 10 Serbian and Albanian Kosovar prisoners in secret camps in northern Albania, removed their organs, and sold the parts abroad for transplantation.*
>
> *The KLA also murdered, kidnapped, and detained people illegally, and in general oversaw a reign of terror against its non-Albanian and Albanian opponents after the group won Kosovo's independence from Serbia in 1999.* ~ John Dyer, Vice.com[976]

This identical barbarism would be used against Russian Orthodox dissidents in Eastern Ukraine, 15 years later.

> *On the outskirts of Donetsk, militia fighters discovered new mass graves of civilians. Representatives of the People's Republic of Donetsk believe that the civilians were killed by National Guard soldiers, as the Ukrainian troops had been staying in the settlement, where the graves were found, since April, whereas Donetsk militia*

occupied the village only on September 21, RIA Novosti reports.

However, Kiev officials deny the information. Earlier, a representative of the Council of National Security and Defense of Ukraine, Andrey Lysenko, said that "no soldier of the National Guard was ever staying in the location."

Prime Minister of the People's Republic of Donetsk Alexander Zakharchenko told the Russian News Service that there were three burials of civilians found - about 40 dead bodies of civilians, prisoners of war and Ukrainian militia soldiers.

According to Zakharchenko, an examination of the bodies showed that the victims lacked internal organs. However, he noted, it remains unclear whether the organs had been harvested at the time when the victims were alive or dead.

OSCE observers confirmed reports about the discovery of three mass graves in the Donetsk region, in the village of Nizhnyaya Krynka and its surroundings on September 23. ~ Pravda[977]

The Bosnian War didn't do much for Christian Serbs but it was a tremendous boon for Islamic terror. Most Americans don't know that National Guardsmen that should be home digging citizens out of weather emergencies are still deploying on this mission today.[978]

In fact, the Pentagon has used state national guards to completely surround Russia in "partnerships" with Poland (IL National Guard), Lithuania (PA), Latvia (MI), Estonia (MD), Romania (AL), Ukraine (CA), Moldova (NC), Bulgaria (TN), Georgia (GA), Azerbaijan (OK), Armenia (KS), Kosovo (IA), Macedonia (VT), Albania (NJ), Montenegro (ME), Serbia (OH), Bosnia (MD), Croatia (MN), Slovenia (CO), Hungary (OH), Slovakia (IN) and the Czech Republic (TX, NE)[979]. These partnerships include *permanent* personnel stationed "in-country" on full-time status paid for with *Federal*, not state dollars.

It was this very conflict that made NATO expansion (against assurances given Russian leaders) the excuse the Luciferian Elite needed. After the Soviet Union was ordered to collapse in 1991, the shock troops of the Company (radical Islam) jumped into the vacuum. [italics suspended]

> ...in February 1990, as East Germany began wobbling, Secretary of State James Baker journeyed to Moscow to discuss German unification. According to James Goldgeier, author of Not Whether But When, the definitive history of NATO expansion, Baker

promised Soviet leader Mikhail Gorbachev that if the Soviets allowed Germany to reunify, NATO—the U.S.-led Western military alliance that took form after World War II—would not expand "one inch" further east, not even into the former East Germany itself. But as the year progressed, the White House developed different ideas, and by the fall it was clear that a unified Germany would enter NATO, no matter what the Russians thought.

The idea of admitting other Eastern European countries into NATO, however, was still considered recklessly provocative toward Russia. The New York Times editorial board and its star foreign-affairs columnist, Thomas Friedman, strongly opposed the idea. The eminent Cold War historian John Lewis Gaddis wrote that, "[H]istorians—normally so contentious—are in uncharacteristic agreement: with remarkably few exceptions, they see NATO enlargement as ill conceived, ill-timed, and above all ill-suited to the realities of the post-Cold War world." ...

For his part, Russian President Boris Yeltsin warned that extending NATO violated the "spirit of conversations" between Baker and Gorbachev, and would produce a "cold peace" between Russia and the West. It didn't matter. In 1995, NATO went to war against Serbia, and then sent peacekeepers to Bosnia to enforce the peace agreement that followed. This new, Eastern-European mission paved the way for further expansion. By 1997, it was clear Poland, Hungary, and the Czech Republic would enter the alliance. In 2004, NATO admitted another seven former Soviet bloc countries, three of which—Lithuania, Latvia, and Estonia—had been part of the USSR. In 2009, Croatia and Albania joined the club. Six former Soviet republics—Ukraine, Georgia, Moldova, Kazakhstan, Armenia, and Azerbaijan—now link their militaries to NATO's via the "Partnership for Peace" program. All five former Soviet republics in Central Asia—Kyrgyzstan, Tajikistan, Turkmenistan, Kazakhstan, and Uzbekistan—provide NATO countries with some basing, transit, refueling, or overflight rights for use in the Afghan war. ~ *No, American Weakness Didn't Encourage Putin to Invade Ukraine: In fact, we've pushed U.S. power further east than anyone could have imagined when the Soviet Union collapsed.* Peter Beinart, the Atlantic[980]

But the war against Christian Serbs was a war that conveniently created a terrorist haven right in the heart of Europe. They would be an endless pool of jihadis to inject chaos wherever the leaders of the West were told to put them. [italics suspended]

For 78 days in 1999, we bombed Christian Serbia and their forces in Kosovo, ostensibly as a humanitarian move to prevent Serbian ethnic cleansing of Kosovo's Albanian population. Our real motive was to cripple the troublesome anti-multiculturalist Serbs and to enhance our standing with the oil-rich Muslim world. We bombed bridges, selected buildings, railroads, even passenger trains, and other targets in the Serbian capital of Belgrade. Unfortunately, the Chinese Embassy was also hit. According to John Pilger, writing in the Guardian, many of the bombs dropped from a relatively safe altitude (for us) of 15,000 feet, also hit schools, hospitals, and homes. Total Serbian dead amounted to about two thousand. Pope John Paul II described the bombing as an "act of diabolical retribution." Many conservative and liberal American leaders agreed, but the Serbs eventually had to yield to our more advanced technology and vastly superior force. ...

The results of our alliance with the KLA and establishing an Albanian base of Muslim power in Kosovo have been horrific. The Albanians have driven 277 thousand Serbs from Kosovo. Hundreds have been murdered. Thousands have been robbed and brutalized as their homes and property were destroyed. Muslim multiculturalists have destroyed 135 Orthodox churches, monasteries, and shrines. All this was done under the noses of UN security forces.

Bill Clinton's great military achievement was a humanitarian disaster, and it established a dangerous Muslim foothold in Europe that is exporting terror and crime. ~ Mike Scruggs, the Ashville Tribune[981]

Unfortunately for Milosevic and the Christians of Serbia, their most important ally, Russia (lead at the time by Boris Yeltsin) was weak and unable to do much more than pick up the pieces for the embattled nation.

Russia has fiercely opposed the NATO bombing and acted as almost the sole ally of Milosevic as the conflict played out. But it has limited its support to hot rhetoric and criticism of NATO, offering no military assistance to the Belgrade government.

The Kremlin is in an uncomfortable position that requires it to play a tough theme to keep nationalist political opponents in Moscow in check even as it works to become a peacemaker on the world stage, where it depends on Western economic support to prop up its faltering economy. ~ Terry Atlas and Charles Madigan, Chicago Tribune[982]

But this conflict did set the stage for a paradigm shift that would place Russia and Christ on one side and America and Mohammad on the other.

Constantine Rising

If there were a polar opposite to Barack Obama, it would be the current leader of the former Communist Russia—Vladimir Vladimirovich Putin.

Putin has either been the President or Prime Minister of the Russian Federation since 1999. Today's Russia indelibly has his finger prints on her, but are they around her hand or her throat?

Putin certainly fits the mold of a pre-selected world leader. Inspired by spy movies he watched while growing up[983], he attempted to join the KGB at 16[984] and was later accepted after graduating from his hometown's university, Leningrad State, eventually rising to the rank of Lieutenant Colonel.[985]

www.kremlin.ru

Brian Warner of Celebrity Networth claims that Putin took advantage of the Russian privatization of vital natural resources to net him astounding wealth.

> *While many previously state-owned industries were privatized, Putin allegedly has used his power to build large secret ownership stakes several multi-billion dollar commodity firms. His most vocal critics assert that Putin has leveraged his power to acquire a 4.5% ownership stake in natural gas producer Gazprom, a 37% stake in oil company Surgutneftegas and 50% stake in Swiss oil-trader Guvnor. Gazprom alone does over $150 billion in revenue annually, Guvnor does $80 billion and Surgutneftegas over $20 billion. Using their most recent market capitalizations, Putin's combined ownership stakes would give him a personal net worth of $70 billion!*[986]

Warner also fairly points out that Barack Obama has done quite well since rising from his humble beginnings as a "community organizer".

> *By comparison, Obama's reported net worth has increased from $200,000 when he first stepped into the Oval Office to nearly $12 million today. That's a 5900% increase in net worth between 2000*

and 2014 (the same time period Putin has essentially ruled Russia).[987]

Putin's position as a wealthy Intelligence insider has all of the earmarks of being an Elite puppet politician. But it would appear that, at some point, Vladimir Putin became his own man.

Putin compares well to the "Conservative" Prime Minister of Britain, David Cameron who most certainly answers to authorities that have little to do with the best interests of Britons. [italics suspended]

> David Cameron is the younger son of stockbroker Ian Donald Cameron ...
>
> Cameron's great-great-grandfather, Alexander Geddes,[12] ... made a fortune in the grain trade in Chicago and returned to Scotland in the 1880s.[13]
>
> Through his paternal grandmother, Enid Agnes Maud Levita, Cameron is a lineal descendant of King William IV by his mistress Dorothea Jordan. This illegitimate line consists of five generations of women starting with Elizabeth Hay, Countess of Erroll, née FitzClarence, William and Jordan's sixth child,[14] through to Cameron's grandmother (thereby making Cameron a 5th cousin of Queen Elizabeth II).[15]
>
> Cameron's paternal forebears also have a long history in finance. His father Ian was senior partner of the stockbrokers Panmure Gordon, in which firm partnerships had long been held by Cameron's ancestors, including David's grandfather and great-grandfather,[3] and was a Director of estate agent John D. Wood. David Cameron's great-great-grandfather Emile Levita, a German Jewish financier (and descendant of Renaissance scholar Elia Levita), who obtained British citizenship in 1871, was the director of the Chartered Bank of India, Australia and China which became Standard Chartered Bank in 1969.[15] His wife, Cameron's great-great-grandmother, was a descendant of the wealthy Danish Jewish Rée family on her father's side.[16][17]
>
> One of Emile's sons, Arthur Francis Levita (died 1910, brother of Sir Cecil Levita),[18] of Panmure Gordon stockbrokers, together with great-great-grandfather Sir Ewen Cameron,[19] London head of the Hongkong and Shanghai Bank, played key roles in arranging loans supplied by the Rothschilds to the Japanese Central Banker (later Prime Minister) Takahashi Korekiyo for the financing of the

Japanese Government in the Russo-Japanese war.[20] ~ Wikipedia[988]

Hong Kong and Shanghai Banking Corporation is one biggest banks in the world. HSBC has also been accused of laundering $15 *trillion* for unknown organizations connected to a "rogue" agency within the United States government and going to an unknown source.[989]

HSBC also launders money for petty drug dealers and arms traffickers, as well.

> *Britain's biggest bank HSBC has been dragged into yet another potential scandal over claims that it set up offshore accounts in Jersey for suspected drug-dealers and fraudsters.*
>
> *HM Revenue & Customs launched an investigation after a whistleblower leaked details of £700million allegedly held in more than 4,000 accounts hidden in the island tax haven. ...*
>
> *Those whose account details were leaked to HMRC are said to include Daniel Bayes, a suspected drug-dealer now living in Venezuela. ...*
>
> *The list also includes a man convicted of owning 300 weapons at a property in Devon, three bankers facing fraud allegations, and a man known as London's "number two computer crook", according to the Daily Telegraph.* ~ Rob Davies, the Daily Mail[990]

Vladimir Putin was installed into power by the same band of wealthy, mostly Jewish, billionaires who installed Boris Yeltsin.[991]

Known as "the Family", the majority of their polices were for their *own* best interests, not those of common Russians. Their lines of influence spider-webbed from London through the Rothschilds[992] to Rome (more on this and turncoat Jews exploited by Luciferians in Chapter 17).

"The Family" assumed that Putin would be their stooge just like Yeltsin was. At the time, Putin was Yeltsin's Prime Minister.

They assumed wrong. [italics suspended]

> On July 28, 2000, Vladimir Putin gathered the 18 most powerful businessmen in Russia for an unprecedented discussion. This was the beginning of Putin's campaign to undermine and reduce the power of a group of men who had made titanic fortunes from reforms designed to pave the way for a transformation of the Soviet planned economy into a free market economy. Russian President

Vladimir Putin was rewriting the rules again. In no uncertain terms, Putin told Russia's wealthiest that the jig was up, and he denounced them as creators of a corrupt state.

A very small number of people — known now as the oligarchs— were able to concentrate a very large portion of the Russian people's wealth into their hands through backroom deals and insider connections. Some who read this essay might condemn me because I point out the Jewish identity of the majority of these oligarchs. My reason for doing so is not to be unfair to Jews or to increase hostile feelings towards them. The reason is the simple fact that their Jewishness is a factor and must be taken into consideration when dealing with Russian politics. In Russia, everyone is aware of the Jewish identity of these men, and the acts of the Jewish oligarchs themselves have done quite a bit to increase anti-Jewish feelings there. The oligarchs themselves recognize this, as do many Russian Jews, who blame the oligarchs for giving Jews a bad name. In my opinion, it is much better to be honest about it than try to pretend that this factor doesn't exist. ~ Justin Cowgill, NationalVanguard[993]

The ringleader of this wealthy cartel was Boris Berezovsky. He was intimately entwined with anything that happened in Russia from running the state television channel ORT[994] to being Deputy Secretary of Russia's National Security Council.[995]

However, after Putin was made President courtesy of Berezovsky's media empire, he quickly found out that Vladimir Vladimirovich was no man's puppet. Berezovsky was forced to flee Russia and it is fascinating to note that it was in London where he was given asylum.[996]

When NSA whistleblower Edward Snowden ended up in Russia, talking heads in Washington, DC *demanded* his extradition.[997]

No such request was made by Russian heads of state regarding Boris Berezovsky. He later died there under "mysterious circumstances".[998]

These circumstances were not to be confused with those of spy Alexander Litvinenko who died 8 years earlier, also in London, when an assassin slipped plutonium into the foreign agent's sushi.[999]

It turned out that Litvinenko was actually working for 3 different intelligence agencies[1000] and had spread himself a little too thin.

Man of the Decade

Putin's detractors alternatively accuse him of being a "wimp" *and* a "thug".

Boris Yeltsin's daughter, Tatyana (herself, a wealthy oligarch, double divorcee, friend of Boris Berezovsky and beneficiary of graft and corruption[1001]), claimed that when Putin was first approached with the idea of being nominated to the presidency by Yeltsin, he asked for a reconsideration. This, she took as proof that his "toughguy" image was fabricated.[1002]

Russia's indomitable leader has admitted, himself, that the majority of his wildlife photos are staged[1003] which shows that, although the Soviet State propaganda machine still works in full form, perhaps the man it props is a man of some integrity.

Barack Obama has his own propaganda machine and it puts as much on his plate as he can handle.

It is interesting to note the direction of the propaganda in Russia and who the target audience is. [italics suspended]

> Vladimir Putin was born and raised in Leningrad, U.S.S.R., now known as St. Petersburg, Russia.
>
> Putin had, in classic Soviet fashion, a secular upbringing. His father was a "model Communist" and a "militant atheist," though his mother was a devout Eastern Orthodox Christian[1] and she had young Putin secretly baptized into that church.[2]
>
> It was merely symbolic, however, as Putin went through the bulk of his adult life–rising through the ranks of the KGB and the Soviet Communist Party–conforming to Soviet secular convention.
>
> It wasn't until the double-whammy of 1) his wife's car accident in 1993 and 2) a life-threatening house fire in 1996 that Putin began questioning his atheism. During a vulnerable moment before Putin departed for a diplomatic trip to Israel, his mother gave him a baptismal cross. He said of the occasion:
>
>> I did as she said and then put the cross around my neck. I have never taken it off since.[3]
>
> Now, Putin has become a bit of a zealot. He seems to want to reestablish a pre-Soviet combination of church and state, saying:

> First and foremost we should be governed by common sense. But common sense should be based on moral principles first. And it is not possible today to have morality separated from religious values.[4]

Furthermore, Putin has proposed compulsory religion and ethics classes for Russian students.[5]

There are many reports of collusion between the Russian Orthodox clergy and the Russian government, with each of them fighting the other's battles for them. The most recent example to receive worldwide attention was the Pussy Riot debacle, in which the girl-punk band sang at a church in Moscow: "Mother of God, Blessed Virgin, drive out Putin."[6] Both the church and the government were outraged and the band was sentenced to two years of prison labor.[7]

The western world erupted in outrage and, recalling Soviet oppression of artists and intellectuals, condemned the sentence as theocratic totalitarianism. Even the Obama administration weighed in...

Still, Putin's religiosity is a blessing to some in the international community. The Eastern Orthodox Church has asked him to protect Christians worldwide, and he has agreed. Russia's controversial support of Bashar al-Assad's regime in Syria is due to Putin's concern that the Christian minority in that country will be persecuted if Assad is toppled.[9] ~ Tom Kershaw, The Hollowverse[1004]

Putin has recently divorced his wife of 30 years, Lyudmila, and the marriage is survived by two rarely-seen daughters. It has been speculated that he holds a mistress who is an Olympic Gymnast and Russian MP—Alina Kabaeva.[1005]

If that is the extent of Putin's misdeeds, they pale in comparison to, say, George "Magog" Bush.[1006,1007]

But Mr. Kershaw has dramatically downplayed the extent of the "Pussy Riot" controversy.

There are strong signs that they are part of a complex foreign subversive plot to destabilize the new Christian Russia with extreme feminism, porn and depravity.

Pussy Riot is not a rock band. They have never recorded a CD, never played in a show. ~ Henry Makow[1008]

On Amazon.com, a search for music from "Pussy Riot" will give you a *book* written on nothing more than their infamous cathedral "protest"[1009] and a single "Pussy Riot" CD with a cover that combines cartoonish porn with a picture of Vladimir Putin's face. However, a close examination of the product reveals, it's not a "Pussy Riot" CD and the top customer feedback (as of this writing) is a single-star review.

a fraud

By Amazon Customer *on March 18, 2014*

The band is 'Nutgun'. The name of the album is 'Pussy Riot'. There is one song. A man says 'pussy riot' over and over on top of some repetitive generic punk/thrash-sounding mess.

There are no Russian freedom-fighting ladies associated with this album. There are no negative-star options, but this fraud deserves worse than 1-star.

I have found many people attempting to profit from their name. I have found no way to actually support Pussy Riot—nothing that the members of the band profit from. If you figure out how to do that, please post it here.[1010]

What did the invisible "punk girl band" do?

To "protest" against the administration of Vladimir Putin, they dawned masks and interrupted a solemn Orthodox mass inside Moscow's Cathedral of Christ the Savior in February of 2012.

They've had support from an unbelievable source; the Wittenberg, Germany town council has nominated the non-existent band to receive the prestigious "Fearless Speech" award that is given each year to commemorate the courage of Martin Luther in

FEMEN activist in front of Sofia Kievska (Saint Sophia Cathedral in Kiev) in protest against Moscow Patriarch Kirill who is on official visit to Ukraine 26-28 July 2010. FEMEN Women's Movement; Wikimedia Commons

defying Rome.[1011] [italics suspended]

> The group is called Pussy Riot, and they were arrested for hooliganism and desecration of the Moscow Cathedral, singing blasphemous verses, and attacking president Putin. Last week, they have been sentenced to two years in jail. They were not condemned for their political views, which they have freely expressed many times before.
>
> Pussy Riot is not a band. They have never recorded a CD, never played in a show. In fact, they are a radical communist group, that loves Karl Marx and performs in honor of Che Guevara's birthday. They are a branch of the extremist group "Voina", (the word means war), that is known for many disgusting and even dangerous agit-prop actions since 2002. Here is an article describing their obscene stunts.[1012] Now there is strong evidence that they have been supported by agencies from the western elite.[1013]
>
> It is interesting to notice that most countries have similar laws against attacks on religion, including England, where the penalty is even more severe, the US and even Brazil, where the action can result in one year of jail time.
>
> Pussy Riot now joins the bare-breasted Ukrainian Femen group, the "March of the Sluts" groups and the Gay Parades that have been in the news lately. Always well funded, their agenda is extreme feminism, cultural marxism and the destruction of all traditional relgious and family values. The use of "frontmen", agents provocateurs who end up as "victims" after intentional confrontation is an old tactic of Cultural Marxists.
>
> Russia is now a special target since the country has turned to more nationalist, conservative ways. Recently, Russia has forbidden gay parades for 100 years, and Saint Petersburg does not allow propaganda that may expose children to the gay lifestyle. They also regulated and controlled foreign-funded NGOs, thus cutting the arms of foreign influence in Russia. ~ Henry Makow[1014]

Perhaps it's no surprise that these efforts have the direct support of even Hillary Clinton[1015], herself—a great promoter of "women's rights"...unless it's a woman that's been raped by her husband.[1016]

In solidarity to "Pussy Riot", the Leftist Feminist group "Femen" tore off their shirts and cut down a large wooden cross that was in a park in Kiev, Ukraine.

The cross—erected during Ukraine's 2004-05 Orange Revolution in memory of the victims of communism—was located near the International Center for Culture and Arts in Kyiv. ~ Radio Free Europe/Radio Liberty[1017]

In Belgium, the Communist performers tore off their shirts and conducted lewd acts with sex paraphernalia in another anti-Putin "protest"[1018]. With such actions spanning from Ukraine to Belgium, they seem to have an unusually long reach—almost as if a powerful organization is helping them.

The European Broadcasting Union is an alliance of useless public broadcasting services that uses taxpayer funding from 56 countries all around the world[1019] via "licensing fees" and direct taxation[1020]. Their flagship event is the "Eurovision Song Contest"—a facsimile of "American Idol".

The 2014 winner was the transgender performer that goes by the name "Conchita Wurst" (Spanish and German slang for "vagina penis").

uploaded by BambooBeast
Wikimedia Commons

Russia was not amused. [italics suspended]

> Russian Minister of Culture Vladimir Medinsky has said it is not within his jurisdiction to ban this year's Eurovision song contest winner, the Austrian transvestite Conchita Wurst, from performing in Russia. His remarks came in response to a plea from Vitaly Milonov, the politician who initiated the "gay propaganda" law in St Petersburg, to prohibit Wurst from travelling to Russia. A spokesperson from the Ministry of Culture said the department was unable to ban "visits from bearded men or women to Russia".
>
> Milonov said of Wurst: "This creature of indeterminate gender is an insult to the majority of the Russian population, and any other country in fact. To allow him to enter our country is more than criminal negligence."
>
> President Vladimir Putin's United Russia party added to the public outcry, with Olga Batalina, the first deputy head of the Duma's Committee on Family, Women and Children, attributing Wurst's victory to the "propaganda of non-traditional and gay culture". She

added: "To win at the Eurovision today, it's not enough to have talent and a good voice. We must also abandon our nature, identity and traditions."

A number of posts from cultural and political figures on social media have supported Russia's official stance, with popular Russian rapper Timati among them. Attributing Wurst's victory to a "mental illness of contemporary society", he added: "I wouldn't like one fine day to have to explain to my child why two guys are kissing or a woman is walking around with a dyed beard and that it's supposed to be normal." Nationalist politician Vladimir Zhirinovsky also echoed Batalina's concern, telling state television channel Rossiya-1: "There's no limit to our outrage. It's the end of Europe. It has turned wild. They don't have men and women anymore. They have 'it'." Russia gave Wurst five points for his performance, one more point than it awarded Ukraine. ~ the Calvert Journal[1021]

Sergei Glazyev is a key economic advisor to President Putin as well as a subject matter expert on relations with Ukraine. His voice carries much weight around the Kremlin. In an interview with the magazine *Rusinform*, he said this about Russia's past and present:

Europe is a post-Christian civilization in which the norms of Christian morality and ethics are rejected. The Europeans practically made the cornerstone of their ideology that which we call moral disintegration and what they call tolerance. Relations between the sexes, between parents and children – these are the foundations of human living. Undermining them, Europe condemns itself to ruin, and we don't feel like taking part in this self-destruction. In Russia for only the last twenty years has there been a restoration of Christian values. Although we must say that even in the Soviet Union "people lived without God, but in a godly fashion," as our Patriarch has said. If you compare the moral codex of a "builder of Communism," to which all members of the Komsomol swore when entering the organization, with the basic principles of Christianity, they coincide in content. Although without faith in God, as the experience of the socialist enterprise showed, they work badly. ~ Mark Hackard, Soul of the East[1022]

Compare Glazyev's statement to anything coming from America's *pulpits* today.

Carl Bildt, Sweden's Minister for Foreign Affairs and one of the architects of the European Union's Eastern policy, has stated that Russia's

Orthodoxy is a "threat to western civilization".

> *In the words of Mr Bildt, Vladimir Putin demonstrates attachment not to world but to Eastern Orthodox values...*
>
> *"The new anti-west and anti-decadent line* [of conduct] *of Putin is based on the deep conservatism of Eastern Orthodox ideas," Carl Bildt is convinced.* ~ REX[1023]

Russia's Foreign Minister agrees.

> *Russian Foreign Minister Sergey Lavrov states that Russia returns to traditional spiritual values and it is one of the reasons why the West distances from it.*
>
> *"Surprisingly, they start operating the thesis that the Soviet Union with its Communist doctrine at least stayed in the system of ideas worked out in the West, while modern Russia returns to its traditional values rooted in Orthodoxy and thus becomes even less understandable," Lavrov said at his meeting with members of the Russian International Affairs Council in Moscow.*
>
> *According to him, the contradiction "between objectively strengthening multipolarity and the USA and historical West strive to keep their usual dominating positions, between modern world's cultural and civilization diversity and attempts to impose everyone Western scale of values."*
>
> *The latter, as the Minister said, "more and more tears apart from their own Christian roots and becomes less susceptible to religious feeling of people belonging to other confessions and religions."* ~ Interfax[1024]

As the Elite continue to close in on Russia, two countries remain as reliable allies: Belarus and Kazakhstan.

Belarus President Alexander Lukashenko stated in June of 2014:

> *"Today we should be united as never before as there is a serious strike made against the most important thing that have always united us and brought us up. It is a strike against the foundation, on which we based our lives, against Christian values," the President said at a meeting with participants in the European Orthodox-Catholic Forum.*
>
> *"We should stand for Christian values, whatever it costs. If we lose*

them, we lose everything," the head of the state said.

He assures that Byelorussians have always been and will be one of the basic cores in the foundation of Christianity as these values are in the foundation of country's development. ~ Pravmir[1025]

Of course, politicians are always pandering to the public. But what does this say of today's Slavs when their leaders make statements such as these?

Certainly, Russia has made controversial alignments and has recently committed to building two nuclear power plants for Iran.[1026]

Russia has also conducted massive military maneuvers with Red China[1027] and is looking into creating a new currency alternative to the U.S./Saudi "petro-dollar" with fellow "BRICS" nations (Brazil, Russia, India, China and South Africa).[1028]

Much of this, however, can be understood as "self preservation".

One thing Russia isn't doing is extending military influence to the detriment of indigenous Christians. This has been the case everywhere the United States military has been sent by George Bush 41, Bill Clinton, George Bush 43 and Barack Obama.

As Jesus Christ warned, "a tree is known by its fruit".

In Afghanistan, not a single Christian church remains open.[1029]

In Libya, Islamists have imposed Sharia law[1030] and gone door-to-door to murder Christian families.[1031]

After a CIA-steered "Arab Spring" installed the Muslim Brotherhood in Egypt, Christians were forced to leave all they had and flee in large numbers[1032]. Their homes were marked by radicals for future terror operations.[1033]

The suffering of Christians in Iraq has not only continued since the Bush Wars 1 & 2 but has gotten unspeakably worse.

In 2003, open season on Christians was declared with a "fatwa" making it "permissible to spill the blood of Christians."[1034]

This is a carefully-planned progression of destabilizing Middle Eastern countries like dominoes that has been planned out for years in advance[1035]. Its purpose is to put the Pope in Jerusalem and we'll look more at that in

Chapter 18.

But Barack Obama has been lagging on the scheduled overthrow of Syria and Putin is one of the main reasons.[1036]

Putin's Russia

The number of Right-minded political leaders willing to stand up against the "New World Order" is extremely limited. If you only include those in office, it is fewer still. As a result, Vladimir Putin has stepped into the gulf and become somewhat of a Right-wing folk hero.

> *While Obama has remained silent on the subject of the ethnic cleansing of Christians going on throughout the Middle East, Russian President Vladimir Putin has not been.*
>
> *On August 1, 2013, Putin said world leaders must come together to stop the violent persecution of Christians in the Middle East.*
>
> *Something is wrong when Putin is a greater champion for freedom and liberty than the President of the United States is.* ~ Judson Philips, Washington Times[1037] [unofficial head of the Tea Party]

Is a rough Communist preferable to Western metrosexuals?

Perhaps a better question is; is Putin a Soviet or is he Russian?

There are those in "Conservative" media who consider Putin a clandestine comrade of the worst order.

> *For nearly a decade, even before he became Russia's "president,"* The New American *has been reporting on Putin's KGB pedigree and his steady implementation of a long-range Soviet deception strategy, including the public rehabilitation and refortifying of the KGB-FSB.*
>
> *We reported in 1999, for instance, on Putin's ominously revealing speech for Security Organs Day, celebrating the accomplishments of Dzerzhinsky and the Cheka. We reported in 2002 on Putin's restoration of important communist symbols:*
>
> - *the Red Star, as Russia's official military emblem;*
> - *the Red Banner, as Russia's military flag;*
> - *the music of the old Soviet anthem, albeit with new words;*

- *and his attempt, along with Moscow Mayor Yuri Luzhkov, to restore the giant statue of Dzerzhinsky to its former place of honor in Moscow's Lubyanka Square.*

Public opposition to the glorification of "Iron Felix" have (temporarily) scotched Putin's plans for Dzerzhinsky's statue. Nevertheless, as we have reported, in 2005, Putin did restore a smaller bust of the mass-murdering Chekist to a pedestal at the infamous Lubyanka headquarters of the KGB-FSB. ~ William F. Jasper, New American[1038]

In 1988, Putin was a mid-level agent assigned to harangue then-President Ronald Reagan over his "human rights" record during a visit to Moscow[1039]. It seemed to have been a prophetic moment.

If Putin is still a Communist, it is possible that he wrongfully convolutes Russian power and prestige with the hammer and sickle.

Petter Strandmark – Wikimedia Commons

Regardless, resurrecting Felix Dzerzhinsky is indefensible.

It is interesting to note that, when querying a popular search engine for "Felix Dzerzhinsky atrocities" the first usable, historical hit is from one of Russia's "propaganda outlets"; *Russia Today*. [italics suspended]

> In 1918 the Cheka orchestrated the campaign of mass arrests and executions that came to be known as Red Terror. A Red Army newspaper wrote: "Let there be floods of blood of the bourgeoisie – more blood, as much as possible". The arrests didn't stop at deserters and rioting workers. Anyone could fall under Cheka's suspicion based on religious beliefs or social standing.
>
> The Cheka also initiated the infamous system of labour camps and conducted a terrifying campaign against the peasantry. According to Lenin's orders, peasants had to sell their excess grain to the state at fixed prices. Because of uncontrolled inflation these payments were virtually worthless so many refused to obey. The full fury of

the Cheka was unleashed on them in what was later called the "Bread War". Entire families were executed and villages wiped out.

The organization turned into a giant man-killing machine. At Cheka's headquarters in Moscow lights glared every night as hundreds were brought in for interrogations. Here Dzerzhinsky spent days on end, keen to take part in questioning and studying files. He virtually lived in his office, where a bed's been fitted for him.

Mass murders left Dzerzhinsky unfazed. During party meetings, Lenin would often send short notes to some of his colleagues. A story goes that at one gathering in 1918, a note went to Dzerzhinsky, asking how many enemies of the revolution were currently jailed. Dzerzhinsky replied with a number of about 1,500. After reading it, Lenin put a cross next to the number and returned the paper to Dzerzhinsky who immediately stood up and left.

Nobody paid any attention to this sudden departure and only the following day did the result of this correspondence become known: Dzerzhinsky had all of the 1,500 inmates shot that very night, having interpreted Lenin's cross as an execution order. Lenin apparently didn't mean it – a cross was his usual way of showing he's read and considered the information. 1,500 people fell victim of Dzerzhinsky's misinterpretation – something nobody dared criticize. ~ Russiapedia, RT[1040]

Russian athletes petitioned their president to change the national anthem. It was less than inspiring. The Soviet anthem was resurrected with new, more positive lyrics and was an immediate success amongst the Russian people.[1041]

Vladimir Putin is a complex man and a simplistic analysis is an incomplete one.

Corporate Russia—both media and government—have shown humble willingness to examine the excesses of Communism. This is the mark of mature citizens who can tell the difference between "Russia" and "the Soviet Union."

One of Russia's most famous dissidents was author Alexander Isayevich Solzhenitsyn.

A man with a proud Imperial Russian military past, both he and his father served in the Russian military. It only took criticizing Joseph Stalin in a private letter to a friend to get him arrested and imprisoned.[1042]

Eventually released, he was exiled from the Soviet Union though his works were already popular and well-read. He took residence in the United States and was an outspoken critic of the Communist Police State.[1043]

But, after living in Vermont for 20 years, Solzhenitsyn felt compelled to return to his beloved homeland, having become disillusioned by the decadence of the West. Solzhenitsyn was a man of true Christian conviction.

> *Besides being credited as one of the most prominent figures in bringing about the demise of Soviet communism, Solzhenitsyn is considered to be one of the most articulate critics of the materialistic decadence of the West and post-communist Russia, a position most famously elucidated in his devastating 1978 "Harvard Address."*
>
> *In that Address, delivered to some 10-15 thousand listeners, and which ultimately served to put him out of favor with many of the West's intelligentsia, Solzhenitsyn denounced the West for its lack of courage and personality, its legalism, moral decadence, intellectual and social shallowness, enslavement to fashion, passivity, short-sightedness, and more. The writer traced these Western sicknesses to the embrace of the materialistic humanism of the Enlightenment, which he defined as "the proclaimed and practiced autonomy of man from any higher force above him." ~* John Jalsevac, Catholic Culture[1044]

Vladimir Putin has embraced both Solzhenitsyn and his legacy.

In response, honest pundits have been forced to re-examine their assessments of Russia's most powerful personality. [italics suspended]

> In these days of acrimonious political mud-slinging, there seems to be almost nothing upon which the radicals on the left and the reactionaries on the right can agree. There is, however, one thing on which both ends of the political spectrum are in absolute agreement, and that's their univocal and unadulterated disdain for Russian President Vladimir Putin.
>
> For those on the left, Putin is beyond the pale because of his failure to endorse the homosexual agenda. Over the past couple of years, Putin has supported the passing of laws in Russia banning

"homosexual propaganda." For those on the right, Putin represents the resurrection of the Soviet bogeyman, a sort of reincarnation of Joseph Stalin or Nikita Khrushchev.

Considering the universal condemnation and demonization of the Russian president, it might seem foolish and perhaps perilous to seek a more balanced perspective. ...

Like Obama's America, Putin's Russia also has a state - "encouraged" common core curriculum. It is intriguing, however, that three of the major works of the anti-Communist dissident and Nobel Prize winner Alexander Solzhenitsyn are required reading at all Russian high schools. These three works are the novella "One Day in the Life of Ivan Denisovich," a harrowing account of the cruelty and barbarism of the Soviet labor camps; "The Gulag Archipelago," a monumental history of the Soviet prison system and its inherent and endemic injustices; and "Matryona's House," a short story about the heroine's retention of traditional Christian virtue in the face of Communist tyranny.

It is worthy of note that Putin is a great admirer of Solzhenitsyn. He met him in September 2000 and was at pains to emphasize that he had Solzhenitsyn's approval for his education policies. In August 2001, Putin stated that, prior to his education reforms, he had contacted eminent people "known and respected by the country, including Alexander Solzhenitsyn." In October 2010, after it was announced that Solzhenitsyn's works would become required reading for all Russian high school students, Putin described "The Gulag Archipelago" as "essential reading": "Without the knowledge of that book, we would lack a full understanding of our country and it would be difficult for us to think about the future." ...

In June 2007, Putin signed a decree honoring Solzhenitsyn (who died in 2008) "for exemplary achievements in the area of humanitarian activities." This apparent rapprochement between the apparatchik and the dissident, between Putin, the former KGB operative, and Solzhenitsyn, the former victim of a failed KGB assassination attempt, has understandably puzzled many observers. Endeavoring to explain the seemingly inexplicable, Daniel Mahoney, author of "Aleksandr Solzhenitsyn: The Ascent from Ideology" and co-editor of "The Solzhenitsyn Reader," saw the solution to the conundrum in Solzhenitsyn's frank appraisal of Putin's political achievements:

Solzhenitsyn, Mahoney wrote, "surely credits Putin for taking on the most unsavory of the oligarchs, confronting the demographic crisis (it was Solzhenitsyn who first warned in his speech to the Duma in the fall of 1994 that Russians were in danger of dying out), and restoring Russian self-respect (although Solzhenitsyn adamantly opposes every identification of Russian patriotism with Soviet-style imperialism)." ~ Joseph Pearce, International Business Times[1045]

It would appear that Vladimir Putin loves Russia almost as much as Barack Obama hates America.

A Look Inside Putin's Brain

Since the fall of the Soviet Union in 1991, Russians have been cynical and disillusioned. Some, especially those who fell prey to it like Solzhenitsyn, saw Communism as a totalitarian beast of the devil, but most Russians saw the Soviet Union as just strong, centralized power. It left a terrible vacuum in that society that has been filled with an amalgam of Orthodox Christian virtue, a drive for renewed nationalistic pride and even Tsarist imperialism.

Vladimir Putin and Alexander Solzhenitsyn
Kremlin.ru

Few men embody this better than Aleksandr Gelyevich Dugin.

Dugin is a political scientist with some revolutionary ideas about putting "truth to power".

It is nearly impossible to find reputable, objective sources of information on him.

Those on the American Left attack Dugin in support of Barack Obama's expansionist foreign policy (a policy shockingly similar to his predecessors). "Conservatives" seem forever stuck in the Cold War and attack Dugin for his Russian nationalism.

As Rasputin was the mystic advisor to the Romanovs, Dugin is purported to have the attention of Vladimir Putin (hence "Putin's Brain") but to what extent no one knows or even if he has any influence at all.

Certainly the West is terrified of him. [italics suspended]

> Alexander (also spelled Aleksandr) Gel'yevich Dugin (Russian: Александр Гельевич Дугин) (born January 7, 1962) is a Russian political activist and ideologue of the contemporary Russian school of geopolitics often known as "neo-Eurasianism". Dugin's so-called "Fourth Political Theory" should be read with caution. Dugin's philosophy mixes a number of both positive and negative ideas, due to his interest in dubious occult and possibly masonic-derived ideas from banned books during the Soviet Era.
>
> He has been embraced by the Kremlin to some extent, mainly because of his geopolitical theories of how to destroy the American Empire. Unlike traditional Russian nationalists of the Black Hundred cloth, he claims to be opposed to "anti-Semitism". Some suspect that this is perhaps due to sharing a common ideological basis with the Jews in their Kabbalah (he openly glorifies Gershom Scholem as "the greatest traditionalist thinker"). ...
>
> Dugin comes from a military family. His father was a high-ranking officer of the Soviet military intelligence; his mother is a doctor. In 1979 he entered the Moscow Aviation Institute, but never graduated. His father helped him to get a job in KGB archives, where he found eventually what he was really interested in – forbidden for the general Soviet population works on fascism, eurasianism, world religions and mysticism.
>
> Dugin worked as a journalist, before becoming involved in politics just before the fall of communism. In 1988 he and his friend Geidar Dzhemal joined the nationalist group Pamyat. He helped to write the political programme for the newly refounded Communist Party of the Russian Federation under the leadership of Gennady Zyuganov, producing a document that was more nationalist in tone than Marxist. ~ Metapedia[1046]

Dugin's *The Fourth Political Theory*[1047] appears to be a transcendent roadmap to handling the post-fascist, post-communist, post-liberal world—fascism having been conquered in 1945 (Dugin claims), Communism having been vanquished in 1991 (with Dugin slotting remaining Communist nations to fail soon) and liberalism morphing into a "global financial oligarchy" that has turned democracy on its head and gives world power to a globalist Elite that is riding the United States into a One World Order.

As a result of sentiments like these, Dugin is finding some surprised Tea Party allies.

But he is not Evangelical, he is Russian Orthodox with a very strong smattering of the occult. His detractors use this to denounce his theories.

Dugin's push for a greater "Eurasia" is gaining popularity amongst the most dangerous demographic possible: young people.

On his blog, he gave a somewhat paranoid denunciation of the two sides of Vladimir Putin and whether or not the Russian President was behind the efforts to oust Dugin from Moscow State. In the post, he mentioned the "Solar Putin" who bravely lead Russia against the Chechen insurgency verses the "Lunar Putin" who succumbs to liberalism and compromise. [1048]

He even has his own flag; 6 outward-pointing gold arrows on a black field.[bb]

And yet, when interviewed by the "Larry King of Russia", Vladimir Pozner, shortly after Easter, Dugin responded to Pozner's formal "good evening" with an immediate, "Good evening. He is risen!" Pozner, son of a Soviet Jew who spied for the Communists while working for Metro-Goldwyn Mayer in Europe[1049], immediately chided Dugin that he was not Christian.

Posner was once a Party "political observer" for Mikhail Gorbachev and had multiple collaborative efforts during the Cold War with Norte Dame-educated Irish Catholic media mogul Phil Donahue in 1985 and again in 1989.[1050]

Donahue is now worth an astounding $23.5 million[1051]. Are these the fruits of Rome's agenda?

When Pozner criticized Dugin for the militancy of his views in countering the London/Washington anti-Christ hegemony, he brought up the "peaceful" teachings of Jesus Christ and how incongruous they were with Dugin's passion (non-Christians use this as a tactic often).

Dugin's response was "Christ was perfect man and perfect God" but even He chased out the money-changers and proclaimed, "'I come not to bring peace, but the sword'..."

Can I get an "Amen!"?

Dugin also uses the metaphor of Russia being the "land" empire and America being the "water" or Atlantean empire. This connection has far more application than he realized and we'll examine it more in Chapter 15.

[bb] This may be a reference to the intersecting of two triangles in opposite directions: the occultic emblem for a desire to make a "Heaven on Earth"—"as above, so below".

In this fascinating interview Dugin also was quick to point his acrimony, not at the American people, but at the United States Elite, stating that if America were following the policies of Ron Paul or Pat Buchanan, she would at worst be neutral towards Russia and at best, fast friends.[1052]

Saint George's Lance

During his 2012 Presidential election victory speech with new Prime Minister Dmitry Medvedev, a tearful Vladimir Putin thanked all of the citizens of Russia.

> *I once asked, "Would we prevail?" We **have** prevailed. ...*
>
> *This was not just a presidential election. This was a very important test for all of us, for our whole nation. ...*
>
> *We have shown indeed, that no one can enslave us.*
>
> ***No one** and **nothing** can enslave us.*
>
> *We have shown that our people are truly able to easily distinguish between the desire for progress and renewed political provocation that has only one objective—to destroy Russian sovereignty and usurp power.*
>
> *The Russian people have now shown that in our country such choices and scenarios will not pass.*
>
> *THEY SHALL NOT PASS.*[1053]

Some have considered this a veiled warning to the "New World Order".

The state propaganda outlet "Russia Today" regularly tackles issues of actual import from genetically-modified food to false flags—always with a pro-Russian spin, of course.

Putin is one of the very few world leaders who is in no hurry to dive into economy-crippling changes for the sake of "global warming"[1054]. In a 2010 visit to the Arctic circle he noted that the climate is changing but he was still unsure if it was as a result of direct human influence or the Earth's own "living and breathing".[1055]

In 2009, British journalist James Delingpole broke a scandal that should've broke "Climate Change". Delingpole released a series of e-mails that showed most un-scientific collusion and conspiracy amongst "Climate Change scientists" to fudge data in their favor. The releases have come to be called "Climategate". [italics suspended]

> The conspiracy behind the Anthropogenic Global Warming myth (aka AGW; aka ManBearPig) has been suddenly, brutally and quite deliciously exposed after a hacker broke into the computers at the University of East Anglia's Climate Research Unit (aka CRU) and released 61 megabytes of confidential files onto the internet.
>
> These alleged emails – supposedly exchanged by some of the most prominent scientists pushing AGW theory – suggest:
>
>> Conspiracy, collusion in exaggerating warming data, possibly illegal destruction of embarrassing information, organised resistance to disclosure, manipulation of data, private admissions of flaws in their public claims and much more.
>
> One of the alleged emails has a gentle gloat over the death in 2004 of John L Daly (one of the first climate change sceptics, founder of the Still Waiting For Greenhouse site), commenting:
>
>> "In an odd way this is cheering news."
>
> But perhaps the most damaging revelations – the scientific equivalent of the Telegraph's MPs' expenses scandal – are those concerning the way Warmist scientists may variously have manipulated or suppressed evidence in order to support their cause. ~ James Delingpole, the Telegraph [emphasis his][1056]

It was later disclosed that said scientists were actually targeted by a sophisticated hacking effort. At the bottom of the effort was the Russian Secret Service.[1057]

It is interesting to note that one of the biggest political figures who stand opposed to Vladimir Putin on "climate change" is Jorge Mario Bergoglio, the Jesuit Pope Francis.

> *VATICAN CITY — Tackling the problem of climate change is a serious ethical and moral responsibility, Pope Francis told negotiators from around the world meeting for a climate summit in Lima, Peru.*
>
> *"The time to find global solutions is running out. We can find adequate solutions only if we act together and unanimously," he said in a written message to Manuel Pulgar-Vidal, Peru's minister of the environment and host president of the 20th UN Climate*

Change Conference.

Thousands of negotiators from 195 countries gathered for the meeting in Lima Dec. 1-12 to hammer out details of a new international agreement to reduce emissions of greenhouse gases that cause global warming. ...

The Pope encouraged the leaders in their discussions because their decisions will "affect all of humanity, especially the poorest and future generations. What's more, it represents a serious ethical and moral responsibility." ~ Carol Glatz, Catholic News Service[1058]

Indeed.

Those most affected will be the dwindling Western Middle Class whose cost of living will cast them into the "poorest generations" of the future—which appears to be Bergoglio's intent.

In late October of 2014, Putin gave what some are calling the most powerful speech of his career at the Valdai International Discussion Club regarding foreign policy[1059]. It has been completely ignored by all Western media. The below summary was presented in English by Club Orlov. [italics suspended]

> 1. Russia will no longer play games and engage in back-room negotiations over trifles. But Russia is prepared for serious conversations and agreements, if these are conducive to collective security, are based on fairness and take into account the interests of each side.
>
> 2. All systems of global collective security now lie in ruins. There are no longer any international security guarantees at all. And the entity that destroyed them has a name: The United States of America.
>
> 3. The builders of the New World Order have failed, having built a sand castle. Whether or not a new world order of any sort is to be built is not just Russia's decision, but it is a decision that will not be made without Russia.
>
> 4. Russia favors a conservative approach to introducing innovations into the social order, but is not opposed to investigating and discussing such innovations, to see if introducing any of them might be justified.
>
> 5. Russia has no intention of going fishing in the murky waters

created by America's ever-expanding "empire of chaos," and has no interest in building a new empire of her own (this is unnecessary; Russia's challenges lie in developing her already vast territory). ...

6. Russia will not attempt to reformat the world in her own image, but neither will she allow anyone to reformat her in their image. Russia will not close herself off from the world, but anyone who tries to close her off from the world will be sure to reap a whirlwind.

7. Russia does not wish for the chaos to spread, does not want war, and has no intention of starting one. However, today Russia sees the outbreak of global war as almost inevitable, is prepared for it, and is continuing to prepare for it. Russia does not war—nor does she fear it.

8. Russia does not intend to take an active role in thwarting those who are still attempting to construct their New World Order—until their efforts start to impinge on Russia's key interests. Russia would prefer to stand by and watch them give themselves as many lumps as their poor heads can take. But those who manage to drag Russia into this process, through disregard for her interests, will be taught the true meaning of pain.

9. In her external, and, even more so, internal politics, Russia's power will rely not on the elites and their back-room dealing, but on the will of the people. ...

To sum it all up: play-time is over. Children, put away your toys. Now is the time for the adults to make decisions. Russia is ready for this; is the world? ~ Зазеркалье/ClubOrlov[1060,1061]

The Eye of Sauron

In December of 2014, Hollywood promoters attempted to put a large display up in downtown Moscow. To hype the opening of the third "Hobbit" film in the "Lord of the Ring" series, a large facsimile of the Eye of Sauron was to be placed on one of Moscow's tallest buildings. The Orthodox Church rode a wave of public concern and discontent with Archpriest Vsevolod Chaplin stating that the Eye of Sauron was a demonic symbol and Russians did not want such a symbol of the "triumph of evil" rising up over the city[1062]. No one should be surprised if something went wrong in Moscow after that.[cc]

The promotion was cancelled.[1063]

With nearly $18,000,000,000,000 of debt and hundreds of trillions in unfunded liabilities—promised payments and benefits for the future that the United States government will collapse under long before they can be realized—the Republican House enabled Barack Obama to build a $1.7 *billion* NSA data storage facility in the safe mountains of Utah that "will employ around 200 technicians, span 1 million square feet and use 65 megawatts of power."[1064]

The year the facility was unveiled (2013), former Defense Intelligence Agency, Central Intelligence Agency and National Security Agency analyst Edward Snowden began leaking highly classified documents to the American public regarding the extent of how much they were being spied upon by their own government. With the new data storage facility in Utah, nearly every piece of electronic communication can be archived for decades to come.

Congress and the FAA have paved the way for 30,000 government surveillance drones to fill American skies by 2020.[1065]

Vladimir Putin says that "drones aren't toys" and has vowed not to use them as the West does.[1066]

Snowden was forced to leave the country.

Disparate actors from all over the United States rushed to condemn what he had done.

Bill Gates told Rolling Stone that Snowden "broke the law" and he was "not admired".[1067]

Republican John Boehner and Democrat Diane Feinstein Called Snowden a "traitor".[1068]

Dick Cheney also called him a traitor.[1069]

Republican Senator Kelly Ayotte joined Democrats Chuck Schumer and Harry Reid in calling Snowden a traitor.[1070]

[cc] Perhaps one will laugh at the superstitions of Muscovites but what was the goal with this agenda? Would it truly have encouraged Russians to see the latest Hobbit movie, or would it have elicited thoughts and emotions quite different from that...?

Lindsey Graham adjured Barack Obama to "follow Mr. Snowden to the ends of the earth to bring him to justice."[1071]

On David Gregory's *Meet the Press*, former Congresspersons Newt Gingrich (R) and Jane Harmon (D) both agreed that Snowden was "dangerous" and needed to "serve prison time".[1072]

Gingrich is no stranger to controversy. He told one wife with recently-diagnosed multiple sclerosis on Mother's Day that he wanted a divorce. Another wife he divorced after she was hospitalized with cancer.[1073]

Harman was caught promising favors to Israeli officials on their espionage efforts.

> *Rep. Jane Harman, the California Democrat with a longtime involvement in intelligence issues, was overheard on an NSA wiretap telling a suspected Israeli agent that she would lobby the Justice Department to reduce espionage-related charges against two officials of the American Israeli Public Affairs Committee, the most powerful pro-Israel organization in Washington.* ~ Glenn Greenwald, Salon[1074]

Rather than push for her prosecution for espionage and sedition, George W. Bush used the "political capital" to propel his Police State.

> *In 2009, it was revealed NSA wiretaps reportedly intercepted a 2005 phone call between Harman and an agent of the Israeli government, in which Harman allegedly agreed to lobby the Justice Department to reduce or drop criminal charges against two employees of AIPAC in exchange for increased support for Harman's campaign to chair the House Intelligence Committee.[13] The NSA transcripts reportedly recorded Harman ending the phone call after saying, "this conversation doesn't exist."[14] It was reported that Alberto Gonzales, Attorney General at the time of the phone call, blocked Justice Department lawyers from continuing the investigation into Harman (in spite of the alleged crime) because the Bush administration "needed Jane" to support their warrantless wiretapping program, which was soon to be revealed to the public by the New York Times.[15]* ~ Wikipedia[1075]

The founder and president of the Center for Security Policy, Frank Gaffney, also called Edward Snowden a "traitor".[1076]

Gaffney is a frequent favorite of Conservative media and CIA propagandists on the dangers of radical Islam[1077]...except when those radical

Islamists can be used to destabilize Russia. Gaffney has been directly connected to Chechen terrorists intent upon that purpose.[1078]

Russian Intelligence sent warnings to the FBI about Boston Marathon bombing suspects, Tamerlan and Dzhokhar Tsarnaev[1079] but they were ignored—probably because the two were on the U.S. Intelligence payroll.[1080,1081]

Donald Trump told Fox News that Snowden should be executed.[1082]

In 2011, Trump had attempted to exploit popular support for any public figure who would question Barack Obama's Constitutional eligibility. He played the role up for weeks, implying he would use the popularity to run for President, himself.

In the end, he quickly folded on all issues and was rewarded with a lucrative deal by Obama insiders, the Emanuel brothers[1083]. It later turned out that he was feigning interest only to get intelligence from Obama birth investigators to turn over to government insiders.[1084]

After a short stay in Red China, Snowden ended up running to Vladimir Putin[1085]. This only embellished Putin's status as an anti-Establishment folk hero.

Arizona Republican Senator John McCain stated that he had "no doubt in his mind" that Snowden was working for Vladimir Putin.[1086]

That we know of, Edward Snowden has not released a state secret that has compromised the security of the American people. But he has shown them that their own government considers them the enemy. Perhaps not by coincidence, that is exactly how Rome feels.

Living Clean

Although Russia lacks the same sophistication or high incomes of the West, it is a nation that also lacks the West's banker-driven debt. Mark Adomanis of Forbes wanted to have 2012 Presidential hopeful Mitt Romney take some cues from the Russian Federation but, alas, he did not.

> *As he is preparing for the next debate maybe Romney can spend some time reading about "Russia's flat tax miracle" or perhaps he could learn that Russia was part of the "global flat tax revolution" or perhaps even how Russia "more than doubled revenues from income taxes" after implementing a flat-tax. Romney could also stand to take a look at the Economist's Global Debt Clock which*

shows that Russia is one of the most fiscally responsible countries in the entire world. ~ Forbes[1087]

In Russia "food patriots" blow up bottles of soda[1088] and President Putin has vowed to protect Russians from genetically-modified organisms ("GMO's")[1089]. At least one source is claiming there is a complete ban on GMO's in Russia.[1090]

In Russia, pedophilia is not protected as a "sexual orientation"[1091] and it is illegal to entice children with homosexual recruiting propaganda.[1092]

One area Russia figures quiet well with the West, unfortunately, is in abortions. The Russian population is literally dying out. If only for sheer necessity, Vladimir Putin has vowed to push back the abortion culture, to give tax bonuses to couples who have kids[1093] and a recent Duma initiative outlawed abortion advertising in public.[1094]

Russia is the only major industrialized nation in the world that is actually *liberalizing* her strict gun laws. A recent move now allows all licensed citizens to carry firearms for personal protection.[1095]

Russia is starting to become wary of radicalized Islam and has prohibited the building of new mosques.[1096]

When terrorists threatened to disrupt the 2014 Winter Olympics in Sochi, authorities acted and several bodies showed up in vehicles wired with explosives. They had been shot and left to be found by police.[1097]

When Chechen warlord Doku Umarov threatened to drown the Sochi Olympics in Russian blood, he was killed.[1098]

Russians are many things but "inefficient" is not one of them. When an enemy is targeted, they are dealt with.

When a Russian oil tanker was seized in 2010 by Somali pirates, they were immediately captured but then "released".

> *The 10 pirates were captured last week after seizing a Russian oil tanker but were then unexpectedly released, with Russian officials saying there was insufficient legal basis to keep them in detention.*
>
> *"According to the latest information, the pirates who seized the Moscow University oil tanker failed to reach the shore. Evidently, they have all died," the high-ranking source was quoted as saying by all Russia's official news agencies.* ~ the Herald Sun[1099]

"The" Ukraine

If it seems like Russia is on the outside of the New World Order, what has been going on at her doorstep should confirm it.

Since 1991, Ukraine has been an independent, sovereign nation. Putting the article "the" in front relegates the nation to ancillary status and, according to the Ukrainian Declaration of Independence[1100] and Constitution[1101], it's incorrect.

Ukrainians still remember when Jesuit priest Joseph Stalin was killing 2,500 men, women and children each week by starving them to death[1102]. They want little to do with Communism and rightly so.

But the Slavic people of modern Ukraine, Russia and Belarus all share the common ancestry of Kievan Rus'—a territory started by the Varangians. The Varangians were a Germanic people who included Scandinavians and Anglo-Saxons.

In the late 9th century, a Varangian warrior named Oleg moved south from Novgorod and pushed the Turkish Khazars out as far as Kiev. This established the boundaries of Kievan Rus'.[1103]

Lithuania and Poland would later rule over the territory of Ukraine until the Turks reasserted themselves through the Ottoman Empire. The Tartars regularly raided Ukrainian and Russian villages to make slaves of their captives. They were opposed by a Slavic version of Greek Spartans known as Cossacks—a hearty rural community of warrior people.

During this time, Russia was growing in strength and eventually pushed the Ottomans back out, taking Crimea and its access to the Black Sea in 1783. There was tension between the two peoples but also co-operation amongst the kindred of Kievan Rus'.

> *After the Russians annexed the Crimean Khanate in 1783, the region called New Russia was settled by Ukrainian and Russian migrants.[49] Despite promises of autonomy in the Treaty of Pereyaslav, the Ukrainian elite and the Cossacks never received the freedoms and the autonomy they were expecting. However, within the Empire, Ukrainians rose to the highest Russian state and church offices.[a]* ~ Wikipedia[1104]

Then the Jesuits enacted their Red October revenge and in 1922, the Union of Soviet Social Republics was born. In it, the nation that had become "Ukraine" was now "the Ukrainian Soviet Socialist Republic".

The oppression of Communism was horribly exacerbated by Stalin's 1932-33 *Holodomor* ("extermination by hunger") purge.

The rise of Nazi Germany created an opportunity for some Ukrainians to break free of Stalin with the help of Adolf Hitler.

When WWII started, Hitler and Stalin were allies. But in 1941, Hitler launched an invasion of Russia and its origin can be found in the name he chose for the effort: "Operation Barbarossa".

FREDERICK I BARBAROSSA, ROMAN EMPEROR

Reign: March 4, 1152, to June 10, 1190; b.1122 or 1123, the son of Frederick II, Duke of Swabia, and Judith, the daughter of Henry the Black. His reddish-blond hair earned him the sobriquet "Barbarossa," which means "Red Beard" in Italian. In 1147 he became Duke of Swabia upon the death of his father and accompanied his uncle, Conrad III, on the unsuccessful Second Crusade. Frederick was elected king of Germany on March 4, 1152 after Conrad's death. His lineage made him an ideal choice to bring reconciliation to Germany...

Frederick hoped to reestablish the power of empire, which had been weakened during the struggle between popes and emperors during the eleventh and early twelfth centuries. After his coronation he predicted the restoration of the greatness of imperial Rome. He considered himself the heir of the caesars and had no difficulty including his own legislation with that of Justinian and the emperors of antiquity. He saw Roman law as a vehicle for extending his power, especially in regard to the papacy. Frederick called his state the sacrum imperium, or "Holy Empire," and he believed himself to have been chosen by God to foster an institution that was the cornerstone of world order, the source of peace and justice. ~ the New Catholic Encyclopedia[1105]

When he attacked, Ukrainians and Russians joined hands in Kiev, but they were outclassed. Prussians like Carl von Clausewitz had turned war into a fine science and it had become lightning-fast ("Blitzkrieg") thanks to technological innovations that were literally *generations* past other nations.

650,000 under-equipped and poorly-trained soldiers were surrounded in Kiev because Stalin refused to send help or allow them to fall back. The Siege of Kiev lasted from July until September of 1941. By August, the 1st Panzer Group of Generalfeldmarschall Ewald von Kleist joined the 2nd Panzer Group of Generaloberst Heinz Guderian and there was no way out.

Considered sub-human by the Germans, the captured soldiers were rarely fed, put to hard labor, and left to die of exposure.

Their hair became stuffing for mattresses. Skin became gloves. ...

In early 1945 the Red Army liberated many camps, often singing songs as they marched in. What was initially a joy for the surviving Soviet prisoners quickly turned bitter.

"Two Soviet officers approached, and one asked, 'So how did you live it up here, you whore?' He didn't even ask us how we survived. He grabbed a pistol and signaled me to get out." Tatiana Nanieva, Soviet Prisoner of War.

Officially, the USSR did not recognize it had any captured soldiers in German hands. In the eyes of the Soviet regime, a prisoner was both a coward and a traitor. Paranoia and shame motivated Stalin to order all two million Soviet POWs liberated in Germany to be tried. They were accused under article 58B: "Betrayal to the Motherland", and sent to the Gulags in Siberia. An estimated half of them died. ~ The Battle of Kiev, Jan Smith[1106]

Caught between Hitler and Stalin, the victims paid dearly.

The pro-Nazi, anti-Communist movement in Ukraine was led by Stepan Bandera. Bandera had been interred in a German concentration camp but was released in order to help win Ukraine for the Nazis. Bandera, himself, however ran the rebellion from Germany and never returned to Ukraine.

The Organization of Ukrainian Nationalists: Bandera faction (OUN-B), and later the Ukrainian Insurgent Army (*Ukrayins'ka Povstans'ka Armiya* or UPA), began committing genocide against ethnic Poles and Jews of any nationality.

The Soviets reacted just as viciously and may have slaughtered up to 100,000 Ukrainian nationalists, many of whom were not Nazis but simply wanted a free and independent Ukraine.

Bandera was assassinated by the KGB in 1959, poisoned in Germany where he lived and he has been a flawed symbol of Ukrainian independence ever since.[1107]

Today, any movement for a self-determinate Ukraine is indelibly linked to this Nazi past from the red and black flags of the "Right Sector" to the Wolfsangel of the Svoboda Party.

These are the forces Western Intelligence agencies and governments have gotten in bed with repeatedly in order to attack and destabilize Russia from her soft underbelly.

Bankers' Holiday

After the Soviet Union fell in 1991, sober-minded pols thought it best to secure nuclear weapons held in former Soviet protectorates like Ukraine. The new Russian Federation, U.S. and U.K. signed the Budapest Memorandum in 1994 which made provisions for Ukraine to send her nukes back to Russia to be dismantled and, in return, have her sovereignty respected by all of the signatories.[1108]

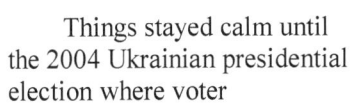

Ivan Bandura – Wikimedia Commons

The derivation of the Ukrainian Nationalist "Wolfsangle" (far right).

Things stayed calm until the 2004 Ukrainian presidential election where voter intimidation, corruption and electoral fraud drove many Ukrainians into the streets for mass demonstrations known as the Orange Revolution. Subsequent run-off elections reversed the winners, taking the presidency from Viktor Yanukovych and giving it to Viktor Yushchenko. Both men were former Communists and wealthy oligarchs, Yushchenko being a banker[1109], Yanukovych a career politician who's questionable business acquisitions brought him opulent wealth reminiscent of a Middle Eastern Sultan.[1110]

Yanukovych had played his cards well and had excellent relations with Russia and he was chosen by powerful players to win the '04 election Chicago style.[1111]

It was during the election that Yanukovych's opponent, Yushchenko, fell deathly ill from dioxin poisoning. The trail led back to Moscow.[1112]

Yushchenko survived (though his complexion was disfigured) and won the run-off election with 52% of the vote to Yanukovych's 44% thereby ending the Orange Revolution.

Yushchenko, however, would prove to be just as much a puppet, dancing on the strings of Western bankers.

> *Opposition candidate Viktor Yushchenko in the Ukrainian presidential elections is firmly backed by the Washington Consensus.*
>
> *He is not only supported by the IMF and the international financial community, he also has the endorsement of The National Endowment for Democracy (NED), Freedom House and the Open Society Institute, which played a behind the scenes role last year in helping "topple Georgia's president Eduard Shevardnadze by putting financial muscle and organizational metal behind his opponents." (New Statesman, 29 November 2004).* ~ Michel Chossudovsky, Global Research[1113]

"NED" is a CIA front operation.

> *Among the numerous Western foundations, the National Endowment for Democracy (NED), although not officially part of the CIA, performs an important intelligence function in shaping party politics in the former Soviet Union, Eastern Europe and around the World.*
>
> *NED was created in 1983, when the CIA was being accused of covertly bribing politicians and setting up phony civil society front organizations. According to Allen Weinstein, who was responsible for establishing the NED during the Reagan Administration: "A lot of what we do today was done covertly 25 years ago by the CIA." (Washington Post, Sept. 21, 1991).* ~ Chossudovsky[1114]

In short order, Yushchenko had Ukraine swimming in debt and prostrate before the International Monetary Fund[1115]. His treachery and connections to IMF puppeteers went back to the 90's.

Who is Viktor Yushchenko? He was the IMF-Sponsored Candidate.

> *In 1993, Viktor Yushchenko was appointed head of the newly-formed National Bank of Ukraine. Hailed as a "daring reformer", he was among the main architects of the IMF's deadly economic medicine which served to impoverish The Ukraine and destroy its economy.*
>
> *Following his appointment, the Ukraine reached a historical agreement with the IMF. Mr Yushchenko played a key role in*

negotiating the 1994 agreement as well as creating a new Ukrainian national currency, which resulted in a dramatic plunge in real wages. ~ Chossudovsky[1116]

In humiliating defeat, Yushchenko flubbed his re-election 6 years later in 2010 and allowed Yanukovych to "retake" the presidency. Ukrainians ousted the Western puppet in favor for the Eastern one and many had buyer's remorse after they fought so hard to put Yushchenko in power. Not even blatant U.S. propping could save him.

A U.S. university should reconsider a leadership award it recently presented to former President Viktor Yushchenko. The decision by the University of Kansas' Dole Institute of Politics to award ex-President Viktor Yushchenko with its 2011 "Leadership Prize" is puzzling.

In his citation for the $25,000 prize, institute director William Lacy notes that Yushchenko is "a great cultural and revolutionary icon," adding that "Yushchenko and the Orange Revolution ignited a fire for the people of Ukraine."

Missing from the text posted on the institute's website last week is that Yushchenko was voted out of office with a miserable 5 percent of the vote in January 2010 after spending his presidency fighting to destroy political rivals rather than fixing the nation. ~ Kyiv Post[1117]

Yanukovych quickly cashed in his chips and asked for "a favor" from President Putin in the vicinity of some $15,000,000,000 to start bailing out Ukraine's debt.[1118]

The second order of business for Yanukovych was to take care of Orange Revolution rival and two-time Prime Minister Yulia Volodymyrivna Tymoshenko.

Tymoshenko is a wealthy authoritarian who believes she's Eva Perón...literally. She's also a former Communist.

If Ukrainians were looking for "change", they weren't going to get it.

Kicking off her campaign this fall, Tymoshenko made sure, as always, to invoke her impoverished roots. "When I was starting out, there were seven of us living in one apartment," she said. "We dreamed of getting on our feet and getting our first apartment–our first personal square meters." She then assured the crowd that she could lead Ukraine through the current economic crisis. "I know

> *quite well what it means to live without water, gas, or heat. And that's why I will put an end to this."*
>
> *The story of a poor childhood is a stumping staple for Tymoshenko, whose fortune of several hundred million dollars is said to be squirreled away in British offshore accounts and gold bullion, and whose mansion is protected by an army of personal bodyguards.* ~ Julia Ioffe, New Republic[1119]

It wasn't hard for her political opponents to find crimes with which to charge her.

> *The criminal taint cited by detractors involves her stewardship of United Energy Systems, which in the middle-late 1990s controlled the supply of natural gas to Dnepropetrovsk, an important industrial city. U.S. charges brought in 2009 against Pavlo Lazarenko, a former Ukrainian prime minister, alleged that from 1995 to 1997, Tymoshenko funneled him about $97 million from the gas sales (pdf page 7). She herself may have received up to $40 million although that is spelled out nowhere. Everyone agrees, however, that she became wealthy.* ~ Steve LeVine, Quartz.com[1120]

In November 2013, Ukraine's Russian-minded Parliament voted against Tymoshenko receiving special medical treatment outside the country and then eschewed the extended banker hand of the European Union, moving instead to shore up ties with Russia.[1121]

Feeding on the unrest, Svoboda nationalists painted the trade agreement with the EU as a cure-all, which it couldn't possibly be.

The EU stepped in and offered to cover Ukraine's debt[1122] and U.S. Secretary of State John Kerry promised an additional $1,000,000,000 courtesy of the U.S. taxpayer.[1123]

What the hapless Ukrainians didn't realize was that, although they might be taken advantage of with Russia, they would be pilfered by the West.

> *According to a report in Kommersant—Ukraine, the finance ministry of Washington's stooges in Kiev who are pretending to be a government has prepared an economic austerity plan that will cut Ukrainian pensions from $160 to $80 so that Western bankers who lent money to Ukraine can be repaid at the expense of Ukraine's poor. It is Greece all over again.*

> *Before anything approaching stability and legitimacy has been obtained for the puppet government put in power by the Washington orchestrated coup against the legitimate, elected Ukraine government, the Western looters are already at work. Naive protesters who believed the propaganda that EU membership offered a better life are due to lose half of their pension by April. But this is only the beginning.*
>
> *The corrupt Western media describes loans as "aid." However, the 11 billion euros that the EU is offering Kiev is not aid. It is a loan. Moreover, it comes with many strings, including Kiev's acceptance of an IMF austerity plan.* ~ Paul Craig Roberts[1124]

As Western "aid" came in, Ukraine's gold went out.

> *...just as the State Department-facilitated coup against former president Victor Yanukovich was concluding...we reported of a strange incident that took place...namely that according to at least one source, "in a mysterious operation under the cover of night, Ukraine's gold reserves were promptly loaded onboard an unmarked plane, which subsequently took the gold to the US."*
>
> *In an interview on Ukraine TV, none other than the head of the Ukraine Central Bank made the stunning admission that "in the vaults of the central bank there is almost no gold left. There is a small amount of gold bullion left, but it's just 1% of reserves."* ~ Zero Hedge[1125]

Where There Is Unrest, There Is the CIA

After that vote against the EU in late 2013, the nationalist Svoboda Party was again enabled by foreign interference.

A video plea for help from a pretty Ukrainian protester went viral on YouTube. Later, it was found to have been created by the CIA.[1126]

The degree to which the CIA controls even mainstream media is disturbing. [italics suspended]

> In 1953, Joseph Alsop, then one of America's leading syndicated columnists, went to the Philippines to cover an election. He did not go because he was asked to do so by his syndicate. He did not go because he was asked to do so by the newspapers that printed his column. He went at the request of the CIA.
>
> Alsop is one of more than 400 American journalists who in the past

twenty-five years have secretly carried out assignments for the Central Intelligence Agency, according to documents on file at CIA headquarters. Some of these journalists' relationships with the Agency were tacit; some were explicit. There was cooperation, accommodation and overlap. Journalists provided a full range of clandestine services—from simple intelligence gathering to serving as go-betweens with spies in Communist countries. Reporters shared their notebooks with the CIA. Editors shared their staffs. Some of the journalists were Pulitzer Prize winners, distinguished reporters who considered themselves ambassadors without-portfolio for their country. Most were less exalted: foreign correspondents who found that their association with the Agency helped their work; stringers and freelancers who were as interested in the derring-do of the spy business as in filing articles; and, the smallest category, full-time CIA employees masquerading as journalists abroad. In many instances, CIA documents show, journalists were engaged to perform tasks for the CIA with the consent of the managements of America's leading news organizations.

The history of the CIA's involvement with the American press continues to be shrouded by an official policy of obfuscation and deception... ~ Carl Bernstein[1127]

Agent Provocateured

As with the reaction to the Snowden leaks, Machine insiders from both political parties showed they all answered to the same authority.

Republican John McCain joined with Democrat Dick Durbin[1128] and several other United States Senators and visited Kiev where they told Nazi rabble-rousers there that they were "inspiring the world".[1129]

After weeks of fighting, the elected Ukrainian leaders were ousted and the interim Prime Minister, Arseniy Yatsenyuk, was quickly given the royal carpet treatment by Barack Obama[1130]. Yatsenyuk is also a banker.

> *"Recall the phone exchange between the Ukraine ambassador and Victoria Nuland (Assistant Secretary of State for European Affairs) that got leaked out, where she basically said 'we want Yats in there.' They like him because he's pro Western," says Vladimir Signorelli, president of boutique investment research firm Bretton Woods Research LLC in New Jersey. "Yatsenyuk is the kind of technocrat you want if you want austerity, with the veneer of*

professionalism," Signorelli said. "He's the type of guy who can hobnob with the European elite. A Mario Monti type: unelected and willing to do the IMFs bidding," he said. ~ Kenneth Rapoza, Forbes[1131]

The political unrest so close to Russia's southern border did not elicit the same response as decades past.

In 1956, the CIA facilitated a revolt in Hungary against the Soviet Union promising aid to Hungarian Patriots. They were betrayed and brutally crushed.[1132]

With much more of an overt threat, Russia is under new management and not behaving as the Soviets of old.

After repeated trips to Kiev, handing out cookies to Nazis[1133], Barack Obama's Assistant Secretary of State for European and Eurasian Affairs at the State Department, Victoria Nuland, spoke for Chevron. Nuland admitted that the United States government has spent $5,000,000,000 helping to destabilize Ukraine.[1134]

Why Chevron? —Because they had just signed a large contract with Western bankers[1135] to rake the Ukrainian countryside with fracking.[1136,1137]

As things began to heat up in Kiev, the "protests" turned deadly.

The Russian news outlet RT reported on a phone conversation that was leaked to the network between EU Foreign Affairs chief Catherine Ashton and Estonia's Foreign Minister Urmas Paet. In the conversation, Paet stated that the snipers who did the killing were doing so on behalf of the "protestors" and killing on both sides.[1138]

Estonia is a Baltic state buffered from Ukraine by 3 other nations and 1,300 kilometers but is now a member of NATO and seems intensely interested (perhaps foolishly so) in poking at the very large neighbor on her eastern border.

Western boots were on the ground, from the Israeli Defense Forces[1139] to military contractors like Blackwater[1140] (now known as "ACADEMI").

At least one cellphone video purports to show Ukrainian Berkut Police interrogating a CIA agent from "Special Activities Division".[1141]

MH-17...Or Was It MH-370?

The idea that, today, a modern passenger jetliner could "disappear" from the military observation systems of all the major nations is patently absurd[1142]—yet that is what we were told regarding Malaysian Airlines flight 370.

A month before the "disappearance", CNN's "foremost international business correspondent" Richard Quest interviewed MH-370's First Officer, Fariq Ab Hamid as he made his transition flight in a Boeing 777 with a different crew.

Quest is an excellent example of a CNN professional journalist. In 2008, he was "busted in Central Park ... with some drugs in his pocket, a rope around his neck that was tied to his genitals, and a sex toy in his boot.[1143]" Crack reporters aren't needed, just crackpots that can make the Company line look good.

19 weeks later, almost to the day, another Malaysian Boeing 777, flight MH-17, was lost on July 17th, 2014—"7/17/2014".

It must again be stressed that the Luciferian world Elite are not normal human beings. They put great stock in numerology and time events to significant numbers in an effort to curry interdimensional favor.

International Monetary Fund Managing Director Christine Lagarde made this bizarre statement before the National Press Club on January 15th of 2014: [italics suspended]

> As you can tell, I do as I'm told and I thought I had to stand up at the time when my immediate predecessor would sit down and clearly I failed.
>
> Good afternoon, and thank you very much for having me with you. I would like to thank the National Press Club and especially President Angela Greiling Keane, for not only inviting me to this prestigious venue, but essentially presenting the outline of what I want to talk to you about now. So it's as if we had prepared that together, which we have not.
>
> Now, let me first of all, of course, begin by wishing you all a happy new year. I guess it's still time to do that, given that we are just exactly halfway through between our western new year and the lunar new year, which will loom in a few weeks' time.
>
> I think it's also appropriate to wish ourselves a happy new year given what I would like to talk to you about, which has to do with the global economy and what we should expect for 2014.

Now, I'm going to test your numerology skills by asking you to think about the magic seven, okay? Most of you will know that seven is quite a number in all sorts of themes, religions. And I'm sure that you can compress numbers as well. So if we think about 2014, all right, I'm just giving you 2014, you drop the zero, 14, two times 7. Okay, that's just by way of example, and we're going to carry on.

So 2014 will be a milestone and hopefully a magic year in many respects. It will mark the hundredth anniversary of the First World War back in 1914. It will note the 70th anniversary, drop the zero, seven— of the Breton Woods conference that actually gave birth to the IMF. And it will be the 25th anniversary of the fall of the Berlin Wall, 25th, okay. It will also mark the seventh anniversary of the financial market jitters that quickly turned into the greatest global economic calamity since the Great Depression.

The crisis still lingers. Yet, optimism is in the air. We've left the deep freeze behind us and the horizon looks just a bit brighter. So my hope and my wish for 2014 is 4 that after those seven miserable years, weak and fragile, we have seven strong years. I don't know whether the G7 will have anything to do with it, or whether it will be the G20.

I certainly hope that the IMF will have something to do with it.[1144]

This is a financial professional–the director of one of the most powerful institutions in the world—talking like a Wiccan priestess to a room full chuckling journalists. None of them pressed her on her statements.

Western governments in general and the United States in specific seem fixated on backing the Bear into the smallest most desperate corner they can.

War atrocities were committed by Western agents and literal Nazis on Russian citizens and sympathizers in Ukraine. Then Russia was expelled from the G8 Summit (formerly the G7) and the intent was to expel Russia from the G20, as well, but "BRICS" nations stopped it from happening.[1145]

MH-17 seemed to be the final false flag needed to light the fuze.

Was that what Lagarde was trying to communicate to anyone "in the know"?

As if on cue, Arizona Republican Senator John McCain stated provocatively that "Putin should pay" for MH-17.[1146]

Vice President Joe Biden said MH-17 "apparently had been shot down. Shot down. Not an accident. Blown out of the sky."[1147]

Biden's son, R. Hunter Biden would be rewarded for his father's loyalty with a seat on the Board of Directors of Burisma Holdings—Ukraine's largest gas producer.[1148]

Soon, however, the Western accusation that Russia had shot MH-17 down was shot full of holes. [1149]

- The Ukrainian government claimed to have intercepted "phone conversations" between pro-Russian rebels and uploaded their evidence to the premier venue for any investigative body—instantly recognized by any court of law: YouTube. There was only one problem, the time stamp was different from the supposed date and time of the conversation.
- A pile of brand-new, unscathed victim passports were found at the crash site, yet many of them had been punched or notched; what officials do to invalidate them.
- One rebel on-site remarked how bodies found didn't seem "fresh".
- The event occurred within hours of the Israeli invasion of Gaza, effectively blacking it out of the news cycle.
- The 10 previous MH-17 flights were all scheduled to travel well-clear of the off-limits warzone. That day, they flew right where they were not supposed to be and even lowered their elevation over the dangerous area to increase their vulnerability.
- Ukraine's SBU security service quickly confiscated recordings between air traffic control and the MH-17 crew.
- At least one, possibly 2, Ukrainian military aircraft were seen in close proximity to MH-17.
- A video of the supposed crash site shows streamers floating that appear to be radar chaff countermeasures implying military aircraft were there to either trick rebels into shooting or to down MH-17 directly.

This was on the heels of an unprecedented war atrocity in Odessa, Ukraine.

A tent city of pro-Russian protestors was attacked and driven into the Trade Union House and then sealed off. They were methodically tortured, women were raped, a pregnant woman was strangled. All of them were burned but some of them were likely burned alive.[1150,1151]

The Associated Press listed the dead at "dozens"[1152] though real numbers will never be known.

This despicable crime was carefully planned by Ukrainian Nazis and their CIA backers.

It had the clear purpose of goading Vladimir Putin into war, but Russians play chess, not checkers.

The Rise of Saint George

Today's official flag of the Russian Federation depicts the Imperial Coat of Arms of the Romanovs and the Czars—the double-headed eagle.

It is a symbol adopted by the Roman and Byzantine Empires to acknowledge the dual authority of the herald—both temporal and spiritual.[1153]

As with all powerful symbols, it has been appropriated by the Freemasons.

> *As a Masonic symbol this device is time honoured and appropriate. It is no less the badge of the Grand Inspector and Sublime Prince than that of the Grand Elect Knight. As the symbol of the Inspector it suggests an equal contemplation of both sides of a question-and thus, judicial balance. It is seen as the fitting emblem of an elect knight in ancient religious engravings, and to the exclusion of the cross itself, it appears upon the banners of the knight and prince who behold the apparition of the virgin and child of the rosary. And, as in ancient Mesopotamia, the double eagle is here associated with the sun symbol in the form of the Chaldean Elu, which the knight and prince wear, evidently with the same ancient meaning: "The light toward which my eyes are turned."*
>
> *Thus does the double-headed eagle stand today for that which it stood in ancient days, its two heads, facing the Ultimate Sun, reminding men and Masons that there is yet even "more light" for the pilgrim who travels East, and in whose heart is the motto,*
>
> *"SPES MEA IN DEO EST.*[dd]*"* ~ the Masonic Dictionary[1154]

[dd] "God is your only hope." Luciferian mocking or "loyalty amongst thieves"?

These associations are troubling.

Yet, on the chest of the eagle is a shield upon which is the likeness of Saint George who, according to the *Golden Legend* of Jacobus de Voragine, saved the daughter of the king of Silene by slaying a dragon that the townspeople were feeding their children to for appeasement.

Will George rise again from the heart of Kievan Rus' to slay the power of the Dragon?

Does the Dragon feed on children today...?

Endnotes

[919] *Catholic and Libertarian? Pope's Top Adviser Says They're Incompatible*, David Gibson, 3 June 2014, Religion News Service
http://www.religionnews.com/2014/06/03/catholic-libertarian-popes-top-adviser-says-theyre-incompatible/

[920] *David*, William Hoffman, Dell (1971), p. 29

[921] *Catholicism and Libertarianism Clash Over Property and the Common Good*, Elizabeth Stoker Bruenig, 12 September 2014, the National Catholic Reporter
http://ncronline.org/blogs/distinctly-catholic/catholicism-and-libertarianism-clash-over-property-and-common-good

[922] *ibid*

[923] Litterae Encyclicae, *Studiorum Ducem*, Pius PP. XI, 29 June 1923, vatican.va
http://www.vatican.va/holy_father/pius_xi/encyclicals/documents/hf_p-xi_enc_19230629_studiorum-ducem_lt.html

[924] *Ex Cathedra*, Catholic Encyclopedia
http://www.newadvent.org/cathen/05677a.htm

[925] *The Humanities and Social Sciences Network* online, h-net.org
http://www.h-net.org/

[926] Robert H. Jackson *Curriculum Vitae*
http://www.bu.edu/polisci/files/people/faculty/jackson/CV.pdf

[927] *The Jesuit Missions of Paraguay, Argentina, and Brazil*, Robert H. Jackson
http://www.h-net.org/~latam/powerpoints/JesuitMissions.pdf

[928] *Liam Neeson Interview: Hard Man Actor on Bono, Ralph Fiennes and His Fear of Guns*, Gill Pringle, 12 September 2014, the Independent
http://www.independent.co.uk/arts-entertainment/films/features/liam-neeson-interview-hard-man-actor-on-bono-ralph-fiennes-and-his-fear-of-guns-9728838.html#

And what do we have here? This Euro-tard has taken up with Irish Catholic propped-up poop star Bone-O. The piece of shit isn't "afraid" of all the f__king *money* "guns" make for him.

[929] To date, I have no hard evidence (barring an official Knight of Malta roll) but De Niro's career certainly has a Jesuit smell to it—particularly wafting with a CIA stench into the nostrils.

De Niro was to have a starring role alongside *"Sir"* Anthony Hopkins in a movie project about the siege of Malta but it was put on hold in 2005:
Knights of Malta on Hold, Robert Micallef, 12 February 2005, MaltaMedia.com
http://www.dailymalta.com/wt/2005/02/knights-of-malta-on-hold.html

De Niro is also extremely intimate with the Catholic Intelligence Agency.
De Niro's Go-To CIA Guy, Daniel Epstein, 2 April 2007, the Constantine Report
http://www.constantinereport.com/three-stars-on-friendly-terms-with-the-cia-jennifer-garner-rachael-seymour-robert-de-niro/

[930] *Robert De Niro on Movie Violence, Gun Control, and Newtown*, Jennifer Vineyard, 21 December 2012, NY Magazine
http://nymag.com/daily/intelligencer/2012/12/robert-de-niro-gun-control-newtown-movie-violence.html

[931] *The Jesuit Missions of Paraguay, Argentina, and Brazil*, Robert H. Jackson
http://www.h-net.org/~latam/powerpoints/JesuitMissions.pdf

[932] *ibid*
[933] *Jesuit Reduction > History*, Wikipedia.org
http://en.wikipedia.org/wiki/Jesuit_reduction#History
[934] *The Enemy Unmasked*, Bill Hughes, Truth Triumphant (2004), p. 5
[935] *Real Social Justice*, Ryan Messmore, 26 November 2010, the "interreligious, nonpartisan research and education institute" First Things.com
http://www.firstthings.com/web-exclusives/2010/11/real-social-justice
[936] *Luigi Taparelli and Catholic Economics*, Thomas C. Behr, Faculty Director of Liberal Studies, University of Houston, Journal of Markets & Morality, Volume 14, Number 2 (Fall 2011), pp. 607–611
[937] *Rerum Novarum*, Encyclical of Pope Leo XIII on Capital and Labor, Vatican.va
http://www.vatican.va/holy_father/leo_xiii/encyclicals/documents/hf_l-xiii_enc_15051891_rerum-novarum_en.html
[938] *Prominent Russians: Peter III*, Alyona Kipreeva, Russiapedia, RT
http://russiapedia.rt.com/prominent-russians/the-romanov-dynasty/peter-iii/
[939] The American Historical Review > Vol. 21, No. 1, Oct., 1915 > *Catherine II and The American Revolution*, Frank Golder, Oxford University Press, p. 93-96
[940] *Blood and Treasure for the Benefit of Private Interests?* Bob Djurdjevic, 4 May 1997, the Washington Times, archived at Bob's blog, here:
http://www.truthinmedia.org/Columns/Blood%20Treasure%20for%20Private%20Interests.html
[941] *Kasata Zakonu*, Jezuici.pl, the Official Website of the Society of Jesus in Poland
http://jezuici.pl/kasata-zakonu/
[942] *Alexander I*, Linda DeLaine, 17 October 2005, Russian Life
http://www.russianlife.com/blog/alexander-i/
[943] History of Russia Heads of the State > The Romanovs > Emperor Nicholas I (1796-1855), RuHistory
http://ruhistory.narod.ru/history/tsar/romanovs/Nikolay1.html
[944] *Biographies - Alexander II The Tsar Liberator*, Nick Nicolason, the Alexander Palace Time Machine
http://www.alexanderpalace.org/palace/AlexIIbio.html
[945] *St Petersburg: Paris of the North or City of Bones?* Andrew Osborn, 8 July 2006, the Independent
http://www.independent.co.uk/news/world/europe/st-petersburg-paris-of-the-north-or-city-of-bones-407069.html
[946] *Union of Liberation*, Encyclopædia Britannica
http://www.britannica.com/EBchecked/topic/339206/Union-of-Liberation
[947] *Karl Marx*, Biography.com
http://www.biography.com/#!/people/karl-marx-9401219
[948] *Social Justice: Theft to All*, Carl Teichrib, 23 February 2011, Forcing Change
http://forcingchange.wordpress.com/2011/02/23/social-justice-theft-to-all/
[949] *Karl Marx: A Life*, Francis Wheen, W. W. Norton & Company (2001), p. 8
[950] *Union of Liberation*, Wikipedia.org
http://en.wikipedia.org/wiki/Union_of_Liberation
[951] Russian Review > Vol. 33, No. 1, January 1974 > The Statutes of the Union of Liberation, Terence Emmons

http://www.jstor.org/discover/10.2307/127623?uid=2129&uid=2&uid=70&uid=4&sid=2 1104797393313

[952] *Mass Grave in Moscow Suburbs is Among Russia's Holiest Sites*, Alexander Annin, 6 May 2014, The Moscow Times
http://www.themoscowtimes.com/art_n_ideas/article/mass-grave-in-moscow-suburbs-is-among-russias-holiest-sites/499598.html

[953] *Peter Berngardovich Struve*, Wikipedia.org
http://en.wikipedia.org/wiki/Peter_Struve

[954] *"Bloody Sunday" in St Petersburg*, Richard Cavendish, History Today, Volume: 55, Issue: 1, 2005
http://www.historytoday.com/richard-cavendish/%E2%80%98bloody-sunday%E2%80%99-st-petersburg

[955] *Descent Into Darkness*, James Zatko, University of Notre Dame Press (1963), p. 111

[956] *Herod the Great: A Life of Intrigue, Architecture, and Cruelty*, Staff, Forerunner magazine, May-June 2008, posted here:
http://www.cgg.org/index.cfm/fuseaction/Library.sr/CT/ARTB/k/1387/Herod-Great.htm

[957] *Napoleon Bonaparte*, Robert Wilde, About.com
http://europeanhistory.about.com/od/bonapartenapoleon/a/bionapoleon.htm

[958] *The Rise of Adolf Hitler*, the History Place.com
http://www.historyplace.com/worldwar2/riseofhitler/born.htm

[959] *Joseph Stalin*, Stephanie L. McKinney, About.com
http://history1900s.about.com/od/people/ss/Stalin_2.htm

[960] *History, Lies, FDR, and Stalin*, Mark Stoval, 10 January 2013, On The Mark blog
http://markstoval.wordpress.com/2013/01/10/history-lies-fdr-and-stalin/
Not a good news or history citation but this gets the point across from someone other than me, which is why I rely so heavily on citing. Opinions are like a-holes.

[961] *Joseph Stalin*, One-Evil.org
http://one-evil.org/content/people_20c_stalin.html

[962] *How Many People Did Joseph Stalin Kill?* Palash Ghosh, 5 March 2013, International Business Times
http://www.ibtimes.com/how-many-people-did-joseph-stalin-kill-1111789

[963] *Mao: The Unknown Story*, Jung Chang and Jon Halliday, Jonathan Cape (2005)
These authors err on the side of conservatism putting the death toll at 70 million but my next citation proves that's too low.

[964] *Madman Who Starved 60 Million To Death: Devastating Book Reveals How Mao's Megalomania Turned China Into A Madhouse*, Tony Rennell, 22 July 2011, the Daily Mail
http://www.dailymail.co.uk/news/article-2017839/Madman-starved-60-million-death-Devastating-book-reveals-Maos-megalomania-turned-China-madhouse.html

[965] *Stalin's Forced Famine 1932-33*, The History Place
http://www.historyplace.com/worldhistory/genocide/stalin.htm

[966] *The Iron Curtain Over America*, John Beaty, Angriff (1951), p. 40

[967] *Chronological Tables: Comprehending the Chronology and History of the World, from the Earliest Records to the Close of the Russian War, Volume 2*, R. Griffin, Richard Griffin and Company (1857), p. 21

[968] *What If An Ex-KGB Officer Predicted That The USSR Would Fake Its Own Collapse To Ultimately Defeat The West...And No One Listened?* Benjamin Weingarten, 19 March 2014, The Blaze

http://www.theblaze.com/blog/2014/03/19/what-if-an-ex-kgb-officer-predicted-that-the-ussr-would-fake-its-own-collapse-to-ultimately-defeat-the-west-and-no-one-listened/

[969] *German Adviser Andreas Gives His Views on the CIA's KGB Officer Anatoli Golitsyn*, Eric Jon Phelps, 18 April 2011, Vatican Assassins.org
http://vaticanassassins.org/2011/04/18/german-adviser-andreas-gives-his-views-on-the-cias-kgb-officer-anatoli-golitsyn/

[970] *The Catholic Church in Crisis*, John McManus, 9 June 1997, The New American, archived here:
http://www.fisheaters.com/forums/index.php?topic=2940508.0

[971] *San Francisco History*, San Francisco.com
http://www.sanfrancisco.com/history/

[972] *Representative John Murtha*, AND NOW HE'S DEAD, "the longest-serving member of Congress in Pennsylvania history", Gawker.com
http://gawker.com/5466935/representative-john-murtha
    Reap what you have sown, spawn.

[973] *Nancy Pelosi: One of Mikhail Gorbachev's Most Useful Idiots*, Judi McLeod, 16 November 2006, Canada Free Press
http://www.canadafreepress.com/2006/ans-cover-news111506.htm

[974] *Rewarding Terrorism, Deception in Kosovo*, Andy Wilcoxson, 14 January 2008, World Net Daily
http://www.wnd.com/2008/01/45527/

[975] *How a President, Distracted by Scandal, Entered Balkan War*, Elaine Sciolino and Ethan Bronner, 18 April 1999, New York Times
http://partners.nytimes.com/library/world/europe/041899kosovo-recap1.html

[976] *Kosovo Leaders Have Been Accused of Killing and Harvesting Organs*, John Dyer, 30 July 2014, Vice.com
https://news.vice.com/article/kosovo-leaders-have-been-accused-of-killing-and-harvesting-organs

[977] *Victims Found In Mass Graves In Ukraine Lack Internal Organs*, unattributed, 25 September 2014, Pravda
http://english.pravda.ru/hotspots/crimes/25-09-2014/128612-ukraine_organ_trafficking-0/

[978] *New Rotation Of Soldiers Heads To Kosovo*, Steven Beardsley, 5 September 2012, Stars and Stripes
http://www.stripes.com/news/new-rotation-of-soldiers-heads-to-kosovo-1.188162

[979] *National Guard State Partnership Program*, United States European Command
http://www.eucom.mil/key-activities/partnership-programs/national-guard-state-partnership-program

[980] *No, American Weakness Didn't Encourage Putin to Invade Ukraine*, Peter Beinart, 3 March 2014, the Atlantic
http://www.theatlantic.com/international/archive/2014/03/no-american-weakness-didnt-encourage-putin-to-invade-ukraine/284168/
    It's funny because this guy is a Libtard running to defend his messiah but the truth serves us in a different way here.

[981] *Creating Another Muslim Foothold In Europe*, Mike Scruggs, undated, the Tribune Papers, archived here:

http://www.ashevilletribune.com/asheville/terrorism/MUSLIM-FOOTHOLD.htm
[982] *Russia Presses For Diplomatic Role In Conflict*, Terry Atlas and Charles M. Madigan, 14 April 1999, the Chicago Tribune
http://articles.sun-sentinel.com/1999-04-14/news/9904140098_1_russian-leaders-russian-role-nato-strikes
[983] *Vladimir Putin's Early Life*, YourNation.org
http://yournation.org/vladimir-putins-early-life/
[984] *Media Talk; Putin's Memoirs Set for Publication in U.S.*, Doreen Carvajal, 20 March 2000, New York Times
http://www.nytimes.com/2000/03/20/business/media-talk-putin-s-memoirs-set-for-publication-in-us.html
[985] Presidents of Russia. Biographies: Vladimir Vladimirovich Putin, Kremlin.ru
http://eng.state.kremlin.ru/president/allbio
[986] *How Vladimir Putin Stashed Away A Secret $70 Billion Personal Fortune*, Brian Warner, 23 July 2014, Celebrity Networth
http://www.celebritynetworth.com/articles/celebrity/how-vladimir-putin-stashed-away-a-secret-70-billion-personal-fortune/
[987] *ibid*
[988] *David Cameron > Family*, Wikipedia.org
http://en.wikipedia.org/wiki/David_Cameron#Family
[989] *Lord James of Blackheath questions $15 trillion scam in House of Lords on February 16, 2012*, Johnny Cirucci YouTube
https://www.youtube.com/watch?&v=-mL97np0PlM
[990] *HSBC "Held Offshore Accounts For Criminals"*, Rob Davies, 9 November 2012, Mail
http://www.dailymail.co.uk/news/article-2230349/HSBC-accused-setting-thousands-tax-evading-accounts-Jersey-including-drugs-arms-dealers.html
[991] *Boris Yeltsin's Daughter Attacks Vladimir Putin*, Andrew Osborn, 23 January 2010, the Telegraph
http://www.telegraph.co.uk/news/worldnews/europe/7063201/Boris-Yeltsins-daughter-attacks-Vladimir-Putin.html
[992] *Oligarchs, Mandelson and Osborne*, Jeremy Warner, 22 October 2008, The Independent [taken down but archived at the Patriot Post]
http://johnnycirucci.com/wp/blog/2015/01/02/oligarchs-mandelson-and-osborne/
[993] *The Silent Coup: Putin vs. the Oligarchs*, Justin Cowgill, 28 July 2000, National Vanguard
http://nationalvanguard.org/2012/05/the-silent-coup-putin-vs-the-oligarchs/
[994] *Russian State TV Channel Says Let's Make a Deal*, Alessandra Stanley, 26 July 1995, New York Times
http://www.nytimes.com/1995/07/26/world/russian-state-tv-channel-says-let-s-make-a-deal.html?n=Top%2fReference%2fTimes%20Topics%2fSubjects%2fT%2fTelevision
[995] *Profile: Boris Berezovsky*, unattributed, 31 May 2007, BBC News
http://news.bbc.co.uk/2/hi/europe/6708103.stm
[996] *Britain Gives Berezovsky Political Asylum*, Catherine Belton, 11 September 2003, The Moscow Times
http://www.themoscowtimes.com/news/article/britain-gives-berezovsky-political-asylum/235961.html

Interesting date for this event. I guess the little Jewish oligarch was a Luciferian Weapon of Mass Destruction that had petered out.
[997] *U.S. Officials Challenge Putin Over Snowden Claims, Push For Extradition*, unattributed, 25 June 2013, Fox News
http://www.foxnews.com/politics/2013/06/25/russian-official-balks-at-us-extradition-demand-for-snowden/
[998] *Boris Berezovsky Inquest Returns Open Verdict On Death*, Ian Cobain, 27 March 2014, The Guardian
http://www.theguardian.com/world/2014/mar/27/boris-berezovsky-inquest-open-verdict-death
[999] *Radiation Poisoning Killed Ex-Russian Spy*, Alan Cowell, 24 November 2006, New York Times
http://www.nytimes.com/2006/11/24/world/europe/25spycnd.html?_r=0
[1000] *Triple Agent! Poisoned Russian Spy Alexander Litvinenko Was Working for British AND Spanish Intelligence, Says Wife*, Ryan Kisiel and Sam Greenhill, 13 December 2012, the Daily Mail
http://www.dailymail.co.uk/news/article-2247486/Alexander-Litvinenko-Poisoned-Russian-spy-working-British-AND-Spanish-intelligence-says-wife.html
[1001] *Ex-KGB in Russia Probe*, unattributed, 27 August 1999, CNN Money
http://money.cnn.com/1999/08/27/worldbiz/russia_probe/
[1002] *Boris Yeltsin's Daughter Attacks Vladimir Putin*, Andrew Osborn, 23 January 2010, the Telegraph
http://www.telegraph.co.uk/news/worldnews/europe/7063201/Boris-Yeltsins-daughter-attacks-Vladimir-Putin.html
[1003] *Russia's Vladimir Putin Admits Wildlife Stunts Are Staged*, Gleb Bryanski and Denis Dyomkin, 13 September 2012, Reuters
http://www.reuters.com/article/2012/09/13/us-russia-putin-critic-idUSBRE88C17T20120913
[1004] *The Religion And Political Views Of Vladimir Putin*, Tom Kershaw 16 January 2013, The Hollowverse
http://hollowverse.com/vladimir-putin/
[1005] *Vladimir Putin: the Mysterious Love Life of Russia's President*, unattributed, 3 April 2014, the Week
http://www.theweek.co.uk/people/57992/vladimir-putin-mysterious-love-life-russias-president
[1006] George W., Knight of Eulogia, Alexandra Robbins, 1 May 2000, the Atlantic
http://www.theatlantic.com/magazine/archive/2000/05/george-w-knight-of-eulogia/304686/
"Magog" was Bush President #1's Skull and Bones name.
[1007] *George Bush Picture with Johnny Gosch 2 years after he was Kidnapped*, Let's Roll Forums
http://letsrollforums.com/george-bush-picture-johnny-t16214.html
Has HW been implicated in the kidnapping of little boys who are tortured by the CIA and turned into sex slaves for men like him? Read on!
[1008] *Pussy Riot - Band or Propaganda Ploy?* Henry Makow, 21 August 2012, HenryMakow.com
http://www.henrymakow.com/medi-whores-go-ape-over.html

[1009] *Pussy Riot!: A Punk Prayer For Freedom*, Paperback– February 5, 2013 by Pussy Riot (Author), Amazon.com
http://www.amazon.com/Pussy-Riot-Punk-Prayer-Freedom/dp/1558618341/ref=pd_bxgy_m_text_z

[1010] *Pussy Riot*, Nutgun (Artist) Format: Audio CD, Amazon.com
http://www.amazon.com/Pussy-Riot-Nutgun/dp/B00F9JFIR2

[1011] *Pussy Riot Nomination Splits Politicians, Scholars*, Jennifer Stange, 9 November 2012, DW.de
http://www.dw.de/pussy-riot-nomination-splits-politicians-scholars/a-16338892

[1012] **WARNING: GRAPHIC**
The VOINA Art-Group («War»). Actions 2006 – 2013, plucer.LiveJournal.com
http://plucer.livejournal.com/266853.html

[1013] *Pussy Riot Connections to Soros*, Jonathon Blakeley 18 August 2012, deLiberation.info
http://www.deliberation.info/pussy-riot-connections-to-soros/

[1014] *Pussy Riot - Band or Propaganda Ploy?* Henry Makow, 21 August 2012, HenryMakow.com
http://www.henrymakow.com/medi-whores-go-ape-over.html

[1015] *Tweeted Pic of Hillary Clinton and Pussy Riot Goes Viral*, 5 April 2014, EDGE Publications
http://www.edgeboston.com/news/national/News/157444/tweeted_pic_of_hillary_clinton_and_pussy_riot_goes_viral

For a "viral" pic, this article from "EDGE"—the same nice Boston perverts who bring you "Homotech" and "YouShoot"—there are ZERO "likes" and ZERO comments.

[1016] *An Open Letter To Hillary Clinton By Juanita Broaddrick*, apfn.org
http://www.apfn.org/apfn/juanita.htm

[1017] *Femen Activists Cut Down Cross In Kyiv*, unattributed, 17 August 2012, Radio Free Europe/Radio Liberty
http://www.rferl.org/content/ukraine-femen-cross-pussy-riot/24679942.html

[1018] *Belgium: FEMEN Suck Dildos in Putin's Name*, LiveLeak
http://www.liveleak.com/view?i=ff1_1401887364

[1019] *European Broadcasting Union*, Wikipedia.org
http://en.wikipedia.org/wiki/European_Broadcasting_Union

[1020] *European Broadcasting Union: Seeking An Alternative To Licence Fee Funding?* the London School of Economics and Political Science, 3 May 2013
http://blogs.lse.ac.uk/mediapolicyproject/2013/05/03/european-broadcasting-union-seeking-an-alternative-to-licence-fee-funding/

[1021] *Russian Backlash Over Transvestite Eurovision Winner Intensifies*, 12 May 2014, the Calvert Journal
http://calvertjournal.com/news/show/2479/russia-expresses-outrage-over-transvestite-singer-winning-eurovision

[1022] *Putin's Advisor on Ukraine*, Mark Hackard, 25 July 2014, Soul of the East.org
http://souloftheeast.org/2014/07/25/a-putin-advisor-speaks-ukraine/

[1023] *REX: Carl Bildt Thinks Eastern Orthodoxy Is Main Threat To Western Civilization*, reposted at Agora Dialogue
http://agora-dialogue.com/rex-carl-bildt-thinks-eastern-orthodoxy-is-main-threat-to-western-civilisation/

[1024] *West Moves Away From Russia as the Country Returns to Orthodoxy, Lavrov Believes*, Interfax, 5 June 2014
http://www.interfax-religion.com/?act=news&div=11308
[1025] *Lukashenko: If We Lose Christian Values – We Lose Everything*, Interfax, 5 June 2014, Pravmir
http://www.pravmir.com/lukashenko-lose-christian-values-lose-everything/
[1026] *Russia to Build Two Nuclear Plants in Iran*, unattributed, 30 August 2014, World Bulletin
http://www.worldbulletin.net/news/143437/russia-to-build-two-nuclear-plants-in-iran
[1027] *China and Russia Conduct Military Drills Together in Northern China*, Leon Siciliano, 29 August 2014, the Telegraph
http://www.telegraph.co.uk/news/worldnews/asia/china/11063276/China-and-Russia-conduct-military-drills-together-in-Northern-China.html
[1028] *BRICS Establish $100bn Bank And Currency Pool To Cut Out Western Dominance*, unattributed, 15 July 2014, Russia Today
http://rt.com/business/173008-brics-bank-currency-pool/
[1029] *Not a Single Christian Church Left in Afghanistan*, Says State Department, Edwin Mora, 10 October 2011, CNS News
http://www.cnsnews.com/news/article/not-single-christian-church-left-afghanistan-says-state-department
[1030] *Libya Imposes Sharia Laws*, Ekaterina Ryzhkova, 12 December 2013, New Eastern Outlook
http://journal-neo.org/2013/12/12/rus-liviya-vvodit-shariat/
[1031] *Gunmen Go Door-to-Door to Find and Execute Christians in Libya*, Morgan Lee, 25 February 2014, the Christian Post
http://www.christianpost.com/news/gunmen-go-door-to-door-to-find-and-execute-christians-in-libya-115136/
[1032] *Pope Tawadros II Says Christians Continue to Flee Egypt, Urges Against "Foreign Interference"*, unattributed, 30 August 2014, the Christian Post
http://www.christianpost.com/news/pope-tawadros-ii-says-christians-continue-to-flee-egypt-urges-against-foreign-interference-103334/
[1033] *Brotherhood Supporters Place X Marks on Coptic Homes*, Raymond Ibrahim, 29 August 2013, Raymond Ibrahim.cob
http://www.raymondibrahim.com/muslim-persecution-of-christians/brotherhood-supporters-place-x-marks-on-coptic-homes/
[1034] *The Silent Extermination of Iraq's "Christian Dogs"* Raymond Ibrahim, 19 April 2011, Frontpage magazine
http://www.frontpagemag.com/2011/raymond-ibrahim/the-silent-extermination-of-iraq%E2%80%99s-%E2%80%98christian-dogs%E2%80%99/
[1035] *Wesley Clark: U.S. Military Plan To Overthrow 7 Countries In 5 Years*, Johnny Cirucci YouTube
https://www.youtube.com/watch?v=Xmms5Eoixfs&
[1036] *Putin Stands Up To G8 Warmongers On Syria, Reaffirming Support For Assad Govt.*, unattributed, 19 June 2013, Press TV
http://www.presstv.com/detail/2013/06/19/309757/putin-draws-red-line-on-syria/
[1037] *While Obama Plays Golf, Putin Defends Liberty*, Judson Philips, 16 August 2014, Washington Times

http://communities.washingtontimes.com/neighborhood/judson-phillips-cold-hard-truth/2013/aug/16/playing-golf-and-helping-americas-enemies/#!
[1038] *Putin's Russia*, William F. Jasper, 22 January 2007, New American
http://www.thenewamerican.com/world-news/europe/item/8420-putins-russia
[1039] *Did Vladimir Putin meet Ronald Reagan as an Undercover KGB Man?* Adrian Blomfield, 19 March 2009, the Telegraph
http://www.telegraph.co.uk/news/worldnews/northamerica/usa/5017264/Did-Vladimir-Putin-meet-Ronald-Reagan-as-an-undercover-KGB-man.html
[1040] *Prominent Russians: Felix Dzerzhinsky*, Russiapedia, RT
http://russiapedia.rt.com/prominent-russians/politics-and-society/felix-dzerzhinsky/
[1041] *National Anthem of Russia*, Wikipedia.org
http://en.wikipedia.org/wiki/National_Anthem_of_Russia
[1042] *Gale Encyclopedia of Biography: Alexander Isayevich Solzhenitsyn*, Answers.com
http://www.answers.com/topic/aleksandr-solzhenitsyn
[1043] *Warning to the West (Words of Warning to the Western World)*, Alexander Solzhenitsyn, 17 January 2007, Orthodoxy Today.org
http://www.orthodoxytoday.org/articles7/SolzhenitsynWarning.php
[1044] *Alexander Solzhenitsyn – Modern Day Prophet, Moral Crusader, Critic of Both West and East*, John Jalsevac, undated, Catholic Culture
http://www.catholicculture.org/culture/library/view.cfm?recnum=8372
Yes, I cited a Catholic source. We're against the *institution* of Rome, not the people beguiled by her wiles.
[1045] *Russian Revelations: Putting Putin In Perspective*, Joseph Pearce, 13 March 2014, International Business Times
http://www.ibtimes.com/russian-revelations-putting-putin-perspective-1561224
[1046] *Alexander Dugin*, Metapedia
http://en.metapedia.org/wiki/Alexander_Dugin
"Metapedia" bills itself as the "electronic encyclopedia about culture, art, science, philosophy and politics..."
[1047] *The Fourth Political Theory*, Alexander Dugin, Arktos Media Ltd (2012)
[1048] Alexander Dugin, 29 June 2014, vk.com
http://vk.com/duginag?w=wall18631635_3186
If you've come to check this reference, you'll need to translate it. My current favorite is the Microsoft engine that is available via Bing Translator. Just paste the hyperlink in the "translate" field and hit the "translate" button.
[1049] *Vladimir Pozner*, Wikipedia.org
http://en.wikipedia.org/wiki/Vladimir_Pozner
[1050] *Two Titans Meet: Can This Be Democracy?* The Russia Project
http://www.russiaproject.org/part2/titans/pozner.html
[1051] *Phil Donahue Net Worth*, Celebrity Networth.com
http://www.celebritynetworth.com/richest-celebrities/phil-donahue-net-worth/
[1052] Interview of Alexander Dugin by Vladimir Pozner for his Russia Channel 1 show "Pozner", can currently be found on the YouTube channel of Ariano Grau with English subtitles under the title of *Vladimir Pozner Interviews Alexander Dugin*:
https://www.youtube.com/watch?&v=tPkEDRSYUpo
[1053] *First English Translation of Putin's Victory Speech*, Max Atkinson, 3 July 2012, the Huffington Post

http://www.huffingtonpost.co.uk/max-atkinson/first-english-translation_b_1324966.html

    The speech can be watched with what appears to be YouTube-added subtitles that aren't as forceful, at *isselman2000's channel* YouTube, *Putin's Victory Speech 2012 (With English Subtitles)*:
https://www.youtube.com/watch?&v=3oMuEo4eDw

[1054] *Putin's New Climate Taskforce Debates Russian Policy Options*, Olga Dobrovidova, 22 February 2013, Responding to Climate Change
http://www.rtcc.org/2013/02/22/putins-new-climate-taskforce-debates-russian-policy-options/

[1055] *Putin Ponders Climate Change in Arctic*, Darya Korsunskaya, 23 August 2010, The Globe and Mail
http://www.theglobeandmail.com/news/world/putin-ponders-climate-change-in-arctic/article1213134/

[1056] *Climategate: The Final Nail In The Coffin Of "Anthropogenic Global Warming"?* James Delingpole, 20 November 2009, the Telegraph
http://blogs.telegraph.co.uk/news/jamesdelingpole/100017393/climategate-the-final-nail-in-the-coffin-of-anthropogenic-global-warming/

[1057] *Climategate: Was Russian Secret Service Behind Email Hacking Plot?* unattributed, 6 December 2009, the Telegraph
http://www.telegraph.co.uk/earth/copenhagen-climate-change-confe/6746370/Climategate-was-Russian-secret-service-behind-email-hacking-plot.html

[1058] *Time to Tackle Global Warming Running Out, Pope Tells Climate Summit*, Carol Glatz, 11 December 2014, Catholic News Service
http://www.catholicregister.org/home/international/item/19357-time-to-tackle-global-warming-running-out-pope-tells-climate-summit

[1059] *Putin at Valdai - World Order: New Rules or a Game without Rules* (FULL VIDEO), RussiaToday YouTube
https://www.youtube.com/watch?v=9F9pQcqPdKo

[1060] *Гейм овер, или как Путин отправил мировую политику на пенсию.* chipstone.livejournal.com
http://chipstone.livejournal.com/1219546.html

[1061] *Putin to Western elites: Play-Time Is Over*, 29 October 2014, ClubOrlov
http://cluborlov.blogspot.com/2014/10/putin-to-western-elites-play-time-is.html

[1062] *Moscow Won't Get Evil Eye of Sauron After All*, Dan Peleschuk, 11 December 2014, the GlobalPost via USA Today
http://www.usatoday.com/story/news/world/2014/12/11/globalpost-moscow-russia-tolkin-lord-of-rings/20238253/

[1063] *Moscow Eye of Sauron Closed After Church Kicks The Hobbit PR*, RT YouTube
https://www.youtube.com/watch?v=lEksOafSRJ4&

[1064] *Welcome to Utah, the NSA's Desert Home For Eavesdropping On America*, Rory Carroll, 14 June 2013, the Guardian
http://www.theguardian.com/world/2013/jun/14/nsa-utah-data-facility

[1065] *FAA: Look For 30,000 Drones To Fill American Skies By The End Of The Decade*, Robert Johnson, 8 February 2012, Business Insider
http://www.businessinsider.com/robert-johnson-bi-30000-drones-by-2020-2012-2

[1066] *Putin Says Drones Aren't Toys, Russia Won't Use Them Like Other Nations*, unattributed, 28 November 2013, RT
http://rt.com/news/putin-drones-not-toys-457/
[1067] *Bill Gates: The Rolling Stone Interview*, Jeff Goodell, 13 March 2014, Rolling Stone
http://www.rollingstone.com/culture/news/bill-gates-the-rolling-stone-interview-20140313
[1068] *Boehner, Feinstein: Snowden's A Traitor*, Ed Morrissey, 11 June 2013, Hot Air
http://hotair.com/archives/2013/06/11/boehner-feinstein-snowdens-a-traitor/
[1069] *Cheney Defends NSA, Calls Snowden A "Traitor"*, Chris Wallace, 16 June 2013, Fox News Sunday
http://nation.foxnews.com/2013/06/16/cheney-defends-nsa-calls-snowden-traitor
[1070] *Senators Demand Repercussions For Russia In Wake Of Snowden Asylum*, Rosie Gray and John Stanton, 1 August 2013, BuzzFeed
http://www.buzzfeed.com/rosiegray/senators-demand-repercussions-for-russia-in-wake-of-snowden#1v3wzwo
[1071] *Lindsey Graham Follow Mr. Snowden To Ends Of Earth Bring Him To Justice*, 10 June 2013, Fire Andrea Mitchell
http://www.fireandreamitchell.com/2013/06/10/lindsey-graham-follow-mr-snowden-to-ends-of-earth-bring-him-to-justice/
[1072] *Meet the Press's Snowden Debate: Traitor or Criminal?* Peter Hart, June 2013, Fair.org
http://www.fair.org/blog/2014/06/02/meet-the-presss-snowden-debate-traitor-or-criminal/
[1073] *Ex-Wife: Newt Knew I Was Ailing*, Brian Blomquist, 19 July 2000, The New York Post
http://nypost.com/2000/07/19/ex-wife-newt-knew-i-was-ailing/
[1074] *Major Scandal Erupts Involving Rep. Jane Harman*, Alberto Gonzales and AIPAC, Glenn Greenwald, 20 April 2009, Salon
http://www.salon.com/2009/04/20/harman/
[1075] *Jane Harman, 2009 Wiretap/AIPAC Allegations*, Wikipedia.org
http://en.wikipedia.org/wiki/Jane_Harman#2009_Wiretap.2FAIPAC_Allegations
[1076] *Edward Snowden, Traitor*, Frank Gaffney 7 March 2014, the Center for Security Policy.org
http://www.centerforsecuritypolicy.org/2014/03/07/edward-snowden-traitor/
[1077] *Frank Gaffney and Allen West discuss Obama, Hillary, Islam, Russia and more LISTEN!*, 14 August 2014, Allen West Republic
http://allenwestrepublic.com/2014/08/15/frank-gaffney-and-allen-west-discuss-obama-hillary-islam-russia-and-more-listen/
[1078] *The Chechens' American Friends*, John Laughland, 8 September 2004, The Guardian
http://www.theguardian.com/world/2004/sep/08/usa.russia
[1079] *"FBI Incompetent To Ignore Russia's Warning Over Chechen Brothers"*, unattributed, 22 April 2013, RT
http://rt.com/op-edge/tsarnaev-us-russia-fbi-222/
 Not "incompetent"...just TREASONOUS and DUPLICITOUS SCUM.
[1080] *News – Was Tamerlan Tsarnaev an FBI Informant?* Diane and David Munson, 29 April 2013, ExFeds
http://www.dianeanddavidmunson.com/blog/?p=293

This is a blog with no citations but skip to the bottom for the resumes of this insider couple.
[1081] *From Boston to the New World Order*, Johnny Cirucci, 15 May 2013, The Patriot Press
http://johnnycirucci.com/wp/johnnys-latest-columns/from-boston-to-the-new-world-order/
[1082] *Donald Trump Attacks "Terrible" Edward Snowden On Fox: "There Is Still A Thing Called Execution"*, 24 June 2013, Financial Armageddon
http://financearmageddon.blogspot.com/2013/06/donald-trump-wants-edward-snowden.html
[1083] *Donald Trump and the Emanuel Brothers—What's the Deal?* Carol Felsenthal, 29 April 2011, Chicago magazine
http://www.chicagomag.com/Chicago-Magazine/Felsenthal-Files/April-2011/Donald-Trump-and-the-Emanuel-Brothers-Whats-the-Deal/
[1084] *Trump Pumps Corsi for Latest on Obama*, Bob Unruh, 24 May 2011, WorldNetDaily
http://www.wnd.com/2011/05/303049/
[1085] *Obama Cancels Meeting With Putin Over Snowden Asylum Tensions*, Dan Roberts and Alec Luhn, 7 August 2013, The Guardian
http://www.theguardian.com/world/2013/aug/07/obama-putin-talks-canceled-snowden
[1086] *John McCain: "No Doubt In My Mind" That Edward Snowden is Working for Vladimir Putin*, Charlie Spiering, 26 March 2014, the Washington Examiner
http://washingtonexaminer.com/john-mccain-no-doubt-in-my-mind-that-edward-snowden-is-working-for-vladimir-putin/article/2546317#!
[1087] *Attention Mitt Romney: Russia Has a Flat Tax and Almost no Debt*, Mark Adomanis, 20 January 2012, Forbes
http://www.forbes.com/sites/markadomanis/2012/01/20/attention-mitt-romney-russia-has-a-flat-tax-and-almost-no-debt/
[1088] *Coca Cola Protest, Russia*, Michael Pizzi, 9 June 2014, RESIST!
http://www.popularresistance.org/russian-food-patriots-blow-up-bottles-of-coke-in-protest/
[1089] *Russia To Protect Citizens From Genetically Modified Food*, unattributed, 27 March 2014, ITAR-TASS
http://en.itar-tass.com/russia/725594
[1090] *It's Official – Russia Completely Bans GMOs*, Arjun Walia, 15 April 2014, Collective Evolution
http://www.collective-evolution.com/2014/04/15/its-official-russia-completely-bans-gmos/
[1091] *Pedophilia Not A "Sexual Orientation" – Duma-Proposed Bill*, unattributed, 26 November 2013, RT
http://rt.com/politics/russia-pedophilia-orientation-ban-312/
[1092] *Putin Signs "Gay Propaganda" Ban And Law Criminalizing Insult Of Religious Feelings*, unattributed, 30 June 2013, RT
http://rt.com/politics/putin-law-gay-religious-457/
[1093] *The One Thing Putin Wants Russians To Do Like Americans*, Susan Yoshihara, 2 March 2012, FoxNews

http://www.foxnews.com/opinion/2012/03/02/one-thing-putin-wants-russians-to-do-like-americans/
[1094] *Russia Outlaws Abortion Ads*, unattributed, 25 November 2013, RT
http://rt.com/politics/russia-abortion-advertising-ban-266/
[1095] *Russians Can Now Carry Guns For "Self-Defense"*, 19 November 2014, RT
http://rt.com/news/206703-russia-guns-self-defense/
[1096] *Russia Outlaws The Building of Mosques, Will Get Tougher On Islam*, Theodore Shoebat, 3 December 2013, Shoebat.com
https://shoebat.com/2013/12/03/russia-outlaws-building-mosques-will-get-tougher-islam/
[1097] *Olympic Fear: Six Men Found Dead In Cars Booby-Trapped With Bombs In Russia*, Associated Press, 9 January 2014, the NY Daily News
http://www.nydailynews.com/news/national/men-found-dead-cars-booby-trapped-bombs-russia-article-1.1570760
[1098] *Chechen Warlord Doku Umarov Who Threatened Sochi Olympics Is "Killed By Russian Special Forces"*, Emma Thomas, 17 January 2014, the Daily Mail
http://www.dailymail.co.uk/news/article-2541319/Chechen-warlord-Doku-Umarov-threatened-Sochi-Olympics-killed-Russian-special-forces.html
[1099] *Captured Somali Pirates "Dead" – Russia*, unattributed, 12 May 2012, the Herald Sun
http://www.heraldsun.com.au/news/breaking-news/captured-somali-pirates-dead-russia/story-e6frf7jx-1225865290897?nk=39e98925d6153afcffb1f5a33ad3fa06
[1100] *Independence Act of Ukraine*, Wikisource
http://en.wikisource.org/wiki/Independence_Act_of_Ukraine
[1101] *The Ukrainian Constitution*, Johnny Cirucci, Scribd
https://www.scribd.com/doc/242072136/The-Ukrainian-Constitution
[1102] *Holocaust By Hunger: The Truth Behind Stalin's Great Famine*, Simon Montefiore, 25 July 2008, the Daily Mail
http://www.dailymail.co.uk/news/article-1038774/Holocaust-hunger-The-truth-Stalins-Great-Famine.html
[1103] *History of Russia: IX - XVIIth Centuries*, Parallel Sixty.com
http://www.parallelsixty.com/history-russia.shtml
[1104] *Ukraine > History > The Ruin*, Wikipedia
http://en.wikipedia.org/wiki/Ukraine#The_Ruin
[1105] *Frederick I Barbarossa*, Roman Emperor, T. E. Carson, 2003, excerpted at Encyclopedia.com
http://www.encyclopedia.com/article-1G2-3407704278/frederick-barbarossa-roman-emperor.html
[1106] *Battle of Kiev 1941 – The Red Army in Ukraine*, 26 September 2011, Jan Smith photography blog
http://smithjan.com/blog/2011/09/26/red-army-in-ukraine/
[1107] *A Fascist Hero in Democratic Kiev*, Timothy Snyder, 24 February 2010, the New York Review of Books
http://www.nybooks.com/blogs/nyrblog/2010/feb/24/a-fascist-hero-in-democratic-kiev/
[1108] *Explainer: The Budapest Memorandum And Its Relevance To Crimea*, Ron Synovitz, 28 February 2014, Radio Free Europe/Radio Liberty

http://www.rferl.org/content/ukraine-explainer-budapest-memorandum/25280502.html

[1109] *Viktor Yushchenko Biography*, Encyclopedia of World Biography
http://www.notablebiographies.com/news/Sh-Z/Yushchenko-Viktor.html

[1110] *House Fit For A Tyrant: Protestors Storm The Sprawling, Luxury Estate Of Ukraine's Fugitive President Which Has Its Own Private Zoo, Golf Course And Is Half The Size Of Monaco*, Wills Robinson, 22 February 2014, the Daily Mail
http://www.dailymail.co.uk/news/article-2565697/House-fit-tyrant-Protestors-storm-sprawling-luxury-estate-Ukraines-fugitive-president-private-zoo-golf-course-half-size-Monaco.html

[1111] *How Putin Lost Ukraine*, Anders Åslund, 21 August 2013, the Moscow Times
http://www.themoscowtimes.com/opinion/article/how-putin-lost-ukraine/484823.html

[1112] *Yushchenko to Russia: Hand Over Witnesses*, unattributed, 28 September 2009, the Kyiv Post
http://www.kyivpost.com/content/ukraine/yushchenko-to-russia-hand-over-witnesses-49610.html

[1113] *IMF Sponsored "Democracy" in The Ukraine*, Professor Michel Chossudovsky, 31 January 2014, Global Research
http://www.globalresearch.ca/imf-sponsored-democracy-in-the-ukraine-2/5360920

[1114] *ibid*

[1115] *IMF Mission Starts Talks With New Ukrainian Government On Fresh Loan Package*, Ivan Verstyuk, 3 March 2014, Kyiv Post
https://www.kyivpost.com/content/business/imf-mission-starts-talks-with-new-ukrainian-government-on-fresh-loan-package-338238.html

[1116] Chossudovsky

[1117] *Bad Choice*, unattributed, 9 September 2011, Kyiv Post
http://www.kyivpost.com/opinion/editorial/bad-choice-112478.html

[1118] *Russia Says Will Honour $15 Billion Loan Pledge To Ukraine*, Alexei Anishchuk and Justyna Pawlak, 28 January 2014, Reuters
http://uk.reuters.com/article/2014/01/28/uk-eu-russia-idUKBREA0R0FM20140128

[1119] *Kiev Chameleon*, Julia Ioffe, 5 January 2010, the New Republic
http://www.newrepublic.com/article/world/kiev-chameleon

[1120] *Why Critics Are Piling On Ukraine's Former Prime Minister Yulia Tymoshenko*, Steve LeVine, 27 February 2014, Quartz.com
http://qz.com/181662/why-critics-are-piling-on-ukraines-former-prime-minister-yulia-tymoshenko/#181662/why-critics-are-piling-on-ukraines-former-prime-minister-yulia-tymoshenko/

[1121] *Tymoshenko Stays: Ukraine Halts Plan to Sign EU Trade Deal*, unattributed, 21 November 2013, der Spiegel
http://www.spiegel.de/international/europe/ukrainian-parliament-votes-against-bills-to-release-tymoshenko-a-934887.html

[1122] *EU Offers Ukraine $15 Billion, But Help Hinges On IMF Deal*, Luke Baker, 5 March 2014, Reuters
http://www.reuters.com/article/2014/03/05/us-eu-ukraine-support-idUSBREA240V020140305

[1123] *Kerry Lands In Kiev, Sanctions Against Russia "In Matter Of Days", US Prepares $1 Billion Loan For Ukraine*, Tyler Durden, 4 March 2014, Zero Hedge http://www.zerohedge.com/news/2014-03-04/kerry-lands-kiev-sanctions-against-russia-matter-days-us-prepares-1-billion-loan-ukr

[1124] *The Looting Of Ukraine Has Begun*, Paul Craig Roberts, 6 March 2014, Paul Craig Roberts.org
http://www.paulcraigroberts.org/2014/03/06/looting-ukraine-begun/

[1125] *Ukraine Admits Its Gold Is Gone: "There Is Almost No Gold Left In The Central Bank Vault"*, Tyler Durden, 18 November 2014, Zero Hedge
http://www.zerohedge.com/news/2014-11-18/ukraine-admits-its-gold-gone

[1126] *Exposed: Ukrainian "Protesters" Backed by Kony 2012-Style Scam*, Paul Watson, 30 February 2014, InfoWars
http://www.infowars.com/exposed-ukrainian-protesters-backed-by-kony-2012-style-scam/

[1127] *The CIA and the Media*, Carl Bernstein, undated, Carl Bernstein.com
http://www.carlbernstein.com/magazine_cia_and_media.php
  I'm not a fan but this is a fantastic piece by a renowned journalist—a flaming Leftist but a journalist none-the-less.

[1128] *McCain, Durbin Urge Obama to Send Weapons to Ukraine*, Brian Bonner, 15 March 2014, the Kyiv Post
http://www.kyivpost.com/content/ukraine/mccain-durbin-say-they-will-urge-obama-to-send-weapons-to-ukraine-339474.html

[1129] *McCain, in Kiev, Tells Protesters That Ukraine Is "Inspiring The World"*, David Eldridge, 15 December 2013, Washington Times
http://www.washingtontimes.com/news/2013/dec/15/john-mccain-kiev-tells-protesters-ukraine-inspirin/#!

[1130] *Obama To Host Ukrainian Pm At White House As Crimea Referendum Nears*, AP, 12 March 2014, FoxNews
http://www.foxnews.com/politics/2014/03/12/obama-to-host-ukrainian-pm-at-white-house-as-crimea-referendum-nears/?intcmp=latestnews

[1131] *Washington's Man Yatsenyuk Setting Ukraine Up For Ruin*, Kenneth Rapoza, 27 February 2014, Forbes
http://www.forbes.com/sites/kenrapoza/2014/02/27/washingtons-man-yatsenyuk-setting-ukraine-up-for-ruin/

[1132] *Betrayal "Made in the U.S.A."*, John F. McManus, 13 November 2006, The New American reposted at the Patriot Press
http://johnnycirucci.com/wp/blog/2014/11/24/betrayal-made-in-the-u-s-a/

[1133] *U.S.' Nuland Treating Ukrainian Protesters to Cookies on Maidan*, unattributed, 11 December 2013, the Voice of Russia
http://voiceofrussia.com/news/2013_12_11/US-s-Nuland-treating-Ukrainian-protesters-to-cookies-on-Maidan-1129/

[1134] *U.S. Undersecretary of State for Europe: Washington Has Spent $5 Billion on Ukraine Unrest*, Johnny Cirucci, YouTube (skip ahead to around 7:25)
https://www.youtube.com/watch?&v=qc45C—xq4k

[1135] *Ukraine Signs $10 Billion Shale Gas Deal With Chevron*, Pavel Polityuk and Richard Balmforth, 5 November 2013, Reuters
http://www.reuters.com/article/2013/11/05/us-ukraine-chevron-idUSBRE9A40ML20131105

[1136] *Potential Health and Environmental Effects of Hydrofracking in the Williston Basin, Montana*, Joe Hoffman, 26 June 2014, the National Science Foundation (NSF) Carleton College
http://serc.carleton.edu/NAGTWorkshops/health/case_studies/hydrofracking_w.html

[1137] *4 States Confirm Water Pollution From Drilling*, Kevin Begos, 5 January 2014, AP, USA Today
http://www.usatoday.com/story/money/business/2014/01/05/some-states-confirm-water-pollution-from-drilling/4328859/

[1138] *Kiev Snipers Hired by Maidan Leaders - Leaked EU's Ashton Phone Tape*, unattributed, 5 March 2014, RT
http://rt.com/news/ashton-maidan-snipers-estonia-946/

[1139] *In Kiev, An Israeli Army Vet Led A Street-Fighting Unit*, Cnaan Liphshiz, 28 February 2014, Jewish Telegraphic Agency
http://www.jta.org/2014/02/28/news-opinion/world/in-kiev-an-israeli-militia-commander-fights-in-the-streets-and-saves-lives

[1140] *"Blackwater" Members In Ukraine's Donetsk*, unattributed, 9 March 2014, Press TV
http://www.presstv.ir/detail/2014/03/09/353918/blackwater-members-in-ukraine/

[1141] *CIA Agent Captured Helping Ukrainian Rebels in Kiev?* Johnny Cirucci YouTube
https://www.youtube.com/watch?v=m1WX27wM_Vk&

[1142] *"MH370: 9/11-Style False Flag Gone Awry?"* unattributed, 31 March 2014, Press TV
http://www.presstv.com/detail/2014/03/31/356688/mh370-911-false-flag-gone-awry/

[1143] *Malaysia Airlines MH370: A Story Created By CNN?* Johnny Cirucci, 24 March 2014, the Patriot Press
http://johnnycirucci.com/wp/blog/2014/03/24/malaysia-airlines-mh370-created-by-cnn/

[1144] *Managing Director of the IMF Christine Lagarde's Illuminati Numerology Message*, Johnny Cirucci, YouTube
https://www.youtube.com/watch?v=Sx_IZ-AcQ_I&

[1145] *Russia Expelled From G8, but G20? Not So Fast*, Thalif Deen, 1 April 2014, International Press Service
http://www.ipsnews.net/2014/04/russia-expelled-g8-g20-fast/

[1146] *McCain: Putin Should Pay if Separatists Shot Down Malaysia Airlines Plane*, unattributed, 9 October 2014, Roll Call
http://www.rollcall.com/multimedia/-234924-1.html

[1147] *Joe Biden On Airline Crash*, Andrew Kaczynski, 17 July 2014, BuzzFeed
http://www.buzzfeed.com/andrewkaczynski/joe-biden-on-airline-crash-apparently-shot-down-not-an-accid#1v3wzwo

[1148] *White House Claims No Conflict of Interest in Biden's Son on Ukraine Gas Company Board*, Mary Chastain, 14 May 2014, Breitbart.com
http://www.breitbart.com/Big-Peace/2014/05/14/Biden-s-Son-Kerry-s-Family-Friend-Joins-Ukraine-Gas-Company-White-House-Claims-No-Conflict-of-Interest

[1149] *MH-17: The Illuminati Push For Final World War*, Johnny Cirucci, 20 July 2014, the Patriot Press
http://johnnycirucci.com/wp/johnnys-latest-columns/mh-17/

[1150] *False Flag in Odessa: The Pathetic U.S. Media Coverage*, Mike Whitney, 8 May 2014, Global Research http://www.globalresearch.ca/false-flag-in-odessa-the-pathetic-u-s-media-coverage/5381326

[1151] **WARNING GRAPHIC:** *How the thugs killed Odessa inhabitants in the Trade Unions House - the details of bloody scenario*, ersieesist, 5 May 2014, Live Journal
http://m.livejournal.com/read/user/ersieesist/813

These pictures are beyond disturbing.

[1152] *Ukrainian Unrest Spreads; Dozens Dead In Odessa*, Jim Heintz and Peter Leonard, 2 May 2014, AP
http://bigstory.ap.org/article/gunfire-blasts-insurgent-held-ukraine-city

[1153] *Double-Headed Eagle*, Wikipedia.org
http://en.wikipedia.org/wiki/Double-headed_eagle

[1154] *The Double-Headed Eagle And Whence It Came*, Arthur Parker, (original) April 1923, the Masonic Dictionary
http://www.masonicdictionary.com/doubleeagle.html

Chapter 12
Movie Magic & Media Menageries

Most people don't appreciate that the Los Angeles district known as "Hollywood" has, in its very name, a dedication to paganism and "magic" as holly was used in both pagan fertility rites and to ward off unwanted spirits[1155]. Each Christmas, Christians decorate with holly and mistletoe in honor of sex magick[ee] rituals that call unclean spirits. They also glorify the burning of a child sacrifice by commemorating the placing of a "Yule Log" in the fire.[1156,1157,1158]

You might be just as surprised to find that the Jesuits have considerable influence in Tinseltown.

Is there anyone around the world who has not seen the 1987 romance fantasy *The Princess Bride*?

We watch enraptured as the Spanish swash-buckler "Inigo Montoya" (played so well by Mandy Patinkin) follows his burning quest for revenge upon "the six-fingered man".[ff]

My name is Inigo Montoya. You killed my father. Prepare to die.

Do you think there is any resemblance to the Spanish soldier who had undying passion to serve his Pope by the name of Íñigo Loyola? Interesting that writer Bill Goldman and director Rob Reiner (two nominal Jews) would put any effort into immortalizing the founder of the Jesuits.

Actor Hugh Jackman has starred in several Company films and his personal views on spirituality probably track well with what the Jesuits prefer is promoted.

> *Jackman was raised by his father, who is a devout born-again Christian. His mother deserted the family when he was 8 and moved back to her native England. Hoping his son would also have*

[ee] "Magick" or "sex magick" are purposeful misspellings coined by satanist Aleister Crowley to describe reproductive rituals designed to open doors for malignant interdimensional entities. See Chapter 15.

[ff] Having 6 digits is the Biblical mark [II Samuel 21:20] of creatures called "Nephilim" [Genesis 6;4] fabricated by fallen angels to be organic portals for unclean spirits called *Rephaim* to interact in our world without having to possess a willing human host. Not all 6-fingered people are Nephilim and not all Nephilim have 6 fingers. Read on!

a born-again experience, his father took Hugh to Billy Graham crusades every time the famed evangelist came to Australia.

"He takes his religion very seriously and would prefer I go to church," Jackman says of his father. "We've had discussions about our separate beliefs. I just find the evangelical church too, well, restrictive. But the School of Practical Philosophy is nonconfrontational. We believe there are many forms of Scripture. What is true is true and will never change, whether it's in the Bible or in Shakespeare. It's about oneness. Its basic philosophy is that if the Buddha and Krishna and Jesus were all at a dinner table together, they wouldn't be arguing. There is an essential truth. And we are limitless." ~ Kevin Sessums, Parade[1159]

With good reason do Christians believe that wealth and power cloud sound judgment. [Matthew 19:23-24]

Jackman played the lead role in the 2004 action thriller *Van Helsing*. In it, he is Gabriel Van Helsing, the Catholic superhero who wears an Illuminist All-Seeing Eye mask as he vanquishes monsters for the Church. A veritable Vatican James Bond, Van Helsing gets his ancient high-tech[gg] gadgets from both Catholic and muslim "scientists"—or are they magicians? Van Helsing must temporarily become a werewolf to stop Count Dracula as he saves the Shakespeare-quoting Frankenstein monster.[hh]

Jackman appeared in another movie with Catholic influence but in a much more subtle way.

In the 2013 film *Prisoners*, Jackman plays "Keller Dover", the survivalist/prepper carpenter who loses his daughter to a kidnapper. Implicated in the crime is near-invalid "Alex Jones" (played by Paul Dano) who is released by police Detective Loki[ii] (Jake Gyllenhaal) on lack of evidence. Dover is then compelled to kidnap the apparent kidnapper to learn of where is daughter was. He tortures "Alex Jones" and the scene calls to mind the debate over what the CIA labels "enhanced interrogation techniques". Dover beats Jones into bloody disfigurement, forces him into a sweatbox and intermittently scalds him.

Prison Planet

In the end, though, "Alex Jones" proves to be an innocent victim of

---

[gg] Might we call ancient advanced technology "Atlantean"?

[hh] Mimicking YHWH in the ability to bring life from lifelessness is a timeless rebellion.

[ii] "Loki"—as if the explosion of Marvel Avengers and Thor movies all over theaters doesn't glorify pagan demigods enough.

circumstance.

The real predators turn out to be Jones' adoptive parents, his aunt and uncle.

They lost their son to cancer and had decided to wage war against God ever since, by stealing, torturing and murdering other people's children.

Sadly, the movie depicts a crisis in America that is all too real. 800,000 children go missing in the United States every year[1160]. That's about 5,000 each day.

What could possibly have such a voracious appetite for America's children?

You will be shocked to know that your own government, the CIA, the Jesuit order and the Vatican have all been implicated in this epidemic (Chapter 14).

In *Prisoners*, the Jones' were traveling Pentecostal snake-charmers before turning into satanic pedophiles.

As Detective Loki[jj] tracks suspects, he comes across a convicted sex offender Catholic priest. The priest is drunk and Loki searches the house to discover a grisly find in the basement—it's Uncle Jones.

Apparently, the pedophile predator priest rose to heroic proportions when the Pentecostal perpetrator came seeking penance for having abducted and murdered so many children. "Father Dunn" (Len Cariou) then locked the monster in the basement where he died, leaving Aunt Holly to carry on her satanic work alone.

She did this from a house with the number "1634" on it.

In 1534, Ignatius Loyola started his Jesuit order[1161], later to be officially sanctioned by the "Holy See" in 1540.

In 1634, Sir Cecilius Calvert, Lord Baltimore, commissioned the Catholic colony of Maryland in America for Rome and managed it from England.[1162]

In spite of all his toughness, our male lead Hugh Jackman, "Dover",

---

[jj] Gyllenhaal looks ludicrous in this movie. Riddled with tattoos, he wears a button dress shirt cinched to his neck. His demeanor is unprofessional as he searchers frantically for the missing children.

allows himself to get handcuffed, drugged and shot by Holly Jones and then voluntarily slithers into a well. She also manages to shoot our other male hero, Detective Loki, before he does her in and rescues Dover's child.

What are the Elites telling you with movies like this?

—Your enemies fear and respect you. As much as they lampoon "preppers", "Bible thumpers" and backwoodsmen, they are terrified by them.

They also secretly loath the evil in themselves which is why it's so easy for them to purge their own ranks.

Controlled Conspiracy

Alex Emerick Jones is the Conspiracy King. On his radio show, you'll hear it all...but will you?

Jones fearlessly covers issues corporate media won't touch, from gun rights, to abortion, to false flags, to "chemtrails", to fluoride, illegal alien invasions, vaccines, "global warming" and the Federal Reserve.

However, Jones also has a delivery that can be so buffoonish as to make you question if he is purposely trying to discredit himself and, by extension, his subject matter.

It has been alleged that Jones' well-to-do dentist father is a Knight of Malta. Is that a source of control for his program?

Jones has an above-average media operation reputable enough to be frequently found on the Drudge Report, so why does he regularly employ apparent tactics of gross exaggeration and hammy over-acting? Is he an entertainer, a journalist or an instrument of disinformation?

Jones has allowed the Constitutional ineligibility of Barack Obama to be discussed on his program but then gives Obama cover by endorsing Canadian-born Ted Cruz[1163] for Vice President[1164]. According to the 12th Amendment, adopted in 1804 — *no person constitutionally ineligible to the office of President shall be eligible to that of Vice-President of the United States.*

The summary of a Ted Cruz presidency would be that the Elite mitigate what good he can do, ride it out for 4 or even 8 years and insure that all of the harm Barack Obama has done will be written in stone.

This is an outcome that is either unseen or not a problem for Alex

Jones, the Tea Party, and "Conservative" pundits like Ann Coulter.[1165,1166]

There is at least one instance of Jones and his crew crashing a pro 2nd Amendment rally in Austin with an apparent attempt to discredit it[1167]. While the hosts of the rally begged Jones to come to the microphone, he stomped up and down the street with a bullhorn in aggressive disruption.

Jones will frequently bring on insiders like "former" CIA case worker Robert Steele who would claim that the Benghazi scandal occurred because Leon Panetta "lost his nerve" and Barack Obama "dithered".[1168]

This is textbook damage control—start off admitting a sensational truth that had long-ago been broken and then finish with the propaganda spin so that the audience will associate the lie with the truth.

In the latter half of 2014, Jones focused excessive amounts of time needlessly stoking fears of an Ebola epidemic and then actually invested in sending reporters to show civil unrest in Ferguson, Missouri.

During this time, the "King of Conspiracy" completely avoided not one but three questionable mass-shooting events.

On October 22nd, 2014, Canadian media reported a shooting at Parliament Hill in Ottawa. Canadian soldier Corporal Nathan Cirillo was dead as was the "gunman" Michael Zehaf-Bibeau. Canada being a gun-free paradise, Bibeau apparently shot up the capital with a pre-1964 lever-action .30-30[1169]. The supposed hero of the shooting, Kevin Vickers, the capital Sergeant-at-Arms, completed a series of mid-air shots while tumbling in what must've looked like something out of the Matrix. He was then showcased at the Israeli Knesset, of all places, for his exploits[1170]. Questions regarding the official story immediately arose regarding "bullet holes" found in the Central Block in the Hall of Honor that were actually present a year before from construction[1171]. Police tape and barricades were seen at the National War Memorial *before* the shooting[1172]. First responders were photographed conducting Cardio-Pulmonary Resuscitation ("CPR") on Corporal Cirillo yet paramedics were reaching *over* his body, not touching it as his white-gloved hands were seen clearly interfering with direct access to his chest[1173]. At stake was a *massive* increase in Canadian Security Intelligence Service powers—a move interestingly considered just days before the shooting[1174]. After the shooting, Canadian Prime Minister Stephen Harper vowed to "fast-track" these powers (lest anyone examine them too closely)[1175]. A dear friend of the American Police State, NY Republican Representative Peter King suggested, due to the Ottawa shootings, the United States beef up *their* surveillance[1176]—because there certainly hasn't been enough of it.

In Marysville, Washington a school shooting took place at Pilchuck High School where a 15 year old boy named Jaylen Fryberg apparently shot 4 students before killing himself. This incident, also occurred in late October 2014 just before elections and referendums were voted on. Prior to the shooting, billionaires Michael Bloomberg and Bill Gates had spent $8 million promoting gun control legislation, "Initiative 594", that would make it illegal to have a friend watch a firearm without a background check[1177]. Just one day before, Marysville police held an "active shooter" SWAT training drill[1178]. "By coincidence" (words actually in the news King 5 report), grieving Sandy Hook mother Nicole Hockley was in Seattle to support Initiative 594 at the time of the shooting[1179]. I-594 miraculously passed.[1180]

There there's the case of Florida State alum Myron May—a Bible-quoting "Conspiracy theorist" who supposedly shot up the FSU campus in November of 2014[1181]. Perhaps as proof of the ubiquitous nature of "mind control" as a subject, controlled mainstream media reported that May had posted on social media the question "Has anyone here ever been encouraged by your handler to kill with a promise of freedom?" just before the shooting, and that he knew he was targeted by the government[1182]. Florida is a bloody battleground over gun rights. After the Trayvon Martin shooting, NY Democrat Senator Chuck Schumer asked for a Federal probe into "stand your ground" laws around the country, when such laws had nothing to do with the Sanford, Florida incident[1183]. Florida is one of the few states where open carry of a firearm is illegal and an initiative to make open carry legal on school grounds was killed in committee in 2011[1184]. Are awake citizens being openly played with incidents like this?

One would think that, not only are these subjects fertile ground for the King of Conspiracy but critical issues to bring into the open—unless he was directed to allow the legislative wins to take place.

It was during this time that Alex Jones spoke with both Robert Steele and CIA/State Department negotiator Steve Pieczenik. Pieczenik would claim that there was nothing manufactured about the Ebola outbreak.[1185]

Pieczenik would go on in the same program to brag about how the military and the CIA (with help from the Saudis) were now crushing the Russian economy. Even if someone considered this a true strategic accomplishment the open aggression towards the Russian Federation has caused Vladimir Putin to threaten nuclear retaliation[1186]. How could it *possibly* be considered an accomplishment for the American people?

Both Pieczenik and Steele do give admonitions of government misdeeds but are clearly still on the payroll.

Jones has also interviewed guests who froth up racial hatred against Jews and "Zionists" such as questionable Christians like Texe Marrs and Fritz Springmeier[kk] and New Age guru David Icke.

Anti-Semitism has been one of the most effective shields the Jesuits and New World Order Luciferians stand behind for anonymity in their machinations.

Jones joined Texe Marrs in excoriating Jesuit critic Eric Phelps (without naming him).[1187]

Is Alex Jones a Jesuit "coadjutor"—a secret friend of the Society of Jesus?

In my correspondence with author William Dean Garner it was disclosed that he was offered a radio slot by Jones' promoter and gold broker, Ted Anderson, on the Genesis Communication Network. Garner would be an improvement over Jones, but on one proviso: he was never to discuss the Company of Loyola.

According to *The Richest*, in 2010 Alex Jones' net worth was an astounding $5 million with total earnings topping $1.5 *billion*[1188]. If it's true that only those who are vetted by the Machine are allowed to taste success, Jones has gotten his reward.

Mark Dice, author of *The Illuminati: Facts & Fiction* began his "Truther" career with Jones then broke away to become a vehement critic of Jones. Dice has claimed that Jones lives on a palatial ranch anywhere from 7 to 9 acres in size.[1189]

Dice has since been welcomed back into the fold and no-longer attacks Jones. It is a shrewd partnership as is the Jones connection with WorldNetDaily chief editor Joseph Farah and nationally-syndicated talk show host Michael Savage.

Jones' success is in direct contrast to the career of Conspiracy shock-jock and author, Milton William "Bill" Cooper.

[kk] We will discuss the topic at length in Chapter 17 but I defend the description "questionable" in this manner: any Christian who vehemently hates the nation of Israel is likely to harbor secret hatred of all Jews and I'll wager this is something the King of the Jews will not truck lightly.

Cooper did reference Jesuit secret agendas often on his program and in his writing, along with other conspiratorial topics.

A decorated Vietnam veteran, Cooper was killed in what was painted as a "shoot-out" with police in 2001. Media portrayed Cooper as a desperate "militia" nut who would "never be taken alive"[1190]. Cooper died 2 months after 9/11.

Hollywood actor Martin Sheen narrated the opening prologue to Oliver Stone's *JFK*.

The Sheen family is popular with Stone who used son Charlie for the starring role in *Platoon* (1986) and *Wall Street* (1987). Stone would bring in Tom Cruise for another Left-leaning film, *Born on the 4th of July* (1989).

Cruise and the Sheens have surprising secret ties to the Catholic Church.

Oliver Stone is a radical Leftist who literally embraces Communist dictators like Hugo Chavez.[1191]

However, *JFK* was a unique accomplishment with excellent historical accuracy.

Alex Jones is very close with the Sheen family, particularly actor Charlie Sheen.

Martin Sheen is a much-lauded hard-Left Catholic activist who has received the "Laetare Medal" from Notre Dame university, "Peacemaker of the Year" by Pax Christi, Metro New York chapter and the Isaac Hecker Award for Social Justice from the Paulist Center in Boston.[1192]

Sheen has claimed to be against abortion[ll] but also vehemently against the death penalty[1193]. Sheen also supports homosexual marriage.[1194]

Sheen's real name is Ramón Estevez but he took the idea for a stage

---

[ll] Activists who equate the unborn with convicted perpetrators of capital crime have no moral compass.

Sheen is best known for substance-less stunts like sleeping one night on a sewage grate to show solidarity with the homeless before returning home to his Beverly Hills mansion.
Chilly Night On A Sidewalk Grate Teaches Lesson About Homeless, NY Times 5 March 1987
http://www.nytimes.com/1987/03/05/us/chilly-night-on-a-sidewalk-grate-teaches-lesson-about-homeless.html

name from two people: CBS casting director Robert Dale Martin and Catholic bishop Fulton J. Sheen.

Like Ignatius Loyola, Martin Sheen can trace his Catholic father's side of the family to Spain.[1195]

On his mother's side is uncle Michael Phelan, a terrorist with the Irish Republican Army and Sheen often sings his praises.[1196]

In 2010 Sheen and son Emilio Estevez worked together on *The Way*; a story about a man's "religious" pilgrimage after the death of his son.

> *Written, produced, and directed by Estevez, The Way follows the journey of Tom Avery (Martin Sheen), an insulated eye doctor whose adventurous son, played by Estevez, dies while hiking El Camino de Santiago—a Christian pilgrimage route to the Cathedral of Santiago de Compostela in Galicia, Spain. To honor his son's memory, Tom embarks on his own adventure across the Camino, scattering his son's ashes along the way, and in the process, discovers vast truths about himself, and his son. ...*
>
> **Religion is, in a way, responsible for both of your careers. Mr. Sheen, I read that it was a Catholic priest who lent you the money to move to New York and pursue acting?**
>
> **Sheen:** *That's true. He was my first supporter. He gave me about $500 over a three-month period. That was big money in those days! You could buy a new Chevy for about $2,500, and he was a parish priest living off a stipend. My father did not want me to go to New York to be an actor, and Father Al had the authority to get between us and make the situation a little easier with my Dad.*
>
> **And Emilio, your first film role was actually produced by the Catholic Paulist order?**
>
> **Estevez:** *That's right. The first lead I had was a show called Insight, and it was an afterschool special. ...*
>
> **Does it bother you the way the Michele Bachmanns and Rick Perrys of the world have co-opted religion to back their own political agendas?**
>
> **Estevez:** *Yeah. That's all they got!*
>
> **Sheen:** *I used to feel very uncomfortable with that but I don't anymore. They appeal to people who have been pretty much shut*

out of everything else. ...

Now, as a fan of* The West Wing, *I must ask: what would President Josiah Bartlet do to fix America?

Sheen: *I would do exactly what President Obama is doing. He's going after the fat cats who have abused their privilege.* ~ Marlow Stern, the Daily Beast[1197]

Given that the Sheen/Estevez family was a creation of, and continues to be enabled by the Catholic Church, their Leftist agenda is interesting to say the least.

Although Sheen still promulgates the idea that Barack Obama is "takin' it to 'the rich'" (like him), others on the Left were immediately deflated when they realized that the Obama presidency has been bankrolled by Wall Street. [italics suspended]

Obama's Big Sellout

The president has packed his economic team with Wall Street insiders intent on turning the bailout into an all-out giveaway.

Barack Obama ran for president as a man of the people, standing up to Wall Street as the global economy melted down in that fateful fall of 2008. He pushed a tax plan to soak the rich, ripped NAFTA for hurting the middle class and tore into John McCain for supporting a bankruptcy bill that sided with wealthy bankers "at the expense of hardworking Americans." ...

Then he got elected.

What's taken place in the year since Obama won the presidency has turned out to be one of the most dramatic political about-faces in our history. Elected in the midst of a crushing economic crisis brought on by a decade of orgiastic deregulation and unchecked greed, Obama had a clear mandate to rein in Wall Street and remake the entire structure of the American economy. What he did instead was ... pack the key economic positions in his White House with the very people who caused the crisis in the first place. This new team of bubble-fattened ex-bankers ... then proceeded to sell us all out, instituting a massive, trickle-up bailout...

Whatever the president's real motives are, the extensive series of loophole-rich financial "reforms" that the Democrats are currently pushing may ultimately do more harm than good. In fact, some parts of the new reforms border on insanity, threatening to vastly amplify Wall Street's political power by institutionalizing the taxpayer's role as a welfare provider for the financial-services industry. At one point in the debate, Obama's top economic advisers demanded the power to award future bailouts without even going to Congress for approval — and without providing taxpayers a single dime in equity on the deals. ~ Matt Taibbi, Rolling Stone[1198]

Estevez' other son, Charlie Sheen, was the highest-paid star on television before his porn-star secret life was outed.[1199]

The misdeeds of those in power are carefully catalogued by the Elite and can be used as punishment at any time.

In Charlie Sheen's case the "crime" may have been his spouting off about having an "army of assassins",[1200] to protect him. Specifically, *Vatican* assassins.

In an interview with Alex Jones in February of 2011, Sheen made the following statement;

> *Guys, it's right there in the thing, duh! We work for the Pope, we murder people. We're Vatican assassins. How complicated can it be? What they're not ready for is guys like you and I and Nails and all the other gnarly gnarlingtons in my life, that we are high priests, Vatican assassin warlocks. Boom. Print that, people. See where that goes.*[1201]

Alex Jones shot into conspiracy stardom when he crashed the Luciferian retreat for the rich and shameless known as the Bohemian Grove. It was an impressive coup that should've been impossible given that the Grove is frequented by the most powerful people in the world and has extremely strict access. We will discuss the Grove at length in Chapter 16.

Jones later confronted political advisor David Gergen[mm] on his attendance at the Grove—another impressive security breach coup.

Subterfuge is a successful counter-intelligence technique. An excellent example is the "conspiracy" that the Conspiracy King Alex Jones is actually

---

[mm] Gergen is a political chameleon of multiple party affiliations—a power aparatchik whose services were rendered to 4 different administrations across the political spectrum from Nixon to Ford to Reagan to Clinton. Such utilitarianism in Washington bespeaks of all answering to a higher authority.

Texas comedian Bill Hicks, who died in 1994. It's a great farce that, even if true, changes nothing of substance. It has the powerful benefit of relegating anyone who questions Jones' authenticity as an even worse "nut" than those already slandered as wearers of tinfoil hats within his audience. Jones, himself, makes great sport of this foolishness[1202]. Was it manufactured by the Elite to shield Jones from scrutiny?

Was Alex Jones given help to break the Bohemian Grove story? Were these incidents engineered[1203] to empower and then control him?

Perhaps we can just say "he is one of them" as Jones was raised in Rockwall, TX, a hotbed of UFO activity.[1204]

Action Assassinated

There are a rare few in Hollywood that question government and media authorities in a way that *isn't* subversive.

Steven Seagal is one of them.

Seagal's first big movie *Above the Law* (1988) is a must see. It portrays a conspiracy between the CIA and FBI to cover up an illicit narcotics trade fostered by the American government and it is basically dead accurate, no pun intended.

In 2010, Steven Seagal's former 23 year-old assistant, Kayden Nguyen, filed a million-dollar lawsuit alleging the then-58 year old actor frequently harassed her and was guilty of sex trafficking and sex slavery with two other women. However, no other women joined her lawsuit or substantiated her claims.

Perhaps indicative of its questionable legitimacy, the lawsuit was dropped and no information has surfaced regarding exactly what happened, since.[1205]

The action star may have made himself a target as he has openly supported the impeachment of Barack Obama[1206] and even questioned the official story regarding many of the mass shootings America has suffered since Obama has taken office.[1207]

But what may have really elevated him on the hit-list was his connections to post-Communist Russia—he has enough pull to personally train with Vladimir Putin, which was a public relations boost for the judo-practitioning president.[1208]

Seagal recently paved the way for a Congressional delegation of

Conservative Congressmen Dana Rohrabacher (R, CA) and Steve King (R, IA) to visit the Russian Federation[1209] to find out why Russian intelligence warnings regarding Boston bombing suspect Tamerlan Tsarnaev weren't taken more seriously by U.S. government agencies.[1210]

Steven Seagal may or may not have been targeted for persecution, but it calls to mind a similar incident from the other side of the political spectrum regarding former Minnesota Governor Jesse "the Body" Ventura.

Highly-lauded Navy SEAL sniper Chris Kyle made headlines and garnered lots of attention for his newly-published book *American Sniper*, by claiming on both radio and TV that he knocked Jesse Ventura to the floor at a SEAL wake for fallen comrade Mike Mansoor. Kyle said Ventura told him "we deserved to lose a few guys" in his criticism of the Iraq war[1211] but Ventura vehemently stated that none of it ever happened, nor would he defame a fellow SEAL.

The war agenda is one that is sustained by lies and make-believe that includes using Hollywood director Jerry Bruckheimer to stage the rescue of Jessica Lynch[1212] and having Americans assassinate folk hero Pat Tillman.

Chris Kyle may have been embroiled in a propaganda scandal. We'll never know because Kyle was murdered.

He was shot in the back by a man whom he was helping cope with Post Traumatic Stress Disorder—by taking him shooting.[1213]

It is surprising, to say the least, that there has been next to no response from the Special Operations community.

Ventura pressed on with his suit against the Kyle estate and, bolstering his claim that the incident was a fabrication, he later won $1.8 million dollars in damages.[1214]

Crusin

Another Hollywood favorite of Rome appears to be Tom Cruise.

Cruise's Scientology certainly compares well with Jackman's "School of Practical Philosophy". Both are equally strange (and identifiably pagan).

The founder of Scientology, L. Ron Hubbard, has been linked to Aleister Crowley, the self-proclaimed "Beast" of John's Revelation.[1215]

It's been reputed that Cruise is a Knight of Malta, though the rolls are not published publicly so this is hard to track down.

What is somewhat more substantive was the location of Cruise's latest failed marriage to actress Katie Holmes: the family fortress of the Orsini clan—the *Castello Orsini-Odescalchi*[1216].

The power, wealth and reach of the Orsinis is one of the best-kept secrets in the world.

> *One of the most ancient and distinguished families of the Roman nobility, whose members often played an important rôle in the history of Italy, particularly in that of Rome and of the Papal States.*
>
> *The Roman or principal line of the family, from which branched off a series of collateral lines as time went on, may be traced back into the early middle Ages, and a legendary ancestry goes back even as far as early Roman times. ... In Rome, the Orsini were the hereditary enemies of the equally distinguished Colonna: in the great medieval conflict between papacy and empire, the latter were for the most part on the side of the emperor and the leaders of the Ghibelline party, while the Orsini were ordinarily champions of the papacy and leaders of the Guelph party. The Orsini gave three popes to the Church — Celestine III, Nicholas III, and Benedict XIII — as well as many cardinals and numerous bishops and prelates. ... The wars between the Orsini and Colonna form an important part of the medieval history of Rome and of Central Italy. Forming as they did a part of the conflicts waged by the emperors in Italy, they influenced in a very prominent manner the general historical development of that time.* ~ The Catholic Encyclopedia[1217]

Castello Orsini is not a location even a Hollywood actor can secure easily, but Tom Cruise did.

It is interesting to note that *Van Helsing* (2004) already appears to be getting a reboot just over 10 years later and is slated to star Cruise who is six years *older* than Hugh Jackman.[1218]

The Orsinis are a clan reputed to be major players amongst the world Elite as are the Aldobrandinis.

> *ALDOBRANDINI. A noble family of Florence, raised to princely dignity by Pope Clement VIII. Salvestro Aldobrandini (1499-1588). A famous teacher of law at Pisa. He led a successful revolt against the Medici in Florence, defended the city against the imperial army of Charles V, and upon capture was condemned to death, but the intervention of a powerful friend of the Medici caused the change of his sentence to that of banishment in 1530. He went to Rome,*

Naples and Bologna, where, in 1538, he became Papal Vice-Legate and Vice-Regent. Realizing the futility of a return to Florence, he went to Ferara, whence he was called to Rome as fiscal advocate of Pope Paul III. ~ New International Encyclopedia[1219]

From time immemorial Elites have assured their ruling oligarchies by arranged marriages. This practice also creates some unusual inbred bloodlines. Today, even Western "elected" leaders share surprisingly similar ancestry[1220]. Do such bloodlines harbor genetic markers that make these people easily accessible by entities from another dimension? We will explore this in Chapter 20.

The name of "Rothschild" frequently comes up in the examination of who the Luciferian World Elite are, but the names of "Orsini" or "Aldobrandini" do not. This may be by design as reputed Jewish lineage of the Rothschilds immediately invokes vehement, mindless anti-Semitism within the Truth movement community. It is an effective shield to hide behind.

Although no one has heard of the Aldobrandini clan, they are attached to the Rothschilds by just such an arranged marriage between "Baron David René James de Rothschild" and "Princess Olimpia Anna Aldobrandini" in 1974.[1221]

Controlled Opposition

Are the Jesuits powerful enough to both create and control their own opposition?

The most ubiquitous symbol of resistance to the New World Order is the Guy Fawkes mask. From the hacker collective known as "Anonymous" to "Occupy Wall Street", anyone who wishes to strike a blow for freedom while in public demonstration is wearing one.

The masks were popularized by the 2005 movie "V for Vendetta."

Starring Natalie Portman and Hugo Weaving, it's another dystopic future set in England.

The movie was written by the brother/brother (sister) team of Andy and Laurence/Lana Wachowski (before Larry's "gender reassignment"). The Wachowskis also masterminded *The Matrix* and wrote, rather appropriately, *Assassins* starring Sylvester Stallone and Antonio Banderas.

"V for Vendetta" portrays an odd love/hate dynamic with Christian and Crusader imagery. The setting was a dark fantasy future but the person of

Guy Fawkes comes from a real English past.

In the movie, "Evey Hammond" (Portman) states;

> "Remember, remember, the Fifth of November, the Gunpowder Treason and Plot. I know of no reason why the Gunpowder Treason should ever be forgot..." But what of the man? I know his name was Guy Fawkes and I know, in 1605, he attempted to blow up the Houses of Parliament. But who was he really? What was he like? We are told to remember the idea, not the man, because a man can fail. He can be caught, he can be killed and forgotten, but 400 years later, an idea can still change the world. I've witnessed firsthand the power of ideas, I've seen people kill in the name of them, and die defending them... but you cannot kiss an idea, cannot touch it, or hold it... ideas do not bleed, they do not feel pain, they do not love... And it is not an idea that I miss, it is a man... A man that made me remember the Fifth of November. A man that I will never forget.

This vague reference is all we get to help us answer the question: Who was Guy Fawkes?

The Gunpowder Plot of 1605 was an effort by a Jesuit cabal of Catholics[1222], lead by Fawkes to assassinate James I of England[1223]. Jesuit priests Henry Garnet and John Gerard were implicated during the subsequent investigation.[1224]

Sharkface217 – Wikimedia Commons

It was just one of many targeting Protestant England.

> *The Babington Plot* [of 1580] *was probably the greatest of the many plots of the pope and the Jesuits during the reigns of Queen Elizabeth I and* [King] *James I designed to bring about the downfall of Protestant England, the overthrow of the Reformation in England, Scotland and Ireland, and to place some other claimant upon the Throne who would be acceptable to Rome, and committed to bring the English in submission to the sovereignty of Rome.*
>
> *Between 1569 and 1605 (of Gunpowder Plot infamy) there were no less than eleven great plots against Elizabeth and English*

Protestantism, working toward assassination, rebellion and invasion. Each is known by the name of the leader of the treachery: Ridolfi, Sanders, [Pope] *Gregory XIII,* [Jesuit priest] *Campion,* [Jesuit priest Robert] *Parsons, the Duke of Guise,* [Cardinal] *Allen, Throgmorten, Parry,* [Anthony] *Babington,* [Pope] *Sixtus V,* [King] *Philip II of Spain, Yorke, Walpole, Southwell, and Guy Fawkes.*

...There can be no doubt whatsoever but that the Pope of Rome was very much interested as well as vitally involved in all of these attempts.

...The Babington Plot [to invade England, to assassinate Queen Elizabeth I, to incite rebellion, and then to place Roman Catholic Mary Stuart on the throne] *took its name from Anthony Babington, a young English gentleman...but the real brains behind the conspiracy were the pope* [Gregory XIII], *Cardinal Allen, the Jesuits, and the Roman Catholic priest named John Ballard... ~ The Babington Plot,* J.E.C. Shepherd[1225]

Every protestor that dawns a Guy Fawkes mask unknowingly glorifies Jesuit assassination—almost certainly by their design.

Endnotes

[1155] *Pagan Meaning of Evergreen & Holly*, April Sanders, undated, Demand Media
http://classroom.synonym.com/pagan-meaning-evergreen-holly-6416.html
[1156] *Christmas Traditions Yule Log*, Ziggy Thomas, 26 April 2009, Spiritual Living 360
http://www.spiritualliving360.com/index.php/christmas-traditions-yule-log-19276/
[1157] *The Occult in Your Living Room! Christmas, Yule and the Winter Solstice*, Clayton Luce, 21 December 2012, the Examiner
http://www.examiner.com/article/the-occult-your-living-room-christmas-yule-and-the-winter-solstice-1
[1158] *Pagan Orgies to Human Sacrifice: The Bizarre Origins of Christmas*, Kristi Harrison, 18 December 2007, Cracked.com
http://www.cracked.com/article_15719_pagan-orgies-to-human-sacrifice-bizarre-origins-christmas.html
[1159] This quote was originally from a Parade Magazine exposé on the actor; *Hugh Jackman's Essential Truth*, Kevin Sessums, 26 April 2009, Parade
http://parade.condenast.com/130535/kevinsessums/hugh-jackman-2/
However it seems to have been edited out. The original is still referenced here; *The Religion and Political Views of Hugh Jackman*, The Hollowverse
http://hollowverse.com/hugh-jackman/#footnote_0_3881
And page 2 of the Parade Mag piece can be found with the quote at MSN (which is where my citation comes from); *PU: Hugh Jackman Page 2*, Entertainment News, MSN.com,
http://entertainment.msn.com/news/article.aspx?news=405789
[1160] *"Missing" to "Recovered": Finding Abducted Kids*, Blair Soden, 13 January 2007, ABC News
http://abcnews.go.com/US/story?id=2793130&page=1
[1161] Sep 27, 1540: Jesuit Order Established, This Day In History, History.com
http://www.history.com/this-day-in-history/jesuit-order-established
The Jesuit movement was founded by Ignatius de Loyola, a Spanish soldier turned priest, in August 1534. The first Jesuits—Ignatius and six of his students—took vows of poverty and chastity...
[1162] *Encyclopedia of North American Immigration*, John Powell, Infobase Publishing (2009), p. 186
[1163] *Ted Cruz's Origins Continue To Haunt Him*, Steven Lubet, 20 September 2013, Salon.com
http://www.salon.com/2013/09/20/ted_cruzs_origins_continue_to_haunt_him/
[1164] *Alex Jones Endorses Paul-Cruz 2016: "I Trust Rand Paul"*, 24 August 2013, MoFoPolitics.com
http://www.mofopolitics.com/2013/08/24/alex-jones-endorses-paul-cruz-2016-i-trust-rand-paul/
[1165] *Ann Coulter's Political Crush on Ted Cruz*, Rick Klein, Richard Coolidge and Jordyn Phelps, 28 October 2013, Yahoo!News
http://news.yahoo.com/blogs/power-players/ann-coulter%E2%80%99s-political-love-affair-with-ted-cruz-205120061.html

I watched Coulter on Hannity answer if she would support Cruz for president "yes". She rightfully calls out Cruz on illegal immigration and then says she's going to resurrect Machine mannequin Mittens Romney. See next endnote.

[1166] *Coulter: Mitt Romney in 2016; "Cruz A Disaster On Illegal Immigration"*, unattributed, 3 April 2014, RealClearPolitics
http://www.realclearpolitics.com/video/2014/04/03/ann_coulter_mitt_romney_in_2016.html

[1167] On 25 January 2010, Texans' for Accountable Government held a rally in Austin at the police building and there are several videos on YouTube showing Jones crashing the rally while the hosts beg him to stop disrupting and even adjuring Jones to join them on the platform, but to no avail. At this writing, a great version with informative subtitles is *Alex Jones Acted Like An Ass To Other Pro 2nd Amendment Activist At Their Rally*, by PsychoRocketRanger on YouTube
https://www.youtube.com/watch?v=9uyIVzdvGi4

[1168] *Former CIA Spy: Benghazi Was CIA Operation*, TheAlexJonesChannel, YouTube
https://www.youtube.com/watch?v=wwR7ss2r8Ek

What an insider scoop that headline is!

[1169] *What Gun Did the Ottawa Terrorist Use?* 25 October 2014, Gun Watch
http://gunwatch.blogspot.com/2014/10/what-gun-did-montreal-terrorist-use.html

[1170] *Kevin Vickers, Sergeant-At-Arms, Meets With Israeli Lawmakers, PM*, 12 November 2014, CBC News
http://www.cbc.ca/news/world/kevin-vickers-sergeant-at-arms-meets-with-israeli-lawmakers-pm-1.2832283

[1171] *Ottawa Shooting: Evidence of a Staged False Flag Attack 51*, Dario Di Meo, 31 October 2014, Memory Hole
http://memoryholeblog.com/2014/10/31/ottawa-shooting-evidence-of-a-staged-false-flag-attack/

[1172] *Ottawa Shooting False Flag - Barricades + Police Tape Prior to Shooting*, freeradiorevolution YouTube
https://www.youtube.com/watch?v=_5T1EfiSXiE&

[1173] *TFM002-The Case of the Corporal's White Gloves & the CPR Fail*, TruthFreqMedia YouTube
https://www.youtube.com/watch?v=ZShsQHWeoWY

[1174] *Government to Give CSIS More Powers in Fight Against Homegrown Radicals*, Dylan Robertson, 16 October 2014, the Ottawa Citizen
http://ottawacitizen.com/news/politics/government-to-give-csis-more-powers-in-fight-against-homegrown-radicals

[1175] *Harper Vows To Fast-Track Boost To Spy, Policing Powers After Shooting*, Steven Chase, 24 October 2014, MSN News
http://www.msn.com/en-ca/news/world/harper-vows-to-fast-track-boost-to-spy-policing-powers-after-shooting/ar-BBaQGgb

[1176] *Canadian And American Politicians Use Ottawa Shootings As Excuses To Demand More Surveillance, Greater Policing Powers*, 24 October 2014, techdirt
https://www.techdirt.com/articles/20141024/15082428934/canadian-american-politicians-use-ottawa-shootings-as-excuses-to-demand-more-surveillance-greater-policing-powers.shtml

[1177] *New Trend: Billionaires "Buying Gun Control"*, Leo Hohman, 12 October 2014, WND

http://www.wnd.com/2014/10/new-trend-billionaires-buying-gun-control/#!
[1178] *SWAT Training Drill During Marysville School Shooting?* 24 October 2014, Activist Post
http://www.activistpost.com/2014/10/swat-training-drill-during-marysville.html
[1179] *Sandy Hook Mom's Message To Marysville*, Heather Graf, 28 October 2014, NBC King 5
http://www.king5.com/story/news/local/marysville-shooting/2014/10/28/sandy-hook-moms-message-to-marysville/18043043/
[1180] *Washington Voters Approving I-594 To Expand Gun Background Checks*, 4 November 2014, Fox Q 13
http://q13fox.com/2014/11/04/washington-voters-approving-i-594-to-expand-gun-background-checks/
[1181] *Police Identify Shooter In Florida State Tragedy*, Sean Rossman, Karl Etters and John Bacon, 20 November 2014, USA Today
http://www.usatoday.com/story/news/nation/2014/11/20/fsu-guman/19310741/
[1182] *FSU Shooter Myron May Feared Government Was Targeting Him: Cops*, Tracy Connor, 20 November 2014, NBC News
http://www.nbcnews.com/news/us-news/fsu-shooter-myron-may-feared-government-was-targeting-him-cops-n252731
[1183] *Schumer Calls For Federal Probe Of "Stand Your Ground" Laws After Florida Shooting*, 25 March 2012, FoxNews
http://www.foxnews.com/politics/2012/03/25/schumer-calls-for-federal-probe-stand-your-ground-laws-after-florida-shooting/
[1184] *Florida Open Carry Bill – Stuck and Gutted*, Luke McCoy, 10 March 2011, USA Carry
http://www.usacarry.com/florida-open-carry-bill-stuck-and-gutted/
[1185] *Dr. Steve Pieczenik: Americans Should Prepare For Ebola Martial Law*, THEINFOWARRIOR, YouTube
https://www.youtube.com/watch?v=pKbou42rthw
[1186] *Putin Warns Of "Nuclear Power Consequences" If Attempts To Blackmail Russia Don't Stop*, Tyler Durden, 15 October 2014, Zero Hedge
http://www.zerohedge.com/news/2014-10-15/putin-warns-nuclear-power-consequences-if-attempts-blackmail-russia-dont-stop
[1187] At this writing, there is the YouTube video *Texe Marrs Exposes Eric Jon Phelps on the Alex Jones Show* posted by "Reasonable Doubtt"
https://www.youtube.com/watch?v=HQnG2wfvsJE

Phelps is a wealth of information, however, he is also highly unstable. I have reached out to him and he has refused to respond. I have spoken at length with his pastor and the diagnosis is that he has great insight on this topic but is a devout racist.

Phelps self-published his book Vatican Assassins can be a useful tool in research although a publisher would've helped with issues that make the work appear sophomoric such as the use of multiple fonts such as Old English.

To his credit, there are extensive references and citations and most of his radio and internet appearances will leave the audience informed.

As always, be a good Berean.

[1188] *Alex Jones Net Worth*, Richest Radio Personality, TheRichest
http://www.therichest.com/celebnetworth/celeb/radio-personality/alex-jones-net-worth/

[1189] As of this writing, there is a Mark Dice Facebook post from 18 October 2012 where Dice references the Jones ranch and its size although the Mark Dice video attached to the post mocking the Jones "money bomb" has been taken down.
https://www.facebook.com/MarkDice/posts/124776211005155
[1190] *Arizona Militia Figure Is Shot to Death*, Times Wire Services, 7 November 2001, LA Times
http://articles.latimes.com/2001/nov/07/news/mn-1182
[1191] *Oliver Stone Laughs Over the Ashes of Venezuela*, Alex Chafuen, 6 March 2014, the Blaze
http://www.theblaze.com/contributions/oliver-stone-laughs-over-the-ashes-of-venezeula/
[1192] *PEOPLE*, 21 March 2008, Nation Catholic Reporter (a periodic summary of the "achievements" of famous Catholics)
http://natcath.org/NCR_Online/archives2/2008a/032108/032108g.htm
[1193] *Martin Sheen Interview*, David Kupfer, July 2003, The Progressive magazine
http://www.progressive.org/news/2003/06/1155/martin-sheen-interview
[1194] *Catholic Actor Martin Sheen: 'the Church is not God' on Gay "Marriage" Issue*, Kathleen Gilbert, 3 April 2012, LifeSiteNews
http://www.lifesitenews.com/news/catholic-actor-martin-sheen-the-church-is-not-god-on-gay-marriage-issue
[1195] *Martin Sheen: Being a Dad*, Joanna Moorhead, 25 March 2011, The Guardian
http://www.theguardian.com/lifeandstyle/2011/mar/25/martin-sheen-emilio-estevez-charlie-sheen
[1196] *I'm Proud Of Jailed Uncle's IRA Past, Says Movie Star Martin Sheen*, James Fielding, the Express
http://www.express.co.uk/news/world/300148/I-m-proud-of-jailed-uncle-s-IRA-past-says-movie-star-Martin-Sheen
[1197] *Sheen Family's Epic Journey*, Marlow Stern, 6 October 2011, the Daily Beast
http://www.thedailybeast.com/articles/2011/10/06/the-way-martin-sheen-emilio-estevez-on-charlie-sheen-occupy-wall-street.html
[1198] *Obama's Big Sellout*, Matt Taibbi, 9 December 2009, Rolling Stone, expunged from their site but reposted at the Patriot Press
http://johnnycirucci.com/wp/blog/2014/12/20/obamas-big-sellout/
[1199] *Forbes Highest Paid TV Actors: Unemployed Charlie Sheen Tops The List!* unattributed, 14 October 2011, Radar online
http://radaronline.com/exclusives/2011/10/forbes-highest-paid-actors-charlie-sheen-ray-romano/
[1200] *Charlie Sheen's 10 Worst Quotes, from Anti-Semitism to Alcoholism*, unattributed, 25 February 2011, the Daily Beast
http://www.thedailybeast.com/articles/2011/02/25/charlie-sheens-anti-semitism-and-alcoholism-his-10-worst-quotes.html#
[1201] *"We are High Priests, Vatican Assassin Warlocks": 14 Bizarre Things Charlie Sheen Said Today*, Meghan Carlson, 24 February 2011, BuddyTV
http://www.buddytv.com/articles/two-and-a-half-men/we-are-high-priests-vatican-as-39499.aspx
[1202] *Twilight Zone: Texas Monthly Investigates if Alex Jones is Really Bill Hicks*, 26 November 2014, InfoWars

http://www.infowars.com/twilight-zone-texas-monthly-investigates-if-alex-jones-is-really-bill-hicks/

[1203] *Bohemian Grove Roster Sent Anonymously to Infowars*, Aaron Dykes, 22 June 2007, JonesReport
http://www.jonesreport.com/articles/210607_bg.html

[1204] *Alex Jones Travels from Texas to CNN to Warn Piers Morgan*, Robert Wilonsky, 8 January 2013, Dallas News
http://thescoopblog.dallasnews.com/2013/01/alex-jones-travels-from-texas-to-cnn-just-barely-to-warn-1776-will-commence-again-if-you-try-to-take-our-firearms.html/

The examples of UFO action in Rockwall are too numerous to cite. Just internet query "UFO Rockwall Texas" and enjoy the ride. I believe there is at least one very creepy "Close Encounter of the Third Kind".

[1205] *Former Personal Assistant Drops Lawsuit Against Steven Seagal*, unattributed, 14 July 2010, NBC Los Angeles
http://www.nbclosangeles.com/news/local/Former_Personal_Assistant_Drops_Lawsuit-98457679.html

[1206] *Steven Seagal: If The Truth Came Out, Obama Would Be Impeached*, Johnny Cirucci YouTube
https://www.youtube.com/watch?v=L-mhU8kVlbc&

[1207] Russia Today's Oksana Boyko interviews Steven Seagal for her program Worlds Apart, reposted on the Johnny Cirucci YouTube under the title; STEVEN SEAGAL: TEA PARTY PATRIOT AND CONSPIRACY THEORIST?!
https://www.youtube.com/watch?v=L-mhU8kVlbc&

[1208] *Vladimir Putin Wants all Russians to be Tough Like Steven Seagal*, Terrence McCoy, 26 March 2014, the Washington Post
http://www.washingtonpost.com/news/morning-mix/wp/2014/03/26/vladimir-putin-wants-all-russians-to-be-tough-like-steven-seagal/

[1209] *Lawmakers in Russia Learn Little About Tsarnaev, Bond With Steven Seagal*, Margaret Hartmann, June 2013, NY Magazine
http://nymag.com/daily/intelligencer/2013/06/congress-in-russia-seagal-bonding-few-facts.html

[1210] *Lawmakers Traveling to Russia to Investigate Boston Bombing*, Congressman Dana Rohrabacher press release, 21 May 2013
http://rohrabacher.house.gov/lawmakers-traveling-russia-investigate-boston-bombing

[1211] *America's Deadliest Sniper Killed 255 Iraqi "Savages" To Protect His Friends... But He Punched Out Jesse Ventura Because He "Bad-Mouthed The Troops"*, Michael Zennie, 6 January 2012, the Daily Mail
http://www.dailymail.co.uk/news/article-2083235/Americas-deadliest-sniper-killed-255-Iraqi-savages-protect-friends—punched-Jesse-Ventura-bad-mouthed-troops.html

[1212] *The Truth About Jessica*, John Kampfner, 15 May 2003, the Guardian
http://www.theguardian.com/world/2003/may/15/iraq.usa2

[1213] *Ex-Navy Sniper, Another Military Vet Killed At Texas Gun Range*, Greg Botelho and Josh Levs, 4 February 2013, CNN
http://www.cnn.com/2013/02/03/justice/texas-sniper-killed/

[1214] *Jesse Ventura Wins $1.8M In Defamation Lawsuit Against Ex-SEAL Sniper*, Ashley Fantz, 31 July 2014, CNN
http://www.cnn.com/2014/07/30/us/ventura-chris-kyle-suit/

[1215] *Hubbard and Aleister Crowley*, Jeff Jacobsen, 1992
http://www.spaink.net/cos/essays/jacobsen_magic.html
[1216] *Cruise, Holmes Marry in Italian Castle*, Maria Sanminiatelli, Associated Press, 28 November 2006, the Denver Post
http://www.denverpost.com/aerospace/ci_4683889
[1217] *Orsini*, The Catholic Encyclopedia, New Advent.org
http://www.newadvent.org/cathen/11325b.htm
[1218] *Tom Cruise To Star In Van Helsing Reboot With Kristen Stewart's Ex Lover At The Helm?* Limara Salt, 12 October 2012, EntertainmentWise
http://www.entertainmentwise.com/news/90838/Tom-Cruise-To-Star-In-Van-Helsing-Reboot-With-Kristen-Stewarts-Ex-Lover-At-The-Helm
[1219] *New International Encyclopedia, Volume 1*, Dodd and Mead (1914), p. 366
[1220] It is my contention that maintaining bloodlines amongst the Elite keeps some trace genetic imperfections there that help the technology of interdimensional possession.
I hope to prove this for you in later chapters. For your consideration there is this: *Is Ruling In The Genes? All Presidents Bar One Are Directly Descended From A Medieval English King*, Snejana Farberov, 4 August 2012, the Daily Mail
http://www.dailymail.co.uk/news/article-2183858/All-presidents-bar-directly-descended-medieval-English-king.html
[1221] *Rothschild Bachelor Toes* [sic] *Line At Last*, The Australian Women's Weekly (1933 - 1982), Wednesday 17 July 1974, page 5
http://www.scribd.com/doc/236352292/Rothschild-Marries-Aldobrandini
[1222] *The Gunpowder Plot*, Bruce Robinson, 29 March 2011, BBC History
http://www.bbc.co.uk/history/british/civil_war_revolution/gunpowder_robinson_01.shtml
[1223] *The Gunpowder Plot: A Detailed Account*, David Herber, Britannia History
http://www.britannia.com/history/gunpowder2.html
[1224] *The Gunpowder Plot: A Detailed Account*, David Herber, no date, Britannia.com
http://www.britannia.com/history/gunpowder2.html
Special thanks to my friend Philip Wylie for the names of the Jesuits involved in the Gunpowder Plot.
[1225] *The Babington Plot: Jesuit Intrigue in Elizabethan England*, J.E.C. Shepherd, Wittenburg Publications (1987), pp. 118, 123

Chapter 13

Boiling Frogs

The Elite hate and fear the common people. Their highest priority is to dumb-down, distract, impoverish, poison, enslave and kill us. The very air we breathe and water we drink is laden with toxins for that purpose.

These poisons are being handed to us openly. Like frogs in slowly boiling water, we breathe, drink and eat them willingly, guaranteeing our own demise.

Vaccine Vectors

Vaccines can be equated with technology. When they are wielded by ethical, compassionate people, they save lives.

But when malignant or malicious people are behind the needle (or, at least, what goes *into* the needle), there are few better vectors for getting poison or nanobots or whatever is desired into oblivious, trusting citizens.

When injecting agents directly into the body, there is little room for error.

In Syria, a measles vaccine administered by the United Nations caused at least 15 children to go into allergic shock and die[1226]. With nearly 200,000 dead in Syria (many of them Christians) as the current running tally of victims of the Western-backed civil war, the world has but shrugged at the deaths.[1227]

A child in France was crippled by a 5-in-1 vaccination and her family waged a 17-year war for justice that finally ended in a settlement in 2012.[1228]

Some experts fear that certain batches of smallpox vaccines are triggering dormant Human Immunodeficiency Virus (HIV) to mature into Acquired Immunodeficiency Syndrome (AIDS).[1229]

Causal links between vaccinations like Hepatitis C and autism in children are so overwhelming that the Center for Disease Control is now actively covering them up. One of their top scientists—Dr. William Thompson—recently turned whistleblower and released a public statement about CDC obfuscation and disinformation.[1230]

Thompson has received no real media coverage.

A Bill Gates Foundation-funded meningitis vaccine paralyzed 50 children in Chad.[1231]

Attorney Walter Kyle is fighting an uphill battle and winning against a myriad of alphabet soup agencies from the Food and Drug Administration to the Department of Health and Human Services to the Center for Disease Control to even the Department of Justice regarding vaccine injuries. It is a battle Americans know little of.

Catherine Frompovich of the Activist Post interviewed Kyle.

> *I began representation of vaccine-injured clients in Arkansas in 1977. My first case out of law school was representing a paraplegic mother who acquired paralytic polio from mutated Sabin live trivalent oral polio vaccine [TOPV] viruses shed from her three-month-old infant's diapers. Centers for Disease control classified the woman in the "immune deficient" category of "vaccine associated contact cases" from Type 2 Sabin vaccine.*
>
> *Walter, you just mentioned the phrase "vaccine viruses shed." For those who are not familiar with such terminology I'd like to say it means certain types of vaccines contain certain viruses that are alive and once injected into [orally administered to] an individual can infect others via contact with bodily fluids, excrement, and sometimes coughing or sneezing. In your first vaccine case, the mother contracted paralytic polio from viruses "shed" in her infant's diapers soiled with urine and feces.* ~ Activist Post[1232]

A common vaccine preservative is mercury-based Thimerosal whose cumulative effects are essentially the same as being poisoned with mercury.

> *Mercury exposure at high levels can harm the brain, heart, kidneys, lungs, and immune system. High levels of methylmercury in the bloodstream of unborn babies and young children may harm the developing nervous system, making the child less able to think and learn.*
>
> *Symptoms of methylmercury poisoning may include impairment of peripheral vision; disturbances in sensations ("pins and needles" feelings); lack of coordination; impairment of speech, hearing, walking; and muscle weakness.* ~ Dr. John P. Cunha, MD, Medicine.net[1233]

These toxins are insidious and work slowly over time. Victims are only aware of the symptoms, not the causes or who is behind them.

Many vaccines contain the chemical compound *squalene*, ostensibly to increase the immune-response from the host body. This defines squalene as an "adjuvant".

Dr. Viera Scheibner noted this about oil-in-water adjuvants like squalene:

> *The adjuvant activity of non-ionic block copolymer surfactants was demonstrated when given with 2% squalene-in-water emulsion. However, this adjuvant contributed to the cascade of reactions called "Gulf War syndrome", documented in the soldiers involved in the Gulf War. The symptoms they developed included arthritis, fibromyalgia, lymphadenopathy, rashes, photosensitive rashes, malar rashes, chronic fatigue, chronic headaches, abnormal body hair loss, non-healing skin lesions, aphthous ulcers, dizziness, weakness, memory loss, seizures, mood changes, neuropsychiatric problems, anti-thyroid effects, anaemia, elevated ESR (erythrocyte sedimentation rate), systemic lupus erythematosus, multiple sclerosis, ALS (amyotrophic lateral sclerosis), Raynaud's phenomenon, Sjorgren's syndrome, chronic diarrhea, night sweats and low-grade fevers.*
>
> *This long list of reactions shows just how much damage is done by vaccines, particularly when potentiated by powerful "immunoenhancers" such as squalene and other adjuvants.*[1234]

Although squalene (like *calcium* fluoride) is naturally-occurring, the difference between ingestion and injection is critical.

> *Oil-based vaccination adjuvants like squalene have been proved to generate concentrated, unremitting immune responses over long periods of time.[vi]*
>
> *A 2000 study published in the American Journal of Pathology demonstrated a single injection of the adjuvant squalene into rats triggered "chronic, immune-mediated joint-specific inflammation," also known as rheumatoid arthritis.[vii]*
>
> *The researchers concluded the study raised questions about the role of adjuvants in chronic inflammatory diseases.*
>
> *Your immune system recognizes squalene as an oil molecule native to your body. It is found throughout your nervous system and brain.*

> *In fact, you can consume squalene in olive oil and not only will your immune system recognize it, you will also reap the benefits of its antioxidant properties.*
>
> *The difference between "good" and "bad" squalene is the route by which it enters your body. Injection is an abnormal route of entry which incites your immune system to attack all the squalene in your body, not just the vaccine adjuvant.*
>
> *Your immune system will attempt to destroy the molecule wherever it finds it, including in places where it occurs naturally, and where it is vital to the health of your nervous system.[viii]* ~ Dr. Joseph Mercola[1235]

Fatal Fluoride

Sodium fluoride reduces mental acuity and debilitates the reproductive system yet large corporations make tremendous amounts of money putting it in your drinking water.

> [sodium] *Fluoride is a waste by-product of the fertilizer and aluminum industry and it's also a Part II Poison under the UK Poisons Act 1972.*
>
> *Fluoride is one of the basic ingredients in both PROZAC (FLUoxetene Hydrochloride) and Sarin nerve gas (Isopropyl-Methyl-Phosphoryl FLUoride).*
>
> *USAF Major George R. Jordan testified before Un-American Activity committees of Congress in the 1950's that in his post as U.S.-Soviet liaison officer, the Soviets openly admitted to "Using the fluoride in the water supplies in their concentration camps, to make the prisoners stupid, docile, and subservient."*
>
> *The first occurrence of fluoridated drinking water on Earth was found in Germany's Nazi prison camps. The Gestapo had little concern about fluoride's supposed effect on children's teeth; their alleged reason for mass-medicating water with sodium fluoride was to sterilize humans and force the people in their concentration camps into calm submission. (Ref. book: "The Crime and Punishment of I.G. Farben" by Joseph Borkin.)* ~ *Scientific Study Finds Fluoride Horror Stories Factual*, Paul Watson[1236]

Even if fluoride had a beneficial quality when ingested, it is not within the bounds of government to put it in drinking water.

It is a basic tenet of natural law[nn] that patients are to give their consent before being medicated.

In fact, it is *calcium* fluoride that has reputed to have been of use hardening and protecting tooth enamel and even then it is strictly for topical application. No dentist asks you to drink a tall glass of fluoride. After a topical application, patients are always told "Rinse and spit!"

It should cause Americans great concern that their governments would be so all-inclusive in their scope as to provide them "medicated" drinking water. Those who attempt to pull themselves out of government-provided water, sewage or electricity are dealt with harshly.

In Oregon, a man who was collecting rain water for his personal use was sentenced to 30 days in jail.[1237]

The effects of fluoride on mental acuity are becoming so well documented it is forcing corporate media to peripherally acknowledge them as this report did from FoxNews:

> *...questions about the impact of fluoride on mental health are growing and can no longer be ignored.*
>
> *A recently published Harvard study showed that children living in areas with highly fluoridated water have "significantly lower" IQ scores than those living in areas where the water has low fluoride levels. In fact, the study analyzed the results of 27 prior investigations and found the following, among other conclusions:*
>
> - *Fluoride may be a developmental neurotoxicant that affects brain development (in children) at exposures much below those that cause toxicity in adults.*
> - *Rats exposed to (relatively low) fluoride concentrations in water showed cellular changes in the brain and increased levels of aluminum in brain tissue.*[1238]

Of course this is only when water is "*highly*" fluoridated."

In Rochester, IL, a toxic spill outside of a plant was so severe, HAZMAT crews were dispatched from multiple surrounding precincts and, by the time they arrived, the chemical was burning into the concrete

---

[nn] "Natural Law" is the innate morality within human beings that *should* be common sense in an argument. Having a patient give consent before medicating them is common sense but I'm sure there are some hard-Left bastion jurisdictions where this is already legal.

surrounding the Rock Island facility.

It was fluoride destined for public water supply.[1239]

The Love of Money is the Root of All Evil

Because the masses are feared by the Elite, wherever billionaires gather, they plot in secret to do us harm.

> *Some of America's leading billionaires have met secretly to consider how their wealth could be used to slow the growth of the world's population and speed up improvements in health and education.*
>
> *They attended a summit convened on the initiative of Bill Gates, the Microsoft co-founder, discussed joining forces to overcome political and religious obstacles to change.*
>
> *...[which] included David Rockefeller Jr, the patriarch of America's wealthiest dynasty, Warren Buffett and George Soros, the financiers, Michael Bloomberg, the mayor of New York, and the media moguls Ted Turner and Oprah Winfrey. ...*
>
> *They gathered at the home of Sir Paul Nurse, a British Nobel prize biochemist and president of the private Rockefeller University, in Manhattan on May 5. The informal afternoon session was so discreet that some of the billionaires' aides were told they were at "security briefings".* ~ John Harlow, the Sunday Times [1240]

They are hoping that, soon, they will be able to skip needles altogether and use genetically-engineered mosquitoes to deliver whatever they chose whether the population wants it or not. The "Bill and Melinda Gates Foundation" started funding that research back in 2009[1241]. Do you wonder how far along they are?

—And there are no lack of scientists willing to help them.

In 2006, University of Texas professor Eric Pianka told an auditorium full of students that he longed for Ebola to wipe out 90% of the Earth's population.

He wasn't speaking at the University of Texas, he was speaking at neighboring Catholic St. Edward's.[1242]

More recently, Dr. Charles Arntzen at Arizona State University joked about using a genetically-modified virus to "cull" the human population.[1243]

Arntzen is a key figure in the latest efforts to create an Ebola vaccine[1244]. I trust him, don't you?

Going Viral

Ebola is a viral disease that occurs in humans and primates. It begins with muscle pain and runs through vomiting, diarrhea, and disfiguring rashes, and ends with liver failure, kidney failure and severe bleeding both internally and externally.

On September 19th, 2014, Sierra Leone's President Ernest Koroma announced that his entire nation was on quarantine as a result of an apparent Ebola outbreak—six million people.[1245]

Both the U.S. government and U.S. media continued to assure Americans that the virus was not airborne. The only way to contract it was by coming into contact with infected bodily fluids.[1246]

In 2012, a study proved that Ebola could be passed from pigs to monkeys without either coming into contact[oo].[1247]

In July of 2014, it was declared that the lead doctor handling the outbreak in Sierra Leon became a victim of the virus despite the precautions he was taking.[1248]

That same month, media stated that Christian aid worker Kent Brantly also contracted the disease. Sky News reported on the troubling knowledge that fully-protected doctors and scientists were still getting the virus.

> *"I'm praying fervently that God will help me survive this disease," Dr Brantly wrote on Monday, asking for co-worker and fellow American Nancy Writebol, who has also fallen ill, to be included in the prayers.*
>
> *As the Texas-trained doctor continued to fight for his life, another doctor treating Ebola patients in Sierra Leone succumbed to the deadly virus.*
>
> *A medical colleague confirmed on Tuesday that Dr Shek Umar, who was credited with treating more than 100 sufferers, died in the far*

[oo] Citizens should be deeply concerned over the type of "scientists" who inflict animals with deadly diseases for nefarious purposes. It is difficult enough to stomach the rare instances that can be legitimized as truly in the "best interest" of humanity. The lack of compassion required for doing such experimentation may, in and of itself, disqualify such "doctors".

> *north of the country a week after being diagnosed with the infection.*
>
> *More than 670 people have died in the West African outbreak.*
>
> *Dr Brantly, who remains in an isolation unit in Monrovia, travelled to Liberia last October to work with a Christian aid group.*
>
> *He and his wife, Amber, decided to remain with their two small children after the Ebola virus moved from neighbouring Guinea into Liberia and Dr Brantly took charge of the mission hospital's Ebola clinic.*
>
> *He contracted the disease despite wearing full-body protective clothing.*[1249]

As if in answer to prayer, Mapp Biopharmaceutical arrived on the map with a secret serum to bring both Kent and fellow infected aid worker Nancy Writebol back from certain death.[1250]

The media actually reported it as a "secret serum".[1251]

Researchers were shocked to learn that the Ebola virus is patented, as are any related cures.

Investigative reporter Dave Hodges found three entities that hold the title: the Center for Disease Control, the National Institute of Health and Bill Gates.[1252]

The National Institute of Allergy and Infectious Diseases (NIAID) has one of those patented vaccines and is giving it to eager volunteers.[1253]

As of 2014, the man running NIAID is Anthony Fauci. Fauci is an Italian Catholic who went to Jesuit-run Regis High School and Jesuit-run Holy Cross college before receiving his MD at Cornell.[1254]

EboLie

Barack Obama appointed Ronald Klain as "Ebola Czar". He was doing this in response to what Republican legislators demanded.

> *President Obama on Friday appointed former White House official Ron Klain to serve as the "Ebola czar," following calls from a number of lawmakers for a single point person in the administration to oversee the government's response to the virus.*
>
> *"There has to be some kind of czar," Sen. John McCain, R-Arizona,*

said Sunday—even though he once maligned the Obama administration for having "more czars than the Romanovs." Similarly, Sen. Jerry Moran, R-Kansas, called on the president to appoint an Ebola czar, even though five years ago he introduced a bill that would have stymied Mr. Obama from appointing more czars.

Those Republicans and others loudly decried the so-called "czars" populating the White House at the start of the Obama administration... ~ Stephanie Condon, CBS News[1255]

Klain has *no* medical or healthcare experience. He does, however, have ties to the housing bubble scandal.[1256]

More importantly, he was Joe Biden's Chief of Staff, and an alumnus of Georgetown.[1257]

But Klain's not just any Georgetown alum, he teaches there.[1258]

Jesuit-trained Ron Klain believes that "Climate Change" and "over population" (particularly in Africa) are the world's top problems.[1259]

This doesn't sound like the man best suited to defend us from, or help stop, an African pandemic.

In West Africa, American soldiers are using a high-tech device to screen for Ebola similar to the one at Texas Health Presbyterian Hospital where America's first Ebola patient—Thomas Eric Duncan was seen, treated, then released. However, at Texas Presbyterian, the unit stayed in the closet as the hospital is forbidden to use it for anything other than research.[1260]

An "Eric Duncan" was found on the professional profile database "LinkedIn" from Liberia that worked with the Peace Corps as a District AIDS Coordinator and as an officer for the Bank of America[1261]. Was it the same man?

These would be some strange associations for the "first, random Ebola victim."

Interestingly, that profile has been taken down.[1262,1263]

Clipboard Guy

The second reported victim of Ebola was a nurse named Amber Vinson who looked after Eric Duncan. Vinson was seen being loaded onto an aircraft for treatment when, like an on-the-set director, an official was caught by local news, standing over her HAZMAT suited body, next to HAZMAT suited attendants, without protective clothing.[1264]

Quickly dubbed "clipboard-guy" for the clipboard he had, the media was forced to scramble for a reason why an unprotected director would be standing over an Ebola patient without fear of catching a deadly hemorrhagic virus that makes you bleed through your eyes, nose, mouth and other orifices before you die.

The response was not very convincing: it was necessary for clipboard guy to direct the other attendants without his HAZMAT suit because they couldn't see where to go.[1265]

Dallas County Judge Clay Jenkins called Amber Vinson "heroic". Then he added something unusual.

> *"Let's remember that as we do our work that this is a real person who is going through a great ordeal, and so is that person's family." ~* WFAA ABC 8[1266]

Soon, work crews in Africa were wearing bright green t-shirts and even using green rakes assuring us that "EBOLA IS REAL!"[1267] If people were blistering blood and bleeding from their eyes in the streets, would any of that be necessary?

Eric Duncan was flown in to Dallas, the same location that signaled the ultimate CIA/Jesuit coup; the broad-daylight slaughter of America's sitting President.

Duncan arrived in Dallas having flown a very circuitous route from Monrovia, the capital of Liberia. Monrovia was founded in 1822 as a colony with the intent of allowing emancipated black slaves an opportunity to return to Africa. These were *true* "African-Americans", most of whom were kidnapped by Arab muslims and displaced from their homeland.

> *It is true that slavery had been written into the basis of the classical world. Periclean Athens was a slave state, and so was Augustan Rome. Most of their slaves were Caucasian. The word slave meant a person of Slavic origin. By the 13th century slavery spread to other Caucasian peoples. But the African slave trade as such, the black traffic, was an Arab invention, developed by traders with the enthusiastic collaboration of black African ones, institutionalized with the most unrelenting brutality, centuries before the white man appeared on the African continent, and continuing long after the*

slave market in North America was finally crushed.

Naturally this is a problem for Afrocentrists, especially when you consider the recent heritage of Black Muslim ideas that many of them espouse. Nothing in the writings of the Prophet [Muhammad] *forbids slavery, which is why it became such an Arab-dominated business. And the slave traffic could not have existed without the wholehearted cooperation of African tribal states, built on the supply of captives generated by their relentless wars. The image promulgated by pop- history fictions like Roots — white slavers bursting with cutlass and musket into the settled lives of peaceful African villages — is very far from the historical truth. A marketing system had been in place for centuries, and its supply was controlled by Africans. Nor did it simply vanish with Abolition. Slave markets, supplying the Arab emirates, were still operating in Djibouti in the 1950s; and since 1960, the slave trade has flourished in Mauritania and the Sudan. There are still reports of chattel slavery in northern Nigeria, Rwanda and Niger.* ~ Robert Hughes, Time[1268]

Perhaps it's only a coincidence that the main hospital in Monrovia is "John F. Kennedy Medical Center".[1269]

International Cartel of Malignancy

One side effect of the Ebola scare is that obedience conditioning has been taken to the next level.

During the height of the Ebola panic, previous conditioning of citizens walking through a humiliating naked body scanner with hands in the air (like a prisoner of war) had the added training of a government official pointing a temperature-gauging "gun" directly at their head.

Fear over Ebola made previously skeptical citizens more willing to receive a government vaccine.

One of the most disturbing stories to come out of Liberia claimed men were being arrested for poisoning the Liberian water supply while children were dying after receiving vaccinations related to protecting them from Ebola. [italics suspended]

> A man in Schieffelin, a community located in Margibi County on the Robertsfield Highway, has been arrested for attempting to put formaldehyde into a well used by the community.
>
> Reports say around 10 a.m., he approached the well with powder in

a bottle. Mobbed by the community, he confessed that he had been paid to put formaldeyde into the well, and that he was not the only one. He reportedly told community dwellers, "We are many." There are agents in Harbel, Dolostown, Cotton Tree and other communities around the country, he said.

State radio, ELBC, reports that least 10 people in the Dolostown community have died after drinking water from poisoned wells.

The man also alleged that some water companies, particularly those bagging mineral water to sell, are also involved. The poison, he said, produces Ebola-like symptoms and subsequently kills people.

The Observer had previously been informed that people dressed as nurses were going into communities with "Ebola Vaccines". Once injected, it reportedly produces Ebola-like symptoms and sends victims into a coma. Shortly thereafter, victims expire. Communities are now reportedly chasing vaccine peddlers out of their communities. After 10 children reportedly died from the "vaccine" in Bensonville, the peddlers were reportedly chased out of the community upon their next visit.

It is possible that the "vaccine" is/was composed of the same formaldehyde-water mixture. This publication has received reports from families whose loved ones' organs were missing upon return of the bodies to the families. Families suspect an organ trafficking operation is capitalizing on the outbreak of the Ebola virus in Liberia. ~ the Liberian Observer[1270]

When asked by e-mail about this, molecular biology expert and author Sharon Gilbert stated that, although a doctor would notice mucosa of the mouth and esophagus appearing corroded, the victim would suffer from nausea and vomiting, two symptoms of viral hemorrhagic fevers.

The untrained eye would indeed think the victim was suffering from the same pandemic they were watching hyped on the local news.

Satan In Charge

Are we in good hands under the Center for Disease Control and Prevention; the CDC?

Kimberly Quinlan Lindsey, the deputy director for the CDC's Laboratory Science Policy and Practice Program Office, was arrested in 2010 for forcing a 6 year old boy and several of her pets to perform and be subject to, perverse sex acts with her and her "live-in boyfriend". She was removed from her position but was quickly reinstated.[1271]

Shockingly, this is a familiar pattern found by those who closely inspect the secret lives of the world's Elite.

In an interview for TruNews on 1 October 2014, Atlanta physician Dr. Elaina George was at a total loss as to the apparent U.S. government incompetence regarding travel to and from African nations who were dealing with thousands of deaths from Ebola.[1272]

She noted that Ebola's 21 day gestation would allow for more contact between infected persons before their symptoms would become evident and they could be quarantined.

Experts and honest journalists remain perplexed as to why the United States would leave access to the effected African nations like Sierra Leone and Liberia wide open.

> *Several African nations have restricted or banned air travel from Ebola-stricken countries, and airlines including Kenya Airways, British Airways, Air Cote D'Ivoire and Nigeria's Arik Air have suspended flights from the countries. ...*
>
> *Others airlines have greatly reduced air travel in the region.*
>
> *...other suspensions reflect a widespread fear that a person sick with Ebola could get on a plane and potentially infect other passengers and airline crew members.* ~ Washington Post[1273]

In 2010, Barack Obama "quietly" dissolved Federal power to quarantine travelers who showed symptoms of having dangerous communicable diseases.

> *The Obama administration has quietly scrapped plans to enact sweeping new federal quarantine regulations that the Centers for Disease Control and Prevention touted four years ago as critical to protecting Americans from dangerous diseases spread by travelers.*
>
> *The regulations, proposed in 2005 during the Bush administration amid fears of avian flu, would have given the federal government additional powers to detain sick airline passengers and those exposed to certain diseases. They also would have expanded requirements for airlines to report ill passengers to the CDC and mandated that airlines collect and maintain contact information for fliers in case they later needed to be traced as part of an investigation into an outbreak.*

Airline and civil liberties groups, which had opposed the rules, praised their withdrawal. ~ USA Today[1274]

Barack Obama's Director for the Center of Disease Control, Tom Frieden, made the astounding statement that closing off travel from Ebola-stricken West African countries will actually make the spread of Ebola *worse*[1275]. Perhaps lacking any foundation in logic or good sense, Frieden attempted to use the Gaslighting techniques already well-tested by the administration.

The last day in July of 2014, it was "recommended" to Barack Obama by his Secretary of Health and Human Services Kathleen Sebelius as well as Acting Surgeon General Boris Lushniak[pp] that he amend a Bush "Executive Order"[1276] regarding communicable diseases to now include—

> *Severe acute respiratory syndromes, which are diseases that are associated with fever and signs and symptoms of pneumonia or other respiratory illness, are capable of being transmitted from person to person, and that either are causing, or have the potential to cause, a pandemic, or, upon infection, are highly likely to cause mortality or serious morbidity if not properly controlled.*[1277]

It is extremely ironic that each "Executive Order" starts with the words

---

Republican-Approved

The former female governor of the state of Kansas, Kathleen Sebelius, is who Barack Obama picked to be his Secretary of Health and Human Services.

The most noteworthy aspect of her career is also the most disturbing.

She is so dedicated to abortion that she gave safe harbor to one of the most vicious 3rd Trimester child executioners in America, George Tiller.

Third Trimester abortion "doctors" make Nazi eugenicists blush. They do no less than birth a fully-formed baby and kill the infant in unspeakable ways while they hold the child.

Tiller was ushering at the Reformation Lutheran Church in Wichita when Pro-Life activist Scott Roeder couldn't take it anymore and shot him through the eye in the church parking lot on May 31, 2009.

[pp] Admiral Lushniak is a Ukrainian specialist in biological warfare. A rather interesting "interlock", as Professor Sutton would say.

"By the authority vested in me as President by the Constitution..."

No such Constitutional authority exists.

A California Emergency Response Twitter account disclosed that Golden State Fire/EMS "tweeted" they were warned months before to prepare for an Ebola outbreak[1278]. Since then, the Golden State EMS Twitter account has disappeared[1279]. They were replying to another account in correspondence and that account—Future Money Trends—is still up and they have the exchange still posted as of this writing.[1280,1281]

ABC dispatched their Chief Health and Medical Editor, Dr. Richard Besser, to Monrovia where he submitted an emotional report of a man laying dead in the streets from Ebola—until the victim showed signs of life minutes before being carted away for burial.[1282]

Collusion leading to outright propaganda between the government and media became apparent as, in 2009 Dr. Richard Besser was the head of Barack Obama's Centers for Disease Control and Prevention—the CDC.[1283]

The travel arrangements that the first infectee Eric Duncan, a.k.a. "Patient 0", made kept casual inspectors from getting suspicious.

> *Details of the man's 28-hour trip from western Africa emerged Wednesday. He flew on two airlines, took three flights, and had lengthy airport layovers before reaching Texas on Sept.*

To paraphrase Ann Coulter; "Babies: 1, abortionists: 50 million."

Barack Obama's Attorney General, Eric Holder, immediately dispatched Federal Marshalls to protect all remaining abortionists.

Holder had the added impetus of losing money—his wife and sister-in-law co-own the building where "Doctor" Tyrone Cecil Malloy preyed on black pregnant women.

Malloy was sentenced to 4 years in prison for taking Medicaid funds as payment for his services.

This has the added benefit of keeping him away from the one or two brave journalists that might ask an uncomfortable question.

SOURCES:

Sebelius Unfit For HHS Post – Facts About Her Connections To The Abortion Cartel, Operation Rescue
http://www.operationrescue.org/noblog/sebelius-unfit-for-hhs-post-facts-about-her-connections-to-the-abortion-cartel/

20. ...

Thomas Eric Duncan left Monrovia, Liberia, on Sept. 19 aboard a Brussels Airlines jet to the Belgian capital, according to a Belgian official. After layover of nearly seven hours, he boarded United Airlines Flight 951 to Dulles International Airport near Washington, D.C. After another layover of nearly three hours, he then flew Flight 822 from Dulles to Dallas-Fort Worth International Airport, the airline confirmed. ~ ABC affiliate WFAA 8[1284]

When he began falling ill, Duncan was treated at a local hospital and then discharged back out into public circulation. This was in spite of telling officials that he had no Social Security Number.

On Sept. 26, he sought treatment at the hospital after becoming ill but was sent back to the northeast Dallas apartment complex where he was staying with a prescription for antibiotics. Duncan's sister, Mai Wureh, said he notified health-care workers that he was visiting from Liberia when they asked for his Social Security number and he told them he didn't have one. ~ USA Today[1285]

Hospital authorities should've immediately questioned a man with no SSN, especially if there was a risk that he had traveled from Ebola-infected Liberia[1286]. In today's illegal-alien friendly America, that is not the case.

Media reported that a second person was being monitored for symptoms[1287] and Mr. Duncan had been in contact with school children before being reinterred into the hospital[1288]. Sources stated he was vomiting profusely.[1289]

The hospital that treated Duncan apologized for its criminal negligence.

---

49 Million To Five, Ann Coulter
http://www.anncoulter.com/columns/2009-06-03.html

Abortionist "Took A Utensil And Stabbed [baby born alive], And Twisted": Allegation, LifeSite News
https://www.lifesitenews.com/news/abortionist-took-a-utensil-and-stabbed-baby-born-alive-and-twisted-allegati

Holder's Family Papers Over His Ties To Abortion Doctor, Human Events
http://humanevents.com/2012/10/31/eric-holders-family-papers-over-his-ties-to-abortion-doctor/

DeKalb Physician Sentenced to Prison for Medicaid Fraud, the Attorney General of Georgia
http://law.ga.gov/press-releases/2014-03-21/dekalb-physician-sentenced-prison-medicaid-fraud

The first person to be diagnosed with Ebola on American soil went to the emergency room last week, but was released from the hospital even though he told staff he had traveled from Liberia.

"A travel history was taken, but it wasn't communicated to the people who were making the decision. ... It was a mistake. They dropped the ball," said Dr. Anthony Fauci, director of the National Institute of Allergy and Infectious Diseases.

"You don't want to pile on them, but hopefully this will never happen again. ... The CDC has been vigorously emphasizing the need for a travel history," Fauci told CNN's "The Lead with Jake Tapper." ~ CNN[1290]

There are few facilities in America capable of handling a pandemic[1291]. It is a foregone conclusion that any official or leader seditious enough to invite one with purposefully malignant policies would be committing an act of high treason. Why would they do such a thing unless they were being ordered to by a higher authority?

—A decidedly malignant one.

In response to the Ebola scare, Barack Obama has called in the Army, and his Secretary of Defense, Georgetown Professor Charles "Chuck" Hagel, would not disappoint.

The Obama/Hagel solution to the West African Ebola outbreak was to send 3,000 American soldiers to the affected

---

Friend or Foe?

Both retired Generals William "Jerry" Boykin and Paul E. Vallely are favorites for Christian Conservative media as they are both vocal and critical of the Obama Administration's self-destructive policies—traits not found in any active duty flag grade officers.

Although retired, General Vallely was recently filmed in Syria helping train Islamist rebels to overthrow the stable government of Bashar al Assad. These are the same rebels who have been torturing and murdering Syria's Christians.

Jerry Boykin is listed as a "Born Again" Christian. Boykin is renowned in the Special Warfare community as a founding member of "Delta Force". One of Boykin's many responsibilities in retirement is Executive Vice President for the Christian advocacy group, the Family Research Council.

He's also "Grand Chancellor" of the "Knights Hospitallers of the Sovereign Order of

location.[1292]

> ...consider the difference between the president's response to ISIS and his response to the Ebola outbreak. He's sending a large force, much larger than ISIS is getting, to deal with this Ebola outbreak.
>
> *Why is he doing* [that]*?* ~ Brit Hume, Fox News Senior Political Analyst[1293]

In a subsequent press release, Obama's Pentagon spokesperson Rear Admiral John Kirby increased the number of troops deploying to *four* thousand and said, "There's no ceiling on this."[1294]

Retired Generals Jerry Boykin and Paul Vallely blasted the decision[1295] although no active duty flag officers have made comment.

The move was so counter-intuitive most experts assumed whomever was guiding Obama's foreign policy was exploiting the outbreak to extend the influence of the United States military into a continent ripe with important resources.

However, there is a precedent for a motive more sinister; soldiers returning home from WWI were carriers for the disease that killed more than bullets did— the Spanish Flu. [italics suspended]

> The first World War was of a short duration, so the vaccine makers were unable to use up all their vaccines. As they were (and still are) in business for profit, they decided to sell it to the rest of the population. So they drummed up the largest vaccination campaign in U.S. history.

Saint John of Jerusalem; Knights of Malta, the Ecumenical Order."

Some may see a conflict of interest between the two.

SOURCES:

"Retired" U.S. General Paul Vallely Helping Islamist "Rebels" in Syria, Johnny Cirucci, YouTube
https://www.youtube.com/watch?v=unRIzIIwysk&feature=youtu.be

FRC Staff: Jerry Boykin, Executive Vice President ~ the Family Research Council
http://www.frc.org/jerryboykin

William G. Boykin>Religious/Political Views and Comments, ~ Wikipedia
http://en.wikipedia.org/wiki/William_G._Boykin#Religious.2FPolitical_views_and_comments

Knights Hospitallers of the Sovereign Order of Saint John of Jerusalem Knights of Malta, the Ecumenical Order > Leadership
http://www.theknightshospitallers.org/leadership

There were no epidemics to justify it so they used other tricks. Their propaganda claimed the soldiers were coming home from foreign countries with all kinds of diseases and that everyone must have all the shots on the market. ...

— the 1918 Spanish Influenza was a vaccine-induced disease caused by extreme body poisoning from the conglomeration of many different vaccines. ...

All the doctors and people who were living at the time of the 1918 Spanish Influenza epidemic say it was the most terrible disease the world has ever had. Strong men, hale and hearty, one day would be dead the next. The disease had the characteristics of the black death added to typhoid, diphtheria, pneumonia, smallpox, paralysis and all the diseases the people had been vaccinated with immediately following World War 1. Practically the entire population had been injected "seeded" with a dozen or more diseases — or toxic serums.

When all those doctor-made diseases started breaking out all at once it was tragic.

That pandemic dragged on for two years, kept alive with the addition of more poison drugs administered by the doctors who tried to suppress the symptoms. As far as I could find out, the flu hit only the vaccinated. Those who had refused the shots escaped the flu.

...the 1918 flu epidemic killed 20,000,000 people throughout the world. ...

There was seven times more disease among the vaccinated soldiers than among the unvaccinated civilians, and the diseases were those they had been vaccinated against. One soldier who had returned from overseas in 1912 told me that the army hospitals were filled with cases of infantile paralysis and he wondered why grown men should have an infant disease. Now, we know that paralysis is a common after-effect of vaccine poisoning. Those at home didn't get the paralysis until after the worldwide vaccination campaign in 1918. ~ *Swine Flu Exposé*, Eleanora I. McBean, Ph.D., N.D.[1296]

Actually, the numbers are closer to **50** million.

—And "science" is working to bring this threat back to life.

Sir Mark Sykes, 6th baronet and owner of historic Sledmere House in Yorkshire, was killed by the Spanish flu virus in 1919, aged 39.

> *Sir Mark was buried in a lead coffin which scientists believe may have helped to preserve the virus...*
>
> *In order to dig up Sir Mark's body from the church in the Sledmere estate, the researchers had to get permission from all of his living relatives as well as relatives of his wife Lady Edith Violet Sykes, who was buried with him.*
>
> *A church court covering the Diocese of York has authorised the exhumation of the body of Sir Mark, after permission was given by his grandchildren.* ~ Urmee Khan, the Telegraph[1297]

It is not a coincidence that the long-dead host of this would-be zombie horror was a member of the Elite.

This unbelievable undertaking was couched in terms of "helping to understand how pandemics like bird flu spread", but not every expert was buying that.

> *Scientists at the University of Wisconsin-Madison used a technique called reverse genetics to build the virus from fragments of wild bird flu strains. They then mutated the virus to make it airborne to spread more easily from one animal to another.*
>
> *"The work they are doing is absolutely crazy. The whole thing is exceedingly dangerous," said Lord May, the former president of the Royal Society and one time chief science adviser to the UK government.* ~ Ian Sample, The Guardian[1298]

What In the World Are They Spraying?

When commercial aircraft travel through the atmosphere at 30,000 they leave a trail of condensation behind—water vapor—which dissipates in a short period of time.

La Responsible – Wikimedia Commons

In the past few decades, however, Americans have increasingly emerged from their homes to find a network of non-dissipating aircraft trails crisscrossing across their horizon.

Euphemistically called "chemtrails", these are *not* the result of normal aircraft operations though few citizens question them.

Who is spraying what and why?

Perhaps a better question is, "What's at stake?"

If a way could be found to manipulate weather, a weapon would result that is nothing short of a doomsday device. The damage, loss of life and destruction of property that could be accomplished with complete anonymity would be unspeakable.

There are some who say such a weapon exists and has already been used.

In 1952, Lynmouth, England experienced a deluge of ninety million tons of water in an over-night flash flood that killed 35. It was later revealed that the RAF was conducting "experiments" that caused the flood, though not a single officer or official was ever reprimanded.[1299]

Nikola Tesla may have been the most brilliant inventor of his era. Some 700 patents are connected to Tesla dealing in everything from alternating current to remote control. Yet few around the globe have ever heard his name. Perhaps that's because his claim to be able to effect weather by electricity and to pull electricity from the atmosphere (providing basically free energy anywhere in the world) were revelations that got Tesla erased from the pages of history by big-monied interests.[1300]

Tesla found that if the atmosphere could be heated, weather fronts could be manipulated in ways that made them many times worse or all but disappear.

Massive antenna arrays such as the High Frequency Active Auroral Research Program (HAARP) in Alaska[1301], Puerto Rico and elsewhere can do that but lacing the atmosphere with refractive particulate makes such facilities many times more effective. Aluminum, barium and strontium have all been suggested as to what has been sprayed with aluminum being the top contender.

A 2010 study of whales found a shockingly high amount of heavy metals in their systems[1302]. The same can be said of soil and water tables in any number of locations around the world.[1303]

Researchers and alternative media journalists have suggested that the devastation that was hurricane Katrina was manipulated by "geoengineering". A chemtrail watchdog blog claims to have satellite image proof.[1304]

In late October 2012, hurricane Sandy was described by meteorologists as a "hybrid" and a "frankenstorm".

> *The name may be funny—Frankenstorm—but be advised: Hurricane Sandy is no joke. Over the weekend meteorologists were running out of frightening things to say about Sandy, which by the time it makes landfall on Monday evening—most likely in New Jersey—will almost certainly be the largest storm to ever hit the East Coast, with a reach that extends some 450 miles beyond its core. Sandy truly will be the perfect storm—not just because a hurricane is meeting a northern blockage that will fuel its strength as it hits land as well as another western storm system, but because Sandy is set to strike the richest and most populated part of the U.S.*
> ~ Time[1305]

The disaster seemed to be timed perfectly for Barack Obama to be showcased as a leader who got things done. NJ Republican Governor Chris Christie provided excellent fodder for Obama supporters as the two worked hand-in-hand for the cameras.

Chuck Kennedy – Wikimedia Commons

> *On the six-month anniversary of Hurricane Sandy, New Jersey Gov. Chris Christie on Monday dismissed GOP criticism of his kind words for President Barack Obama in the aftermath of the storm and said that the president has delivered everything he promised.*
>
> *"No," he said flatly on MSNBC's "Morning Joe," when asked whether he regretted working with and lauding Obama after the devastating storm — something that occurred right ahead of the 2012 election and outraged some conservatives.*

"Listen, the president has kept every promise that he made," Christie said. ~ POLITICO[1306]

Leftist pundits like Chris Matthews actually gave thanks for the storm.[1307]

Sandy turned out to be the ultimate "October surprise"—one brought about solely by "nature".

> *Amidst a blizzard of last-minute polls, I'm still working on my final calls for the electoral map, which I'll post later today. But first a quick heads-up about Hurricane Sandy and its aftermath. I know that some readers find it distasteful to cast such a human tragedy in terms of electoral politics, but there's no getting away from the fact that President's adroit response to the storm has had a significant effect on public opinion. After being behind in the national polls for most of October, he has now reëstablished a narrow lead. While there are a number of possible explanations for this turnaround, the most convincing is the simplest: his handling of Sandy has raised his standing, and his poll ratings.* ~ the New Yorker[1308]

Geoengineering

"Geoengineering" is any process by which human beings effect the climate or environment. It is a massive undertaking that skeptics claim is impossible without a significant infrastructure. "If they're really spraying, where are the whistleblowers?" is the frequent barb.

Although whistleblowers are rare they aren't non-existent. Former Air Force Senior Industrial Hygienist and Environmental Specialist, Kristen Meghan has recounted overseeing large quantities of "chemtrail" particulate frequently delivered to posts she has worked at.[1309]

Military operation secrecy can account for most of the silence. The rest can be seen as willful collusion by soldiers of the Left.

For many Leftists, "climate change" has become their religion. Not having one of their own, they proselytize like Jesuits, even to the extreme that those who disagree with their "obvious" reality are considered dangerous and criminal.

> *Accurately understanding our natural environment and sharing that information can be a matter of life or death. When it comes to global warming, much of the public remains in denial about a set of facts that the majority of scientists clearly agree on. With such high*

> stakes, an organised campaign funding misinformation ought to be considered criminally negligent.
>
> The earthquake that rocked L'Aquila Italy in 2009 provides an interesting case study of botched communication. This natural disaster left more than 300 people dead and nearly 66,000 people homeless. In a strange turn of events six Italian scientists and a local defence minister were subsequently sentenced to six years in prison. ...
>
> More deaths can already be attributed to climate change than the L'Aquila earthquake and we can be certain that deaths from climate change will continue to rise with global warming. Nonetheless, climate denial remains a serious deterrent against meaningful political action in the very countries most responsible for the crisis.
> ~ Lawrence Torcello, Assistant Professor of Philosophy at Rochester Institute of Technology[1310]

The Left imagine the unseen killer of "climate change" stacking bodies like cordwood. As a result, simply disagreeing with them is probable cause.

> Man-made climate change happens. Man-made climate change kills a lot of people. It's going to kill a lot more. We have laws on the books to punish anyone whose lies contribute to people's deaths. It's time to punish the climate-change liars. ~ Adam Weinstein, Gawker[1311]

These are people who would happily participate in dumping millions of tons of particulate into the atmosphere without your say. The plans are openly discussed.

> A controversial proposal to create artificial white clouds over the ocean in order to reflect sunlight and counter global warming could make matters worse, scientists have warned.
>
> The proposed scheme to create whiter clouds over the oceans by injecting salt spray into the air from a flotilla of sailing ships is one of the more serious proposals of researchers investigating the possibility of "geoengineering" the climate in order to combat global warming.
>
> Geoengineering – deliberately altering the global climate – was dismissed as outlandish fantasy a decade ago but has recently been seen as a serious topic of study, given the international failure to curb global emissions of carbon dioxide and the possibility of

extreme climate change. ~ Steve Connor, the Independent[1312]

Day after day, month after month, year after year, people are being poisoned from above and it is having a devastating effect.

The exact causes of Alzheimer's disease are still unknown, but experts have identified a host of contributing factors: diabetes, smoking, saturated fats. Now a theory points the finger in a different direction: a variety of metals that can build up in the body over time. Look inside the brains of people with Alzheimer's who have died and you'll find protein clogging the brain's signaling system, along with tiny clusters called beta-amyloid plaques. "When researchers tease those plaques apart, they find metals, including iron, copper, and aluminum," says Neal Barnard, MD, an adjunct associate professor of medicine at the George Washington University School of Medicine. ~ Leslie Goldman, Huffington Post[1313]

With so much foreign material in the soil, the "cure" has actually been the cause as CO_2-consuming trees are dying off at alarming rates.[1314]

Each streak of white across the sky is one more string of evidence which implies that billionaires believe the "useless eaters" must die.

TED

The annual "Technology, Entertainment & Design" Conference is a gala event where the world Elite gather to push their latest hotbutton propaganda issues. The inexplicable confluence of those 3 words tells you all you need to know about who is behind the conference, or why mainstream media simply calls it "TED" without explaining what the acronym stands for.

The 2007 guest speaker was Bill Clinton and he spoke on the necessity for population control in Africa.[1315]

In 2010, Microsoft billionaire Bill Gates spoke[1316] on how Americans are producing 20 metric tons of "deadly" carbon dioxide every year and how their standard of living must plummet if the world is to be saved.

During Gates' presentation, he put up on screen an equation with CO_2 on one side and 4 variables on the other, representing "people", "services per person", "energy per service" and "CO_2 per unit energy" and then told his enraptured audience "One of these numbers is gonna have to get pretty-near to '0'."

So said one of the richest men on the planet whose every move entails a massive coterie of CO_2-exhaling attendants.

Gates, (whose father, Bill Gates, Senior, was a former president of Planned Parenthood[1317]) continued:

> *The world today has 6.8 billion people, that's headed up to about 9 billion. Now if we do a really great job on new vaccines, health care, reproductive health services, we could lower that by perhaps 10 or 15%.*[1318]

We call the above a "non sequitur"—a conclusion that is illogically disconnected from its premise.

We also call that a "Freudian slip".

How is doing "a really great job on new vaccines" going to get one of the Elite's variables of world population to "near zero"?

The latest outbreak of Ebola could be a test run.

Endnotes

[1226] *15 Syrian Children Dead Following UN Measles Vaccination Campaign*, unattributed, 18 September 2014, RT
http://rt.com/news/188580-syria-children-dead-vaccinations/

[1227] *Death Toll in Syria Estimated at 191,000*, Nick Cumming-Bruce, 22 August 2014, New York Times
http://www.nytimes.com/2014/08/23/world/middleeast/un-raises-estimate-of-dead-in-syrian-conflict-to-191000.html?_r=0

[1228] *After a 17 Year Struggle, Baby Disabled From Vaccines Wins 3 Million Euros in Compensation*, Christina England, 18 May 2012, VacTruth.com
http://vactruth.com/2012/05/18/baby-disabled-from-vaccines/

[1229] *Smallpox Vaccine "Triggered Aids Virus"*, Pearce Wright, 11 May 1987, the London Times, reposted at Want To Know.info
http://www.wanttoknow.info/870511vaccineaids

[1230] *CDC Whistleblower Admits Suppressing Information Regarding Vaccines and Autism*, Ben Swann, 2 September 2014, BenSwann.com
http://benswann.com/cdc-whistleblower-admits-suppressing-information-regarding-vaccines-and-autism/

[1231] *At Least 50 African Children Paralyzed After Receiving Bill Gates-Backed Meningitis Vaccine*, Ethan Huff, 23 January 2013, Natural News
http://www.naturalnews.com/038796_meningitis_vaccine_children_paralyzed.html

[1232] *Exposing the FDA's Vaccine Injury Cover-up: An Interview With Walter Kyle, Esq.*, Catherine Frompovich, 30 August 2012, Activist Post
http://www.activistpost.com/2012/08/exposing-fdas-vaccine-injury-cover-up.html

[1233] *Mercury Poisoning*, John P. Cunha, DO, FACOEP, 18 April 2014, Medicine.net
http://www.medicinenet.com/mercury_poisoning/article.htm

[1234] *Adverse Effects Of Adjuvants In Vaccines*, Viera Scheibner, Ph.D., Nexus Dec 2000 (Vol 8, No1) & Feb 2001 (Vol 8, Number 2)
http://www.whale.to/vaccine/adjuvants.html

[1235] *Squalene: The Swine Flu Vaccine's Dirty Little Secret Exposed*, Joseph Mercola, Ph.D., 4 August 2009, Mercola.com
http://articles.mercola.com/sites/articles/archive/2009/08/04/squalene-the-swine-flu-vaccines-dirty-little-secret-exposed.aspx

[1236] *Scientific Study Finds Fluoride Horror Stories Factual*, Paul Joseph Watson, 15 January 2008, Prison Planet
http://www.prisonplanet.com/articles/january2008/011508_fluoride_horror.htm

[1237] *Man Sentenced to Jail for Collecting Rainwater in Oregon*, 30 July 2012, RT
http://rt.com/usa/rain-water-harrington-oregon-439/

[1238] *Does Fluoride In Drinking Water Hurt Your Brain?* Dr. Keith Ablow, 22 August 2012, FoxNews
http://www.foxnews.com/health/2012/08/22/does-fluoride-in-drinking-water-hurt-your-brain/

[1239] A report from local news WQAD Moline, Illinois reposted on the Johnny YouTube channel titled *Fluoride Spill In Rochester, IL Burned Through Concrete*
https://www.youtube.com/watch?&v=y04CNZJ6HkA

[1240] *Billionaire Club In Bid To Curb Overpopulation*, John Harlow, 24 May 2009, the Sunday Times
http://www.thesundaytimes.co.uk/sto/news/world_news/article169829.ece
    If, like me, you're not efféte enough to subscribe to the Times, you can find the article reposted at Global Research:
http://www.globalresearch.ca/billionaire-club-in-bid-to-curb-overpopulation/13736
[1241] *Bill Gates Funds Research Into "Flying Syringe" Mosquitoes to Deliver Vaccines*, unattributed, 23 October 2008, AFP, reposted at Cryptogon.com
http://www.cryptogon.com/?p=4601
[1242] *UT Professor Says Death Is Imminent*, Jamie Mobley, 2 April 2006, The Gazette-Enterprise, reposted here;
http://forums.macresource.com/read.php?2,76663
[1243] *Edible Vaccine Inventor Jokes about Culling Population with GMO Virus*, TRUTHstreammedia, YouTube
https://www.youtube.com/watch?v=stGT6NcxVRQ
[1244] *Did the Creator of the Experimental Ebola Drug Joke About Culling 25% of the World's Population?* Michael Krieger, 6 August 2014, Liberty Blitzkrieg blog
http://libertyblitzkrieg.com/2014/08/06/did-the-creator-of-the-experimental-ebola-drug-joke-about-culling-25-of-the-worlds-population/
[1245] *"One Of Biggest Tragedies": Ebola Triggers Sierra Leone Lockdown*, 19 September 2014, RT YouTube
https://www.youtube.com/watch?v=XmrlbJsOCYc&
[1246] *Ebola (Ebola Virus Disease)>Transmission*, Centers for Disease Control and Prevention, 18 September 2014, CDC.gov
http://www.cdc.gov/vhf/ebola/transmission/
[1247] *Ebola from Pigs to Monkeys*, Ed Yong, 15 November 2012, The Scientist.com
http://www.the-scientist.com/?articles.view/articleNo/33277/title/Ebola-from-Pigs-to-Monkeys/
[1248] *Sierra Leone's Chief Ebola Doctor Contracts The Virus*, unattributed, 23 July 2014, Reuters via the NY Daily News
http://www.nydailynews.com/life-style/health/sierra-leone-chief-ebola-doctor-contracts-virus-article-1.1877739
[1249] *U.S. Doctor Stricken With Ebola "Is Terrified"*, unattributed, 29 July 2014, Sky News
http://news.sky.com/story/1309462/us-doctor-stricken-with-ebola-is-terrified
[1250] *Experimental Drug Likely Saved Ebola Patients*, Dr. Sanjay Gupta and Danielle Dellorto, 5 August 2014, CNN
http://www.cnn.com/2014/08/04/health/experimental-ebola-serum/
[1251] *Ebola and ZMapp: What is the "Secret Serum" That "Cured" American Doctor Kent Brantly?* Hannah Osborne, 5 August 2014, International Business Times
http://www.ibtimes.co.uk/ebola-zmapp-what-secret-serum-that-cured-american-doctor-kent-brantly-1459856
[1252] *The CDC, NIH & Bill Gates Own the Patents On Existing Ebola & Related Vaccines: Mandatory Vaccinations Are Near*, Dave Hodges, 17 September 2014, the Common Sense Show.com
http://www.thecommonsenseshow.com/2014/09/17/the-cdc-nih-bill-gates-own-the-patents-on-existing-ebola-related-vaccines-mandatory-vaccinations-are-near/

[1253] *Scientists: "Positive" Results In 1st Human Trial of Experimental Ebola Vaccine*, Laura Spark, 27 November 2014, CNN
http://www.cnn.com/2014/11/27/health/ebola-outbreak/
[1254] *Anthony S. Fauci > Education and Career*, Wikipedia
https://en.wikipedia.org/wiki/Anthony_S._Fauci#Education_and_career
[1255] *Obama Adds "Ebola Czar" to Contentious List of White House Czars*, Stephanie Condon, 17 October 2014, CBS News
http://www.cbsnews.com/news/obama-adds-ebola-czar-to-contentious-list-of-white-house-czars/
[1256] *New Ebola Czar: A Bureaucrat with Zero Healthcare Experience Who Helped Fuel Housing Bubble*, Melissa Melton, 17 October 2014, the Daily Sheeple
http://www.thedailysheeple.com/new-ebola-czar-bureaucrat-and-lobbyist-with-zero-healthcare-experience-helped-fuel-housing-bubble_102014
[1257] *Who Is Ron Klain, Who Will Lead The Obama Administration's Response To Ebola?* Katie Zezima, 17 October 2014, the Washington Post
http://www.washingtonpost.com/blogs/post-politics/wp/2014/10/17/who-is-ron-klain-who-will-lead-the-obama-administrations-response-to-ebola/
[1258] *Klain Appointed Ebola Czar*, Suzanne Monyak, 21 October 2014, The Hoya
http://www.thehoya.com/klain-appointed-ebola-czar/
[1259] *Ebola Czar Ron Klain: African Overpopulation, "Climate Change" Top Concerns*, Johnny Cirucci YouTube
https://www.youtube.com/watch?v=CwlT46XlxU0&
[1260] *Dallas Hospital Had the Ebola Screening Machine That the Military Is Using in Africa*, Patrick Tucker, 16 October 2014, Defense One
http://www.defenseone.com/threats/2014/10/dallas-hospital-had-ebola-screening-machine-military-using-africa/96713/
[1261] screen shot from the blog of Glenn Canady of purported "Eric Duncan" LinkedIn profile, reposted at the Patriot Press
http://johnnycirucci.com/wp/?attachment_id=3057
[1262] screenshot of my Bing search shows there *was* such a profile (why the hell is "Catholic.org" the #4 hit with something *completely* unrelated???)
http://johnnycirucci.com/wp/?attachment_id=3058
[1263] "Profile Not Found"...note the hyperlink address of "eric-duncan"
http://johnnycirucci.com/wp/?attachment_id=3059
[1264] *Ebola Crisis: "Clipboard Man" Seen Without Any Protective Gear Standing With Workers In Full Hazmat Suits Transporting Patient*, Heather Saul, 16 October 2014, the Independent
http://www.independent.co.uk/news/world/americas/clipboard-man-seen-without-any-protective-gear-stood-with-workers-in-full-hazmat-suits-transporting-ebola-patient-9798637.html#
[1265] *Here's Why "Clipboard Guy" Wasn't Wearing A Hazmat Suit While Moving The Ebola Patient*, Kevin Loria, 16 October 2014, Business Insider
http://www.businessinsider.com/man-with-clipboard-didnt-need-hazmat-2014-10
[1266] *Dallas Officials Urge Calm After Second Ebola Diagnosis*, WFAA and AP, 12 October 2014, WFAA ABC 8
http://www.wfaa.com/story/news/health/2014/10/12/presbyterian-hospital-worker-ebola/17147507/

[1267] *NBC News Freelance Journalist Tests Positive for Ebola*, Joshua Barajas, 3 October 2014, PBS
http://www.pbs.org/newshour/rundown/nbc-news-freelancer-tests-positive-ebola/
[1268] *The Fraying Of America*, Robert Hughes, 24 June 2001, Time
http://content.time.com/time/magazine/article/0,9171,158947,00.html
[1269] *Intro to JFKMC*, JFKMC Doctors
http://jfkmcdoctors.wordpress.com/jfk-medical-center/
[1270] *BREAKING: Formaldeyde in Water Allegedly Causing Ebola-like Symptoms*, Observer Staff, 2 September 2014, the Liberian Observer
http://www.liberianobserver.com/security/breaking-formaldeyde-water-allegedly-causing-ebola-symptoms
[1271] *CDC Official Back To Work Amid Child Molestation, Bestiality Charges*, unattributed, 1 December 2011, CBS Atlanta
http://atlanta.cbslocal.com/2011/12/01/cdc-official-back-to-work-amid-child-molestation-bestiality-charges/
[1272] *Wednesday October 1, 2014 – Dr. Elaina George & Bill Fleckenstein*, TruNews.com
http://www.trunews.com/wednesday-october-1-2014-dr-elaina-george-bill-fleckenstein/
[1273] *Why Hasn't The U.S. Closed Its Airports To Travelers From Ebola-Ravaged Countries?* Abby Phillip, 1 October 2014, the Washington Post
http://www.washingtonpost.com/news/to-your-health/wp/2014/10/01/why-hasnt-the-u-s-closed-its-airports-to-travelers-from-ebola-ravaged-countries/
[1274] *Obama Administration Scraps Quarantine Regulations*, Alison Young, 1 April 2010, USA Today
http://usatoday30.usatoday.com/news/washington/2010-04-01-quarantine_N.htm
[1275] *CDC Director Doubles Down on Lack of Flight Restrictions From Ebola Stricken Countries*, Katie Pavlich, 3 October 2014, Townhall
https://townhall.com/tipsheet/katiepavlich/2014/10/03/cdc-director-doubles-down-on-lack-of-flight-restrictions-from-ebola-stricken-countries-n1900450
[1276] 42 United States Code 264: Regulations to Control Communicable Diseases
http://uscode.house.gov/view.xhtml?req=granuleid:USC-prelim-title42-section264&num=0&edition=prelim
[1277] *Executive Order—Revised List of Quarantinable Communicable Diseases, Amendment to Executive Order 13295*, Office of the White House Press Secretary
http://www.whitehouse.gov/the-press-office/2014/07/31/executive-order-revised-list-quarantinable-communicable-diseases
[1278] *"Disaster Teams Were Notified Months Ago They Would Be Activated in October"*, Mac Slavo, 1 October 2014, SHTF plan
http://www.shtfplan.com/headline-news/report-disaster-teams-were-told-months-ago-they-would-be-activated-in-october_10012014
[1279] *Sorry, that page doesn't exist!*
https://twitter.com/goldenstateems
[1280] #goldenstateems @goldenstateems twitter account removed. Here's a re-post of their almost shocking tweet #Ebola: @FutureMoneyTren
https://twitter.com/FutureMoneyTren/status/518084153993330688
[1281] I took a screen shot…just in case. :)
http://johnnycirucci.com/wp/?attachment_id=3035

[1282] *Man Thought to Have Died From Ebola Awakens After Burial Team Wraps Him Up*, Richard Besser, 2 October 2014, ABC News
http://abcnews.go.com/Health/man-thought-died-ebola-awakes-burial-team-arrives/story?id=25915800
[1283] *Dr. Richard Besser*, bio, ABC News
http://abcnews.go.com/News/dr-richard-besser-abc-news-official-biography/story?id=8214676
[1284] *Man With Ebola Flew Roundabout Trip To U.S.*, David Koenig and Scott Mayerowitz, 1 October 2014, WFAA 8, ABC affiliate
http://www.wfaa.com/story/news/health/2014/10/01/ebola-patient-airlines-united-brussels/16555277/
[1285] *Officials: Second Person Being Monitored for Ebola*, Marjorie Owens, 1 October 2014, WFAA-TV
http://www.usatoday.com/story/news/nation/2014/10/01/texas-ebola-patient/16525649/
[1286] *Who Is Thomas Eric Duncan? Ebola In US Victim Identified As Liberia Citizen*, Maria Vultaggio, 1 October 2014, International Business Times
http://www.ibtimes.com/who-thomas-eric-duncan-ebola-us-victim-identified-liberia-citizen-1698074
[1287] *ibid*
[1288] *Schoolchildren Have Come Into Contact With Texas Ebola Patient, Officials Say*, Ryan Gorman, 1 October 2014, AOL
http://www.aol.com/article/2014/10/01/schoolchildren-have-come-into-contact-with-texas-ebola-patient/20970709/
[1289] *Dallas Ebola Patient "Throwing Up All Over The Place" On Way To Hospital*, Reuters, 2 October 2014, the Chicago Tribune
http://www.chicagotribune.com/lifestyles/health/chi-ebola-patient-america-20141002-story.html#page=1
[1290] *Hospital "Dropped The Ball" With Ebola Patient's Travel History, NIH Official Says*, Catherine Shoichet, Ashley Fantz and Holly Yan, 1 October 2014, CNN
http://www.cnn.com/2014/10/01/health/ebola-us/index.html
[1291] *After First Ebola Case, Red Flags Emerge That U.S. Unprepared For Pandemic*, Kelly Riddell, 30 September 2014, Washington Times
http://www.washingtontimes.com/news/2014/sep/30/after-first-ebola-case-fears-turn-us-pandemic-prep/?page=all#!
[1292] *U.S. To Deploy Up To 3,000 Military Personnel To Fight Ebola in West Africa*, unattributed, 16 September 2014, Fox News
http://www.foxnews.com/politics/2014/09/16/ebola-crisis-us-sending-3000-military-personnel-west-africa/
[1293] *Reps. King, Schiff on if President Obama's ISIS Strategy Will Succeed*, Chris Wallace 21 September 2014, Fox News
http://www.foxnews.com/on-air/fox-news-sunday-chris-wallace/2014/09/21/reps-king-schiff-if-president-obamas-isis-strategy-will-succeed#p//v/3797934051001
[1294] *U.S. Ramps Up Ebola Troop Deployments, Total May Near 4,000*, Phil Stewart, 3 October 2014, Reuters
http://www.reuters.com/article/2014/10/03/us-health-ebola-usa-pentagon-idUSKCN0HS1MQ20141003

[1295] *Generals Blast Obama's Order Of Troops To Fight Ebola*, Michael Maloof, 6 October 2014, WorldNetDaily
http://www.wnd.com/2014/10/generals-blast-obamas-order-of-troops-to-fight-ebola/
[1296] *Swine Flu Exposé*, Eleanora I. McBean, Ph.D., N.D., Health Research Books (1975), pp. 32, 34, 35, 36
[1297] *Body of Dead Aristocrat Who Died of Spanish Flu Exhumed*, Urmee Khan, 16 September 2008, the Telegraph
http://www.telegraph.co.uk/health/2967801/Body-of-dead-aristocrat-who-died-of-Spanish-flu-exhumed.html
[1298] *Scientists Condemn "Crazy, Dangerous" Creation Of Deadly Airborne Flu Virus*, Ian Sample, 11 June 2014, The Guardian
http://www.theguardian.com/science/2014/jun/11/crazy-dangerous-creation-deadly-airborne-flu-virus
[1299] *Rain-Making Link to Killer Floods*, 30 August 2001, BBC
http://news.bbc.co.uk/2/hi/uk_news/1516880.stm
[1300] *Phenomenon: Nikola Tesla*, Johnny Cirucci, YouTube
https://www.youtube.com/watch?v=HRrXC9ldgaU&
[1301] *HAARP Ionospheric Research Program Set To Continue*, Brian Dodson, 24 July 2013, Gizmag
http://www.gizmag.com/haarp-operations-on-hold/28383/

As with all "mainstream" media coverage of forbidden subjects jizzmag is filled with disinformation. Of course you can manipulate humans with powerful ELF waves blasted at them from the atmosphere.

[1302] *"Jaw-Dropping" Levels Of Heavy Metals Found In Whales*, Arthur Max, 25 June 2010, AP, the Boston Globe
http://www.boston.com/news/science/articles/2010/06/25/jaw_dropping_levels_of_heavy_metals_found_in_whales/
[1303] *Is Aluminium Really a Silent Killer?* Liz Bestic, 5 March 2012, the Telegraph
http://www.telegraph.co.uk/health/9119528/Is-aluminium-really-a-silent-killer.html

"Liz" seems to be a bit of a dullard. Here's what you need to walk away with from this article:
But while 50 years ago we may have ingested minute amounts from vegetables (and possibly from some of the pots they were cooked in), today aluminium is found in almost everything.

[1304] *HURRICANE KATRINA: Satellite Images Confirm Aerosol Geoengineering and EM Modification of CAT-3 Storm*, 31 October 2012, ChemtrailsPlanet
http://chemtrailsplanet.net/2012/10/31/hurricane-katrina-satellite-images-confirm-aerosol-geoengineering-and-em-modification-of-cat-3-storm/
[1305] *Frankenstorm: Why Hurricane Sandy Will Be Historic*, Bryan Walsh, 29 October2012, Time
http://science.time.com/2012/10/29/frankenstorm-why-hurricane-sandy-will-be-historic/
[1306] *Chris Christie: President Obama Delivered on Hurricane Sandy Aid*, Katie Glueck, 29 April 2013, POLITICO
http://www.politico.com/story/2013/04/chris-christie-hurricane-sandy-aid-president-obama-90729.html

[1307] *MSNBC's Matthews: "I'm So Glad We Had That Storm Last Week"*, 7 November 2012, Breitbart
http://www.breitbart.com/Breitbart-TV/2012/11/07/MSNBCs-Matthews-Im-So-Glad-We-Had-That-Storm-Last-Week

[1308] *How Much Did Hurricane Sandy Help Obama?* John Cassidy, 4 November 2012, the New Yorker
http://www.newyorker.com/rational-irrationality/how-much-did-hurricane-sandy-help-obama

[1309] *Geoengineering Whistleblower ~ Ex-Military ~ Kristen Meghan, Hauppauge, NY, January 18th, 2014*, 27 January 2014, Natural News TV
http://tv.naturalnews.com/v.asp?v=aef1f19c4ab1d064ecfdf66b39dfa1fa

[1310] *Is Misinformation About the Climate Criminally Negligent?* Lawrence Torcello, 13 March 2014, the Conversation
https://theconversation.com/is-misinformation-about-the-climate-criminally-negligent-23111

[1311] *Arrest Climate-Change Deniers*, Adam Weinstein, 28 March 2014, Gawker
http://gawker.com/arrest-climate-change-deniers-1553719888

[1312] *Radical Plan to Combat Global Warming "May Raise Temperatures"*, Steve Connor, 07 June 2010, the Independent
http://www.independent.co.uk/news/science/radical-plan-to-combat-global-warming-may-raise-temperatures-1993281.html#

[1313] *3 Metals That Might Cause Memory Problems*, Leslie Goldman, 18 December 2013, Huffington Blows
http://www.huffingtonpost.com/2013/12/18/metal-dangers-memory-loss-alzheimers-disease_n_4413511.html

[1314] *Trees Dying in the West at Record Rate*, David Perlman, 23 January 2009, the San Francisco Chronicle
http://www.sfgate.com/green/article/Trees-dying-in-the-West-at-record-rate-3253763.php

[1315] *Clinton Health Access Initiative: Rwanda - Bill Clinton*, TED.com
https://www.ted.com/participate/ted-prize/prize-winning-wishes/chai-rwanda-bill-clinton

[1316] *Bill Gates: We Need Global "Energy Miracles"*, John D. Sutter, 12 February 2010, CNN
http://www.cnn.com/2010/TECH/02/12/bill.gates.clean.energy/?hpt=T2

[1317] *Bill Gates' Planned-Parenthood-President Dad Inspired Pro-Abort Funding*, unattributed, 9 May 2003, LifeSite News
http://www.lifesitenews.com/news/bill-gates-planned-parenthood-president-dad-inspired-pro-abort-funding#./bill-gates-planned-parenthood-president-dad-inspired-pro-abort-funding?&_suid=141140016726906311548198831841

[1318] *Bill Gates: Innovating to Zero!* TED 2010
http://www.ted.com/talks/bill_gates?language=en
    Yeah. That "zero!" is YOU.

Chapter 14

The Eaters of Children: Sex Slavery Is a Government Industry

"You are of your father the devil, and you want to do the desires of your father. He was a murderer from the beginning, and does not stand in the truth because there is no truth in him. Whenever he speaks a lie, he speaks from his own nature, for he is a liar and the father of lies." ~ John 8:44

"The thief comes only to steal and kill and destroy; I came that they may have life, and have it abundantly." ~ John 10:10

What normal citizens and good hard-working Americans need to understand is that the Elite who manipulate world affairs live in a world that is so foreign to us it is shocking and instantly repugnant.

The world system of "Mystery Babylon" delivers to them any evil they desire.

If you did not believe in a "devil" and you respect the sources I am about to cite, you will believe by the end of this chapter.

The malignant force that feeds the Elite yearns to defile and cause pain to the innocent, the vulnerable. Defenseless animals and children are preferred targets. They *feed* off of them emotionally, sexually and even cannibalistically.

> *As if China needed any more negative press on their barbaric One Child Policy after blind human rights activist Chen Guangcheng's dramatic escape from house arrest, multiple news outlets are now reporting that South Korean officials have seized thousands of capsules and pills that reportedly contain the powdered flesh of fetuses and babies. The stomach-turning story reports that, since August, over 17,000 of these capsules have been seized from smugglers attempting to bring them in from—you guessed it—China.*
>
> *First it was details of forced sterilizations, grotesque forced abortions that included women being strapped to chairs while the butchers of Chinese officialdom tore their offspring from their womb, and babies being drowned in buckets. Now reports indicate*

that cannibalistic capsules were created in factories where the corpses of Chinese babies were chopped like meat, dried out on stoves, and ground into powder. The purpose of these capsules? In a myth akin to the idea that sex with a virgin could cure AIDs, apparently some believe that consuming a dead child can ward off disease. Another report that I desperately hope is inaccurate indicates that they could be used as sexual performance enhancers, grotesquely completing this hellish horror story—have sex, kill the resulting baby, and then use the killed baby to enhance sex. ~ Jonathon Van Maren, Unmasking "Choice"[1319]

When Western culture dehumanizes the unborn with terms like "fetus", unspeakable barbarism is much easier to accomplish. [italics suspended]

> A British citizen has been arrested in Bangkok after six foetuses were found stuffed into travel bags.
>
> Hok Kuen Chow, 28, a Briton born in Hong Kong of Taiwanese parents, was held in the city's Yaowarat area after police received a tip-off.
>
> He is suspected of trying to smuggle the foetuses – from two to seven months – back to Taiwan to sell to wealthy customers online.
>
> Chow has reportedly admitted buying the bodies, which had been roasted dry and painted in gold leaf, for 200,000 baht (£4,040).
>
> Back in Taiwan he could have sold them for six times that amount to rich clients who believe the foetuses will bring them good fortune. "The bodies are between the ages of two and seven months," said Wiwat Kumchumnan, of the police's children and women protection unit.
>
> "Chow said he planned to sell the foetuses to clients who believe they will make them lucky and rich."
>
> "Some were found covered in gold leaf."
>
> Police said the bodies also had a variety of religious decoration and tattoos on them.
>
> The corpses had a number of religious threads on them and they are thought to have undergone a black magic ritual
>
> It was not clear yesterday where the bodies, which had been stored in six travel bags, came from or who had handed them over to

Chow.

It is possible they had undergone the grisly Thai practice "Kuman Thong", in which unwanted babies are surgically removed from their mother's womb before being subjected to a ceremonial ritual.

Instead of being buried, the bodies are roasted dry and covered with a lacquer before being painted with gold leaf. ~ Paul Sims, the Daily Mail[1320]

The "Bible Belt" state of Kansas is reaping what it has sown by empowering extreme abortion defenders like former woman Governor Kathleen Sebelius, outrageously chosen by Barack Obama and confirmed by Republicans in the Senate to be his first Health and Human Services Secretary.

A Kansas City abortionist is out of business after investigators discovered a grisly house of horrors at his clinic – with fetuses kept in Styrofoam cups in his refrigerator and one employee accusing him of microwaving one and stirring it into his lunch.

The unsanitary conditions in Krishna Rajanna's clinic prompted legislative approval of new abortion regulations in Kansas, a bill that was vetoed by the governor. Rajanna's activities have reportedly been the subject of law-enforcement investigations for nearly two years. ~ WorldNetDaily[1321]

This is who the Elite are. With good reason have I termed them "Luciferians".

In April 2014, Sebelius would be replaced by Clinton retread Sylvia Burwell and, like Bill Clinton, conditioned in Communism as a "Rhodes Scholar".

She is best known as having proved her loyalty to the Machine by going dumpster-diving to grab any incriminating documents from the trash of White House Counsel Vince Foster after his death[1322]. Foster's very high-profile "suicide" was investigated by the Washington DC Park Police[1323]. Their crack facilities and team were instrumental in assuring no hint of foul play.

Their investigation was conducted under the watchful eye of the FBI which destroyed crime scene photos, switched out the weapon found on Foster's body and falsified the testimony of key on-scene eyewitnesses.[1324]

Again, and again, and again, we see that in cases of national import, the

FBI can be consistently counted upon to cover up and obfuscate crime. There is no explanation for this except to say *they don't work for the American people.*

The Franklin Coverup

Lawrence King sang the national anthem at the 1984 Republican National Convention.

He was also a serial pedophile who regularly violated young boys and trafficked them to state and national Elites.

In 1994, ITV Yorkshire[1325] (then "Yorkshire Television") did an on-site investigation, traveling from the UK to Omaha, to cover this shocking conspiracy. The documentary was supposed to air on the Discovery Channel but, at the last minute, was pulled from the schedule. A rough-edit of the program still exists[1326], though, and it paints an unbelievable story of the satanic appetites who roam the halls of power in America.

Who can forget the Oscar-winning 1938 classic "Boys Town" with Spencer Tracy and Mickey Rooney?

If the Catholic Church needed to make its image wholesome and valuable, that movie most certainly did.

But Rome doesn't have a good track record when it comes to "celibate" priests coming in contact with children.

> *Almost every day across the world there is a new accusation of child sex abuse or yet another court case filed against a paedophile Catholic priest. These horrors of violence continue to haunt the Vatican with every sign of increasing, and many of the allegations stemmed from Pope John Paul II's 27-year reign. During this time, thousands of family members were called upon to help victims cope with a callous and even malicious Vatican system, while John Paul II caressed, protected and promoted one of Catholicism's worst child abusers, Fr. Marciel Maciel Degollado. In the outrage that followed the Pope's beatification in Vatican City on May 1st, 2011, Boston Globe reporter Kevin Cullen extended the view that Blessed John Paul II "presided over a church that was guilty of one of the biggest institutional cover-ups of criminal*

activity in history". He added that, "Priests were raping children all over the world with impunity", and by studying the growing evidence, we can see the accuracy of Kevin Cullen's statements. ~ Tony Bushby, Vati Leaks[1327]

Requiring celibacy of all her leadership had little to do with Christian doctrine—

> *...if they do not have self-control, let them marry; for it is better to marry than to burn with passion.* ~ I Corinthians 7:9, NASU

—and everything to do with a political entity insuring that property would return to Church leadership. Consequently perversion abounds.

> *The Roman Catholic Church ... has insisted upon celibacy even though many popes, among them Sergius III (904-11), John X (914-28), John XII (955-63), Benedict V (964), Innocent VIII (1484-92), Urban VIII (1623-44), and Innocent X (1644-55), as well as millions of cardinals, bishops, archbishops, monks, and priests throughout history, have repeatedly violated such vows. Not only has celibacy made sinners of the clergy who engage in fornication, but it makes harlots out of those with whom they secretly cohabit. Rome is indeed "the mother of harlots"! Her identification as such is unmistakable. No other city, church, or institution in the history of the world is her rival in this particular evil.*
>
> *History is replete with sayings that mocked the church's false claim to celibacy and revealed the truth: "The holiest hermit has his whore" and "Rome has more prostitutes than any other city because she has the most celibates" are examples. Pius II declared that Rome was "the only city run by bastards" [sons of popes and cardinals]. Catholic historian and former Jesuit Peter de Rosa writes:*
>
>> *Popes had mistresses of fifteen years of age, were guilty of incest and sexual perversions of every sort, had innumerable children, were murdered in the very act of adultery [by jealous husbands who found them in bed with their wives]. ... In the old Catholic phrase, why be holier than the pope?[16]*
>
> *As for abominations, even Catholic historians admit that among the popes were some of the most degenerate and unconscionable ogres in all of history.* ~ *A Woman Rides The Beast*, Dave Hunt[1328]

In Oregon during the 50's, a Jesuit priest preying on teenage boys could get himself shot.

That's almost what happened to Reverend Michael Toulouse. Unfortunately, Oregonians permitted the Catholic/Jesuit leadership to handle the matter and Toulouse was allowed to sneak off to another diocese where he was unknown. [italics suspended]

> Lawyer Timothy D. Kosnoff, who represents some of the men claiming abuse by Toulouse, said the forthcoming bankruptcy resolution — and the money it means for him and his clients — is secondary to exposing Jesuit leadership. For years, some of the Northwest's Jesuit leaders — much like the bishops who headed some of the nation's Catholic dioceses — quietly protected pedophile priests by moving them from place to place, victim to victim.
>
> "They're into protecting their wealth and their image from scandal, even at the expense of harming — gravely harming — children," Kosnoff said. "To me, that was the real evil."
>
> Toulouse was first accused of sex abuse in late 1950, when the father of a 14-year-old boy stalked into the office of the Rev. Francis Corkery, president of Gonzaga University in Spokane, carrying a pistol.
>
> The distraught dad told Corkery he intended to kill Toulouse and tell the press how the priest had sexually abused his son for two years. Corkery jumped up, according to a witness account in court papers, and said, "No, you can't do that. I'll take care of it."
>
> ...Toulouse, then 39, told superiors the boy had been the aggressor.
>
> Jesuit leaders didn't question the boy or consult police...
>
> The Jesuits sent Toulouse to a teaching job at Seattle University...
>
> No one, it appears, warned Seattle's children.
>
> By 1953, Toulouse was planting his feet under the table of a working-class family in Seattle. He won their hearts with his philosophical orations, and took a special interest in their 10-year-old son.
>
> Now in his middle 60s, the son and two younger brothers accuse Toulouse of worming his way into their home and molesting them,

one after another, until the youngest told his mother in 1965.

In interviews with *The Oregonian*, the eldest brother recalled that Toulouse would abuse him and then give him absolution for his sins. ...

His mother, after learning of her youngest son's abuse, complained to the Rev. James B. McGoldrick, a prominent faculty member at Seattle University [such naiveté approaches criminal negligence]. Jesuit officials paid her son a settlement in exchange for signing an agreement that forbid him from suing them or disclosing the allegations.

But the abuse didn't end, according to a lawsuit filed in King County, Wash., by eight men. In one instance, McGoldrick paired Toulouse with a teenage boy who had gotten in trouble with the law to help get the boy back on track. Toulouse is accused of molesting him, too. ~ Bryan Denson, the Oregonian[1329]

Surely Jesuit leadership knew this would be the ultimate outcome—Toulouse would violate young boys again. One can only draw the conclusion that Catholic leadership was purposely serving up American children for the satanic appetites of these fiends.

Boys Town

The Catholic teenage retreat of Boys Town would be the starting point for one of the most notorious sex slave rings in America.

Boys Town had several accounts at Lawrence King's Franklin Federal Credit Union and would frequently hire graduates from the Catholic institution to work there.

During the 1980's, allegations of abuse by King were submitted to the Nebraska State Foster Care Review Board. The Board then sent extensively-documented complaints of pedophilia to Nebraska governmental and law enforcement authorities but there was no follow up and no investigation. The response the Board received was that they had given "insufficient evidence" for one.

Review Board members were dumbfounded.

Larry King lived a lavish lifestyle courtesy of money that he had embezzled from the FFCU. He used that money to court political favor all the way to the White House. He gave extravagant parties for political figures and sometimes pimped out young boys to them.

In 1988, King became the subject of an IRS/FBI sting for his theft of FFCU funds. Extensive testimony regarding his child sex slave ring involvement was reviewed but only the embezzlement was officially addressed.

As a result of inaction, the Nebraska State Legislature conducted its own inquiry and hired professional investigator Gary Caradori.

The reason for the lack of action by authorities soon became apparent when names like that of prominent businessman Alan Baer[1330] and Omaha World-Herald (the premier Nebraska newspaper) entertainment reporter Peter Citron[1331] surfaced as frequent abusers of young boys.

When contacted by Yorkshire TV for an interview, the Boys Town representative refused any participation in the documentary stating over the phone that the scandal was "Something we don't even care to delve into." *click*

Private Investigator Gary Caradori was able to find three teenagers willing to come forward with evidence that they were abused by this slave ring.

One of them, Paul Bonacci, stated that he had turned in complaints to the authorities but neither the FBI nor the Omaha Police Department took any action.

The Nebraska State Legislature swore out a special committee to investigate the scandal and put local corn farmer and stalwart Republican Loran Schmit, in as chairman.

Schmit was shocked to find that the FBI had responded to the claims of the possible victims by treating them as if *they* were the offenders. It was soon clear that the FBI's agenda was to get the victims to change their story. This charade of treason was depicted very well in Oliver Stone's *JFK* where FBI agents interrogated key Kennedy assassination witnesses and bullied them into making their testimony fit the Warren Commission cover-up.

The Federal Bureau of Obfuscation hit paydirt when they got to Caradori's other male whistleblower, Troy Boner. Boner later admitted that he was coerced by the FBI to change his story. Agents told him that if he didn't say what they wanted him to, he would be convicted of perjury and sent to prison. Apparently, they knew they had a lock on the Grand Jury.

Boner subsequently rescinded his testimony which left the third victim, Alisha Owen, to be put on trial for perjury.

She refused to recant and was subsequently sent to prison for an astounding *twenty five years*.

In her interview with Caradori in 1984, Owen implicated Robert "Robbie" Wadman, the Omaha Nebraska Police Chief, as one of her abusers.[1332]

Amazingly, the grand jury sidestepped pedophilia charges against Larry King, Peter Citron and Alan Baer, indicting them for lesser charges such as soliciting a minor for sex but avoided the more obvious allegations of kidnapping and sex slave racketeering.

They acknowledged that Boner, Bonacci and Owen *had* been abused but not by the people they identified.

Nebraska State Senator John DeCamp went on the record stating that the FBI was the *architect* of the Franklin cover-up.

On July 11th 1990, Gary Caradori died with his son, 8 year old AJ, when his small private plane broke up in midair[1333]. The FBI immediately impounded all of Caradori's documents.

Nebraska State Senator Loren Schmit was visibly distraught when interviewed by Yorkshire TV stating that the system had failed both the victims and the citizenry. After a long pause he remarked "It has shaken my faith in government."

Nebraska State Senator John DeCamp exclaimed, "I can't find an instance *anywhere* where a child was sentenced to 25 years for perjury. ... They had to send a signal to any future children who might come forward."

Larry King was given 15 years for embezzlement, 10 years less than his victim, Alisha Owen.

Interestingly, DeCamp happened to be friends with former CIA Director William Colby who advised him to be careful for his personal safety.

Colby passed DeCamp's evidence to the Justice Department and, ironically, *he* later died in a "boating accident".[1334]

It was obvious to DeCamp that Troy Boner's recanted testimony was key to the cover-up.

Troy's brother Shawn would later be found dead from a gunshot wound. Law enforcement claimed that it was caused by a negligent discharge as a result of playing "Russian Roulette".[1335]

During a second trial involving Alisha Owen's conviction review and probation, the Nebraska District Attorney threatened Boner with a subpoena for perjury and he disappeared.

John DeCamp speculated that the FBI was protecting some very prominent politicians up to and including the highest offices in the country.

Child victim and whistleblower Paul Bonacci told DeCamp that he had accompanied Larry King to Washington DC for illicit sex "parties" where other young boys and hard narcotics were offered to DC Elites.

Bonacci identified Republican Lobbyist Craig Spence and stated that Spence took Bonacci on exclusive tours of the White House, into areas the public wasn't allowed to see.

Already the suspect of a Federal investigation into male prostitution, Spence was arrested in July of 1989 for possession of cocaine and an illegal firearm[1336]. Spence was released on bail and found dead in his hotel room 4 months later from apparent suicide. Authorities disclosed a note which included the admonition—

> *All this stuff you've uncovered (involving call boys, bribery and the White House tours), to be honest with you, is insignificant compared to other things I've done. But I'm not going to tell you those things, and somehow the world will carry on.* ~ Michael Hedges and Jerry Seper, the Washington Times [1337]

Bonacci told DeCamp that Larry King had a special stable of "golden boys" under the age of 10, that he presented to the Elite.

Nationwide

Omaha wasn't the only hub of child sex slaves.

Alternative Views News Magazine's Frank Morrow produced a similar documentary in 1983 that paralleled an exposé appearing on local Texas television with the title *Boys for Sale*.

Morrow featured the investigative work of University of Texas history professor Tom Philpott who stated that, in 1979, there existed a "Call Boy" network with phone hookups to all the major cities that would receive "orders" by credit card to send a young boy to a certain location anywhere around the country. He estimated 350 boys a year were murdered in Houston, alone, to cover up the child sex ring. Many more die from drug overdose, abuse or commit suicide from being emotionally distraught.[1338]

Going the Extra Mile

Vampiric pedophiles were showing up everywhere; Nebraska, Texas, New York, even Pennsylvania.

In 2011, an assistant football coach for Pennsylvania State University named Jerry Sandusky was indicted on fifty two counts of child molestation for a period spanning 1994 to 2009.[1339]

Sandusky would've been arraigned sooner but the Centre County District Attorney that was handling the investigation in 2005, Ray Gricar, "disappeared".[1340]

The level of influence necessary to murder a District Attorney entails massive power. It included muzzling the press on a clearly sensational story.

Later it was leaked that Sandusky was "pimping out" little boys to powerful people.[1341]

In 1990, George H.W. Bush would give Sandusky a "Point of Light" award for his "2nd Mile" foundation[1342]. It was through that organization that Sandusky chose his future victims.[1343]

"Devout, practicing Catholic[1344]," Republican United States Senator from the Commonwealth of Pennsylvania, Richard "Rick" Santorum sponsored Sandusky for a "Congressional Angels in Adoption" award in 2002.[1345]

There was nothing "angelic" about what Sandusky was doing to his adopted boys.

To date, Santorum has not been accused of wrongdoing and maintained a solid "Conservative" voting record while in the Senate.

The same, however, can not be said of George Herbart Walker Bush.

House of Horrors

Cathleen Ann O'Brien is a Michigan woman who has published a book that made the shocking accusation that she was sold into sex slavery by her father and tortured to become a sex robot for America's most powerful people in the 80's and 90's.

Trance Formation of America[1346], will, at the very least, bother you and at worst, darken your soul.

Criticisms about O'Brien and what she has claimed are that the CIA projects she mentions don't exist[1347], or that they're just too shocking to exist. This is known as a "normalcy bias"—when something is so beyond your experience you assume it can't be real.

Such a bias has no place in the rational examination of facts.

What takes O'Brien's book out of the realm of "fantasy/horror" and into "autobiography" are corroborating facts found in other sources.

It makes what she has written, that much more troubling. [italics suspended]

> *Trance Formation of America* is quite strange and disturbing, and is written in the form of almost a narrative, including long passages of dialog that O'Brien claims to have remembered. She says that during the mind control sessions she developed dissociative identity disorder, which used to be classified as multiple personality disorder, and that one of her "alters" had a photographic memory and could recall every conversation that occurred in her presence during the years of her captivity and abuse.
>
> O'Brien claims that some of her abusers were George H.W. Bush, Ronald Reagan, Gerald Ford, Jimmy Carter, Dick Cheney, and Hillary Clinton. She says that she was rescued in 1988 by a man named Mark Phillips who claims to be a former CIA operative. Also a part of the story is O'Brien's daughter Kelly who was also said to be a victim of this program.
>
> What makes O'Brien's allegations seem believable to some, is the fact that mind control programs like MK-ULTRA have been exposed, and that the aims of such experiments included some unthinkable practices including torture, mind-altering drugs, sexual abuse, and hypnotism. Some of the actual goals of this program were to create mind controlled slaves or Manchurian Candidates, who would willingly accept and carry out any order given to them regardless of what it was. There are authentic declassified documents which outline these horrific practices and several victims have been awarded financial settlements for their abuse, so some believe that Cathy O'Brien could be another actual victim of such programs. During a press conference, President Bill Clinton publicly admitted that, "thousands of government sponsored

experiments did take place, at hospitals, universities and military bases around our nation. Some were unethical, not only by today's standards, but by the standards of the time in which they were conducted."[1] ...

In her speeches, O'Brien has claimed that a smiley face was carved on the inside of her vagina using an X-Acto knife for the pleasure of her abusers. In a documentary film called *The Most Dangerous Game*, produced by the Guerilla News Network in 2002, the film makers took her to a gynecologist and had her examined, and to the doctor's surprise, there did appear to be such a thing. The film showed extremely graphic video and photos of the examination in an attempt to prove her allegations.

... O'Brien says that her father Earl O'Brien was a pedophile and had been involved in selling her into child pornography when she was a little girl. In her book she includes a photo of him, along with her family and names them all, including her siblings. While the claims she makes are extremely disturbing and farfetched, similar activities have been uncovered by congressional hearings and declassified documents. Serious investigations need to be made into O'Brien's claims and her background. ~ Mark Dice[1348]

One of the first perpetrators O'Brien identified was Michigan Republican Congressman Guy Vander Jagt. O'Brien implied a strong Catholic influence from Vander Jagt yet he is supposedly a Presbyterian.

But Vander Jagt began a law degree at *Georgetown* and stopped, transferring to the University of Michigan for his actual diploma[1349]. This would give him full secular education credentials.

I caution the reader to proceed with care as these excerpts from O'Brien's book are upsetting. However, they are also critical in understanding just who it is runs the United States and the masters who sit above them.

> *Immediately after my father's return from Boston, I was routinely prostituted to then Michigan State Senator Guy VanderJagt. VanderJagt later became a U.S. Congressman and eventually chairman of the Republican National Congressional Committee that put George Bush in the office of President. I was prostituted to VanderJagt after numerous local parades which he always participated in, at the Mackinac Island Political Retreat, and in my home state of Michigan, among other places.* ~ O'Brien[1350]

O'Brien then states that a priest abused her in the confessional[1351] and, later, both Vander Jagt and Gerald Ford raped her as well.[1352]

According to O'Brien, Vander Jagt's strongest connection to what happened to her was through the local Catholic Church. The co-operative was openly satanic. [italics suspended]

> VanderJagt unlocked the rectory door of the old church across the street from the new St. Francis structure, explaining that we had to "have a very important talk now that I had eaten the body of Christ." The talk, blood trauma, and sexual abuse that ensued conditioned my mind to readily accept programming throughout the years that deliberately merged both U.S. Government and Jesuit mind-control efforts for New World Order controls.
>
> "I work for the Vatican, and now, so do you," VanderJagt told me. "You have just entered into a covenant with the holy Catholic church. You must never break that covenant." ...
>
> VanderJagd's pedophile comrade in Project Monarch, Father Don, joined us, reaching deep into the pocket of his robes to present me with a delicate blue charm of the Holy Mother. It was to be worn in conjunction with the rosy cross "to symbolize your service to the holy Catholic church," Father Don told me, which I would "promise to serve and obey".
>
> Father Don joined VanderJagt in a ritual which bathed me in the blood of a slaughtered lamb, and subsequently, through this hideous blood trauma, locked their stated perceptions and a basis for mind-control programming deep in my mind. This basis for programming was anchored in the Vow of Silence which the Jesuit monks take "not only to keep secrets, but so they can still their mind and hear their inner guidance." Certain that the "Rite to Remain Silent" which they had performed would ensure that I keep their secret Father Don and Guy VanderJagt subjected me to their pedophile perversions. ~ O'Brien[1353]

O'Brien then linked Catholic/French Canada and one of their heads of state to the satanic scheme.

> *When Pierre Trudeau was elected Prime Minister of Canada in 1968, I often heard it said, "Pierre Trudeau is one of Ours, you know." I first heard this phrase cryptically referring to Trudeau's loyalty to the Vatican when Father Don was discussing him with my famer one Sunday after mass. This fact circulated quickly among*

those I knew who were involved in the Catholic/Jesuit aspect of Project Monarch.

"When I was at the Vatican," VanderJagt began, "I was told that Prime Minister Trudeau is a friend of the Pope. He thinks like one of us. A true Catholic. ~ O'Brien[1354]

O'Brien said that Trudeau was also one of her rapists. Her description of Trudeau shows him to be a true Luciferian.

Had I been capable of fear, I would have been afraid of Pierre Trudeau.

Trudeau's slow, deliberate movements masked the brutal power of his body much the way his smooth, soft voice pierced my mind and intruded on my thoughts. The icey [sic] *cold touch of his effeminate, manicured long fingers contrasted with the heat of his perversion...* ~ O'Brien[1355]

It was at this point that she was "given" to another Protestant puppet, "Baptist" Robert C. Byrd, who raped her often. According to O'Brien, Byrd sadistically pushed her pain threshold to near-death limits.

...I was forced to take more pain than any human could logically withstand. I was dedicated to Byrd at age thirteen which meant he would be directing my future in Project Monarch, and my father would raise me according to his specifications. ~ O'Brien[1356]

Perhaps almost as bad as being his sex slave was being forced to admire his musical "talent".

Byrd fancied himself a country music fiddler and it was "my duty to love what he did", I was ordered to listen to country music or no music at all. Music was my psychological avenue for escape, a dissociative tool. But this, too, was used in setting the stage for my future as a Project Monarch "Presidential Model" mind-controlled slave. ~ O'Brien[1357]

O'Brien states that her father used her slavery to earn him both political power and wealth that is derived from the military / industrial complex—to include her serving military personnel.

My father took advantage of his new political connections and advanced himself occupationally, manufacturing camshaft auto parts at a local factory.

> *Soon he was promoted to a sales management position due to his connections within the Pentagon Procurement Office and General Services Administration, coupled with what he had learned about double bind hypnotic persuasion. He continued to supplement his income by sexually exploiting us children* [O'Brien claims her father also sold her siblings]. *This I now included brazenly prostituting me to Muskegon Coast Guard officials while on cocaine runs to and from the base. Meanwhile, my father took us all to church every Sunday, and my mother stayed busy having babies to raise in the Project. In true pedophile fashion, he surrounded himself with children by coaching little league sports, chaperoning school and Catechism activities, and becoming involved with the Boy Scouts. All of this made him appear to be a model citizen and "pillar of the community".* ~ O'Brien[1358]

This is corroborated by outside sources. Military contractors Dyncorp and Dick Cheney's Halliburton were the subject of a sex slave ring investigation. [italics suspended]

> Almost a year after Representative Cynthia McKinney was told by Donald Rumsfeld that it was not the policy of the Bush administration to reward companies that engage in human trafficking with government contracts, the scandal continues to sweep up innocent children who are sold into a life of slavery at the behest of Halliburton subsidiaries, Dyncorp and other transnational corporations with close ties to the establishment elite.
>
> On March 11th 2005, McKinney grilled Secretary Rumsfeld and General Myers on the Dyncorp scandal.
>
> "Mr. Secretary, I watched President Bush deliver a moving speech at the United Nations in September 2003, in which he mentioned the crisis of the sex trade. The President called for the punishment of those involved in this horrible business. But at the very moment of that speech, DynCorp was exposed for having been involved in the buying and selling of young women and children. While all of this was going on, DynCorp kept the Pentagon contract to administer the smallpox and anthrax vaccines, and is now working on a plague vaccine through the Joint Vaccine Acquisition Program. Mr. Secretary, is it [the] policy of the U.S. Government to reward companies that traffic in women and little girls?"
>
> The response and McKinney's comeback was as follows.
>
> Rumsfeld: "Thank you, Representative. First, the answer to your

first question is, is, no, absolutely not, the policy of the United States Government is clear, unambiguous, and opposed to the activities that you described. The second question."

McKinney: "Well how do you explain the fact that DynCorp and its successor companies have received and continue to receive government contracts?"

Rumsfeld: "I would have to go and find the facts, but there are laws and rules and regulations with respect to government contracts, and there are times that corporations do things they should not do, in which case they tend to be suspended for some period; there are times then that the—under the laws and the rules and regulations for the—passed by the Congress and implemented by the Executive branch—that corporations can get off of—out of the penalty box if you will, and be permitted to engage in contracts with the government. They're generally not barred in perpetuity."

McKinney: "This contract—this company—was never in the penalty box." ~ *Republicanism - the Dark Night of the America Dream*, G. P. Geoghegan[1359]

The official position of the United States government is that it's too cumbersome to prosecute human trafficking.

> *Three years ago, President Bush declared that he had "zero tolerance" for trafficking in humans by the government's overseas contractors, and two years ago Congress mandated a similar policy.*
>
> *But notwithstanding the president's statement and the congressional edict, the Defense Department has yet to adopt a policy to bar human trafficking.*
>
> *A proposal prohibiting defense contractor involvement in human trafficking for forced prostitution and labor was drafted by the Pentagon last summer, but five defense lobbying groups oppose key provisions and a final policy still appears to be months away, according to those involved and Defense Department records.*
>
> *The lobbying groups opposing the plan say they're in favor of the idea in principle, but said they believe that implementing key portions of it overseas is unrealistic.* ~ Cam Simpson, the Chicago Tribune[1360]

Behind the horrors of O'Brien's experiences lies the Beast of Rome.

> *In 1973, Senator Byrd instructed my father to send me to Muskegon Catholic Central High School which was overseen by the director of St. Francis of Assisi Church, Father Lepre. The Catholic church, of course, has its own political structure, with the Pope presiding over all. The strong political ties between the Catholic church and the U.S. Government was overtly evidenced by the much publicized relationship between the President and the Pope during the Reagan Administration. Of course, I had been privy to this political relationship ever since my First Communion-a relationship that the Rite to Remain Silent was intended to cover. My experience with Catholic Central's direct involvement in Project Monarch's physical and psychological conditioning further confirmed the union between the U.S. Government and the Catholic church. ~ O'Brien*[1361]

O'Brien appears to have dealt with her ordeal by becoming an atheist. This has had the unfortunate side effect of clouding her judgment on just how important Ritual Satanic Abuse (RSA) is in the mind-control process.

It is difficult imagining anyone enduring what Cathy O'Brien has and coming out of it with any spiritual faith what-so-ever but that is just what is claimed by Susan Lynne Ford (also known as "Brice Taylor"), who dedicated her book to "Jesus—the love of [her] life, [her] Lord and Savior.[1362]" Ford would make claims very similar to O'Brien's in regard to sex slavery and torture at the hands of the CIA.

In early 2014, another devout Christian made an equally shocking accusation in her book *What Witches Don't Want Christians to Know*.

Mary Lou Lake claims that her entire Missouri town was turned into a black hole of witchcraft experimentation and satanic ritual by military authorities from nearby Fort Leonard Wood. She was victimized by both rituals and subsequent military experiments that tested her abilities to conduct supernatural feats.[1363]

It is important to note that Christian pastors fail miserably at any of these subjects, not least of which is coping with pain and trail. Everyday pain (not Satanic Ritual Abuse) is guaranteed in the Bible and is even necessary for the development of true, deep character. [Ecclesiastes 7:1-6]

The Christian Holy Spirit knows what it means to be defiled by sin. [Matthew 11:12]

It was the ultimate, willing sacrifice of Jesus Christ. [II Corinthians 5:21]

Human beings need this anchor of faith to survive. Cathy O'Brien did not have one and the weakness was exploited by her tormentors.

> *In my required religion class, Sister Ann Marie had been leading us in study on the topic of Confession. This was to prepare us for the kind of Confessions we were to be giving Father Vesbit, who was also our school principal. The day Sister ordered us to Confession, I refused to go. I unconsciously feared I would be sexually assaulted again in the Confessional, this time while my teenage peers waited impatiently outside the door. Sister made an example out of me to the class, saying I was a "Satanist" and that I was "going to hell".*
>
> *With seemingly no escape from the occultism that proliferated at the school, I could no longer differentiate between Catholicism and Satanism.* ~ O'Brien[1364]

Satanism is what mind-control "scientists" used to create trauma that forces a victim to undergo dissociative personality disorder—to create alternate personalities for programming to please sexually, to memorize photographically or to kill without remorse; whatever the programmer designs.

> *Satanism is often used as an extreme pain/violence trauma base in Project Monarch Mind Control, reportedly due to the previous German Nazi Himmler's Research...* ~ O'Brien[1365]

O'Brien stated that her collaborating Catholic high school exploited her mind control conditioning.[1366]

Technology is now providing a shortcut for this programming. Days, months, years of trauma-based mind interface are being replaced by microchips.

With unspeakable ease, "scientists" write of the torture of simians for these breakthroughs in MIT's "Technology Review".

> *Researcher Jose Carmena has worked for years training macaque monkeys to move computer cursors and robotic limbs with their minds. He does so by implanting electrodes into their brains to monitor neural activity. Now, as part of a sweeping $70 million program funded by the U.S. military, Carmena has a new goal: to use brain implants to read, and then control, the emotions of mentally ill people.*

> *This week the Defense Advanced Research Projects Agency, or DARPA, awarded two large contracts to Massachusetts General Hospital and the University of California, San Francisco, to create electrical brain implants capable of treating seven psychiatric conditions, including addiction, depression, and borderline personality disorder.* ~ Antonio Regalado, MIT Technology Review[1367]

O'Brien notes that many local cops and officials are either corrupted or complicit in the child sex slave trade and one abusive priest implied that the usual victims are foreign children.[1368]

O'Brien mentioned the use of NAFTA and the child sex trade crossing America's non-existent southern border.[1369]

Perhaps this is why a United States Congressman was being barred from investigating the allegation that Army leaders at Fort Sill, Oklahoma were displacing soldiers from barracks in order to house "Unaccompanied Alien Children". [italics suspended]

> Following reports that soldiers were booted from their barracks at an Oklahoma Army base to make room for a wave of illegal immigrant minors, the Obama administration is refusing to give the federal lawmaker who represents the state in Congress access to the facility.
>
> Could it be that the administration is hiding something? The facility, Ft. Sill, is located in Lawton about 85 miles southwest of Oklahoma City. It serves as the United States Army and Marine Corps' Field Artillery School and houses nearly 9,000 soldiers along with 62,621 family members, according to its official Army website. Last week Judicial Watch received reports that single enlisted soldiers were transferred from their barracks to tents in order to accommodate the flood of Unaccompanied Alien Children (UAC) coming from Central America. ...
>
> One of the state's representatives in Congress, Jim Bridenstine, tried to visit but was denied access to the facility. In a statement issued this week Congressman Bridenstine's office says Ft. Sill is housing up to 1,200 UACs, but the lawmaker couldn't offer any more information because he wasn't allowed inside. He says a fence covered with material that totally obscures any view has been erected around the barracks housing the UACs "There is no excuse for denying a Federal Representative from Oklahoma access to a federal facility in Oklahoma where unaccompanied children are

being held," said Bridenstine, a former Navy pilot.

This crisis has been cloaked in secrecy from the start and the administration has withheld crucial information from the American public. For instance JW reported that a Texas military base is being covertly used as an illegal immigrant processing/holding location. A hangar at the El Paso facility, Ft. Bliss, is quietly being used by the Department of Homeland Security (DHS) to process, house and transition the influx of illegal immigrant minors that have arrived in the U.S. in recent weeks, a high-level inside source told JW. A Pentagon official demanded JW pull the story three days after it got published but backed off when we requested he put it in writing. ~ Judicial Watch[1370]

There is a similar admonition by Susan Ford, stating that her father prostituted her to a local cop when she was only 4 years old so that he could receive a police "courtesy card".[1371]

Cathy O'Brien states that the Catholic Church exploits the confessional in its manipulation of American affairs.

> *My Uncle Bob Tanis was visiting our house soon after that. He had flown in from what he claimed was a "black ops" Air Force Intelligence operation. I know now that in typical CIA mode of operations, he was relating a story of lies salted with some truth. His point was to inform me that the Catholic Church is "justified" in its involvement with our government due to the Priests' "hearing confessions from mobsters and spies". He also explained that Exchange Students were "spies in the making" that Priests found, through Confession, were problems.* ~ O'Brien[1372]

Satanic Panic

Susan Ford claims that her initial programming was conducted via a Baptist Church whose hierarchy doubled as a satanic cult—she, too, states that attempts were made by the satanists to have her directly associate Jesus with her trauma. Children were picked from the Church daycare for ritual abuse.[1373]

This was not an uncommon accusation in the 1980's and soon reports were coming in from all over the country regarding children left in daycare facilities assaulted and involved in satanic rituals.

One such example involved the Fells Acres Day School in Malden, Massachusetts.

> *On Labor Day 1984, 60-year-old Violet Amirault—proprietor of the thriving Fells Acres Day School in Malden, Mass.—received a call about a child abuse accusation against her son. Two days later the police arrested 31-year-old Gerald (who worked at Fells Acres) on charges of raping a five-year-old boy, a new pupil.*
>
> *In short order, the hideous crimes supposedly committed by Gerald began to multiply—as did the number of the accused. Soon, Violet Amirault herself and her newly married 26-year-old daughter, Cheryl, were also charged with having perpetrated monstrous sexual crimes against children ages three to five.*
>
> *Children had supposedly been raped with knives ... and sticks, and been assaulted by a clown (allegedly Gerald) in a "magic room." Some children told—after interrogations by investigators—of being forced to drink urine, of watching the Amiraults slaughter blue birds, of meeting robots with flashing lights. Violet Amirault was accused of shoving a stick into the rectum of a child while he was standing up, and of raping him with "a magic wand." Mrs. Amirault was convicted of these charges. The child also testified he was tied naked to a tree in the schoolyard, in front of all the teachers and children, while "Miss Cheryl" cut the leg off a squirrel.* ~ Dorothy Rabinowitz, the Wall Street Journal[1374]

This incident has been mitigated by propaganda spin as "daycare ritual abuse hysteria". The "debunking" of the accusations revolved around lack of physical evidence, yet those who study mental conditioning understand that humans can be trained to overcome extreme pain via strong focus, even if that focus is induced by trauma.

Susan Ford recounts several sessions with her pedophile slave-handler father where she says he conditioned her to be tortured yet neither felt the torture nor saw evidence of it afterward.[1375]

Ford also states that, although her initial conditioning took place via "Baptist" satanists, it was solidified for her via her Catholic master, Leslie Townes "Bob" Hope.

> *Throughout my formative years, I was molded to be extremely sexual through the sexual abuse with my father and others. The personalities that were created from that abuse didn't always experience the encounters as abusive, because that is all they knew. Bob later told my father through an instilled message delivered through me during an incestual encounter with my father...*

Bob was Catholic and so was the part of me that performed. She was my "inner twin sister" for programming purposes, to keep that part of me separate from my created "normal" reality and her name was Sharon. Bob said he liked Catholic girls because they were easy and he liked "em like that."

Bob was always racy until he got to acting old around 1987. I had a lifetime of Bob Hope and his antics, and over the years, he lost his funny and happy persona and became just a mean and nasty old man. And then, he became cruel to me, there wasn't anything fun left in him. He was just real old and mean. ~ Ford[1376]

Although Leslie "Bob" Hope's religious affiliation was kept secret, his wife Dolores was a devout Catholic and they, as a couple, gave generously to multiple Catholic charities. [1377]

Both Disney Land and ancient pagan and/or Catholic rituals like repetitive prayer by rote were mentioned frequently by Ford as being used in her conditioning. [italics suspended]

> ...my inner twin sister Sharon also had to have programming experiences at Disneyland. To accomplish that our neighbor Mary took me to Disneyland with her daughter Peggy, who was my age. At one point we visited the beautiful Magic Castle that is located in the middle of the Magic Kingdom. As I walked through the Castle, exploring the area, I rounded a corner and as I stepped into a darkened area, a man in a black cape that had been hiding in a dark corner of the castle stepped forward and grabbed me. He put his hand over my mouth so I wouldn't scream and he elbowed me in the stomach before he raped me. Then he took me in the direction of the dog kennels in the front of Disneyland where other bad things happened. Every year, Sharon had to watch the "President Show with Lincoln" that played in a theatre on Main Street and in order to keep her secret experiences hidden from her conscious mind, this twin sister part of me also had to be exposed to many of the same kinds of trauma.
>
> Sharon was created to be Catholic, and Mary and Peggy often took me with them to Catholic mass.
>
> (They didn't know about my connection to Henry Kissinger.) I was taught about Holy Water and genuflecting and the Stations of the Cross and Confession and Hail Marys and saying the Rosary. Peggy let me borrow her rosary beads that had a little blue enamel picture of the Blessed Mary on it. I learned to say, "Hail Mary full

of grace the Lord is with thee," over and over again for each bead. We always had to wear a hat or a scarf. They had a lot of rules you had to follow. Had to get that Holy Water and dab it on yourself at your Stations of the Cross; forehead, heart then each shoulder, before you genuflected upon entering the pews. Then we knelt down and said the Rosary for a very long time. ...

Now of course, in order to insure that Sharon's memory was kept separate from my conscious mind, trauma had to be induced to create the dissociative barrier. Among other traumas, I was taken to St. Mel's Catholic Church in Woodland Hills and was molested by a short fat "Father," at the back of the church in a side room. This priest who spoke with an Irish accent and smelled like alcohol, pulled my hair while he sexually satisfied himself in my mouth. When he was finished with me, two men in suits escorted me to an awaiting limousine. I had short hair and wore a felt poodle skirt, flats, white socks and a white blouse. It wasn't unusual to see limousines lined up in front of this large Catholic church for use at funerals or weddings. It was nearing dark and once out of sight of the public, these men were very rough with me. They threw me into the back seat and once inside the limo I laid on the seat in a fetal position, rocking myself, terrified out of my mind. ~ Ford[1378]

Cathy O'Brien was frequently taken to military bases like MacDill Air Force Base in Florida in 1974 for increased conditioning.

Another base she mentioned was Offutt Air Force Base in Nebraska—a location that has come up in the testimony of boys taken during the "Franklin Coverup".

O'Brien mentions Richard Bruce "Dick" Cheney as one of her primary torturers.

Cheney was Gerald Ford's White House Chief of Staff. His connections got him a seat in the House of Representatives and he was then made the Secretary of Defense by his friend George H.W. Bush. He would be returned to power by Bush's son to become Vice President—a position H.W. Bush knew secretly ran the Administration from behind the scenes. [italics suspended]

> Dick Cheney, then White House Chief of Staff to president Ford, later Secretary of Defense to President George Bush, documented member of the Council on Foreign Relations (CFR), and Presidential hopeful for 1996, was originally Wyoming's only Congressman. Dick Cheney was the reason my family had traveled

to Wyoming where I endured yet another form of brutality— his version of "A Most Dangerous Game," or human hunting.

It is my understanding now that A Most Dangerous Game was devised to condition military personnel in survival and combat maneuvers. Yet it was used on me and other slaves known to me as a means of further conditioning the mind to the realization there was "no place to hide," as well as traumatize the victim for ensuing programming. It was my experience over the years that A Most Dangerous Game had numerous variations on the primary theme of being stripped naked and turned loose in the wilderness while being hunted by men and dogs. In reality, all "wilderness" areas were enclosed in secure military fencing whereby it was only a matter of time until I was caught, repeatedly raped, and tortured.

Dick Cheney had an apparent addiction to the "thrill of the sport". He appeared obsessed with playing A Most Dangerous Game as a means of traumatizing mind-control victims, as well as to satisfy his own perverse sexual kinks. ~ O'Brien[1379]

Cheney demanded she voice her desire to be used by him. In shock from being "hunted" and from loss of blood, she was unable to respond to his liking.

Cheney's face turned red with rage. He was on me in an instant, slamming my back into the wall with one arm across my chest and his hand on my throat, choking me while applying pressure to the carotid artery in my neck with his thumb. His eyes bulged and he spit as he growled, "If you don't mind me, I will kill you. I could kill you—Kill you—with my bare hands. You're not the first and you won't be the last. I'll kill you any time I goddamn well please,"

He flung me on the cot-type bed that was behind me. There he finished taking his rage out on me sexually. ~ O'Brien[1380]

In 2006, Cheney would make headlines for having "accidentally" shot lawyer and real estate broker Harry Wittington in the face while "quail hunting." Wittington will carry some 30 pieces of birdshot in his face and neck to his grave.[1381]

That same year, a book was published that would later be made into a major motion picture titled "The Hunger Games" that pitted a male and female teenager in controlled death-matches. Hunger Games authoress Suzanne Collins rarely gives interviews[1382]. Is that because her book isn't really hers and she is uncomfortable keeping up the façade?

Disney's Nightmare

Cathy O'Brien says that the work and facilities of Walter Elias "Walt" Disney was frequently helpful to those who tortured her.

Disney, himself, was the victim of abuse as a child[1383] and would later hold a very distinctive honor—that of being a member of DeMolay International.

> *Disney was kind of a big deal in Demolay—he was only the 107th member to join the organization, and a member of the Mother Chapter. He was later inducted into Demolay's Legion of Honor, and the Hall of Fame. He was very fond of the Demolay organization, and spoke out favorably about it often. In fact, he made his creation, Mickey Mouse, a member of Demolay!* ~ Todd Creason, From Labor to Refreshment[1384]

DeMolay International is an institution for teenage boys, run by Freemasons, in honor of Catholic legend and "Grand Master" of the "Knights Templar", Jacques de Molay.[1385]

O'Brien states that her father was richly rewarded for selling his children to the military/industrial complex and was protected from prosecution by the CIA. Robert Byrd was the benefactor of this transaction.

Byrd started his career in the West Virginia legislature and continued to rise to hold unprecedented power in the United States Senate, not the least of which was to chair the Senate Appropriations Committee. Byrd was one of the longest-serving politicians in American history and only gave up his seat in death at 92.

O'Brien states that she was then given to "Wayne Cox" who's brutality and barbarism was beyond description. She claims he would ritually impregnate her and kill the baby, sometimes consuming the tiny body.

While at Barksdale Air Force Base, O'Brien says she was taken to an area secured for General Dynamics where she was raped by Democrat United States Senator John Bennett Johnston from Louisiana. General Dynamics did, indeed, figure prominently in the financing of Bennett's campaigns.[1386]

O'Brien says that one of her assignments was to help run guns and drugs through the state of Arkansas, where she came in contact with another Jesuit creation, Bill Clinton.

Clinton was clearly "in the know" about the secret slave agenda and got her to complete her courier mission by manipulating her with trigger words.

> *Using standard Jesuit hand signals and cryptic language, he triggered/switched me and accessed a previously programmed message.*
>
> *"Senator Johnston sent me to give this to you." I handed Clinton a thin, large brown envelope, "And I have some fairy dust guaranteed to make you fly high." I took the personal stash of cocaine that Johnston was sharing with Clinton from my pocket.* ~ O'Brien[1387]

During her decompression, sex slave victim Susan Ford recounted countless rapings from the top names in the public spotlight.

> *After I fled from California and was no longer living in the midst of my programmed abuse base, nor was I in therapy, I began having vivid, detailed memories of being used both as a sex slave and human mind file computer to some of our nation's highest level governmental officials in and out of the White House. Among them: John F. Kennedy (sex and delivered messages). Lyndon Baines Johnson (sex and delivered messages), Henry Kissinger (masterminded my U.S. Government and international mind file use), Nelson Rockefeller (mind file use coordinated in conjunction with Henry Kissinger), Gerald Ford (sex and delivered messages), Jimmy Carter (delivered messages), Ronald Reagan (sex and delivered messages), George Bush (mind file use; he is a known pedophile and had sex with my programmed daughter Kelly[qq]), and top entertainment professionals, such as my "owner" Bob Hope (sex and message courier).* ~ O'Brien[1388]

Another one of Cathy O'Brien's handlers was chosen from the entertainment industry. He was connected to the United Services Organization, otherwise known as "the USO".

> *My new mind-control handler, CIA operative and country music ventriloquist/ stage hypnotist Alex Houston...Houston was 26 years older than I, and claimed to have gained his knowledge of stage hypnosis and government mind-control methods from the military while entertaining overseas in Bob Hope's USO tours.* ~ O'Brien[1389]

[qq] Cathy O'Brien also has a daughter Kelly, who she claims was preyed upon by George H.W. Bush. This could be proof of unreliable stories or memories, however, both daughters exist, both are named "Kelly" and I think it more than likely George H.W. Bush is truly that evil.

There was such a person and he did tour with the USO.[1390,1391]

Another USO showgirl by the name of Jessica Arline Wilcox came to light as a possible victim of "MK Ultra". In *The C.I.A. Doctors*, Dr. Colin Ross, M.D., tells her story.

> *The Control of Candy Jones*[23] *is about the creation of a Manchurian Candidate by U.S. mind control doctors... The story has not been independently corroborated... However, hypnosis expert Dr. Herbert Spiegel*[296]*, who examined Candy Jones in person is quoted*[23] *(p. 201) as saying, "I have no doubt that she's been brainwashed." ~ The CIA Doctors*, Ross[1392]

Ross then states that Jones (born Jessica Wilcox) was recruited for mind control by boxer Gene Tunney through British spy William Stephenson to J. Edgar Hoover, himself. Jesuit plant and founder of the OSS William Donovan would say of Stephenson, "[he] taught us all we ever knew about foreign intelligence."[1393]

Wilcox's mother would frequently beat Jessica with a riding crop and subject her to sensory deprivation in an unlit closet. Wilcox was also isolated, personally, which had the same effect as direct torture, forcing her to create alternate identities to keep her company. Her "Arlene" identity was later amplified for use by Projects BLUEBIRD/ARTICHOKE "Doctor" Gilbert Jensen.

During therapy, she would recount her use as mind-controlled courier "Arelen Grant", taking an envelope to an unknown American in Taiwan.

Wilcox's husband, radio talk show host "Long" John Nebel became suspicious of secrets in her past. In July of 1973, he was notified that a Japan Airlines ticket was being held for his wife to fly from Kennedy Airport to Tokyo, however, the booking had been made for "Cynthia". Dr. Ross believed this was Amy Elizabeth Thorpe, an OSS operative code-named "Cynthia" who died in 1963.

During more therapy, it was discovered that mind control doctor Gilbert Jensen had programmed Wilcox to kill herself, but because the method was to jump from a cliff while visiting the Bahamas (a trip that was cancelled), she did not complete the instruction.[1394]

Jessica Wilcox—whose stage name was "Candy Jones"—was apparently chosen for mind control after contracting malaria while on tour with the USO in the Pacific in 1945. It was there that Gilbert Jensen (a pseudonym) decided to induct her into the program. She appears to have been brought in at an experimental stage of MK Ultra while Cathy O'Brien was later given more complete conditioning.

It was John Nebel who had noticed that sometimes his wife Jessica ("Candy") would get up in the middle of the night and become an alternate personality. Nebel found that she had been contacted by FBI agents in 1959 to ostensibly help them with surveillance of an unknown location and to allow her apartment to be used as a mail dead-drop.

While working to rehabilitate Jessica, Nebel discovered that this "Dr. Jensen" worked for the CIA and had subjected Wilcox to hypnotherapy aided by narcotics. He attempted a crude form of hypnosis in his own efforts to help but was shocked to discover a mental memory barrier Jensen had erected in Wilcox's mind that was quite effective.

> *Under John's hypnosis, Candy revealed that she had been given a number of drugs by Jensen: possibly aminazin, reserpine, and sulfazin, as well as the "truth drugs" sodium amytal and sodium pentothal. She was programmed not to allow any doctor except Jensen to treat her, and never to allow anyone to give her thorazine, the powerful tranquillizer. ~ Operation Mind Control*, Walter Bowart[1395]

Candy Jones/Jessica Wilcox appeared to have fared better than women like Sue Ford ("Brice Taylor") or Cathy O'Brien in that she was not repeatedly raped but her programming was tested on several occasions, perhaps purposely. On her trips to Taiwan, she was intercepted by Chinese operatives who tortured her. She was sent more than once to the same location and tortured by the same people and it makes one believe that it was all part of the CIA proving what they could accomplish—almost as if the Chinese were in on it.

On at least one occasion, it was discovered that Wilcox was being both conditioned and paraded at the CIA's headquarters in Langley, Virginia. She was placed naked on an examining table and "Dr. Jensen" shoved a lit candle into her privates to prove the reality of "mind control" to his audience of military brass and intelligence spooks.[1396]

Hypno-tarts

The music and entertainment industries are fertile grounds for mind control of both audiences and performers. The outrageous antics of Britney Spears, Lindsay Lohan, Miley Cyrus and Katy Perry are all carefully scripted and it is possible that many of these people may not be in full control of themselves at all times.

It is an insight into who their masters are when Katy Perry performs a witchcraft ritual complete with a Knights Templar cross across her body for the 2014 "Grammys"[1397] or when Madonna Louise Ciccone (known only as "Madonna") hangs on a cross while performing on stage.[1398]

In May of 2014, Catholic nun Cristina Scuccia was awarded the winner of Italy's "The Voice" competition. The chaste sister will be covering *Like A Virgin* in her upcoming album.

Madonna Ciccone was extremely supportive.[1399]

It is not coincidental that these pagan magick sex rituals on stage should include Catholic iconography.

Rose "Kesha" Sebert recently sued her handler, Polish media producer Lukasz Gottwald, alleging that he sexually assaulted her and injected her with narcotics to keep her senseless[1400]. Although this is all too common in Los Angeles, it also has the earmarks of "mind control".

The Groves of Molech

These are not just "mind control" experiments. They are demonically-driven pagan rituals and timeless in their rebellion. It is no coincidence that victims would be transported to locations of ancient rite demon worship.

Susan Ford summarized the experiences of Franklin Cover-up whistleblower Paul Bonacci as his Luciferian/Jesuit/CIA handlers took him from Boys Town to Bohemian Grove.

> *Paul Bonaci, a courageous survivor who endured almost two decades of degradation under Project MONARCH, has disclosed strong corroborating evidence of widescale crimes and corruption from the municipal/state level all the way up to the White House.[17] He has testified about sexually-abused males selected from Boy's Town in Nebraska and taken to nearby Offutt AFB, where he says they were subjected to intense MONARCH programming, directed mainly by Commander Bill Plemmons and former Lt. Col. Michael Aquino.[18] After thoroughly tormenting the young boys into mindless oblivion, they were used (along with girls) for pornography and prostitution with several of the nation's political and economic power-brokers. Bonaci recalled being transported from the Air Force base via cargo planes to McClelland AFB in California. Along with other unfortunate adolescents and teenagers, he was driven to the elite retreat, Bohemian Grove. The perpetrators took full advantage of these innocent victims,*

committing unthinkable perversions in order to satisfy their deviant lusts. Some victims were apparently murdered, further traumatizing already terrified and broken children. ~ Thanks for the Memories, Brice Taylor[1401]

We will devote much of the next chapter on United States Army officer Michael Aquino and the role the devil has played in Western Intelligence since the 17th century.

Generational Curse

According to Cathy O'Brien, her daughter was sired by sadistic handler Wayne Cox to be brought into the CIA sex slave operation. [italics suspended]

> In the early 1980s, my base programming was instilled at Fort Campbell, Kentucky by U.S. Army Lt. Colonel Michael Aquino. Aquino holds a TOP SECRET clearance in the Defense Intelligence Agency's Psychological Warfare Division (Psy Ops). He is a professed Neo-Nazi, the founder of the Himmler inspired satanic Temple of Set, and has been charged with child ritual and sexual abuse at the Presidio Day Care in San Francisco, California. But like my father and Cox, Aquino remains "above the law" while he continues to traumatize and program CIA destined young minds in a quest to reportedly create the "superior race" of Project Monarch Mind-Controlled slaves. ...
>
> In 1981, [United States Senator Robert] Byrd personally joined Aquino in Huntsville, Alabama during one of our programming sessions. NASA cooperated fully with Byrd on any and everything, since it was Byrd's Senate Appropriations Committee that determined how much and/or whether NASA received government funding. ...
>
> Byrd was providing Aquino with specific details of certain perversions he wanted me equipped to fulfill or perform. Additionally, they talked about scrambling my immediate memory with two private porn films they were arranging to have produced locally. These were titled *How To Divide a Personality* and *How To Create a Sex Slave*. These films are the kind NASA became involved in producing for the dual purpose of "scrambling" memory and documenting their mind-control procedures. The resident Huntsville, Alabama pornographers were two local cops, one of which was (and is) a Sergeant.[5] This served NASA and the CIA well when cover-up was necessary. ...

Although Byrd periodically sexually abused Kelly throughout her Project Monarch victimization, the horrific incident in West Virginia was the last time I was able to instinctively think to respond at all. Aquino's mind-control programming further insured it, as did Byrd's access to high tech mind-control equipment via West Virginia's Jesuit College [Wheeling Jesuit University], where he claimed the role of "Head Friar".[6] ~ O'Brien[1402]

O'Brien then goes on to implicate a member of the Mellon bank family as well as Governor of Pennsylvania and later U.S. Attorney General, and finally Under-Secretary General for the United Nations, Dick Thornburgh as being rapists allowed access to her by the CIA.

Also on O'Brien's list was James Traficant who was then an Ohio county Sheriff, later to become a quirky Catholic Democrat Congressman.

In 2002, he was indicted on racketeering and corruption charges. Traficant represented himself. When brought under similar charges in 1983, Traficant represented himself and was the only defendant to win against Racketeer Influenced and Corrupt Organizations (RICO) in such fashion[1403]. It didn't work the second time around and he went to prison. He received support from White Supremacist David Duke and Traficant wrote Duke a letter claiming he had inside information on events like Ruby Ridge, Waco and the Kennedy Assassination. He was released from prison and died on September 23rd, 2014 when his tractor flipped and pinned him beneath it[1404]. It was an unusual accident.

His unstable honesty had made him a bit of a folk hero in the "Truth" movement and independent journalist Luke Rudkowski noted that Traficant had received death threats.[1405]

O'Brien stated that porn scion Larry Flynt (whom she called "the Official White House Pornographer") was part of the operation and the satanists would even conduct mock "weddings" where slaves were bonded to slave owners.

> *I was "made of honor" for my friend's "wedding," which was no more a marriage than mine to* [ventriloquist Alex] *Houston. As was customary with Project Monarch slaves, her marriage to her handler equated to marriage to her mind-control owner, U.S. Senator Arlen Spector.*
>
> *The "wedding" I was forced to participate in was for pornography purposes only, and it took place in Arlen Spector's Conneaut Lake house in Pennsylvania.*

> *Spector's stone house was located in a wooded, remote setting and was masculine in decor. Side rooms were either designated for perverse sex or were furnished with antiquated NASA virtual reality and programming equipment.*
>
> *The musty smell of Spector's playhouse was overpowered by the scent of roses, which he symbolically presented to his slave on their "wedding" day.*
>
> *My friend's "wedding" photos included Catholic themes, and the crucifix featured was rose cut crystal similar to the one I received from Byrd...* ~ O'Brien[1406]

This was not the first time the "Grand Old Party" was connected to the porn industry.

> *RNC Chief Ken Mehlman accepted political contributions from gay porn king? ...*
>
> *It turns out that the Republican National Committee is a regular recipient of political contributions from Nicholas T. Boyias, the owner and CEO of Marina Pacific Distributors, one of the largest producers and distributors of gay porn in the United States. This recent article on Marina Pacific's new marketing campaign form XBiz, a porn industry trade sheet, notes that, in addition to producing its own material, the "company acts as a distribution house to hundreds of lines, mostly gay, 40 of which can be purchased only through MPD."*
>
> *The company actually seems to be a trendsetter in the industry. As Boyias recently noted, "We have always modeled ourselves after a Fortune-style company. They are the models of exceptional customer service. We have formed strategic alliances with our vendors and customers alike, offering them tools and marketing to assist them in succeeding with their business models. Our one-on-one interpersonal relationships have never been duplicated in the distribution industry."* ... ~ Josh Marshall, Talking Points Memo[1407]

Cathy O'Brien also connected the dots back to Boys Town.

> [Alex Houston] *"had business at Boys Town in Omaha, Nebraska" where the wayward boys were being traumatized and sexually abused in accordance with the Catholic involvement in Project Monarch. Survivor Paul Bonacci of the infamous Franklin Cover-up case has named Alex Houston as one of his abusers there in Boys*

> *Town. Houston often went to Boys Town or other similar "vacation resorts" while I was on covert government business.* ~ O'Brien[1408]

O'Brien's experiences presaged today's Police State as she claimed that, while at Offut Air Force Base, being subjected to "you can run but you can't hide" conditioning, an Air Force officer promised her that high-tech satellite surveillance would track her if she ever tried to escape.

Presidential Model

Cathy O'Brien states that Marilyn Monroe was the first so-called "Presidential Model" mind-controlled sex slave. The odd circumstances surrounding Monroe's life and death strengthens this accusation.

> *On August 5, 1962, Marilyn Monroe's body was found in the bedroom of her home in Brentwood. According to the autopsy, the investigation came to the conclusion that the death was caused by an acute barbiturate poisoning. Monroe's house was filled with listening devices, and surveillance was conducted on the day of her death. ...*
>
> *At 4:25 am on Sunday, August 5, the Los Angeles Police received a call. The caller introduced himself as Dr. Hyman Engelberg, Marilyn's personal physician. He said that the actress Marilyn Monroe committed suicide. When the police arrived at the house of the movie star, they found Marilyn's naked body next to a bottle of sedatives. According to the description of the scene, she was lying face down, her face buried in a pillow, her arms stretched out along her body, the right arm slightly bent, her legs straight.*
>
> *The investigation immediately suggested that she was put this way by someone, because, in spite of the general concept, an overdose of sleeping pills usually causes cramps in the victim's leg and vomiting, and the position of the body is distorted. Witness evidence was very strange. They claimed that Marilyn's body was found before four o'clock, but they could not go to the police until so permitted by the advertising department of the "20th Century Fox Film Corporation."*
>
> *The preliminary autopsy determined that Marilyn died of an overdose of barbiturates. Traces of pentobarbital (sleeping pills) were found in her liver, and chloral hydrate in her blood. The reason of Marilyn's death was identified as a "probable suicide."*
>
> *The coroner based his determination of the cause of death as a*

> *"suicide" on traces of sedatives present in her blood, her previous suicide attempts, and lack of signs of violence. Some forensic experts did not agree. They argued that there were no traces of Nembutal in Monroe's stomach or intestines, and only in her liver, suggesting that Marilyn died of a rectally administered barbiturate enema.* ~ Sergei Vasilenkov, Pravda[1409]

Monroe's early life had all the earmarks of her being targeted, living in both an orphanage and foster care. Her first marriage was supposedly arranged to keep her from having to return to either one, at 16 years old.

> *After experiencing foster homes and an attempt by Gladys* [her mentally unstable mother, abandoned by Norma Jeane's father], *to provide a home for herself and her young daughter, eventually Norma Jeane was admitted to the Los Angeles Orphanage for care, despite the fact that she had a living mother (and most probably a living father out there somewhere!) after leaving the orphanage sometime in June 1936 Norma Jeane lived between the homes of Grace Goddard and her Great Aunt Ida Mae Martin until 1938, when at the age of 12, Norma Jeane was returned to the full time care of her legal guardian Grace Goddard. Grace was Gladys's best friend and had over seen the care of Norma Jeane throughout her young life. Having married a gentleman by the name of Erwin (Doc) Goddard, Grace felt that she was now well placed to provide stability for Norma Jeane.*
>
> *In 1942 Doc was promoted and required to move to West Virginia. However, the Goddard's were unable to take Norma Jeane. There is a great deal of uncertainty and debate as to why Norma Jeane was unable to move with them.* ~ "Shar", Loving Marilyn[1410]

Supposedly, foster parent Erwin Goddard had made a drunken pass at the teenager and all agreed it was best not to allow that to happen again. Conversely, the two stayed in close contact until Goddard threatened to defend his reputation via a printed insider account of Mortenson's first marriage. She had claimed it was only a marriage of convenience that she felt pressured to enter into as a result of being semi-abandoned by the Goddards.

She divorced Jim Dougherty as soon as she started her glamour career. Dougherty is reported to have been a good man. Had Mortenson stayed with him, she would have missed both fame as well as exploitation and an early death.

> *In order to avoid having to go back to an orphanage, she married her first husband, 21 year old Jimmy Dougherty in June of 1942; apparently not entirely by choice, though this point has been disputed. Monroe herself stated about it, "Grace McKee arranged the marriage for me, I never had a choice. There's not much to say about it. They couldn't support me, and they had to work out something. And so I got married."*
>
> *Doughtery soon went off to fight in WWII, leaving Monroe at home. Before he left, she tried to convince him to get her pregnant, as she was afraid he'd die, but he refused because he thought she was too young to be pregnant. This worked out for her, though, in some respects, as she found herself working in a Radioplane plant where she was discovered by a photographer. Before her husband returned from the war, she already had a successful career in modeling and would very soon launch her movie career. Shortly after he returned, they got a divorce partially due to the fact that he did not approve of her new career and how scantily clad she was in many of the photos.* ~ StrangeCosmos[1411]

She is said to have suffered from severe performance anxiety which doesn't comport with the image of a woman who used her sex appeal to get what she wanted.

> *Marilyn Monroe suffered from severe stage fright, even late in her career. Producer Henry Weinstein remarked that he saw her on many occasions near physically ill from stage fright while preparing to film her scenes. He further stated of her stage fright, "Very few people experience terror. We all experience anxiety, unhappiness, heartbreaks, but that was sheer primal terror."* ~ StrangeCosmos[1412]

In the authorized biography of famed Church of Satan founder Howard Levey (who changed his name to "Anton Szandor LaVey") there is the claim that Levey briefly dated and had sex with Monroe while she was "struggling".

They supposedly met in Los Angeles, 1948, at the Mayan Burlesque Theater when Mortenson was making $12 a day as a stripper and Levey was making $10 a day as a singer and organist/piano player.

The book lists Levey's parents as "Augusta LaVey and her husband Joe" however their real names were Michael Joseph Levey (1903–1992), from Chicago, who married the former Gertrude Augusta Coultron.[1413]

The biography is greatly embellished for effect so the account can only be taken with a grain of salt.

> *Anton LaVey is uniquely qualified to speak of that part of Marilyn's life which has generally been conceded as the "lost" period. ...*
>
> *While Marilyn had no trouble charming men, she didn't have as much luck with her automobile. "She was a terrible driver," Anton confirms. "She hit a minister, you know. Rear-ended him when he was waiting at a stoplight. Of course, he couldn't cuss but you could see he was visibly agitated. Some people have read a lot of significance into that incident. Maybe there was. She had totally soured on religion just before I met her. She'd been told all her life that she was no good and sinful and bad. The final straw came just about two weeks before she hit that minister. She went into a Christian Science Reading Room and really tried to read that stuff. Finally she came out and decided you couldn't read it – it didn't make any sense."*
>
> *Anton supposed that was one reason why they got along so well – their mutual disdain for religion. ...*
>
> *Marilyn was fascinated with Anton's stories of his life in the carnival and his ever-deepening study of the Black Arts.*
>
> *While they drove along the night-misted streets of L.A., she always wanted to hear more about occultism, about death – to explore the provinces of the strange and bizarre that Anton was becoming more and more familiar with. ... ~ The Secret Life of a Satanist*, Blanche Barton[1414]

In his thousand-page tome, *The Church of Satan* Michael Aquino calls Levey's facts into question.[1415]

The end of Monroe's career was so erratic that her circumstances point accusingly at sinister manipulation and control. [italics suspended]

> As a Beta Slave, she was also used by industry people. In June DiMaggio's book *Marilyn, Joe and Me* the author describes how she was forced to service old men and that she had to completely dissociate from reality (an important aspect of MK programming) to be able to go through the disgusting acts. ...
>
> In the last months of her life, Marilyn was reportedly very difficult to work with and her behavior caused observers to worry about her situation. During the shooting of her last completed movie, *The*

Misfits, Monroe had a "serious illness" that was never disclosed but was reportedly treated by a ... psychiatrist. In other words, mind control. ...

In 1962, Marilyn began filming *Something's Got to Give*, but she was so ill and unreliable that she ultimately got fired and sued by the studio 20th Century Fox for half a million dollars. The movie's producer Henry Weinstein stated that Marilyn's behavior during the filming was horrifying...

Weinstein observed that Marilyn's was not having regular "bad days" or mood swings. She was feeling "sheer primal terror" – something that products of trauma-based Mind Control often end up experiencing. ~ Vigilant Citizen[1416]

Turn On, Tune In, Drop Out

Marilyn Monroe's life and death confirmed the use of narcotics as a weapon by the CIA, through the entertainment industry, *aimed at the American people*.

> *CIA covert drug operations had permeated the industry. Entertainers were used to buy, sell, and distribute cocaine brought into this country by the U.S. government for the purpose of funding the Pentagon's and CIA's Black Budgets. Nashville's local government, from my perspective, was totally corrupted by these criminal covert operations. Cover-up, murder, drugs, and white slavery prevailed.*
>
> *Entertainers usually made it big only when they participated in CIA operations and/or were slaves themselves. ...*
>
> *The drug business was booming for the CIA, and the only "War on Drugs" I witnessed was that launched by the CIA against its competition.* ~ O'Brien[1417]

Eric Holder's "Operation: Fast and Furious" had the agenda of empowering the Sinaloa cartel over their competitors and as use in propaganda in disarming the American people. The government / trafficking connection insures a steady flow of poison to harm America with.

Cathy O'Brien stated that 9/11 co-conspirators in the House of Saud—the Royal Ruling Elite of Saudi Arabia—were also beneficiaries of CIA sex slaves like her.

O'Brien wrote that George H.W. Bush preferred little girls as young as

3 years old and created his "Fred Rogers" (of "Mr. Rogers' Neighborhood") persona as part of his sickness in enticing toddlers.

O'Brien says that not only is Hillary Clinton a lesbian but Bill is bisexual and both are perfectly at home with the CIA's sex slave program and what it does to its victims.

Hillary Clinton has long lusted after America's children.

It Takes a Village to Steal Your Child

In 1996, Clinton published *It Takes A Village* (to raise a child). Rightly has it been characterized by critics as deceptive campaign rhetoric. Even the title is put forth under false pretenses—there are no reputable African sources for the "African" phrase.[1418] [italics suspended]

> If you were to pick up Hillary Clinton's book and begin reading it, you would no doubt be surprised by what you found. Christians will find lots of areas of agreement. ...
>
> I believe this is precisely the reaction Mrs. Clinton intended. She spends countless pages analyzing the social problems facing our children and providing constructive ideas for parents and communities to follow. Not only is she critical of drugs, violence, illegitimacy, and the plight of American education, she is also critical of such things as the impact of no-fault divorce laws. People looking for a clearly stated liberal agenda will not easily find it in this book. ...
>
> Even though Mrs. Clinton attempt to soft-pedal some of the more radical aspects of her agenda, controversy inevitably slips through. For example, many of what she claims are the President's successes can hardly be considered successes, programs such as: Goals 2000 and Parents as Teachers. Many of her other favorites indicate a clear endorsement of socialist programs by Mrs. Clinton.
>
> Let's look at just one example. Mrs. Clinton believes that the best way to solve what she believes is the problem of adequate day care facilities, is to adopt the French model of day care. She asks us to "imagine a country in which nearly all children between the ages of three and five attend preschool in sparkling classrooms, with teachers recruited and trained as child care professionals." She goes on to say this exists where "more than 90 percent of French children between ages three and five attend free or inexpensive preschools called *écoles maternelles*. Even before they reach the age of three,

many of them are in full-day programs."

Her desire is to replicate this system in the United States so that the state can have an early maternal influence on the children of America. She envisions a country in which "Big Brother" essentially becomes "Big Momma."

But is this really what we want in the United States? A nationally subsidized day care system that puts three-years-olds (even two-year-olds) in institutionalized care? Throughout the book Mrs. Clinton seems to be making the tragic assumption that the state can do a better job of raising children than parents. She proposes a system in which the First Lady becomes the "First Mom" —a system in which children are no longer the responsibility of the parents, but become instead wards of the state. ~ Kerby Anderson, Leadership University[1419]

Having a monopoly on your children remains a high priority for the Luciferian Left. In April of 2014, MSNBC host Melissa Harris-Perry cut a commercial promoting the idea that Americans should have a more "collective" mindset regarding how parents raise their children.[1420]

Barack Obama has proposed to spend $75 *billion* on Hillary Clinton's "universal pre-school" agenda.[1421]

A powerful voice behind it is Jorge Mario Bergoglio, Rome's Jesuit Pope. [italics suspended]

In a scene that is sure to disturb many a conservative and thrill many a liberal, on Sunday Pope Francis addressed a massive crowd of over 300,000 school students from schools all over Italy. He had them all chant together over and over again this saying: "It takes a village to raise a child."

Most conservatives will recall that phrase as the title of Hillary Clinton's 1996 book and the memorable debate over her vision for the child as the charge of the state rather than being in the primary care of their parents. The origin of the phrase though is attributed to an African proverb. ...

The mantra of "it takes a village to raise a child," has been used to assist in the erosion of parents' rights, especially in schools. Under the guise of giving "rights" to children and adolescents the state has pushed its anti-moral agendas on children in schools all over the world. In public and Catholic schools alike.

For instance in 2005 when a California school district was introducing disturbing and explicit sex information to students, parents sued, arguing that they had the sole right "to control the upbringing of their children by introducing them to matters of and relating to sex in accordance with their personal and religious values and beliefs."

The Ninth Circuit Court ruled however that "there is no fundamental right of parents to be the exclusive provider of information regarding sexual matters to their children. ... Parents have no due process or privacy right to override the determinations of public schools as to the information to which their children will be exposed while enrolled as students."

All over North America and Europe the push is on to have parents denied the right to opt their children out of controversial sex-education programs that promote homosexual "marriage". ~ John Westen, *LifeSite*[1422]

Controlled

Are world leaders as controlled as some of the sex slaves they sleep with?

Young Barry Soetoro was manipulated from an early age by perversion and maintained there, from the "transgender" nanny he was given while in Indonesia[1423] to the astounding collection of pagan-demonic jewelry and talismans he always keeps on his person.

- A ring resembling a wedding band on his left ring finger with the inscription, "There is no god but Allah!"[1424] He's been wearing it since a single homosexual at college.[1425]
- A small pendant of "Hanuman", the Indian monkey god.[1426]
- A Catholic "miraculous medal" and Virgin with Child pendant.[1427]
- A picture of the Virgin Mary in his wallet.[1428]

Worst of these is the medallion Obama is seen wearing during a "family picture" taken in Jakarta, Indonesia with stepfather Lolo Soetoro.[1429]

What exactly the pendant is depicting defies description but it would appear to be a humanoid mantis, a "Reptilian" or even a tall "alien grey".

The origin of the medallion is difficult to surmise. Most Hindu gods are depicted as having a human upper-half and an animal lower-half such as the half-human/half-snake *Nāga*, or the half-human/half-crocodile (or fish)

Makara.

The predominant religion in Indonesia is Islam which frowns upon ostentatious jewelry for men.

Even more fascinating is that Hawaiian native and resident of Indonesia Ron Mullers, chairman of the "Friends of Obama" organization, commissioned a bronze statue to be built and emplaced in Jakarta[1430]. It is supposed to depict a 10 year old Obama in near life-sized dimensions. It could be any black child except in one respect—that same medallion is on the statue.

The child is holding a butterfly but not looking at it. Butterfly symbolism was used in mind control experimentation such as the CIA's Project Monarch.[1431]

Interestingly, the nationalistic people of Indonesia were offended by this publicity stunt and forced the removal of the statue from the park in the nation's capital where it was placed, believing that such an honor should go to true Indonesians.[1432]

Experts on the subjects of sorcery, necromancy and the occult will attest that talismans like young Obama's humanoid mantis pendant are a controlling point for spirits, especially if the wearer has been conditioned for such control.

Victims of ritual satanic and sexual abuse are easily manipulated and Obama shows the signs, according to WorldNetDaily's Jerome Corsi.

> *The intimate, fatherly relationship with pornographer and card-carrying communist Frank Marshall Davis that Barack Obama captured in a disturbingly graphic poem has led many to speculate Obama was sexually abused as a teen. ...*
>
> *Speculation about Obama's sexuality has roiled beneath the radar of establishment media, fed, among other things, by Larry Sinclair's sensational claims of cocaine-fueled homosexual acts with Obama in Chicago and reports of Obama's "transgender nanny" in Indonesia.*
>
> *Now, the former radical activist from Occidental College who has recounted a 1980 encounter in which Obama affirmed revolutionary Marxist views tells WND in an interview his strong impression at the time was that Obama and the wealthy Pakistani roommate who accompanied him were homosexual lovers.* ~ Corsi,

WND[1433]

The Jesuit-managed CIA learned this from Nazis scientists whom they brought over illegally[1434] after WWII via "Operation: PAPERCLIP".[1435]

Satanism, sexual abuse and torture are applied to the victim who is kept from blacking out by narcotics. Their mind has only one place to go—create another personality. This personality is then trained to be a sex slave, spy, courier or assassin and triggered at the will of the oppressor.[1436]

Two-Card Monte

Like Terry Reed, Cathy O'Brien experienced the sophistry that was America's political party system.

> *I met up with Bill Clinton again in 1982 at a county fair in Berryville, Arkansas. Alex Houston was "entertaining" there due to the close proximity of the CIA Near Death Trauma Center (aka slave conditioning and programming camp) and drug distribution point at Swiss Villa in Lampe, Missouri. ...*
>
> *From my perspective, those who were actively laying the groundwork for implementing the New World Order through mind conditioning of the masses made no distinction between Democratic and Republican Parties. Their aspirations were international in proportion, not American. Members were often drawn from, among other elitist groups, the Council on Foreign Relations. Like George Bush, Bill Clinton was an active member of the CFR, Bilderbergers, and Tri-Lateral Commission. Based on numerous conversations I overheard, Clinton was being groomed and prepared to fill the role of President under the guise of Democrat in the event that the American people became discouraged with Republican leaders. This was further evidenced by the extent of Clinton's New World Order knowledge and professed loyalties.* ~ O'Brien[1437]

America's traitor puppet politicians have absolutely rationalized what they are doing, and the worst is yet to come.

> *Byrd "justified" mind-control atrocities as a means of thrusting mankind into accelerated evolution, according to the Neo-Nazi principles to which he adhered. He "justified" manipulating mankind's religion to bring about the prophesied biblical "world peace" through the "only means available"—total mind control in the New World Order." After all," he proclaimed, "even the Pope and Mormon Prophet know this is the only way to peace and they*

cooperate fully with The Project." ~ O'Brien[1438]

At Bohemian Grove, the blackmailing of prominent people via any conceivable perversion and horror wasn't the worst thing O'Brien says she experienced, it was what she overheard they intend to do to all of us. [italics suspended]

> Among these internationally scandalous tapes are numerous videos covertly produced at the supposedly secure political sex playground in northern California, Bohemian Grove. According to Houston, Dante's high tech undetectable cameras used fiber optics, and fish-eye lens were in each of the elite club's numerous sexual perversion theme rooms. My knowledge of these cameras was due to the strategically compromising positions of the political perpetrators I was prostituted to in the various kinky theme rooms.
>
> I was programmed and equipped to function in all rooms at Bohemian Grove in order to compromise specific government targets according to their personal perversions. "Anything, anytime, anywhere with anyone" was my mode of operation at the Grove. I do not purport to understand the full function of this political cesspool playground as my perception was limited to my own realm of experience. My perception is that Bohemian Grove serves those ushering in the New World Order through mind control, and consists primarily of the highest Mafia and U.S. Government officials.
>
> There was a triangular glass display centered in a main through way where I was locked in with various trained animals, including snakes. Members walking by watched elicit sex acts of bestiality, women with women, mothers with daughters, kids with kids, or any other unlimited perverse visual display.
>
> From the owl's roost to the necrophilia room, no memory of sexual abuse is as horrifying as the conversations overheard in the Underground pertaining to implementing the New World Order. I learned that perpetrators believed that controlling the masses through propaganda mind manipulation did not guarantee there would be a world left to dominate due to environmental and overpopulation problems. The solution being debated was not pollution/population control, but mass genocide of "selected undesirables." ~ O'Brien[1439]

Don't Give Up Yet!

Depressed? Don't be.

Not only will we win, I've seen signs that a secret Resistance is already striking back.

Endnotes

[1319] *They're Not Human Beings—So Welcome to the Buffet*, Jonathon Van Maren, 8 May 2012, Unmasking "Choice".ca
http://www.unmaskingchoice.ca/blog/2012/05/08/theyre-not-human-beings-so-welcome-buffet

[1320] *Thai Police Arrest Man With Suitcase Full Of Gold Plated Babies Set To Be Used In Black Magic Ritual*, Paul Sims, 18 May 2012, the Daily Mail
http://www.dailymail.co.uk/news/article-2146396/British-man-arrested-Thailand-suitcase-dead-babies-used-religious-ritual.html

[1321] *Abortionist Accused of Eating Fetuses*, 14 June 2005, WorldNetDaily
http://www.wnd.com/2005/06/30815/

[1322] *Obama's HHS Nominee Proved Her Loyalty to Clinton by Digging Through a Dead Man's Trash*, Andrew Stiles, 11 April 2014, the Washington Free Beacon
http://freebeacon.com/blog/obamas-new-hhs-secretary-proved-her-loyalty-by-clinton-by-digging-through-a-dead-mans-trash/

[1323] *Whitewater: The Foster Report, II. BACKGROUND, A. 1993 Park Police Investigation*, the Washington Post
http://www.washingtonpost.com/wp-srv/politics/special/whitewater/docs/fosterii.htm

[1324] *Vince Foster's Death: An FBI Cover-Up?* 19 August 2000, WorldNetDaily
http://www.wnd.com/2000/08/4230/

[1325] *ITV Yorkshire*, Wikipedia.org
http://en.wikipedia.org/wiki/ITV_Yorkshire

[1326] *Conspiracy of Silence*, Yorkshire Television (1994), Johnny Cirucci, YouTube
https://www.youtube.com/watch?v=C3dE3tC7uRo&

[1327] *"The Pope Who Fooled the World … Blessed John Paul II"*, Tony Bushby 1 July 2011, Vati Leaks
http://www.vatileaks.com/_blog/Vati_Leaks/post/Pope_John_Paul_II's_international_paedophile_ring_of_Catholic_priests/

[1328] *A Woman Rides The Beast*, Dave Hunt, Harvest House (1994), p. 78

[1329] *Jesuit Priest Who Abused Boys Casts Shadow In The Northwest Long After His Death*, Bryan Denson, 27 February 2010, the Oregonian
http://www.oregonlive.com/portland/index.ssf/2010/02/jesuit_priest_who_abused_boys.html

[1330] *Philanthropist Alan Baer Dies - Nov 6, 2002 - Omaha World-Herald*, Franklin Case.org
http://www.franklincase.org/index.php?option=com_content&view=article&id=171:king-expands-into-food-service-something-on-every-burner-jan-12-1985-&catid=6:news-articles&Itemid=14

[1331] *Ex-WH Writer Peter Citron Dies - June 28, 2003 - Omaha World-Herald, 28 June 2003*, Franklin Case.org
http://www.franklincase.org/index.php?option=com_content&view=article&id=172:king-expands-into-food-service-something-on-every-burner-jan-12-1985-&catid=6:news-articles&Itemid=14

[1332] *Investigator Gary Caradori's Interview of Child Sex Slave Victim Alisha Owen*, Johnny Cirucci, YouTube
https://www.youtube.com/watch?v=1Ml-mHxqiZ0&

[1333] *SPECIAL REPORT: FBI Killed Franklin Scandal Investigator*, Wayne Madsen, 20-22 June 2014, the Wayne Madsen Report
http://www.roseanneworld.com/blog/2014/06/special-report-fbi-killed-franklin-scandal-investigator-wayne-madsen-report/
[1334] *William Colby > Death*, Wikipedia.org
http://en.wikipedia.org/wiki/William_Colby#Death
[1335] *The Beast at Work*, Gyeorgos Ceres Hatonn, Phoenix Source Distributors (1993), p. 45
[1336] *Lobbyist Is Arrested in New York*, 10 August 1989, NY Times
http://www.nytimes.com/1989/08/10/us/lobbyist-is-arrested-in-new-york.html
[1337] *In Death, Spence Stayed True To Form*, Michael Hedges and Jerry Seper, 13 November 1989, the Washington Times, reposted here
http://johnnycirucci.com/wp/blog/2014/10/11/in-death-spence-stayed-true-to-form/
[1338] *Boys for Sale*, Alternative Views News Magazine, 1983
https://www.youtube.com/watch?v=5aEcFY_c6Ds&
[1339] *What Are The Charges Against Jerry Sandusky?* CNN Wire Staff, 21 June 2012, CNN
http://www.cnn.com/2012/06/21/justice/pennsylvania-sandusky-charges/
[1340] *DA Who Never Charged Sandusky Has Been Missing Since 2005*, Teresa Masterson, 10 November 2011, NBC Philadelphia
http://www.nbcphiladelphia.com/news/local/DA-Who-Never-Charged-Sandusky-Has-Been-Missing-Since-2005-133615093.html
[1341] *SHOCKING PENN STATE RUMOR: Jerry Sandusky "Pimped Out Young Boys To Rich Donors"*, Tony Manfred, 10 November 2011, Business Insider
http://www.businessinsider.com/jerry-sandusky-donors-2011-11
[1342] *Bush Names Local Group As "Daily Point Of Light"*, John Hirokawa, 12 November 1990, the Daily Collegian
http://www.collegian.psu.edu/archives/article_64ba0c7d-87f4-5b6d-bb7f-35409c4de4a7.html
[1343] *PSU's Jerry Sandusky "Found His Victims" At Second Mile Group Home*, Timothy McNulty and Janice Crompton, 6 November 2011, the Pittsburgh Post-Gazette
http://www.post-gazette.com/sports/psu/2011/11/06/PSU-s-Jerry-Sandusky-found-his-victims-at-Second-Mile-group-home/stories/201111060201
[1344] *Rick Santorum*, Wikipedia.org
http://en.wikipedia.org/wiki/Rick_Santorum
[1345] *Santorum Sponsored Honor For Accused PSU Coach*, Thomas Fitzgerald, 9 November 2011, the Philadelphia Inquirer
http://www.philly.com/philly/blogs/big_tent/Santorum-honored-accused-PSU-Coach-as-angel.html
[1346] *Trance Formation of America*, Cathy O'Brien and Mark Phillips, Reality Marketing (1995)
[1347] *Cathy O'Brien > Criticisms of O'Brien*, Wikipedia.org
http://en.wikipedia.org/wiki/Cathy_O'Brien#Criticisms_of_O.27Brien
[1348] *Cathy O'Brien's Claims of Being an MK-ULTRA Victim*, Mark Dice, undated, Mark Dice.com
http://www.markdice.com/index.php?option=com_content&view=article&id=126:cathy-obriens-claims-of-being-an-mk-ultra-victim
[1349] *Guy Vander Jagt (1931-2007) Papers*, Grand Valley State University Archives

http://www.gvsu.edu/cms3/assets/00D0CC14-A2F1-C75D-7C8E7587D95C099E/pdf/RHC-11%20VanderJagt.pdf
[1350] *Trance Formation of America*, Cathy O'Brien and Mark Phillips, Reality Marketing (1995), p. 86
[1351] *ibid*, p. 86
[1352] *ibid*, p. 87
[1353] *ibid*, pp. 89-90
[1354] *ibid*, p. 91
[1355] *ibid*, p. 92
[1356] *ibid*, p. 93
[1357] *ibid*, p. 95
[1358] *ibid*, p. 95
[1359] *Republicanism - the Dark Night of the America Dream*, G. P. Geoghegan, Lulu.com (2008), pp, 81-82
[1360] *U.S. Stalls On Human Trafficking*, Cam Simpson, 27 December 2005, the Chicago Tribune
http://www.chicagotribune.com/chi-0512270176dec27-story.html#page=1
[1361] *Trance Formation of America*, p. 96
[1362] *Thanks For The Memories ... The Truth Has Set Me Free! The Memoirs of Bob Hope's and Henry Kissinger's Mind-Controlled Slave*, Brice Taylor, Brice Taylor Trust (1999), p. 5
[1363] *VFTB 208: What Witches Don't Want Christians to Know*, Derek Gilbert, 4 December 2014, View From The Bunker
http://vftb.net/?p=5530
[1364] *Trance Formation of America*, pp. 96-97
[1365] *ibid*, p. 97
[1366] *ibid*, p. 97
[1367] *Military Funds Brain-Computer Interfaces to Control Feelings*, Antonio Regalado, 29 May 2014, MIT Technology Review
http://www.technologyreview.com/news/527561/military-funds-brain-computer-interfaces-to-control-feelings/
[1368] *Trance Formation of America*, p. 99
[1369] *Trance Formation of America*, p. 162
[1370] *Lawmaker Denied Ft. Sill Entry After Reports of Displacing Soldiers to Accommodate Illegal Aliens*, 2 July 2014, Judicial Watch
http://www.judicialwatch.org/blog/2014/07/lawmaker-denied-ft-still-entry-reports-displacing-soldiers-accommodate-illegal-aliens/
 What kind of ball-less, spineless Caspar Milquetoasts is America putting into office?
[1371] *Thanks for the Memories*, p. 50
[1372] *Trance Formation of America,*, p. 99
[1373] *Thanks for the Memories*, pp. 45-46
[1374] *A Darkness in Massachusetts*, Dorothy Rabinowitz, 9 July 2001, the Wall Street Journal
http://online.wsj.com/articles/SB122635300174815027
[1375] *Thanks for the Memories*, p. 48
[1376] *Thanks for the Memories*, p. 51

[1377] *Dolores Hope Supported Catholic Causes*, Catholic News Service, 22 September 2011, the Catholic Herald
http://catholicherald.com/stories/Dolores-Hope-supported-numerous-Catholic-causes,16782
[1378] *Thanks for the Memories*, pp. 61-62
[1379] *ibid*, p. 101
[1380] *ibid*, p. 101-102
[1381] *Since Dick Cheney Shot Him, Harry Whittington's Aim Has Been To Move On*, Paul Farhi, 14 October 2010, Washington Post
http://www.washingtonpost.com/wp-dyn/content/article/2010/10/13/AR2010101307173.html
[1382] *"Hunger Games" Author Suzanne Collins, In Rare Interview, Muses On War And The Cycle Of Violence*, Molly Driscoll, 20 November 2013, the Christian Science Monitor
http://www.csmonitor.com/Books/chapter-and-verse/2013/1120/Hunger-Games-author-Suzanne-Collins-in-rare-interview-muses-on-war-and-the-cycle-of-violence
[1383] *Walt Disney Biography*, Encyclopedia of World Biography
http://www.notablebiographies.com/De-Du/Disney-Walt.html
[1384] *Walt Disney: Freemason Or Not?* Todd E. Creason, 26 October 2011, From Labor to Refreshment
http://toddcreason.blogspot.com/2011/10/walt-disney-freemason-or-not.html
[1385] *DeMolay International*, Wikipedia.org
http://en.wikipedia.org/wiki/DeMolay_International
[1386] *General Dynamics, Campaign Finance*, Influence Explorer.com
http://influenceexplorer.com/organization/general-dynamics/4438cca4c4ae4715b1bf348629b68cc0?cycle=1990
[1387] *Trance Formation of America*, p. 109
[1388] *Thanks For The Memories*, pp. 41-42
[1389] *ibid*, p. 111
[1390] *Alex Houston and Elmer – Nashville's Best*, 29 August 2006, Waxidermy.com
http://waxidermy.com/alex-houston-and-elmer-nashvilles-best/
[1391] *The Porter Wagoner Show: Season 1, Episode 270, Alex Houston and Elmer(8 Sep. 1969)*, the Internet Movie Database
http://www.imdb.com/title/tt3097502/
[1392] *The C.I.A. Doctors: Human Rights Violations by American Psychiatrists*, Colin Ross, Greenleaf (2006), p. 58
[1393] *William Stephenson, British Spy Known as Intrepid, Is Dead at 93*, Albin Krebs, 3 February 1989, the NY Times
http://www.nytimes.com/1989/02/03/obituaries/william-stephenson-british-spy-known-as-intrepid-is-dead-at-93.html
[1394] *The C.I.A. Doctors*, pp. 59-60
[1395] *Operation Mind Control*, Walter Bowart, Dell (1978), p. 121
[1396] *Operation Mind Control*, Walter Bowart, Dell (1978), p. 126
[1397] *Even E! Was Spooked: "Katy Perry Performs 'Satanic Ritual' at the Grammys"*, WTF News, 27 January 2014, WTFRLY.com
http://wtfrly.com/2014/01/27/even-e-was-spooked-katy-perry-performs-satanic-ritual-at-the-grammys/

[1398] *Madonna Hangs On A Cross, Knocks World Leaders In Tour Kickoff*, Corey Moss, 22 May 2006, MTV.com
http://www.mtv.com/news/1532204/madonna-hangs-on-a-cross-knocks-world-leaders-in-tour-kickoff/

[1399] *Madonna Reacts To Nun Sister Cristina's "Like A Virgin" Cover With A Pair Of Instagram Photos*, Robbie Daw, 23 October 2014, Idolator
http://www.idolator.com/7567656/madonna-nun-sister-cristina-like-a-virgin-cover-reaction

[1400] *Kesha Sues Producer, Alleges Years Of Sex Abuse And Forced Drugging*, Richard Winton, 14 October 2014, the LA Times
http://www.latimes.com/local/lanow/la-me-ln-kesha-sues-producer-sexual-abuse-drugging-20141014-story.html

[1401] *Thanks For The Memories ... The Truth Has Set Me Free! The Memoirs of Bob Hope's and Henry Kissinger's Mind-Controlled Slave*, Brice Taylor, Brice Taylor Trust (1999), p. 21

[1402] *Trance Formation of America*, Cathy O'Brien and Mark Phillips, Reality Marketing (1995), pp. 113, 114, 115

[1403] *James Traficant Jr., Expelled from Congress in 2002, Dies at 73*, Neela Banerjee, 27 September 2014, the LA Times
http://www.latimes.com/local/obituaries/la-me-james-traficant-20140928-story.html

I'm not a Traficant sycophant but was it necessary for the slime at the Times to headline his worst moment for his ___ing *obituary*?!

When Traficant was charged with bribery the first time, he was still a sheriff. Did he have access to information that helped him get acquitted?

These are the questions corporate media won't ask.

[1404] Another good entry from Wikipedia: *James Traficant*
http://en.wikipedia.org/wiki/James_Traficant

[1405] *The Death Of James Traficant*, WeAreChange, YouTube
https://www.youtube.com/watch?v=LjTdpqTsqZ8

[1406] *Trance Formation of America*, p. 118

[1407] *RNC Chief Ken Mehlman*, Josh Marshall, 29 October 2006, TalkingPointsMemo
http://talkingpointsmemo.com/edblog/--91702

If you use satan's official search engine, "Google", this hit will not pop up in Internet Explorer. I had to use FireFox.

[1408] *Trance Formation of America*, p. 150

[1409] *Mystery of Marilyn Monroe's Death Unveiled?* Sergei Vasilenkov, 7 March 2013, Pravda
http://english.pravda.ru/society/stories/03-07-2013/125016-marilyn_monroe_death-0/

[1410] *Loving Marilyn*, undated, "Shar", LovingMarilyn.com
http://lovingmarilyn.com/dougherty.html

A helpful summary of the autobiography of Norma Jeane Mortenson's first husband, Jim Dougherty.

[1411] *Strange Marilyn Monroe Facts*, StrangeCosmos.com
http://www.strangecosmos.com/content/item/182843.html

[1412] *ibid*

[1413] *Anton LaVey > Ancestry and Early Life*, Wikipedia
http://en.wikipedia.org/wiki/Anton_LaVey#Ancestry_and_early_life

Again, Wikipedia at its best!

[1414] *The Secret Life of a Satanist*, Blanche Barton, Feral House (1992), my electronic copy showed pages 12, 13 and 14 but that is likely different in print.

I have forced to give a hat tip to the always acerbic Mark Dice for having covered this in one of his YouTube videos, thus pointing me in a direction to look.

[1415] *The Church of Satan*, Michael A. Aquino, self-published trash (1983), pp. 17 – 19

Although the dork couldn't get his ridiculous tome published, I found what little I read of it disturbingly thorough and well-written. Clearly, this was a United States government official that was useful to the Luciferian Machine after he got as much as he could from that clown Howard Levey, a.k.a. "Anton LaVey!"

[1416] *The Hidden Life of Marilyn Monroe, the Original Hollywood Mind Control Slave (Part-II)*, 5 June 2013, the Vigilant Citizen
http://vigilantcitizen.com/vigilantreport/the-hidden-life-of-marilyn-monroe-the-original-hollywood-mind-control-slave-part-ii/

[1417] *Trance Formation of America*, pp. 123, 124

[1418] *It Takes a Village > Proverb Question*, Wikipedia
http://en.wikipedia.org/wiki/It_Takes_a_Village

[1419] *It Takes a Village: An Analysis of Hillary Clinton's Book*, Kerby Anderson, Leadership University
http://www.leaderu.com/orgs/probe/docs/village.html

[1420] *Melissa Harris-Perry: Your Kids Aren't Yours!* Tami Jackson, 8 April 2014, the Black Sphere
http://theblacksphere.net/2013/04/know-your-kids-arent-yours/

[1421] *Obama Proposes $75 Billion for Universal Preschool*, Dylan Scott, 10 April 2013, Governing.com
http://www.governing.com/news/federal/gov-obama-proposes-66-billion-over-10-years-for-universal-preschool.html

[1422] *"It Takes A Village To Raise A Child": Did Pope Francis Quote Hillary Clinton?* John Westen, 14 May 2014, LifeSite
https://www.lifesitenews.com/blogs/it-takes-a-village-to-raise-a-child-did-pope-francis-quote-hilary-clinton

[1423] *President Barack Obama's Transgender Former Nanny Living In Indonesia, Overwhelmed By Celebrity*, Associated Press, 8 March 2012, New York Daily News
http://www.nydailynews.com/news/politics/president-barack-obama-transgender-nanny-living-indonesia-overwhelmed-celebrity-article-1.1035331

[1424] *Obama's Ring: "There Is No God But Allah"*, Jerome Corsi, 10 October 2012, WorldNetDaily
http://www.wnd.com/2012/10/obamas-ring-there-is-no-god-but-allah/

[1425] *Tea Party Activist: Evidence Obama Was Married to Pakistani Man*, Eric Dolan, 8 August 2012, Raw Story
http://www.rawstory.com/rs/2012/08/08/tea-party-activist-evidence-obama-was-married-to-pakistani-man/

[1426] *Obama to Get Hanuman Idol*, unattributed, 24 June 2008, the Times of India
http://timesofindia.indiatimes.com/India/Obama_to_get_Hanuman_idol/rssarticleshow/3160730.cms

[1427] *President Obama Carries Miraculous Medal*, Crown of Stars blog, 23 January 2009
http://crownofstars.blogspot.com/2009/01/president-obama-carries-miraculous.html

[1428] *Obama's Devotion to the Virgin Mary: Who Knew?* David Gibson, at this writing, listed date was simply "3 years ago"...Huffington Post is such a useless rag, "Politics Daily", the Huffington Post
http://www.politicsdaily.com/2010/09/28/obamas-devotion-to-the-virgin-mary-who-knew/
[1429] Barack Obama Childhood Photo Pages, Barack Obama Photos.com
http://www.barack-obama-photos.com/Obama-Childhood-Photos.html
[1430] *Statue Of Young Obama Unveiled In Indonesia*, Kathy Quiano, 10 December 2009, CNN
http://www.cnn.com/2009/WORLD/asiapcf/12/10/indonesia.obama.statue/
[1431] *Origins and Techniques of Monarch Mind Control*, 12 December 2012, the Vigilant Citizen
http://vigilantcitizen.com/hidden-knowledge/origins-and-techniques-of-monarch-mind-control/
[1432] *Controversial Obama Statue In Indonesia Removed From Park After Protests*, Douglas Stanglin, 15 February 2010, USA Today
http://content.usatoday.com/communities/ondeadline/post/2010/02/controversial-obama-statue-in-indonesia-removed-from-park-after-protests/1
[1433] *Occidental Activist: I Thought Obama Was "Gay"*, Jerome Corsi, 15 August 2012, WorldNetDaily
http://www.wnd.com/2012/08/occidental-activist-i-thought-obama-was-gay/
[1434] *The NASA Nazis*, unattributed, no date, Rocketry South Carolina, excellent YouTube on the page by the same title, featuring Bruce k. Gagnon of the *Global Network Against Weapons and Nuclear Power in Space*
http://www.rocketrysouthcarolina.com/youtube_browser.php?do=show&vidid=zkEUv6z20qo
[1435] *Nazi Technology*, History Detectives Special Investigations, no date, PBS
http://www.pbs.org/opb/historydetectives/feature/nazi-technology/
[1436] *Origins and Techniques of Monarch Mind Control*, Vigilant Citizen, 12 December 2012
http://vigilantcitizen.com/hidden-knowledge/origins-and-techniques-of-monarch-mind-control/
[1437] *Trance Formation of America*, p. 154
[1438] *ibid*, pp. 120-121
[1439] *ibid*, pp. 171, 173

Chapter 15

The Light of Lucifer:
How the Devil Gives Nations He Rides Their Edge

...such men are false apostles, deceitful workers, disguising themselves as apostles of Christ.

No wonder, for even Satan disguises himself as an angel of light.

Therefore it is not surprising if his servants also disguise themselves as servants of righteousness, whose end will be according to their deeds. ~ II Corinthians 11:13-15

Intelligence and technology are the two endeavors that can put a nation state in a winning position.

War is a tool of domination by the Elite and never serves the best interest of the common people.

Americans will be shocked to know that it is the devil who has given the United States her technological edge to wield by his servants in Rome, just as they wielded Hitler, Napoleon and many others before us.

The Nazification of American Technology

At the end of WWII, the U.S. and U.S.S.R. descended on Berlin like it was Christmas morning, eagerly snatching up the most diabolical minds in the German military.

The Office of Strategic Services (OSS) then secreted these Nazi scientists to the United States where they helped build the same empire but under different masters. In many ways, post WWII America was turned into the Fourth Reich by United States politicians and leaders.

**The grandfather of NASA, Wernher von Braun.
German Federal Archive**

The most notable and perhaps best known of these Nazis was Wernher von Braun, the mastermind behind the American Space program.

Before helping create the National Aeronautics and Space Administration, von Braun was busy building V2 rockets to kill Britons with.[1440]

A far less well-known name is that of Erich Traub.

> *Erich Traub (1906–1985) was a German veterinarian and scientist/virologist who specialized in foot-and-mouth disease, Rinderpest and Newcastle disease. Traub was a member of the National Socialist Motor Corps (NSKK), a Nazi motorist corps, from 1938 to 1942. He worked directly for Heinrich Himmler, head of the Schutzstaffel (SS), as the lab chief of the Nazi's leading bio-weapons facility on Riems Island.[1]*
>
> *Traub was rescued from the Soviet zone of Germany after World War II and brought to the United States in 1949 under the auspices of the United States government program Operation Paperclip, meant to exploit the post-war scientific knowledge in Germany, and deny it to the Soviet Union.[2]* ~ Wikipedia[1441]

Traub had actually been chosen *before* the war to work biological warfare for one of America's richest families, the Rockefellers.

> *During the 1930s, he studied on a fellow-ship at the Rockefeller Institute for Medical Research in Princeton, New Jersey mentored by Richard Shope, performing research on vaccines and viruses, including pseudorabies virus and lymphocytic choriomeningitis virus (LCM).[3][4][5] During his stay in the United States, Traub and his wife were listed as members of the German American Bund, a pro-nazi German-American club just thirty miles west of Plum Island in Yaphank, Long Island, from 1934 to 1935.[6]* ~ Wikipedia[1442]

Traub would go on to mirror the Nazi biological warfare facility on Riems Island for his American keepers on Plum Island, New York.

> *Dr. Traub is known as the father of the Plum Island biological research lab, located 6 miles from Old Lyme, Connecticut. According to the book Lab 257, by author Michael Carroll, Dr. Traub was chief of Insel Riems, a virological research institute in the Baltic sea now known as the Friedrich Loeffler Institute.*
>
> *Traub worked directly for Adolf Hitler's second in charge, Heinrich*

> *Himmler. At Insel Riems, Dr. Traub's interests included personally collecting Rinderpest virus from Anatolia, and packaging weaponized foot and mouth disease for dispersal onto cattle and reindeer in Russia. Dr. Traub also experimented with the glanders bacteria and had a particular fascination for organisms that voraciously devour the brain.* ~ Erich Traub and Lyme Disease, tech-archive[1443]

That was Traub's specialty—getting biological agents spread into a populace via parasitic insects.

> *...insects of all types, particularly the biting and stinging kinds, can be used as disease vectors in a biological warfare program. Germany, Japan, Britain, Russia and the U.S. all conducted experiments along these lines during the Second World War, and the Japanese used such insect-borne diseases against both soldiers and civilians in China. This was one reason that Franklin Roosevelt and Secretary of War Henry Stimson ordered the creation of an American biological warfare program in 1942...* ~ Wikipedia[1444]

In case that doesn't sound familiar to you, it's how Lyme Disease is spread; via ticks. Left untreated, Lyme disease can affect the joints, eyes, heart, nerves and brain, leading to loss of sensory or motor functions in the extremities. It was first discovered in 1975 around Lyme Connecticut, less than 20 miles from Plum Island.

> *An important chapter in ... the possible link between Plum Island, Erich Traub's work on behalf of the U.S.* [government] *and the spread of Lyme Disease concerns the work of former Justice Department prosecutor John Loftus. In his book The Belarus Secret, Loftus referred to work done on Plum Island in the early 1950's in which Nazi scientists were experimenting on diseased ticks. Might that have referred to Traub?!* " *... Attorney John Loftus was hired in 1979 by the Office of Special Investigations, a unit set up by the Justice Department to expose Nazi war crimes*

> *and unearth Nazis hiding in the United States. Given top-secret clearance to review files that had been sealed for thirty-five years, Loftus found a treasure trove of information on America's postwar Nazi recruiting. In 1982, publicly challenging the government's complacency with the wrongdoing, he told 60 Minutes that top Nazi officers had been protected and harbored in America by the CIA and the State Department. 'They got the Emmy Award,' Loftus wrote. 'My family got the death threats.'"*
>
> *"In the preface of The Belarus Secret, Loftus laid out a striking piece of information gleaned from his spy network: 'Even more disturbing are the records of the Nazi germ warfare scientists who came to America. They experimented with poison ticks dropped from planes to spread rare diseases. I have received some information suggesting that the U.S. tested some of these poison ticks on the Plum Island artillery range off the coast of Connecticut during the early 1950's. ... Most of the germ warfare records have been shredded, but there is a top secret U.S. document confirming that 'clandestine attacks on crops and animals' took place at this time." ~ Patricia Doyle, Ph. D., Rense.com*[1445]

America's burgeoning Intelligence apparatus received a distinctly Nazi touch. It would eventually lead to "mind control" technology breakthroughs that were chilling. [italics suspended]

> After WWII, the U.S. Department of Defense secretly imported many of the top German Nazi and Italian Fascist scientists and spies into the United States via South America and the Vatican. The code name for this operation was Project PAPERCLIP.[4] One of the more prominent finds for the U.S. was German General Reinhard Gehlen. Hitler's Chief of Intelligence against Russia. Upon arriving in Washington D.C. in 1945, Gehlen met extensively with President Truman, General William "Wild Bill" Donovan, Director of the Office of Strategic Services(OSS) and Allen Dulles, who would later become the stalwart head of the CIA. The objective of their brain-storming sessions was to reorganize the nominal American intelligence operation, transforming it into a highly-efficient covert organization. The culmination of their efforts produced the Central Intelligence Group in 1946, renamed the Central Intelligence Agency(CIA) in 1947.
>
> Reinhard Gehlen also had profound influence in helping to create the National Security Council, from which the National Security Act of 1947 was derived. This particular piece of legislation was implemented to protect an unconscionable number of illegal

government activities, including clandestine mind control programs.

The Evolution of Project MK Ultra

With the CIA and National Security Council firmly established, the first in a series of covert brain-washing programs was initiated by the Navy in the fall of 1947. Project CHATTER was developed in response to the Soviet's "successes" through the use of "truth drugs." This rationale, however was simply a cover story if the program were to be exposed. The research focused on the identification and testing of such drugs for use in interrogations and the recruitment of agents.[5] ...

The CIA decided to expand their efforts in the area of behavior modification, with the advent of Project BLUEBIRD, approved by director Allen Dulles in 1950. Its objectives were to; (1) discover a means of conditioning personnel to prevent unauthorized extraction of information from them by known means, (2) investigate the possibility of control of an individual by application of special interrogation techniques, (3) investigate memory enhancement and (4) establish defensive means for preventing hostile control of agency personnel. In August 1951, Project BLUE BIRD was renamed Project ARTICHOKE, which evaluated offensive uses of interrogation techniques, including hypnosis and drugs. The program ceased in 1956. Three years prior to the halt of Project ARTICHOKE, Project MKULTRA came into existence on April 13, 1953 along the lines proposed by Richard Helms, Deputy Director of Central Intelligence (DDCI) with the rationale of establishing a "special funding mechanism of extreme sensitivity."[6]

The hypothetical etymology of "MK" may possibly stand for "Mind Kontrolle." The obvious translation of the German word "Kontrolle" into English is "control."[7] A host of German doctors, procured from the post war Nazi talent pool, were an invaluable asset toward the development of MKULTRA. The correlation between the concentration camp experiments and the numerous sub-projects of MKULTRA are clearly evident. The various avenues used to control human behavior under MKULTRA included radiation, electroshock, psychology, psychiatry, sociology, anthropology, graphology, harassment substances and paramilitary devices and materials "LSD" being the most widely dispensed "material". A special procedure, designated MKDELTA, was established to govern the use of MKULTRA abroad. MKULTRA/DELTA materials were used for harassment, discrediting or disabling purposes.[8] Of the 149 subprojects under the umbrella of MKULTRA having been identified, Project MONARCH, officially begun by the U.S. Army in the early 1960's (although unofficially implemented much earlier) appears to be the most prominent and is still classified as TOP SECRET for "National Security" reasons.[9] MONARCH may have culminated from MKSEARCH subprojects, such as operation SPELLBINDER, which was set up to create "sleeper" assassins (i e. "Manchurian candidates") who could be activated upon receiving a key word or phrase while in a post-hypnotic trance. Operation OFTEN, a study which attempted to harness the power of occultic forces was possibly one of several cover programs to hide the insidious reality of Project MONARCH. ~ Ron Patton, The Conspiracy Reader [1446]

Satan's Army

A man who figures prominently in Cathy O'Brien's mind control narrative is Michael Aquino.

There is no Wikipedia entry for "Michael A. Aquino".[1447]

"Truther" blogs around the internet will alternatively label him as "Lieutenant Colonel" Aquino or "General" Aquino of the United States Army Reserve and sometimes as a "Green Beret". This is probably an exaggeration based upon Aquino's work in Special *Operations* and not the Special *Forces*.

Aquino received a commission in the United States Army and did time in "Psychological Operations" during the Vietnam war as an administrator.

In 1980, while at the Catholic/Army fortress retreat of the Presidio, Aquino wrote a short paper for his boss titled *From PSYOP to MindWar: The Psychology of Victory*.

His superior was then Colonel Paul E. Vallely, darling of today's Conservative Christian movement and frequent contributor to FoxNews.

Psychological Operations have always been a part of large groups of men warring on each other and it was Pope Urban II during the Siege of Antioch 1097-1098 that inspired his Catholic Crusaders to lob the severed heads of vanquished muslims over the battlement walls into the city.[1448]

War is a vicious, brutal enterprise and even good men should wage it ruthlessly but problems arise when militaries are told their own citizenry is now "the enemy".

In that light, the paper United States Army Major Michael Aquino wrote is disturbing. [italics suspended]

> LTC John Alexander's Military Review article in support of "psychotronics" — intelligence and operational employment of ESP — was decidedly provocative.[3] ...
>
> Psychotronic research is in its infancy, but the U.S. Army *already* possesses an operational weapons systems designed to do what LTC Alexander would like ESP to do — except that *this* weapons system uses *existing* communications media. It seeks to map the minds of neutral and enemy individuals and then to change them in accordance with U.S. national interests. It does this on a wide scale, embracing military units, regions, nations, and blocs. In its present form it is called *Psychological Operations* (PSYOP). ...
>
> What the Army now considers to be the most effective PSYOP — tactical PSYOP — is actually the most limited and primitive effort, due to the difficulties of formulating and delivering messages under battlefield constraints. Such efforts must continue, but they are properly seen as *reinforcement* of the main MindWar effort. If we do not attack the enemy's will until he reaches the battlefield, his nation will have strengthened it as best it can. We must attack *that will before* it is thus locked in place. We must instill in it a predisposition to inevitable defeat.
>
> Strategic MindWar must begin the moment war is considered to be inevitable. It must seek out the attention of the enemy nation through every available medium, and it must strike at the nation's potential soldiers *before* they put on their uniforms. It is in their homes and their communities that they are most vulnerable to MindWar. Was the United States defeated in the jungles of Vietnam, or was it defeated in the streets of American cities?
>
> To this end MindWar must be strategic in emphasis, with tactical applications playing a reinforcing, supplementary role. In its strategic context, MindWar must reach out to friends, enemies, and neutrals alike across the globe — neither through primitive "battlefield" leaflets and loudspeakers of PSYOP nor through the weak, imprecise, and narrow effort of psychotronics[11] — but through the media possessed by the United States which have the capabilities to reach virtually all people on the face of the Earth. ~ *From PSYOP to MindWar*, Colonel Paul E. Valley with Major Michael A. Aquino, [emphasis in the original][1449]

Aquino would show up 6 years later in 1988 as one of the accused in a scandal centered on a Presidio daycare center where as many as 60 toddlers claimed to have been molested in sado / satanic sex rituals.

Although this was spun as "hysteria" based upon the over-active imagination of the children, the NY Times reported that at least 4 of the little girls (who hadn't even been through puberty) were diagnosed with the sexually-transmitted disease chlamydia.[1450]

This was on the heels of another Army scandal where parents had been shocked to learn that their children from 3 years old down to *three months old* had been sexually assaulted on the other side of the country in a West Point daycare facility. Even more upsetting to the parents; officers, administrators and commanders at West Point were all claiming they bore no responsibility for the outrage[1451]. United States Attorney Rudolph Giuliani was the man entrusted by the Elite to make it go away.

U.S. Attorney Will Not Reopen West Point Sex Case
Tim McGlone
Staff Writer for the Newburgh-Beacon Evening News
Tuesday, July 14, 1987

WEST POINT — U.S. Attorney Rudolph W. Giuliani will not reopen an investigation into alleged incidents of child sexual abuse at the West Point Child Development Center from 1984 to 1985.

U.S. Representative Hamilton Fish, Jr. had asked Giuliani to reopen the investigation and reconvene a grand jury, but Giuliani reiterated to Fish in a letter to him Friday that the case would only be reopened if new, substantive evidence were discovered.

"I am disappointed that criminal prosecution seems to have reached its conclusion, at least for the time being," Fish, R-Millbrook said.

Although he had no new evidence to present to Giuliani, Fish had asked him in a letter May 28 to reopen the investigation because the alleged child abuse incidents continued to be of great concern to him and those families involved.

A petition of 5,000 signatures started by one of the parents of one of the children allegedly abused was also included in Fish's request to reopen the case.[1452]

Giuliani was a loyal Loyola insurgent, educated at (Catholic) Christian

Brothers' Manhattan College[1453] with an honorary degree from Loyola. His pro-abortion stance may have bothered a bishop or two, but it didn't bother the Jesuits.[1454]

In 2002 he was made *Sir* Rudolph Giuliani by Dame of Malta[1455], Queen Elizabeth II.[1456]

When pedophile priest and personal friend Monsignor Alan Placa (who had officiated at Giuliani's wedding) needed a place to run to and be hired with, "Giuliani Partners in New York" was there for him.[1457]

Giuliani seems to fit right in with such perversion. He has appeared in public dressed as a woman no less than four different times since 1997—the last time was for the homosexual TV show *Queer As Folk*.[1458]

When Georgetown alum George Tenet (then Director of the CIA) would oversee the most treasonous mass-killing in America on September 11th, 2001, Giuliani was the man in NYC to see it done on his end.

Giuliani would later be hired by video game manufacturer Activision to defend them from a lawsuit initiated by ousted Panamanian dictator Manuel Noriega. While in jail, the aging autocrat found out that the video game "Call of Duty: Black Ops II" used his image without acquiring the rights to do so.[1459]

The *Call of Duty* series of video games has been a great recruitment tool for America's future out-of-touch with reality button-pushing killers and there has been close collaboration with the Pentagon for just that purpose.[1460]

Satan's Society

Michael Aquino was the protégé of "Church of Satan" founder Howard Levey ("Anton LaVey").

They have both been used extensively by the United States government for the purposes of mass and individual "mind control". As a result, Aquino was able to appear on the Oprah Winfrey show in 1988, shortly after being accused of raping and torturing the children of soldiers at the Presidio, and walk away unscathed.

> *The Army did not suspend his clearance when he joined the Church of Satan, founded by Anton LaVey, in 1969. Nor when Aquino founded his own satanic church in 1975. Nor when Aquino while on a NATO tour of Europe in 1982 performed a satanic ritual in the*

Westphalian castle that had been used as an occult sanctuary by Heinrich Himmler's SS elite in Nazi Germany. Nor did the Army move to suspend Aquino's top security

clearance during the sex abuse investigation. "The nature of the investigation that prompted the search of his house, and I understand some of his belongings were taken by police, really is a question for the San Francisco Police Department," Maj. Greg Rixon, spokesman at the Pentagon said Aquino, who now works as a program analyst at the Army Reserve Personnel Center in St Louis, has vehemently denied ever meeting or having in his house the young girl who has alleged he abused her. ~ Linda Goldston, the San Jose Mercury News[1461]

Aquino has become so arrogant that he even sued the Secretary of the Army in 1992 to protect his "reputation". However, not even Michael Aquino can sue the Federal government.[1462]

Aquino gathered as much information from "Anton LaVey" as he could (which wasn't very much) and then "broke off" from the Church of Satan to start his "Temple of Set" in 1975. That was the platform that the CIA found extremely useful.

But the co-operative of spooks and satan goes back much further.

"Mr. Crowley"

Edward Alexander "Aleister" Crowley (1845-1947) called himself alternatively "the Beast" and "the World's Most Wicked Man". A pagan/satanist, he was and remains one of the most influential men of the 20th century. Immortalized by propagandists, he was sung about by Black Sabbath's lead vocalist Ozzy Osbourne in his second single "Mr. Crowley", released in 1980. In the song, the hint at child sacrifice is unmistakable.

Mr. Crowley, what went down in your head?
Mr. Crowley, did you talk to the dead
Your lifestyle to me seems so tragic
With the thrill of it all
You fooled all the people with magic
You waited on Satan's call

Mr. Charming, did you think you were pure
Mr. Alarming, in nocturnal rapport
Uncovering things that were sacred, manifest on this earth
Conceived in the eye of a secret

Yeah, they scattered the afterbirth

Mr. Crowley, won't you ride my white horse?
Mr. Crowley, it's symbolic of course
Approaching a time that is classic
I hear that maidens call
Approaching a time that is drastic
Standing with their backs to the wall

Was it polemically sent?
I wanna know what you meant
I wanna know
I wanna know what you meant...

"Was it polemically sent?"

For a man who is barely intelligible in human speech, these were well-written lyrics.[1463]

On the cover of the Beatles album "Sgt. Pepper's Lonely Hearts Club Band", Crowley can be seen in the top row, second from the left.

In a documentary on the creative genius of Shawn Carter (a.k.a. "Jay-Z") for the music video "Run This Town", Carter is shown wearing a "hoodie" sweatshirt emblazoned with Crowley's worshipful phrase of supreme hedonism, "Do What Thou Wilt".[1464]

Crowley took over the British chapter of "Ordo Templi Orientis"—a secret society based upon an amalgamation of the Templars and the Freemasons.

The Beast remolded the O.T.O. in his own satanic image. It was an image that soon took over the whole, sordid organization.

> *Although officially founded at the beginning of the 20th century e.v., O.T.O. represents a surfacing and confluence of the divergent streams of esoteric wisdom and knowledge which were originally divided and driven underground by political and religious intolerance during the dark ages. It draws from the traditions of the Freemasonic, Rosicrucian and Illuminist movements of the 18th and 19th centuries, the crusading Knights Templars of the middle ages and early Christian Gnosticism and the Pagan Mystery Schools. Its symbolism contains a reunification of the hidden traditions of the East and the West, and its resolution of these traditions has enabled it to recognize the true value of Aleister Crowley's revelation of The*

Book of the Law. ~ U.S. Grand Lodge, Ordo Templi Orientis[1465]

The daughter of Bob Geldof (former lead singer of the "Boomtown Rats" and now world peace-maker along with Paul "Bono" Hewson) Peaches Geldof, was a devotee of the O.T.O.[1466] until her death on April 7th, 2014 at the age of 25.

Although rumored to have been a cult ritual sacrifice (perhaps for making the seemingly-extinct O.T.O. headline news), the death was officially listed as an "accidental heroin overdose"[1467]—sadly, a quite plausible explanation given the lifestyle of the out-of-wedlock mother of two.

Her father Bob Geldof told Gabriel "Gay" Byrne for RTE's "The Meaning of Life" television program that Jesus was a charismatic "pain in the ass" who was turned into an icon by the Apostle Paul.

Geldof vehemently denies the Divinity of Jesus of Nazareth. Byrne asked him during the interview; "Was He Divine?" Geldof, "No." "Was He the Son of God?" Geldof, "No." During the program, while mocking the language of religious adherents, Geldof said to his audience, "'Lord'? Fuck off 'Lord'."[1468]

To complete the laughing stock that is an English knighthood, Dame of Malta Queen Elizabeth II made the propped up pop personality "*Sir*" Bob Geldof in 1986[1469]—probably for the miracle of being such a public figure when his actual musical accomplishments are non-existent.

Geldof joined Mick Jagger, Elton John, Paul McCartney and Paul "Bono" Hewson as some of the most ridiculous figures in pop culture ever to be knighted.[1470]

However, as purveyors of perversion and destroyers of decency, they are true "Defenders of the Realm".

Swiss journalist and author Peter-Robert Koenig has written extensively on the Ordo Templi Orientis.

The O.T.O. has a hierarchy of attainment by "degrees", as the Freemasons do, but in the O.T.O. there are only 12 degrees.

The perverse tie-in to Rome is shocking and unmistakable.

> *While the O.T.O.'s initiatory system is a sort of Kafkaesque bureaucratic club game, it has a religious association under its obedience: The Gnostic Catholic Church—one of the*

O.T.O.groups—intends "to restore Christianity to its real status as a solar-phallic religion." ~ Koenig[1471]

The VI° of the O.T.O. is the "Illustrious Knight Templar of the Order of Kadosch, Companion of the Holy Grail" and a "Grand Inquisitor Commander"[1472]. Does Aleister Crowley sound like a satanist Beast to you...or a Papal one?

The VIII° is the "Perfect Pontiff of the Illuminati"[1473]—the Pope of the Jesuit-created Freemason super-sect.

The "working" of the degrees within the O.T.O. is meant to usher in the "Aeon of Horus".

Crowley asserted that man was first civilized under the Gaia-like "Aeon of Isis" where he worshipped "Mother Nature" in harmony with the Earth.

What we understand as medieval history, Crowley calls the "Aeon of Osiris" and submission to the "Father god".

The offspring of Osiris and Isis is Horus and he is to be coaxed into this world by a series of satanic sex rituals Crowley called "sex magick" instituted in geographic locations called "workings" that are perceived to be interdimensional portals...or the most convenient apartment.

This was all catalogued in Crowley's "Thelema" religion (which he pulled entirely out of his "eye of Horus" with the help of his interdimensional friends Aiwass, Choronzon and Lam).

Needless to say, to call such "workings" dangerous is beyond understatement.

We don't know if Crowley was successful or not but at least one source puts Pauline Pierce, mother of Barbara Pierce (later the wife of George H.W. Bush) in France with Crowley circa 1924 during his

Aleister Crowley 1929, Barbara Bush 1992
[public domain]

"Eroto-Comotose Lucidity" rite, with her being the possible result in June of 1925.[1474]

This "ECL" rite was designed to overcome the demon entity "Choronzon", so that the adherent could attain final enlightenment.

Choronzon was supposedly first encountered by English mystic and magician John Dee.

Dumble-dalf 007

If you've never heard of Dr. John Dee, you should have. He was advisor to Elizabeth I and an advanced occult adept. He was the impetus for the Harry Potter character of "Dumbledore" and the Tolkien magician "Gandalf" in Lord of the Rings.

Henry VIII was King of England from 1509-1547 and, although a licentious autocratic tyrant, his 6 marriages actually helped England break free of the power of Rome. His son Edward VI was the first English king to be raised Protestant but he died at the young age of 15.

As England's first true Protestant King, Edward was most certainly a Jesuit target for assassination. Author Susan Higginbotham brings up the astounding accusation that, not only was Edward poisoned, his body was switched before burial to hide the evidence.[1475]

Edward tried to have his cousin Jane Grey rule instead of Mary I but Lady Jane was quickly deposed and Bloody Mary took over the throne. She and her husband Philip of Spain immediately repealed the protections Henry and Edward had extended to Protestants. She reaffirmed England's subservience to the Pope and then began a reign of terror that saw nearly 300 Protestants executed, most by being burned alive.

Even as "reformers", both Henry VIII and Edward VI did little to help Protestants.

> *Protestants were martyred during persecutions against Protestant religious reformers for their faith during the reigns of Henry VIII (1509-1547) and Mary I of England (1553–1558). Radical Protestants were also executed during the reigns of Edward VI (1547-1553), Elizabeth I (1558-1603) and James I (1603-1625). The excesses of this period were recorded in Foxe's Book of Martyrs.*
>
> *Protestants in England and Wales were executed under legislation that punished anyone judged guilty of heresy against the Roman*

Catholic faith. ~ Wikipedia[1476]

Mercifully, Mary died in 1558 after only a brief rule and her half-sister Elizabeth I, whom she had had imprisoned, ascended to the throne as a Protestant Queen.

While in prison, Elizabeth had made the acquaintance of a magician who had fallen out of favor with Bloody Mary; John Dee.

Once on the throne, the Jesuit threats to Elizabeth's life were very real and a cordon of British Royalists formed around her lead by Francis Walsingham. They created an intelligence network to ferret out Papists with designs against their Queen and Dr. John Dee was part of their network. When he wrote to her, he knew she had an eye fetish so he signed his name in code to resemble eyes: "007".

Aeon of Horus

Creating a demonic offspring must've been difficult for Crowley because the man was absolutely *obsessed* with sodomy, being, himself, a bisexual.

The XI° of the O.T.O. is supposedly unknowable. It is likely portrayed as such because it dealt with sodomy and the violation of young boys.

Here we return to Koenig but I caution the reader to proceed with care, we're dealing with satanists here and the content is depraved.

I include this so that you know what you're dealing with and you will see the connection to Rome. [italics suspended]

> Aleister Crowley: "Of the Eleventh Degree [of the Ordo Templi Orientis], its powers, privileges, and qualifications, nothing whatever is said in any grade. It has no relation to the general plan of the Order, is inscrutable, and dwells in its own palaces." (Liber CXCIV, 1919)

> Crowley: "I am inclined to believe that the XIth degree is better than the IXth degree", diary entry 26 August 1916.

> "Oh, how superior is the Eye of Horus to the Mouth of Isis!". Diary 1913 about a boy showered with "foaming seed": "While the other in his orgasm receives the waters." "Let it be no sin to us to have buggered the virile bum." "While the priest thrusts his thyrsus between boyish buttocks, All is accomplished; come Holy Dove!". "The Equinox" IV;2, Maine 1998, 405. ...

In 1909 Aleister Crowley met the poet Victor Benjamin Neuburg "Frater Lampada Tradam, Omnia Vincam" (6.5.1883-1940), and in December made use of him as his magical partner, when he allowed himself to become possessed by the Thelemic 'Devil' Choronzon, and receive "The Vision and the Voice". In 1910 Crowley produced the "Bagh-I-Muattar" in which the joys of homosexuality were poetically extolled (the book has been widely reproduced in facsimile [e.g. the Morton Press edition] although initially copyrighted by Marcelo Ramos Motta in his "Sex and Religion", published in Nashville in 1981; this copyright was renewed by Martin P. Starr in 1991.)

Neuburg was Crowley's sexual partner again around the end of 1913 in the "Paris Working", which was performed "to reconstitute the OTO."[1] On the basis of these experiments, Crowley wrote the homosexually oriented sex-magical instructions for his branch of the O.T.O., the "Mysteria Mystica Maxima". So, for example there was not only a 'Venereal' version of "Liber C" (one dedicated to Venus), but also a Mercurial one. He now signed the more important O.T.O. documents, like the "Statutes", with an "XI°" as his title. Neuburg soon separated himself from his Master, and died May 31st 1940.

SUMMARY OF CROWLEY'S SEX MAGICK SYSTEM

VII° Adoration of the phallus as Baphomet, both within and without

VIII° Interaction with something outside the closed vessels of the vagina and the anus

IX° Interaction inside the vagina with either the blood or the secretions of a woman when excited

X° Impregnation + fertilisation of an egg + the act of creation or succession (e.g. election of the OHO)

XI° Two-folded: i) Isolation in the anus [per vas nefandum] where it is considered unable to interact with anything at all ii) interaction with excrement (one of Crowley's preferred ingredients) and small amounts of blood (where small wounds occur through the intercourse), mucus and of course the mucous membranes that lead directly into the blood supply, etc., etc. Crowley dreamt of giving birth to a foetus per anum. "... a mass of blood & slime." ~ Koenig[1477]

Secret Agent 666

Certainly a man this perverse needed to serve a role in British government and he did—as a spy and international provocateur.

From mass-killing to mind control, Crowley was there to serve the King. [italics suspended]

> Referencing documents in British, American, French and Italian archives, [University of Idaho's Department of History chair Richard] Spence discovered that Crowley was connected to the sinking of the Lusitania, a British luxury liner that was torpedoed off of Ireland, killing 1,198 of the people aboard; the sinking turned public opinion in many countries against Germany in World War I. ...
>
> Later in his life, Crowley claimed that he came to the U.S. as a British undercover agent with a mission to infiltrate and undermine the German propaganda effort. "He did undermine that effort," said Spence. "His writing was an over-the-top parody of saber-rattling German militarism."
>
> He actively encouraged German aggressiveness, such as the attack on the Lusitania, with the ultimate aim of bringing America into the war. In doing so, "Crowley followed precisely the wishes of Admiral Hall, chief of British Naval Intelligence," said Spence.
>
> "Crowley was an adept amateur psychologist, had an uncanny ability to influence people and probably utilized hypnotic suggestion in his undercover work," Spence added. "The other thing he made good use of was drugs. In New York, he carried out very detailed studies on the effects of mescaline (peyote). He would invite various friends over for dinner, fix them curry and dose the food with mescaline. Then he observed and took notes on their behavior."
>
> Mescaline, Spence noted, was later used by intelligence agencies for experiments in behavior modification and mind control. ~ the University of Idaho[1478]

Crowley had traveled from Britain to the U.S. on the Lusitania in

1914[1479]. He was, apparently, her passenger of doom—her Mothman.[ᵣᵣ]

"The Beast" would then turn his obsession with the male genitalia toward helping the Allies achieve victory over the Nazis. [italics suspended]

> Around this time [1941], Crowley contributed his expertise in magick to the war effort. If the Nazis could wield crushing power through the ancient symbol of the swastika, then England could certainly use more powerful magick to win the war. Hence a magical antidote to the swastika became his quest. Crowley's first suggestion was the poem "Thumbs Up!" The corresponding gesture, popular among pilots, was phallic, and Crowley wished to publish the poem with an equally phallic pentacle on the cover. However, he desired a more potent symbol. "How can I put It over pictorially or graphically?" he pondered. "I want positive ritual affirmation, like Liber Resh, 'saying will,' and so on."[44]
>
> Soon afterward, he found this even more poetnet formula "to bring victory ... [and] a way to put it across."[45] Crowley decided on the letter V: in Hebrew, *vav* is phallic in both image and meaning; it literally meant "nail," and Crowley thought this symbolized the nails in Hitler's coffin. Furthermore, V suggested AC's Magester Templi motto, V.V.V.V.V. And, according to the GD formula of LVX, V also designated the Egyptian deities of Apophis and Typhon; these deities suggested the tarot card "The Devil," appropriate since the V also symbolizes a pair of horns. The V for Apophis sign occurred in the Adeptus Minor ($5°=6^\square$) ritual, which is appropriate since V is the number five in the Roman numeral system but six in gematria. It also suggested the famous "Veni, vidi, vici" ("I came, I saw, I conquered"). But most importantly, Crowley recognized "V for Victory." "Seabrook should be thrilled, " he wrote, "in view of his story about 'Wow!'"[46]
>
> Although "V for Victory" has been attributed to BBC broadcasts by Victor de Lavaleye or David Ritchie, Crowley maintained he invented the gesture as a magical counterattack to the Nazi swastika; then, using his MI5 connections, he suggested it to NID [Naval Intelligence Division] and had it accepted by Churchill. ~ *Perdurabo: The Life of Aleister Crowley*, Richard Kaczynski [1480]

[ᵣᵣ] "Mothman" is an apparition that supposedly appeared as a harbinger of the collapse of the Silver Bridge between West Virginia and Ohio. 46 people died on that day, December 15th, 1967. It has been connected to other disasters as well.

It is a gesture that survives to this day and a recent photograph of child actress turned purveyor of perversion to preteens, Miley Cyrus, flashed it after the 2013 MTV Video Music Awards performance that spoke overtly to violation of little girls by mind control.[1481]

One anonymous "insider" source claims her father, Billy Ray Cyrus, used to rape her as a leading attraction at the Bohemian Grove.[1482]

Crowley has "connections in MI5"?!

This only barely scratches the surface.

On Her Majesty's Secret Service

The tradition of utilizing the demonic realm for intelligence advantages is as old as Babylon but the British solidified it under John Dee and it was passed from Dee to a man named Francis Bacon, the founder of America (or, at least, the visionary behind "the New World").

Dee and Bacon were little-reported contemporaries though Bacon was a young man as Dee was aging.

> *Little has come down to us in terms of records of Francis Bacon and John Dee knowing each other but on the afternoon of August 11, 1582 there was an entry in Dee's journal that they met at Mortlake. Bacon was 21 years old at the time and was accompanied by a Mr. Phillipes, a top cryptographer in the employ of Sir Francis Walsingham who headed up the early days of England's secret service. They were there according to Ewen MacDuff, in an article, "After Some Time Be Past" in 'Baconiana', (Dec.1983)" to find out the truth about the ancient Hebrew art of the Gematria—one of the oldest cipher systems known, dating from 700 B.C. They were seeking to discuss this with Dee because he was not only one of the leading adepts of this field, but a regular practitioner in certain levels of Gematria."* ~ D.W. Cooper and Lawrence Gerald, Sir Bacon.org[1483]

This is a connection the Freemasons seized upon—eager to exploit anything that might appear to give them more legitimacy and ancient power. [italics suspended]

> Manly P. Hall [Canadian author and mystic, best known for his work *The Secret Teachings of All Ages: An Encyclopedic Outline of Masonic, Hermetic, Qabbalistic and Rosicrucian Symbolical*

Philosophy which he astoundingly wrote at 25] had a book, *Orders of Universal Reformation* in which a woodcut from 1655 by Jacob Cats, shows an emblem of an ancient man bearing likeness to John Dee, passing the lamp of tradition over an open grave to a young man with an extravagantly large rose on his shoe buckle. In Bacon's sixth book of the *Advancement of Learning* he defines his method as, *Traditionem Lampadis*, the delivery of the lamp. ~ Cooper and Gerald[1484]

Although Bacon is considered the "father of modern science", Cooper and Gerald believe that it was cover to keep him out of trouble with superstitious Christians.

> *There is no doubt of John Dee's ubiquitous influence during the Elizabethan age. When James became King, Dee's ideas on magic were no longer appreciated. James unfavorable and fearful attitude toward the occult was the opposite of Elizabeth's. Bacon became well aware that it was necessary to be very careful while advancing his scientific ideas to James and that any trace of Dee's weird angelic-alchemical study could jeopardize his own projects from taking hold. Bacon's observation of the mistreatment bestowed upon Dee by James served to reinforce that it was a different era and that the need to practice that Shakespeare maxim, "Discretion is the better part of valor" was imperative to anyone with a sweet disposition toward magic and mathematics or a secret society. Dee was even derided in the Ben Jonson play The Alchemist perhaps to placate James, yet another signal that this was an end of the liberal Elizabethan attitude toward Hermeticism. So it's not surprising that Bacon chose to hold back his Rosicrucian utopia The New Atlantis from publication until after his death as it portrayed a future world in which man could co-exist with his fellow man without the divine right of kings and the new tools that the magic of science would one day bring could also be in harmony with nature as well. But it was Dee's colonization dream many years before who referred to the new world as "Atlantis." He would have been proud to have read Bacon's New Atlantis and seen Bacon's sympathetic portrayal of him as the magician Prospero, of* The Tempest. ~ D.W. Cooper and Lawrence Gerald, Sir Bacon.org[1485]

In the Marvel Comic movie adaptation of "Thor" (2011), a human scientist witnesses things she can't explain and the god of thunder (Chris Hemsworth) tells her probably what the "Watcher" angels have told and are telling their modern human partners.

> *Your ancestors called it "magic" ... but you call it "science." I come from a land where they are one and the same.*

The Watchers

Via all of his perversion and dedication to satan, Crowley was apparently able to speak and hear across dimensions.

His breakthrough was chronicled in *The Book of the Law* which was supposedly given to him by an interdimensional being.

> *Aiwass: An alleged superhuman intelligence contacted by Aleister Crowley in 1904, Aiwass dictated to Crowley a work called "Liber Al" or the "Book of the Law," which prophesied wars and revolutions leading to the collapse of Christian civilizations and the dawn of the Aeon of Horus. Liber Al also proclaims the Law of Thelema, usually summed up in three mantra-like aphorisms: "Do what thou wilt shall be the whole of the law," "Love is the law, love under will," and "Every man and every woman is a star." ~ Everything Is Under Control*, Robert Wilson and Miriam Hill[1486]

It was during his time in America, working for British Intelligence, that he conducted more rituals and made more interdimensional connections. [italics suspended]

> By 1914 Crowley was living a hand-to-mouth existence, relying largely on donations and the membership fees from the O.T.O. and A∴A∴.[114] ... During this time the First World War broke out.[116] After recuperating from a bout of phlebitis, Crowley set sail for the United States aboard the RMS Lusitania in October 1914.[117] Arriving in New York City, he moved into a hotel and began earning money writing for the American edition of Vanity Fair and undertaking freelance work for the famed astrologer Evangeline Adams.[118] In the city, he continued experimenting with sex magic, through the use of masturbation, female prostitutes, and male clients of a Turkish bathhouse; all of these encounters were documented in his diaries.[119]

> Professing to be of Irish ancestry and a supporter of Irish independence from Great Britain, Crowley began to espouse views

supporting Germany in their war against Britain. He became involved in New York's pro-German movement, and in January 1915 German spy George Sylvester Viereck employed him as a writer for his propagandist paper, *The Fatherland*, which was dedicated to keeping the U.S. neutral in the conflict.[121] In later years, detractors denounced Crowley as a traitor to Britain for this action.[122] In reality, Crowley was a double agent, working for the British intelligence services to infiltrate and undermine Germany's operation in New York. Many of his articles in *The Fatherland* were hyperbolic, for instance comparing Kaiser Wilhelm II to Jesus Christ; in July 1915 he orchestrated a publicity stunt – reported on by *The New York Times* – in which he declared independence for Ireland in front of the Statue of Liberty; the real intention was to make the German lobby appear ridiculous in the eyes of the American public.[123] It has been argued that he encouraged the German Navy to destroy the Lusitania, informing them that it would ensure the U.S. stayed out of the war, while in reality hoping that it would bring the U.S. into the war on Britain's side.[124]

Crowley entered into a relationship with Jeanne Robert Foster, with whom he toured the West Coast. In Vancouver, headquarters of the North American O.T.O., he met with Charles Stansfeld Jones and Wilfred Talbot Smith to discuss the propagation of Thelema on the continent. In Detroit he experimented with anhalonium at Parke-Davis, then visited Seattle, San Francisco, Santa Cruz, Los Angeles, San Diego, Tijuana, and the Grand Canyon, before returning to New York.[125] There he befriended Ananda Coomaraswamy and his wife Alice Richardson; Crowley and Richardson performed sex magic in April 1916, following which she became pregnant and then miscarried.[126] Later that year he took a "magical retirement" to a cabin by Lake Pasquaney owned by Evangeline Adams. There, he made heavy use of drugs and undertook a ritual after which he proclaimed himself "Master Therion". He also wrote several short stories based on J.G. Frazer's *The Golden Bough* and a work of literary criticism, *The Gospel According to Bernard Shaw*.[127]

In December he moved to New Orleans, his favourite U.S. city, before spending February 1917 with evangelical Christian relatives in Titusville, Florida.[128] Returning to New York, he moved in with artist and A∴A∴ member Leon Engars Kennedy, in May learning of his mother's death.[129] After the collapse of *The Fatherland*, Crowley continued his association with Viereck, who appointed him contributing editor of arts journal *The International*. Crowley used it to promote Thelema, but it soon ceased publication.[130] He then moved to the studio apartment of Roddie Minor, who became his partner and Scarlet Woman. Through their rituals, Crowley believed that they were contacted by a preternatural entity named Alamantrah. The relationship soon ended.[131]

In 1918, Crowley went on a magical retreat in the wilderness of Esopus Island on the Hudson River. Here, he began a translation of the Tao Te Ching and experienced past life memories of being Ge Xuan, Pope Alexander VI, Alessandro Cagliostro, and Eliphas Levi, also painting Thelemic slogans on the riverside cliffs.[132] Back in New York, he moved to Greenwich Village, where he took Leah Hirsig as his lover and next Scarlet Woman.[133] He took up painting as a hobby, exhibiting his work at the Greenwich Village Liberal Club and attracting the attention of the New York Evening World.[134] With the financial assistance of sympathetic Freemasons, Crowley revived *The Equinox* with the first issue of volume III, known as "The Blue Equinox."[135] He spent mid-1919 on a climbing holiday in Montauk before returning to London in December.[136] ~ Wikipedia[1487]

It was his time in New York that was most important. Many believe that Crowley succeeded in opening a portal that should've remained closed. [italics suspended]

At the outbreak of WWI, Crowley set sail from his native England aboard the Lusitania, bound for the USA. Arriving in high spirits, he took up residence in an apartment on New York's bustling West 36th street and there divided his time more or less equally between acts of sex magic and the composition of crackpot pro-German propaganda for *The Fatherland*.

Following an expedite to Vancouver via San Francisco and New Orleans he returned to New York and moved into furnished rooms on Central Park West. Roddie Minor, a married woman living apart from her husband, joined him there circa September/ October 1917 and together they set about exploring the wilder shores of magica sexualis.

Crowley's personal record for October 1, 1917 describes Minor as "big, muscular, (and) sensual." John Symonds adds that she was "broad-shouldered and pleasant-faced." In addition to these homely attributes, she also possessed a well-developed clairvoyant faculty.

Under the influence of hashish and opium she described to Crowley a series of archetypal visions involving (among others) a king, a small boy and a wizard who introduced himself as "Amalantrah" — who delivered exhortations to "find the egg." The reaction of most people would no doubt be to view these accounts as nothing more than drug-induced hallucinations having no wider significance, but Aleister Crowley was no ordinary man. According to Symonds, he "made no attempt to interpret this material in terms of unconsciousness. To him the characters and incidents of mescal visions were more real than anything reality or the ego could provide. He would not have been surprised to meet...Amalantrah strolling up Fifth Avenue. The wizard would have descended onto the plane of illusion, that is all."

At length, feeling that Amalantrah had nothing further to impart, Crowley decamped for Europe, leaving Roddie Minor to her own devices.

But the story doesn't end there. It would be beyond my competence to provide a complete and faithful account of the Amalantrah Working and its aftermath. ... The details are unclear, but it seems that at some stage during the proceedings he underwent a form of contactee experience involving a large-headed entity now known to occultists as Lam.

Lam, (whose name derives from the Tibetan word for "way" or "path") later became the subject of a portrait by Crowley, drawn from life and imbued with a haunting inner quality of its own. The original was first exhibited in New York in 1919 and has been reproduced several times since then, most recently in the third issue of "Starfire" magazine. Although lacking the crude power of Crowley's more extravagant canvases and murals, it is nevertheless a remarkable piece of work. The subject is depicted in extreme close-up and appears somehow dwarfish, despite the fact that there is no indication of scale in the overall composition. The head is large, smooth and hairless, tapering to a pointed chin. The mouth is slitlike; the eyes extend part-ways around the sides of the face. There is no suggestion of clothing beyond what appears to be a cloak buttoned at the neck, nor does the entity have any ears. In short, Lam resembles nothing so much as a typical UFO occupant of the "examiner" type (what Americans would call "greys".) ~ *Aleister Crowley and the LAM Statement*, Ian Blake[1488]

Although Crowley did little with "Lam" in public at the time, the proliferation of "grey aliens" has brought Crowley's drawing back into public scrutiny. Writer Kenneth Grant made the connection in 1973. [italics suspended]

> When Aleister Crowley was living in New York, doing various magickal experiments in a place on West 9th, he did what's called the Amalantrah Working. It's theorized this process created a deliberate channel in ephemeral cosmic influences so that extra-dimensional entities could enter our universe. In short, he likely created a portal for what we know as gray aliens to come visit us.
>
> Eventually Crowley made contact with an entity known as Lam and drew its portrait, and damn if it doesn't look like the pictures we see of Grays now. (Incidentally, "lam" is the mantra linked to the root chakra, which is associated with survival.) This was around 1917. While there are possibly ancient accounts of extra-terrestrial visitations in other parts of the world, this was one of the first-known Grays to have popped into Western consciousness, although Crowley didn't explicitly say this.
>
> Crowley introduced Lam for the first time in his commentary on the Voice of the Silence by Theosophy founder ... [Helena] Blavatsky. Founded or not, he basically tears that classic to shreds without ever really explaining why he started it off with his portrait of Lam. Since then, Lam's been expounded on by a writer named Kenneth Grant who knew Crowley personally and is his acknowledged successor. ~ Liz Armstrong, VICE[1489]

In a way, Aleister Crowley is the father of the American space program.

JPL

Nick Redfern is a prolific author and outstanding researcher. When whistleblowers inside the United States government wanted to get word out that the U.S. was in bed with malignant entities from another dimension, they came to him. [italics suspended]

> At his birth in 1914, Jack Parsons was given the memorable and unusual name of Marvel Whiteside Parsons and had a truly extraordinary life. An undoubted genius, he indirectly led NASA to send the Apollo astronauts to the Moon in 1969. Moreover, the Aerojet Corporation—which Parsons personally founded—today produces solid-fuel rocket boosters for the Space Shuttle that are based on Parsons' very own, decades-old innovations. For his accomplishments, a large crater on the far side of the Moon was named in his honor, and each and every year, on Halloween no less, NASA's Jet Propulsion Laboratory holds an open-house memorial, replete with mannequins of Jack Parsons and his early JPL cohorts

known as "Nativity Day." And, within the aerospace community, there is a longstanding joke that JPL actually stands for "Jack Parsons Laboratory" or "Jack Parsons Lives."[1]

In fact, however, this man Parsons, who was so revered and honored by very senior figures within the U.S. space-program, was an admitted occultist, a follower of Aleister Crowley, and someone who topped even Crowley himself by engaging in bestiality with the family dog and sexual relations with his own mother, perhaps at the same time, no less. Moreover, before each rocket test, Parsons would undertake a ritual to try and invoke the Greek god, Pan.[2]

It was perhaps inevitable that his path would eventually cross with that of Aleister Crowley. In 1942, after the two had become acquainted as a result of their like-minds and pursuits, Crowley chose Parsons to lead the Agape Lodge of the Thelemic Ordo Templi Orientis (O.T.O.) in California, after Crowley expelled one Wilfred Smith from the position. The devoted Parsons eagerly practiced Aleister Crowley's Thelemic Rituals, the goal of which was the creation of a new breed of human being that, if the ritual proved successful, would lead to the destruction of Christianity.

A figure from the science-fiction community who came to know Parsons in this same period was none other than L. Ron Hubbard of Church of Scientology fame. And it was in front of Hubbard that Parsons engaged in his Babylon rituals—with which Hubbard quickly became fascinated and near obsessed. And, in turn, the Jack Parsons of the mid-1940s was favorably impressed by L. Ron Hubbard's personal interest in, and support of, the ways of Aleister Crowley. Parsons penned a letter to the Great Beast that, in part, said: "I deduced that [Hubbard] is in direct touch with some higher intelligence. He is the most Thelemic person I have ever met and is in complete accord with our own principles.

In the wake of this glowing statement, Hubbard moved in to live with Parsons, was brought into Crowley's Ordo Templi Orientis, and soon had his eyes set on Parsons' girlfriend, a 19-year-old named Sara Northrup. In early 1946, Parsons and Hubbard began an extensive, magical ritual that has become known as the Babalon Working, the ultimate goal of which was to try and manifest an elemental entity in much the same way that Crowley had succeeded in doing with the very alien-looking Lam several decades earlier. Parsons was overwhelmingly convinced that the complicated ritual had worked when, approximately two weeks later, a beautiful woman, a certain Marjorie Elizabeth Cameron, came upon the scene.

> On February 26, 1946, a very pleased and infinitely proud Parsons told Crowley: "I have my elemental!" Two months later, Parsons, Cameron, and Hubbard tackled the next stage of the Babalon Working, the aim of which, this time, was to attempt to summon up a "moonchild" just as had been portrayed within the pages of Crowley's novel of the same name. ~ *Final Events*, Nick Redfern[1490]

Unfortunately for Parsons, however, Hubbard would prove to be a less-than-trustworthy partner—he stole $10,000 and absconded with Jack's girlfriend.

Crowley was not pleased.

Despite the buffoonery, many believe that what they did in the "Babylon Working" ushered in a new Luciferian era.

> *Regardless of the precise nature, intent, and outcome of the strange relationship between Parsons and Hubbard, many students of Parsons' work believed that the portal of entry that Crowley opened in 1918—when he successfully invoked Lam—may have been further enlarged by Parsons and Hubbard in the 1940s with the commencement of the Babalon Working, which resulted in something wicked coming this way. Perhaps those same students were correct, as soon after Parsons' occult actions reached their tipping point, pilot Kenneth Arnold had that historic UFO encounter over Mt. Rainier, Washington, followed a little more than a week later by the legendary flying saucer crash outside of Roswell, New Mexico.* ~ Redfern[1491]

In 2000, French science writer Pierre Kohler broke the story that Russian and American astronauts were conducting sex experiments in space, ostensibly to see how interstellar couples could propagate the species in zero gravity.[1492]

The story was later "debunked" when NASA claimed that the leaked documents in Kohler's possession were forged.[1493]

Treasonous Intelligence

The Whore of Babylon is *Rome*; the Vatican. Satan's stormtroopers are the Company of Loyola.

They have accomplished a coup d'état over *generations* of insurgency in the United States via America's institutions of banking, education and media and the enterprise that they control the most is the one that is killing America the fastest—her Intelligence apparatus lead by the FBI and CIA.

The Nazis had shown that shattering a person's identity with shock, torture and narcotics was the fastest route to controlling their mind but it was a sloppy process that required a lot of experimentation.

That's just what the CIA conducted. [italics suspended]

> ...the first major group to examine the potential use of LSD was, of course, the CIA. In the 1950s and '60s the CIA had several top secret initiatives under the names BLUEBIRD, ARTICHOKE and MK-ULTRA, which sought to develop mind control techniques or "brainwashing" à la Manchurian Candidate as an aid to the interrogation of subjects as part of their Cold War activities. These programs had been inspired by, among other things, documents that the CIA had obtained after World War II describing experiments with mescaline performed by Nazi doctors on the inmates of the Dachau concentration camp. LSD was first brought to the United States in 1949 by Dr. Max Rinkel, who carried out research using the drug on a population of 100 volunteers. Together with his colleague Dr. Paul Hoch they noted that LSD produced effects that mimicked schizophrenic psychosis. Indeed, they postulated that LSD produced a model psychosis—that is, it was "psychotomimetic." As we have seen, similar ideas circulated about the properties of mescaline. Such ideas were very influential and stimulated a great deal of subsequent research, which ultimately fell out of favor but has recently been revived.
>
> The idea that LSD could produce mental disorganization encouraged the CIA to start using it in experiments similar to those carried out by the Nazi doctors. CIA operatives began administering the drug in secret to different subject populations (or indeed to each other). Like the Nazis, the CIA used different populations of helpless individuals such as prisoners, drug addicts, and mental patients in their experiments, often with appalling results. The CIA not only performed experiments on individuals but also came up with schemes for contaminating the water supply of potential enemies with LSD so as to incapacitate entire hostile populations. For this they would need large amounts of the drug, at one point ordering the equivalent of 100 million doses from Sandoz. When they found out that obtaining such a large amount as this might be somewhat problematic they turned to Eli Lilly and Company, whose capable chemists broke the secret Sandoz patent

and assured the CIA that they could produce LSD in tons or similar amounts. Thankfully for the future of humanity, this eventuality never came to pass. In the end the CIA concluded that the effects of hallucinogenic drugs like LSD were just too unpredictable for general use in the Cold War, and should just be reserved for very specific circumstances. Nevertheless, in the atmosphere of general paranoia that pervaded the postwar era, the CIA maintained an important role in manipulating the developing drug culture. CIA operatives acted as drug suppliers if they were interested in observing drug effects under particular circumstances, and infiltrated different drug-using groups with political points of view deemed to be of "interest" so as to relay information back to Washington. ~ Richard Miller, Salon[1494]

Experimenting on unwitting victims with narcotics to aid in mind control is, in fact, verified by several "mainstream" sources including a class-action lawsuit by veterans. Soldiers and minorities seemed to be the preferred victims. [italics suspended]

> The army and CIA experimented on thousands of soldiers with dangerous drugs during the Cold War, dosing them with mescaline and other chemicals that left them with lasting impairments, the Vietnam Veterans of America says. With the help of Nazi scientists recruited through "Project Paperclip," the Army and CIA used at least 7,800 veterans as human guinea pigs at the Edgewood Arsenal alone, the federal complaint states.
>
> Similar experiments were conducted at Fort Detrick, Md.
>
> The experiments, whose true nature often was not disclosed to the human guinea pigs, left many of them with medical problems for decades.
>
> Individual soldiers and the Vietnam Veterans of America claim the consent forms they signed at Edgewood Arsenal are invalid because they do not conform to international law and the Wilson Directive, which calls voluntary consent "essential." The soldiers claim the Army trained them to follow orders and as such they could not consent freely.
>
> The Army covered up the experiments, started in the 1950s with names such as Bluebird, Artichoke and MKUltra, and denied medical care to the soldiers suffering from a number of maladies including post-traumatic stress disorder, bipolar disorder and memory loss, according to the complaint.

> Soldiers were given mescaline, LSD, barbiturates and other drugs to test the effects. The army wanted to find ways to paralyze, confuse, hypnotize and secretly kill enemies, and promised the soldiers they would get medals for participating, according to the complaint. ~ Chris Marshall, Courthouse News Service[1495]

A San Francisco newspaper ran the details of one such terrible story. [italics suspended]

> It's been over 50 years, but Wayne Ritchie says he can still remember how it felt to be dosed with acid.
>
> He was drinking bourbon and soda with other federal officers at a holiday party in 1957 at the U.S. Post Office Building on Seventh and Mission streets. They were cracking jokes and swapping stories when, suddenly, the room began to spin. The red and green lights on the Christmas tree in the corner spiraled wildly. Ritchie's body temperature rose. His gaze fixed on the dizzying colors around him.
>
> The deputy U.S. marshal excused himself and went upstairs to his office, where he sat down and drank a glass of water. He needed to compose himself. But instead he came unglued. Ritchie feared the other marshals didn't want him around anymore. Then he obsessed about the probation officers across the hall and how they didn't like him, either. Everyone was out to get him. Ritchie felt he had to escape.
>
> He fled to his apartment and sought comfort from his live-in girlfriend. It didn't go as planned. His girlfriend was there, but an argument erupted. She told him she was growing tired of San Francisco and wanted to return to New York City. Ritchie couldn't handle the situation. Frantic, he ran away again, this time to the Vagabond Bar where he threw back more bourbon and sodas. From there, he hit a few more bars, further cranking up his buzz. As he drank his way back to Seventh and Mission, Ritchie concocted a plan that would change his life.
>
> Now in his mid-eighties and living in San Jose, Ritchie may be among the last of the living victims of MK-ULTRA, a Central Intelligence Agency operation that covertly tested lysergic acid diethylamide (LSD) on unwitting Americans in San Francisco and New York City from 1953 to 1964. ~ Troy Hooper, San Francisco Weekly[1496]

Cultural icons like Aldus Huxley and Timothy Leary encouraged

Americans to "turn on, tune in, drop out" with LSD.

—That's Holy Cross Jesuit-educated Catholic Irishman Timothy Francis Leary.[1497]

Leary and Crowley had a special relationship across the grave.

> *1960's – Crowley wrote how the new age would bring about free sex and free drugs. Through spiritual guidance he wrote in "The Book of the Law," "I am the Snake that giveth bright glory, and stir the hearts of men with drunkenness. To worship me take wine and strange drugs whereof I will tell my prophet and be drunk thereof! They shall not harm ye at all."*
>
> *The editor of Playboy from 1967-1971 was Robert Anton Wilson. He was the heart of the hippie movement and a follower of Aleister Crowley. He also wrote, "Cosmic Trigger – The Final Secret of the Illuminati." He writes how Timothy Leary thought he was sent to fulfill what Crowley had started. "In Switzerland during his exile, Leary was shown a deck of Crowley's tarot cards. To test his divinatory power he asked who am I and what is my destiny. Then he cut to a single card and got the ace of disc. This shows a large disc bearing the Greek letter "tomake atherion" (this is spelled phonetically, I have no idea how to spell what he said). Therion is the great beast. "Leary interpreted this to mean he is Crowley reborn and is suppose to complete the work Crowley began, preparing humanity for cosmic consciousness."*
>
> *The musical "Hair" had songs entitled, "Age of Aquarius," "Sodomy," "LSD." Crowley taught sodomy as a mystical rite. He also wrote in his book, "Every man and every woman is a star...This means that each of us stars is to move on our true orbit, as marked out by the nature of our position." This is astrology prohibited in the Bible.* ~ Rock & Roll Sorcerers of the New Age, Hegewisch Baptist[1498]

This cancerous culture was *absolutely* engineered for America's harm.

The Marriage Between Drugs and Pop Culture

Two of the famous individuals who had discovered the supernatural powers of drugs were the late Timothy Leary, formerly of Harvard and an ardent follower of Aleister Crowley, and British intellectual Aldous Huxley, known for popular books such as Brave New World and The Doors of Perception. (It is said that it was Crowley who introduced Huxley to mescaline.[36]) After he heavily induced himself with psilocybin, Huxley told Leary in a chilling conversation:

"'Your role is quite simple. Become a cheerleader for evolution. That's what I did and my grandfather before me. These brain-drugs, mass-produced in the laboratories, will bring about vast changes in society. All we can do is spread the word. The obstacle to this evolution, Timothy, is the Bible.'"[37]

The late British psychiatrist William Sargant wrote, "Aldous Huxley, in his writings and in talking to me personally, insisted that mescaline had taken him into the presence of God."[38] Leary declared, "I am a revolutionary, and the faster this system [the culture and the Christian ideals upon which it was built] goes down the happier I'll be."[39] ~ Jonas Alexis, Veterans Today[1499]

It was a message that was injected into American culture via the magick of Tinseltown. [italics suspended]

> The famous Hollywood director Oliver Stone was no stranger to drugs.

> "Stone loosely based Scarface on his own addiction to cocaine which he had to kick while writing the screenplay. Stone has been rumored to use drugs while making films. On the DVD of Natural Born Killers: The Director's Cut, one of the producers, Jane Hamsher, recounts stories of taking psilocybin mushrooms with Stone and some of the cast and crew and almost getting pulled over by a police officer—a situation which Stone later wrote into the film.

> "In 1999, Stone was arrested and pleaded guilty to drug possession and no contest to driving under the influence. He was ordered into a rehabilitation program. He was arrested again on the night of May 27, 2005, in Los Angeles for possession of a small amount of marijuana."[58]

Stone admitted, "It was a wild time. I was doing a lot of drugs. Grass and acid. I was into Timothy Leary…"[59]

Stone declared, "I'm seeing someone separately where I work in a trance state…I believe in meditation. I believe in prayer; you should go to deeper levels... I'm trying to reshape the world through movies"[60]

What has Stone learned from all of this drug trips? Stone declared back in 1987:

"I think America has to bleed. I think the corpses have to pile up. I think American boys have to die again. Let the mothers weep and mourn."[61]

Stone continued, "I believe in [Jim] Morrison's incantations. Break on through. Kill the pigs. Destroy. Loot. Fuck your mother. All that fuck. Anything goes. Anything."[62] ~ Alexis[1500]

It was during that time that Howard Levey and Michael Aquino were tapping in to sex, drugs and satan for the CIA.

The popular culture push for LSD and satan was so successful during the 60's and 70's it snared no less a figure than the Rat Pack's own, Sammy Davis Jr.[1501]

Davis would eventually renounce affiliation with the "Church of Satan" and be granted an honorary membership as a Knight of Malta.

Mind control researcher Walter Bowart interviewed Timothy Leary on the counter-culture.

Bowart put MK Ultra on the map with his book *Operation Mind Control*. By a twist of fate, he was born in Omaha, Nebraska but his family relocated to Enid, Oklahoma where he attended the University of Oklahoma.[1502]

Bowart died at a relatively young 68 years of age.[1503]

In working with Leary, Bowart found that Leary was not treated well for all he had done on behalf of the Company (either "Company"). Bowart found CIA memos seeking intelligence from both Leary and Aldus Huxley regarding the effects of hallucinogenic drugs for their applications in mind control programs like MKUltra.

He also found government grants sending Leary money from 1953 to

1958 through the National Institute of Mental Health, a front organization for mind control experiments.

Leary was eventually imprisoned for drug possession and interned into the Vacaville California Medical Facility where he was subjected to mind control medical procedures—perhaps some his "research" helped perfect. One of the trauma-based procedures was "anectine therapy" which makes the victim feel as if they are dying through loss of control of their respiratory system.

Upon his release, Browart met with Leary and interviewed him. Leary shocked Browart by telling him he knew he was working for the CIA the whole time. [italics suspended]

> "I like the CIA!" he said. "The game they're playing is better than the FBI. Better than the Saigon police. Better than Franco's police. Better than the Israeli police. They're a thousand times better than the KGB. So it comes down to: who are you going to work for? The Yankees or the Dodgers?" ...
>
> I couldn't believe my ears. The CIA had created the "Psychedelic Sixties" with Timothy Leary's help?
>
> "You were wittingly used by the CIA?" I asked again. "...During the sixties? You knew you were being used by the CIA?" ...
>
> —"I knew I was being used by the intelligence agents of this country." "I'm a witting agent in that I think Roosevelt was a disaster, but historically necessary.... So, pin me down and I'll tell you exactly what I'm doing for the CIA," he said.
>
> "What are you doing for the CIA?" I said, disbelieving everything he said.
>
> "I'm raising the intelligence of an elite... a very elite group of Americans," he said. ...
>
> While LSD was banned by the federal government on October 6, 1966, it has made its comeback among the young as the recreational drug of choice. As if to prove its own failure in the "War on Drugs" a 1993 survey made by the federal government showed a substantial upswing in the use of acid by the nation's eighth-graders. The report recorded the highest level of LSD use by high school seniors since 1985 and it said the teen-agers preferred LSD to cocaine. ~ Bowart[1504]

Americans would be furious if they knew that their own government, via the CIA, had been trying to destabilize the nation for generations by being the biggest drug pushers this side of the Rio Bravo.

Porn Nation

Another avenue of destabilization is lust.

Disciplined and Godly, married men able to shoulder responsibility are the most dangerous demographic to the Luciferian Elite.

The male population of the West is enticed to go one of two directions; to become hormone-driven beasts who are controlled by lust or emasculated metrosexual mama's boys who cower in fear in the face of adversity.

Their willing accomplices are in Hollywood where the myth of the woman sex object with man-like strength attacks traditional masculinity.

It is not a coincidence that men of the Christian faith are particularly assaulted as Christianity teaches the delicate balance between strong male leadership and yet proper deference to women—especially when bonded in marriage. [Ephesians 5:25-31, I Peter 3:7]

The discipline that leads to self control is what makes an individual truly focused and that focus is deeply powerful.

There are few sources for such discipline as most see no need for it. Aleister Crowley's dictum, "Do what thou wilt shall be the whole of the law," is the requiem for hedonism.

Yet discipline is demanded by the Founder of Christianity.

> *Then Jesus said to His disciples, "If anyone wishes to come after Me, he must deny himself, and take up his cross and follow Me. For whoever wishes to save his life will lose it; but whoever loses his life for My Sake will find it."*
>
> *"For what will it profit a man if he gains the whole world and forfeits his soul?"*
>
> *"Or what will a man give in exchange for his soul?"*
>
> *"For the Son of Man will return in the Glory of His Father with His angels, and He will repay every man according to what he has done."* ~ Matthew 16:24-27

As a result, Christians in general and Christian men in specific are targeted by the same forces that have taken over America.

> *Gloria Steinem, editor of Ms. magazine made this statement: "By the year 2000 we will, I hope, raise our children to believe in human potential, not God..."* Dr. MaryJo Bane, associate director of Wellesley College's Center for Research on Women, made this statement: *"We really don't know how to raise children. ... The fact that children are raised in families means there's no equality ... in order to raise children with equality, we must take them away from families and raise them..."* ~ Reaction to the Modern Women's Movement, 1963 to the Present, Angela Howard, Sasha Tarrant[1505]

Gloria Steinem is a paid agent of the CIA.

This was leaked to the public and a story was then fabricated that the vitriolic feminist was actually a Patriot who was helping the male-dominated country she despised fight her Communist comrades in the Soviet Union.

> *What of the patriotic volunteers? Gloria Steinem, the future feminist, has acknowledged that she worked for a CIA front, the amusingly named Independent Service for Information, whose purpose was to undermine a Soviet-bloc youth festival in Vienna.* ~ Charles Trueheart, Bloomberg[1506]

Are you gullible enough to go for that?

Crushed Dreams

The Peace movement of the 1960s had powerful and potent messages, yet it devolved into "sex, drugs and rock & roll" that destroyed the hopes of several generations. This destruction was finalized for many of them with the public slaughter of the youthful President John F. Kennedy.

Mae Brussell was a housewife who was so devastated by Kennedy's assassination, she did what few other people (save prosecutor Jim Garrison) have ever done: she read the entire Warren Commission report[1507]. The information she gleaned showed her just what entity it was that destroyed the hopes of the 60's. [italics suspended]

> Everything was beautiful until the insanity began.
>
> The CIA got into the business of altering human behavior in 1947.
>
> "Project Paperclip," an arrangement made by CIA Director Allen Dulles and Richard Helms, brought one thousand Nazi specialists and their families to the United States. They were employed for

military and civilian institutions.

Some Nazi doctors were brought to our hospitals and colleges to continue further experimentations on the brain.

American and German scientists, working with the CIA, then the military, started developing every possible method of controlling the mind.

Lysergic Acid Diethylmide, LSD, was discovered at the Sandoz Laboratories, Basel, Switzerland, in 1939 by Albert Hoffman. This LSD was pure. No other ingredients were added.

The U.S. Army got interested in LSD for interrogation purposes in 1950. After May, 1956, until 1975, the U.S. Army Intelligence and the U.S. Chemical Corps "experimented with hallucinogenic drugs."

The CIA and Army spent $26,501,446 "testing" LSD, code name EA 1729, and other chemical agents. Contracts went out to forty-eight different institutions for testing. The CIA was part of these projects. They concealed their participation by contracting to various colleges, hospitals, prisons, mental hospitals, and private foundations. ...

Valuable documentation of LSD experiments should not have been in the hands of CIA Director Richard Helms. January 31, 1973, one day before he retired from the CIA, he removed some possible answers as to the fate of persons minds the past ten years.

Helms had been behind all the types of experimentations since 1947.

Mind altering projects went under the code names of Operation Chatter, Operation Bluebird/Artichoke, Operation Mknaomi, Mkultra, and Mkdelta.

By 1963, four years before Monterey Pop, the combined efforts of the CIA's Directorate of Science and Technology, Department of U.S. Army Intelligence, and U.S. Chemical Corps were ready for any covert operations that seemed necessary.

U.S. agents were able to destroy any persons reputation cause by inducing hysteria or excessive emotional responses, temporary or permanent insanity, suggest or encourage suicide, erase memory, invent double or triple personalities inside one mind, prolong lapses of memory, teach and induce racism and hatred against specific groups, cause subjects to obey instructions on the telephone or in person, hypnotically assure no memory remains of the assignments.

The CIA has poison dart guns to kill from far away, tranquilizers for pets so the household or neighborhood is not alerted by entry or exit.

While pure LSD is usually 160 micrograms, the CIA was issuing 1600 micrograms. Some of their LSD was administered to patients at Tulane University who already had wired electrodes in their brain. ... ~ *Operation: CHAOS*, Mae Brussell[1508]

After the Battle of Lake Erie, Commodore Oliver Hazard Perry said to General William Henry Harrison, "We have met the enemy and he is ours!" Later, a cartoonist named Walt Henry put the perfect twist on the quote that sums up the malignancy that has been running America (interestingly, Kelly was writing about the war in Vietnam).

"We have met the enemy and he is us."

In September 1967, precisely as [Operation] CHAOS was launched by the CIA and the White House, Dr. Timothy Leary, tossed out of the Army for erratic behavior, abandoned experimenting with LSD on prisoners for the CIA in upstate New York, dropped a reading of the Tibetan Book of the Dead and donned the robes of designated LSD media prelate.

"In addition to this long mainstream tradition of far-out Sufi gnostic experimentation," Leary told religious historian Rick Fields in 1983, "there was another branch of drug research."[18] While still at Harvard, Leary was approached by Henry Murray, chief of psychological operations for William Donovan's Office of Strategic Services during WWII (and after the war a mind control researcher at Harvard who enlisted as a subject of experimentation one Ted Kaczynski, the Unabomber[19]. At the 1950 spy trial of Alger Hiss, Murray openly testified: "The whole nature of the functions of OSS were particularly inviting to psychopathic characters; it involved sensation, intrigue, the idea of being a mysterious man with secret knowledge."[20] And so Leary was fascinated with psychedelic compounds, "like most intelligence men," he added, and volunteered early on for the psilocybin trials, surreptitiously sponsored by the Company. ~ The Covert War Against Rock, Alex Constantine[1509]

How can pro-Communists and anti-Communists stand in solidarity to do harm to America? —When they are both controlled by the same malignant entity.

> *"Dropping out," ditching the corporate warfare state, was postulated by the emerging leadership of the anti-war subculture. And the philosophical direction of the swelling drop-out class was influenced by metaphysical, counter-cultural spokesmen with CIA support, each talking a blue streak about self, transcendence, consciousness expansion and equally high-minded, apolitical flights of mental expatriation.*
>
> *On the East Coast, Ira Einhorn, an eclectic new-age quack, and his friend Andrija Puharich, inventor of the tooth implant and a CIA-Army mind control researcher, lectured the counter-culture on drug reveling and "alien" visitations. Among the business sponsors of Ira Einhorn (currently a fugitive living in France, wanted for the alleged murder of his girlfriend Holly Maddox),* [were] *the Bronfman family of Seagram's fame; Russell Byers, a HUD director; John Haas, president of Rohm and Haas chemical conglomerate; Bill Cashel, Jr., a former Marine and president of Bell Pennsylvania. Einhorn wrote a chapter for a book edited by Humphrey Osmond, the infamous LSD chemist, Tim Leary and Alan Watts. His attorney was Arlen "Magic Bullet" Spector.*[7] ~ Constantine[1510]

Specter was the Warren Commission lawyer who came up with the solution for how Lee Oswald could fire 3 shots in 6 seconds with one missing completely and the final shot creating 7 wounds between Jack Kennedy and Texas Governor John Connally—and then miraculously reappearing in nearly perfect form on a gurney for use as an exhibit.[1511]

Specter was rewarded (having shown his loyalty) with a United States Senate Seat representing the Commonwealth of Pennsylvania for *thirty years*. Specter's Leftist voting record as a Republican finally caught up with him and there was a hard-fought primary in 2004, but then-President George W. Bush along with then-Pennsylvania Senator Rick Santorum rallied support and Specter was granted 6 more years.[ss]

[ss] No power in Hollywood? In *X-Men: Days of Future Past* (2014), Specter's ridiculous theory is bolstered by make-believe. It was Magneto's manipulation that made the bullet *obviously curve* because "he was one of us."

It fits so well with the rest of the Warren Report it should be added as an addendum.

> ...when I say Specter is a far-Left extreme Liberal, I'm not just name-calling. He supports the Roe v. Wade decision which "legalized" abortion and has destroyed the lives of more than 40 million innocent, unborn children. He has voted against banning the hideous procedure known as partial-birth abortion — which is really infanticide. He's for taxpayer-funding of abortion. He's against parental notification before abortions.
>
> In addition, Specter led the effort to stop Robert Bork from becoming a U.S. Supreme Court justice. But he voted for the far-Left extreme Liberal Ruth Bader Ginzburg to become a high-court justice. He refused to vote for the impeachment of Bill Clinton. And he opposed giving the Boy Scouts access to schools and Federal buildings unless they agreed to allow homosexuals Scout leaders.
>
> So, because this was one of those times when principle should have been put over party, President Bush should never have campaigned for Specter (but he did). Pennsylvania's other GOP Senator Rick Santorum should never have campaigned for Specter (but he did). Republicans should never have re-nominated Specter (but they did). And certainly, if nothing else, Rep. Pat Toomey should never, ever have said he will now support Specter (but he did). ~ the Constitution Party's Michael Peroutka[1512]

What Patriotic Americans have seen as an inexplicable strangle-hold on the Republican Party by poisonous Elites via "Party loyalty" has actually been a much more comprehensive plan of destruction coming from an outside source.

As Americans go through the theater of national elections each year, they little-realize that the game is rigged and the outcome all but guaranteed minus a mass uprising. Thanks to the influx of *millions* of illegal immigrants, that may never happen in America again until *radical* changes are accomplished...

—and they will be.

Endnotes

[1440] *The V-2 Rocket*, About.com
http://inventors.about.com/library/inventors/blrocketv2.htm
[1441] *Erich Traub*, Wikipedia.org
http://en.wikipedia.org/wiki/Erich_Traub
[1442] *ibid*
[1443] *Erich Traub and Lyme Disease*, 31 July 2007, tech-archive.net
http://sci.tech-archive.net/Archive/sci.med.diseases.lyme/2007-08/msg00037.html
[1444] *Erich Traub > Bio-Weapon Research*, Wikipedia.org
http://en.wikipedia.org/wiki/Erich_Traub#Bio-weapon_research
[1445] *Plum Island, Lyme Disease And Operation Paperclip - A Deadly Triangle*, Patricia Doyle, PhD, 21 August, 2005, Rense.com
http://www.rense.com/general67/plumislandlyme.htm
   Jeff Rense is about as big a doofus as there is in the "Truther" community, between that hair he cultivates and his rabid hatred of Jews but this was a good article that he had nothing to do with.
[1446] *Project Monarch: Nazi Mind Control*, Ron Patton, 1999, PARANOIA: The Conspiracy Reader
http://www.whale.to/b/patton.html
[1447] As of the date of this writing—14 October 2014—there is only this entry for "Michael A. Aquino" on Wikipedia:
This page has been deleted. The deletion and move log for the page are provided below for reference.
   00:37, 20 January 2009 Wizardman (talk | contribs) deleted page Michael A. Aquino (per OTRS ticket #2008073010004644; subject requests deletion, plus was AfD'd before)
   Wikipedia does not have an article with this exact name.
http://en.wikipedia.org/wiki/Michael_A._Aquino
[1448] *The Greatest Story Ever Forged (Curse of the Christ Myth)*, David Hernandez, Dorrance Publishing (2009), p. 141
[1449] *From PS YOP to MindWar: The Psychology of Victory*, -by- Colonel Paul E. Valley, Commander - with - Major Michael A. Aquino, PSYOP Research & Analysis Team Leader, Headquarters, 7th Psychological Operations Group, United States Army Reserve, Presidio of San Francisco, California, 1980
https://www.scribd.com/doc/242961753/From-PS-YOP-to-MindWar-The-Psychology-of-Victory
[1450] *Army Will Close Child-Care Center*, AP, 16 November 1987, NY Times
http://www.nytimes.com/1987/11/16/us/army-will-close-child-care-center.html
[1451] *Child Abuse Alleged at West Point*, AP, 8 December 1984, the New Hanover/Brunswick Morning Star, reposted at the Patriot Press
http://johnnycirucci.com/wp/?attachment_id=3054
[1452] *U.S. Attorney Will Not Reopen West Point Sex Case*, Tim McGlone, 14 July 1987, the Newburgh-Beacon Evening News, reposted at the Patriot Press
http://johnnycirucci.com/wp/?attachment_id=3055
[1453] *Rudy Giuliani, President (of Phi Rho Pi)*, Paul Schwartzman, 15 May 2007, Salon
http://www.salon.com/2007/05/15/giuliani_66/

[1454] *Cardinal Denounces Honor for Giuliani*, Nick Anderson and Alan Cooperman, 20 May 2005, the Washington Post
http://www.washingtonpost.com/wp-dyn/content/article/2005/05/19/AR2005051901733.html
[1455] *Is the Queen of England a Dame of Malta?* Yahoo! Answers
https://answers.yahoo.com/question/index?qid=20090923183147AALGO5U
   There is an entry for the Order of the Garter in Wikipedia and it very helpfully shows the cloak and crest and that is *not* the case.
Order of the Garter, Wikipedia
http://en.wikipedia.org/wiki/Order_of_the_Garter
   Worse for the doubters, the "Order of the Garter" has clear Templar roots and Jesuit Fordham University's seal is, itself, similar in design!
Jesuit Fordham University Has A Witchcraft Order Of The Garter Logo, The Unhived Mind, 14 April 2013
http://theunhivedmind.com/UHM/jesuit-fordham-university-has-a-witchcraft-order-of-the-garter-logo/
[1456] *Giuliani Joins A Distinguished Club*, Dylan Reynolds, 13 February 2002, CNN
http://edition.cnn.com/2002/WORLD/europe/02/13/knighthoods/
[1457] *Giuliani Defends, Employs Priest Accused of Molesting Teens*, Brian Ross and Avni Patel, 23 October 2007, ABC News
http://abcnews.go.com/Blotter/story?id=3753385&page=1
[1458] *Mayoralty of Rudy Giuliani > Drag Appearances*, Wikipedia.org
http://en.wikipedia.org/wiki/Mayoralty_of_Rudy_Giuliani#Drag_appearances
   Another great entry at Wikipedia—nowhere else was it concisely gathered that this pervert had come out in drag 4 different times.
[1459] *Activision Hires Rudy Giuliani to Fight Noriega's "Call of Duty" Suit*, Paresh Dave (pronounced "Duh-vay"), 22 September 2014, the LA Times
http://www.latimes.com/business/technology/la-fi-tn-activision-rudy-giuliani-noriega-20140922-story.html
[1460] *Call of Duty Creator Helps Defense Experts Predict Future Of War*, Chris Perez, 29 September 2014, the New York Post
http://nypost.com/2014/09/29/ex-pentagon-official-calls-on-call-of-duty-creator-to-predict-future-of-warfare/
[1461] *Child Abuse At The Presidio*, Linda Goldston, 24 July 1988, the San Jose Mercury News, archived here
http://web.archive.org/web/20130118004343/http://web.archive.org/web/20050301093215/http://www.outpost-of-freedom.com/aquino01.htm
[1462] *AQUINO v. STONE* No. 91-1164. 957 F.2d 139 (1992) Michael A. AQUINO, Plaintiff-Appellant, v. Michael P.W. STONE, Secretary of the Army, Defendant-Appellee. United States Court of Appeals, Fourth Circuit. Decided February 26, 1992, Leagle.com
http://leagle.com/decision/19921096957F2d139_11068.xml/AQUINO%20v.%20STONE
[1463] There is actually a Wikipedia entry for this song that gives credit to Osbourne, guitarist Randy Rhoads and bass guitarist Bob Daisley for the lyrics, however, use of the music industry for the Luciferian agenda is undeniable and, thanks to who populates it, little engineering is needed! Just take a look at the cover of Osbourne's "Blizzard of Ozz" album. Really?!!
Mr. Crowley, Wikipedia

http://en.wikipedia.org/wiki/Mr_Crowley
[1464] *The Making of JAY Z's "Run This Town" Video*, JAY Z's Life+Times, YouTube
https://www.youtube.com/watch?v=4KImMZQiX9I&
[1465] U.S. Grand Lodge, Ordo Templi Orientis, History, OTO USA.org
http://oto-usa.org/oto/history/
[1466] *From Scientology to Libertine Cult Ordo Templi Orientis (OTO): How Peaches Was Obsessed With The Occult And Spiritual Study*, Harriet Arkell, 8 April 2014, the Daily Mail
http://www.dailymail.co.uk/news/article-2599517/From-Scientology-libertine-cult-Ordo-Templi-Orientis-OTO-How-Peaches-obsessed-occult-spiritual-study.html
[1467] *Peaches Geldof Died of Heroin Overdose: Coroner*, Stephen Silverman, 23 July 2014, People
http://www.people.com/article/peaches-geldof-died-heroin-overdose-coroner
[1468] I wasn't kidding when I said "adoring public". Check out the title from this moron: *Bob Geldof on religion- "Jesus was a pain" & " fuck off Lord". Classic quotes!* from the YouTube channel of skyzthelimi7
https://www.youtube.com/watch?v=ueZOHTCXBxs
   Don't worry, moron...it's a "dry" heat and you can see your atheist icon there along with GAY Byrnes.
[1469] *Queen Knights Bob Geldof, but Don't Call Him Sir Bob*, AP, 10 June 1986, the LA Times
http://articles.latimes.com/1986-06-10/news/mn-10030_1_sir-bob-geldof
[1470] *10 Music Stars Knighted By The Queen Of England*, Alison Hill, 7 April 2011, Listosaur.com
http://listosaur.com/entertainment/10-music-stars-knighted-by-the-queen-of-england/
[1471] *GNOSTIC CATHOLIC CHURCHES, Ecclesia Gnostica Catholica, Wandering Bishops, Episcopi Vagantes, Eglise Gnostiqe Catholique, Eglise Gnostique Universelle, A compilation by Peter-R. Koenig*, undated, parareligion.ch
http://www.parareligion.ch/church.htm
[1472] *Degrees of the O.T.O.* geocities.ws
http://www.geocities.ws/nu_isis/degrees.html
[1473] *ibid*
[1474] *George W. Bush, Barbara Bush, and Aleister Crowley*, 1 April 2006, the Cannonfire blog
http://cannonfire.blogspot.com/2006/04/george-w-bush-barbara-bush-and.html
[1475] *From Hearsay to History: The Fate of Edward VI's Body*, Susan Higginbotham, 14 August 2011, Susan Higginbotham.com
http://www.susanhigginbotham.com/blog/posts/from-hearsay-to-history-the-fate-of-edward-vis-body/
[1476] *List of Protestant martyrs of the English Reformation*, Wikipedia
http://en.wikipedia.org/wiki/List_of_Protestant_martyrs_of_the_English_Reformation
[1477] **WARNING: GRAPHIC CONTENT** *XI° – Rocket to Uranus, Anal Intercourse and the O.T.O.*, Peter-Robert Koenig, undated, parareligion.ch
http://www.parareligion.ch/sunrise/xi.htm
   Trust me. I'm good at research.
   Is this trip really necessary???
[1478] *Aleister Crowley Was A British Agent*, 2008, the University of Idaho, reposted at the Patriot Press

[1478] http://johnnycirucci.com/wp/blog/2014/10/15/aleister-crowley-was-a-british-agent/
[1479] *Aleister Crowley > United States: 1914–19*, Wikipedia.org
http://en.wikipedia.org/wiki/Aleister_Crowley#United_States:_1914.E2.80.9319
[1480] *Perdurabo: The Life of Aleister Crowley*, Richard Kaczynski, North Atlantic Books (2010), p. 511
[1481] *MTV VMAs 2013: It Was About Miley Cyrus Taking the Fall*, 27 August 2013, the Vigilant Citizen
http://vigilantcitizen.com/musicbusiness/mtv-vmas-2013/
[1482] *Satanists Control Britain With Blackmail, "Red Ox"*, 12 May 2013, Henry Macow.com
http://henrymakow.com/2013/05/Satanists-Blackmail-Britain%20%20.html
[1483] *Sir Francis Bacon and John Dee : the Original 007*, D.W. Cooper and Lawrence Gerald, undated, Sir Bacon.org
http://www.sirbacon.org/links/dblohseven.html
[1484] *ibid*
[1485] *ibid*
[1486] *Everything Is Under Control*, Robert Wilson and Miriam Hill, William Morrow Paperbacks (1998), p. 42
[1487] *Aleister Crowley > United States: 1914–19*, Wikipedia.org
http://en.wikipedia.org/wiki/Aleister_Crowley#United_States:_1914.E2.80.9319
[1488] *Aleister Crowley and the LAM Statement*, Ian Blake, 1996, Rutgers.edu
http://paul.rutgers.edu/~mcgrew/ufo/crowley
[1489] *Magickal Stories - Lam*, Liz Armstrong, 19 January 2012, VICE
http://www.vice.com/read/magickal-stories-lam
[1490] *Final Events and the Secret Government Group on Demonic UFOs and the Afterlife*, Nick Redfern, Anomalist Books (2010), pp. 44-46
[1491] *ibid*, p. 47
[1492] *If You Could, Would You Like To Experiment By Having Sex In Space?* Grace Bush, 03 December 2007, Sodahead
http://www.sodahead.com/united-states/if-you-could-would-you-like-to-experiment-by-having-sex-in-space/question-30714/?link=ibaf&q=Pierre+Kohler++The+experiments+carried+out+so+far+relate+to+missions+planned+for+married+couples+on+the+future+International+Space+Station%2C+the+successor+to+Mir.+Scientists+need+to+know+how+far+sexual+relations+are+possible+without+gravity.
[1493] *Sex in Space. Or Not*, Jon Henley, 6 December 2007, the Guardian
http://www.theguardian.com/news/blog/2007/dec/06/sexinspaceornot
Someone please bitch-slap this guy's parents. People who do stupid, cutsie things with the name of their child should be sterilized. Really!
http://www.theguardian.com/news/blog/2007/dec/06/sexinspaceornot
[1494] *Timothy Leary's Liberation, and the CIA's Experiments! LSD's Amazing, Psychedelic History*, Richard J. Miller, 14 December 2013, Salon
http://www.salon.com/2013/12/14/timothy_learys_liberation_and_the_cias_experiments_lsds_amazing_psychedelic_history/
Note the subheading of this stooge's piece, "The U.S. psychedelic drug scene was kickstarted by spies and spooks, just as much as Timothy Leary and Jerry Garcia."
No moron! The poisonous drug culture was *all* top-down.

[1495] *Vets Sue CIA & Army for Cold War Drug Experiments*, Chris Marshall, 8 January 2009, Courthouse News Service
http://www.courthousenews.com/2009/01/08/12414.htm
[1496] *Operation Midnight Climax: How the CIA Dosed S.F. Citizens with LSD*, Troy Hooper, 14 March 2012, San Francisco Weekly
http://www.sfweekly.com/sanfrancisco/operation-midnight-climax-how-the-cia-dosed-sf-citizens-with-lsd/Content?oid=2184385
[1497] *FLASHBACK: Stories from Mount St. James; Timothy Leary '42*, James Dempsey, 2005, Holy Cross Magazine
http://www.holycross.edu/departments/publicaffairs/hcm/spring07/GAA/gaa8.html
[1498] *Rock & Roll Sorcerers of the New Age*, admin, 19 October 2011, Hegewisch Baptist
http://hbcdelivers.org/rock-roll-sorcerers-of-the-new-age/
[1499] *Aleister Crowley and the Drug Revolution*, Jonas Alexis, 24 June 2013, Veterans Today
http://www.veteranstoday.com/2013/06/24/aleister-crowley-and-the-drug-revolution-part-i/
[1500] *ibid*
[1501] *5 Beloved Famous People With Creepy Secret Obsessions*, Jake Flores, 14 March 2013, Cracked.com
http://www.cracked.com/article_20302_5-beloved-famous-people-with-creepy-secret-obsessions.html
[1502] *Walter Howard Bowart*, Wikipedia.org
http://en.wikipedia.org/wiki/Walter_Bowart
[1503] *Walter Bowart, Alternative Journalist, Dies at 68*, Margalit Fox, 14 January 2008, the NY Times
http://www.nytimes.com/2008/01/14/arts/14bowart.html?n=Top/Reference/Times%20Topics/Subjects/M/Media&pagewanted=all&_r=0
[1504] *Lords of the Revolution: Timothy Leary and the CIA*, Walter H. Bowart, undated, reposted at the Patriot Press
http://johnnycirucci.com/wp/blog/2014/10/16/lords-of-the-revolution/
[1505] *Reaction to the Modern Women's Movement, 1963 to the Present, Volume 3*, Angela Howard, Sasha Tarrant, Taylor & Francis (1997), p. 153
[1506] *What Gloria Steinem, Henry Kissinger Have in Common: CIA Pay*, Charles Trueheart, 22 February 2008, Bloomberg
http://www.bloomberg.com/apps/news?pid=newsarchive&sid=a1M9EAly2hog
[1507] *Mae Brussell*, Wikipedia.org
http://en.wikipedia.org/wiki/Mae_Brussell
[1508] Mae, God love her, simply drew the wrong conclusions. She saw the hand of the CIA and decided that the CIA had *ruined* the Peace movement. What she didn't understand was that it was *behind the entire movement, itself* (or, co-opted the movement at a very early stage).
OPERATION CHAOS; The CIA's War Against the Sixties Counter-Culture, Mae Brussell, November 1976, Mae Brussell.com
http://www.maebrussell.com/Mae%20Brussell%20Articles/Operation%20Chaos.html
[1509] *The Covert War Against Rock*, Alex Constantine, Feral House (2000), p. 38
[1510] *ibid*, pp. 37-38

[1511] *The Magic Bullet: Even More Magical Than We Knew?* Gary Aguilar and Josiah Thompson, 16 July 1999, History Matters
http://www.history-matters.com/essays/frameup/EvenMoreMagical/EvenMoreMagical.htm

[1512] *Bush, Santorum, Toomey Support For Specter Demonstrates Moral Bankruptcy Of Republican Party And Need For Constitution Party*, Michael Peroutka, 2004, the American View
http://archive.theamericanview.com/index.php?id=78

Chapter 16

Ancient Hate: Pagan Mysticism Behind The One World Order

Why?

Why do the Rulers of the world harbor so much hate for the common people?

Empirically, this is nearly impossible to answer.

There is, however, a Christian extrapolation available given the facts of who the Elite are and what they have done.

Adam was placed in Eden to steward YHWH's Creation [Genesis 1:15, Psalm 8, Psalm 24:1] and fellowship with Him. [Genesis 5:24, Exodus 33:11] Eve was made from Adam to help him in this and be a companion for him.

But they shared Eden with an adversary, cast out of Heaven for wishing to aspire to "be like unto the Most High". [Isaiah 14:13-14]

Consumed with jealousy and hatred, this adversary longs to rebuild on Earth what he could not attain in Heaven and his mantra became "As above, so below!"

But the adversary could not take from man what was his, he was forced to steal it. He built a system of power in secret and seduced those who shared his flaws (greed, lack of compassion, arrogance, selfishness and weakness) to partake of it. [Matthew 4:8-10, Ephesians 2:1-2]

Secrecy is paramount to the adversary as he fears the strength of the righteous. [I Corinthians 10:6, Hebrews 2:5-8] So he creates cells of quisling human beings to rise above their brethren or appropriates groups and people that rose on their own.

This seems to be what happened during the first rebellion against YHWH by man; Babylon.

Fallen Ones

Although Nimrod only receives passing mention as becoming a "mighty one" and a "mighty hunter before the Lord" in the Bible, in lore and literature, he is credited for having lead the first rebellion.

> *...it was Nimrod who excited them to such an affront and contempt of God. He was the grandson of Ham, the son of Noah, a bold man, and of great strength of hand. He persuaded them not to ascribe it to God, as if it was through his means they were happy, but to believe that it was their own courage which procured that happiness. He also gradually changed the government into tyranny, seeing no other way of turning men from the fear of God, but to bring them into a constant dependence on his power.*
>
> *He also said he would be revenged on God, if he should have a mind to drown the world again; for that he would build a tower too high for the waters to be able to reach! and that he would avenge himself on God for destroying their forefathers!*
>
> *Now the multitude were very ready to follow the determination of Nimrod, and to esteem it a piece of cowardice to submit to God; and they built a tower, neither sparing any pains, nor being in any degree negligent about the work: and, by reason of the multitude of hands employed in it, it grew very high, sooner than any one could expect; but the thickness of it was so great, and it was so strongly built, that thereby its great height seemed, upon the view, to be less than it really was. It was built of burnt brick, cemented together with mortar, made of bitumen, that it might not be liable to admit water. When God saw that they acted so madly, he did not resolve to destroy them utterly, since they were not grown wiser by the destruction of the former sinners; but he caused a tumult among them, by producing in them divers languages, and causing that, through the multitude of those languages, they should not be able to understand one another. The place wherein they built the tower is now called Babylon...* ~ Josephus[1513]

As a result of this, "Babylon" became a euphemism for rebellion against the Lord—especially when it was an organized, corporate effort.

When the Dragon fell from Heaven, he took $1/3$ of the angelic host with him in disloyalty. [Revelation 12:4]

The Bible implies that the price of this disloyalty was the inability to freely walk amongst the Creation as loyal angels do. [Genesis 18:1-19:29, Hebrews 13:2]

There are two ways for disloyal spiritual entities to interact with Earthly existence: to possess a living host as a result of its acquiescence (particularly a human host); or to *create* an organic host or hosts, *nephilim* (נְפִילִים), devoid of Divine spirit and inhabit it.

We will get into this in more detail in Chapter 20 but suffice it to say the latter method is preferable to the former in that created organic hosts can be endowed with advantages over humanity that makes them ascend to positions of leadership easily.

There is a third way that appears to be rare, requiring advanced knowledge and skill that may have been lost when the offending beings were imprisoned [Jude 6, II Peter 2:4]: that is to take an already living human and turn him *in* to an altered organic portal to be possessed as one created for that purpose.

This may have happened to Nimrod.

Genesis 10:8 tells us that Nimrod "began to be a mighty one":

הֵחֵל לִהְיוֹת גִּבֹּר

chalal hayah gibbor

It is interesting to note that "chalal" (Strong's OT 2490) has this breakdown in the Blue Letter Bible:

I. to profane, defile, pollute, desecrate, begin
   A. (Niphal)
      i. to profane oneself, defile oneself, pollute oneself
         a. ritually
         b. sexually
      ii. to be polluted, be defiled
   B. (Piel)
      i. to profane, make common, defile, pollute
      ii. to violate the honour of,

Fallen Angels vs. Demons

It has become *chic* in Christian circles for some expositors to wow their audiences by differentiating between a "fallen angel" and a "demon" but very few describe what they mean.

There is no precedent in the Bible for such a differentiation, especially if one defines the two to be completely different entities.

There is precedent, however, for an angelic hierarchy; Seraphim [Isaiah 6:1-7] and Cherubim [Genesis 3:24, etc] and "archangels" with special authority. [I Thessalonians 4:16]

The spirits that animate the unholy union between disloyal angels and humans are called *rephaim* (רְפָאִים).

Only YHWH can breathe the Breath of Life into His creation *ex nihilo*, "out of nothing".

If there are differences between "fallen angels", "demons" and the *rephaim* it is most likely that they are all angelic beings but of different strata.

        dishonor
        iii. to violate (a covenant)
        iv. to treat as common
    C. (Pual) to profane (name of God)

Was Nimrod defiled in his disobedience to become a willing organic portal of spiritual entity possession? Is this happening today via electromagnetic radiation and experimentation?

> *Experts in the area of the biological effects of electromagnetic frequencies (EMF) and wireless technologies believe there's virtually **no doubt** that cell phones and related gadgets are capable of causing not only cancer but contributing to a wide variety of other conditions, from depression and diabetes to heart irregularities and impaired fertility. Researchers have now identified numerous mechanisms of harm, which explain how electromagnetic fields impact your cells and damages [alters] your DNA.* ~ Dr. Joseph Mercola [emphasis his][1514]

Interdimensional interaction is key to understanding who, or *what* the world Ruling Elite are.

Drawn to Power

These interdimensional entities are drawn to power and oppression is always their ultimate goal. Whether they create organizations for this purpose or take them over is academic. One may make the case for a particular secret society having originally altruistic designs but men may be philanthropists without cavorting in secret. Secrecy is used to gain an advantage over others and that always entails a negative outcome for those "others".

Centralization of power is fertile ground for hostile demonic takeover and nowhere is this more apparent than in the practice of "religion".

Roman Catholicism, in particular, is this ancient pagan rebellion greatly enhanced by Christian truths and the Jesuit order are the wizards and knights within that whirlwind.

Bohemian

Proof that Luciferians run the world system of "Mystery Babylon" can be found in their secret assemblies like the Bohemian Grove and the Bilderberg Group.

Both Bohemian Grove and the Bilderberg Group are gatherings of the most powerful people in the world that are completely free of media scrutiny—never a good sign.

Named for their inaugural meeting at the Hotel de Bilderberg in Oosterbeek, Netherlands in May of 1954, a shocking number of Elites gather at Bilderberg without the slightest media scrutiny each year (which is useful, as many media moguls also attend).

Experts have surmised that Bilderberg is where the Luciferian Super Class give their instructions to their agents and political puppets without having to mingle with them.

In 2008, journalists that were following Barack Obama to cover his presidential campaign were lured onto Obama's jetliner and forcibly locked there in flight—literally kidnapped—while the future president, along with his future Secretary of State, Hillary Clinton, got their marching orders at Bilderberg in Chantilly, Virginia.[1515]

In 2014, the guest list included,

- the Belgian Minister of State
- the Professor of Medicine, Canada's McGill University (very helpful for answering questions on "population control")
- the CEO of TD Bank Group
- the Canadian Minister of Employment and Social Development
- the Governor of the Bank of Canada
- the Yiping Professor of Economics at the National School of Development, Peking University, China
- the Chairman of Royal Dutch Shell
- the CEO of Royal Dutch Shell
- French Member of Parliament and Mayor of Troyes, François Baroin
- the French Deputy Secretary General of the Presidency
- the Chairman of the Supervisory Board of Deutsche Bank
- the Former CEO of Deutsche Bank
- the German State Secretary of Labour and Social Affairs
- the Chairman of the Foreign Affairs Committee of the German Bundestag
- the Chairman of the Board of the National Bank of Greece
- the Former Prime Minister of Hungary (NATO since 1999)
- the Chairman of Fiat
- the NATO Supreme Allied Commander Europe
- the Secretary General of NATO
- Member of the Executive Board, European Central Bank Benoît Coeuré
- the Managing Director of the International Monetary Fund (she was

there to talk numbers)
- the Vice President and Commissioner for Justice, Fundamental Rights and Citizenship of the European Commission (now THAT'S someone I trust)
- the Minister for Agriculture, Food and the Marine of Ireland
- the Chairman, Goldman Sachs International
- Princess Beatrix of the Netherlands
- the Minister of Health of Portugal
- Portugal's Member of Parliament for the Socialist Party, Inês de Medeiros
- the Spanish Minister of Foreign Affairs and Cooperation
- the Queen of Spain
- the Swedish Minister for Foreign Affairs and founder of the European Union, Carl Bildt
- the President and CEO of Saab (also a military contractor)
- the British Shadow Chancellor of the Exchequer
- the British Chancellor of the Exchequer (the Minister of Finance/Secretary of the Treasury)
- the Editor-in-Chief of *The Economist*
- the British Secretary of State for International Development
- the Group Chairman of HSBC Holdings
- the Former Commander of U.S. Cyber Command and Former Director of the National Security Agency
- the Chairman of the Board of International Advisors of Goldman Sachs Group
- the Professor of Economics at Harvard University
- the CEO of Palantir Technologies, a surveillance specialist
- the Vice President and Co-Director of Metropolitan Policy Program at The Brookings Institute
- the Executive Chairman of Google
- Henry Kissinger (always a crowd-pleaser)
- Former U.S. National Security Advisor Thomas Donilon (Irish Leftist Catholic and personal friend of Joe Biden)
- the Co-Chair, Council on Foreign Relations and Former U.S. Secretary of the Treasury
- the Principal Research Scientist at Massachusetts Institute of Technology
- the President of Thiel Capital, Libertarian icon Peter Thiel
- Harvard Professor Larry Summers
- the Professor of Economics at New York University.[1516]

This is not an exhaustive list!

Although the names may vary each year, the gravity of their position does not.

Every year since 1954 these meetings take place without a hint of coverage from corporate news media.

As a result of this reality, when "Conservative" pundits like Glenn Beck mock concerns or questions regarding Bilderberg[1517], many begin to wonder if he, too, isn't controlled opposition.

Who "They" Are

Bohemian Grove is a scenic retreat located in Monte Rio, California and has been frequented by every Republican in high office in the past 100 years and more than a few Democrats as well.[1518] [italics suspended]

> Founded just after the Civil War by Henry Harry Edwards as a private camp where bohemians, artists and writers could go to relax and recuperate from the rigors of the work-a-day world, over time the club's membership evolved to include the rich and powerful, which now numbers over 2,400. The secrecy imposed about the annual meetings has led many to speculate as to the purposes and impact such a conclave might have on the nations affairs, especially when membership lists included every Republican President since 1923 (and some Democrats), many cabinet officials, and CEOs of large corporations including the major financial institutions. Military contractors, oil companies, banks (including the Federal Reserve) and national media all have high-ranking officials as either members or guests.
>
> Despite the club's motto: Weaving Spiders Come Not Here, ... plenty of business, both economic and political, has been done there. As noted in Peter Phillips dissertation for his doctorate in philosophy at the University of California, Davis, The Bohemian Grove has long been a political networking point for Republicans along with significant numbers of cabinet members and White House officials. [Dwight] Eisenhower gave a premier political address at the Grove in 1950, setting himself on the path to the presidency. In addition, he noted,
>
>> Presidential hopeful Nelson Rockefeller flew into the Grove [to give a] Lakeside Chat in 1963 and [Richard] Nixon and [Ronald] Reagan sat down informally at the Grove in 1967 to work a political deal wherein Reagan was to run [for President] only if Nixon faltered.

> The Grove became famous when word leaked out about a Manhattan Project meeting that took place there in September of 1942, which led subsequently to the development of the atom bomb. Attending that meeting were a number of high-ranking military officers, the president of Harvard University, and representatives of Standard Oil and General Electric. ~ Bob Adelmann, The New American[1519]

Here, too, we see that the predilections of the power-elite span the sophistry of feuding nation-states. [italics suspended]

> Monte Rio is a depressed Northern California town of 900 where the forest is so thick that some streetlights stay on all day long. Its only landmark is a kick-ass bar called the Pink Elephant, but a half-mile or so away from "the Pink," in the middle of a redwood grove, there is, strangely enough, a bank of 16 pay telephones. In midsummer the phones are often crowded. On July 21 of this year Henry Kissinger sat at one of them, chuffing loudly to someone—Sunshine, [he] called her, and Sweetie—about the pleasant distractions of his vacation in the forest.
>
> "We had jazz concert," Kissinger said. "We had rope trick. This morning we went bird-watching."
>
> Proudly Kissinger reeled off the names of some of his fellow campers: "Nick Brady and his brother is here." (Brady was the U.S. Treasury Secretary at the time.) "Tom Johnson is here." (Then the publisher of the Los Angeles Times, who had copies of his newspaper shipped up every day.) "That Indian is here, Bajpai." (He meant Shankar Bajpai, former ambassador to the U.S.) "Today they had a Russian."
>
> The Russian was the physicist Roald Sagdeev, a member of the Soviet Supreme Council of People's Deputies, who had given a speech to Kissinger and many other powerful men too. George Shultz, the former secretary of State, wearing hiking boots, had listened while sitting under a tree. Kissinger had lolled on the ground, distributing mown grass clippings across his white shirt, being careful not to set his elbow on one of the cigar butts squashed in the grass, and joking with a wiry, nut-brown companion.
>
> The woman on the line now asked about the friend. "Oh, Rocard is having a ball." Kissinger was sharing his turtleneck with Rocard, for nights amid the redwoods grew surprisingly cool. The two of them were camping in Mandalay, the most exclusive bunk site in

> the encampment, the one on the hill with the tiny cable car that carries visitors up to the compound.
>
> Meanwhile, Kissinger had been offering Rocard advice: "I told him, 'Do anything you want, hide in the bushes—just don't let them see you.'" Rocard was Michel Rocard, the prime minister of France, and this was a secret trip. No one was supposed to know he was peering up at ospreys and turkey vultures and hearing Soviet speakers along with former American secretaries of State and the present secretary of the Treasury. And David Rockefeller too. And Dwayne Andreas, the chairman of Archer-Daniels-Midland. Merv Griffin. Walter Cronkite.
>
> No one was supposed to know that Rocard himself would be speaking the next day down at the lake, under the green speakers' parasol. ~ Philip Weiss, Spy Magazine[1520]

The Grove has been explained as a place where powerful men smoke, drink alcohol constantly, make secret deals and urinate where-ever they please.[1521]

But the reality is that it is a pagan/satanic place of worship as timeless as the first rebellion against YHWH.

Tacitus wrote of the barbarian "Suabians" (Swabia) of southern Germany who sacrificed animals and even human beings to "Isis" in groves because it was offensive to consider their deities as being confined within walls.[1522]

For good reason is Bohemian Grove located just outside of San Francisco. The term "Bohemian" is related to the gypsies of central and eastern Europe[1523] who regularly conducted pagan rituals and sexual hedonism. These practices made it easy for Adolf Hitler to target for extermination many gypsies during his ethnic cleansing genocide.[1524]

The Grove mascot is the owl; an animal revered by pagans.[1525]

Conducting perverse sex "magick" in wooded groves has a long past. [italics suspended]

> Every time a primitive man engaged in a sexual act he believed that he was playing his role in stirring up the passion of his chief Father God and Mother Goddess in order to insure the fertility of his fields and flocks. The primitive peoples believed that if their

God and Goddess abstained from sexual union sterility was all around. To insure fertility and everyday survival, the ancient religious hierarchy implemented various phallic rites and celebrations of vile nature to insure that their God and Goddess would continually perform their love making and so pass on fertility onto everything else. As a result, both male and female reproductive organs came to be venerated and worshipped. The male reproductive organ or phallus was called "The Staff" while the female "The Door Of Life."

The male and female organs in conjunction were displayed in every major shrine. At other smaller and more portable shrines "pillars" and "groves" were erected near the sacrificial altars. At times bald and enormous phallic figurines were paraded through public streets during certain festive occasions—as was the practice during the Dionysian rites of ancient Greece. Triangle was associated with sex and the triune God of the pagans. It stood for the Father God, Mother Goddess, and their firstborn Son—the result of their first sexual act. The triangle was also associated by a primitive man to a triangle of the "pubic hair" found on both male and female sexually mature bodies. The famous "Star Of David" is nothing more than a symbol of male and female pubic triangles in conjunction during the sexual intercourse. Throughout the ancient world the "cross" was an object of veneration and worship. It was the "sign" and "seal" of baptism of ancient initiates who were inaugurated into the ancient Mystery Religion. Church Father Tertulian wrote that the initiates of his day who were still initiated into the Mystery Religion were signed with the sign of the "cross" on their foreheads in the same way as his Christian countrymen of Africa. The "cross" was a visible image which always reminded the initiates of the very purpose of their religion. It was purely of phallic nature and with an intent to insure fertility of the land. ~ John Vujicic, Beware Deception.com[1526]

Following on the heels of sex magick involving children is to kill them after they've been exploited. This gives the perpetrator a false sense of having covered his tracks but, more importantly, sheds innocent blood for unclean entities.

> *The Cremation of Care ceremony was first conducted in the Bohemian Grove at the Midsummer encampment in 1881, devised by James F. Bowman with George T. Bromley playing the High Priest.*[19] *It was originally set up within the plot of the serious "High Jinks" dramatic performance on the first weekend of the summer encampment, after which the spirit of "Care", slain by the*

> *Jinks hero, was solemnly cremated. The ceremony served as a catharsis for pent-up high spirits, and "to present symbolically the salvation of the trees by the club ..."[20] The Cremation of Care was separated from the Grove Play in 1913 and moved to the first night to become "an exorcising of the Demon to ensure the success of the ensuing two weeks."[21] The Grove Play was moved to the last weekend of the encampment.[22]*
>
> *The ceremony takes place in front of the Owl Shrine, a 40-foot (12 m) hollow owl statue made of concrete over steel supports. The moss- and lichen-covered statue simulates a natural rock formation, yet holds electrical and audio equipment within it. For many years, a recording of the voice of club member Walter Cronkite was used as the voice of The Owl during the ceremony.[1] Music and pyrotechnics accompany the ritual for dramatic effect. ~* Wikipedia[1527]

There is no positive way to spin the most powerful men in the world even just *imitating* ancient demonic child-sacrifice.

> *Indeed the sons of Israel and the sons of Judah have been doing only evil in My Sight from their youth; for the sons of Israel have been only provoking Me to anger by the work of their hands," declares the Lord. "Indeed this city has been to Me a provocation of My Anger and My Wrath from the day that they built it, even to this day, so that it should be removed from before My Face, because of all the evil of the sons of Israel and the sons of Judah which they have done to provoke Me to anger—they, their kings, their leaders, their priests, their prophets, the men of Judah and the inhabitants of Jerusalem. They have turned their back to Me and not their face; though I taught them, teaching again and again, they would not listen and receive instruction. But they put their detestable things in the house which is called by My Name, to defile it. They built the high places of Baal that are in the valley of Ben-hinnom to cause their sons and their daughters to pass through the fire to Molech, which I had not commanded them nor had it entered My Mind that they should do this abomination, to cause Judah to sin." ~* Jeremiah 32:30-35 NASB (some capitalization added to correct lack of respect)

During his foray into the Grove, Alex Jones secretly filmed this event.[1528]

But there are sources that claim far worse happens at the Grove including real child sacrifice. Investigative journalist Anthony Hilder interviewed a man who claimed to have witnessed the killing of young Kevin Andrew Collins[1529], kidnapped as a child over 30 years ago.[1530]

In an enclave completely isolated from prying eyes, the Elite are said to partake of any sexual perversion their heart desires.

Reputed attendee Bill Clinton mocked a critic who asked him about the Grove; "That's where all those rich Republicans stand naked against redwood trees, right?"[1531]

Richard Nixon said that Bohemian Grove was "the most faggy goddamned thing you could imagine."[1532]

Isis Unveiled

Helena Petrovna Blavatsky (1831-1891) was a Russian mystic and occultist whose writings line the shelves of the world's secret society lodges.

In-fighting amongst rival Elites will often bring hidden truths to the surface. Even criticism of Christian leaders, groups and behaviors by honest enemies will show sincere Believers where to examine themselves.

Although Blavatsky was an apologist for the darkest of pagan ritualism, she was unafraid to call out false Christians for what they were and was also surprisingly frank about rivals like the Jesuits.

> [Secret "Christian" societies all] *have an immediate connection ... they are of kabalistic parentage and have once held to the secret "Wisdom Religion," recognizing as the One Supreme, the Mystery-God of the Ineffable Name.*
>
> *...are more or less connected with magic—practically, as well as theoretically...*
>
> *To term them Christians, is wholly unwarranted. They neither believe in Jesus as Christ, nor accept his atonement, nor adhere to his Church, nor revere its "Holy Scriptures."*
>
> *Neither do they worship the Jehovah-God of the Jews and Christians, a circumstance which of course proves that their founder, John the Baptist, did not worship him either.* ~ Blavatsky[1533]

While the uninitiated see the Company of Loyola as a very dedicated group of Catholic teachers and missionaries, Blavatsky accused them and their Papal hierarchy of paganism, black magic, murder and chaos. [italics suspended]

> The origin of the Roman Catholic amulets and "relics" blessed by the Pope, is the same as that of the "Ephesian Spell," or magical characters engraved either on a stone or drawn on a piece of parchment; the Jewish amulets with verses out of the Law, and called phylacteria, Fulakthria , and the Mahometan charms with verses of the Koran. All these were used as protective magic spells; and worn by the believers on their persons. Epiphanius, the worthy ex-Marcosian, who speaks of these charms when used by the Manicheans as amulets, that is to say, things worn round the neck (Periapta), and "incantations and such-like trickery," cannot well throw a slur upon the "trickery" of the Pagans and Gnostics, without including the Roman Catholic and Popish amulets.
>
> But consistency is a virtue which we fear is losing, under Jesuit influence, the slight hold it may ever have had on the Church. That crafty, learned, conscienceless, terrible soul of Jesuitism, within the body of Romanism, is slowly but surely possessing itself of the whole prestige and spiritual power that clings to it. For the better exemplification of our theme it will be necessary to contrast the moral principles of the ancient Tanaïm and Theurgists with those professed by the modern Jesuits, who practically control Romanism to-day, and are the hidden enemy that would-be reformers must encounter and overcome. Throughout the whole of antiquity, where, in what land, can we find anything like this Order or anything even approaching it? We owe a place to the Jesuits in this chapter on secret societies, for more than any other they are a secret body, and have a far closer connection with actual Masonry — in France and Germany at least — than people are generally aware of. The cry of an outraged public morality was raised against this Order from its very birth.*
>
> Barely fifteen years had elapsed after the bull approving its constitution was promulgated, when its members began to be driven away from one place to the other. Portugal and the Low Countries got rid of them, in 1578; France in 1594; Venice in 1606; Naples in 1622. From St. Petersburg they were expelled in 1815, and from all Russia in 1820.
>
> It was a promising child from its very teens. What it grew up to be every one knows well. The Jesuits have done more moral harm in this world than all the fiendish armies of the mythical Satan.

Whatever extravagance may seem to be involved in this remark, will disappear when our readers in America, who now know little about them, are made acquainted with their principles (principia) and rules as they appear in various works written by the Jesuits themselves.

We beg leave to remind the public that every one of the statements which follow in quotation marks are extracted from authenticated manuscripts, or folios printed by this distinguished body. Many are copied from the large Quarto* published by the authority of, and verified and collated by the Commissioners of the French Parliament. The statements therein were collected and presented to the King, in order that, as the "Arrest du Parlement du 5 Mars, 1762," expresses it, "the elder son of the Church might be made aware of the perversity of this doctrine. ... A doctrine authorizing Theft, Lying, Perjury, Impurity, every Passion and Crime, teaching Homicide, Parricide, and Regicide, overthrowing religion in order to substitute for it superstition, by favoring Sorcery, Blasphemy, Irreligion, and Idolatry ... etc." Let us then examine the ideas on magic of the Jesuits. Writing on this subject in his secret instructions, Anthony Escobart† says:

> "It is lawful ... to make use of the science acquired through the assistance of the Devil, provided the preservation and use of that knowledge do not depend upon the Devil, for the knowledge is good in itself, and the sin by which it was acquired has gone by."‡ Hence, why should not a Jesuit cheat the Devil as well as he cheats every layman?

> "Astrologers and soothsayers are either bound, or are not bound, to restore the reward of their divination, if the event does not come to pass. I own," remarks the good Father Escobar, "that the former opinion does not at all please me, because, when the astrologer or diviner has exerted all the diligence in the diabolic art which is essential to his purpose, he has fulfilled his duty, whatever may be the result. As the physician ... is not bound to restore his fee ... if his patient should die; so neither is the astrologer bound to restore his charge ... except where he has used no effort, or was ignorant of his diabolic art; because, when he has used his endeavors he has not deceived."§

> Further, we find the following on astrology: "If any one affirms, through conjecture founded upon the influence of the stars and the character, disposition of a man, that he

will be a soldier, an ecclesiastic, or a bishop, this divination may be devoid of all sin; because the stars and the disposition of the man may have the power of inclining the human will to a certain lot or rank, but not of constraining it."*

~ Blavatsky[1534]

Blavatsky confirmed that Jesuit insurgency was as insidious as John Adams had stated, "Shall we not have Swarms of them here? In as many shapes and guises as ever the king of the Gypsies ... assumed? In the shape of Printers, Editors, Writers School masters, etc."

> *Says Mackenzie: "The Order has secret signs and passwords, according to the degrees to which the members belong, and as they wear no particular dress, it is very difficult to recognize them, unless they reveal themselves as members of the Order; for they may appear as Protestants or Catholics, democrats or aristocrats, infidels or bigots, according to the special mission with which they are entrusted. Their spies are everywhere, of all apparent ranks of society, and they may appear learned and wise, or simple or foolish, as their instructions run. There are Jesuits of both sexes, and all ages, and it is a well-known fact that members of the Order, of high family and delicate nurture, are acting as menial servants in Protestant families, and doing other things of a similar nature in aid of the Society's purposes. We cannot be too much on our guard, for the whole Society, being founded on a law of unhesitating obedience, can bring its force on any given point with unerring and fatal accuracy."* ~ Blavatsky[1535]

They used their Christian trappings to excuse sexual perversion, robbery and murder.

> *Let, then, all pious Christians listen and acquaint themselves with this alleged "rule of life" and precepts of their God, as exemplified by the Jesuits. Peter Alagona (St. Thomae Aquinatis SummæTheologiæ Compendium) says: "By the command of God it is lawful to kill an innocent person, to steal, or commit ... (Ex mandato Dei licet occidere innocentem, furari, fornicari); because he is the Lord of life and death, and all things, and it is due to him thus to fulfil his command" (Ex prima secundæ, Quæst., 94).* ~ Blavatsky[1536]

As an apologist for Masonry, Blavatsky ties the Jesuits and the Vatican in with the sect by claiming that Vatican treasurer-knights, the Templars, were unfairly persecuted. It is interesting that she made such a connection.

> As to the modern Knights Templar and those Masonic Lodges which now claim a direct descent from the ancient Templars, their persecution by the Church was a farce from the beginning. They have not, nor have they ever had any secrets, dangerous to the Church. Quite the contrary; for we find J. G. Findel saying that the Scottish degrees, or the Templar system, only dates from 1735-1740, and "following its Catholic tendency, took up its chief residence in the Jesuit College of Clermont, in Paris, and hence was called the Clermont system."
>
> Count Ramsay, a Jesuit, was the first to start the idea of the Templars being joined to the Knights of Malta. Therefore, we read from his pen the following: "Our forefathers (! ! !), the Crusaders, assembled in the Holy Land from all Christendom, wished to unite in a fraternity embracing all nations, that when bound together, heart and soul, for mutual improvement, they might, in the course of time, represent one single intellectual people."
>
> This is why the Templars are made to join the St. John's Knights, and the latter got into the craft of Masonry known as St. John's Masons. ~ Blavatsky[1537]

In fact, Blavatsky quotes a contemporary of hers as stating that the Jesuits were behind nearly *all* of the secret societies of their day!

> In this connection, place may well be given to a letter from Mr. Charles Sotheran, Corresponding Secretary of the New York Liberal Club, which was received by us on the day after the date it bears. Mr. Sotheran is known as a writer and lecturer on antiquarian, mystical, and other subjects. In Masonry, he has taken so many of the degrees as to be a competent authority as regards the Craft. ...
>
>> "It is curious to note too that most of the bodies which work these, such as the Ancient and Accepted Scottish Rite, the Rite of Avignon, the Order of the Temple, Fessler's Rite, the 'Grand Council of the Emperors of the East and West — Sovereign Prince Masons,' etc., etc., are nearly all the offspring of the sons of Ignatius Loyola. The Baron Hundt, Chevalier Ramsay, Tschoudy, Zinnendorf, and numerous others who founded the grades in these rites, worked under instructions from the General of the Jesuits. The nest where these high degrees were hatched, and no

> *Masonic rite is free from their baleful influence more or less, was the Jesuit College of Clermont at Paris.*
>
> *"That bastard foundling of Freemasonry, the 'Ancient and Accepted Scottish Rite,' which is unrecognized by the Blue Lodges was the enunciation, primarily, of the brain of the Jesuit Chevalier Ramsay. It was brought by him to England in 1736-38, to aid the cause of the Catholic Stuarts.*
>
> ~ Blavatsky[1538]

At the minimum, they know virtually every move of organizations they might share power with but it is far more likely they are at least working together on those agendas and even guiding them.

The similarities between them all alone is final proof, as Edith Starr Miller, the Lady Queenborough noted.

> *The well-known authority on theocratic organizations, Heckethorn, writes the following concerning the Jesuits:*
>
> *"There is considerable analogy between Masonic and Jesuitic degrees..."* ~ Edith Starr Miller[1539]

According to Miller, there are echelons in the Jesuit order just like in the Masons.

> *"It has six grades. These are novices, scholastics, temporal, coadjutors, professed of the three vows, and professed of the four vows, the latter two grades being the only ones which confer a share in the government and eligibility for the offices of the society. Its head, virtually a commander-in-chief, is known as The General. He wields absolute power over the members who are pledged to blind obedience. The General claims his authority from The Pope."*
> ~ Miller[1540]

Perhaps these structuring similarities come from having a mutual founder(s).

Miller believed (falsely) that "the Illuminati" was a "Protestant organization created to fight the Jesuits" and yet their methods are virtually identical.

> *Its members were pledged to blind obedience to their superiors and this was insured by a strict system of secret confessions, and*

monthly reports checked by mutual espionage. ~ Miller[1541]

Illuminating

The most infamous secret society to date is "the Illuminati". It is a sect of Freemasonry that was founded the same year America declared her independence.

To judge whether the two events are related, we must look at the creator of the Illuminati, Adam Weishaupt.

The *Allgemeine Deutsche Biographie* contains the biographical information of some 26,500 Bavarians of the 18th, 19th and 20th centuries. It lists Jewish Adam Weishaupt as starting his education with the Jesuits at the tender age of 7.[1542]

Like Karl Marx to Communism, the Jesuits cunningly manufactured a Jew as the figurehead of this infamous movement.

Not only was Weishuapt Jesuit-educated, he so excelled that he eventually became a Professor of Canon Law at the Jesuit-run University of Ingolstadt.[1543]

> *From the Jesuit College at Ingolstadt is said to have issued the sect known as "The Illuminati of Bavaria" founded by Adam Weishaupt under the guidance of* [Friedrich] *Nicolai, in 1776. Weishaupt, its nominal founder, however, seems to have played a subordinate though conspicuous role in the organization of this sect. ...* ~ Edith Starr Miller[1544]

Weishaupt would go on to create his secret order on May 1st, 1776[1545]: "May Day"—one of the most sacred days of the year for pagans and Communists alike.

Weishaupt is quoted as having said,

> *At a time, however, when there was no end of making game of and abusing secret societies, I planned to make use of this human foible for a real and worthy goal, for the benefit of people. I wished to do what the heads of the ecclesiastical and secular authorities ought to have done by virtue of their offices...* ~ *Quest for Mysteries*, Heinrich Schneider[1546]

Any "expert" who talks of "the Illuminati" yet doesn't acknowledge Weishaupt being surrounded by Jesuits all his life is at best a charlatan and at worst a Papal coadjutor.

In a letter dated January 31st, 1800, the author of the Declaration of Independence—Thomas Jefferson—wrote the author of the Constitution—James Madison—that he believed Weishaupt to be on the side of human liberty, decentralized government and Jesus Christ and that he was going to put Freemasonry back on track.

> *Wishaupt believes that to promote this perfection of the human character was the object of Jesus Christ. That his intention was simply to reinstate natural religion, & by diffusing the light of his morality, to teach us to govern ourselves. His precepts are the love of god & love of our neighbor. And by teaching innocence of conduct, he expected to place men in their natural state of liberty & equality. He says, no one ever laid a surer foundation for liberty than our grand master, Jesus of Nazareth. He believes the Free masons were originally possessed of the true principles & objects of Christianity, & have still preserved some of them by tradition, but much disfigured. The means he proposes to effect this improvement of human nature are "to enlighten men, to correct their morals & inspire them with benevolence. Secure of our success, sais he, we abstain from violent commotions. To have foreseen, the happiness of posterity & to have prepared it by irreproachable means, suffices for our felicity. The tranquility of our consciences is not troubled by the reproach of aiming at the ruin or overthrow of states or thrones." As Wishaupt lived under the tyranny of a despot & priests, he knew that caution was necessary even in spreading information, & the principles of pure morality. He proposed therefore to lead the Free masons to adopt this object & to make the objects of their institution the diffusion of science & virtue. He proposed to initiate new members into his body by gradations proportioned to his fears of the thunderbolts of tyranny. ~ The Works of Thomas Jefferson, edited by Paul Ford*[1547]

Weishaupt was no "victim" of tyrannical priests, but Jefferson most certainly was.

This was proof of the success of Jesuit guile for a great many of the Founding generation knew of the Society's efforts to undermine legitimate government.

Just before the turn of the 19th century, a young Protestant minister named George Washington Snyder wrote to his beloved namesake about a terrible conspiracy he was concerned with. The former president responded at length.[1548]

Snyder was a German émigré who was deeply impassioned to protect his new American home. He had read a book[1549] that outlined the plans of a "Society of Freemasons"—

> ...that distinguishes itself by the Name "of Illuminati," whose Plan is to overturn all Government and all Religion, even natural; and who endeavour to eradicate every Idea of a Supreme Being, and distinguish Man from Beast by his Shape only. A Thought suggested itself to me, that some of the Lodges in the United States might have caught the Infection, and might cooperate with the Illuminati or the Jacobine Club in France. Fauchet is mentioned by Robison as a zealous Member: and who can doubt of Genet and Adet? Have not these their Confidants in this Country?

President Washington responded to Snyder that, although he was sure that the poison had not reached any of the lodges in America, he, himself, was no-longer regularly attending any of them.

> I have heard much of the nefarious, & dangerous plan, & doctrines of the Illuminati, but never saw the Book until you were pleased to send it to me. The same causes which have prevented my acknowledging the receipt of your letter, have prevented my reading the Book, hitherto; namely—the multiplicity of matters which pressed upon me before, & the debilitated state in which I was left after, a severe fever had been removed. And which allows me to add little more now, than thanks for your kind wishes and favourable sentiments, except to correct an error you have run into, of my Presiding over the English lodges in this Country. The fact is, I preside over none, nor have I been in one more than once or twice, within the last thirty years. I believe notwithstandings, that none of the Lodges in this Country are contaminated with the principles ascribed to the Society of the Illuminati.
>
> With respect I am Sir Your Obedt Hble Servt Go: Washington

The letters are a great read and can be found in their entirety in Appendix B.

Perverse Prophecy

Secret Societies, Communism, war; man's greatest blights for the past 5 centuries can all be traced back to the Company of Loyola and, over a longer period of time, to Rome.

Canadian Naval Officer William Guy Carr[tt] (1895 - 1959) was enticed at a young age into Bolshevism but rather than become a Communist, Carr investigated the movement and found many a secret passage.

According to Carr, the notable head of "the Illuminait" after Adam Weishaupt was Italian revolutionary Giuseppe Mazzini. Carr drew lines between Mazzini and Scottish Rite Freemason Grandmaster and founder of the KKK, Albert Pike. [italics suspended]

> In 1800, Captain Wm. Morgan took upon himself the duty of informing other Masons how and why the Illuminati were using their lodges for subversive purposes. The Illuminati delegated one of their members, Richard Howard, to execute Morgan as a traitor. Morgan tried to escape to Canada. He failed. ...
>
> In 1829, an English Illuminist named "Fanni" Wright lectured to a carefully selected group of Illuminists in the new Masonic Temple in New York. She explained the Luciferian ideology regarding "free love" and "sexual liberty." She also informed the American Illuminists it was intended to organize, and finance, Atheistic-Communism for the purpose of fathering their own secret plans and ambitions. Among those who helped put this phase of the Luciferian conspiracy into effect were Clinton Roosevelt, (a direct ancestor of F D Roosevelt), Horace Greeley, and Charles Dada. ...
>
> In 1834, the Illuminati appointed Guiseppe Mazzini their "Director of Political Action". This title was a cover up for the office of "Director of Revolutionary Activities." ~ *The Conspiracy To Destroy All Existing Governments and Religions*, William Guy Carr[1550]
>
> He held this post until he died in 1872.
>
> In 1840, General Albert Pike was brought under the influence of Mazzini because he became a disgruntled officer when President Jefferson Davis disbanded his auxiliary Indian troops on the grounds they had committed atrocities under the cloak of legitimate warfare. Pike accepted the idea of a one world government and ultimately became head of the Luciferian Priesthood.
>
> Between 1859, and 1871, he worked out the details of a military

---

[tt] Carr never looked past the "Illuminati" or Freemasons either because of true short-sighted zeal or because he was a coadjutor. In this book you will see the *whole* picture...and it encompasses seven hills.

blue-print, for three world wars, and three major revolutions which he considered would further the conspiracy to its final stage during the twentieth century. ~ *Pawns in the Game*, William Guy Carr[1551]

This "plan" for three world wars is acknowledged by multiple sources based upon a letter from Mazzini to Pike. [italics suspended]

> In a letter dated January 22, 1870, Italian revolutionary and Illuminati leader Giuseppe Mazzini wrote this to Albert Pike, 33-degree Freemason:
>
>> We must allow all of the federations to continue just as they are, with their systems, their central authorities and diverse modes of correspondence between high grades of the same rite, organized as they are at present, but we must create a super rite, which will remain unknown, to which we will call those Masons of high degree whom we shall select. With regard to our brothers in Masonry, these men must be pledged to the strictest secrecy. Through this supreme rite, we will govern all Freemasonry which will become the one International Center, the more powerful because its direction will be unknown.[vi]
>
> Albert Pike wrote a letter to Mazzini on August 15, 1871, in which he outlined plans for three world wars that were seen as necessary to bring about the One World Order. For a short time, this letter was on display in the British Museum Library in London and it was copied by William Guy Carr, former Intelligence Officer in the Royal Canadian Navy.
>
>> We shall unleash the nihilist and the atheists, and we shall provoke a formidable social cataclysm which in its horror will show clearly to the nations the effect of absolute atheism, origin of savagery and the most bloody turmoil. Then everywhere, the citizens, obliged to defend themselves against the minority of revolutionaries, will exterminate those destroyers of civilization, and the multitude, disillusioned with Christianity...will receive the pure light through the universal manifestation of the pure doctrine of Lucifer...the destruction of Christianity and atheism. Both conquered and exterminated at the same time.[vii]
>
> According to threeworldwars.com, these were the purposes of the three world wars Pike and Mazzini had in mind:

The First World War: To overthrow the power of the Czars in Orthodox Russia and bring about an atheistic communist state.

The Second World War: To originate between Great Britain and Germany. To strengthen communism as antithesis to Judeo-Christian culture and bring about a Zionist State in Israel.

The Third World War: A Middle Eastern War involving Judaism and Islam and spreading internationally.[viii]

Dr. Dennis L. Cuddy agrees:

> Mazzini, with Pike, developed a plan for three world wars so that eventually every nation would be willing to surrender its national sovereignty to a world government. The first war was to end the czarist regime in Russia, and the second war was to allow the Soviet Union to control Europe. The third world war was to be in the Middle East between Moslems and Jews and would result in Armageddon.[ix]
>
> ~ *Jesuits Behind Politics*, Amazing Discoveries[1552]

Although Carr rightfully saw these puppet masters as Luciferians, he assumed that middlemen like Pike had the vision to plot out three world wars. [italics suspended]

> Pike's plan was as simple as it has proved effective. He required that Communism, Naziism, Political Zionism, and other International movements be organized and used to foment the three global wars and three major revolutions. The first world war was to be fought so as to enable the Illuminati to overthrow the powers of the Tzars in Russia and turn that country into the stronghold of Atheistic-Communism. The differences stirred up by agentur of the Illuminati between the British and German Empires were to be used to foment this war. After the war ended, Communism was to be built up and used to destroy other governments and weaken religions.
>
> World War Two, was to be fomented by using the differences between Fascists and Political Zionists. This war was to be fought so that Naziism would be destroyed and the power of Political Zionism increased so that the sovereign state of Israel could be established in Palestine. During world war two International Communism was to be built up until it equaled in strength that of

united Christendom. At this point it was to be contained and kept in check until required for the final social cataclysm. Can any informed person deny Roosevelt and Churchill did not put this policy into effect?

World War Three is to be fomented by using the differences the agentur of the Illuminati stir up between Political Zionists and the leaders of the Moslem world. The war is to be directed in such a manner that Islam (the Arab World including Mohammedanism) and Political Zionism (including the State of Israel) will destroy themselves while at the same time the remaining nations, once more divided against each other on this issue, will be forced to fight themselves into a state of complete exhaustion physically, mentally, spiritually and economically. Can any unbiased and reasoning person deny that the intrigue now going on in the Near, Middle, and Far East isn't designed to accomplish this devilish purpose? ~ Carr[1553]

These wars only make sense if one places *Rome* and *satan* as the agents with the vision, power and patience to carry out such an agenda.

All war is used to bleed the world's populations and enrich the Elite.

WWI was to punish Jesuit/Papal enemies like Prussia and birth Communism to be used against the Russian people.

WWII was to punish expulsioners of the Jesuits in Japan and the birthplace of the Reformation; Germany. It was used to both slaughter Jews and give political rebirth to Israel.

WWIII will be to further punish both Jewish and Muslim "heretics" and install One World Government.

Rose & Cross

The apocryphal *Book of Enoch* gives the details of why YHWH judged the Earth with a great flood. With advanced technology, fallen angels who constantly watched and yearned to interfere with men—"Watchers"—brought to mankind implements of war, the martial arts of both armed and unarmed combat, the use of female accoutrements for seduction, the ability to write, metallurgy, the hybridization of species and even abortion.[1554]

In the Book of Genesis we find both of Adam's sons Seth and Cain having boys named "Lamech". The Cainite Lamech was the first to take two wives in rebellion against the Divine ideal of one man and one woman. He was also a murderer like his great grandfather. The Cainite Lamech sired

Tubal-Cain by his second wife Zillah. Tubal-Cain was "the forger of all instruments of bronze and iron." [Genesis 4:22]

The Freemasons attached themselves to Tubal-Cain and elevated him in their mythology.

> *He was the inventor of edge-tools, and introduced many arts into society which tended towards its improvement and civilization. Tubal Cain is the Vulcan of the Pagans, and is thought to have been closely connected with ancient Freemasonry. Faber says that "all the most remarkable ancient buildings of Greece, Egypt, and Asia Minor, were ascribed to Cabirean or Cyclopean Masons," the descendants of Vulcan, Dhu Balcan, the god Balcan, or Tubal Cain. Oliver says, "In after times Tubal Cain, under the name of Vulcan and his Cyclops, figured as workers in metals and inventors of the mysteries; and hence it is probable that he was the hierophant of a similar institution in his day, copied from the previous system of Seth, and applied to the improvement of schemes more adapted to the physical pursuits of the race to which he belonged."*
>
> *For these reasons Tubal Cain has been consecrated among Masons of the present day as an ancient brother. His introduction of the arts of civilization having given the first value to property. Tubal Cain has been considered among Masons as a symbol of worldly possessions. ~ Lexicon of Freemasonry*, Albert Mackey[1555]

Who exactly are the Freemasons?

> *Freemasonry is a fraternal organisation that traces its origins to the local fraternities of stonemasons, which from the end of the fourteenth century regulated the qualifications of masons and their interaction with authorities and clients. The degrees of freemasonry, its gradal system, retain the three grades of medieval craft guilds, those of Apprentice, journeyman or fellow (now called Fellowcraft), and Master Mason. These are the degrees offered by craft, or blue lodge Freemasonry. There are additional degrees, which vary with locality and jurisdiction, and are now administered by different bodies than the craft degrees.*
>
> *The basic, local organisational unit of Freemasonry is the lodge. The lodges are usually supervised and governed at the regional level (usually coterminous with either a state, province, or national border) by a Grand Lodge or Grand Orient. There is no international, worldwide Grand Lodge that supervises all of Freemasonry. Each Grand Lodge is independent, and they do not*

necessarily recognise each other as being legitimate. ~ Wikipedia[1556]

Freemasonry, like any secret society, is a gateway organization. If aspiring men wish access to power, they must prove they will be dedicated to the agenda of the Luciferian Elite by being inducted into such a society and showing as they rise through the degrees that they will dutifully serve satan. That may sound inflammatory but that is, essentially, the truth and it is born out in the ancient rituals memorized and conducted by the acolytes.

In this, the Freemasons sound very much like the Jesuits and perhaps with good reason. Secret societies not connected to Rome provide the Church with both plausible deniability as well as the comfort of keeping heretics at arm's length. [italics suspended]

> Masons often claim that Freemasonry is not a secret organization, but an organization with secrets. ...the only real secrets in Freemasonry are the "modes of recognition", which include due guards, signs, tokens (which are the handshakes or secret grips), and passwords. ...
>
> ...most Masons will refuse to divulge anything and will "forever conceal, and never reveal any of the art or arts, part or parts, point or points of the hidden mysteries of Freemasonry, which they have received, may be about to receive, or may be hereafter be instructed in, to any person unless it shall be to a worthy Brother Mason." This is, in part, the result of the fear so indelibly embedded on one's mind when they enter the lodge for the very first time; being "received on the point of a sharp instrument piercing their naked left breast, which is to teach them that as this is an instrument of torture to the flesh, so should the recollection thereof be to their minds and consciences, should they ever reveal the secrets of Freemasonry unlawfully."
>
> What's more, after taking the bloody oath that reinforces this fear, the candidate is told that "the penalty of their oath (or obligation) is ... symbolic of what an honest man would rather undergo then to violate his solemn vow." ...either you fear that some over zealous Mason just might hold you accountable by fulfilling the penalty on behalf of the Craft, or else your pride and honor are at risk of being destroyed. In either case, most Masons choose to take the safest route and keep their mouths shut entirely, rather than risk either consequence.
>
> However, as Ex-Masons for Jesus we fear (reverence) God not man,

and therefore we're not obligated to an oath which was rendered to us under false pretenses. As far as we are concern, the oaths which we took are null and void. ...

While Masonic Rituals and Modes of Recognitions vary slightly from one jurisdiction to another, they are all true to "due and ancient form" in every duly constituted regular lodge. This means that the variation in wording found in one ritual when compared to another may be minor, yet in essence you will find that they all basically say the same thing. The same holds true for Modes of Recognition. Masons can recognize these signs even if their own jurisdiction performs them slightly differently. ~ the Order of Former Freemasons[1557]

The Jesuit guidebook *Secreta Monita* gives instructions regarding the use of front groups and on how to hide behind prominent individuals.

The society can also usefully trade, under the name of rich merchants attached to us; but certain and abundant gain is to be looked at, as in the Indies, which have furnished the society not only souls but thus far also much wealth through the favor of God. ~ Secreta Monita[1558]

But what makes these efforts so successful is that the adherents within the secret societies so willingly conform to their Luciferian agendas.

For Freemasons, Bacon's "New Atlantis" was a powerful ideal of gnostic nirvana; Salvation by secret knowledge. It is this reason that causes them to parse "the devil" from "Lucifer, the bearer of light" yet they serve one and the same.

"Atlantis" first comes to us via the Socratic dialogue of *Timaeus*, by Plato in 360 BC. In it, Plato appears to create a fictional adversary of advanced warrior prowess that attacks noble Athens but is staved off. Falling out of favor with the gods, the island was shaken by earthquakes and engulfed by the ocean. Was this an allegory of the antediluvian Earth or was it something more?

Atlantis would return in a much more positive light 1700 years later thanks to British occultist Francis Bacon.

Bacon is considered the "father of empiricism" and a great practitioner of the scientific method. His processes of examining the environment would quell spiritualism and superstition but would also quench reverence for God and fear of His Wrath at injustice and unrighteousness.

Wielded by unscrupulous men, this methodology would usher in the Enlightenment and Darwinian Evolution—rationalization the Elite used for racism, slave labor and genocide.

Bacon would rekindle ideas of an "Enlightened" utopia and pick Plato's "Atlantis" to do it with. In his work *New Atlantis*, Bacon laid out his vision, replete with copious amounts of Christian imagery.

In this "New Atlantis" (which was actually a small novel he left unfinished in 1627), the citizens have been Christianized via a copy of the Bible that has miraculously appeared on their island of Bensalem—Hebrew for "son of peace". They are chaste and pious and the political officials act without compensation. It is a society founded on "science". These ideas strongly influenced men of the Founding Generation both in America and in Britain. More than a few, on both continents, thought they were creating Bacon's "New Atlantis" here. [italics suspended]

> American Masonry can be traced to England during the time of Sir Francis Bacon (1561–1626), who is considered the first grand master of modern masonry. Even at this time, the inner doctrine of embracing all the world religions alongside Christianity existed, but they did not publish such things in formal declarations, for fear of persecution.
>
> Sir Francis Bacon's close associate during this time was Dr. John Dee, who was the court astrologer for Queen Elizabeth I. It is well known that Dee was a sorcerer who summoned demonic spirits to obtain secret knowledge; a practice used by Rosicrucians (of whom Dee was the chief in England) for centuries. The root word for "demon" means "a knowing one." The Rosicrucians desired to know secrets of science (i.e., knowledge) and consulted demons to get information. Bacon also made contact with demonic spirits, including the goddess Pallas Athena, whom he claimed was his muse or inspiration. In time, Dee handed off the leadership of the Rosicrucian Society to Bacon, who would enfold the secrets of Rosicrucianism into the system of Freemasonry.
>
> Little wonder that Sir Francis Bacon would become the father of the modern scientific method, and that men like Benjamin Franklin and Thomas Jefferson would follow his example in their scientific endeavors. Franklin and Jefferson are both claimed by modern Rosicrucians as being of their order.
>
> Like the Gnostics, the Rosicrucians craved knowledge; it was this desire that led them to worship Lucifer. ...

> In 1793 when George Washington sanctioned the laying of the capital building's cornerstone, he did so wearing a Masonic apron emblazoned with the brotherhood's symbols. For occult expert and 33rd Degree Freemason Manly P. Hall, this made perfect sense. "Was Francis Bacon's vision of the 'New Atlantis' a prophetic dream of the great civilization, which was so soon to rise upon the soil of the New World?" he asked in The Secret Teachings of All Ages. "It cannot be doubted that the secret societies…conspired to establish [such] upon the American continent. …'" Hall continued that historical incidents in the early development of the United States clearly bore "the influence of that secret body, which has so long guided the destinies of peoples and religions. By them nations are created as vehicles for the promulgation of ideals, and while nations are true to these ideals they survive; when they vary from them, they vanish like the Atlantis of old which had ceased to 'know the gods.'" ~ *Apollyon Rising 2012*, Thomas Horn[1559]

In Freemasonry, the intersecting of the compass and square are meant to call to mind the Luciferian desire to create a "paradise on Earth" and to "be like unto God" [Isaiah 14:14] with their mantra "as above, so below". The so-called "Star of David" is a more symmetrical rendition of this. The hermaphroditic "Baphomet" shows the combining of man, woman and animal into one satanic being, pointing above and below.

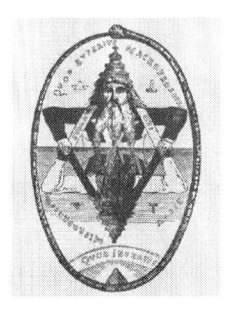

Author Richard Allan Wagner would show in his book *The Lost Secret of William Shakespeare* the trail that lead from the Templars through Bacon, through Masonic / Rosicrucianism to the New World. [italics suspended]

> The ... suppression of the Knights Templar in 1307 had driven European philosophy and science completely underground. The progressive minds from the Templar ranks proficient in the arts and sciences found refuge in small, secret enclaves throughout Europe. The clandestine "movement" was generically known to its

adherents as "The Invisible College," and "The Great Society."[uu]

It is not certain when such terms as "Rosicrucian" and "Freemason" began to take root. But it is certain that the Movement lacked any semblance of cohesive organization and purpose. ...

Dr. John Dee, the immanent authority on Hermeticism and Kabbalism in England laid the ground-work for the formation of the "Rosicruician Order." He most certainly initiated young Bacon into the Order, as evidenced by Jacob Cats' engraving (1655) of Dee passing the "Lantern of Rosicrucian Light" to Bacon—over an open grave.

For all intents, Bacon was now the leader of the Rosicrucian movement. ...

As a measure to insure that Rosicrucianism wouldn't become Baconism, Bacon invented a mythical Rosicrucian founder whom he cleverly dubbed Christian Rosenkreutz or Brother CRC—some sources make references to Father CRC (Rosenkreutz is German for Rose Cross). As had been the case with Shakespeare, the names were carefully crafted as encryption devices corresponding to the powerful Kabbalistic number 13. ...

As had been the case with the Rosicrucians, Operative Freemasonry was stagnating without direction or purpose. The old order had adopted the practice of accepting worthy men such as Bacon into their ranks who were not employed in the trade of masonry. As descendants of the Knights Templar, the Rosicrucians and the Operative Freemasons both made use of the same symbols and rituals. On a deeper level, the Chymical Wedding reflected Bacon's desire to (alchemically) transmute the two orders into one, unified society sharing the same ideals, goals and philosophy. ...

The year 1606 saw the establishment of several Rosicrucian colonies, the most prominent taking root in what is now Pennsylvania. Later, Benjamin Franklin (who was greatly influenced by Bacon's work) would emerge as the highest ranking Rosicrucian-Masonic figure from that colony. Likewise, other Rosicrucian-Masonic founding fathers of the new American nation such as George Washington, Thomas Jefferson, and Thomas Paine were avid readers of Bacon. Jefferson is said to have carried a

---

[uu] Lyndon Johnson named his socialist utopian socialist welfare state "The Great Society". It was no more realized than New Atlantis has been.

picture of Bacon with him wherever he went. In his book The Secret Destiny of America, Manly P. Hall writes: "Franklin spoke for the Order of the Quest, and most of the men who worked with him in the early days of the American Revolution were also members. The plan was working out, the New Atlantis was coming into being, in accordance with the program laid down by Francis Bacon a hundred and fifty years earlier." ~ Wagner[1560]

The rebellion of technological nirvana, free from the restrictions of the Creator, continued through the ages and in 1882, *Atlantis: The Antediluvian World* was published by Ignatius Loyola.

Ignatius Loyola Donnelly, that is—Lieutenant Governor of Minnesota and 3-term Republican Congressman, holding those offices collectively from 1860 to 1868. Those were critical years for America.

T.E. Wilder, in his review of David Stevenson's *The Origins of Freemasonry*, noted the questionable agenda of "Lutherans" obsessed with alchemy as well as the man credited with creating Freemasonry being a Catholic.

> *...the fact that the most interesting Mason of the 17th century, Sir Robert Moray, was a Covenanter general, and that one stream of influence on freemasonry was the hermetic Lutheranism of the Rosicrucians (which was present in the military arm of German protestantism) should make us reexamine the goals and methods of this generation of reformers.*
>
> *First responsible for the transformation of what was still basically a trade guild into an esoteric society was the royal master of works William Schaw, apparently a "moderate", i.e. unprincipled, Roman Catholic. "Apparently" is a key word here as much of what Stevenson's can discover about him is inferential. His office of Master of Works put him in charge of all royal castles and palaces, and acting in that capacity and as warden of the craft of "maister maissounis within this realme" ... he issued statutes regulating the mason's guild. ...*
>
> *The Rosecrucian order, supposedly founded by Christian Rosencreutz (probably actually an allegorical figure), drew its name partly from Luther's coat of arms with its rose from which a cross emerges. Arising from Lutheran mystics and a partly cleaned up Hermeticism (believed to be the secrets of the Ancient Egyptians) the Rosicrucians expected the dawn of a great new age.*[1561]

The Catholic Church teaches vehement opposition to Freemasonry, as Jesuit priest Robert Bradley tells us;

What is the truth regarding the present official attitude of the Catholic Church toward Freemasonry? To begin this inquiry into that which is now in effect, we should go back to what was stated in the Church's canon law before there was any doubt about where the Church stood on Masonry. The former code (which, incidentally, was promulgated on Pentecost, May 27, 1917, just two weeks after Our Lady's first apparition at Fatima) contained a canon which definitely capped all the previous papal condemnations of it. Canon 2335 reads as follows:

Persons joining associations of the Masonic sect or any others of the same kind which plot against the Church and legitimate civil authorities contract <ipso facto> excommunication simply reserved to the Apostolic See. ~ EWTN[1562]

How is it possible for a Catholic to have initiated Freemasonry if the Masons are Rome's "mortal enemies"?

Does the "G" in the center of the masonic compass and square stand for "gnosticism", or "Gesu" as in the Italian of "Society of Jesus": *Compagnia di Gesù*?

Author John Daniel considers the Illuminati and the Freemasons to be the Jesuits' greatest weapons. [italics suspended]

The truth is, the Jesuits of Rome have perfected Freemasonry to be their most magnificent and effective tool, accomplishing their purposes among Protestants, yet remaining completely hidden and unknown. But when you decipher their Occult symbols of the Illuminati and Freemasonry that you see in Washington D.C. and on the U.S. Great Seal, then you discover the workings and intentions of Rome that she so secretly and amazingly works behind. One of the most startling, when you understand what it mears, is the pyramid and its capstone, "not sitting in place" , that makes up the reverse of the American Great Seal and as seen on the back of one dollar bills. That 'Pyramid', which represents the heart and soul of Babylonian Sun Worship, and its 'Great Work', that is carried on by Romanism, is unfinished! Why? Because the "Capstone", which represents the *Novus Ordo Seclorum*, or New World Order, is not yet in place. Which also means however, that Rome's timeclock, ever since the birth of this nation, has been ticking; anticipating for over two hundred years, the date when the Capstone "will" be put into place.

This special event, will "signal" or herald the "beginning" of the so called triumph of Mary which proclaims the victory of Rome for dominating the whole world. The Virgin Mary, who is actually Rome's Isis, will become Rome's central figure, used to deceive and rally the earth's inhabitants; compelling them to submit to the New Order of things. Consequently, it will bring on the need to immediately revive the diabolical Holy Inquisition with unprecedented powers and brutality to rid the earth of dissenters. ~ *The Grand Design Exposed*, John Daniel[1563]

Enlightened

The triumph of "reason" over "religion" was a seed planted by Francis Bacon and harvested at the Enlightenment.

It is generally understood that the Enlightenment was a movement that was vehemently fought by Rome[1564] as so many "Enlightened" thinkers like François-Marie Arouet ("Voltaire") were openly critical of the Catholic Church.

But much as the Church has steered, used and even created enemies such as the "Illuminati" and the Freemasons, the power behind Voltaire was the Company of Loyola. [italics suspended]

> The Jesuit *Journal de Trévoux* could see nothing that was not praiseworthy in the project of 'M. de Voltaire, de se rendre philosophe et de rendjre, s'il est possible, tout l'univers newtonien'.[31] The lively resistance Voltaire did encounter was almost entirely from entrenched groups of philosophically inclined érudits, dismissed by him as 'Cartesians', among the academies and the intellectual avant-garde. Acknowledging that Newton always speaks of the Creator and his attributes 'avec décence', the Jesuits, by contrast, were now willing to endorse [Voltaire's teachings] in the colleges, universities, and academies of France and, with it, the spread of Voltaire's national influence.[32]

> As far as major sections of the French establishment of church and state were concerned, Voltaire's Enlightenment based on 'English ideas' had in fact, by 1738, won the battle. At Paris, by the end of the 1730s and beginning of the 1740s, it was almost automatic for both Catholics interested in natural philosophy and students like Diderot (who was aged 25 when Voltaire's book appeared), aspiring to the status of *philosophe*, to be enthusiasts for ... Voltaire.[33]

Having warmly welcomed the first edition of Voltaire's work on Newton, the Jesuits were even more positive in their reception of the second edition of June 1744. ...

The Jesuits regularly praised Voltaire's philosophical efforts, plays, and poetry during these years, continuing to support him also after Guillatnne-Francois Berthier (1704~82), the pre-eminent Jesuit intellectual strategist of the mid eighteenth century, became editor-in-chief of the *Mémoires de Trevoux* in1745.[35] Once the machinery of Jesuit publicity had set this fateful course, the initially welcoming clerical response to Voltaire and his allies was indeed to take many years to reverse. ~ *Enlightenment Contested*, Jonathan I. Israel[1565]

"Enlightened" writers like Voltaire weren't just lashing out at the Catholic Church, they were excoriating the Bible and Jesus Christ.

Edith Starr Miller—the Lady Queenborough—made the same accusation of a Jesuit front movement called "Illuminism"; the ideals behind Weishaupt's movement.

> *According to Le Forestier, Illuminism was just as much Masonry as the system of the Rose Croix, that of the Templars or the crowd of Masonic French degrees...*
>
> *[Charles Frederic] Bahardt and [Johann Bernard] Basedow, at the same time, in cheap and popular tracts, scattered among the lower classes the poison of infidelity ; and they, as well as [Christoph Friedrich] Nicola'i, were in close communication with Weishaupt, carrying on with the most reckless violence, and with the weapons of a most shameless ribaldry, the warfare against Christianity.*
>
> *The great critic [Gotthold Ephraim] Lessing, the founder of the modern German literature, lent his powerful support to the anti-Christian League. While librarian at Wolfenbuttel he edited a work, composed by [Hermann Samuel] Reimarus, consisting of various irreligious essays entitled Fragments of Wolfenbuttel, and which, from the tone of earnestness and dialectic acuteness wherein they were written, exerted a very prejudicial influence over public opinion.[3]* ~ Edith Starr Miller[1566]

Another Jesuit creation—Communism—would have a similar anti-Christ/anti-family agenda.

> *Abolition [Aufhebung] of the family! Even the most radical flare up at this infamous proposal of the Communists.*

On what foundation is the present family, the bourgeois family, based? On capital, on private gain. In its completely developed form, this family exists only among the bourgeoisie. But this state of things finds its complement in the practical absence of the family among the proletarians, and in public prostitution.

The bourgeois family will vanish as a matter of course when its complement vanishes, and both will vanish with the vanishing of capital.

Do you charge us with wanting to stop the exploitation of children by their parents? To this crime we plead guilty.

But, you say, we destroy the most hallowed of relations, when we replace home education by social.

And your education! Is not that also social, and determined by the social conditions under which you educate, by the intervention direct or indirect, of society, by means of schools, &c.? The Communists have not invented the intervention of society in education; they do but seek to alter the character of that intervention, and to rescue education from the influence of the ruling class.

The bourgeois clap-trap about the family and education, about the hallowed co-relation of parents and child, becomes all the more disgusting, the more, by the action of Modern Industry, all the family ties among the proletarians are torn asunder, and their children transformed into simple articles of commerce and instruments of labour. ~ Marx and Engels[1567]

Jesuits weren't just supporting the attacks on Christianity by the Enlightenment, they were helping write them. [italics suspended]

> There can be little doubt that Voltaire was the great voice in 18th century France, the witty, sarcastic, intellectual oracle of the Enlightenment that would lead to the French Revolution. It was Voltaire who set the stage for an irreverent, and often mocking view of the Bible and its teachings. The French philosopher famously said:
>
>> "It took twelve ignorant fishermen to establish Christianity; I will show the world how one Frenchman can destroy it."
>
> It was Voltaire who also said:

> "The son of God is the same as the son of man; the son of man is the same as the son of God. God, the father, is the same as Christ, the son; Christ, the son, is the same as God, the father. This language may appear confused to unbelievers, but Christians will readily understand it."

This same attitude against the Trinity can likewise be found in the writings of the American revolutionaries, as we show in our film. Voltaire's writings and view of the Bible, Christianity and the Church became known as Voltarianism – the particular spirit of which permeates the writings of men like Paine, Jefferson, Adams and Franklin. Many other examples could be given, but our intention here is to be concise and to the point.

We think it no coincidence that Voltaire was educated for seven years by Jesuit priests at their College Louis-le-Grand. From them he undoubtedly learned to question the divine inspiration of Scripture (for which the Jesuits are legend, who prefer their Papal idol that they call "infallible" to the authority of God's Holy Word). With this in mind, we now refer to a quote from an early 19th century book on the Jesuit conspiracy to take over the world for the Pope. It was penned by a former Jesuit initiate named Jacopo Leone, who claimed to have left the order after learning of their dreadful ambitions, and who was compelled to warn others of their intent. At the very end of his writing, he related the following:

> "The fact, which I will make known in special publications, concerns the seventeenth century and a part of the eighteenth. I will demonstrate that Voltarianism prevailed in Italy during a whole century before Voltaire; that those who attacked mysteries and dogmas with language and sarcasms like his, were not libertines repudiated and condemned by the religious authority, or a handful of savans whose incredulity was confined to the circle of the cultivated class; but that the attack on the foundations of religion and morality was made in the very churches, from the pulpit, and by numerous preachers; that the numbers who flocked to hear them were immense, and that they enjoyed the countenance of the bishops and prelates. This horrible disorder was practiced in the most celebrated churches of Rome; it resisted the few feeble efforts made to put it down, and was still in existence when Voltaire appeared. The sacred buildings rang with loud shouts of laughter in approval of the most shameless commentaries. The acts of the patriarchs were held up to ridicule; the Song

of Songs afforded an ample theme for obscene jesting; the visions of the prophets were turned into derision, and themselves treated as addle-headed and delirious. The Apostles were not spared, and it was taught that everything concerning them was mere fable. Finally, Christ himself was outraged worse than he had ever been by his most rancorous enemies, and was accused of criminal intercourse with the Magdalene, the woman taken in adultery, and the woman of Samaria. Thus was absolute irreligion preached, and for so long a time did this poison flow from the pulpits. The Bible was scoffed at, and Christianity likened to a mythology." (*The Jesuit Conspiracy*, by Jacopo Leone, pp. 260-261)

~ *The Jesuits, Voltaire & The Founding Fathers*, Pinto[1568]

Even today, the first Jesuit Pope, Jorge Mario Bergoglio, is using cunning tactics of two steps forward, one step back, to inch civilization toward acceptance of what most consider "perverse".

Pope Says Church Is "Obsessed" With Gays, Abortion and Birth Control

Six months into his papacy, Pope Francis sent shock waves through the Roman Catholic church on Thursday with the publication of his remarks that the church had grown "obsessed" with abortion, gay marriage and contraception, and that he had chosen not to talk about those issues despite recriminations from critics. ~ Laurie Goodstein, NY Times[1569]

At the Vatican, a Shift in Tone Toward Gays and Divorce

In a marked shift in tone likely to be discussed in parishes around the world, an assembly of Roman Catholic bishops convened by Pope Francis at the Vatican released a preliminary document on Monday calling for the church to welcome and accept gay people, unmarried couples and those who have divorced, as well as the children of these less traditional families. ~ Elisabetta Povoledo and Laurie Goodstein, NY Times[1570]

When the recent Papal "Synod on the Family" extended overtures to accepting homosexuality, there was immediate reaction against the move and it was retracted.

Interestingly, a Jesuit took to the Liberal Huffington Post and explained that, if readers were angry or frustrated, they didn't understand what was going on.

> ...this has simply been the first formal phase of a longer conversation... So if you're overly energized about the synod, if this is for you an ecclesial soap-opera, or if you have used the word "revolution" in the context of describing this whole process, please, I beg you, relax. You likely haven't really understood what this synod actually is, anyway. ~ The Vatican's Synod on the Family, and Why You've Missed the Point, Rev. Michael Rogers, S.J.[1571]

Looking Behind the Curtain

Nimrod can be seen in the Sumerian epic of the giant Gilgamesh, and again as the Egyptian god Osiris and the Greek god Apollo.

Genesis 10:6-7 tell us that Nimrod was the son of Cush, son of Ham, the accursed son of Noah who at the very least looked upon and mocked his drunk and naked father and perhaps worse. [Genesis 9:21-22]

Who was the wife of Nimrod? Some say Enéh but many say Semiramis.[1572]

One legend surrounding them both is that Nimrod was executed by his great uncle Shem for his blasphemy and heresy. He was subsequently chopped up and scattered as a sign to others. His wife somehow managed to impregnate herself with his severed body part to conceive and birth their son Tammuz who was Nimrod reincarnated. Many presuppose that if there was ever any truth to the myth it was spun by this "Semiramis", herself, to cover the birth of an illegitimate child by another father.

When Nimrod was scattered upon the waters, it was Dagon the fish god that responded. Some legends state Dagon found the missing phallus for Semiramis, others that Dagon emerged from the waters as a reincarnated Nimrod.

> *One of the many sacred names by which Tammuz or Nimrod was called, when he reappeared in the Mysteries, after being slain, was Oannes.**

>> ** BEROSUS, BUNSEN'S Egypt. To identify Nimrod with Oannes, mentioned by Berosus as appearing out of the sea, it will be remembered that Nimrod has been proved to be Bacchus. Then, for proof that Nimrod or Bacchus, on being overcome by his enemies, was fabled to have taken refuge in the sea, see chapter 4, section i. When, therefore,*

> *he was represented as reappearing, it was natural that he should reappear in the very character of Oannes as a Fish-god. Now, Jerome calls Dagon, the well known Fish-god Piscem moeroris (BRYANT), "the fish of sorrow," which goes far to identify that Fish-god with Bacchus, the "Lamented one"; and the identification is complete when Hesychius tells us that some called Bacchus Ichthys, or "The fish."*
>
> ~ *The Two Babylons*, Alexander Hislop[1573]

"Oannes" is also a "bearer of light".

> *Oannes (Ὠάννης) was the name given by the Babylonian writer Berossus in the 3rd century [BC] to a mythical being who taught mankind wisdom. Berossus describes Oannes as having the body of a fish but underneath the figure of a man. He is described as dwelling in the Persian Gulf, and rising out of the waters in the daytime and furnishing mankind instruction in writing, the arts and the various sciences. Oannes and the Semitic god Dagon were considered identical.[3]* ~ Wikipedia[1574]

For many experts the similarity between the Catholic miter and the ancient fish garb worn by priests of Dagon is unmistakable. Often there are even occultic symbols where the eyes of the fish would be expected.

An interesting wood carving from Assyria connects Dagon to the All-Seeing Eye—an image Masons claim is of YHWH but is clearly a *Watcher*.

Figure 1.

> *This Figure represents Assyrian priests offering in the presence of what is supposed to be Baal-or the representative of the sun-and of the grove. The first is typified by the eye, with wings and a tail, which make it symbolic of the male triad and the female unit. The eye, with the central pupil, is in itself emblematic of the same. The grove represents mystically* le verger de Cypris. *On the right, stands the king; on the left are two priests, the foremost clothed with a fish's skin, the head forming the mitre, thus showing the origin of modem Christian bishops' peculiar head-*

dress. Arranged about the figures are, the sun ; a bird, perhaps the sacred dove, whose note, coa *or* coo, *has, in the Shemitic, some resemblance to an invitation to amorous gratification; the oval, symbol of the yoni; the basket, or bag, emblematic of the scrotum, and apparently the lotus.* ~ Ancient Pagan and Modern Christian Symbolism, Thomas Inman and John Newton[1575]

Another ancient depiction is even more curious, linking fish worship to the Virgin and Child.

This is taken from a photograph of a small bronze image in the Mayer collection of the Free Museum, in Liverpool. The figure stands about nine inches high, and represents Isis, Horus, and the fish. It is an apt illustration of an ancient custom, still prevalent amongst certain Christians, of reverencing a woman, said to be a virgin, giving suck to her child, and of the association of Isis, Venus, and Mary with the fish. Friday, for example, is, with the Romanists, both "fish day," and "dies Veneris." Fish are known, to be extraordinarily prolific. There was a belief that animals, noted for any peculiarity, imparted their virtues to those who ate them; consequently, tigers flesh was supposed to give courage, and snails to give sexual power. The use of fish in connubial feasts is still common. Those who consider it pious or proper to eat fish on Venus day, or Friday, proclaim themselves, unconsciously, adherents to those heathen ideas which deified parts about which no one now likes to talk. The fish has in one respect affinity with the mandrake. ~ Inman and Newton[1576]

Today's Catholic "Madonna and Christ" has a clear lineage back to Semiramis and Tammuz, Isis and Horus.[vv]

In Papal Italy, as travellers universally admit (except where the Gospel has recently entered), all appearance of worshipping the King Eternal and Invisible is almost extinct, while the Mother and the Child are the grand objects of worship. Exactly so, in this latter respect, also was it in ancient Babylon. The Babylonians, in their popular religion, supremely worshipped a Goddess Mother and a

---

[vv] It is now in vogue to claim Hislop has been "debunked" and these images clearly prove what authority makes such a claim. I have yet to hear *details* of why Hislop was wrong and that is always a sign of subterfuge.

> Son, who was represented in pictures and in images as an infant or child in his mother's arms. From Babylon, this worship of the Mother and the Child spread to the ends of the earth. In Egypt, the Mother and the Child were worshipped under the names of Isis and Osiris.* In India, even to this day, as Isi and Iswara; ** in Asia, as Cybele and Deoius; in Pagan Rome, as Fortuna and Jupiter-puer, or Jupiter, the boy; in Greece, as Ceres, the Great Mother, with the babe at her breast, or as Irene, the goddess of Peace, with the boy Plutus in her arms...
>
>> * Osiris, as the child called most frequently Horus. BUNSEN.
>>
>> ** KENNEDY'S Hindoo Mythology. Though Iswara is the husband of Isi, he is also represnted as an infant at her breast.
>
> ~ Hislop[1577]

Pagan obsession with sex and genitalia are more than simple licentious fixations; they are the means by which genetic experimentation by the Watchers can produce demigod world leaders.

These messages are clearly sent via the oldest architecture and have been frequently replicated in Catholic structures.

> We find it rather unwise on the part of Catholic writers to pour out their vials of wrath in such sentences as these: "In a multitude of pagodas, the phallic stone, ever and always assuming, like the Grecian batylos, the brutally indecent form of the lingham ... the Maha Deva."* Before casting slurs on a symbol whose profound metaphysical meaning is too much for the modern champions of that religion of sensualism par excellence, Roman Catholicism, to grasp, they are in duty bound to destroy their oldest churches, and change the form of the cupolas of their own temples. The Mahody of Elephanta, the Round Tower of Bhangulpore, the minarets of Islam — either rounded or pointed — are the originals of the Campanile column of San Marco, at Venice, of the Rochester Cathedral, and of the modern Duomo of Milan. All of these steeples, turrets, domes, and Christian temples, are the reproductions of the primitive idea of the lithos, the upright phallus. "The western tower of St. Paul's Cathedral, London," says the author of The Rosicrucians, "is one of the double lithoi placed always in front of every temple, Christian as well as heathen."† ~ Blavatsky[1578]

The Middle Eastern veil—taken to barbaric extremes by Islam—also has the same roots. An accusation has been levied by a Jesuit insider that Islam was created by the Vatican (we will examine that more closely in Chapter 18) and there is historical evidence that hints at this.

The Egyptian Isis was also represented as a Virgin Mother by her devotees, and as holding her infant son, Horus, in her arms. In some statues and basso-relievos, when she appears alone she is either completely nude or veiled from head to foot. But in the Mysteries, in common with nearly every other goddess, she is entirely veiled from head to foot, as a symbol of a mother's chastity.
~ Blavatsky[1579]

The Egyptian version of the legend of Nimrod has a fascinating twist; the good god Osiris (Nimrod) is murdered by his evil brother Set (Shem) while his wife Isis (Semiramis) manages to conceive his son Horus with him, posthumously.

It is this undead body part of Osiris that sprouts up the many obelisks around the world and the most significant of them are erected across from domed structures that represent the womb of Isis.

There are two very important places where this connection of obelisk and dome are made: Washington DC and Rome. [italics suspended]

Unrecognized by the vast majority of peoples around the world is the greatest conspiracy of all time, sitting right out in the open in Washington DC and at the Vatican. It is an ancient, magical, talismanic diagram—the Lost Symbol—based on the history and cult of Isis, Osiris, Horus, and the prophecy of the deity's return.

The primeval concept was designed in antiquity for the express purpose of regeneration, resurrection, and apotheosis, for deity incarnation from the underworld to earth's surface through union of the respective figures—the Dome (ancient structural representation of the womb of Isis) and the Obelisk (ancient representation of the erect male phallus of Osiris). ...

The U.S. capital has been called the "Mirror Vatican" due to the strikingly similar layout and design of its primary buildings and streets. This is no accident. In fact, America's forefathers first named the capital city "Rome." And, like Rome, Washington DC has seven hills corresponding to the heavenly layout of the stars of Pleiades. But the parallelism between Washington and the Vatican is most clearly illustrated by the Capital building and Dome facing the Obelisk known as the Washington Monument, and at St. Peter's Basilica in the Vatican by a similar Dome facing a familiar Obelisk—both of which were, I according to their own official records, fashioned after the Roman Pantheon, the circular domed Rotunda "dedicated to all pagan gods." This layout—a domed temple facing an Obelisk—is an ancient, alchemical blueprint that holds significant esoteric meaning.

In ancient times, the Obelisk represented the god Osiris' "missing" male organ, which Isis was not able to find after her husband/brother was slain and chopped into fourteen pieces by Seth. Isis replaced the missing organ with an Obelisk and magically impregnated herself with Horus, the resurrected Osiris. This legend formed the core of Egyptian cosmology and was fantastically venerated on the most imposing scale throughout all of Egypt by towering Obelisks, including at Karnak where the upright Obelisks (of Osiris) were "vitalized" or "stimulated" from the energy of the masturbatory Sun god Ra shining down upon them. Modern people, especially in America, may view these symbols as profane or pornographic, but they were in fact ritualized objects the ancients believed could produce tangible reactions, properties, or "manifestations" within the material world. The Obelisk and Dome as imitations of the deities' male and female reproductive organs could, through government representation, invoke into existence the being or beings symbolized by them. This is why inside the temple or Dome, temple prostitutes representing the human manifestation of the goddess were also available for ritual sex as a form of imitative magic...

The Obelisk in St. Peter's Square in Rome is not just any Obelisk, but one removed and transferred there from ancient Heliopolis, the city of "On" in the Bible dedicated to Ra, Osiris and Isis. ...

When visitors to Washington DC tour the Capitol, one of the

unquestionable highlights is to visit the womb of Isis—the Capitol Dome—where, when peering upward from inside Isis' continuously pregnant belly, tourists can see hidden in plain sight Brumidi's 4,664-square-foot fresco, *The Apotheosis of George Washington*. The word "apotheosis" means to "deify" or to "become a god," and explains part of the reason U.S. presidents, military commanders, and members of Congress lay in state in the Capitol Dome. The womb of Isis is where they go to death to magically reach apotheosis and transform into gods. ~ *Apollyon Rising: 2012*, Thomas Horn[1580]

Constantino Brumidi helped insure the stamp of the Vatican on America's future. He was imprisoned as a thief of Vatican treasures but his exile to the United States resulted in extremely loyal work for Rome.

Brumidi was born in Rome before Italy was a nation. ...

At the Roman villa of the wealthy Torlonia family, he was in

"As above, so below."

charge of decorating the new theater with murals including trompe l'oeil architectural forms and classical motifs that he later adapted for the Capitol. Brumidi also worked extensively for the Vatican, restoring frescoes for Pope Gregory XVI and painting the official portrait of Pope Pius IX. His last murals in Rome were in a small church dedicated in 1851.

Brumidi helped support his family with the coffee shop inherited from his father. He also served as captain in the civic guard authorized by Pius IX, but when the pope fled the city, and a republic was declared in 1849, Brumidi was caught up in the revolution when he removed valuable objects from church buildings for safekeeping. After the pope returned to power, Brumidi was among many arrested and accused of serious crimes. Despite numerous testimonies in his favor, and after 13 months of incarceration, he was sentenced to 18 years in prison. The pope pardoned him with the understanding that he would be leaving for America, where he was promised work in planned churches. ~

Explore Capitol Hill, Architect of the Capitol.gov[1581]

"As above, so below."

For this reason, Washington, DC, has a great many "reflecting pools" scattered around the city.

One of the most renown of these is the Lincoln Memorial pool. Both the pool and the Memorial were designed by American Architect Henry Bacon, Jr. Bacon was deeply influenced by his brother Francis Henry Bacon who was one of the leaders of the Greek Assos excavation.[1582]

These American Bacons were related through their father, Captain Henry Bacon, Sr. of Massachusetts to esoteric English philosopher Sir Francis Bacon.[1583,1584]

While standing at the top of the Memorial stairs and looking at the reflecting pool one's gaze is to the massive Phallus of Osiris, known to the uninitiated as the "Washington Monument".

When George Washington first learned of an expensive effort to commemorate him in stone, he scrapped the project but it was later resurrected with a decidedly pagan twist.

> *Gaslighting Communication*
>
> When you see the "Washington Monument" do you think of George Washington?
>
> When you see the "All-Seeing Eye" do you think of the God of the Bible?
>
> When a Freemason tells you they worship "the Great Architect of the Universe" do you think they mean YHWH?
>
> These are all tools of propaganda to mask who the Luciferians are and whom they serve.
>
> The negative side is they have been completely successful and no one questions them.
>
> The positive side is that they do this out of fear; fear of *you* and how you'd react if you knew the truth.

> *In 1783, the Continental Congress voted to erect a statue of Washington, commander-in-chief of the American army during the Revolutionary War, in the nation's yet-to-be constructed permanent capital city. However, after Washington became president, he scrapped the plans for his memorial, as federal government funds were tight and he didn't want to use public money for the project. After Washington died in 1799, Congress considered building him a pyramid-shaped mausoleum to be housed in the Capitol rotunda; however, the plan never came to fruition. ...*

> *Robert Mills' winning design called for a pantheon (a temple-like building) featuring 30 stone columns and statues of Declaration of Independence signers and Revolutionary War heroes. A statue of Washington driving a horse-drawn chariot would reside above the main entrance and a 600-foot-tall Egyptian obelisk would rise from the pantheon's center.* ~ Elizabeth Nix, History.com[1585]

Although some sources list the width of each side at the base of the obelisk at 55 feet and 1 inch, others list it as 55.5 feet (next time you visit, take a tape measure). If the 55 ½ foot measurement is correct, the number in inches is 666.

What is in less dispute is the overall height: 555.5 feet and that exchanges to 6,666 inches as listed on this helpful-but-anonymous web site below.

> *The sides of the monument are aligned with the cardinal directions. At ground level the sides are 55.5 feet (666 inches) long and the monument is 555.5 feet high. The 10 to one ratio between the sidelength and the height was modeled after ancient Egyptian obelisks that have this same ratio.*
>
> *The 555.5 foot height of the monument converts to 6666 inches.*[1586]

Egypt has been more than the source of inspiration for such structures. There are three similar obelisks in London, Paris and New York City, all of them mislabeled "Cleopatra's Needle".

> ***Cleopatra's Needle*** *is the popular name for each of three Ancient Egyptian obelisks re-erected in London, Paris, and New York City during the nineteenth century. The obelisks in London and New York are a pair, the one in Paris, also part of a pair came from a different site in Luxor where its twin remains. Although all three needles are genuine Ancient Egyptian obelisks, their shared nickname is a misnomer, as they have no connection with Queen Cleopatra VII of Egypt, and were already over a thousand years old in her lifetime.* ~ Wikipedia[1587]

The mislabeling is almost certainly as a result of the true meaning behind these structures being instantly offensive to the uninitiated: pagan/demonic phallic symbols for sex magick.

> *It's 70 feet tall, 220 tons and the city's oldest artifact — but many New Yorkers don't know it exists.*

> *Cleopatra's Needle, a 3,500-year-old obelisk from Ancient Egypt, survived a voyage to Central Park more than a century ago and has been a park treasure ever since.*
>
> *Nestled behind the Metropolitan Museum of Art, the -hieroglyph-covered column was commissioned by one of Egypt's most powerful pharaohs and reigns as among the last of its kind.*
>
> *"It's our oldest inhabitant," says Dr. Bob Brier, a renowned Egyptologist at Long Island University's C.W. Post Campus in Brookville, LI.*
>
> *"When it was erected, everyone went bananas," he adds. "Then it was forgotten. Trees grew up around the knoll and obscured it. People just stopped thinking about it."*
>
> *Still, Brier says the artifact's history has enough twists and turns to make a Hollywood film.*
>
> *Erected in Heliopolis around 1450 BC, the obelisk was toppled centuries later by Persian invaders. It was buried in the dust for 500 years more until the Romans snatched it for Julius Caesar.* ~ Kate Briquelet, New York Post[1588]

The muslim "Khedive of Egypt", Ismail Pasha was convinced[1589] to gift it to the United States where railroad magnate William Vanderbilt[1590] brought it. His great, great grandson is CNN host Anderson Cooper[1591], a homosexual[1592] trained by the CIA.[1593]

A Sign

Alberto Rivera claimed to be an ex-Jesuit priest and convert to Evangelical Christianity. He joined with Christian publisher Jack Chick and used comic books to give inside information on the Company from a position of safety the same way "faction" gives insiders a venue to give up secrets—because they're telling stories *based* on fact that are still considered "fiction".

The comic series Chick published was titled "Alberto" and Monsterwax gave an excellent summary of the "Godfather" issue. [italics suspended]

> According to Alberto, both the Nazi and Communist parties were started by the Vatican. The Vatican has supposedly wanted to move to Jerusalem and set up shop there, since that is where Christianity started. However, the Orthodox Jews have stopped her, and that's why they are on "Rome's hit list." During the Crusades in the

Middle Ages, children from Jewish and Roman Catholic unions were later recruited to serve as crusaders to capture the Holy Land from Islamic control. Of course, this effort failed. The Vatican had another rival to contend with: the Greek and Russian Orthodox churches. Under Vatican influence, the Communist party was created for the sole purpose of destroying the Czar of Russia since he protected the Russian Orthodox Church. The Communist revolutionaries were nothing but a tool to wipe out these rivals. Later, the Vatican bankrolled the beginning of the Nazi party to destroy the Jews so the Vatican could realize it's dream of moving to Jerusalem. In the 20th century, various popes from Pius X, Benedict XV, and Pius XII supported World Wars I and II to wipe out Jews. Alberto says that Hitler's seminal work "Mein Kampf" was ghost-written by a Jesuit priest named Staempfle. This book served to fuel the Nazi party in Germany, but what history books don't record is that the Holocaust was another Inquisition orchestrated by the Vatican. During World War II, the Jesuits propped up Hitler, Mussolini, and Franco as "The Defenders of the Faith" to conquer the world for the Vatican, since she wasn't satisfied with merely taking over the city of Jerusalem alone. The Vatican wanted to take over the whole world, but Protestants, Jews and democracy got in their way.

The other rival, the Greek Orthodox churches, were subjugated in Yugoslavia by the Ustachi killing squads made up of Roman Catholic priests. While all of the killing and maiming occurred during the 20th century, the Vatican also plotted to cover itself in the event that the Nazis lost World War II. This plot included making everybody believe the Vatican had nothing to do with the war, and in time convince the world the Holocaust never happened. In America, the Vatican's agents were at work to wipe out the Protestant movement through ecumenism. The secret sign to be given to the Jesuits worldwide when this was accomplished by the Vatican was when a President of the United States took his oath of office facing an obelisk (a four sided pillar that resembles the Washington Monument and the one in St. Peter's Square in the Vatican). ~ Monsterwax[1594]

In investigating the assassination of Abraham Lincoln, so many ties were found to the Vatican that the United States severed relations with the "sovereign entity" in 1867[1595]. The man to change that in late 1983 was Ronald Reagan[1596]. Perhaps knowingly or unknowingly, it was his administration that signaled the complete control of America by "the Unseen Hand".

United States Diplomatic Relations With the Vatican

Pub. L. 98–164, title I, §134, Nov. 22, 1983, 97 Stat. 1029, provided that: "In order to provide for the establishment of United States diplomatic relations with the Vatican, the Act entitled 'An Act making Appropriations for the Consular and Diplomatic Expenses of the Government for the Year ending thirtieth June, eighteen hundred and sixty-eight, and for other purposes', approved February 28, 1867, is amended by repealing the following sentence (14 Stat. 413): 'And no money hereby or otherwise appropriated shall be paid for the support of an American legation at Rome, from and after the thirtieth day of June, eighteen hundred and sixty-seven.'." ~ Management of Foreign Affairs, United States Code[1597]

On January 20th, 1981, Ronald Wilson Reagan was the first President of the United States to conduct his inauguration on the west front of the Capitol instead of the east front. As Alberto Rivera predicted, he was facing the Washington Monument.[1598]

Reagan was handled by Vatican agents as soon as he had a future on the national stage...perhaps sooner. [italics suspended]

> For all of [Michael] Deaver's expertise in running the campaign, when Reagan lost the 1980 Iowa caucus, William J. Casey was appointed as campaign director. A Knight of Malta, Casey had worked for the OSS in Germany. ...
>
> After Casey was named head of the CIA, the agency employed undercover operatives to lobby members of the Curia[ww]... In addition, private and charitable organizations continually fed information to the Vatican from around the world at the same time American intelligence officials in Rome were providing their appraisals of people and events to the Vatican. This flow of information only increased when the US established full diplomatic relations with the Vatican in 1984. ...
>
> Within a month of Reagan's election, Archbishop (later Cardinal) Pio Laghi was assigned to Washington DC directly from his service in Buenos Aires. Described as a "charming if ambitious career diplomat... conservative because he is ambitious for his career,"

[ww] *The Roman Curia is the administrative apparatus of the Holy See and the central governing body through which the Roman Pontiff conducts the business of the entire Catholic Church.* ~ *Roman Curia*, Wikipedia
http://en.wikipedia.org/wiki/Roman_Curia

Laghi was mentioned as a candidate for Vatican Secretary of State.[29] The US had used Argentina as a training ground for right-wing militias and the archbishop had also served in Managua in the 1950s, so Laghi already had high level contacts in the Reagan administration.

In Washington, a close relationship developed between Laghi, Casey and fellow Knight of Malta Judge William Clark, Reagan's National Security Advosir and one of his earliest California supporters. Clark was referred to as Reagan's "closest spiritual partner."[30] "'Casey and I dropped into his [Laghi's] residence early mornings during critical times to gather his comments and counsel' said Clark. ... On at least six occasions Laghi came to the White House and met with Clark or the president; each time, he entered the White House through the southwest gate in order to avoid reporters."[31] ~ *The Neo-Catholics*, Betty Clermont[1599]

National Treasure

It was signer of the Declaration of Independence Francis Hopkinson—a banker and judge—who originally designed the reverse side of the Great Seal of the United States in all its esoteric glory.[1600]

Hopkinson also designed the first American flag but with 13 *six*-pointed stars[1601]: "as above, so below".

Hopkinson died young and there are few records allowed regarding who is on the Freemasonic rolls but at least one Mason claims him.[1602]

Although whether Hopkinson was or wasn't a Mason is hotly contested, his work does speak for itself. His original seal was a 13-stepped, unfinished pyramid with the Latin *PERENNIS* above it, "FOREVER". During the 3rd Committee for the Great Seal, heraldist William Barton added the All-Seeing Eye and "DEO FAVENTE" to Hopkins' design, "FOREVER, (with) GOD'S FAVOR"[1603]—yet nowhere is there a Christian precedent for depicting the Presence of YHWH as an "All-Seeing Eye".

All of those mottos were done away with and replaced with what we have today by the Secretary of the Continental Congress from 1774 to 1789, Charles Thomson.

Immigrating from Ireland with his father, Thomson is oddly described as an "Irish Catholic Presbyterian"[1604]. Thomson is reported to have been orphaned at 10. He was adopted by benefactors and immersed himself in Greek and Latin—at the time, the Holy Bible was the foundation for these studies.[1605]

But was Thomson a Christian? [italics suspended]

> Between the years of 1774-1789 a positioned role of Congressional Secretary was held by none other than, Charles Thomson. Thomson's role as secretary to Congress was not limited to clerical duties, from the words of Boyd Schlenther, "Thomson took a direct role in the conduct of foreign affairs." It has also been suggested by Fred S. Rolater that Charles Thomson was essentially the "Prime Minister of the United States".[1] Leader in the revolutionary crisis of the 1770s, Thomson was also revered by John Adams as the "Samuel Adams of Philadelphia".
>
> In later time Thomson joined efforts with William Barton where both works brought about the designing of the Great Seal of the United States.
>
> Charles Thomson is clearly a name that's hidden within the shadows of our founding fathers.
>
> But he, himself is reckoned as a founder.
>
> Holding all official Governmental records of the Continental Congress and the Government of the United States, Thomson had an educated inside view of such matters that arose through the real life character of our forming day.
>
> Of all who engaged in America's Revolution, Charles Thomson is said to have been the closest to the work and the people of this time.
>
> As the events of America's Revolution unfolded Charles Thomson documented a detailed account which he then found the encouragement of many to publish, Thomson with his own reasoning declined.
>
>> No, for I should contradict all the histories of the great events of the Revolution, and show by my account of men, motives and measures, that we are wholly indebted to the agency of providence for its successful issue. Let the world admire the supposed wisdom and valor of our great men. Perhaps they may adopt the qualities that have been ascribed to them, and thus good may be done. I shall not undeceive future generations.
>
> ~ *Mirror of Daze*, Phillip Garncarz[1606]

Thomson is said to have then destroyed his personal journal and notes; evidence of this so-called "deception".

What was the deception?

Perhaps it can be found in the Latin phrases he added to the reverse of the Great Seal.

ANNUIT CŒPTIS

NOVUS ORDO SECLORUM

"The undertaking has been approved: a New Order of the Ages!"

But exactly *who* "approved the undertaking"?

At least one blogger believes that Thomson's allusion to "Providence" was a typical 18th century dodge used by men who lived in a Christian society and feared to speak of Luciferian influence.[1607]

As I have mentioned before: Latin is the language of *Rome* and used often by her emissaries to mask her influence.

The large Roman Numeral at the bottom of the pyramid equates to the number "1776"—either the year of America's Declaration of Independence, *or* the year that Jesuit Adam Weishaupt created the Secret Society within the Freemason Secret Society (the "Illuminati").

Shrine On You Crazy Diamond

The reverse of the Great Seal, itself, remained hidden until 1934. [italics suspended]

> In 1934, Secretary of Agriculture, soon-to-be Vice-President (1940-44) and 32nd degree freemason Henry Wallace submitted a proposal to the president to mint a coin depicting the seal's obverse and reverse. ...Franklin D. Roosevelt, also a 32nd degree freemason, liked the idea but opted to instead place it on the dollar bill. ...
>
> "Roosevelt as he looked at the colored reproduction of the Seal was first struck with the representation of the 'All-Seeing Eye,' a Masonic representation of Great Architect the Universe. Next he was impressed with the idea that the foundation for the new order of

the ages had been laid in 1776 (May 1st, 1776, founding of the Illuminati) but would be completed only under the eye of the Great Architect. Roosevelt like myself was a 32nd degree Mason. He suggested that the Seal be put on the dollar bill rather that a coin."

Besides being a high ranking freemason and having the distinction of introducing socialism into the American political system, Roosevelt was a member of a secret society called the Ancient Arabic Order of Nobles of the Mystics Shrine (Shriners), attaining the grade of a Knight of Pythias. The Order of Nobles and Mystics claimed to be an offshoot of the Illuminati.

Freemasons, Walter Flemming and William Florence founded an American branch in New York, 1872. Membership in the order was open only to Freemasons who had reached the 32nd degree of the Ancient and Accepted Scottish Rite or those who've attained the last degree of the York Rite, the thirteenth degree (Knight Templar).

The Order of Nobles and Mystics have origins which date back to the seventh century – apparently founded by a descendent of Mohammed. Author Michael Howard describes the Order's symbols.

"The symbol of the Order is a crescent moon, made from the claws of a Bengal tiger, engraved with a pyramid, an urn and a pentagram. The crescent is suspended from a scimitar and in the Order is a representation of **the Universal Mother worshipped in ancient times as Isis**. The horns of the crescent point downwards because it represents the setting moon of the old faith at the rising of the Sun of the new religion of the brotherhood of humanity." — *The Occult Conspiracy*, p.93 [emphasis mine] [xx]

According to Anton LaVey, founder of the Church of Satan, Roosevelt's Shriner's have a ritual similar to a satanic ritual called "The Ceremony of the Stifling Air", or better known as "L'air Epais." LaVey says that this rite was originally performed "when entering the sixth degree of the Order of the Knights Templar." Remember that if the Masonic candidate chooses to follow the York Rite, after he completes the 13th degree called the Knight Templar, he can apply to become a Shriner. ~ *The All-Seeing Eye*, Terry

---

[xx] Does not the face of the Pharaoh resemble Barack Hussein Obama?!

Melanson[1608]

History does not record the fact that Roosevelt had a direct line of communication with the Vatican and Papal authorities were extremely pleased with his agenda to yank America to the Left via a new Socialist order.

> *President Franklin D. Roosevelt sent Myron C. Taylor as his personal representative to the Holy See in 1939. Taylor served until 1950. Roosevelt had the support of two American cardinals from different ends of the political spectrum. Chicago's Cardinal George Mundelein supported the New Deal and its call for social action. When Mundelein died, Taylor, under orders from Roosevelt asked Vatican Secretary of State Cardinal Luigi Maglione to consider Bishop Bernard Sheil, another social liberal as Mundelein's replacement. ~ The Neo-Catholics*, Betty Clermont[1609]

Two popular Shriners of Roosevelt's generation were Douglas MacArthur[1610] and Roosevelt's successor Harry Truman.[1611]

Some have claimed Dwight Eisenhower was a quiet Shriner but he was a frequent attendee of Bohemian Grove.[1612]

Eisenhower's wartime rise to power was unprecedented as he was nothing more than an aide to Douglas MacArthur and had never held an active duty command[1613]. Not an impressive resumé for the Supreme Allied Commander—unless, of course, he wasn't really in charge.

Washington: Demonically-Controlled

The layout of Washington DC was originally designed by Pierre Charles "Peter" L'Enfant. L'Enfant was recruited[1614] by the "playwright, watchmaker, inventor, musician, diplomat, fugitive, spy, publisher, horticulturalist, arms dealer, satirist, financier, and revolutionary (both French and American)"[1615] and all-around Renaissance man Pierre-Augustin Caron de Beaumarchais.

What is most notable about Beaumarchais is that he came from a family of Huguenots but had converted to

Catholicism[1616], many assume as a result of Papal persecution. As Beaumarchais recruited men to fight in the American Revolution, it appears that he favored men who shared his Catholic faith such as L'Enfant. Few historians remark on L'Enfant's religious beliefs although as late as 1949, it was proudly proclaimed in a Catholic comic book entitled, *Design For A Democracy: Pierre L'Enfant, Catholic Architect.*

Another well-kept secret is that L'Enfant was also a Mason, belonging to Holland Lodge No. 8 in New York City[1617]. L'Enfant was yet another example of the supposedly at-odds Catholic Mason.

Whether an agent for Rome or not, L'Enfant strikes a sympathetic character. He was a military engineer during the Revolutionary War and was wounded at the Siege of Savannah in 1779.

As L'Enfant built his Masonic capital, he crossed the one man that had the power to cause his downfall.

No less an authority than George Washington dismissed L'Enfant because he had demolished the home of Daniel Carroll[1618], the premier Catholic patriarch of the New World.[yy]

The Carrolls were thoroughly invested in the American Revolution. Cousin Charles Carroll signed the Declaration of Independence and Daniel was one of only two Catholics to sign the Constitution and one of only 5 men to have signed both Constitution and the Articles of Confederation.[1619]

Daniel Carroll's brother John was a Jesuit and the first Arch Bishop of Baltimore[1620]. John Carroll founded a private school for boys, and named it "Georgetown".[1621]

Tolerating Treason

Nearly all of America's moral and ethical woes can be traced to the failure of Christian citizens to claim preeminence for their Faith.

Interestingly, there is no basis for the idea that "all religions are equal" either in America's founding or the Bible.

Although America was torn between the ancient pagan mystics of Masonry and passionate, devout Christians, Believers gave a good showing and non-Christians openly acknowledged the ascendance of the Christian Faith.

[yy] Was this a secret message of resistance against the Carroll Clan? Read on to find out just how powerful they were.

> *"It can not be emphasized too strongly or too often that this great nation was founded, not by religionists, but by Christians; not on religions, but on the Gospel of Jesus Christ. For this very reason peoples of other faiths have been afforded asylum, prosperity and freedom of worship here."* ~ Patrick Henry, March 23, 1775 at the Second Virginian Convention given at St. John's Church in Richmond, Virginia.

In response to Secretary of State John Marshall regarding the prospect of an influx of atheist devotees to Thomas Paine, President John Adams stated;

> *The German letter proposing to introduce into this country a company of schoolmasters, painters, poets, &c., all of them disciples of Mr. Thomas Paine, will require no answer. I had rather countenance the introduction of Ariel and Caliban* [Shakespearian demons], *with a troop of spirits the most mischievous from fairy land.*[1622]

As far as "tolerance" in the Bible for all religions goes, the opposite is found therein. Access to the Father and to Heaven is only through Jesus Christ [John 14:6]. It is in His Name, alone, that there is Salvation [Acts 4:12]. The entirety of all Creation was made through Jesus Christ and for him [Colossians 1:16]. And after telling Pontius Pilate *at that moment*, His Kingdom was "not of this world", three days later He would ascend to His Throne as King of the Universe [Mark 16:19] and the subjugation of His enemies is ongoing! [Psalm 110:1]

Today, "tolerance" and religious relativism is now taken to such an extreme that satanists have required equal consideration in the capital of Florida and have been allowed to erect a Christmas display for Lucifer.[1623]

In Conservative Oklahoma, satanists have installed a children's shrine to Baphomet in Oklahoma City.

Once equal consideration was given, the competition was smashed—literally.

On October 24th, 2014, a satan worshipper drove his car into the now highly controversial marble replica of the Ten Commandments on the Oklahoma City Capitol grounds, destroying it. He claims he urinated on it first.[1624]

This universal religious pluralism was all started by Jesuit John Carroll.

Instrumental in obtaining religious tolerance for Catholics, [John] Carroll worked to preserve the Church property which had belonged to the Jesuits before the order was disbanded. In 1784 he was appointed Supreme of Missions. Pius VI named him bishop of Baltimore in 1789... ~ the Encyclopedia of World Biography[1625]

Protesting

In Virginia, not everyone was comfortable with the overbearing presence of the Carroll family.

Jesuit Archbishop John Carroll was forced to take to newspapers to defend Rome[1626] and more than one Protestant American was questioning whether "Papal Infallibility" would cause Catholic clergy to commit acts against the best interest of the new nation.

Charles Wharton was an English Jesuit until he began to be troubled by what he had found in the Bible regarding how to treat "heretic" Protestant brethren in Christ and his own Catholic hierarchy. Wharton left the Company of Loyola and departed from England so that he could return to his native state of Maryland where he dawned the vestal sash of a Protestant preacher and began to counter John Carroll.

> *"There was a time, when, like you, I gloried in my religion; I daily thanked God, that I was not, like other men, heretics, scizmatics and infidels; I subscribed with unfeigned sincerity to that article of your belief; That the Roman church is the mother and mistress of all churches, and that out of her communion no salvation can be obtained."**
>
> ** See the famous creed of Pope Pius IV. the present standard of orthodoxy in the Roman church. ~ The Principal Points of Controversy Between the Protestant and Roman Churches,* Reverend Charles Henry Wharton[1627]

Although Wharton was taught, as a Jesuit, to be blindly obedient to the Pope, Scripture suggested to him otherwise.

> *To "prove all things, and hold fast that which is good," was the important advice of an inspired apostle. 1 Thess. v. I regarded it as an essential duty of a minister of religion " to be ready always to give an answer to every man that asketh him a reason of the hope that is in him, with meekness and fear." 1 Pet. iii. 15. In a word, the positive injunction of the beloved disciple of Jesus, " not to believe every spirit, but try the spirits, whether they be of God," 1*

John iv. 1. was a sufficient voucher for the lawfulness and expediency oft inquiry.

Neither transubstantiation, nor the infallibility of the Roman church, are taught more explicitly as articles of faith, than the impossibility of being saved out of the communion of this church. That Roman Catholics profess some tenets supernumerary, and inimical to Christian faith, may be the opinion of a Protestant: but that Protestants of sense and education are in a state of damnation, must be the religious belief of a consistent Roman Catholic.

The absurdity and uncharitableness of believing with the assent of faith, that the members of no Christian church but our own can be saved, is, therefore, to me quite palpable and evident.

If a man's belief be not rational; if he submit to human authority without weighing or understanding the doctrines which it inculcates, this belief is not faith—it is credulity; it is weakness. With equal merit might he be a Jew, a mussulman, or an idolater, as each of these grounds his principles upon authority, whose decrees he deems sacred, whilst he neglects to examine them. ~ Reverend Wharton[1628]

A Walk Around the Park

Despite Pierre L'Enfant's dismissal, his original plans for Washington, DC were kept loyal to his Masonic vision—so much so that he later demanded an astounding $95,500 from Congress given that he was dismissed without being paid for services rendered.[1629]

L'Enfant was replaced by Andrew Ellicott and his surveyor, Benjamin Banneker—a talented free black farmer. Although he had left with his plans, Ellicott and Banneker stayed true to the Mason's intent.[1630]

As a result of Dan Brown's *da Vinci Code* and follow up novel *The Lost Symbol*, the Washington Post addressed the question of Masonic architecture in the capital.

1. The Temple of the Supreme Council of the 33rd and Last Degree of the Ancient and Accepted Scottish Rite of Freemasonry for the Southern Jurisdiction of the United States

Or House of the Temple, for short. It's the massive edifice 13 blocks north of the White House, guarded by two sphinxes.

Inside are vast halls with ancient motifs and Masonic symbols —

> *the double-headed eagle, the famous square-and-compass with the letter G (for God and Geometry). The number 33 is big: There are 33 columns on the outside, 33 chairs in a ceremonial room. There's also a 33 on the cover of Brown's book, stamped inside a triangle above the Latin motto: "Order out of Chaos." ...*
>
> **2. The L'Enfant Street Plan**
>
> *Let's drive south on 16th Street toward the White House — straight into the heart of the Pentagram.*
>
> *Brown and his publisher have been issuing riddles and ciphers for fans to solve on Facebook and Twitter. One was the word "L'Enfant."*
>
> *Another consisted of five pairs of numbers, which turned out to be the latitude and longitude for the White House, Washington Circle, Dupont Circle, Logan Circle and Mount Vernon Square. Draw lines on the avenues connecting the points (pretend Rhode Island doesn't stop at Connecticut) and you get a five-pointed star.*
>
> *For years Masons have wasted a lot of breath pointing out that five-pointed stars may be demonic, but they aren't particularly Masonic.*
>
> *But wait: It's also possible to divine a six-pointed star on the map east of the Capitol; and a square-and-compass centered on the Capitol. Those are Masonic symbols. Busted!?*
>
> *A couple of problems: Pierre L'Enfant, who conceived the street design in 1791, was not a Mason...* ~ David Montgomery and Monica Hesse, the Washington Post[1631]

We've already shown he was on the rolls of Holland Lodge No. 8 in NY.

And as for a broken pentagram, it is actually a potent symbol of black magic.

> *The pentagram is used extensively in black magic, but when so used its form always differs in one of three ways: The star may be broken at one point by not permitting the converging lines to touch; it may be inverted by having one point down and two up; or it may be distorted by having the points of varying lengths. When used in black magic, the pentagram is called the "sign of the cloven hoof," or the footprint of the Devil. The star with two points upward is also called the "Goat of Mendes," because the inverted star is the*

same shape as a goat's head. When the upright star turns and the upper point falls to the bottom, it signifies the fall of the Morning Star. ~ The Secret Teachings of All Ages, Manly Palmer Hall[1632]

We've also already suggested the "G" could be a reference to the Italian *la Compagnia di Gesù*.

And the "double-headed eagle" is certainly a kindred of the two keys on the Vatican "Coat of Arms" symbolizing both spiritual and temporal authority. [italics suspended]

> Did we mention that 16th Street is Washington's "Rose Line"? [the Rosicrucians] Thomas Jefferson ... conceived that 16th Street would be the prime meridian for the new world. The meridian line would pass through the White House. He imagined that a monument to George Washington would be placed on the spot where the meridian line intersected a straight line drawn west from the U.S. Capitol. Unfortunately, the Washington Monument had to be located slightly off the Rose Line where the ground was firmer.
>
> Continue the intersecting line from the Capitol across the Potomac River and you hit a place called Rosslyn, which, as "Code" readers know, is also the name of the sacred Templar chapel in Scotland. According to Brown's fiction, Rosslyn and Rose Line are linguistically connected: Rosslyn-Roslin-Rose Line.
>
> So the Masonic headquarters — built more than a century after L'Enfant went to work — is on Washington's Rose Line. And at the foot of the Rose Line, in Lafayette Park, the key statues depict Masons, according to Hodapp: Andrew Jackson, Lafayette, Kosciusko, Von Steuben and Rochambeau.

3. Statue of Albert Pike

> Hiding in plain site [sic] in Judiciary Square is said to be the only outdoor statue of a Confederate general in Washington.
>
> ...He was also a sovereign grand commander of the Scottish Rite Masons.
>
> His big, bearded likeness is almost lost in the canopy of trees. At his feet is a woman holding a banner with the double-headed eagle, the triangle and the number 33. The 33 is a specific reference to the Scottish Rite. Most Masons are not Scottish Rite. Washington wasn't. The Scottish Rite was founded in 1801 — two years after Washington died, a decade after the city was laid out. ...

4. The Capitol

In September 1793, Washington donned a ceremonial Masonic apron and helped lay the cornerstone of the Capitol, a ritual complete with a silver trowel, marble gavel and the sprinkling of corn, wine and oil.

Washington's participation was special for Masons. He was the president of the country, but he was simultaneously being a Mason.
...

High on the Capitol Rotunda's domed ceiling is Brumidi's dramatic portrayal of the "Apotheosis of Washington" — the Mason ascending to heaven. Of 100 or so statues in Statuary Hall and elsewhere in the building, Hodapp counts at least 30 Masons. And he found a panel on the doors of the Senate depicting the cornerstone ceremony, Washington wearing his apron.

5. George Washington Masonic National Memorial

[Completely unreliable account already countered in these pages.]

6. Kryptos, Central Intelligence Agency, Langley

...The public can't visit, but the agency has a little Web tour we can call up on our laptops.

Created in 1990 by sculptor James Sanborn, the copper and stone Kryptos has four panels inscribed with letters, concealing four coded messages. Three have been solved. Still encrypted is a message with about 97 characters. What does it say?

Shugarts was among those who spotted the almost-exact coordinates of Kryptos's location on the jacket of "The Da Vinci Code." Shugarts also found on the jacket the phrase "only WW knows," which is part of one of the decoded messages of Kryptos. WW is generally believed to refer to former spy chief William Webster... — unless WW stands for William Wirt, who ran on the Anti-Masonic Party ticket in 1832, and whose skull was supposedly stolen from his grave. The skull and bones were reunited by Smithsonian anthropologists. ~ Montgomery and Hesse, Washington Post[1633]

Also in the article is a "debunking" of how the Seal and the back of the $1 bill are not Masonic.

But perhaps the strongest example of success in Masons communing with interdimensional intelligences is the fact that all of the major colonial Eastern Seaboard cities line up on a "ley line"—a significant alignment of locations for tapping in to hidden energies...or entities.

> ...the cities of Boston, New York, Philadelphia, Baltimore, and Washington D.C. are all on a perfect diagonal that continues down to Teohitican and all the way up to Stonehenge, Troy, and Baalbak. London to Giza and Paris to Dendera are almost equidistant parallel lines as well. ~ Eric Dubay, the Atlantean Conspiracy[1634]

Moths to the Flame of "Knowledge"

Whether the Jesuits created other secret societies may be up for debate but one thing is for certain and another not far from that; the United States of America was founded by Masons and the Company of Loyola has swallowed up many of them. [italics suspended]

> At least fifty out of the fifty-six signers of the Declaration of Independence, including John Hancock, Benjamin Franklin, and Thomas Jefferson, were Freemasons. Franklin and Jefferson had both been ini-tiated into a French Masonic lodge, and Washington was initiated into the Masonic Lodge of Fredericksburg, VA.[10] At the time of America's founding, the Masonic lodges were very different from the social clubs they've become today. They had a strong metaphysical orientation, which developed common values and purposes among members, as well as deep bonds of loyalty. The tradi-tional secrecy preserved in Masonic lodges allowed members to communicate and organize the American Revolution with little fear of exposure. Several significant non-American contributors to the revolution were also Masons, such as the Marquis de Lafayette of France.
>
> The Boston Tea Party was the work of the Masons of the St. Andrews Lodge while taking a "recess."[11] Paul Revere began his famous ride after he left an adjourned meeting of a Masonic lodge.[12] ...
>
> The cornerstone of the U.S. Capitol Building was laid in a Masonic ceremony, with George Washington presiding as Grand Master. Masonic architects also laid out the city of Washington, D.C., in a meta-physical design to make the best use of the earth energies-called "ley lines," or "dragon lines," for creating healing or harmony. The original de-sign of Pierre-Charles L'Enfant was later modified by Washington and Jefferson to produce the specifically

octagonal patterns incorporating the particular cross used by the Masonic Templars.[15] ~ *Spiritual Politics: Changing the World from the Inside Out* McLaughlin and Davidson[1635]

Send In the Marines

It has been repeatedly said that the Society of Ignatius Loyola is "the Pope's Marines". Perhaps, when considering the Masonic/Jesuit connection, that's not as trite a euphemism as one would think. [italics suspended]

> Ask any Marine. ... He will tell you that the Marine Corps was born in Tun Tavern on 10 November 1775. But, beyond that the Marine's recollection for detail will probably get fuzzy. ...
>
> In the year 1685, Samuel Carpenter built a huge "brew house" in Philadelphia. He located this tavern on the waterfront at the corner of Water Street and Tun Alley. ...
>
> Beginning 47 years later in 1732, the first meetings of the St. John's No. 1 Lodge of the Grand Lodge of the Masonic Temple were held in the tavern. ...Benjamin Franklin, was its third Grand Master. Even today the Masonic Temple of Philadelphia recognizes Tun Tavern as the birthplace of Masonic teachings in America. ...
>
> In 1747 the St. Andrews Society, a charitable group dedicated to assisting poor immigrants from Scotland, was founded in the tavern.
>
> Nine years later, then Col. Benjamin Franklin organized the Pennsylvania Militia. He used Tun Tavern as a gathering place to recruit a regiment of soldiers to go into battle against the Indian uprisings that were plaguing the American colonies. George Washington, Thomas Jefferson, and the Continental Congress later met in Tun Tavern as the American colonies prepared for independence from the English Crown.
>
> On November 10, 1775, the Continental Congress commissioned Samuel Nicholas to raise two Battalions of Marines. That very day, Nicholas set up shop in Tun Tavern. He appointed Robert Mullan, then the proprietor of the tavern, to the job of chief Marine Recruiter—serving, of course, from his place of business at Tun Tavern. ~ *Warrior Culture of the U.S. Marines*, Marion F. Sturkey [1636]

The only shield that has been more effective than the compass and square for Rome to hide behind is the Star of David.

Endnotes

[1513] *The Antiquities of the Jews*, Flavius Josephus, translated by William Whiston, Chapter 4, sections 2-3

[1514] *Warning: 50 Minutes of Cell Phone Use Can Alter Your Brain and DNA*, Joseph Mercola, 19 January 2012, Mercola.com
http://articles.mercola.com/sites/articles/archive/2012/01/19/health-canada-on-cell-phone-use-limitation.aspx

[1515] *Media Kidnapped to Screen Obama Hillary Attending Bilderberg*, Johnny Cirucci YouTube
https://www.youtube.com/watch?v=ipzpf9iOtEE&

[1516] *Bilderberg 2014 : Full List of Official Attendees*, 31 May 2014, the Vigilant Citizen
http://vigilantcitizen.com/latestnews/bilderberg-2014-full-list-official-attendees/

[1517] *Really? Conspiracy Theorist Claims Global Elite Feasting On Roasted Babies Wrapped In Gold*, 4 June 2012, GlennBlech.com
http://www.glennbeck.com/2012/06/04/really-conspiracy-theorist-claims-global-elite-feasting-on-roasted-babies-wrapped-in-gold/
  I've already shown to you that the stories of Luciferians eating babies is quite real so fuck you Glenn Blech, you controlled opposition piece of shit.

[1518] *List of Bohemian Club Members*, Wikipedia
https://en.wikipedia.org/wiki/List_of_Bohemian_Club_members

[1519] *Bohemian Grove: Where the Elite Meet to Eat (and Conspire)*, Bob Adelmann, 13 July 2011, The New American
http://www.thenewamerican.com/usnews/politics/item/9468-bohemian-grove-where-the-elite-meet-to-eat-and-conspire

[1520] *Masters of the Universe Go to Camp: Inside the Bohemian Grove*, Philip Weiss, November 1989, Spy Magazine
http://www2.ucsc.edu/whorulesamerica/power/bohemian_grove_spy.html

[1521] *ibid*

[1522] *The Agricola and Germania of Tacitus*, translated by K. B. Townshend, M.A., Methuen & co., 86 Essex Steeet, W.C., London (1894), pp. 61-62

[1523] *What Is Bohemian?* Andy Walker, 11 March 2011, BBC 4 (gotta love the variety in state-owned Limey media!)
http://www.bbc.co.uk/news/magazine-12711181
  This is still a fluff piece. There's nothing attractive about being an "eccentric" Bohemian "artist". "Unconventional" in the Bohemian sense is synonymous with *uncivilized*.
  Limeys. —apologies to my beloved brother Julian Charles. :)

[1524] *Genocide of European Roma (Gypsies)*, 1939–1945, United States Holocaust Memorial Museum
http://www.ushmm.org/wlc/en/article.php?ModuleId=10005219

[1525] *Exposing The "Secret Owl Society" Soaring Through History*, Richard Cassaro, 19 November 2010, Richard Cassaro.com
http://www.richardcassaro.com/uncovering-the-secret-owl-society

[1526] *Idolatry And Sex Worship In Ancient Israel Part 1*, John Vujicic, 2 May 2009, Beware Deception.com

http://bewaredeception.com/index.php?option=com_content&view=article&id=38:idolatry-and-sex-worship-in-ancient-israel-part-1&catid=1:articles&Itemid=3
   The set-up of this blog looks like a high school student did it—it's *brutal* on the eyes. But the information is good and very thought-provoking. I will hit up vegetarianism and compassion for animals in my next book.
   ...maybe.

[1527] *Bohemian Grove > Cremation of Care*, Wikipedia
https://en.wikipedia.org/wiki/Bohemian_Grove#Cremation_of_Care

[1528] *Dark Secrets: Inside Bohemian Grove (FULL LENGTH ALEX JONES FILM)*, WakeUpToTheNWO1 YouTube
https://www.youtube.com/watch?v=zJgjz4CmyjM
   InfoWars is very liberal with their products, smartly so, and if this link is down there are many others on YouTube.

[1529] *Eye Witness to Murder at Bohemian Grove Americas Satanic HellFire Club - Anthony J Hilder*, Anthony Hilder, YouTube
https://www.youtube.com/watch?v=CvY7thwBVu4

[1530] *I-Team: Did a Serial Killer Take Missing Child Kevin Collins?* Dan Noyes, 26 October 2012, ABC News 7
http://abc7news.com/archive/8860582/

[1531] *Bill Clinton gets asked about the Bohemian Grove club that he and other elites attend.* Standonarock YouTube
https://www.youtube.com/watch?v=u8y-FPQlNfI

[1532] *The Nixon Tapes: Bohemian Grove Was The Most Faggy Goddamned Thing You Could Imagine*, Johnny Cirucci YouTube
https://www.youtube.com/watch?v=6AE6dgYMxlY&

[1533] *Isis Unveiled: A Master-Key to the Mysteries of Ancient and Modern Science and Theology, Volume II – Theology*, H. P. Blavatsky, Theosophical University Press (1877), pp. 267, 268

[1534] *ibid*, pp. 325-327

[1535] *ibid*, pp. 327-328

[1536] *ibid*, p. 328

[1537] *ibid*, pp. 351, 354

[1538] *ibid*, p. 357

[1539] *Occult Theocrasy*, Edith Starr Miller; Lady Queenborough, Imprimerie F. Paillart (1933), p. 313

[1540] *ibid*, p. 308

[1541] *ibid*, p. 372

[1542] *Weishaupt, Adam*, Deutsche Biographie, NDB/ADB
http://www.deutsche-biographie.de/sfz84871.html

[1543] *The Enlightened Ones: The Illuminati and the New World Order*, Michael Howard, 7 April 2010, New Dawn Magazine
http://www.newdawnmagazine.com/articles/the-enlightened-ones-the-illuminati-and-the-new-world-order

[1544] *Occult Theocrasy*, Edith Starr Miller; Lady Queenborough, Imprimerie F. Paillart (1933), p. 313

[1545] *A Bavarian Illuminati Primer*, Trevor McKeown, 16 September 2013, the Grand [Masonic] Lodge of British Columbia and Yukon
http://freemasonry.bcy.ca/texts/illuminati.html
[1546] *Quest for Mysteries: The Masonic Background for Literature in 18th Century Germany*, Heinrich Schneider, Kessinger Publishing (1947), p. 24
[1547] *Thomas Jefferson to Reverend James Madison, January 31, 1800*, The Works of Thomas Jefferson in Twelve Volumes. Federal Edition. Collected and Edited by Paul Leicester Ford. Philadelphia, Jan. 31, 1800. The Library of Congress.
http://memory.loc.gov/cgi-bin/query/r?ammem/mtj:@field%28DOCID+@lit%28tj090050%29%29
[1548] *To George Washington from G. W. Snyder, 22 August 1798*, The Washington Papers, Founders online archive
http://founders.archives.gov/documents/Washington/06-02-02-0435
[1549] *Proofs of a Conspiracy Against All the Religions and Governments of Europe, Carried On in the Secret Meetings of Free Masons, Illuminati, and Reading Societies, Collected from Good Authorities*, John Robison, A.M., Royal Society of Edinburgh, printed and sold by George Forman, No. 64, Water-Street, between Coenties and the Old-Slip (1798)
http://www.conspiracyarchive.com/PROOFS_OF_A_CONSPIRACY_John_Robison.pdf
[1550] *The Conspiracy To Destroy All Existing Governments and Religions*, William Guy Carr, CPA Books (1998), pp. 13-14
  This appears to be a self-published pamphlet, later put into paperback.
[1551] *Pawns in the Game*, William Guy Carr, the Federation of Christian Laymen (1958), p. 10 [digital copy]
[1552] *Jesuits Behind Politics*, 19 August 2010, Amazing Discoveries
http://amazingdiscoveries.org/S-deception-Jesuits_French_Reformation_Hitler
[1553] *Pawns in the Game*, Carr, p. 11 [digital copy]
[1554] See I Enoch, Chapters 6, 7, 8, 68 (some editions show 69). An online version (about as trustworthy as any, I guess) can be found here for Chapters 1 through 60:
http://reluctant-messenger.com/1enoch01-60.htm
—and here for 61-105:
http://reluctant-messenger.com/1enoch61-105.htm
[1555] *Lexicon of Freemasonry*, Albert Gallatin Mackey, (1869), republished by Kessinger (1994), p. 361
[1556] *Freemasonry*, Wikipedia
https://en.wikipedia.org/wiki/Freemasonry
[1557] *The Secrets of Freemasonry*, the Order of Former Freemasons
http://www.formermasons.org/issues/the_secrets_of_freemasonry.php
[1558] *Secret Counsels of the Society of Jesus*, Robert Breckinridge, Baltimore: Edward J. Cole & Co. (1835), p. 68
[1559] *Apollyon Rising 2012: The Lost Symbol Found and the Final Mystery of the Great Seal Revealed*, Thomas Horn Defender (2009), pp. 8-9, 52-53
[1560] *The Lost Secret of William Shakespeare*, Richard Allan Wagner, self-published (2010), pp. 54-58, 68-69
  Whenever someone self-publishes a book you lose the veracity of the publishing process. Is Wagner a reliable and professional writer? You'll have to judge for yourself. This work can be downloaded here:

http://www.fbrt.org.uk/pages/essays/The%20LOST%20SECRET%20of%20William%20Shakespeare.pdf

It is extremely interesting to note that Wagner lists himself in this way: *Richard (Rick) Wagner: Wagner is a 32nd Degree Scottish Rite Freemason and a Frater of the AMORC Rosicrucian Order.*
http://thetruthaboutshakespeare.com/index.php/contact-richard-allan-wagner

[1561] *Review of The Origins of Freemasonry*, T.E. Wilder, *The Origins of Freemasonry: Scotland's Century 1590-1710, by David Stevenson (Cambridge University Press, 1988) xvii, 246 pages, index.*, Contra Mundum, No. 1, Fall 1991
http://www.contra-mundum.org/cm/reviews/tw_masonry.pdf

[1562] *Catholicism vs. Freemasonry—Irreconcilable Forever*, Rev. Robert I. Bradley, S.J., EWTN
http://www.ewtn.com/library/ANSWERS/BACAFM.HTM

[1563] *The Grand Design Exposed*, John Daniel, CHJ Publishing (1999), pp. 302-303

[1564] *The Catholic Church and the Enlightenment*, Tasha Brandstatter, Opposing Views
http://people.opposingviews.com/catholic-church-enlightenment-5697.html

[1565] *Enlightenment Contested: Philosophy, Modernity, and the Emancipation of Man 1670-1752*, Jonathan I. Israel, Oxford University Press (2006)

Another digital online copy where the idiots at Google deprive us of what frigging page we're reading.

Speaking of idiots, how "Jonathan I. Israel" could lump Newton and Locke in with Voltaire and the Jesuits makes me wonder if *he's* a puppet himself.

[1566] *Occult Theocrasy*, Edith Starr Miller; Lady Queenborough, Imprimerie F. Paillart (1933), pp. 371-372

Here Miller is either incredibly shortsighted and mislead or she is actually an agent of disinformation. She states that Weishaupt was Jesuit-educated but that his Secret Society was a Protestant counter to the Counter-Reformation using Jesuit methods. They were also Masonic but arch enemies of all Masons. Huh? She then explains how the Illuminati was overtly anti-Christian. My guess is that she was a doofus. A great source of information, but still a doofus...cut short by the "Society of Jesus".

[1567] *Manifesto of the Communist Party*, Karl Marx and Frederick Engels, February 1848, Marx/Engels Selected Works, Vol. One, Progress Publishers, Moscow, 1969, pp. 25-26

[1568] *The Jesuits, Voltaire & The Founding Fathers*, Christian J. Pinto, 3 May 2011, Noise of Thunder
http://www.noiseofthunder.com/articles/2011/5/3/the-jesuits-voltaire-the-founding-fathers.html

Chris is a little unnecessarily hard on John Adams.

[1569] *Pope Says Church Is "Obsessed" With Gays, Abortion and Birth Control*, Laurie Goodstein, 19 September 2013, NY Times
http://www.nytimes.com/2013/09/20/world/europe/pope-bluntly-faults-churchs-focus-on-gays-and-abortion.html?pagewanted=all&_r=0

[1570] *At the Vatican, a Shift in Tone Toward Gays and Divorce*, Elisabetta Povoledo and Laurie Goodstein, 13 October 2014, NY Times
http://www.nytimes.com/2014/10/14/world/europe/vatican-signals-more-tolerance-toward-gays-and-remarriage.html?_r=0

[1571] *The Vatican's Synod on the Family, and Why You've Missed the Point*, Rev. Michael Rogers, S.J., 17 October 2014, the Sodomite Post

http://www.huffingtonpost.com/rev-mr-michael-rogers-sj/the-vaticans-synod-on-the_b_6002884.html
[1572] *Semiramis, Queen Of Babylon*, Bryce Self, undated, Lambert Dolphin.org http://www.ldolphin.org/semir.html
[1573] *The Two Babylons: Or, the Papal Worship Proved to Be the Worship of Nimrod*, Alexander Hislop, Loizeaux Brothers (1916), p. 102 [digital copy doubtless does not match paper copy]
[1574] *Adapa > As Oannes*, Wikipedia https://en.wikipedia.org/wiki/Adapa#As_Oannes
[1575] *Ancient Pagan and Modern Christian Symbolism*, Thomas Inman and John Newton, M.R.C.S.E, New York J.W. Bouton (1875), p. 13 (digital page 61)
[1576] *ibid*, p. A (digital page 50)
[1577] *The Two Babylons*, pp. 19-21
[1578] *Isis Unveiled*, pp. 16-17
[1579] *ibid*, p. 21
[1580] *Apollyon Rising 2012: The Lost Symbol Found and the Final Mystery of the Great Seal Revealed*, Thomas Horn, Defender (2009), pp. 286, 289, 291, 293
[1581] *Constantino Brumidi*, Explore Capitol Hill, AOC.gov http://www.aoc.gov/constantino-brumidi
[1582] *The Assos Journals of Francis H. Bacon*, edited by Lenore Congdon, 1 December 2006, Archaeology Archive http://archive.archaeology.org/online/features/assos/
[1583] *Architect: Bacon, Henry*, the Pacific Coast Architecture Database https://digital.lib.washington.edu/architect/architects/830/
[1584] *Bacon Family; 1299 – 2005*, Ancestry.com http://freepages.genealogy.rootsweb.ancestry.com/~dav4is/ODTs/BACON.shtml
[1585] *5 Things You Might Not Know About the Washington Monument*, Elizabeth Nix, 9 October 2013, History.com http://www.history.com/news/5-things-you-might-not-know-about-the-washington-monument
[1586] *Washington Monument*, hiwaay.net http://home.hiwaay.net/~jalison/WM.html
[1587] *Cleopatra's Needle*, Wikipedia http://en.wikipedia.org/wiki/Cleopatra's_Needle
[1588] *How Cleopatra's Needle Got to Central Park*, Kate Briquelet, 14 June 2014, New York Post http://nypost.com/2014/06/14/how-cleopatras-needle-a-3500-year-old-egyptian-obelisk-got-to-central-park/
[1589] *An Obelisk for Central Park*, Edmund Whitman, July/August 1975, Saudi Aramco World Magazine https://www.saudiaramcoworld.com/issue/197504/an.obelisk.for.central.park.htm
[1590] *The Oldest Outdoor Manmade Object in New York – Cleopatra's Needle*, Nick Carr, 14 May 2012, Scouting New York http://www.scoutingny.com/the-oldest-outdoor-manmade-object-in-new-york-city-cleopatras-needle/
[1591] *Anderson Cooper*, Biography.com http://www.biography.com/#!/people/anderson-cooper-20851303

[1592] *Anderson Cooper Comes Out: "The Fact Is, I'm Gay"*, Jack Mirkinson, 1 September 2012, Huffington Blows
http://www.huffingtonpost.com/2012/07/02/anderson-cooper-comes-out-gay_n_1643276.html
[1593] *Anderson Cooper's CIA Secret*, Staff, 27 October 2008, Radar Online
http://radaronline.com/exclusives/2008/10/anderson-coopers-cia-secret-php/
[1594] *"The Godfathers"* (Alberto part 3/The Crusaders 14.) Review by Rich Lee, Monsterwax.com
http://www.monsterwax.com/chickcomics3.html
[1595] *Holy See–United States Relations > 1867–1984*, Wikipedia
https://en.wikipedia.org/wiki/Holy_See%E2%80%93United_States_relations#1867.E2.80.931984
   Expunged from the record is *why* relations were cut off in 1867.
[1596] *Reagan Decideds to Reopen Diplomatic Ties With Vatican*, Steven Weisman, 31 December 1983, the NY Times via the Spokane Chronicle
https://www.scribd.com/doc/237221763/Reagan-to-Re-open-Ties-With-Vatican-Spokane-Chronicle-Dec-31-1983
[1597] *22 USC 2656 - Sec. 2656. Management of Foreign Affairs*, United States Code, v|lex: Global Legal Intelligence
http://us-code.vlex.com/vid/sec-management-foreign-affairs-19203755
[1598] *Facts, Firsts and Precedents*, Senate.gov
http://www.inaugural.senate.gov/about/facts-and-firsts
[1599] *The Neo-Catholics: Implementing Christian Nationalism In America*, Betty Clermont, SCB Distributors (2011)
   Another digital wonder from Google with no f___ing page numbers.
[1600] *Francis Hopkinson*, Great Seal.com
http://greatseal.com/committees/secondcomm/hopkinson.html
[1601] *Betsy Ross Homepage Resources: Historic Analysis*, U.S. History.org
http://www.ushistory.org/betsy/flagpcp.html
[1602] *Masons And U. S. Flag*, Andrew Boracci, Master Mason.com
http://www.mastermason.com/hempstead749/theflag.htm
[1603] *Great Seal of the United States > Third Committee*, Wikipedia
https://en.wikipedia.org/wiki/Great_Seal_of_the_United_States#Third_committee
[1604] *The Life Of Charles Thomson, Secretary Of The Continental Congress And Translator Of The Bible From The Greek*, Lewis R. Harley, Philadelphia, G.W. Jacobs & co (1900), p. 163, 3rd footnote
[1605] *Patriot Was Well-Versed In Scripture*, Glenn Rawson, 10 August 2013, the Blackfoot Journal
http://blackfootjournal.com/patriot-was-well-versed-in-scripture/
[1606] *Mirror of Daze: What Does Your Life Reflect?* Phillip Garncarz, CrossBooks (2012), pp. 84-85
[1607] *Novus Ordo Seclorum: the New World Order*, Overlords of Chaos
http://www.overlordsofchaos.com/html/1800-49.html
[1608] *The All-Seeing Eye, The President, The Secretary and The Guru*, Terry Melanson, July 2001, Conspiracy Archive
http://www.conspiracyarchive.com/NWO/All_Seeing_Eye.htm

[1609] *The Neo-Catholics: Implementing Christian Nationalism In America*, Betty Clermont, SCB Distributors (2011)
    Ask the terds at Google what page this is. They are the morons that digitzed the book without them.
[1610] *Douglas MacArthur*, Ararat Shrine Temple
http://www.araratshrine.com/history/famous/macarthur/
[1611] *Harry S. Truman*, Ararat Shrine Temple
http://www.araratshrine.com/history/famous/truman/
[1612] *Bohemian Grove: Where the Elite Meet to Eat (and Conspire)*, Bob Adelmann, 13 July 2011, the New American
http://www.thenewamerican.com/usnews/politics/item/9468-bohemian-grove-where-the-elite-meet-to-eat-and-conspire
[1613] *Military Life of Dwight D. Eisenhower*, Armed Forces History Museum
http://armedforcesmuseum.com/military-life-of-dwight-d-eisenhower/
[1614] *Project Condorcet - Pierre Charles L'Enfant*, American Presence Post: Bordeaux, United States State Department
http://bordeaux.usconsulate.gov/projectcondorcet-pclenfant.html
[1615] *Pierre Beaumarchais*, Wikipedia
http://en.wikipedia.org/wiki/Pierre_Beaumarchais
[1616] *Gioachino Rossini: il barbiere di siviglia*, performed by the Vienna State Opera Wiener Staatsoper, 2012/2013 programme, p. 23
http://www.wiener-staatsoper.at/Content.Node/mobile/progheftenglish/Programm-Barbiere-en.pdf
    Be impressed. I wanted to give you something beside "Wikipedia" and had to really dig this one up.
[1617] *The Masonic Career of Major Pierre Charles L'Enfant*, Pierre F. de Ravel d'Esclapon, 32°, Valley of Rockville Center, N.Y, March-April 2011, Scottish Rite of Freemasonry Supreme Council, 33°, Southern Jurisdiction, U.S.A.
http://scottishrite.org/about/media-publications/journal/article/the-masonic-career-of-major-pierre-charles-lenfant/
    If that doesn't breathe "subversive organization" I don't know what does.
[1618] *George Washington Fires Major Pierre Charles L'Enfant*, George Washington Papers, Library of Congress. View original. 28 February 1792
http://mallhistory.org/items/show/299
[1619] *Soldier-Statesmen of the Constitution: Daniel Carroll*, Robert K. Wright, Jr. and Morris J. MacGregor, Jr., the
Center of Military History, the United States Army, pp. 152-153
http://www.history.army.mil/books/RevWar/ss/carroll.htm
[1620] *Most Rev. John Carroll*, the Archdiocese of Baltimore
http://www.archbalt.org/about-us/the-archdiocese/our-history/people/carroll.cfm
[1621] *Catholic Founding Fathers - The Carroll Family*, Catholic Education.org
http://www.catholiceducation.org/articles/history/us/ah0016.html
[1622] *The Works of John Adams, Second President of the United States: With a Life of the Author, Notes and Illustrations, Volume 9*, edited by Charles Francis Adams, Little and Brown (1854), p. 73
[1623] *Holidays from Hell: Satanic Temple Wins Right to Erect "Fallen Angel" Display in Florida*, 5 December 2014, Russia Today

http://rt.com/usa/211631-satanism-florida-capitol-representation/
[1624] *Car Smashes Ten Commandments Statue, Man Detained*, Sean Murphy, 24 October 2014, San Francisco Gate via AP
http://www.sfgate.com/news/crime/article/Disputed-Oklahoma-Ten-Commandments-statue-smashed-5845127.php
[1625] *John Carroll*, Encyclopedia of World Biography, 2004
http://www.encyclopedia.com/topic/John_Carroll.aspx
[1626] *John Carroll and the Creation of the Catholic Church in America: Part 2*, Stephen Klugewicz, 17 May 2011, The Imaginative Conservative
http://www.theimaginativeconservative.org/2011/05/john-carroll-and-creation-catholic.html
[1627] *A Concise View of the Principal Points of Controversy Between the Protestant and Roman Churches*, Reverend Charles Henry Wharton, David Longworth (1817), p. 7
[1628] *ibid*, pp. 8, 10, 12, 17
[1629] *Pierre Charles L'Enfant*, Encyclopædia Britannica
http://www.britannica.com/EBchecked/topic/335841/Pierre-Charles-LEnfant
[1630] *World Almanac Library of the States*, Acton Figueroa, Gareth Stevens (2003), p. 11
[1631] *Take a Tour of Masonic Washington: What Does It All Mean?* David Montgomery and Monica Hesse, 10 September 2009, the Washington Post
http://www.washingtonpost.com/wp-dyn/content/article/2009/09/09/AR2009090902501.html
[1632] *The Secret Teachings Of All Ages*, Manly P. Hall, H.S. Crocker Company (1928), p. 303
[1633] *Take A Tour With Two Propaganda Clowns of Outrageously Masonic Washington, Demonically-Controlled!* David Montgomery and Monica Hesse, 10 September 2009, the Washington Post
http://www.washingtonpost.com/wp-dyn/content/article/2009/09/09/AR2009090902501.html
    It's late and I'm punchy...had to write my own headline. The real one is on note 63.
[1634] *Freemasonry, Astrology, and the Washington D.C. Street Plan*, Eric Dubay, 2 July 2013, the Atlantean Conspiracy
http://www.atlanteanconspiracy.com/2009/01/freemasonry-astrology-and-washington-dc.html
[1635] *The Deeper, Secret Roots of America's Founding*, Corinne McLaughlin and Gordon Davidson, The Center for Visionary Leadership
http://www.visionarylead.org/articles/am_found.htm
[1636] excerpt from *Warrior Culture of the U.S. Marines*, (2001) Marion F. Sturkey, Heritage Press International, USMC Press.com
http://www.usmcpress.com/heritage/usmc_heritage.htm

Chapter 17

It's The Jews!

The burden of the Word of the L-rd for Israel, saith the L-rd, which stretcheth forth the heavens, and layeth the foundation of the Earth, and formeth the spirit of man within him.

Behold, I will make Jerusalem a cup of trembling unto all the people round about...

And in that day will I make Jerusalem a burdensome stone for all people ... ~ Zechariah 12:1-3, KJV (abbreviation and some capitalization added for respect)

Few topics polarize humanity better than the Jews or the existence of the nation of Israel. Two camps instantly arise to form polar opposite extremes.

"Christian Zionists"

On the one extreme are well-meaning Conservative Christians who innately connect with Israelis. They feel a kindred spirit with them and seek passionately for Israel's political prosperity. Yet, they betray the central tenet of the Christian Faith which states that, apart from Jesus Christ, there can be no true prosperity. [John 15:1-4]

Some take well-meaning outreach to extremes that other Christians might rightfully call "blasphemous" such as bombastic Texas mega-church pastor John Hagee who, in advertising for his book *The Defense of Israel*, denied that Jesus Christ claimed He was the Messiah.[1637]

The Christian Zionists claim Genesis 12:3 as their impetus.

But can there be any greater curse than to insulate a man condemned from the effects of his rebellion, especially when he has time to repent and return home?

"Anti-Zionists"

On the other extreme is mindless, irrational anti-Semitism that destroys sound judgment and discredits truth-seekers. They claim to be lovers of freedom then stand with the worst and most vicious of tyrants from literal cut-throat Islamists to Nazis new and old in their desire to wipe Israel off the map.

The de Rothschilds have been instrumental in the re-founding of modern Israel.

> *Rothschild has a long history in Israel and the Rothschild family has played a significant role in the development of the country.*
>
> *The connection with the region began as early as 1855 with the creation of a hospital and, later, the Rothschild family helped to fund the building of the Knesset and the Supreme Court. Rothschild also helped establish Israel's agricultural industry, mineral extraction industries, and the production of glass and wine.*
>
> *Today, Rothschild has a fully staffed local office in Israel and our activities are supported by the expertise and contact network of our Head of Israel Office, Doron Gurevitz, and our Chairman of Rothschild Israel, Oded Gera. ~ Israel*, Rothschild.com[1638]

"Truthers" see this and the endless bloodshed and distraction of the Middle East as a carefully-planned conspiracy by the Luciferian Elite, which it most certainly is.

But then emotion and prejudice steal their senses and they become deluded into thinking that Jews and the existence of Israel are the problem—just as the Luciferians intend. They spin yarns about who are "real" Jews with just about the entirety of Judaism falling into the "not real" Jew category.

Like mind-controlled sex object pop stars or patsy Islamic militants, many Jews allow the servants of the *nachash* (נָחָשׁ) to use them to hide behind because it temporarily empowers them; but they will all end the same.

There is a "Synagogue of Satan" [Revelation 2:9, 3:9] who actively persecutes Christians but they are nothing compared to the great Beast. The ethnicity of Christian persecutors matters not, only that those who are vehemently opposed to Christian ideals are all in the enemy's camp. [Matthew 12:30]

Such powerful anti-Jewish sentiment has not escaped the notice of the Luciferian Elite and they actively foment it for their advantage.[1639]

The reality lies somewhere in the middle.

Israel and the Jews: a Balanced Perspective

Imagine how the Parable of the Prodigal Son [Luke 15:11-32] would've ended if, just before the prodigal son had been broken by his circumstances, a well-meaning outsider showered him with finances and compliments?

Yet the existence of corporate Israel (despite her Luciferian backers) can be seen much as the Bible Codes or the Shroud of Turin; a Testimony to YHWH.

But how do Christians fit in?

"Gentile" (non-Jewish) Christians are *grafted* in as a botanist grafts in a wild olive branch. [Romans 11:17]

Jesus Christ—*Yeshua ha'Mashiach*—is a Jewish Savior, who's Message was sent to the Jew, first, and then to the Greek (non-Jews). [Romans 1:16]

Corporately, Israel rejected her Messiah; "May His Blood be upon us and our children!" [Matthew 27:25]

This rejection brought the death of the Jewish religion and judgment upon the Jewish people. [Zechariah 13:6, Matthew 23:37]

However, the Jewish religion breathes Yeshua of Nazareth. He can be found on every page of the Old Testament and those who approach their faith with this in mind are richly blessed. The rare Jew who accepts Yeshua as Messiah is even more so. [Matthew 5:18, Luke 24:13-32, Psalm 22, Isaiah 52:13-53:12]

Those who accept Jesus Christ as their Messiah are His "Chosen", His "Elect", irrespective of their past. [Romans 8:33]

In Christ, both Jew and "Gentile" are one. They are *all* His Chosen People. [Galatians 3:23-29, Ephesians 2:11-22]

Promised

If non-believing Jews are *not* "His Chosen People", what are they?

Genesis 12:3 lays out YHWH's Covenant with Abram; "I will bless those who bless you and curse those who curse you and, in you, all the nations will be blessed." Christians believe that, indeed, Abraham's offspring—Yeshua—has blessed the entire world.

Genesis 15:18 commits "Canaan" / "Palestine" to Abraham's descendants but their *maintaining* of that land was *conditional* upon their obedience. [Deuteronomy 32]

Non-Believing Jews remain YHWH's *Covenant* People but await a future restoration and acknowledgement of Yeshua to become one with His *Chosen* People. [Zechariah 12:10, Matthew 3:9, Romans 11:25]

Until then, the only advantages being Jewish will get you is to be chosen by the Luciferian Elite to prosper temporarily until they can garner enough anti-Semitism to elicit a 2nd Holocaust even worse than the first. [Zechariah 13:7-9]

A Captured Operation

The "Gay Pride" parade in the capital of Israel is considered the most extensive anywhere in the world and attracted 100,000 people in 2014.[1640]

Israel is a captured operation just as all the major NATO and Western nations are.

Israel is simply a smaller version of the United States; she fights brutal wars against enemies she has created, herself.

> *All signs indicate that the government of Israeli Prime Minister Benjamin Netanyahu is prepared to wage a protracted battle in the battered Gaza Strip as it seeks to crush the capabilities of the Islamist militant group Hamas. The ongoing conflict has already exacted a bloody toll, with the Palestinian death count approaching the total of Israel's 2008-2009 bombing campaign and ground offensive in Gaza, which led to the deaths of at least 1,383 Palestinians over three weeks. ...*
>
> *The current fighting — a clash between Israel's vastly superior armed forces and Hamas's insurgents — obscures the greater challenges facing Israelis and Palestinians, including the thorny question of how to accord equal rights to millions of Palestinians living under occupation in the event that a separate Palestinian state turns out not to be viable.*
>
> *It also obscures Hamas's curious history. To a certain degree, the Islamist organization whose militant wing has rained rockets on Israel the past few weeks has the Jewish state to thank for its existence. Hamas launched in 1988 in Gaza at the time of the first intifada, or uprising, with a charter now infamous for its anti-Semitism and its refusal to accept the existence of the Israeli state.*

But for more than a decade prior, Israeli authorities actively enabled its rise. ~ Ishaan Tharoor, the Washington Post[1641]

Couched as a "blunder", the Israeli government and Intelligence community aided the rise of vehemently Islamist Hamas over the secular PLO. Essentially, to counter-balance a jackal, a dragon was created.

> *Instead of trying to curb Gaza's Islamists from the outset, says Mr. [Avner] Cohen [listed only as an "Israeli official"], Israel for years tolerated and, in some cases, encouraged them as a counterweight to the secular nationalists of the Palestine Liberation Organization and its dominant faction, Yasser Arafat's Fatah. Israel cooperated with a crippled, half-blind cleric named Sheikh Ahmed Yassin, even as he was laying the foundations for what would become Hamas. Sheikh Yassin continues to inspire militants today; during the recent war in Gaza, Hamas fighters confronted Israeli troops with "Yassins," primitive rocket-propelled grenades named in honor of the cleric.* ~ Andrew Higgins, the Wall Street Journal[1642]

Given the death and destruction this "mistake" has caused, one would think the individuals who committed the "blunder" would be facing the most severe punishments possible but they continue to prosper as does Hamas.

In 1954, the Mossad targeted Americans, Brits and Egyptians to die in a failed false flag terror operation known today as "the Lavon Affair".

> *The Lavon Affair refers to a failed Israeli covert operation, code named Operation Susannah, conducted in Egypt in the Summer of 1954. As part of the false flag operation,[1] a group of Egyptian Jews were recruited by Israeli military intelligence to plant bombs inside Egyptian, American and British-owned civilian targets, cinemas, libraries and American educational centers. ... The attacks were to be blamed on the Muslim Brotherhood, Egyptian Communists, "unspecified malcontents" or "local nationalists" with the aim of creating a climate of sufficient violence and instability to induce the British government to retain its occupying troops in Egypt's Suez Canal zone.[2] ...*
>
> *The operation ultimately became known as the Lavon Affair after the Israeli defense minister Pinhas Lavon was forced to resign as a consequence of the incident. Before Lavon's resignation, the incident had been euphemistically referred to in Israel as the "Unfortunate Affair" or "The Bad Business" (Hebrew: עסק ביש, Esek HaBish). After Israel publicly denied any involvement in the incident for 51 years, the surviving agents were officially honored*

in 2005 by being awarded certificates of appreciation by Israeli President Moshe Katzav.[3] ~ Wikipedia[1643]

Although there were no American casualties, the Egyptian operatives involved were captured, tortured and killed.

But Israelis *did* kill Americans who were aboard the intelligence surveillance ship the U.S.S. Liberty, 13 years later in 1967.

The Liberty was tracking the progress of the Six Day War between Israel and Egypt when she was attacked by Israeli fighter-bombers and torpedo boats. 34 were killed and 171 were wounded but the attack broke off before the Liberty was sunk.

"Remember the Liberty!" have been the calls of the "anti-Zionists" ever since, but the man who ordered the Israelis to attack has been completely shielded from culpability: Lyndon Baines Johnson. [italics suspended]

> Lyndon Baines Johnson is a president who has escaped the scrutiny and judgment of history despite considerable documentation that should make him an outstanding candidate for historical review, critique and analysis.
>
> ... he personally gave the order to Israel to bomb and utterly destroy the USS Liberty and its entire crew of 294 Americans. Astoundingly, when the mission went awry and Sixth Fleet Commanders were ordering the rescue of the besieged and bloodied USS Liberty crew, LBJ ordered that rescue operations be called back, at least twice. Against all odds, the USS Liberty survived but after the attack, 34 Americans lay dead. Except for 4 worthless 50 caliber machine guns, the USS Liberty was unarmed and defenseless against the far superior firing power of the Israeli naval and air force armada that descended upon it with relentless and unspeakable terror. ...
>
> The "official" story of the USS Liberty according to the government and mainstream media version of the event is that on June 8, 1967 the Israelis accidentally bombed the USS Liberty off the coast of Egypt and killed 34 American sailors.
>
> The real story is that President Johnson, who was being battered in the polls over the Vietnam War and facing a general election loss and even losing the DNC primary, ordered the Israelis to bomb the USS Liberty to create a *casus belli* to secure a Gulf of Tonkin style

resolution to explode the world into war because in America everybody loves an outraged and indignant president who will use the full force of the military at the slightest provocation, even a government planned false flag attack.

The USS Liberty, however, encompasses far more than a murderous psychopathic American president resorting to hideously evil deeds to get re-elected. In addition to ordering the total destruction of the USS Liberty and sending 294 Americans to a watery grave in the Mediterranean Sea, LBJ also ordered the nuclear bombing of Cairo, an event specifically designed to create a nuclear war by blaming the entire USS Liberty affair on Russia or Egypt. More horrifying, it's documented that US planes were on emergency standby orders as pilots waited on the runways in their planes armed with nuclear weapons. The nuclear bombing of Cairo was called off only 3 minutes before the nuclear bomb drops. ~ Judy Morris, the Economic Policy Journal[1644]

Investigative journalist Roger Stone credits Johnson as the lynchpin behind the Kennedy assassination and states he was more than corrupt enough to get the job done. In 2013, Stone was interviewed by the Voice of Russia regarding his newly-published book *The Man Who Killed Kennedy: The Case Against LBJ*. [italics suspended]

VOR: For those, who don't know of Lyndon Johnson's personality and demeanor, could you describe why he would be the most logical mastermind behind JFK's assassination?

Stone: I think the reason why he is the most logical murderer of John Kennedy is that in November of 1963 Lyndon Johnson was a man, who was looking into the abyss. He was tangled up in at least two of the major public corruption scandals of the day: the Bobby Baker scandal – Baker was Johnson's right-hand man, who was taking huge bribes on Johnson's behalf in the U.S. Senate and then Billie Sol Estes scandal. Estes was a Texas wheeler dealer businessman who had got millions of dollars in Federal contracts thanks to Lyndon Johnson. Both of those investigations were coming to a head, both of them pointed to corruption by Johnson, corruption of Biblical proportions. And Johnson knew he was going to be dumped from the ticket and probably sent to prison. So, time was running out for Lyndon Johnson. He knew that Life magazine – a very prominent American magazine at the time – planned a major expose of his financial situation and his corruption. A week after the assassination and that the information for the Life magazine article had been sent to them by attorney general Robert

Kennedy who very very much wanted Lyndon Johnson off the national ticket in 1964, so he, Lyndon Johnson is your most likely perpetrator.

VOR: You said in your book that Lyndon Johnson's biographer would panic if he's reminded about Wallace. Who was that man and what role did he play in the assassination?

Stone: I believe that Malcolm Wallace, who was a long-time associate and hitman for LBJ is the actual killer, I tie Johnson to at least eight murders in Texas prior to John F. Kennedy. These were murders to cover up corruption, they were murders to cover up voter fraud through theft of elections. Johnson had murder in his repertoire. In fact I would go so far as to say that Johnson could order a murder the way you and I would order a sandwich. And it is very important historically to understand that in the immediate aftermath of Kennedy's assassination in order to justify the cover-up to many in the government, in order to get them to go along with the fiction that Lee Harvey Oswald had killed Kennedy, Johnson tried to give the impression that the assassination of John F. Kennedy was done by the Russian State. Johnson told this lie repeatedly in order to get people to go along with the cover-up, because you see, if we don't blame Oswald and we don't claim that he is a lone communist acting by himself and people learn that he is really an agent of a foreign government – the Russian government – then it would cause a major national incident, needless to say that's all a lie. In fact the KGB according to declassified documents that we got in 1985 the KGB conducted their own totally independent investigation to determine who killed Kennedy. You know what they determined? They said: it was Lyndon Johnson. ~ Voice of Russia[1645]

This does not absolve the Company from Langley nor the Company of Loyola. Stone could very well be doing them all a service unknowingly or willingly by holding Johnson up as the *only* man behind the conspiracy (a feat quite impossible given its expanse) but his role is unquestionable.

On Johnson's hands, along with the blood of so many other Americans, including her 35th President, is that of the sailors onboard the Liberty.

> *After the Mirages had done their work, the ship was hit by medium bomber [aircraft], carrying Napalm and other munitions like White Phosphorous. The USS Liberty was then attacked by three Israeli torpedo boats, bearing Israeli flags. The torpedo gunboats opened fire with high caliber machine guns and launched torpedoes. A*

single torpedo struck the ship, blowing a hole in both sides—entering the ship and leaving a thirty foot exit hole when it exploded. Then the torpedo boats began strafing life rafts in the water— an international war crime.

While all of this was happening, an oversized American flag flew clearly above the ship. The attack on the Liberty went on for hour after hour after hour.

During the entire attack the USS Liberty continually called the Sixth Fleet that was nearby, begging for air support or rescue. Two [nearby] aircraft carriers responded by launching fighter aircraft. Unbelievably, they were then recalled by the White House. Rear Admiral Geiss, commanding the carrier in the sixth fleet, called Washington personally to confirm the recall order. Secretary of Defense McNamera came on the line, and then President Johnson himself told Geiss: "I want that g..damn ship going to the bottom! No help— recall the wings." Imagine being Admiral Geiss, begging the President to allow you to defend an American ship that is under attack, and being told by him that he wants the ship going to the bottom.

Despite the fact that the U.S. carriers withdrew their help, a Russian spy ship appeared, and witnessed part of the attack. After three hours into the attack, the Israelis withdrew because there were witnesses, allowing the damaged USS Liberty to limp to safety.
~ Terrorstorm[1646]

Surprisingly, it was America's cold war enemy who saved the Liberty.

Few people in America or Russia are aware of the crucial and heroic role played by Destroyer 626/4 of the Soviet Navy during the Six-Day War in June, 1967. The commander and crew of this ship

The infamous wink between TX Democrat Rep. Albert Thomas and his friend Lyndon Johnson while being sworn in as President, standing next to the former First Lady still in shock over her husband having his brains blown out next to her.

> *guarded the American intelligence vessel GTR-4, better known as the USS Liberty, after the attack on it by the combined air and naval branches of the Israeli Defense Force. The [Israeli] attack was coordinated with elements of the U.S. Navy, U.S. intelligence and the White House.*
>
> *The top-secret plan was known as Operation Cyanide and was intended to result in the sinking of the Liberty with all hands, to be blamed on Egypt and exploited to permit the bombing of Cairo and the entry of the United States into the war on Israel's side. The Soviet Union's relationships with Arab countries would have been damaged and perhaps cut, with America and Israel seizing control of all Mid-East oil production. Israel's borders would have expanded from the Nile to the Euphrates Rivers.* ~ Izrail Schmerler[1647]

The Protocols of Zion

In Thomas Jefferson's January 1800 letter to John Adams, he mentions an important name.

> *Dear Sir, I have lately by accident got a sight of a single volume (the 3d.) of the Abbe Barruel's Antisocial conspiracy, which gives me the first idea I have ever had of what is meant by the Illuminatism against which "illuminate Morse" as he is now called, & his ecclesiastical & monarchical associates have been making such a hue and cry. Barruel's own parts of the book are perfectly the ravings of a Bedlamite.*[1648]

Augustin Barruel (1741-1820) was a French publicist and Jesuit priest who may have been the most successful purveyor of propaganda the Company of Loyola has ever had.

"Abbé" ("Father") Barruel brilliantly wove a treatise on the barbaric excesses of the French Revolution by blaming the Illuminati Masons in specific and Freemasons in general[1649], which, given that the "Illuminati" were created by Jesuit Adam Weishaupt and the French nobility was largely masonic, was patently absurd.

The *Mémoires pour servir à l'histoire du Jacobinisme* ("Memoirs Illustrating the History of Jacobinism") were widely circulated and immensely popular though later debunked.

Barruel eventually switched his target of distraction from the Illuminati to the Jews.

> *... in 1806, Barruel circulated a forged letter, probably sent to him by members of the state police opposed to Napoleon Bonaparte's liberal policy toward the Jews, calling attention to the alleged part of the Jews in the conspiracy he had earlier attributed to the Masons. This myth of an international Jewish conspiracy reappeared later on in 19th century Europe in places such as Germany and Poland.* ~ Jewish Virtual Library[1650]

This would set the stage for the dissemination of the greatest anti-Semitic hoax of all time, the purported plan for world Jewish domination—*The Protocols of the Elders of Zion*.

It proved to be quite useful to anti-Semites like Adolf Hitler and Henry Ford.

> The Protocols of the Elders of Zion or The Protocols of the Meetings of the Learned Elders of Zion *is an antisemitic hoax purporting to describe a Jewish plan for global domination.*[1] *It was first published in Russia in 1903, translated into multiple languages, and disseminated internationally in the early part of the 20th century. Henry Ford funded printing of 500,000 copies that were distributed throughout the US in the 1920s.*
>
> *Adolf Hitler and the Nazis publicized the text as though it were a valid document, although it had already been exposed as fraudulent. After the Nazi Party came to power in 1933, it ordered the text to be studied in German classrooms. The historian Norman Cohn suggested that Hitler used the Protocols as his primary justification for initiating the Holocaust—his "warrant for genocide".*[2] ~ Wikipedia[1651]

Using the Jews as targets and shields was extremely appealing to a great many Catholic authorities.

> *No pope hated Jews more than Paul IV (1555-59), whose cruelties defy the bounds of human reason. Catholic historian Peter de Rosa confesses that a whole "succession of popes reinforced the ancient prejudices against Jews, treating them as lepers unworthy of the protection of the law. Pius VII [1800-23] was followed by Leo XII, Pius VIII, Gregory XVI, Pius IX [1846-78]-all good pupils of Paul IV."*[2] *Historian Will Durant reminds us that Hitler had good precedent for his sanctions against the Jews:*
>
>> *The [Roman Catholic] Council of Vienne (1311) forbade all intercourse between Christians and Jews. The Council*

> *of Zamora (1313) ruled that they must be kept in strict subjection and servitude. The Council of Basel (1431-33) renewed canonical decrees forbidding Christians to associate with Jews ... and instructed secular authorities [as the church had herself long enforced in Rome and the papal states] to confine the Jews in separate quarters [ghettos], compel them to wear a distinguishing badge [it had previously been a yellow hat], and ensure their attendance at sermons aimed to convert them.[3] ...*

> *For most of the Jews living in Europe, Church law made it impossible to intermarry without converting to Roman Catholicism. Here again the Roman Catholic Church played an infamous role. For centuries it was a capital offense under the popes for a Jew to marry a Christian, preventing intermarriage even for those who desired it. ~ A Woman Rides The Beast*, Dave Hunt[1652]

The Rothschilds

The Rothschilds are the most notorious family in truth-seeking circles but their connection to the Vatican is both little-known yet critical to what they do.

> *... the Nationalist and Reactionary parties in France desired to counterbalance the "Semitic" influence of the Rothschilds by establishing a banking concern which should be essentially Catholic. Accordingly in 1876 the Union Générale was founded with a capital of 4,000,000 francs, increased to 25,000,000 fraces in 1878 under the direction of a certain Bontoux. After various vicissitudes, graphically described by Zola in his novel "L'Argent," the Union failed, and brought many of the Catholic nobility of France to ruin, leaving the Rothschilds still more absolutely the undisputed leaders of French finance, but leaving also a legacy of hatred which had much influence on the growth of the anti-Semitic movement in France. Something analogous occurred in England when the century-long competition of the Barings and the Rothschilds culminated in the failure of the former in 1893; but in this case the Rothschilds came to the rescue of their rivals and prevented a universal financial catastrophe. It is a somewhat curious sequel to the attempt to set up a Catholic competitor to the Rothschilds that at the present time the latter are the guardians of the papal treasure. ~ Encyclopedia Judaica*[1653]

Although this may seem like an unlikely collaborative effort, it's really quite intuitive given the Luciferian designs of all involved.

Jewish Patriot Emanuel Josephson, writing in 1968, brilliantly put it all together from banking to the Bolsheviks and from Secret Societies to the Society of Loyola.

Most astutely, Josephson described how Jewish bankers were used as an end-around by their crafty Vatican masters to allow the appearance of piety while still cashing in on currency manipulation. [italics suspended]

> Human experience teaches the power of the purse. One may well wonder if it is not Almighty.
>
> Few of the power-mad characters of history who have sought to rule their fellows and to build empires have failed to grab the wealth of lands on which they have design, and usurp the power of purse over those whom they seek to subjugate. This is true even of those who have been more motivated by the lust for power than by simple thievery and brigandage. For money is the lifeblood of commerce and industry. In the form of either cash or credit, money enables the expansion of a nation's economy beyond the narrow limits of crude barter. Since commerce and industry are the livelihoods of nations and their peoples, the control of money is the obvious key to the control of nations and the world.
>
> From time immemorial, rulers of lands have seized and retained control of their monetary systems. The issuance of coins and the control of currency have been cherished throughout the ages as the prime source of wealth, might and power. Roman emperors, for instance, proudly stamped their images on their coins as an expression of their power; and manipulated the content of those coins for their personal profit.
>
> Rome's successor, the Holy Roman Empire, dissimulated its interest in money and its power. This was in accord with its professed tenets of Nazarene, theistic Communism. Under ecclesiastic, Canon Law, even profits in business transactions were decreed to be the cardinal sin and capital offence of "usury". As late as the sixteenth century, one hundred Christian business men who held no Papal dispensation, were burned at the stake in Geneva, as a penalty under Church law, for making profits in their business transactions. Title to all wealth as well as to the persons and lives of all the earth are claimed by the Church, on the ground that their ownership is divinely vested in the Pope as the vicar of Jesus Christ on earth. Thus theistic, Nazarene Communism, and the "modern" religion that goes by the name of Communism and is supposedly atheist, both are basically super-capitalist and both mask

their avid grab for money and wealth.

Title to all wealth was vested in the Church and in its champion "knights," who at the same time assumed the role of so-called "protectors," much like the present-day "labor leaders" of their vassals whom they mercilessly enslaved and looted.

Both Churchmen and lay knights used the despised Jews for the conduct of their usurious financial operations, in order to avoid "sinning" and the death penalty that it involved. The Jews proved very useful and handy for that purpose. ~ *The "Federal" Reserve Conspiracy*, Josephson[1654]

According to Josephson, their Roman masters considered Jews already condemned and, therefore, using them for usury and giving them the onerous reputation that came with it was perfectly acceptable. Those who failed to ruthlessly engage in banking were burned and those who did well were partnered with. If it seemed advantageous to the priests, even successful Jewish bankers were robbed and burned.

It was the inner war waged by the "loyal as a corpse with no will of their own" Jesuits that forced the Vatican into bed with the Rothschilds.

Josephson, as well, recognized that the founder of "the Illuminati" was a loyal Loyola agent and that his apprentice was the author of Communism. [italics suspended]

> Dispensation from the Canon on Usury was ... granted by the Vatican, in the 15th century, to the German Fuggers, the Rockefellers of that era. Their profits from commerce, usury and the sale of Papal dispensations, as agents of the Vatican, grew rapidly, as did their "payoff" to the Church. They were heaped with Papal honors. But their grasping greed and merciless loan-sharking earned for them distrust and terror. When one of their number was elevated to the rank of Cardinal, the Churchmen feared that the Fuggers would reach out and steal the Vatican itself. They then decided that their Jewish pawns were more completely at their mercy, more amenable and safer.

> Trusteeship of the fortune of one of the wealthiest Christian rulers of Europe whose confidence had been earned by honest and trustworthy dealings, during the Napoleonic wars, is the source of the wealth and influence that the Rothschilds acquired in the first decades of the 19th century. Subsequently, after making a large loan to the hard-pressed Vatican, that no Christian would consider

making, they became the fiscal agents of the Vatican, received Papal decorations and preferments, and enforced the policies dictated by the Church. It was largely in this sense that they were "international bankers". And the pillaging dictated by them were in effect the policies dictated by the Church. They enforced those policies through their establishments in many lands.

An amusing story is told of the earliest relations of the Rothschilds with the Vatican. The Vatican found itself short of ready cash after almost half a century of war waged on it for the Jesuit Order by one of its unordained members, Adam Weishaupt, to avenge its abolition, in 1773, as "immoral and a menace to the Church and the Faith" by short-lived Pope Clement XIV in his Papal breve *Dominus Ac Redemptor*. Weishaupt and his fellow Jesuits cut off the income to the Vatican by launching and leading the French Revolution; by directing Napoleon's conquest of Catholic Europe; by the revolt against the Church led by such priests as Father Hidalgo, in Mexico and Latin America; by eventually having Napoleon throw Pope Pius VII in jail at Avignon until he agreed, as the price for his release, to reestablish the Jesuit Order. This Jesuit war on the Vatican was terminated by the Congress of Vienna and by the secret, 1822, Treaty of Verona.(72:8;73) The Jesuits thus so completely impaired the credit of the Vatican that no Christian banker would entrust it with a loan of needed funds.

Only the nouveau riche Jewish upstarts, who had made their fortune in the latter part of the Napoleonic wars, the Rothschilds, would trust the Church with urgently needed 5 million pounds.

Pope Gregory XVI was so grateful to the Rothschilds that he conferred on Kalman [Karl] Rothschild a Papal decoration. In deference to the Jewish faith of the philanthropic banker, the usual cross in the decoration was replaced by a Star of David. Rothschild was incensed at this discriminatory gesture. He demanded, and was awarded, the decoration with a cross. Ever since, the Rothschilds have been the fiscal agents of the Vatican.

The Rothschilds sought to extend their financial and political dominion to the United States, for themselves primarily to serve the interests of their Vatican masters. The Vatican's interest in the U.S. Republic was clearly revealed in the Treaty of Verona, in which the Jesuit Order pledged itself, as the price of its reestablishment, to destroy the "works of Satan" that it had accomplished in setting up, by revolts, representative governments such as republics and so-called "democracies".(72:8) Senator Robert Owen pointed out, in the Senate, that the prime target to which the Vatican and the "Holy Alliance" directed the subversive and destructive activities of the Society of Jesus is the United States (73), as well as other republics of the Western Hemisphere.(72:10) This plot, he related, was the target at which the Monroe Doctrine was directed.

The Rothschild-Vatican cabal unsuccessfully attempted to gain control over the power of the purse in the U.S. through the First and the Second Bank of the United States. They were established under the emergency powers granted the President by the Constitution, as temporary institutions to tide the country through the periods of financial stress occasioned by the Revolutionary and 1812 Wars. But the conspirators failed in their efforts to fasten their hold on the nation's power of the purse through establishment of a privately controlled central bank of permanent character. They were doomed to failure by the stumbling block of fear of a banking monopoly, and by the deliberate barrier against central banking and Federal control and issue of currency that had been embodied in the Constitution...

"Give me control of a nation's money, and I care not who rules it," is an age-old adage, the origination of which is attributed to Amshel Mayer Rothschild. It is a trite expression of the power of the purse that he might well have learned as a familiar nursery rhyme.

Few of the plotters who have conspired to enslave and rule mankind plotted more studied use of the control of money and wealth than did the founders of modern-day Communism: Jesuit Adam Weishaupt, alias Spartacus, and his disciple, Moses Mordecai Marx Levy, alias (Heinrich) Karl Marx. They proposed for the purpose of sneakily stealing control of the world and of looting everyone, three basic measures: First, their control, as rulers, of money and banking. Second, a progressive income tax that would be perverted into a capital tax. Third, a confiscatory inheritance tax. ... ~ *The "Federal" Reserve Conspiracy*, Josephson [1655]

The "Secret Treaty of Verona" is a document said to have been signed by representatives from France, Austria, Prussia and Russia in 1822. Its goal was to solidify Elite control over civil populations by mitigating democracy and the dissemination of information via a free press. Acknowledging that "religion" helped keep the people quelled, Article III specifically thanks the Pope for his help with this agenda.[1656]

The Treaty was leaked to the administration of James Monroe who subsequently published the Monroe Doctrine the following year in 1823 as a result, declaring that any further colonization by European powers (and their Jesuit shock troops) in the Western hemisphere would be seen as an act of war.

This information can be found in the testimony and work of United States Senator Robert Owen. In 1916, Owen introduced the Secret Treaty of Verona into the Congressional record and referenced it in his 1919 book *Where Is God In the European War?*[1657]

Owen is an interesting figure. A banker and the first Senator from Oklahoma, he is the Democrat who sponsored the Federal Reserve Act in the Senate. His aforementioned book has more religious sentiment than a Southern Baptist sermon and appears to attempt to shore up the destructive policies of the Wilson administration while exposing Wilson's masters, (probably unwittingly).

Perhaps Vladimir Lenin would've called him a "useful idiot".

Even When Facts Bear It Out, Bigotry Isn't the Answer

When certain groups of people consistently behave in ways that are detrimental to the nation, it becomes extremely tempting to profile on those grounds.

American blacks have not done well in protecting the nation from the scourge that is Barack Hussein Obama.

In 2008, more registered Democrats voted for John McCain (10%) than did blacks (4%) as they turned out in the highest percentage of lock-step support in electoral history of Obama at nearly 96%.[1658]

Since then, Barack Obama has been *poison* for the black community.

His top priority was to destroy school choice for black families, particularly those in Washington DC.[1659]

While in Johannesburg, South Africa, Obama showed his true colors (those of a Luciferian puppet) by telling Africans:

> ... *if you think about all the youth that everybody has mentioned here in Africa, if everybody is raising living standards to the point where everybody has got a car and everybody has got air conditioning, and everybody has got a big house, well, the planet will boil over ...* ~ Ryan Kierman, CNS News[1660]

Barack Obama supports abortion at levels that, for lack of dispassionate terms, can only be described as "satanic". While as an Illinois State Senator (an office appropriated for him from black Communist Alice Palmer[1661]) Obama repeatedly helped defeat the Infant Born Alive Protection Act and once did it single-handedly as the Health & Human Services Committee chairman[1662]. This is an industry that preys so exclusively on blacks as to rightly be called "genocidal".[1663]

All gains that were made in helping black Americans be freed from the chains of state-sponsored welfare were reversed under Obama[1664] as he insured a skyrocket in suicidal levels of national debt.

Despite all of this, not even dissatisfaction with an incumbent could drop black support of Obama below 93% in his 2012 re-election.[1665]

But it all would've been turned on its head and America would today be as strong and as healthy as with any administration in the past 100 years if the fortunes of Obama and the black Catholic man who ran against him for Illinois Senate seat in 2004 had been reversed.

Ambassador to the United Nations Economic and Social Council and Assistant Secretary of State for International Organization Affairs under Ronald Reagan, Dr. Alan Keyes contested Barack Obama in his meteoric rise in both his 2004 Illinois Senate Seat and in 2008 for the Presidency.[zz]

Two groups of people betrayed him: American blacks and American Conservatives.

Black Americans found his message of family, self discipline and Patriotism so distasteful they couldn't run fast enough to pull the lever for Barack Obama.

renewamerica.us

But the worst betrayal was from the so-called "Conservative" Right.

The "Christian" and "Conservative" Family Research Council lead by Tony Perkins purposefully excluded Keyes from their invitation for all 2008 presidential candidates to address family issues in a debate.[1666]

In 2009, after Obama won the White House, Keyes warned that the

---

[zz] Did Papal powers promote this juxtaposition as validation of their satanic agenda before God? "They deserve us, Lord. Look at how they reacted."

Chosen One was a radical Communist bent on destroying America. He stated Obama's policies and actions on abortion were an "abomination" and that he wasn't even Constitutionally eligible to *be* the President of the United States.[1667]

"Conservative" David Horowitz lambasted Dr. Keyes for National Review.

> *The continuing efforts of a fringe group of conservatives to deny Obama his victory and to lay the basis for the claim that he is not a legitimate president are embarrassing and destructive. The fact that these efforts are being led by Alan Keyes, a demagogue who lost a Senate election to the then-unknown Obama by 42 points, should be a warning in itself.*[1668]

National Review was founded by William F. Buckley, a CIA operative who was a member of Skull and Bones[1669]. He was also a devout Catholic.[1670]

As devastating as Leftist Jews and minorities have been to the good interests of the United States there have been a handful of Patriots who risked all to fight for her and for Truth.

> *The only uniformly loyal moneyed group were the Jewish refugee group fleeing from the Inquisition that had followed them to Brazil, who had settled in Philadelphia. They so highly cherished the freedom that they had found there that some of them had turned over their entire fortunes to finance the [American] Revolution. They were members of the group that are buried in the Jewish Cemetery of the Mikveh Israel Congregation in Philadelphia, at Ninth and Spruce Streets, that has been made a national monument. It included Haym Salomon (who unstintingly gave his entire fortune to the Revolutionary cause and was never repaid a farthing of it), Samuel Hays (the ancestor of a many distinguished servants of our Republic), Philip Moses Russel (a Revolutionary War surgeon and reputed ancestor of the Senator from Georgia), Michael Gratz (in whose grocery Thomas Jefferson is reported to have drafted the Declaration of Independence), and Manuel Josephson, among others. (187) Their loyalty contrasted sharply, with the attitude of another group of Brazilian Jewish refugees who migrated to New York, including some of the van Rosenvelts (now known as Roosevelts) who became ringleaders of the Illuminist Communist conspiracy in Revolutionary days, (7188) and became identified with the Tory moneylenders and merchants.* ~ Josephson[1671]

As America nears what Thomas Jefferson called the "watering of the Tree of Liberty with the blood of Patriots and Tyrants"[1672], it will be men like these who fill the ranks of her III%.

Roughly 100,000 men served in the Continental Army during the Revolutionary War.[1673]

The total population of the Colonies at the time was around 2 million.[1674]

When considering losses and fluctuation in those numbers, the total population of America responsible for ousting the most powerful military in the world leveled off at around 3% with direct aid coming from no more than 10% of the Colonies.

Endnotes

[1637] *John Hagee Denies Christ As Messiah*, Johnny Cirucci YouTube
https://www.youtube.com/watch?v=K2KTfCJGkG4&
[1638] *Israel*, Rothschild.com
http://www.rothschild.com/israel/
[1639] *PROOF: You Are Being Played!* Johnny Cirucci, 27 October 2013, the Patriot Press
http://johnnycirucci.com/wp/blog/2013/10/27/
[1640] *"World's Best Gay City" Shows Off Its Pride With 16th-Annual Gay Pride Parade*, Sarah Gruen, 13 June 2014, the Jerusalem Post
http://www.jpost.com/National-News/Tel-Aviv-celebrates-16th-annual-Gay-Pride-Parade-358170
[1641] *How Israel Helped Create Hamas*, Ishaan Tharoor 30 July 2014, the Washington Post
http://www.washingtonpost.com/blogs/worldviews/wp/2014/07/30/how-israel-helped-create-hamas/
[1642] *How Israel Helped to Spawn Hamas*, Andrew Higgins, 24 January 2009, the Wall Street Journal
http://online.wsj.com/articles/SB123275572295011847
[1643] *Lavon Affair*, Wikipedia
https://en.wikipedia.org/wiki/Lavon_Affair
[1644] *The USS Liberty, Israel & President Johnson's Order to Destroy the USS Liberty*, Judy Morris, 30 January 2014, the Economic Policy Journal
http://www.economicpolicyjournal.com/2013/01/the-uss-liberty-israel-president.html
[1645] *Lyndon B. Johnson Arranged John F. Kennedy's Assassination - Roger Stone*, 8 November 2013, Voice of Russia
http://sputniknews.com/voiceofrussia/2013_11_08/Lyndon-B-Johnson-arranged-John-F-Kennedys-assassination-Roger-Stone-5591/
[1646] Transcript from the documentary *Terrorstorm— Clip: A History of False Flag Attacks*, a well-done video from InfoWars despite their role as Jesuit coadjutors.
http://www.newsofinterest.tv/video_pages_flash/politics/infowars/terrorstorm/false_flag_history.php
[1647] *Operation Cyanide*, Israel Shamir, 22 October 2012, Shamir Readers on Yahoo! Groups
https://groups.yahoo.com/neo/groups/shamireaders/conversations/topics/1928
   Izrail Schmerler, a.k.a. "Israel Shamir" is a fascinating individual. Here is his Wikipedia entry:
https://en.wikipedia.org/wiki/Israel_Shamir
[1648] *Thomas Jefferson to Reverend James Madison, January 31, 1800*, The Works of Thomas Jefferson in Twelve Volumes. Federal Edition. Collected and Edited by Paul Leicester Ford. Philadelphia, Jan. 31, 1800. The Library of Congress.
http://memory.loc.gov/cgi-bin/query/r?ammem/mtj:@field%28DOCID+@lit%28tj090050%29%29
[1649] *Antisemitism: A Historical Encyclopedia of Prejudice and Persecution, Volume 1*, Richard Levy, ABC-CLIO (2005), p. 59
[1650] *History of the "Protocols of the Elders of Zion"*, Jewish Virtual Library
http://www.jewishvirtuallibrary.org/jsource/anti-semitism/protocols.html
[1651] *The Protocols of the Elders of Zion*, Wikipedia

http://en.wikipedia.org/wiki/The_Protocols_of_the_Elders_of_Zion
[1652] *A Woman Rides The Beast*, Dave Hunt, Harvest House (1994), pp. 23, 24
[1653] *ROTHSCHILD, The Union Générale*, JewishEncyclopedia
http://www.jewishencyclopedia.com/articles/12909-rothschild
[1654] *The "Federal" Reserve Conspiracy & Rockefellers: Their "Gold Corner"*, Emanuel M. Josephson, Chedney Press 1968, p. 10
[1655] *ibid*, pp. 4-6
[1656] *The Secret Treaty of Verona*, Johnny Cirucci Scribd
https://www.scribd.com/doc/249050961/The-Secret-Treaty-of-Verona
[1657] *Where Is God In The European War?* Robert L. Own, Centry (1919), pp. 17, 22, etc.
[1658] *Inside Obama's Sweeping Victory*, 5 November 2008, Pew Research Center
http://www.pewresearch.org/2008/11/05/inside-obamas-sweeping-victory/
[1659] *Dems Kow-Tow To Teacher's Union - Kill Successful DC Voucher Program*, Aaron Gee, 21 December 2009, American Thinker
http://www.americanthinker.com/blog/2009/12/dems_kowtow_to_teachers_union.html
[1660] *Obama: "Planet Will Boil Over" If Young Africans Are Allowed Cars, Air-Conditioning, Big Houses*, Ryan Kierman, 1 July 2013, CNS News
http://cnsnews.com/news/article/obama-planet-will-boil-over-if-young-africans-are-allowed-cars-air-conditioning-big
[1661] *Barack Hussein Obama*, Discover the Networks
http://www.discoverthenetworks.org/individualProfile.asp?indid=1511
	Wow! Fantastic and comprehensive. Word search "Alice Palmer" for the details I referenced.
[1662] *Links to Barack Obama's votes on Illinois' Born Alive Infant Protection Act*, February 2008, Jill Stanek.com
http://www.jillstanek.com/2008/02/links-to-barack-obamas-votes-on-illinois-born-alive-infant-protection-act/
[1663] *Abortion: Black Genocide*, Jesse Lee Peterson, 13 February 2008, WND
http://www.wnd.com/2008/02/56202/#!
[1664] *Ending Work for Welfare: An Overview*, Robert Rector and Rachel Sheffield, 29 August 2012, the Heritage Foundation
http://www.heritage.org/research/reports/2012/08/obama-administration-ends-welfare-reform-as-we-know-it
[1665] *Blacks Outvoted Whites in 2012, the First Time On Record*, Dan Merica, 9 May 2013, CNN
http://politicalticker.blogs.cnn.com/2013/05/09/blacks-outvoted-whites-in-2012-the-first-time-on-record/
[1666] *Alan Keyes Excluded From FRC Event*, 22 October 2007, WND
http://www.wnd.com/2007/10/44141/#!
[1667] *Alan Keyes' Prophetic Warning: Obama Is A Radical Communist Who Will Destroy America*, Johnny Cirucci YouTube
https://www.youtube.com/watch?v=4TRxtmtgYPk&
[1668] *Obama Derangement Syndrome: Shut up about the birth certificate.* David Horowitz, 8 December 2008, National Review
http://www.nationalreview.com/articles/226474/obama-derangement-syndrome/david-horowitz#!

[1669] *CIA/Skull-and-Bonesman Wm. F Buckley Jr. Obituary*, Michael Hoffman, 27 February 2008, the Revisionist Review
http://revisionistreview.blogspot.com/2008/02/ciaskull-and-bonesman-wm-f-buckley-jr.html
   This idiot smells like an Ivy League Communist but as long as it's someone else telling you what Buckley was that's all I wanted.
[1670] *The Catholicism of William F. Buckley, Jr.*, Paul Kengor, 01 May 2011, the Catholic World Report
http://www.catholicworldreport.com/Item/504/the_catholicism_of_william_f_buckley_jr.aspx
[1671] *The Federal Reserve Conspiracy*, Emanuel Josephson, p. 10
[1672] *The tree of liberty... (Quotation)*, Monticello.org
http://www.monticello.org/site/jefferson/tree-liberty-quotation#_ref-0
[1673] *Myths of the American Revolution*, John Ferling, January 2010, Smithsonian Magazine
http://www.smithsonianmag.com/history/myths-of-the-american-revolution-10941835/?all&no-ist
[1674] *Reflections on the American Revolution (Part I of II)*, Dan McLaughlin, 28 January 2012, RedState
http://www.redstate.com/2013/01/28/reflections-on-the-american-revolution-part-i-of-ii/

Chapter 18

From Nimrod to al Ilah

Who is it that Rome and her Jesuits truly worship?

For that answer, we need to look up...in the Sistine Chapel.

The world famous fresco that adorns the ceiling of the Sistine Chapel was painted by the Renaissance artist and engineer, Michelangelo di Lodovico Buonarroti Simoni.

For generations, Michelangelo Buonarroti's depiction of the creation has thrilled onlookers with the lackadaisical reach of Adam's hand towards God, encapsulating the struggle of mankind to reach his Divine potential in relationship with YHWH.

But who is Adam really reaching out to?

In the fresco, "God" and His cherubim are encompassed by an odd structure; it's the outline of the human brain (amazing knowledge of anatomy for the early 1500's).

The message of Buonarroti? —"God" is a construct of your mind.

Inside the brain, is a mysterious organ known as the pineal gland. It is thought to secrete the compound Dimethyltryptamine, or "DMT"[1675], which easily crosses the blood-brain barrier and has a psychedelic, hallucinogenic effect. Pagans and mystics believe it actually allows a consciousness to cross into another dimension to communicate with other-worldly intelligences.

There's at least one scientist who agrees with them.

Rick Strassman is a PhD, MD who had a general psychiatry residency at U. C. Davis (with honors) and a private practice at a mental health facility in Alaska. He obtained fellowship training in clinical psychopharmacology research at the University of California San Diego's Veteran's Administration Medical Center, then served on the clinical faculty in the Department of Psychiatry at UC Davis.

But it was Strassman's full-time work at the Department of Psychiatry at the University of New Mexico where his experiments with N,N-Dimethyltryptamine ("DMT") had him asking serious questions about forbidden topics.

In an interview with author, investigator and talk show host Derek Gilbert, Strassman recounted his research administering Dimethyltryptamine to volunteers at UNM in the 1990's.[1676]

According to Strassman, the most effective means of getting DMT into a subject's brain is by injection. If ingested, enzymes in the stomach dissolve it before it enters the blood.

Strassman gave 60 volunteers 400 doses across the breadth of his research at UNM. Not surprisingly, they had already experimented with hallucinogenic drugs and the predominant religious affiliations were wiccans and pagans.

In over half of the experiences, the volunteer claimed to have interacted with intelligent beings that Strassman believes were *not* the constructs of the subject's imagination.

Within a minute of receiving DMT into the bloodstream, subjects experienced a "high-pitched screeching", a kaleidoscope of colors and then their room was overlaid with an alternative world. Quickly, they were confronted with beings

---

A Curious "Discovery"

Dimethyltryptamine is an hallucinogenic compound that occurs both in the human body and in nature.

To date, it is unknown how the human body produces DMT although experiments have shown that tissue from the pineal gland can result in DMT when mixed with other naturally-occurring substances.

South American shamans use a mixture known as *ayahuasca* to bypass the body's digestion of DMT and get it past the blood/brain barrier.

The name Ayahuasca comes from Quechua, a widely spoken South American language found throughout the Amazon: aya means "soul" or "spirits" and huasca means "vine"...

The origin of this mixture and even its full historic background remains a mystery.

that looked like serpents, insects, humans, machines, cyborgs and angels.

The most common was a humanoid praying mantis, probably not too different from the being on the amulet worn by young Barry Soetero, seen in his Indonesian family photo.

The most unique was a subject who interacted with a sentient apartment. His experience presaged by a decade a threat made by short-lived CIA Director David Petraeus in early 2012.

> **SOURCES:**
>
> *Ayahuasca and Amazonian Shamanism*, Temple of the Way of Light
> http://templeofthewayoflight.org/shamanism-ayahuasca/ayahuasca-and-amazonian-shamanism/

> *More and more personal and household devices are connecting to the internet, from your television to your car navigation systems to your light switches. CIA Director David Petraeus cannot wait to spy on you through them.*
>
> *Earlier this month, Petraeus mused about the emergence of an "Internet of Things" — that is, wired devices — at a summit for In-Q-Tel, the CIA's venture capital firm. "'Transformational' is an overused word, but I do believe it properly applies to these technologies," Petraeus enthused, "particularly to their effect on clandestine tradecraft."* ~ Spencer Ackerman, Wired[1677]

Americans continue to "muse" over the steamrolling of the 4th Amendment by traitors who have captured their nation.

As the world's Intelligence Agencies (guided by the Luciferian Papal Elite) continue to build a literal Skynet of Artificial Intelligence ("AI"), are they, in fact, weaving a web of slavery for us all?

Dr. Rick Strasser had abandoned his Jewish faith long ago. He had invested several decades into Zen Buddhism as a personal discipline.

But his research data shocked him. If his subjects actually were experiencing a truly spiritual encounter, there should be a dissolution of the personal ego followed by a collective joining or melding (much as Teilhard de Chardin predicted).

Instead, each volunteer maintained their individuality and had encounters based upon who they were.

As he struggled for answers, Strasser has returned to the Old Testament of the Bible for understanding of the spirit realm.[1678]

In the ancient Egyptian "Eye of Horus" is the unmistakable outline of the inner-workings of the brain, centered around the pineal gland. Did the Egyptians also consider it a "gateway to the gods"? Was their knowledge of human anatomy that good, or was something else at play?

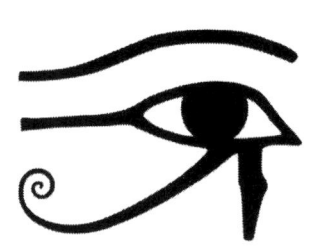

Another "gateway" to alternative dimensions is the human reproductive system.

With good reason did satanists like Aleister Crowley, Jack Parsons, Anton LaVey and Michael Aquino conduct rituals in relation to perverse forms of sex to reach other realms.

—Or let other realms reach them.

Apparently, Michelangelo Buonarroti knew all of this because if you superimpose a schematic of the brain over its outline encompassing "God" you will find the pineal gland lines up roughly with about where "God's" private parts would be.

Is this the dramatic fresco of a brilliant Christian artist, or the secret message of a gnostic adept?

The Goddess of Wisdom

There's something else.

Notice the naked woman that "God" has his arm around. Most assume she is Eve and move on.

This woman is understood by gnostics, not as the bride of Adam, but the bride of God[1679]. She is known as "Sophia" the goddess of wisdom and knowledge.

The "wife of God" has another name, as well.

> *The connection between the Goddess Isis and the Goddess Wisdom (Sophia in Greek; Chokmah in Hebrew) is an interesting one. In fact, some scholars think that the figure of Sophia was patterned after Isis. And they may well be right.*
>
> *In Michelangelo's famous Sistine Chapel painting, Wisdom (Sophia) nestles in the crook of God's left arm...* ~ Isis & Sophia, Isiopolis[1680]

In Iraq, a group of Islamists is slicing its way across the Middle East. Its barbarism has little to do with "wisdom" but its creators may feel they do.

From the beginning, it was known as "the Islamic State of Iraq and Syria": ISIS and it was absolutely a creation of the CIA[1681,1682] and, ultimately, of Rome.

Realizing they had been too clever by half, and that the dumbed-down masses weren't quite that dumb, the Elite quickly had the media re-lable the jihadists as "Islamic State" or "the Islamic State of Iraq and the Levant" but the message had already been received.

> *It's rather ironic that this latest wave of Western armed and financed "Islamic" militants invading Iraq and now conveniently threatening Syria and Iran is named ISIS. Or is it deliberate? It's being used to stand for this oddly anglicised fabricated "Islamic State in Iraq and Syria" full on barbaric movement presently sweeping Iraq, but anyone acquainted with any degree of occult knowledge or esoteric mythology know the goddess Isis is one of the most important figures in the so-called mystery schools and a favorite of Freemasonry and the Illuminati. ~ The ISIS Ploy: Illuminati Sorcery and Sacrifice, Zen Gardner*[1683]

The stable secular nations in the Middle East were scheduled by the Elite to fall one by one[1684], but the dominoes stopped at Syria, held up by one man: Vladimir Putin.[1685]

At every step, Putin moved like a strategic chess master.

> *On Monday, September 9, Russian President Vladimir Putin made a diplomatic move that seemed to catch the entire international community, not just U.S. President Barack Obama and his team, by surprise. He seized the most dramatic moment possible—the eve of what was to be a fateful vote in the U.S. Congress on Obama's decision to launch a targeted strike against Syrian leader Bashar al-Assad—to propose that Syria surrender its chemical weapons to an international commission headed by the United Nations. Assad quickly agreed to the proposal, at least in principle.*

> *By the evening of September 10, after a day full of calls from every imaginable corner to pursue Putin's plan, Obama seemed to back away from threats of imminent military action. In a live address to the nation, he requested a delay in the congressional vote, announced that Secretary of State John Kerry would meet with the Russians to hash things out, pushed for the United Nations to*

maintain the diplomatic pressure on Assad, and put another round of the Syrian game in motion. Putin then further pressed his advantage by demanding a promise from Washington not to attack Assad if the Syrian leader surrenders his chemical weapons. ~ Fiona Hill, Foreign Affairs[1686]

Furious, the Luciferians took their weapon and re-aimed it at Iraqi heretics.

Secretly, Western Intelligence in general and the CIA in specific fueled the bloodshed and barbarism.

In fact, it wasn't so secret.

Iraq Intel Report: US Planes Supplying ISIL with Weapons, Foodstuff

TEHRAN (FNA) Iraqi intelligence sources disclosed that US military planes have been supplying the Islamic State of Iraq and the Levant Takfiri terrorists with weapons and foodstuff under the guise of air raids on militants' positions. ~ FARS News Agency[1687]

The scourge of Muhammad's scimitar at every step has been funded by the American taxpayer to include cutting a 5 year old Christian boy in half[1688], to crucifying, beheading and burning alive Christian adults.[1689]

While this went on, the United States military bombed empty buildings[1690] and operations have exploited the cover of darkness to hide their purposeful ineffectiveness[1691]. Meanwhile *real* missions were conducted in Syria against such targets as a Syrian oil refinery that ISIS miraculously learned how to take over and operate.[1692]

Barbarism In Common

Whenever critics wish to slander or attack Christianity, or to equivocate the dangers of generalized "religion", they point to the Crusades or the Inquisition as evidence of how "Christians" are no better than the worst offenders in Islam. These are *all* resoundingly Catholic institutions.

As you look down upon both Roman Catholicism and Islam there are some startling similarities. In both instances, the real victims have been Bible-believing followers of Jesus Christ.

Chaldean-American businessman Marc Arabo told CNN that "ISIS" was making Iraq a living nightmare for Christians. Children were being beheaded and their little heads placed on sticks. Every Christian that is found is tortured and killed and a religious form of genocide is being systematically conducted.[1693]

The Beast Behind Christian Persecution

In 1620, a Scottish traveler named William Lithgow had the unfortunate experience of being aboard an English merchant vessel that landed at Malaga, Spain.

> *As soon as Mr. Lithgow got on shore, he proceeded towards his lodgings by a private way, (being to embark the same night for Alexandria) when, in passing through a narrow uninhabited street, he found himself suddenly surrounded by nine sergeants, or officers, who threw a black cloak over him, and forcibly conducted him to the governor's house. After some little time the governor appeared when Mr. Lithgow earnestly begged he might be informed of the cause of such violent treatment. The governor only answered by shaking his head, and gave orders that the prisoner should be strictly watched till he (the governor) returned from his devotions; directing at the same time, that the captain of the town, the alcade major, and town notary, should be summoned to appear at his examination, and that all this should be done with the greatest secrecy, to prevent the knowledge thereof reaching the ears of the English merchants then residing in the town. ~ Foxe's Book of Martyrs*[1694]

His Spanish captors were sure that Mr. Lithgow was an English spy, that all Englishmen were Protestants and that nothing Mr. Lithgow vowed in his defense could be trusted.

> *"Wherefore, (said they) these Lutherans, and sons of the devil, ought to have no credit given to what they say or swear." ~* Foxe[1695]

Lithgow asked his Inquisitors to fetch his cloak-bag which contained proof of his identity but the accomplishing of this task only seemed to confirm the suspicions of the Spanish. He was put into holding that was less than comfortable.

> *About midnight, the sergeant and two Turkish slaves released Mr. Lithgow from his then confinement, but it was to introduce him to one much more horrible. They conducted him through several passages, to a chamber in a remote part of the palace, towards the garden, where they loaded him with irons, and extended his legs by means of an iron bar above a yard long, the weight of which was so great that he could neither stand nor sit, but was obliged to lie*

continually on his back. They left him in this condition for some time... ~ Foxe[1696]

For 47 days, William Lithgow was kept in solitary confinement with no relief from his condition.

> *In this wretched and melancholy state did poor Lithgow continue without seeing any person for several days, in which time the governor received an answer to a letter he had written, relative to the prisoner from Madrid; and, pursuant to the instructions given him, began to put in practice the cruelties devised, which they hastened, because Christmas holy-days approached, it being then the forty-seventh day since his imprisonment.*
>
> *About two o'clock in the morning, he heard the noise of a coach in the street, and some time after heard the opening of the prison doors, not having had any sleep for two nights; hunger, pain, and melancholy reflections having prevented him from taking any repose.*
>
> *Soon after the prison doors were opened, the nine sergeants, who had first seized him, entered the place where he lay, and without uttering a word, conducted him in his irons through the house into the street, where a coach waited, and into which they laid him at the bottom on his back, not being able to sit. Two of the sergeants rode with him, and the rest walked by the coach side, but all observed the most profound silence. They drove him to a vinepress house, about a league from the town, to which place a rack had been privately conveyed before; and here they shut him up for that night.* ~ Foxe[1697]

The next morning, the governor and the alcaldé showed up to again force a confession not only of espionage but of crimes committed which William Lithgow refused to give to them.

> *In consequence of this he was conducted by the sergeants to the end of a stone gallery, where the rack was placed. The encarouador or executioner, immediately struck off his irons, which put him to very great pains, the bolts being so close riveted, that the sledge hammer tore away half an inch of his heel, in forcing off the bolt; the anguish of which, together with his weak condition, (not having the least sustenance for three days) occasioned him to groan bitterly; upon which the merciless alcade said, "Villain, traitor, this is but the earnest of what you shall endure."* ...

> *It is impossible to describe all the various tortures inflicted upon him. Suffice it to say, that he lay on the rack for above five hours, during which time he received above sixty different tortures of the most hellish nature; and had they continued them a few minutes longer, he must have inevitably perished.* ~ Foxe[1698]

There were any number of things that could've happened to William Lithgow. A frequent affliction was to slowly pull a victim's arms out of their sockets by hoisting them up via a winch with the victim's arms behind their back so that their weight ripped them out. If they were too light or flexible, further weight could be added.

"The Rack" could slowly rip out specific limbs if they would be so targeted.

Edgar Allan Poe's frightening 1842 short story *The Pit and the Pendulum* is a first-person account of the Inquisition torture where a victim is placed on the rack but kept alive so that a slowly-descending blade could saw them in half by fractions of an inch with each swing of the blade over a prolonged period.

Whenever limbs were meant to be kept in place, iron shackles with spikes that pierced the flesh to the bone were employed.

Hot irons to the feet and other extremities were also frequently applied to Inquisition victims.

Presaging the "enhanced interrogation techniques" of the CIA, water, sometimes boiling, would be poured into a victim perhaps as much as 8 gallons worth. Sometimes vinegar was used. Former Bush #43 Administration Vice President Dick Cheney has claimed that torture of that nature has been essential in "keeping Americans safe"[1699]. Sadly, Americans have no idea that men like Cheney are infinitely more dangerous to them than CIA asset Tim Osman ever was. Osman was more popularly known as Osama bin Laden.[1700,1701]

If the Inquisitor wanted a victim to look at them during torture, a "Heretic's Fork" was stuck into their chest and under their chin that would dig into the flesh and force the victim's head erect.

If a victim's screams were distracting, they could be silenced with a "Mute's Bridle" that covered the lower part of their face and pushed an iron protrusion into their mouth, sometimes attaching to the victim's tongue with a nail.

A device called a "Pear" could be pushed into any bodily opening and expanded until the mouth, uterus or intestines burst.

These were all administered by representatives of the Vicar of Christ.[1702,1703]

Wikipedia, however, seems to list a more sterilized view of history.

> *As with all European tribunals of the time, torture was employed.[60][61] The Spanish inquisition, however, engaged in it far less often and with greater care than other courts.[61][62] Historian Henry Kamen contends that some "popular" accounts of the inquisition (those that describe scenes of uncontrolled sadistic torture) are not based in truth.* ~ The Spanish Inquisition, Wikipedia[1704]

When addressed at all, centuries of outrages are covered in a small paragraph (with a request for further citation).

> *Torture could be used after 1252. On May 15, Pope Innocent IV issued a papal bull entitled Ad extirpanda, which authorized the use of torture by inquisitors. Torture was undoubtedly used in the trial of the Templars, but is in fact not much found in heresy trials until the later fourteenth century. Torture methods that resulted in bloodshed, births, mutilation or death were forbidden. Also, torture could be performed only once. However, it was common practice to consider a second torture session to be a "continuation" of the first. The most commonly employed methods of torture included hanging by the wrists, with weights suspended from the ankles (a form of torture known as strappado); the rack; foot roasting; and the water torture.[citation needed]* ~ Medieval Inquisition, Wikipedia[1705]

According to that source, the most prominent victims of the Inquisition were the poor Templars.

Tell it to William Lithgow.

> *These cruel persecutors being satisfied for the present, the prisoner was taken from the rack, and his irons being again put on, he was conducted to his former dungeon, having received no other nourishment than a little warm wine, which was given him rather to prevent his dying, and reserve him for future punishments, than from any principle of charity or compassion.*
>
> *As a confirmation of this, orders were given for a coach to pass*

every morning before day by the prison, that the noise made by it might give fresh terrors and alarms to the unhappy prisoner, and deprive him of all possibility of obtaining the least repose. ...

In this loathsome prison was poor Mr. Lithgow kept till he was almost devoured by vermin. They crawled about his beard, lips, eye-brows, &c. so that he could scarce open his eyes; and his mortification was increased by not having the use of his hands or legs to defend himself, from his being so miserably maimed by the tortures. ... ~ Foxe[1706]

But it was after the Jesuits arrived that Lithgow's troubles truly began.

Edith Starr Miller noted that the satanic excesses of the Inquisition that were credited to the Franciscans were actually created and initiated by the Jesuits.

"The merited odium which has overtaken the Inquisition, usually officered by Dominicans, has induced the Jesuits, whose own controversial methods had been different, to disclaim all connexion with that tribunal, and to represent their society as free from complicity in its acts. But, in truth, it was Ignatius Loyola himself who procured its erection in Portugal in 1545-6, and F. Nithard, one of the very few cardinals of the society, was inquisitor-general of that kingdom in 1655." ~ Miller[1707]

William Lithgow would find that out. [italics suspended]

Two days after he had received the above information, the governor, an inquisitor, and a canonical priest, accompanied by two Jesuits, entered his dungeon, and being seated, after several idle questions, the inquisitor asked Mr. Lithgow if he was a Roman catholic, and acknowledged the pope's supremacy? He answered, that he neither was the one or did the other; adding, that he was surprised at being asked such questions, since it was expressly stipulated by the articles of peace between England and Spain, that none of the English subjects should be liable to the inquisition, or any way molested by them on account of diversity in religion, &c. In the bitterness of his soul he made use of some warm expressions not suited to his circumstances: "As you have almost murdered me (said he) for pretended treason, so now you intend to make a martyr of me for my religion." He also expostulated with the governor on the ill return he made to the king of England, (whose subject he was) for the princely humanity exercised towards the Spaniards in 1588, when their armada was shipwrecked on the Scotch coast, and thousands of the Spaniards found relief, who must otherwise have miserably perished.

The governor admitted the truth of what Mr. Lithgow said, but replied with a haughty air, that the king, who then only ruled Scotland, was actuated more by fear than love, and therefore did not deserve any thanks. One of the Jesuits said, there was no faith to be kept with heretics. The inquisitor then rising, addressed himself to Mr Lithgow in the following words: "You have been taken up as a spy, accused of treachery, and tortured, as we acknowledge, innocently: (which appears by the account lately received from Madrid of the intentions of the English) yet it was the divine power that brought those judgments upon you, for presumptuously treating the blessed miracle of Loretto with ridicule, and expressing yourself in your writings irreverently of his holiness, the great agent and Christ's vicar upon earth; therefore you are justly fallen into our hands by their special appointment: thy books and papers are miraculously translated by the assistance of Providence influencing thy own countrymen."

This trumpery being ended, they gave the prisoner eight days to consider and resolve whether he would become a convert to their religion; during which time the inquisitor told him he, with other religious orders, would attend, to give him such assistance thereto as he might want. One of the Jesuits said, (first making the sign of the cross upon his breast) "My son, behold, you deserve to be burnt alive; but by the grace of our lady of Loretto, whom you have blasphemed, we will both save your soul and body."

In the morning, the inquisitor with three other ecclesiastics returned, when the former asked the prisoner what difficulties he had on his conscience that retarded his conversion; to which he answered, "he had not any doubts in his mind, being confident in the promises of Christ, and assuredly believing his revealed will signified in the gospels, as professed in the reformed catholic church, being confirmed by grace, and having infallible assurance thereby of the christian faith." To these words the inquisitor replied, "Thou art no christian, but an absurd heretic, and without conversion a member of perdition." The prisoner then told him, it was not consistent with the nature and essence of religion and charity to convince by opprobrious speeches, racks, and torments, but by arguments deduced from the scriptures; and that all other methods would with him be totally ineffectual. ... ~ Foxe [emphasis added][1708]

What happened to William Lithgow? —Nothing short of a miracle.

He was kept alive by his kindly Turkish servant who snuck in figs, raisins and honey and wiped the vermin from his body, whenever he could, until a Spanish gentleman was made appraised of his situation. Having been unfairly accused of espionage, he was rescued and eventually placed in the care of another English ship captain, which is how his story was able to be recounted.

Given that the authority to "stamp out heretics" was granted some 500 years before, many non-Catholics did not fare as well.

Inquiring Minds

It takes a Luciferian to bravely and honestly chronicle the outrages of Rome.

> *Regretting that space should prevent our giving one of the most curious lists in the world of burned witches, we will nevertheless make a few extracts from the original record as printed in Hauber's Bibliotheca Magica. One glance at this horrible catalogue of murders in Christ's name, is sufficient to discover that out of 162 persons burned, more than one-half of them are designated as strangers (i.e., Protestants) in this hospitable town; and of the other half we find thirty-four children, the oldest of whom was fourteen, the youngest an infant child of Dr. Schutz.* ~ Blavatsky[1709]

The Inquisition began with the Synod of Rheims in 1157 AD approving the use of execution for apostasy culminating in the Synod of Verona[1710] in 1184 combining the powers of Pope Lucius III and Emperor Frederick Barbarossa to search out and destroy all heretics.[1711]

In 1835, the Pastor of the Cedar-street Church of New York, Cyrus Mason, was deeply concerned in noting an influx of Jesuits to America after their restoration. What he asserted was that the Inquisition was still in effect after over 700 years.

> *The pope of Rome his recently honoured the United States of America, and shown the deep interest he feels in this country, by the appointment of an ecclesiastical ambassador, a legate with plenary powers to manage the cause of Romanism in the new world. This high officer of the church and state of Rome, has expressed his gratitude and loyalty by appearing before the public (at Baltimore,) as the apologist and defender of the Inquisition.*
>
> *The order of the Jesuits is restored, and, so far as we know, without any change in its constitution and character. The Romish*

> *missionaries to this country are mostly of the order of Jesuits; for it is said by American citizens who have wintered at Rome, that the Jesuits who come, there for commission and patronage, are specially ambitious of appointments to this country. They regard our country as an open field, where they may pursue their schemes without molestation, and with entire success; where they may profit by the toleration enjoyed under our mild and free institutions.*
>
> *Here, then, we have the order of the Jesuits rising and spreading over the fair face of our country, encouraged by vast importations of the least desirable classes of Roman Catholics from the old kingdoms of Europe, and supported by the joint patronage of the Society de Propaganda and the Catholic monarchs of the old world. These sworn servants of a foreign potentate have as a leader an avowed defender of the inquisition.* ~ *A History of the Holy Catholic Inquisition*, Cyrus Mason[1712]

In 1835, it was Pope Gregory IX whom, according to Catholic historian and former Jesuit, Malachi Martin, was, indeed, still presiding over the Inquisition. [italics suspended]

> Pius IX was not yet a cardinal on the death of Pius VI. But he remembers the three popes after Pius VII (Leo XII, Pius VIII, and Gregory XVI); they had done the damage. The legacy of Pius VII was a terrible one: oppression, surveillance, a dictatorship. Between 1823 (death of Pius VII) and 1846 (when Pius IX was elected), almost 200,000 citizens of the papal states were severely punished (death, life imprisonment, exile, galleys) for political offences; another 1.5 million were subject to constant police surveillance and harassment.
>
> There was a gallows permanently in the square of every town and city and village. Railways, meetings of more than three people, and all news papers were forbidden. All books were censored. A special tribunal sat permanently in each place to try, condemn, and execute the accused. All trials were conducted in Latin. Ninety-nine percent of the accused did not understand the accusations against them. Every pope tore up the stream of petitions that came constantly asking for justice, for the franchise, for reform of the police and prison system. When revolts occurred in Bologna, in the Romagna, and elsewhere, they were put down with wholesale executions, sentences to lifelong hard labor in the state penitentiary, to exile, to torture. Austrian troops were always being called in to suppress the revolts. Secret societies abounded. Assassinations, robberies, crime in general increased.

Pope Leo XII kept cats, about three-score cats, as his pets and rebuilt St. Paul's Church with 60,000 francs from King Charles of France. He also forbade the selling of wine and any woman's dress that went above the ankles. He restored the Inquisition and its torture chambers, hated France and all Frenchmen. Pope Pius VIII was pope for twenty months, suffered from violent torticollis, took long placid walks with members of the diplomatic corps, and literally dropped dead on hearing that Charles X of France had died. Pope Gregory XVI published one book, *Triumph of the Church Against the Assaults of Innovators*, took two extended tours through the papal states, each costing 400,000 gold crowns, was a renowned epicurean, created the Egyptian and Etruscan museums in the Vatican, put down a revolution in Rome by wholesale butchery of the rebels, and died suddenly and unaccountably in 1846. Pius IX remembers that he got a full account of it all from Marcantonio Pacelli, who had been head of Gregory XVI's finance department. ~ *The Decline and Fall of the Roman Church*, Malachi Martin[1713]

Pastor Cyrus Mason made an interesting comparison between the Inquisition and practices of another religion.

It was a Mahometan precept to propagate their religion by fire and the sword: but the inquisition, refining upon the former, went still beyond in cruelty; and although they showed as little mercy to the bodies of their enemies, they made war against their very minds; the tortures of the body ... being absolutely nothing compared to the mental agonies to which their victims were subjected. Can any thing be conceived more opposite to Christianity in every feature? But as there is nothing on the face of the earth to which it may be compared, let it not be deemed extravagant if we go further, and liken the inquisition itself to Pandemonium, and its ministers to malignant demons. ~ Mason[1714]

What of "Our Lady of Loretto[aaa]," whom William Lithgow almost lost his life over insulting?

Therein lies a tale.

The Queen of Heaven

The Word that came to Jeremiah for all the Jews living in the land of Egypt, those who were living in Migdol, Tahpanhes, Memphis, and the land of Pathros, saying, "Thus says the Lord of hosts, the

---

[aaa] Actually spelled "Loreto".

> *God of Israel, 'You yourselves have seen all the calamity that I have brought on Jerusalem and all the cities of Judah; and behold, this day they are in ruins and no one lives in them, because of their wickedness which they committed so as to provoke Me to anger by continuing to burn sacrifices and to serve other gods whom they had not known, neither they, you, nor your fathers.'" ...*
>
> *Then all the men who were aware that their wives were burning sacrifices to other gods, along with all the women who were standing by, as a large assembly, including all the people who were living in Pathros in the land of Egypt, responded to Jeremiah, saying, "As for the Message that you have spoken to us in the Name of the Lord, we are not going to listen to you! But rather we will certainly carry out every word that has proceeded from our mouths, by burning sacrifices to the queen of heaven and pouring out drink offerings to her, just as we ourselves, our forefathers, our kings and our princes did in the cities of Judah and in the streets of Jerusalem..."* ~ Jeremiah 44:1-3, 15-17[bbb]

Protestant Christians (with no little Biblical affirmation) believe fervently that the Salvation of the soul is achieved by submissive faith in Jesus Christ and Him alone. [Acts 4:5-12]

As a result, Christian or near-Christian belief systems that deemphasize the singular importance of Jesus or attempt to share His Redemptive Power are considered heresy that endangers souls.

The ancient Babylonian worship of the Mother and Child does just this.

It is a trap that entices with the appeal of a mother's compassion: Semiramis and Tammuz, Isis and Horus and the mortal woman Alcmene who was impregnated by Zeus to give birth to the hybrid god/man hero Heracles ("Hercules" was the Roman version).

From these pagan myths it becomes almost instinctive to ask the "divine mother figure" for intervention, but the Bible speaks against it. [I Timothy 2:5-6, Matthew 12:46-50, Luke 11:27-28]

Protestants see the Catholic doctrine of Mary as "Co-Redemptrix" as causing souls to be damned and, therefore, a literal satanic heresy.

Pope Leo XIII wrote in his Encyclical on the Rosary, *Iucunda Simper Expectatione*:

[bbb] New American Standard Bible translation with some capitalization added to correct lack of reverence.

The recourse we have to Mary in prayer follows upon the office she continuously fills by the side of the throne of God as Mediatrix of Divine grace; being by worthiness and by merit most acceptable to Him, and, therefore, surpassing in power all the angels and saints in Heaven. Now, this merciful office of hers, perhaps, appears in no other form of prayer so manifestly as it does in the Rosary. For in the Rosary all the part that Mary took as our co-Redemptress comes to us, as it were, set forth, and in such wise as though the facts were even then taking place; and this with much profit to our piety, whether in the contemplation of the succeeding sacred mysteries, or in the prayers which we speak and repeat with the lips. ... The Virgin bears Him. And when the Shepherds and the wise men, first-fruits of the Christian faith, come with longing to His cradle, they find there the young Child, with Mary, His Mother. Then, that He might before men offer Himself as a victim to His Heavenly Father, He desires to be taken to the Temple; and by the hands of Mary He is there presented to the Lord. It is Mary who, in the mysterious losing of her Son, seeks Him sorrowing, and finds Him again with joy. And the same truth is told again in the sorrowful mysteries.[1715]

To adherents of this doctrine, Mary is "Co-Redemptrix, Mediatrix of All Graces, and Advocate."[1716]

When it came to blood and treasure, few Popes pursued both as ruthlessly as John XXII. The exploits John XXII (a Frenchman by the name of Jacques Duèze) rivaled even Charlemagne and it was "Mary" to whom he committed his well-being. [italics suspended]

> John XXII's predecessor, Clement V, had given away all of the Church's wealth to his relatives, leaving a bare treasury. That condition the new pope went about to cure with a vengeance. He sold everything for a price, including absolution from sin and eternal salvation. Thus the golden chalice held by the woman riding the beast was refilled with filthy lucre gained by abominable means exactly as the apostle John foresaw in his remarkable vision.
>
> John XXII published a list of crimes and gross sins, together with the individual price for which he, as vicar of Christ, head of the one true Church, would absolve transgressors from each of them. The list left nothing out, from murder and piracy to incest, adultery, and sodomy. The wealthier one was, the more one could sin; the more Catholics sinned, the richer the Church became.
>
> Much of the wealth thus acquired was spent to further John XXII's passion for wars. One of his contemporaries wrote: "The blood he

shed would have incarnadined the waters of Lake Constance [an extremely large lake], and the bodies of the slain would have bridged it from shore to shore."[9]

John XXII's pet doctrine was like that of many who are popular on Christian radio and TV today: that Christ and His apostles had been men of great wealth. So he declared in a papal bull, Cum inter nonnullos (1323). To deny this dogma was heresy punishable by death. John demanded that secular rulers burn at the stake Franciscans who had taken vows of poverty. Those who refused to do so were excommunicated. During his pontificate he handed over 114 Franciscans to the Inquisition to be consumed by the flames for the heresy of purposely living in poverty as Christ had. Thus it became official Roman Catholic dogma that Christ and His disciples were men of considerable wealth, and that all Christians ought to be so-a dogma repudiated by other popes. ...

Millions of Catholics from whom the historical truth has been hidden have looked upon John XXII as an exceptionally holy man. Was he not favored above all popes by "Our Lady of Mount Carmel" with one of her rare personal appearances? John swore that the "Virgin Mary" appeared to him to present the Great Promise: that she would personally go into purgatory the Saturday after their death and take to heaven all those who, having met certain other conditions, died wearing her brown scapular. In reliance upon this special Sabbatine [Saturday] Privilege, which was confirmed by other popes, untold millions of Roman Catholics have since worn (and still wear today) the brown scapular of "Our Lady of Mount Carmel" as their ticket to heaven. ~ *A Woman Rides The Beast*, Hunt[1717]

In regards to utilizing beads to keep track of repetitious prayer, there is strange harmony between Rome and Mecca.

This, too, is strongly contested by Fundamentalist Protestants. Before the most mindlessly-repeated prayer in human history, the "Our Father", Jesus gave this warning;

> *"But when ye pray, use not vain repetitions, as the heathen do: for they think that they shall be heard for their much speaking."* ~ Matthew 6:7, KJV

Nearly all Protestants and a great many Catholics don't know that Papal doctrine teaches that Mary is without sin, that she gave birth to Christ without losing her virginity (and never consummated her marriage with

Joseph[ccc]) and was bodily assumed into Heaven immediately after her death, lest her body decay.

> *The deepening of faith in the virginal motherhood led the Church to confess Mary's real and perpetual virginity even in the act of giving birth to the Son of God made man.*[154] *In fact, Christ's birth "did not diminish his mother's virginal integrity but sanctified it."*[155] *And so the liturgy of the Church celebrates Mary as Aeiparthenos, the "Ever-virgin".*[156]
>
> *The Fathers of the Eastern tradition call the Mother of God "the All-Holy" (Panagia), and celebrate her as "free from any stain of sin, as though fashioned by the Holy Spirit and formed as a new creature".*[158] *By the grace of God Mary remained free of every personal sin her whole life long.* ~ Catechism of the Catholic Church, Vatican.va[1718]

This is direct contravention of Scripture which states that Christ, alone, is without sin [II Corinthians 5:21] and the one who claims otherwise is a liar [I John 1:8].

The Bible implies a bodily assumption of Enoch [Genesis 5:24] and clearly states it happened to Elijah [II Kings 2:11] and the Son of God [Mark 16:19, Acts 1:9] but on pain of excommunication does a Catholic not believe Mary was as well.

> *Celebrated every year on August 15, the Feast of the Assumption of the Blessed Virgin Mary commemorates the death of Mary and her bodily assumption into Heaven, before her body could begin to decay—a foretaste of our own bodily resurrection at the end of time. Because it signifies the Blessed Virgin's passing into eternal life, it is the most important of all Marian feasts and a Holy Day of Obligation. ...*
>
> *The Assumption of the Blessed Virgin Mary into Heaven at the end of her earthly life is a defined dogma of the Catholic Church. On November 1, 1950, Pope Pius XII, exercising papal infallibility, declared in Munificentissimus Deus that it is a dogma of the Church "that the Immaculate Mother of God, the ever Virgin Mary, having completed the course of her earthly life, was assumed body and soul into heavenly glory." As a dogma, the Assumption is a required belief of all Catholics; anyone who publicly dissents from the dogma, Pope Pius declared, "has fallen away completely from the*

[ccc] Matthew 13:55 names the half-brothers and half-sisters of Christ.

divine and Catholic Faith." ~ Scott P. Richert, About Religion[1719]

"Our Lady of Loreto" is a shrine with an incredulous story behind it.

The legend claims that the house where Mary raised Christ was, itself, "bodily assumed" and transported by angels to Loreto, Italy where Mary currently visits worshippers with miracles—"Our Lady of Loreto".

Although this was, at first, embarrassing to Vatican leadership, they eventually supported it with full Papal power.

> *Bulls in favour of the Shrine at Loreto were issued by Pope Sixtus IV in 1491, and by Julius II in 1507, the last alluding to the translation of the house with some caution (ut pie creditur et fama est). While, like most miracles, the translation of the house is not a matter of faith for Catholics, nonetheless, in the late 17th century, Innocent XII appointed a missa cum officio proprio (a special mass) for the Feast of the Translation of the Holy House, which as late as the 20th century was enjoined in the Spanish Breviary as a greater double on 10 December 10.*
>
> *On 4 October 2012, Benedict XVI visited the Shrine to mark the 50th anniversary of John XXIII's visit. In his visit, Benedict formally entrusted the World Synod of Bishops and the Year of Faith to the Virgin of Loreto.*[6][7][8] ~ Wikipedia[1720]

It is taught that, when the muslims invaded the Holy Land in 1090, they miraculously spared the Holy House from brigandage.[1721]

Perhaps they knew that, hundreds of years later, Rome would extend the hand of friendship.

—Or, rather, "Mary" would.

Apparition Apprehensions

In 1916, three Portuguese children were herding sheep when an angel appeared to them on multiple occasions at *Cova da Iria* ("Irene's Cove") just outside of Fátima. Lucia dos Santos was 9 and her cousin Francisco Marto was 8. Francisco's sister, Jacinta Marto, was 6. The angel taught them how to pray[1722] and "sacrifice" on behalf of sinners.[1723]

Ilustração Portuguesa

> *On May 13, 1917, Lúcia described seeing a lady "brighter than the sun, shedding rays of light clearer and stronger than a crystal goblet filled with the most sparkling water and pierced by the burning rays of the sun". While they had never spoken to anyone about the angel, Jacinta divulged her sightings to her family despite Lucia's admonition to keep this experience private. Her disbelieving mother told neighbors as a joke, and within a day the whole village knew.[6] Further appearances were reported on June 13 and July 13. In these, the lady asked the children to do penance and Acts of Reparation and make personal sacrifices to save sinners. According to Lúcia's account, the lady also confided to the children three secrets, now known as the Three Secrets of Fátima.*
>
> *The children subsequently wore tight cords around their waists, performed self-flagellation using stinging nettles, abstained from drinking water on hot days, and performed other works of penance.[6]* ~ Wikipedia[1724]

Despite their claims, they were ridiculed by some and the apparition they saw promised to give them powerful prophecies on the 13th of the month, in October of 1917.

Between May and October of 1917, always on the 13th of the month, the children received three secrets. Lucia eventually disclosed them from the Convent where she became a nun. Francisco and Jacinta died just a few short years later in the Spanish Flu Epidemic of 1918-20.

It is important to note that October 13th 1307 is established by the Luciferian Elite as the day Pope Clement V collaborated with France's King Philip IV and suppressed the Vatican Treasury guardians—the Knights Templar.[1725]

Sister Lucia wrote her account much later in life under orders from the Bishop of Leiria. In 1940, she sent her recollection to Pope Pius XII.

> *Well, the secret is made up of three distinct parts, two of which I am now going to reveal[4].*
>
> *The first part is the vision of hell[5].*
>
> *Our Lady showed us a great sea of fire which seemed to be under the earth. Plunged in this fire were demons and souls in human form, like transparent burning embers, all blackened or burnished bronze, floating about in the conflagration, now raised into the air by the flames that issued from within themselves together with great*

clouds of smoke, now falling back on every side like sparks in a huge fire, without weight or equilibrium, and amid shrieks and groans of pain and despair, which horrified us and made us tremble with fear. The demons could be distinguished by their terrifying and repellent likeness to frightful and unknown animals, all black and transparent. This vision lasted but an instant.

How can we ever be grateful enough to our kind heavenly Mother, who had already prepared us by promising, in the first Apparition, to take us to Heaven. Otherwise, I think we would have died of fear and terror.

We then looked up at Our Lady, who said to us so kindly and so sadly: "You have seen hell where the souls of poor sinners go. To save them, God wishes to establish in the world devotion to my Immaculate Heart[6]." ~ Fátima In Lucia's Own Words: Sister Lucia's Memoirs[1726]

The second secret stated that a very important country would stand in the balance between "good" and "evil": *Russia*.

The war[7] [World War II] *is going to end: but if people do not cease offending God, a worse one will break out during the pontificate of Pius XI[8]. When you see a night illumined by an unknown light, know that this is the great sign 9 given you by God that He is about to punish the world for its crimes, by means of war, famine, and persecutions of the Church and of the Holy Father.*

"To prevent this, I shall come[10] to ask for the consecration of Russia to my Immaculate Heart, and the Communion of reparation on the First Saturdays. If my requests are heeded, Russia will be converted, and there will be peace; if not, she will spread her errors throughout the world, causing wars and persecutions of the Church. The good will be martyred; the Holy Father will have much to suffer; various nations will be annihilated. In the end, my Immaculate Heart will triumph. The Holy Father will consecrate Russia to me[11], and she will be converted, and a period of peace will be granted to the world[12]." ~ Sister Lucia's Memoirs[1727]

When Sister Lucia released her memoirs, Papal authority had passed from Pius XI to Pius XII.

May 13th is celebrated as the first apparition of Mary in 1917 and that was the day the Jesuits made an attempt on the life of John Paul II. He survived after having been shot 4 times and accounted it as a miracle from

Our Lady of Fátima.

> *After the assassination attempt of 13 May 1981, it appeared evident that it was "a mother's hand that guided the bullet's path", enabling "the Pope in his throes" to halt "at the threshold of death" (Pope John Paul II,* Meditation from the Policlinico Gemelli to the Italian Bishops, *Insegnamenti, XVII, 1 [1994], 1061). On the occasion of a visit to Rome by the then Bishop of Leiria-Fátima, the Pope decided to give him the bullet which had remained in the jeep after the assassination attempt, so that it might be kept in the shrine. By the Bishop's decision, the bullet was later set in the crown of the statue of Our Lady of Fátima.* ~ Cardinal Angelo Sodano, Vatican Secretary Of State[1728]

Catholics everywhere awaited with great anticipation for the third secret.

After the nearly-successful attempt on John Paul II's life (a Pole named Karol Józef Wojtyła), there were 3 more[1729]. It was then that the secret was finally released.

> *The third part of the secret revealed at the Cova da Iria-Fátima, on 13 July 1917.*
>
> *I write in obedience to you, my God, who command me to do so through his Excellency the Bishop of Leiria and through your Most Holy Mother and mine.*
>
> *After the two parts which I have already explained, at the left of Our Lady and a little above, we saw an Angel with a flaming sword in his left hand; flashing, it gave out flames that looked as though they would set the world on fire; but they died out in contact with the splendour that Our Lady radiated towards him from her right hand: pointing to the earth with his right hand, the Angel cried out in a loud voice: 'Penance, Penance, Penance!'. And we saw in an immense light that is God: 'something similar to how people appear in a mirror when they pass in front of it' a Bishop dressed in White 'we had the impression that it was the Holy Father'. Other Bishops, Priests, men and women Religious going up a steep mountain, at the top of which there was a big Cross of rough-hewn trunks as of a cork-tree with the bark; before reaching there the Holy Father passed through a big city half in ruins and half trembling with halting step, afflicted with pain and sorrow, he prayed for the souls of the corpses he met on his way; having reached the top of the mountain, on his knees at the foot of the big*

> *Cross he was killed by a group of soldiers who fired bullets and arrows at him, and in the same way there died one after another the other Bishops, Priests, men and women Religious, and various lay people of different ranks and positions. Beneath the two arms of the Cross there were two Angels each with a crystal aspersorium in his hand, in which they gathered up the blood of the Martyrs and with it sprinkled the souls that were making their way to God.* ~ Sister Lucia's Memoirs[1730]

The future Benedict XVI (then Joseph Cardinal Ratzinger) was chosen to give the Doctrinal Response. Even he seemed unenthused.

> *A careful reading of the text of the so-called third "secret" of Fátima, published here in its entirety long after the fact and by decision of the Holy Father, will probably prove disappointing or surprising after all the speculation it has stirred. No great mystery is revealed; nor is the future unveiled.*[1731]

But what was noteworthy is that witnesses claim something *did* show up on October 13th, 1917. From some accounts, it didn't look like Mary.

"Miracle of the Sun"

On the 610th anniversary[ddd] of the Templar suppression, Mary appeared to three children as well as anywhere from 30,000 to 100,000 Portuguese, depending upon which report you believe.

It had been raining but, as the miracle goes, the rain suddenly stopped and there were two visions—one of Mary, Joseph and baby Jesus[eee], seen only by the 3 children of whom only 1 survived into adulthood.

The rest of the people there saw a UFO. [italics suspended]

> While the rain had stopped, dark clouds continued to obscure the sun, which suddenly bursts through them and is seen to be a soft spinning disk of silver. ...
>
> **O Seculo (a pro-government, anti-clerical, Lisbon paper):**
>
> —the sun "danced" according to the typical expression of the people. ...

[ddd] Numbers are significant but they should not be allowed to direct, only to inform. The Luciferian Elite, however, use them for calling upon their interdimensional masters.
[eee] Reducing Christ to a child or infant is a dangerous concept that disconnects humans from responsibility and/or capability of a saving relationship with an adult Yeshua.

O Dia (another Lisbon daily, edition of 17 October 1917):

At one o'clock in the afternoon, midday by the sun, the rain stopped. The sky, pearly grey in colour, illuminated the vast arid landscape with a strange light. The sun had a transparent gauzy veil so that the eyes could easily be fixed upon it. The grey mother-of-pearl tone turned into a sheet of silver which broke up as the clouds were torn apart and the silver sun, enveloped in the same gauzy grey light, was seen to whirl and turn in the circle of broken clouds. ...

The light turned a beautiful blue, as if it had come through the stained-glass windows of a cathedral, and spread itself over the people who knelt with outstretched hands. The blue faded slowly, and then the light seemed to pass through yellow glass. Yellow stains fell against white handkerchiefs, against the dark skirts of the women. They were repeated on the trees, on the stones and on the serra. ...

Ti Marto (father of Jacinta and Francisco):

We looked easily at the sun, which for some reason did not blind us. It seemed to flicker on and off, first one way, then another. It cast its rays in many directions and painted everything in different colors—the trees, the people, the air and the ground. But what was most extraordinary, I thought, was that the sun did not hurt our eyes. Everything was still and quiet, and everyone was looking up. Then at a certain moment, the sun appeared to stop spinning. It then began to move and to dance in the sky until it seemed to detach itself from its place and fall upon us. It was a terrible moment.

Dr. Almeida Garrett, PhD (Coimbra University):

...The sun's disc did not remain immobile. This was not the sparkling of a, heavenly body, for it spun round on itself in a mad whirl. Then, suddenly, one heard a clamor, a cry of anguish breaking from all the people. The sun, whirling wildly, seemed to loosen itself from the firmament and advance threateningly upon the earth as if to crush us with its huge and fiery weight. The sensation during those moments was terrible. ~ *Apparition of 13 October 1917*, EWTN[1732]

Christian author and researcher L.A. Marzulli has suggested that this was an introduction to the "coming great deception"[1733] (an "alien disclosure") and we will see shortly that, if the aliens have an official religion it is Roman Catholicism.

But there has been another purpose exposed for the Fátima apparition and that has been for the Pope to extend the olive branch of "peace" to the Religion of Pieces.

The Blue Army

Did you know that Our Lady of Fátima has an army? —A *blue* army.

> *The Blue Army of Our Lady of Fátima, now mostly known as the World Apostolate of Fátima, is a public international association of the Christian faithful that has as its general purpose "the promotion of the authentic teaching of the Roman Catholic Church and the strict adherence to the tenets of the Gospel; the personal sanctification of adherents through faithful adherence to the Message of Fátima and the promotion of the common good by the spreading of that Message of Fátima". ~ Wikipedia*[1734]

—And they're recruiting muslims.

> *Islam is an Arabic word that can be defined as "to make peace." ... over the centuries, Muslims have engaged in tremendous wars with Christians and Jews. It would seem that there is little hope for peace. However, Heaven's Peace Plan, involving Our Lady, is evidenced at Fatima, Portugal as well as other places around the world.*
>
> *The Moors once occupied Portugal. The village of Fatima was given the Islamic name of the well-loved Princess of the nearby Castle of Ourem. She died at an early age after marrying the Count of Ourem and converting to Catholicism. Baptized with the Christian name of Oureana, she was named at birth "Fatima," like many other Moslem girls, in honor of the daughter of Mohammed. Of his daughter, Fatima, the founder of Islam, Mohammed, said: "She has the highest place in heaven after the Virgin Mary."*
>
> *It is a fact that Moslems from various nations, especially from the Middle East, make so many pilgrimages to Our Lady of Fatima's Shrine in Portugal that Portuguese officials have expressed concern. The combination of an Islamic name and Islamic devotion to the Blessed Virgin Mary is a great attraction to Moslems. God is writing straight with crooked lines, as we will see. Fatima is a part of Heaven's Peace Plan. It is hope for the world.*
>
> *In the Koran, the holy name of the Blessed Virgin Mary is mentioned no less than thirty times. No other woman's name is even*

mentioned, not even that of Mohammed's daughter, Fatima. Among men, only Abraham, Moses, and Noah are mentioned more times than Our Lady. In the Koran, Our Blessed Mother is described as "Virgin, ever Virgin." The Islamic belief in the virginity of Mary puts to shame the heretical beliefs of those who call themselves Christian, while denying the perpetual virginity of Mary. Make no mistake about it, there is a very special relationship between the Blessed Virgin Mary and the Moslems! ~ Fr Ladis J. Cizik, Blue Army National Executive Director[1735]

There are many questions surrounding the apparition at Fátima. Why would it choose a location so easily identified by muslims?

Is the apparition of Fátima a cunningly-divined hoax for the political power of uniting Catholicism with Islam?

- Only the children saw "Mary", even during the October event in 1917. Two of them died shortly thereafter and the third was controlled from a convent. She even admits she was directed to reveal what she saw by Catholic authorities.
- There were supposedly 70,000 people in the Cova da Iria that day in 1917 yet evidence is extremely sparse with only a handful of eyewitness accounts existing.

In Islam, there is no "peace" until you *submit*.

The Myth: *Lesser educated Muslims sometimes claim that the root word of Islam is "al-Salaam," which is "peace" in Arabic.*

The Truth: *An Arabic word only has one root. The root word for Islam is "al-Silm," which means "submission" or "surrender." There is no disagreement about this among Islamic scholars. al-Silm (submission) does not mean the same thing as al-Salaam (peace), otherwise they would be the same word.* ~ The Myths of Islam[1736]

Alberto

The Company of Loyola is a Secret Society. Not only that, but they are the most powerful Secret Society in the world. Their financial resources (which we will discuss in the next chapter) are staggering and their protégés and puppets in Western Intelligence as well as the military/industrial complex make them almost, but not quite, invincible. They are expert in satanism (eliciting demonic alliances), mind control and assassination.

Getting whistleblowers to come forward is exceptionally rare.

Verifying the veracity of the exceptionally-rare whistleblower is near-impossible.

Alberto Rivera was such a man and, at least, he has a Wikipedia entry.

> ***Alberto Magno Romero Rivera*** *(September 19, 1935 – June 20, 1997) was an anti-Catholic religious activist who was the source of many of the conspiracy theories about the Vatican espoused by fundamentalist Christian author Jack Chick.*
>
> *Chick promised to promote Rivera's claims even after he died. Rivera claimed to have been a Jesuit before becoming a Fundamentalist Protestant, and many of the stories Chick published about Rivera involve Jesuit conspiracies.* ~ Wikipedia[1737]

Rivera was a Christian Evangelist. In a way, a clear recounting of the Gospel Message lends credibility to a speaker. Most charlatans end their presentations with the spotlight on them.

Interestingly, Alberto Rivera's Wikipedia entry says only this about his death at the age of 62:

> ***Death*** *:According to cemetery records, Rivera is buried in Section Moore (28) L-14 #3 at Rose Hill Cemetery in Tulsa, Oklahoma.*[9][10] ~ Wikipedia[1738]

The footnotes are to the cemetery records online database (which requires you to manually enter Rivera's information, then gives you nothing) and a very unprofessional, unflattering Catholic blog—the "Catholic Texan"—as a citation.

The "cause of death" is uncharacteristically not addressed.

Rivera certainly made enemies for himself; the most dangerous enemies on the planet.

> *Rivera also alleged that Muhammad was manipulated by the Catholic Church to create Islam and destroy the Jews and other groups of Christians, and that his first wife, Khadijah bint Khuwaylid, was actually a Catholic nun in an Arabian monastery who was told by a bishop to marry him and sow the seeds of what was to become Islam.*[4] *Rivera also alleged that the Vatican staged an apparition at Fatima (named after Muhammed's daughter) to cozy up to Muslims.*[4] *He further claims that it also staged the*

1981 assassination attempt on Pope John Paul II using a Muslim as the marksman "to guilt-induce the Muslim world, bringing them still closer to the Catholic faith!"[4] ~ Wikipedia[1739]

At Red Ice Creations (the internet home of the Swedish George Noory—Henrik Palmgren[fff]) is an article with Alberto Rivera's name and it gets quite specific about how the Jesuits created and use Islam. [italics suspended]

> What I'm going to tell you is what I learned in secret briefings in the Vatican when I was a Jesuit priest, under oath and induction. A Jesuit cardinal named Augustine Bea showed us how desperately the Roman Catholics wanted Jerusalem at the end of the third century. Because of its religious history and its strategic location, the Holy City was considered a priceless treasure. A scheme had to be developed to make Jerusalem a Roman Catholic city.
>
> The great untapped source of manpower that could do this job was the children of Ishmael. The poor Arabs fell victim to one of the most clever plans ever devised by the powers of darkness. ...
>
> On this holy placed today where the temple once stood, the Dome of the Rock Mosque stands as Islam's second most holy place. Sweeping changes were in the wind. Corruption, apathy, greed, cruelty, perversion and rebellion were eating at the Roman Empire, and it was ready to collapse. The persecution against Christians was useless as they continued to lay down their lives for the gospel of Christ.
>
> The only way Satan could stop this thrust was to create a counterfeit "Christian" religion to destroy the work of God. The solution was in Rome. Their religion had come from ancient Babylon and all it needed was a face-lift. This didn't happen overnight, but began in the writings of the "early church fathers".
>
> It was through their writings that a new religion would take shape. The statue of Jupiter in Rome was eventually called St. Peter, and the statue of Venus was changed to the Virgin Mary. The site chosen for its headquarters was on one of the seven hills called "Vaticanus", the place of the diving serpent where the Satanic temple of Janus stood.

[fff] Palmgren covers the same topics on his "Red Ice Radio" that Noory does for "Coast to Coast AM".

The great counterfeit religion was Roman Catholicism, called "Mystery, Babylon the Great, the Mother of Harlots and Abominations of the Earth"- Revelation 17:5. She was raised up to block the gospel, slaughter the believers in Christ, establish religions, create wars and make the nations drunk with the wine of her fornication as we will see. ...

After his mother and grandfather also died, Muhammad was with his uncle when a Roman Catholic monk learned of his identity and said, "Take your brother's son back to his country and guard him against the Jews, for by god, if they see him and know of him that which I know, they will construe evil against him. Great things are in store for this brother's son of yours.

The Roman Catholic monk had fanned the flames for future Jewish persecutions at the hands of the followers of Muhammad. The Vatican desperately wanted Jerusalem because of its religious significance, but was blocked by the Jews. ~ How the Vatican created Islam, Alberto Rivera[1740]

Muhammad's advisor, Waraka ibn Nawfal—the first to believe in him as "the prophet"—was, indeed, an "Ebionite" (Christian) priest.[1741]

Soon Rome realized that it had created a monster when uppity muslims began defaming the Pope as an infidel. Upon asking his new soldiers for Jerusalem the Pope was denied! This required it to be taken by force, hence, the Crusades.

A Whore Rides the Beast

Rome wielding the Scimitar of Mohammad against Christians is, in fact, nothing new. Pagan priestess Helena Blavatsky had more compassion for Protestants than the "religious" of her time (or, sadly, ours). [italics suspended]

> His Holiness the Pope, after exhausting, in a metaphor of self-laudation, every point of assimilation between the great biblical prophets and himself, has finally and truly compared himself with the Patriarch Jacob "wrestling against his God." He now crowns the edifice of Catholic piety by openly sympathizing with the Turks! The vicegerent of God inaugurates his infallibility by encouraging, in a true Christian spirit, the acts of that Moslem David, the modern Bashi-Bazuk; and it seems as if nothing would more please his Holiness than to be presented by the latter with several thousands of the Bulgarian or Servian "foreskins." True to

her policy to be all things to all men to promote her own interests, the Romish Church is, at this writing (1876), benevolently viewing the Bulgarian and Servian atrocities, and, probably, manoeuvring with Turkey against Russia. Better Islam, and the hitherto-hated Crescent over the sepulchre of the Christian god, than the Greek Church established at Constantinople and Jerusalem as the state religion. Like a decrepit and toothless ex-tyrant in exile, the Vatican is eager for any alliance that promises, if not a restoration of its own power, at least the weakening of its rival. The axe its inquisitors once swung, it now toys with in secret, feeling its edge, and waiting, and hoping against hope. In her time, the Popish Church has lain with strange bedfellows, but never before now sunk to the degradation of giving her moral support to those who for over 1200 years spat in her face, called her adherents "infidel dogs," repudiated her teachings, and denied godhood to her God!

The press of even Catholic France is fairly aroused at this indignity, and openly accuses the Ultramontane portion of the Catholic Church and the Vatican of siding, during the present Eastern struggle, with the Mahometan against the Christian. "When the Minister of Foreign Affairs in the French Legislature spoke some mild words in favor of the Greek Christians, he was only applauded by the liberal Catholics, and received coldly by the Ultramontane party," says the French correspondent of a New York paper.

"So pronounced was this, that M. Lemoinne, the wellknown editor of the great liberal Catholic journal, *the Debats*, was moved to say that the Roman Church felt more sympathy for the Moslem than the schismatic, just as they preferred an infidel to the Protestant. 'There is at bottom,' says this writer, 'a great affinity between the Syllabus and the Koran, and between the two heads of the faithful. The two systems are of the same nature, and are united on the common ground of a one and unchangeable theory.' In Italy, in like manner, the King and Liberal Catholics are in warm sympathy with the unfortunate Christians, while the Pope and Ultramontane faction are believed to be inclining to the Mahometans." ~ Blavatsky[1742]

Peter-Hans Kolvenbach is a Dutchman who was "Superior General" of the Company from 1983 to 2008. He served much of his time in the Middle East and is at home in bloodshed.

> *Kolvenbach was born in Druten, Netherlands, in 1928. He lived most of his teen years during the German occupation of the Netherlands. In an interview Kolvenbach later noted that experiencing war was not an uncommon experience in the*

formation of a Superior General. It was the experience of Ignatius at Pamplona, and the experience of his predecessor, Pedro Arrupe, who witnessed the dropping of the atomic bomb. Kolvenbach also lived in the midst of war in Beirut as a professor of linguistics and working with refugees in Lebanon. ~ Loyola Press[1743]

Some believe that Kolvenbach was the man behind 9/11.

According to author Eric Phelps, Peter Hans Kolvenbach, the Jesuit General known as the Black Pope, ordered the 9/11 attacks assisted by a military advisor to warn of any mistakes and a confessor at his side to ease his conscience to absolve any sins.

The deadly plan, claims Phelps, was carried-out with the advice and consent of his general staff, composed of five assistants, each representing a hemisphere with many advisory Provincials, including 10 in the United States.

Further, success was guaranteed by total cooperation and obedience from New York Archbishop Edward Cardinal Egan through his obedient Central Intelligence Agency, the National Security Agency, the Secret Service, Military Intelligence, the Federal Bureau of Investigation, and the Mafia.

Phelps also claims, through decades of research shunned by the press, the same gang of criminals and agencies worked together before in carrying out the Kennedy assassination and cover-up under the control of their former master, Jesuit trained Francis Cardinal Spellman. ~ Greg Szymanski, the Arctic Beacon[1744]

Kolvenbach is still alive today which means in eerie synchronicity, there are now two "white Popes" and two "black Popes"...and three of them are Jesuits.

The Scimitar is being wielded against Americans by the Company at Langley under the Company of Loyola. The CIA is attacking the enemies of Rome.

In Christian, Conservative Oklahoma City, an ex-convict calling himself "Jah'Keem Yisrael", was released from prison early (where he became a proselyte of the "Religion of Peace"). His real name was Alton Nolen and he cut off the head of 50 year old grandmother Colleen Hufford where the two worked at Vaughn Foods.[1745]

As Jah'Keem Yisrael was in the process of attempting to behead a second victim, Vaughn CEO Mark Vaughn grabbed his privately-owned firearm and wounded the killer.[1746]

It is, after all, Oklahoma.

The Federal Bureau of Obfuscation was quick to state that, just like the slaughter of 14 soldiers and civilians at Fort Hood by a man who shouted "Allhu Akbar!" with each pull of the trigger[1747], Jah'Keem Yisrael's jihad was not an act of "terrorism".[1748]

The fact that United States Army Major Nidal Hasan was in frequent communication with senior al Qaeda recruiter Anwar al-Awlaki did not make headlines. They were both closely monitored by the FBI but agents "dropped the ball" yet again and Americans died because of the "miscue".

> *Last Thursday, as the jury in the trial of Nidal Hasan was deliberating, outgoing FBI Director Robert Mueller appeared on CBS News and discussed a string of emails between the Fort Hood shooter and Anwar al-Awlaki, a radical Islamic cleric with ties to the 9/11 hijackers. The FBI had intercepted the messages starting almost a year before Hasan's 2009 shooting rampage, and Mueller was asked whether "the bureau dropped the ball" by failing to act on this information. He didn't blink: "No, I think, given the context of the discussions and the situation that the agents and the analysts were looking at, they took appropriate steps."* ~ Mariah Blake, Mother Jones[1749]

Few people knew that Anwar al-Awlaki was an American, born in New Mexico, who had a mosque very conveniently located in Falls Church, Virginia, just a few minutes from Washington, DC, the Pentagon or CIA Headquarters.[1750]

In fact, al-Awlaki had dinner at the Pentagon just 2 weeks after 9/11.[1751]

Barack Obama reportedly killed al Awlaki with a drone strike in Yemen because, according to him, "drones make me a good killer[1752]".

Al-Awlaki was a "terrorist", therefore he was an American citizen easily executed without due process.

The precedent needed to be set, lest tyranny not follow the "Rule of Law".

It was first reported in January of last year that the Obama administration had compiled a hit list of American citizens whom the President had ordered assassinated without any due process, and one of those Americans was Anwar al-Awlaki. No effort was made to indict him for any crimes (despite a report last October that the Obama administration was "considering" indicting him). Despite substantial doubt among Yemen experts about whether he even had any operational role in Al Qaeda, no evidence (as opposed to unverified government accusations) was presented of his guilt. When Awlaki's father sought a court order barring Obama from killing his son, the DOJ argued, among other things, that such decisions were "state secrets" and thus beyond the scrutiny of the courts. He was simply ordered killed by the President: his judge, jury and executioner. When Awlaki's inclusion on President Obama's hit list was confirmed, The New York Times noted that "it is extremely rare, if not unprecedented, for an American to be approved for targeted killing." ~ Glenn Greenwald, Salon[1753]

Given that this occurred without any supervision or video evidence, al-Awlaki the CIA lackey may very well be basking away in the Maui sun as Grab'ir Boubii, the wealthy, retired owner of a chain of convenience stores.

Either way, Americans lose.

The Purse of Satan

Do the Luciferian Elite need more time to usher in the Aeon of Horus?

The Jesuits have a powerful apparatus. They shield the Elite from view behind the Star of David and attack their enemies with the Sword of Muhammad.

But how do they pay the bills?

Endnotes

[1675] *LC/MS/MS analysis of the endogenous dimethyltryptamine hallucinogens, their precursors, and major metabolites in rat pineal gland microdialysate.* The United States National Library of Medicine.
http://www.ncbi.nlm.nih.gov/pubmed/23881860
 So these Mengeles found DMT in a rodent's brain…I'm starting to think the entire "science" industry is filled with satanists who care nothing of the pain and chaos they inflict as long as it furthers their agenda.

[1676] *VFTB 201: DMT – The Soul of Prophecy?* Derek Gilbert, 9 November 2014, A View From The Bunker
http://vftb.net/?p=5432

[1677] *CIA Chief: We'll Spy on You Through Your Dishwasher*, Spencer Ackerman, 14 March 2012, Wired
http://www.wired.com/2012/03/petraeus-tv-remote/

[1678] *Horizons 2010: Rick Strassman, M.D. - "Old Testament Prophecy – A Western Model of the Psychedelic Experience"*, 2010
http://vimeo.com/16298958

[1679] *In Search Of Sophia*, Dr. Quenten Quesnell, Department of Religion and Biblical Literature, Smith College
http://www.smith.edu/religion/Rel99/quenten.html

[1680] *Isis & Sophia*, "Isidora", 19 January 2013, Isiopolis
http://isiopolis.com/2013/01/19/isis-sophia/

[1681] *Suspicions Run Deep in Iraq That C.I.A. and the Islamic State Are United*, David Kirkpatrick, 20 September 2014, NY Times
http://www.nytimes.com/2014/09/21/world/middleeast/suspicions-run-deep-in-iraq-that-cia-and-the-islamic-state-are-united.html

[1682] *Blowback! U.S. Trained Islamists Who Joined ISIS*, Aaron Klein, 17 June 2014, WorldNetDaily
http://www.wnd.com/2014/06/officials-u-s-trained-isis-at-secret-base-in-jordan/#!
 The only "blowback" about this *purposeful agenda of carnage* is from dupes who aren't paying attention.

[1683] *The ISIS Ploy: Illuminati Sorcery and Sacrifice*, Zen Gardner, 14 June 2014, Zen Gardner.com
http://www.zengardner.com/isis-ploy-illuminati-sorcery-sacrifice/

[1684] *Wesley Clark: U.S. Military Plan To Overthrow 7 Countries In 5 Years*, Johnny Cirucci YouTube
https://www.youtube.com/watch?v=Xmms5Eoixfs&

[1685] *Russia and China Vow to Protect Syria from Becoming Another Libya*, Farooq Yousaf, 25 June 2012, Pravda
http://english.pravda.ru/hotspots/conflicts/25-06-2012/121471-russia_china_syria_libya-0/

[1686] *Putin Scores on Syria: How He Got the Upper Hand—And How He Will Use It*, Fiona Hill, 11 September 2013, Foreign Affairs
http://www.foreignaffairs.com/articles/139905/fiona-hill/putin-scores-on-syria

[1687] *Iraq Intel Report: US Planes Supplying ISIL with Weapons, Foodstuff*, 16 November 2014, FARS

http://english.farsnews.com/newstext.aspx?nn=13930825001416
[1688] *5-Year-Old Christian Boy Cut in Half by ISIS Terrorists*, Melissa Barnhart, 11 August 2014, the Christian Post
http://www.christianpost.com/news/5-year-old-christian-boy-cut-in-half-by-isis-terrorists-124648/
[1689] *Rev. Graham on ISIS: Christians Crucified, Beheaded, Buried Alive*, Michael W. Chapman, 18 August 2014, CNS News
http://www.cnsnews.com/news/article/michael-w-chapman/rev-graham-isis-christians-crucified-beheaded-buried-alive
[1690] *US Bombed "Empty Buildings" in Airstrikes on ISIL in Syria*, Patrick Henningsen, 24 September 2014, 21st Century Wire
http://21stcenturywire.com/2014/09/24/us-bombed-empty-buildings-in-raqqa-in-airstrikes-on-isil-in-syria/
[1691] *Did Obama Bomb Syria At Night to Avoid Actually Killing Terrorists?* Rusty Weiss, 24 September 2014, Headline Politics
http://www.headlinepolitics.com/did-obama-bomb-syria-at-night-to-avoid-actually-killing-terrorists/
[1692] *Pentagon: New Airstrikes Target Refineries Used by ISIS in Syria*, Chelsea J. Carter, Barbara Starr and Gul Tuysuz, 24 September 2014, CNN
http://www.cnn.com/2014/09/24/world/meast/us-airstrikes/
[1693] *Christian Leader: ISIS Beheading Children*, Jonathan Mann, 6 August 2014, CNN
http://www.cnn.com/video/data/2.0/video/world/2014/08/06/idesk-iraq-christians-persecuted-mark-arabo-intv.cnn.html
[1694] *Foxe's Book of Martyrs*, John Foxe, Michael Hobart Seymour (1838), p. 142
[1695] *ibid*, p. 143
[1696] *ibid*, p. 144
[1697] *ibid*, p. 145-6
[1698] *ibid*, p. 146-7
[1699] *Cheney: Enhanced Interrogations "Essential" in Saving American Lives*, Bill Sammon, 30 August 2009, FoxNews
http://www.foxnews.com/politics/2009/08/30/cheney-enhanced-interrogations-essential-saving-american-lives/
[1700] *Osama bin Laden, A.K.A. CIA Asset "Tim Osman"*, What Really Happened
http://whatreallyhappened.com/WRHARTICLES/binladen_cia.html
[1701] *How The CIA Helped Create Osama Bin Laden*, Casey McCalla, 2 May 2011, News One, the BLACK news website for BLACK FOLKS
http://newsone.com/1205745/cia-osama-bin-laden-al-qaeda/

    I shaved off Casey's hyphenated name, the way she shaved off the balls of the moron who married her.

[1702] *How the Spanish Inquisition Worked*, Shanna Freeman, undated, How Stuff Works
http://history.howstuffworks.com/historical-figures/spanish-inquisition3.htm
[1703] *Roman Catholic Satanic Torture Methods!* okcSDRmedia, YouTube
https://www.youtube.com/watch?v=Xl13wMpvj3s

    As a source, alone, this uncited video is questionable but as a visual aid to other sources it is ... disturbing.

    Note the demonic face inscribed on "The Pear" and tell me again whom these Catholics serve.

[1704] *The Spanish Inquisition > Torture*, Wikipedia
http://en.wikipedia.org/wiki/Spanish_Inquisition#Torture
[1705] *Medieval Inquisition > Torture*, Wikipedia
http://en.wikipedia.org/wiki/Medieval_Inquisition#Torture
[1706] *Foxe's Book of Martyrs*, p. 147
[1707] *Occult Theocrasy*, Edith Starr Miller; Lady Queenborough, Imprimerie F. Paillart (1933), p. 311
[1708] *Foxe's Book of Martyrs*, pp. 149-150
[1709] *Isis Unveiled: A Master-Key to the Mysteries of Ancient and Modern Science and Theology, Volume II – Theology*, H. P. Blavatsky, Theosophical University Press (1877), p. 56
[1710] Here, too, Wikipedia gives *nothing* to the researcher—a few sentences and the rest has been sanitized.
Synod of Verona, Wikipedia (as of 28 October 2014)
http://en.wikipedia.org/wiki/Synod_of_Verona
The Synod of Verona was held in 1184 under the auspices of Pope Lucius III. It is most notable for condemning the Waldensians under the charge of witchcraft; the charge was later amended to include heresy. The Synod of Verona condemns Cathars, and Waldensians as heretics. That's the entire entry!!!
[1711] *A Study in the Inquisition*, Clinton D. Hamilton, *The Preceptor*, Vol. 1, No. 4, Feb. 1952, and No. 5. Mar. 1952, reposted by the La Vista Church of Christ
http://lavistachurchofchrist.org/LVarticles/StudyOfTheInquisitions.html
[1712] *A History of the Holy Catholic Inquisition*, Cyrus Mason, H. Perkins (1835), pp. v-vi, entered into the Congressional Record by Henry Perkins in 1835 via the District Court of the Eastern District of Pennsylvania
[1713] *The Decline and Fall of the Roman Church*, Malachi Martin, G.P. Putnam's Sons, NY (1981), pp. 256-257
[1714] Mason, p. 17
[1715] *Iucunda Semper Expectatione Encyclical Of Pope Leo XIII On The Rosary*, Vatican.va
http://www.vatican.va/holy_father/leo_xiii/encyclicals/documents/hf_l-xiii_enc_08091894_iucunda-semper-expectatione_en.html
[1716] *Co-Redemptrix, Mediatrix of All Graces, and Advocate*, Monsignor Charles M. Mangan, May 2007, Catholics United for the Faith
http://www.cuf.org/2007/05/faith-fact-co-redemptrix-mediatrix-of-all-graces-and-advocate/
[1717] *A Woman Rides The Beast*, Dave Hunt, Harvest House (1994), pp. 113-114
[1718] *Catechism of the Catholic Church,* Vatican.va
http://www.vatican.va/archive/ccc_css/archive/catechism/p122a3p2.htm
[1719] *The Assumption of the Blessed Virgin Mary*, Scott P. Richert, undated, About Religion
http://catholicism.about.com/od/holydaysandholidays/p/Assumption.htm
[1720] *Basilica della Santa Casa (Holy House of Loreto) > History*, Wikipedia
http://en.wikipedia.org/wiki/Holy_House_of_Loreto#History
[1721] *The Miracle of the Holy House of Loreto*, Lee Wells, Catholic Tradition.org
http://www.catholictradition.org/Mary/loreto1.htm
[1722] *Fátima: First Apparition of the Angel*, EWTN
http://www.ewtn.com/fatima/apparitions/angel1.htm
[1723] *Fátima: Second Apparition of the Angel*, EWTN

http://www.ewtn.com/fatima/apparitions/angel2.htm
[1724] *Our Lady of Fátima > Initial Apparitions*, Wikipedia
http://en.wikipedia.org/wiki/Our_Lady_of_F%C3%A1tima#Initial_apparitions
[1725] *Why Is Friday The 13th Unlucky? Find Out What Happened On This Day In 1307 To Curse It To Bad Luck*, Amanda Schiavo, 13 December 2013, the Latin Times
http://www.latintimes.com/why-friday-13th-unlucky-find-out-what-happened-day-1307-curse-it-bad-luck-138728
[1726] *Fátima In Lucia's Own Words: Sister Lucia's Memoirs*, Edited by Fr. Louis Kondor, SVD., Fatimæ, Julii (2007), p. 123
[1727] *ibid*, pp. 123-124
[1728] *Announcement Made By Cardinal Angelo Sodano Secretary Of State*, Fátima, 13 May 2000, Congregation For The Doctrine Of The Faith, The Message Of Fátima, Vatican.va
http://www.vatican.va/roman_curia/congregations/cfaith/documents/rc_con_cfaith_doc_20000626_message-fatima_en.html
[1729] *The Attempts To Kill Pope John Paul II*, 22 May 2013, Vati Leaks
http://www.vatileaks.com/_blog/Vati_Leaks/post/the-attempts-to-kill-pope-john-paul-ii/
[1730] *Sister Lucia's Memoirs*, p. 216
[1731] *The Message Of Fátima*, Congregation For The Doctrine Of The Faith, JosephCard. Ratzinger, Prefect of the Congregation for the Doctrine of the Faith, Vatican.va
http://www.vatican.va/roman_curia/congregations/cfaith/documents/rc_con_cfaith_doc_20000626_message-fatima_en.html
[1732] *Fátima: Apparition of 13 October 1917*, undated, EWTN
https://www.ewtn.com/fatima/apparitions/October.htm
[1733] *Politics, Prophecy & the Supernatural*, L.A. Marzulli, Spiral of Life Publishing, pp. 110-123
This was a copy L.A. gifted to me and signed when I went to hear him speak and, given that I was out of work at the time, I was/am deeply greatful for his generosity.
[1734] *Blue Army of Our Lady of Fátima*, Wikipedia
http://en.wikipedia.org/wiki/Blue_Army_of_Our_Lady_of_F%C3%A1tima
[1735] *Our Lady And Islam: Heaven's Peace Plan*, Fr Ladis J. Cizik, Blue Army National Executive Director, EWTN
http://www.ewtn.com/library/mary/olislam.htm
[1736] *The Myths of Islam*, Religion of Peace.com
http://www.thereligionofpeace.com/pages/myths-of-islam.htm#islammeanspeace
Kind of bloggish but I already knew this to be accurate.
[1737] *Alberto Rivera*, Wikipedia
http://en.wikipedia.org/wiki/Alberto_Rivera#Death
[1738] *Alberto Rivera > Death*, Wikipedia [as of 29 October 2014]
http://en.wikipedia.org/wiki/Alberto_Rivera#Death
[1739] *Alberto Rivera > Allegations That The Church Created Islam*, Wikipedia
https://en.wikipedia.org/wiki/Alberto_Rivera#References
[1740] *How The Vatican Created Islam*, Alberto Rivera, 13 April 2006, Red Ice Creations
http://www.redicecreations.com/specialreports/2006/04apr/catholicislam.html
[1741] *The Priest and the Prophet: The Christian Priest, Waraqa Ibn Nawfal's, Profound Influence Upon Muhammad, the Prophet of Islam*, Joseph Azzi, The Pen Publishers (2005)

[1742] *Isis Unveiled: A Master-Key to the Mysteries of Ancient and Modern Science and Theology, Volume II – Theology*, H. P. Blavatsky, Theosophical University Press (1877), pp. 73-74
[1743] *Peter-Hans Kolvenbach, SJ (1928–)*, Ignatian Spirituality, Loyola Press
http://www.ignatianspirituality.com/ignatian-voices/20th-century-ignatian-voices/peter-hans-kolvenbach-sj/
[1744] *Did Black Pope Order And Help Orchestrate 9/11?* Greg Szymanski, 20 April 2006, the Arctic Beacon
http://www.arcticbeacon.com/articles/20-Apr-2006.html
[1745] *Woman Beheaded In Oklahoma Attack Was Grandmother Who Had Just Lost Her Home In Tornado As It Emerges Muslim Attacker Was Let Out Of Jail Early*, Jill Reilly, 28 September 2014, the Daily Mail
http://www.dailymail.co.uk/news/article-2772594/Woman-beheaded-Oklahoma-attack-grandmother-just-lost-home-tornado-emerges-attacker-let-jail-early.html
[1746] *5 Things About the Armed Executive Who Stopped Alton Nolen*, the Oklahoma Terrorist, Rodney Conover, 27 September 2014, Joe for America
http://joeforamerica.com/2014/09/5-things-armed-executive-stopped-alexander-nolen-oklahoma-terrorist/
[1747] *"He Yelled Allahu Akbar": Dramatic New Video Features Fort Hood Victims Demanding Shooting Be Classified as Terrorism*, Madeleine Morgenstern, 19 October 2012, the Blaze
http://www.theblaze.com/stories/2012/10/19/he-yelled-allahu-akbar-dramatic-new-video-features-fort-hood-victims-demanding-shooting-be-classified-as-terrorism/
[1748] *FBI: Oklahoma Beheading Not Linked To Terrorism*, K. Querry, 29 September 2014, KFOR News Channel 4
http://kfor.com/2014/09/25/reports-police-respond-to-possible-shooting-near-moore-grocery-store/
[1749] *Internal Documents Reveal How the FBI Blew Fort Hood*, Mariah Blake, 27 August 2013, Mother Jones
http://www.motherjones.com/politics/2013/08/nidal-hasan-anwar-awlaki-emails-fbi-fort-hood
[1750] *Radical US-Born Cleric Anwar al-Awlaki "Killed"*, Damien McElroy, 30 September 2011, the Telegraph
http://www.telegraph.co.uk/news/worldnews/al-qaeda/8798599/Radical-US-born-cleric-Anwar-al-Awlaki-killed.html
[1751] *Anwar al Awlaki dined at Pentagon after 9/11*, Johnny Cirucci YouTube
https://www.youtube.com/watch?v=X9YIBrSBmU8&
    A FoxNews Alert!
[1752] *"I'm Really Good At Killing People": New Book Claims President Obama Joked To Aides About Using Drone Strikes*, Michael Zennie, 3 November 2013, the Daily Mail
http://www.dailymail.co.uk/news/article-2486809/New-book-claims-President-Obama-bragged-aides-using-drone-strikes.html
[1753] *The Due-Process-Free Assassination Of U.S. Citizens Is Now Reality*, Glenn Greenwald, 30 September 2011, Salon
http://www.salon.com/2011/09/30/awlaki_6/

Chapter 19

The Golden Rule: He Who Owns the Gold, Makes the Rules

Of the outward exhibition of a contempt of riches.

I. To prevent the seculars from charging us with covetousness, it will be occasionally proper to refuse the smaller alms, which are offered for services performed by the society; from those, however, who are entirely devoted to us, it is best to accept even the smallest offerings, lest we exhibit avarice, by admitting of none, but large gifts. ~ Secreta Monita[1754]

"Gold is money, everything else is credit..." is attributed to JP Morgan himself while testifying in front of Congress back in 1912 shortly before his death. ...it was exactly 100% correct back then and even more pertinent today... Morgan ... actually said, "Money is gold, nothing else." ...in 1912 Congress was rarely lied to if ever. Whereas today hearing the truth is as rare as hens teeth. Please recall our past Federal Reserve chairman Ben Bernocchio as he lied to Congress when he replied, "No" when asked if gold was money. ~ Bill Holter, Miles Franklin Brokers[1755]

Year of Infamy

If there was a year where the enemies of America thoroughly took over her finances and thoroughly condemned the average working American to fiscal servitude it would be 1913.

> *This Saturday at a stump speech in Rochester, Minnesota Ron Paul may have outdone even himself. Famous for advocating the repeal of many laws, the elimination of numerous agencies and substantially reducing the size and scope of the federal government Ron Paul recently told the Wall Street Journal "I'd really like to repeal 1913." Why a whole year? Three reasons:*
>
> ■ *On February 3, 1913 the 16th Amendment to the United States Constitution was ratified. The amendment allows Congress to levy an income tax without apportioning it among the states per the Constitution Article I, Sections 2,8, and 9.*

> ■ *On May 31st, 1913 the 17th Amendment was declared part of the Constitution by Secretary of State William Jennings Bryan. It established the direct election of U.S. Senators by popular vote stripping the right away from the state legislators.*
>
> ■ *On December 23, 1913 the Federal Reserve Act was passed. This act grants a consortium of private banks legal authority to issue Federal Reserve Notes.*
>
> ~ Topher Morrison, AMTV[1756]

Most Americans have no idea that their powerful United States Senators were originally chosen by state legislatures. This gave individual states standing against a Leviathan central government and provided a layer of insulation against corruption.

Elihu Root was the Secretary of War[ggg] for William McKinley and Teddy Roosevelt as well as the Secretary of State for Roosevelt. He was also the personal lawyer of steel magnate and robber-baron Andrew Carnegie.

Root led the way to give his masters direct access to U.S. Senators and their long 6-year terms in office.

The 17th Amendment also transferred the power of selecting interim U.S. Senators from the state legislatures and gave it to the state governor—again, much easier to corrupt.

But if the 17th Amendment was a treasonous coup, much more so the 16th.

The very idea that the United States government has the right to take from 40 to 60% and more from your income before you even lay eyes on it via an "Income Tax" is, itself, completely unconstitutional.

Not only is the intent in direct opposition to the founding documents and ideals of this nation, but Bill Benson of Constitutional Research Associates claims he has proof: the 16th Amendment was *not* ratified by the Constitutionally-required three-fourths of states. [italics suspended]

> Article V of the U.S. Constitution defines the ratification process and requires three-fourths of the states to ratify any amendment proposed by Congress. There were forty-eight states in the American Union in 1913, meaning that affirmative action of thirty-

---

[ggg] A title infinitely more honest than "Secretary of Defense".

six was necessary for ratification. In February 1913, Secretary of State Philander Knox proclaimed that thirty-eight had ratified the Amendment.

In 1984 Bill Benson began a research project, never before performed, to investigate the process of ratification of the 16th Amendment. After traveling to the capitols of the New England states and reviewing the journals of the state legislative bodies, he saw that many states had not ratified. He continued his research at the National Archives in Washington, D.C.; it was here that Bill found his Golden Key.

This damning piece of evidence is a sixteen-page memorandum from the Solicitor of the Department of State, among whose duties is the provision of legal opinions for the Secretary of State. In this memorandum, the Solicitor lists the many errors he found in the ratification process.

These four states are among the thirty-eight from which Philander Knox claimed ratification:

- California: The legislature never recorded any vote on any proposal to adopt the amendment proposed by Congress.
- Kentucky: The Senate voted on the resolution, but rejected it by a vote of nine in favor and twenty-two opposed.
- Minnesota: The State sent nothing to the Secretary of State in Washington.
- Oklahoma: The Senate amended the language of the 16th Amendment to have a precisely opposite meaning.

When his project was finished at the end of 1984, Bill had visited the capitol of every state from 1913 and knew that not a single one had actually and legally ratified the proposal to amend the U.S. Constitution. Thirty-three states engaged in the unauthorized activity of altering the language of an amendment proposed by Congress, a power that the states do not possess.

Since thirty-six states were needed for ratification, the failure of thirteen to ratify was fatal to the Amendment. This occurs within the major (first three) defects tabulated in Defects in Ratification of the 16th Amendment. Even if we were to ignore defects of spelling, capitalization and punctuation, we would still have only two states which successfully ratified. ~ Bill Benson[1757]

There's more.

One organization says there is no law on the books *whatsoever* that requires a private American citizen to file a tax return[1758] and they have staked $50,000 to the assertion with no winners.[1759]

What they did win were several IRS Agents turned whistleblower like Joe Banister and Sherry Jackson.

As a result of their integrity, both have been heavily persecuted and prosecuted.

Joe Bannister was charged with tax fraud. After a brutal court battle in 2001, Bannister was acquitted.

> *...an April 2001 email between a Department of Justice lawyer named DiLeonardo, who had worked with Banister while Banister was working at the IRS, and Ron Semino, the chief of the Western Division of the Department of Justice's Tax Division, showed that the government viewed Banister to be the most visible personality in what many people today call "the tax honesty movement." ...*
>
> *...the jury ... saw no crime in what Banister was doing. Two of the jurors, who spoke with AFP right after the trial, related the thinking that led to their decision.*
>
> *They said the false tax return charges were "non-starters with the jury." The jury saw that the IRS might have disagreed with the position of Banister on the tax returns. However, the tax returns contained no false information.*
>
> *The jurors said they were surprised when the testimony part of the case ended, since they had yet to see or hear any evidence of a crime. They said the evidence showed that Banister was honest, straightforward, credible, believed in what he was doing and was trying to follow the law. They also believed that Banister was honestly trying to get answers, but the government consistently refused to answer his questions and address his concerns.* ~ Peymon Mottahedeh, Freedom Law School[1760]

Sadly, he is the exception, not the rule.

A system whose existence depends upon taxation will not stand by while whistleblowers and rebels strike at its heart. If Americans learned their government had no legal authority to summarily tax their personal incomes (businesses are different, I'm afraid), the entire system would collapse under the weight of parasitic fatcats.

Both Joe Bannister and Sherry Jackson were helping private citizens understand the tax trap in their individual finances as well as giving open public classes[1761] about the truth of the "progressive tax code". The Progressive tax code is a weapon that can be fine-tuned to attack specific portions of America's populace (which is why a flat tax will never be allowed by the traitors and subversives currently running our government). It is extremely helpful to Luciferians, globalists and Papists who *despise* America's Middle Class.

Sherry Jackson was convicted of tax fraud in 2008.[1762]

Jackson was heavily persecuted and her health began to fail her in prison when Texas Congressman Ron Paul came to her aid.[1763]

She is still under attack and currently being sued by the government for $150,000. Not being a Rockefeller or Rothschild, losing would destroy her entire family.

Dr. Dino

Kent Hovind was so successful in his defense of Creationism he had his own theme park; Dinosaur Adventure Land. Those who loved his ministry call him "Dr. Dino." He was even inducted into the Creation Science Hall of Fame.[1764]

Unfortunately for Kent, he had just enough information about America's tax scam to get himself into trouble. He interwove the personal finances of himself and his wife with those of his ministry and his foundation[1765], and then utilized his bank account in ways that avoided required Federal reports to be logged; such as repeatedly making withdraws of just under $10,000[1766]. This is known as "structuring" and *any* small business owner can be easily sucked into being guilty of this offense.

Kent has continued to defend himself from prison which seems to have irked the Federal government. In proof of the definition of "tyranny" as having so many over-lapping laws and regulations you need only to have a target and the broken law will appear, new charges are being levied against him due to his "frivolous" counter-suits having "encumbered" Lady Justice. These charges come just as he is being readied to leave prison after 8 years.[1767]

As an enemy of both Orwellian government and Darwinian Evolution,

Hovind[hhh] perfectly fit the profile of a voice powerful enough to sway masses but not quite well-known enough to start an uprising when it is quelled.

From Freedom to Fascism

If you haven't heard of Kent Hovind, you probably haven't heard of Aaron Russo. He, too, had fit the description of someone extremely dangerous yet not public enough to be protected.

> *Aaron Russo ... was an American entertainment businessman, film producer and director... He was best known for producing such movies as* Trading Places, Wise Guys, *and* The Rose. ~ Wikipedia[1768]

Russo had a conversion—he took the Red Pill and started using his considerable Hollywood skills and connections to make a *tour dé force* documentary in 2006 titled *America: Freedom to Fascism.* It was extremely well done and covered subjects like the Income Tax, the Federal Reserve, Radio Frequency Identification ("RFID"), electronic voting machines and the Surveillance State.

Russo died a year later at the young age of 64 of bladder cancer.

Banksters' Rule

The most powerful way to enslave and steer a nation is to control her finances and, on that definition alone, America has been enslaved since 1913.

The battle for a central bank has been waged from America's inception and few in the Founding generation were for it, having witnessed the excesses and criminal activities of powerful bankers elsewhere in the world as well as throughout history.

Alexander Hamilton was a driving force behind both strong centralized government and a central bank. [italics suspended]

> There was always a group of men in American politics who were not opposed to the evil mercantilist system in principle. They recognized it as a wonderful system for accumulating power and wealth as long as they could be in charge of it. Being victimized by it was another matter. These men, led by Alexander Hamilton and

---

[hhh] My support of Kent has no bearing on his insistence of a "young Earth" and dinosaurs co-existing with man. That will be covered in the next book...maybe.

his fellow Federalists, strived to implement an American version of British mercantilism as soon as the Revolution was over. In doing so they were traitors to the American Revolution and the worst kind of corrupt, power-seeking political scoundrels. ...

The Virginia statesman John Taylor of Caroline smoked out these political scoundrels in an 1823 book entitled *New Views of the Constitution of the United States* (reprinted in 2005 by The Lawbook Exchange, Ltd, of Union, New Jersey). Making extensive use of the recently published *Secret Proceedings and Debates of the Constitutional Convention* by Robert Yates, who attended the constitutional convention, Taylor shredded the false notions of "nationalists" like Hamilton (and later, Clay and Lincoln).

Focusing on Hamilton as the chief culprit, Taylor explained how the "nationalists" did try at the constitutional convention to create a completely centralized government, but failed. For example, he quotes Hamilton himself at the convention as proposing a form of government such that "All laws of the particular states, contrary to the constitution or laws of the United States [government], to be utterly void. And the better to prevent such laws being passed, the governor ... of each state shall be appointed by the general government, and shall have a negative upon the laws about to be passed in the state of which he is governor." ...

Taylor understood that the reason why Hamilton and other Federalists wanted a centralized or consolidated government was that states' rights would forever stand in the way of their accumulation of power and wealth through the mercantilist system that they hoped to impose on America. Therefore, states' rights must be crushed, in the eyes of Hamilton and his followers (despite occasional lip service paid to the notion of states' rights). ~ *Traitors to the American Revolution*, Thomas DiLorenzo[1769]

Perhaps we can be a little less judgmental of Col. Hamilton when we think of a nation with no central government and no common national currency. It would be like traveling across old Europe (not the confederated Europe of today, ruled by unaccountable Elites in Brussels), each state acting as its own sovereign nation with different forms of currency of different values, completely vulnerable to a small but serious host of threats.[iii]

[iii] The vast majority of strategic threats today are fabricated, particularly nation-state wars but there is a need for a small but razor-sharp standing military to

However, if Hamilton was attempting to create a "Federal Reserve" as America's first central bank then he was, indeed, a traitor.

> *Though the intent of the Bank was to facilitate government finances, Hamilton had another goal in mind—to function as a commercial bank. At the time of the revolution, there were barely any banks in the colonies; Britain had used its authority to protect its own banks and prevent the development of financial rivals. Hamilton's vision was to create a central source of capital that could be lent to new businesses and thereby develop the nation's economy. So ... in some ways the First Bank prefigured the Federal Reserve...* ~ the Federal Reserve Bank of Minneapolis[1770]

Regardless, he was killed by a traitor of a different stripe; Aaron Burr, who tried to enlist the British to start his own country in America.[1771]

As far as a central bank was concerned, several Founders were overwhelmingly against the idea and having a standardized, national currency was the exclusive power of Congress under the Constitution.

> *"The Congress shall have Power To...coin Money, regulate the Value thereof, and of foreign Coin...."*
> ~ *Article I, Section 8, Clause 5*

> *Congress's power to coin money is exclusive: under Article I, Section 10, the states are not permitted to "coin Money; emit Bills of Credit; [or] make any Thing but gold and silver Coin a Tender in Payment of Debts...." Whereas the prohibitions on the states are clear and detailed, Congress's grant of power under the Coinage Clause is open-ended.*

> *Nonetheless, certain elements are clear. First, Congress is granted the authority to "coin money," which authorizes Congress to coin money from precious metals such as gold and silver. Under the Articles of Confederation, the power to coin money was a concurrent power of Congress and the states. To create a more standardized monetary system and reduce the costs of running mints, the Constitution granted this power to Congress exclusively. The elimination of the states' power to coin money and the exclusive grant to Congress provoked controversy because the power to coin money was traditionally understood as a symbol of political sovereignty. Second, Congress is empowered to regulate the value*

---

actually defend the interests of "We the People". Sadly, such a force would look nothing like the corporatocracy enforcers our military are today.

of the coins struck domestically and to set the value of foreign coins.
~ Todd Zywicki, The Heritage Guide to The Constitution[1772]

We don't need to go any further to understand that *it is not the responsibility of a central bank to coin money.*[iii]

Sadly, there are far worse reasons than that to seek the death of the Federal Reserve.

The First and-not-the-Last Central Bank

Although Hamilton was able to get a compromise central bank signed into law by George Washington, it was not renewed by Congress when the charter expired.

> *The First Bank of the United States was modeled after the Bank of England ... For example, it was partly owned by foreigners, who shared in its profits. ...it was not solely responsible for the country's supply of bank notes. It was responsible for only 20% of the currency supply; state banks accounted for the rest. Several founding fathers bitterly opposed the Bank. Thomas Jefferson saw it as an engine for speculation, financial manipulation, and corruption.*[2] *In 1811 its twenty-year charter expired and was not renewed by Congress.* ~ Wikipedia[1773]

There are several needlessly embellished Jefferson anti-bank quotes floating around the blogosphere that can not be sourced but his provable sentiments are more than enough.

Thomas Jefferson did not like bankers.

In setting the record straight, the Monticello Project (a proud member of the United Nations Educational, Scientific and Cultural Organization; "UNESCO") posted this—

> —*a statement Jefferson made in a letter to John Taylor in 1816... "And I sincerely believe, with you, that banking establishments are more dangerous than standing armies; and that the principle of spending money to be paid by posterity, under the name of funding, is but swindling futurity on a large scale."*[3] ...
>
> —*Jefferson's comment to John Wayles Eppes, "Bank-paper must be*

[iii] Some might split hairs on the words "coin money" to mean that Congress was forbidden from issuing paper currency but the phrase was/is common enough in encompassing *all* forms of currency as to be a mute point.

> *suppressed, and the circulating medium must be restored to the nation to whom it belongs."[4]* ~ Monticello.org[1774]

After the dust settled on the death of the first central bank, banking agents quickly went to work building a second...until they ran into a wall of Old Hickory.

Old Hickory

> *To* [Andrew] *Jackson, the* [presidential runoff between himself and sitting president John Quincy Adams] *was simply the latest stage of the historic struggle against privilege that ran back to the Magna Carta and included the Protestant Reformation of the sixteenth century, the English Revolution of the seventeenth, and the American Revolution of the eighteenth. At each stage the people seized more of what by right belonged to them, from those who intended that power remain the monopoly of the few.* ~ *Andrew Jackson: His Life and Times*, H.W. Brands[1775]

The Jacksonian presidency has been slandered due his uncharitable treatment of American Indians but Jackson was a man familiar with what would happen to those at the mercies of Indians during wartime.

In many ways, Indians at war acted as if they were on a jihad. [italics suspended]

> The Indians' resistance grew more sophisticated. They discovered that the Europeans belonged to more than one tribe, with the French as hostile to the English as either were to any of the Indians. Some Indians sided with the French, others with the English, and when the French and English went to war—as they did once a generation—the various Indian tribes exploited the opportunities to their own advantage. The largest of the conflicts (called the French and Indian War by the English in America) began in 1754 and inspired the Delawares and Shawnees, allies of France, to try to drive the English away from the frontier. To this end they launched a campaign of terror against British settlements in the Ohio Valley. The terror began successfully and over three years threatened to throw the English all the way back to the coast. ...
>
> The assault on a British fort at Mackinac showed the swiftness with which the Indians commenced their attacks and the brutality with which they completed them. Pontiac's campaign was spreading faster than the news of it, and the troops and traders at Mackinac knew of no reason to fear the large group of Ojibwas who

approached the fort in amicable fashion and commenced a game of lacrosse immediately beneath the walls. The British came out to watch, as they did on such occasions. The intensity of the game mounted, until one of the players threw the ball close to the gate. The laughing, cheering Spectators took no alarm when both teams tore after it. But then the players dropped their lacrosse sticks, snatched war axes from under the robes of their women, and rushed through the unguarded gate. The surprise was total and the carnage almost equally so. A trader named Alexander Henry, who managed to hide in a storage closet, left a chilling account:

> Through an aperture, which afforded me a view of the area of the fort, I beheld, in shapes the foulest and most terrible, the ferocious triumphs of barbarian conquerors. The dead were scalped and mangled; the dying were writhing and shrieking under the unsatiated knife and tomahawk; and from the bodies of some, ripped open, their butchers were drinking the blood, scooped up in the hollow of joined hands, and quaffed amid shouts of rage and victory.

~ Brands[1776]

The animosity and barbarism continued long after both the French & Indian War and the Revolution. In the year 1791, Jackson's native Cumberland, Tennessee lost "a man, woman, or child about every ten days, sometimes in the most ghastly fashion."[1777]

During the Revolutionary War, Jackson was only 13 when British dragoons under Banastre Tarleton drove he and his widowed mother from their farm in Charleston and ravaged it. Finding out that his brother Hugh had died on a campaign fighting Redcoats, he tried to enlist and would not take "No!" for an answer. He was put to use as a scout and courier.

Andy and his brother Robert were cornered trying to get supplies from the home of an aunt. They watched in horror as the British ransacked the woman's home, destroying everything she had of value. When ordered to polish an officer's boots, the teen defiantly refused and received a deep gash from the flat of a cutlass. The two brothers were interned at the Camden prison and languished under British maltreatment. Their mother, Elizabeth, courageously sought them out and organized an exchange for two British soldiers the Rebels couldn't afford to keep (given that they were actually receiving food and medicine), but not without a price. What Jackson's brother Robert suffered while in prison took his life the second day he was home and Andy contracted smallpox.

Garnering miraculous strength for a rail-thin teenager, he refused to let the disease take him and was one of the very rare survivors of it, though his recovery was a long one.

On the success of getting back her boys, Elizabeth lit out after two nephews she had raised as sons but the journey took too much out of her. She contracted cholera and died—the third of Andy's immediate family taken by the British.

After the Revolution, Jackson received a modest inheritance from a deceased grandfather in Scotland and used it to pursue law. His iron constitution caused him to exert himself in ways that gave him a bit of a reputation.

> *Around Salisbury Jackson acquired a reputation as a wild thing going quickly wrong. Years after he left, the townsfolk remembered an evening when Jackson and his friends toasted their mutual health and then, lest the glasses be used for less noble purposes, hurled them into the fire. With the logic of apprentice lawyers, they reasoned that the same argument compelled them to hurl the chairs they sat on into the fire. And then the table. And then the drapes, and everything else in the room that wasn't nailed down. The building survived the pyrotechnics, but barely.* ~ Brands[1778]

Jackson had the occasion to take up with Lewis and Rachel Robards when he was in his early twenties. Robards was incessantly jealous over his pretty wife and had already disowned her once (later taking her back) in accusations of infidelity. Sensing a spark between her and Jackson he disowned her again. Another boarder, John Overton, would later fiercely attest to Jackson's good character.

The incident, along with Rachel's beauty and charm, brought the two together and they eloped. Being young and infatuated, they didn't wait for the long process of divorce to finalize (they couldn't have foreseen the drive-thru services available in today's America). Who knew what tomorrow would bring?

"Tomorrow" brought not one, but two campaigns for the presidency. The mere appearance of Jackson having stolen another man's wife played big in the papers. The accusations destroyed Rachel from within. After winning the second run for President in 1828, Rachel died just before Jackson left for office.

Andrew Jackson was a far better soldier then he was a lawyer.

For almost 30 years, Jackson's strong physique and indomitable leadership served him well in the military. He would later prove his worth and take out all of his frustrations against the British in a battle so lopsided it has rightly become legend. [italics suspended]

Jackson was appointed commander of the Tennessee militia in 1801, with the rank of colonel. He was later elected major general of the Tennessee militia in 1802.[17]

TheCustomOfLife, Wikimedia Commons

Creek Campaign and Treaty

During the War of 1812, the Shawnee chief Tecumseh encouraged the "Red Stick" Creek Indians of northern Alabama and Georgia to attack white settlements. He had unified tribes in the Northwest to rise up against the Americans, trying to repel American settlers from those lands north of the Ohio. Four hundred settlers were killed in the Fort Mims massacre—one of the few instances of Native Americans killing a large number of American settlers and their African-American slaves.[18]—which brought the United States into the internal Creek campaign. Occurring at the same time as the War of 1812, the Creek campaign saw Jackson command the U.S. forces, which included the Tennessee militia, U.S. regulars, and Cherokee, Choctaw, and Lower Creek warriors. Sam Houston and David Crockett served under Jackson in this campaign.

Jackson defeated the Red Sticks at the Battle of Horseshoe Bend in 1814. U.S. forces and their allies killed 800 Red Stick warriors in this battle, but spared the chief Red Eagle, a mixed-race man also known as William Weatherford. ...

Battle of New Orleans

Jackson's service in the War of 1812 against the United Kingdom was conspicuous for bravery and success. When British forces threatened New Orleans, Jackson took command of the defenses, including militia from several western states and territories. He was a strict officer but was popular with his troops. They said he was "tough as old hickory" wood on the battlefield, and he acquired the nickname of "Old Hickory". In the Battle of New Orleans on January 8, 1815, Jackson's 5,000 soldiers won a decisive victory over 7,500 British. At the end of the battle, the British had 2,037 casualties: 291 dead (including three senior generals), 1,262 wounded, and 484 captured or missing. The Americans had 71 casualties: 13 dead, 39 wounded, and 19 missing.[21] ~ Wikipedia[1779]

Given the technology of warfare at that time and British combat experience, such a victory was nigh unto miraculous.

When ordered by then Secretary of War, William Crawford, to remove squatters from American Indian lands, General Jackson recalled his memories of Indian barbarism and was instantly sympathetic to the squatters. He considered his assignment as forcing him to become a Royal martial law dictator. Is there a parallel for Israeli settlements in contested areas of "Palestine"? Regardless, Jackson so Indians as a threat to national security.

> *Jackson was no apologist for lawbreakers, but he couldn't escape the irony of being asked to play the role of Britain against Americans. And though he applauded fair-mindedness in principle, he thought the administration overlooked a fundamental difference between whites and Indians on the frontier: the former were citizens of the United States and almost certainly would fight for the Union against any foreign foe, while the latter were noncitizens and might well take the part of Britain or Spain, as they had in the past. Unlike many of his white contemporaries, who asserted a higher claim to the land on grounds that they were civilized Christians, Jackson rarely addressed the cosmic morality of the land question. Instead he asked whether a particular arrangement would make the Union more secure or less. And in nearly every case he concluded that white control served national safety.* ~ Brands[1780]

This does not excuse abuse—especially of American Indians who had become Christians—but it gives us needed perspective completely missing from today's propaganda in Jesuit-influenced history texts and entertainment.

The Jackson presidency was a populist one and he would've easily fit in with today's Libertarians or the Tea Party.

> *The principle Jackson decided on was that rotation in office, rather than permanent tenure, should be the norm in a democracy. As this was a departure from previous practice, and liable to*

misinterpretation, he took care to explain the reasoning behind it. "There are, perhaps, few men who can for any great length of time enjoy office and power without being more or less under the influence of feelings unfavorable to the faithful discharge of their public duties," he said. "They are apt to acquire a habit of looking with indifference upon the public interests and of tolerating conduct from which an unpracticed man would revolt. Office is considered as a species of property." Such thinking was wrong, and it was what Jackson intended to root out. "In a country where offices are created solely for the benefit of the people, no one man has any more intrinsic right to official station than another. Offices were not established to give support to particular men at the public expense. ..." ~ Brands[1781]

On matters of religion, Jackson was non-sectarian Christian, to a fault. He was completely unaware of the wiles of the Company of Loyola and their extensive incognito efforts to subvert America.

I am no sectarian, though a lover of the Christian religion. I do not believe that any who shall be so fortunate as to be received to heaven, through the atonement of our blessed Saviour, will be asked whether they belonged to the Presbyterian, the Methodist, the Episcopalian Baptist, or Roman Catholic [church]. All Christians are brethren, and all true Christians know they are such because they love one another. A true Christian loves all, immaterial to what sect or church he may belong. ~ Brands[1782]

It was during Jackson's presidency that historian Alexis de Tocqueville visited America to catalogue the "Great Experiment". His writing and the populist Jackson Administration highlighted the conflict between full democratic mob-rule (manipulated by the Elite) and aristocratic feudalism.

It was a battle that would pit Jackson against his greatest foe; Nelson Biddle.

Tocqueville knew that Americans had abandoned property qualifications for voting. Didn't their absence cause problems? Finley [a man who hosted de Tocqueville in Baltimore] *acknowledged that it did. "I have seen elections swayed by the paupers from the alms house, whom one of the candidates had had fetched," he said. This was a manifestation of what he considered the worst feature of American politics: that elections could be determined by "those who have no interest in stability, since they possess nothing and have but little understanding."*

> *Tocqueville expressed puzzlement as to how democracy had ever taken hold. "It is yourselves, the members of the upper classes, who have made the existing laws," he said. "You were the masters of society fifty years ago." What had gone wrong? Finley answered succinctly: "Each party, to gain power, chose to flatter the people, and bid for its support by granting new privileges."*
>
> *At Philadelphia, Tocqueville met Nicholas Biddle, the president of the Bank of the United States. Tocqueville had been struck by the lack of defining ideologies between parties in America, at least by comparison with the situation in France, where avowed monarchists denounced republicans and vice versa. In America everyone paid at least lip service to the sovereignty of the people. ~ Brands*[1783]

Tocqueville would go on to note this conflict in the breakdown of America's political parties; who supported the bank verses who supported the President.

> *The President attacks the Bank of the United States; the country gets excited and parties are formed; the educated classes in general l line up behind the bank, while the people are for the President. ~ Brands*[1784]

Wealthy Elites were able to resurrect the central bank and it would eventually fall under the leadership of Nelson Biddle. [italics suspended]

> ...the Bank had come under the direction of Nicholas Biddle who was a formidable adversary to Jackson, not only because of the power of his position, but because of his strong will and sense of personal destiny. He was the archetype of the new Eastern Establishment: wealthy, arrogant, ruthless, and brilliant.
>
> Be had graduated from the University of Pennsylvania at the age of only thirteen, and, as a young man entering business, had fully mastered the secret science of money.
>
> With the ability to control the flow of the nation's credit, Biddle soon became one of the most powerful men in America. This was brought out dramatically when he was asked by a Senate Committee if his bank ever took advantage of its superior position over the state banks. He replied: "Never. There are very few banks which might not have been destroyed by an exertion of the powers of the Bank. None has ever been injured."[1] As Jackson publicly noted a few months later, this was an admission that most of the state banks

existed only at the pleasure of the Bank of the United States, and that, of course, meant at the pleasure of Mr. Biddle.

As Commanding General of the pro-bank forces, Biddle had one powerful advantage over his adversary. For all practical purposes, Congress was in his pocket. Or, more accurately, the product of his generosity was in the pockets of *Congressmen*. Following the Rothschild Formula, Biddle had been careful to reward compliant politicians with success in the business world. Few of them were willing to bite the hand that fed them. Even the great Senator, Daniel Webster, found himself kneeling at Biddle's throne. Galbraith says:

> Biddle was not without resources. In keeping with his belief that banking was the ultimate source of power, he had regularly advanced funds to members of Congress when delay on appropriations bills had held up their pay. Daniel Webster was, at various times, a director of the Bank and on retainer as its counsel. "I believe my retainer has not been renewed or refreshed as usual. If it be wished that my relation to the Bank should be continued, it may be well to send me the usual retainers." Numerous other men of distinction had been accommodated, including members of the press.[1]

Webster is a particularly interesting study in how even socalled "great" men can be compromised by an addiction to wealth. He had always been an advocate of sound money in Congress, yet, as a lawyer on Biddle's payroll, he represented the Bank's position before the Supreme Court in McCulloch v. Maryland. Much of the twisted logic that allowed the Court to end-run the Constitution and destroy sound money came from his pen. ~ *The Creature from Jekyll Island*, G. Edward Griffin [emphasis his][1785]

It was those same Elites who pushed a fight over the 2nd Bank of the United States upon Jackson. In mocking defiance, they sent him the Congressionally-approved renewal charter on July 4th, 1832.

> *The Second Bank of the United States was authorized for a 20-year period during James Madison's tenure in 1816. This was done in order to add stability to the national economy devastated by the War of 1812.*[71] *Jackson who almost went bankrupt by his own earlier speculations, strongly distrusted banks.*[71] *In 1829 and 1830 in his State of the Union Addresses Jackson wanted the Second Bank of the United States to be controlled by the Treasury*

Department.[72] In 1831 Jackson appointed Louis McLane Secretary of Treasury and Edward Livingston Secretary of State, both who supported the Second Bank of the United States.[72] Rather than have another Cabinet split and avoid an election controversy Jackson toned down his rhetoric against the bank in his third State of the Union Address.[72] The bank issue, however, did materialize as part of an 1832 election campaign strategy orchestrated by Henry Clay, that ultimately failed.[72]

On July 3, 1832 Congress passed the bank's recharter bill four years before it was necessary.[72] Jackson, upset that Clay brought the bank issue into the 1832 election, vetoed the bill.[73] ~ Wikipedia[1786]

Supremely Subverted

When Maryland tried to impede the power of the 2nd Bank by taxing notes that entered the state, suit was brought and the Supreme Court spoke through Chief Justice John Marshall in 1819 via *McCulloch v. Maryland*: a Central Bank is Constitutional!

Who gave Marshall the power to be the final arbiter over Constitutional authority? —He did!

Thomas Jefferson had just won the presidency from John Adams. Adams, before leaving office, appointed William Marbury as Justice of the Peace in the District of Columbia. President Jefferson ordered his Secretary of State, James Madison, to withhold the appointment and Marbury brought suit.

Part of the decision of *Marbury v. Madison* came down to "who had the final authority" given that the Judiciary Act of 1789 appeared to give powers not found in Article III of the Constitution. Although Marshall's overall decision was not to expand the powers of the Central Government, he crowned the Supreme Court as the ultimate arbiter in the question of constitutionality. This unprecedented power is today known as "Judicial Review".

It has been the root of treasonous tyranny throughout American history ever since, where as few as 5 Supreme Court Justices can subvert the will of the entire American populace—and why there now sit 6 Catholics on the Court (with the other 3 being puppet Leftist Jews, again shielding the Papists from focus).

In 1962, 5 Justices decided prayer in public schools was

"unconstitutional" despite all of America's history contrary to that point in *Engel v. Vitale*.

In 1972, 5 Justices decided that pornography was protected by the First Amendment—a ludicrous decision in *Miller v. California*.

One year later, seven Justices claimed that a woman has the "Constitutional right" to kill her unborn child in *Roe v. Wade*.

As of January 2014, there have been 56,662,169 abortions since then[1787]. That's 1,382,000 abortions a year, 115,167 abortions per month, 3,838 abortions every day, 159 abortions every hour, 2 abortions every second.

The implements of this industry look as if they came from the Inquisition. "Abortion doctors" burn the innocent and vulnerable unborn with salt solutions, rip them limb-from-limb with suction devices and whirling blades and pull their fully-formed bodies out of their mother just enough to jam scissors into the base of their tiny skull.[1788]

In ages past, satanists called demonic entities by ritual "sex magick" and then taking the bastard offspring born to pagan priestesses threw them alive into bonfires. Sometimes, desperate or deluded parents murdered their legitimate children in the same way.

Today, endless streams of the innocent are ritually slaughtered in the Holy of holies (their mother's womb) for the opening of interdimensional portals for unclean spirits to cause havoc in our realm.

> *Abortions are nothing more than modern day ritualistic, satanic, blood sacrifices. I realize that there are some who will read this and scoff. However, let's remember what the Maya did. We shudder when we think about their version of human sacrifice but are too educated and bolstered by our modernity to see our own version of it.*
>
> *In the Book off Enoch, we are told that one of the fallen angels showed the women how to kill the embryo in the womb. According to that text it would appear that the first abortion came from the Fallen One's emissaries; I believe that there's no way around that. It is a blood sacrifice that has opened the gates of hell. Here's why:*
>
> *In any occult ceremony there is a blood offering. The occultists do this in order to gain power, but also to open a gateway for the demonic spirits to manifest. Abortion accomplishes the same thing. The bloodletting opens up a portal, a gateway, to the demonic. It*

> *allows them to manifest in our dimension. Is this why a UFO is reported once every ten minutes in some part of our globe, because the ritualistic blood sacrifice has literally opened the doors to the second heaven?* ~ L.A. Marzulli[1789]

Don't believe L.A. Marzulli? How about Aleister Crowley—or, rather, the entity "Aiwass" *via* Crowley and his then-wife, Edith.

> *The best blood is ... the fresh blood of a child...* ~ *The Book of the Law*[1790]

That is the legacy of "Judicial Review" and Old Hickory was having none of it. [italics suspended]

> The basic problem with the bank, Jackson said, was that it was unconstitutional. The bank's defenders cited political precedent and Supreme Court decisions as providing constitutional sanction. "To this conclusion I can not assent," he rejoined. "Mere precedent is a dangerous source of authority, and should not be regarded as deciding questions of constitutional power except where the acquiescence of the people and the States can be considered as well settled." If anything, the history of the Bank of the United States showed that the question was far from settled. Congress had approved a bank in 1791 and disapproved it in 1811. It had debated long before reapproving it in 1816. As for the states, Jackson reckoned that the sum of legislative, executive, and judicial opinions from the states ran against the bank by as much as four to one.
>
> Regarding the Supreme Court, Jackson didn't think it had spoken in anything like a definitive tone on the bank. But more to the point, Jackson didn't believe the executive was bound by Supreme Court decisions. Nor, for that matter, was the legislature. To a later generation such a position might appear radical, even anarchic. But in the 1830s decisions of the Supreme Court had yet to acquire the finality they would eventually win, and *Jackson saw no reason to defer to an unelected tribunal.*
>
>> The Congress, the Executive, and the Court must each for itself be guided by its own opinion of the Constitution. Each public officer who takes an oath to support the Constitution swears that he will support it as he understands it, and not as it is understood by others. It is as much the duty of the House of Representatives, of the Senate, and of the President to decide upon the

constitutionality of any bill or resolution which may be presented to them for passage or approval as it is of the supreme judges when it may be brought before them for judicial decision. The opinion of the judges has no more authority over Congress than the opinion of Congress has over the judges, and on that point the President is independent of both.

~ Brands [emphasis mine][1791]

Historian and author H.W. Brands drove the point home further.

There was much more to Jackson's opposition than strict construction. Like Benton and other anti-bankers, the president feared the emergence of a monopoly of money. He didn't oppose monopolies per se. Patents and copyrights were monopolies that were both constitutional and conducive to the general welfare. But a monopoly of money was inherently dangerous. Of the bank's twenty-five directors, only five were chosen by the government, the rest by the stockholders of the bank. Thus the public interest was always outweighed by the interests of the bank's private owners, who must have been saints not to be tempted by the power they held over the nation's economy. "It is easy to conceive that great evils to our country and its institutions might flow from such a concentration of power in the hands of a few men irresponsible to the people," Jackson said. Nor was the economy the sum of what was at risk from the bank's excessive power. "Is there no danger to our liberty and independence? ... Will there not be cause to tremble for the purity of our elections in peace and for the independence of our country in war?" ~ Brands[1792]

If Old Hickory only knew what was planned to replace the 2nd Bank.

"It's the Jews!"

Through these machinations, author Andrew Carrington Hitchcock only sees Jews. In his book *The Synagogue of Satan* he uses the same contortions as other anti-Semites (while masking themselves as so-called "anti-Zionists") of differentiating between "real" Jews and "Khazarian" Jews. To them, the "real Jews" are nowhere to be found while the "Khazarian Jews" are everywhere. You might as well be an anti-Semite.

Hitchcock sees the Vatican's Rothschild accountants as running Rome, and not vice-versa. The case for the reverse pleads itself. [italics suspended]

1821: Kalmann (Carl) Mayer Rothschild is sent to Naples, Italy. He goes on to do a great deal of business with the Vatican and Pope Gregory XVI subsequently confers upon him the Order of St. George.

Also, whenever the Pope receives Kalmann, he gives him his hand rather than the customary toe to kiss, which causes concern with regard to the extent of Kalmann Rothschild's power over the Vatican.

1823: The Rothschilds' take over the financial operations of the Catholic Church, worldwide.

1828: After 12 years during which the Second Bank of the United States, ruthlessly manipulated the American economy to the detriment of the people but to the benefit of their own money grabbing ends, the American people had not surprisingly had enough, and opponents of this bank nominated Senator Andrew Jackson of Tennessee to run for President.

To the dismay of the Rothschilds', Jackson wins the Presidency and makes it quite clear he is going to use his mandate to kill this bank at his first opportunity. He starts out during his first term in office, rooting out the bank's many minions from Senator Andrew Jackson government service. To illustrate how deep this cancer was rooted in government, in order to achieve this end he had to fire 2,000 of the 11,000 employees of the Federal Government. ...

1832: In July, Congress is unable to override President Jackson's veto. President Jackson then stands for re-election and for the first time in American history he takes his argument directly to the people by taking his re-election campaign on the road. His campaign slogan is, "Jackson And No Bank!"

Even though the Rothschilds' pour over $3,000,000 into the campaign of President Jackson's opponent, the Republican, Senator Henry Clays, President Jackson is re-elected by a landslide in November. However, President Jackson knows the battle is only beginning, and following his victory he states,

> "The hydra of corruption is only scotched, not dead!"

1833: President Jackson starts removing the government's deposits from the Rothschild controlled, Second Bank of the United States and instead deposits them into banks directed by democratic bankers.

This causes the Rothschilds' to panic and so they do what they do best, by contracting the money supply and causing a depression. President Jackson knows what they are up to and later states,

> "You are a den of thieves' vipers, and I intend to rout you out, and by the Eternal God, I will rout you out."

1834: The Italian revolutionary leader, Guiseppe Mazzini, is selected by the, "Illuminati," to direct their revolutionary program throughout the world and goes on to serve in that capacity until his death in 1872.

1835: On January 30th, an assassin tries to shoot President Jackson, but miraculously both of the assassin's pistols misfire. President Jackson later claims that he knew the Rothschilds' were responsible for that attempted assassination. He is not the only one. Indeed, even the assassin, Richard Lawrence, who was found not guilty by reason of insanity, later brags that powerful people in Europe had hired him and promised to protect him if he were caught. [kkk] ...

1836: Following his years of fighting against the Rothschilds' and their central bank in America,

---

"The Hydra Is Not Dead!"

Telegraphing their moves is a favorite game of the Luciferian Elite, especially with such a lock on Hollywood. It appears to be a unwritten rule to allow the victims time to become self-aware and jump out of the pot before the boil.

A common movie theme is that in government and espionage there is a hidden hand that works above theatrical conflicts.

Blue-blood banker Elite and intelligence insider Ian Fleming wove the idea into his successful "James Bond" series of books—above the CIA and MI6 on one hand, and the Soviet "Smersh" on the other was "SP.E.C.T.R.E.": *SPecial Executive for Counter-intelligence, Terrorism, Revenge and Extortion*

Their symbol was an octopus because they had tentacles in everything.

In the most recent Daniel Craig Bond reboots, a shadowy organization called

---

[kkk] *The Assassins*, Robert J. Donovan, Harper & Brothers (1952), p. 83

President Andrew Jackson finally succeeds in throwing the Rothschilds' central bank out of America, when the bank's charter is not renewed. It would not be until 1913 that the Rothschilds' would be able to set up their third central bank in America, the Federal Reserve.

On July 28th, Nathan Mayer Rothschild dies and the control of his bank, N. M. Rothschild & Sons is passed on to his younger brother, James Mayer Rothschild.

David Sassoon, the Rothschilds' drug dealer over in China, increases his trade to over 30,000 chests of opium annually and drug addiction in coastal cities becomes endemic. ~ Hitchcock[1793]

> "Quantum" operates with impunity above the CIA and MI6.
>
> In the Marvel Comic incarnation of "Captain America", a timeless organization appropriately called "Hydra" spans evil overwatch from Nazi Germany to America's own "S.H.I.E.L.D." most recently defined as *Strategic Homeland Intervention, Enforcement and Logistics Division*.

But the attempt to assassinate Andrew Jackson was just as astounding as the rest of his life.

Putting aside our suspicions that Presidents John Adams and Thomas Jefferson were poisoned by the Company of Loyola, Andrew Jackson was the first President to have an assassin confront him openly in a bold attempt to murder him.

Truly, by the Hand of God, both of Richard Lawerence's single-shot cap-and-ball pistols failed to ignite.

The Creature from Jekyll Island

> *Q. What are banks for?*
> *A. To make money.*
> *Q. For the customers?*
> *A. For the banks.*
>
> ~ *The Creature from Jekyll Island*,
> G. Edward Griffin[1794]

The hydra did, indeed, rise up again after Old Hickory chopped the neck with Nelson Biddle's head on it.

As anyone who has studied America's current central bank will tell you, the "Federal Reserve" isn't "Federal" (a government agency), and there are no reserves.

Having fought this battle before, the money-changers were more cagey about how to deceive the American people the third time around.

Perhaps it is no coincidence that Judas was the treasurer for the disciples. He also used to skim off the top, like any good banker. [John 12:6]

In researching the Federal Reserve, two names invariably surface; G. Edward Griffin[III] and Eustace Mullins.

Mullins would pre-date Griffin by almost a decade though he received none of the notoriety that Griffin did. He accused Griffin of plagiarizing his 1983 book.[1795]

Griffin did borrow heavily from Mullins but "plagiary" seems more sour grapes than fair.

The story of the Federal Reserve conspiracy starts via a secret rail trip in the private car of Nelson Aldrich.

> *The name of Nelson Aldrich, senator from Rhode Island, was well known even in New Jersey. By 1910, he was one of the most powerful men in Washington, D.C., and his private railway car often was seen at the New York and New Jersey rail terminals during frequent trips to Wall Street. Aldrich was far more than a senator. He was considered to be the political spokesman for big business. As an investment associate of J.P. Morgan, he had extensive holdings in banking, manufacturing, and public utilities. His son-in-law was John D. Rockefeller, Jr. Sixty years later, his grandson, Nelson Aldrich Rockefeller, would become Vice President of the United States.* ~ Griffin[1796]

A group of powerful bankers skulked around in secret just as the Bilderberg Group does every year. [italics suspended]

> On the night of November 22, 1910, a group of newspaper reporters stood disconsolately in the railway station at Hoboken, New Jersey. They had just watched a delegation of the nation's leading

---

[III] Spent *ten minutes* trying to find out what the guy's first name is—it remains a mystery. Proof he's controlled opposition? No, but annoying. I always saw that convention as aristocratic and, as I said, annoying.

financiers leave the station on a secret mission. It would be years before they discovered what that mission was, and even then they would not understand that the history of the United States underwent a drastic change after that night in Hoboken.

The delegation had left in a sealed railway car, with blinds drawn, for an undisclosed destination. They were led by Senator Nelson Aldrich, head of the National Monetary Commission. President Theodore Roosevelt had signed into law the bill creating the National Monetary Commission in 1908, after the tragic Panic of 1907 had resulted in a public outcry that the nation's monetary system be stabilized. ...

Accompanying Senator Aldrich at the Hoboken station were his private secretary, Shelton; A. Piatt Andrew, Assistant Secretary of the Treasury, and Special Assistant of the National Monetary Commission; Frank Vanderlip, president of the National City Bank of New York, Henry P. Davison, senior partner of J.P. Morgan Company, and generally regarded as Morgan's personal emissary; and Charles D. Norton, president of the Morgan-dominated First National Bank of New York. Joining the group just before the train left the station were Benjamin Strong, also known as a lieutenant of J.P. Morgan; and Paul Warburg, a recent immigrant from Germany who had joined the banking house of Kuhn, Loeb and Company, New York as a partner earning five hundred thousand dollars a year.

Six years later, a financial writer named Bertie Charles Forbes (who later founded the Forbes Magazine; the present editor, Malcom Forbes, is his son), wrote:

"Picture a party of the nation's greatest bankers stealing out of New York on a private railroad car under cover of darkness, stealthily hieing hundred of miles South, embarking on a mysterious launch, sneaking onto an island deserted by all but a few servants, living there a full week under such rigid secrecy that the names of not one of them was once mentioned lest the servants learn the identity and disclose to the world this strangest, most secret expedition in the history of American finance. I am not romancing; I am giving to the world, for the first time, the real story of how the famous Aldrich currency report, the foundation of our new currency system, was written. ... The utmost secrecy was enjoined upon all. The public must not glean a hint of what was to be done. Senator Aldrich notified each one to go quietly into a private car of which the railroad had received orders to draw up on an unfrequented platform. Off the party set. New York's ubiquitous reporters had been foiled ... Nelson (Aldrich) [all of the participating scum were told only to use first names] had confided to Henry, Frank, Paul and Piatt that he was to keep them locked up at Jekyll Island, out of the rest of the world, until they had evolved and compiled a scientific currency system for the United States, the real birth of the present Federal Reserve System, the plan done on Jekyll Island in the conference with Paul, Frank and Henry. ... Warburg is the link that binds the Aldrich system and the present system together. He more than any one man has made the system possible as a working reality."[2] ~ *The Secrets of the Federal Reserve*, Eustace Mullins[1797]

Warburg is recognized by most as the personal emissary of the Rothschilds. He would be responsible for repeating the plan that would one day destroy the buying power of the average American and teeter the fiscal stability of the United States on a mountain of unsustainable debt.

It had already been proven to work.

Paul Moritz Warburg was a leading member of the investment banking firm of M.M. Warburg & Company of Hamburg, Germany, and Amsterdam, the Netherlands. He had come to the United States only nine years previously. Soon after arrival, however, and with funding provided mostly by the Rothschild group, he and his brother, Felix, had been able to buy partnerships in the New York investment banking firm of Kuhn, Loeb & Company, while continuing as partners in Warburg of Hamburg.[1] Within twenty years, Paul would become one of the wealthiest men in America with an unchallenged domination over the country's railroad system.

At this distance in history, it is difficult to appreciate the importance of this man. But some understanding may be had from the fact that the legendary character, Daddy Warbucks, in the comic strip Little Orphan Annie, was a contemporary commentary on the presumed benevolence of Paul Warburg, and the almost magic ability to accomplish good through the power of his unlimited wealth.

A third brother, Max Warburg, was the financial adviser of the Kaiser and became Director of the Reichsbank in Germany. This was, of course, a central bank, and it was one of the cartel models used in the construction of the Federal Reserve System. The Reichsbank, incidentally, a few years later would create the massive hyperinflation that occurred in Germany, wiping out the middle class and the entire German economy as well. ~ Griffin[1798]

The gathering represented a sizable portion of all the wealth in the world, and they wanted more.

> *An article appeared in the New York Times on May 3, 1931, commenting on the death of George Baker, one of Morgan's closest associates. It said: "One-sixth of the total wealth of the world was represented by members of the Jekyll Island Club."* ~ Griffin[1799]

The Great Panic

The great "Panic of 1907" is said to have been the impetus for convincing Americans they needed the "stability" of a central bank. What they didn't know was just how easy it was to start a panic when banks never have enough capital to cover all the people's investments (because they spend it like it's their own commodity).

> *John Pierpont Morgan ... used rumor and innuendo to create a panic that would change the course of history. The panic of 1907 was triggered by rumors that two major banks were about to become insolvent. Later evidence pointed to the House of Morgan as the source of the rumors.*
>
> *The public, believing the rumors, proceeded to make them come true by staging a run on the banks. Morgan then nobly stepped in to avert the panic by importing $100 million in gold from his European sources. The public thus became convinced that the country needed a central banking system to stop future panics, overcoming strong congressional opposition to any bill allowing the nation's money to be issued by a private central bank controlled by Wall Street...* ~ Ellen Brown, Global Research[1800]

Because Morgan both created and then solved the panic, he is frequently lauded by dupes and co-conspirators as the literal savior of America.

> *This week we continue our discussion of the Panic of 1907 and the man who, single-handedly, turned things around, J.P. Morgan.*
>
> *As I wrote last week, speculation in the early 1900s was rampant.*

The lack of a central bank became a worrisome topic for many because the banks were intimately involved in the market, either as underwriters or investors. ~ Brian Trumbore, President/Editor, StocksandNews.com[1801]

The destination of the secret party in 1913 was Jekyll Island, Georgia. A special retreat for the rich and shameless.

Like all places where Luciferians gather, it had a history of spiritual significance to natives[1802] until it was stolen for the benefit of the Elite. Jekyll Island still has paranormal activity to this day.[1803]

The goal of their plan was to choke America's prosperity with a private cartel of bankers that could've easily been prosecuted with Federal racketeering charges.

The composition of the Jekyll Island meeting was a classic example of cartel structure. A cartel is a group of independent businesses which join together to coordinate the production, pricing, or marketing of their members. The purpose of a cartel is to reduce competition and thereby increase profitability. This is accomplished through a shared monopoly over their industry which forces the public to pay higher prices for their goods or services than would be otherwise required under free-enterprise competition.

Here were representatives of the world's leading banking consortia: Morgan, Rockefeller, Rothschild, Warburg, and Kuhn Loeb. They were often competitors, and there is little doubt that there was considerable distrust between them and skillful maneuvering for favored position in any agreement. But they were driven together by one overriding desire to fight their common enemy. The enemy was competition.

In 1910, the number of banks in the United States was growing at a phenomenal rate. In fact, it had more than doubled to over twenty thousand in just the previous ten years. Furthermore, most of them were springing up in the South and West, causing the New York banks to suffer a steady decline of market share. ~ Griffin[1804]

Like foxes running the hen-house, the banker Elite planned on showing up to Congress pretending to be the saviors of the American people but, in reality, they were only finishing off the last battle in a meticulously choreographed war against the Middle Class.

> *The "monetary reform" plan prepared at Jekyll Island was to be presented to Congress as the completed work of the National Monetary Commission. It was imperative that the real authors of the bill remain hidden. So great was popular resentment against bankers since the Panic of 1907 that no Congressman would dare to vote for a bill bearing the Wall Street taint, no matter who had contributed to his campaign expenses. The Jekyll Island plan was a central bank plan, and in this country there was a long tradition of struggle against inflicting a central bank on the American people. It had begun with Thomas Jefferson's fight against Alexander Hamilton's scheme for the First Bank of the United States, backed by James Rothschild. It had continued with President Andrew Jackson's successful war against Alexander Hamilton's scheme for the Second Bank of the United States, in which Nicholas Biddle was acting as the agent for James Rothschild of Paris. The result of that struggle was the creation of the Independent Sub-Treasury System, which supposedly had served to keep the funds of the United States out of the hands of the financiers. A study of the panics of 1873, 1893, and 1907 indicates that these panics were the result of the international bankers' operations in London. The public was demanding in 1908 that Congress enact legislation to prevent the recurrence of artificially induced money panics. Such monetary reform now seemed inevitable. ~ Secrets of the Federal Reserve, Mullins*[1805]

Since then, not a single American politician has even questioned the *existence* of the cartel, no less press it to open its books, (with the exception of now-retired Texas Congressman Ron Paul[mmm]).

To deceive the American people via the bankers' willing henchmen in government, the system needed a deceptive name and multiple locations that give the *appearance* of being harmless and decentralized.

> *Everyone knew that the solution to all these problems was a cartel mechanism that had been devised and already put into similar operation in Europe. As with all cartels, it had to be created by legislation and sustained by the power of government under the deception of protecting the consumer. ...*
>
> *The American people did not like the concept of a cartel. The idea of business enterprises joining together to fix prices and prevent competition was alien to the free-enterprise system. It could never*

[mmm] To my knowledge, Ron Paul has never questioned the existence of the Fed but has been the loudest voice calling for it to be audited.

> *be sold to the voters. But, if the word cartel was not used, if the venture could be describe with words which are emotionally neutral—perhaps even alluring—then half the battle would be won.*
> ...
>
> *The first decision, therefore, was to follow the practice adopted in Europe. Henceforth, the cartel would operate as a **central bank**. And even that was to be but a generic expression. For purposes of public relations and legislation, they would devise a name that would avoid the word **bank** altogether and which would conjure the image of the federal government itself. Furthermore, to create the impression that there would be no concentration of power, they would establish regional branches of the cartel and make that a main selling point. Stephenson tells us: "Aldrich entered this discussion at Jekyll Island an ardent convert to the idea of a central bank. His desire was to transplant the system of one of the great European banks, say the Bank of England, bodily to America." ~ Griffin [emphasis his]*[1806]

Once that was accomplished, the saboteurs needed to conceal that Wall Street was the hub of their conspiracy.

> *The next consideration was to conceal the fact that the proposed "Federal Reserve System" would be dominated by the masters of the New York money market. The Congressmen from the South and the West could not survive if they voted for a Wall Street plan. Farmers and small businessmen in those areas had suffered most from the money panics. There had been great popular resentment against the Eastern bankers, which during the nineteenth century became a political movement known as "populism". The private papers of Nicholas Biddle, not released until more than a century after his death, show that quite early on the Eastern bankers were fully aware of the widespread public opposition to them. ~ Mullins*[1807]

The Jesuit/Luciferian Counter-Reformation insurgency to destroy the independent Middle Class of the United States has been a terrible success.

> *The accepted version of history is that the Federal Reserve was created to stabilize our economy. One of the most widely-used textbooks on this subject says: "It sprang from the panic of 1907, with its alarming epidemic of bank failures: the country was fed up once and for all with the anarchy of unstable private banking."*
>
> *Even the most naive student must sense a grave contradiction*

> *between this cherished view and the System's actual performance. Since its inception, it has presided over the crashes of 1921 and 1929; the Great Depression of '29 to '39; recessions in '53, '57, '69, '75, and '81; a stock market "Black Monday" in '87; and a 1000% inflation which has destroyed 90% of the dollar's purchasing power.[3]*
>
> *Let us be more specific on that last point. By 1990, an annual income of $10,000 was required to buy what took only $1,000 in 1914.[4] That incredible loss in value was quietly transferred to the federal government in the form of hidden taxation, and the Federal Reserve System was the mechanism by which it was accomplished.*
> ~ Griffin[1808]

In some states, it's now near-impossible to realize the "American Dream" and start your own business.

Bureaucratic Brutality

"Tyranny" can sometimes be defined as an oppression of endless regulation. [italics suspended]

> Longtime actor and entrepreneur Joseph C. Phillips, a man you might recognize from "The Cosby Show" or "General Hospital" ... discussed "the real" American dream and the difficulties of starting a small business in today's economy — particularly in California.
>
> The "unapologetic Christian and conservative" recently opened a restaurant called Daddy J's Wingshack...
>
> "Given that small businesses represent the quest for the American dream, one might imagine that our governments, local and federal, would support and encourage those attempting to open small businesses. Well — one would be wrong, at least if you live in California," he began.
>
> "When we opened our doors a year and a half ago we were immediately beset by bureaucrats walking in carrying mountains of documents for us to read, lengthy rules, stuff for us to sign obligating us to this tax and that tax, writing check after check after check..." he continued.
>
> "My problem with bureaucrats is...the rules and guidelines and statutes that are enforced are often a matter of who you're talking to — whether they stayed up too late the night before, whether they got some lovin' from their spouse or their loved one, and quite

frankly, whether or not they like the way you look!" he said. "The codes [are] written so that oftentimes they conflict with one another. You go down to the Health Department, the code says one thing, then you go down to the building safety department, the code says something completely different." ...

"If some bureaucrat wants to jam you up — if some guy who's driving a city car, who's never risked anything in his life, never built anything — if he wants to jam you up, wants to flex a little bit, you're going to get jammed up," he said. "And in the same way, if some inspector decides you look cool and wants to cut you some slack, you get to skate." ~ Erica Ritz, *The Blaze*[1809]

One would think that a young black male like Philips would be encouraged to start a business where it can employ other Americans but that is not the Communist/Luciferian/Jesuit agenda.

No less a source than the San Francisco Federal Reserve recently reported that small businesses were hit disproportionately hard during the long recession the international banking cartel facilitated.

> *During the recent recession and recovery, small businesses experienced disproportionate job losses (see Burgen and Aliprantis 2012, Tasci and Burgen 2012, and Sahin et al. 2011). Between 2007 and 2012, their share of total net job losses was nearly double their 30% share of total employment. From the employment peak immediately before the recession through March 2009, the recession low point for private nonfarm employment, jobs at small businesses declined about 11%, according to the Business Employment Dynamics (BED) database of the U.S. Bureau of Labor Statistics. By contrast, payrolls at businesses with 50 or more employees shrank about 7%.*[1810]

Today, in America, raising a single child to the age of 18 will cost a family nearly $245,000[1811]. That's up $50,000 in just two years.[1812]

While Americans get distracted by the political theater of "Democrat vs. Republican", they are both co-operating fully with the cartel that is bleeding us dry.

> *Instead of fighting a phony mommy war over what Hilary Rosen said about Ann Romney, we should face the fact that most families these days cannot afford to have one parent stay home with the kids. This is not about "lifestyle" or "values." This is an economic struggle highlighting yet again the social costs arising from decades*

of stagnating or declining wages and growing income inequality. ~ E.J. Dionne Jr., the Washington Post[1813]

Barack Obama made a speech in Rhode Island on Halloween 2014, recognizing that parents are working and still not making ends meet. His "solution" is to spend *more* taxpayer money to facilitate preschool for all Americans—that way, all the terrible things that can happen to them will have full coverage.

> *Moms and dads deserve a great place to drop their kids off every day...*
>
> *Sometimes, someone, usually mom, leaves the workplace to stay home with the kids, which then leaves her earning a lower wage for the rest of her life as a result.* ***That's not a choice we want Americans to make.*** ~ Sarah Jean Seman, Townhall [emphasis mine; who is "we"?][1814]

The "Aldrich Plan"

When the moneychangers got back from their "duck hunt" they needed to start the propaganda rolling hard and fast. They had the capital and they quickly found both the front men and institutions that would make it happen.

> *The participants in the Jekyll Island conference returned to New York to direct a nationwide propaganda campaign in favor of the "Aldrich Plan". Three of the leading universities, Princeton, Harvard, and the University of Chicago, were used as the rallying points for this propaganda, and national banks had to contribute to a fund of five million dollars to persuade the American public that this central bank plan should be enacted into law by Congress.*
>
> *Woodrow Wilson, governor of New Jersey and former president of Princeton University, was enlisted as a spokesman for the Aldrich Plan. During the Panic of 1907, Wilson had declared, "All this trouble could be averted if we appointed a committee of six or seven public-spirited men like J.P. Morgan to handle the affairs of our country."* ~ Mullins[1815]

Charles Lindbergh, Sr. (father of the daredevil pilot) was the Ron Paul of his day. He opposed the so-called "Aldrich Plan" as well as America's entry into WWI. He would be a lone voice in a sea of sharks.

> *Testifying before the Committee on Rules, December 15, 1911, after the Aldrich plan had been introduced in Congress, Congressman*

Lindbergh stated,

"Our financial system is a false one and a huge burden on the people ... I have alleged that there is a Money Trust. The Aldrich plan is a scheme plainly in the interest of the Trust ... Why does the Money Trust press so hard for the Aldrich Plan now, before the people know what the money trust has been doing?"

Lindbergh continued...

"The Aldrich Plan is the Wall Street Plan. It is a broad challenge to the Government by the champion of the Money Trust. It means another panic, if necessary, to intimidate the people. Aldrich, paid by the Government to represent the people, proposes a plan for the trusts instead. It was by a very clever move that the National Monetary Commission was created." ~ Mullins[1816]

Later, Charles Jr. would pick up his father's mantle and continue the fight. He was a powerful voice and struck a heroic figure for the American people.

The interwar peace movement was arguably the largest mass movement of the 1920s and 1930s, a mobilization often overlooked in the wake of the broad popular consensus that ultimately supported the U.S. involvement in World War II. The destruction wrought in World War I (known in the 1920s and 1930s as the "Great War") and the cynical nationalist politics of the Versailles Treaty had left Americans disillusioned with the Wilsonian crusade to save the world for democracy. Senate investigations of war profiteering and shady dealings in the World War I munitions industry both expressed and deepened widespread skepticism about wars of ideals. On the right wing of the antiwar movement, Charles A. Lindbergh, popular hero of American aviation, was a champion of diehard isolationism and a prominent member of the America-First Committee, organized in September 1940. In this 1941 speech, he drew on a time-honored theme of American exceptionalism as he urged his listeners to avoid entanglements with Europe. ~ History Matters[1817]

It was a fight that would cost the Lindbergh family dearly—their next generation.

On March 1st, 1932, little Charles was taken from his crib in the Lindberghs' New Jersey home and a ransom for $50,000 was demanded. The ransom was exchanged but the note in return led to a dock and a ship that didn't exist. Two months later, the little boy's body was found in a nearby woods.

Now that Charles was dead, would justice be done?

President Herbert Hoover offered the services of J. Edgar Hoover and the FBI. The Governor of New Jersey called the best detective in the state—Ellis Parker (who had previously solved over 200 murders)—but the lead man in the investigation turned it all down.

That man was the Superintendent of the New Jersey State Police: H. Norman Schwarzkopf, father of the West Point graduate of the same name who would be given credit for the success of the first Gulf War.

After two years of inaction, a German immigrant—Bruno Hauptmann—was caught passing one of the marked bills from the ransom money. But the Bronx carpenter had neither the brains nor the means to accomplish a complex, high-profile kidnapping.

Hauptmann was tried and convicted and subsequently given the death penalty back when New Jersey still executed criminals for capital crimes.

> *The man who raped and killed 7-year-old Megan Kanka—the 1994 crime that inspired "Megan's Law"—is one of eight men whose sentences were commuted to life in prison this week as part of New Jersey's new ban on execution.*
>
> *The Garden State on Monday became the first state in more than three decades to abolish the death penalty after a commission ruled the punishment is "inconsistent with evolving standards of decency."*
>
> *Gov. Jon Corzine[nnn] the day before commuted the sentences of eight men sitting on the state's death row. They will now serve life in prison without parole, according to the governor's office.*

[nnn] Only the best from a Goldman Sachs CEO, United States Senator and Governor who can "lose" $1.2 *billion* dollars and stroll away whistling.
Corzine: "Don't Know" Where MF Global Customers' $1.2B Went, Kevin McCoy, 8 December 2011, USA Today
http://usatoday30.usatoday.com/money/industries/brokerage/story/2011-12-08/mf-global-corzine/51732752/1

Among the eight is Jesse Timmendequas, 46, who was sentenced to death in June 1997 for Megan's murder.

Prosecutors said Timmendequas lured Megan to his home by saying he wanted to show her a puppy. He then raped her, beat her and strangled her with a belt. ~ CNN[1818]

The Governor, aware of questions regarding how the prosecutor had conducted himself in the case, ordered more than one stay of execution but Hauptmann was on the hotseat to go to the electric chair and he was executed in an astounding two years from the beginning of the investigation: 1936. Modern stays on "death row" can last up to *40 years* after a conviction and even then have the convict die of natural causes and not state execution as did Gary Alvord who strangled an 18 year old, her mother and her grandmother in Florida.[1819]

Hauptmann's wife Anna would spend the next 60 years vehemently trying to clear his name.

Since then, several books have been written that accuse Charles Lindbergh, Jr. of having murdered his own son. *Crime of the Century: The Lindbergh Kidnapping Hoax* (1993) was written by Gregory Ahlgren and Stephen Monier. Monier would later be appointed U.S. Marshal for New Hampshire by George W. Bush.

Was there a better suspect? A Professor at New York University thinks so.

Alan Marlis wrote *The Lindbergh Baby Kidnap Conspiracy* in which he connected the dots from the Lindberghs to the Warburgs.

James Perloff summarized them[ooo]: [italics suspended]

> In 1932, one man still posed a threat to [Roosevelt]'s election — Charles Lindbergh. Lindy was too young constitutionally to run for President, but his popularity was so universal that his active presence alone might have kept Republican hopes alive. But five months after Morrow's sudden death, Lindbergh's baby was murdered — effectively removing the grieving father from the political scene. Some of the links Marlis draws to James Warburg:
>
> • The Lindberghs and Warburgs had what Marlis calls a "blood feud." In 1913, Charles Lindbergh, Sr. tried to stop creation of the Federal Reserve — which Paul Warburg, its first vice-chairman,

---

[ooo] The above details were taken from Perloff's excellent article.

had designed. In 1917, Lindbergh tried to have Warburg, as well as FDR's uncle Frederic Delano, impeached from the Federal Reserve Board. According to Marlis, Lindbergh "Jew-baited" Warburg at the Fed chairman hearings; Paul told his son, and the insult wasn't forgotten.

• In 1941, the fathers' feud continued between the sons. James Warburg helped found and finance the Freedom First Committee to oppose Lindbergh's America First Committee, debated Lindbergh at Madison Square Garden, and publicly denounced him.

• Paul Warburg died less than two months before the kidnapping.

• The police had suspected the crime was an inside job. The governess in James Warburg's household was the sister of the Morrows' seamstress, Marguerite Junge, who knew about the Lindberghs' change of plans. Junge's alibi for the kidnapping night: She was "out riding" with Red Johnsen — boyfriend of the baby's nurse.

• In April 1932 (just after the kidnapping and ransom payment), James Warburg took a two-month trip to Europe.

• Warburg's estate was in Greenwich, Connecticut — the town where the very first Lindbergh ransom gold certificate was passed, by a well-dressed woman at a bakery. The cashier, checking the serial-number list, exclaimed it was Lindbergh ransom money. The woman snatched it back and ran outside into a chauffeured sedan — which police unsuccessfully searched for. ~ Perloff[1820]

Despite the brutal murder of his little boy, Lindbergh was still a formidable enough America-First isolationist to require 33° Shriner Freemason Franklin Roosevelt to maneuver the Japanese into freely killing 4,000 Americans on December 7th to launch the nation into war.

A Rigged Game

As has repeatedly been the case since, big-monied interests rigged the elections of 1912 to insure that no matter who the people pulled for, the country would be enslaved, regardless. [italics suspended]

> The Presidential campaign of 1912 records one of the more interesting political upsets in American history. The incumbent, William Howard Taft, was a popular president, and the Republicans, in a period of general prosperity, were firmly in control of the government through a Republican majority in both

houses. The Democratic challenger, Woodrow Wilson, Governor of New Jersey, had no national recognition, and was a stiff, austere man who excited little public support. Both parties included a monetary reform bill in their platforms: The Republicans were committed to the Aldrich Plan, which had been denounced as a Wall Street plan, and the Democrats had the Federal Reserve Act. Neither party bothered to inform the public that the bills were almost identical except for the names. In retrospect, it seems obvious that the money creators decided to dump Taft and go with Wilson. How do we know this? Taft seemed certain of reelection, and Wilson would return to obscurity. Suddenly, Theodore Roosevelt "threw his hat into the ring." He announced that he was running as a third party candidate, the "Bull Moose". His candidacy would have been ludicrous had it not been for the fact that he was exceptionally well-financed. Moreover, he was given unlimited press coverage, more than Taft and Wilson combined. As a Republican ex-president, it was obvious that Roosevelt would cut deeply into Taft's vote. This proved the case, and Wilson won the election. To this day, no one can say what Theodore Roosevelt's program was, or why he would sabotage his own party. Since the bankers were financing all three candidates, they would win regardless of the outcome. Later Congressional testimony showed that in the firm of Kuhn Loeb Company, Felix Warburg was supporting Taft, Paul Warburg and Jacob Schiff were supporting Wilson, and Otto Kahn was supporting Roosevelt. The result was that a Democratic Congress and a Democratic President were elected in 1912 to get the central bank legislation passed. ~ Mullins[1821]

Just like today, all of the Parties involved worked for the same malignant Luciferian Elite bent on impoverishing and enslaving the American Middle Class.

Corporately stealing the wealth of the American people while simultaneously destroying their buying power is an agenda to kill for.

> *It is interesting to note how many assassinations of Presidents of the United States follow their concern with the issuing of public currency; Lincoln with his Greenback, non-interest-bearing notes, and Garfield, making a pronouncement on currency problems just before he was assassinated.* ~ Mullins[1822]

To these we can easily add Andrew Jackson in his battle against the 2nd United States Bank and John F. Kennedy who's Executive Order 11110 authorized the Secretary of Treasury to do the job Congress just wouldn't do—issue silver certificates in competition with America's fiat "Federal Reserve Notes".

The Republican "Aldrich Plan" was repackaged by Paul Warburg as the Democrat "Federal Reserve Act" and voted on a week before Christmas when many legislators had already gone home for the holidays. This tactic has been used often to screen the worst of Elite-sponsored poisonous legislation.

Congressman Charles Lindbergh, Sr. stood on the near-empty floor of Congress and railed at the devil fruitlessly.

> *"This Act establishes the most gigantic trust on earth. When the President signs this bill, the invisible government by the Monetary Power will be legalized. The people may not know it immediately, but the day of reckoning is only a few years removed. The trusts will soon realize that they have gone too far even for their own good. The people must make a declaration of independence to relieve themselves from the Monetary Power. This they will be able to do by taking control of Congress. Wall Streeters could not cheat us if you Senators and Representatives did not make a humbug of Congress. ... If we had a people's Congress, there would be stability."* ~ Mullins[1823]

Woodrow Wilson put his signature to the bill on December 23rd, 1913.

Merry Christmas, America.

Wilson is often quoted as having said later in remorse over his treason, "I am a most unhappy man. I have unwittingly ruined my country." But there is no source for this quote and he likely went to his judgment without the slightest change of heart.

Today, the Chairman of the "Federal Reserve" boldly tells journalists that the Fed is "an independent institution" which answers only to the international banking cartel.[1824]

Slipped into the inversely-named "Patriot Act" was a provision for Fed banks to contract their security and throw off the veneer of being a "government institution" altogether[1825]. Now if you protest a "Federal Reserve" branch, well-armed private security throw you off *private* land.

After decades of working it, Congressman Ron Paul finally got a *partial* audit of the Fed for the first time in its history in 2011 and found out that the institution has been sending trillions upon trillions of dollars out around the world in lending and money-making schemes on the backs of the American taxpayer.[1826]

The First Sphere of Influence

> *The richest 1% of the world's population are getting wealthier, owning more than 48% of global wealth, according to a report published on Tuesday which warned growing inequality could be a trigger for recession. ...*
>
> *"Taken together, the bottom half of the global population own less than 1% of total wealth. In sharp contrast, the richest decile hold 87% of the world's wealth, and the top percentile alone account for 48.2% of global assets," said the annual report, now in its fifth year.* ~ Jill Treanor, the Guardian[1827]

Part of the political theater that Americans get played by is the notion that everyone in business is the same and everyone with money is the same.

Controlled opposition talkshow hosts puff on their cigars and tell you that the oligarchy which maintains critical commodities like so-called "fossil fuels" giving you no real capitalist competition and maximizing price-gouging profits is just the "free market" at work. The reality is that those oligarchies have completely subverted true capitalism and there's no "free market" at all.

> *A consumer group is publicizing a series of memos marked "highly confidential" alleging major oil companies – including Mobil, Chevron and Texaco – intentionally limited their refining capacity in order to raise gasoline prices and increase profits.*
>
> *The revelation comes as Americans have seen a major spike in prices at the pump in the immediate aftermath of Hurricane Katrina, while "the oil industry blames environmental regulation for limiting number of U.S. refineries."* ~ Joe Kovacs, WorldNetDaily[1828]

When a hard-working man or family busts their backs and, years later, beat the odds to finally live comfortably, that's part of the "American Dream".

But when a family that has used graft and corruption to amass so much wealth that they can steer the courses of nations, they have become an enemy of mankind.

Let me repeat that: billionaires and trillionaires *are the enemies of mankind*. Perhaps they don't start out that way, but they always wind up that way.

Christians might further speculate that they are all bound to be co-opted by an intricate system of demonic power that rules the world from behind the scenes some label as "Mystery Babylon". [Matthew 4:8-10, Revelation 17:1-13]

This also applies to people who are in the right time and place to be the beneficiary of runaway wealth like Bill Gates.

They are the ones who have secret meetings about how to "reduce world population".

Above them is an even smaller circle of ancient Luciferians who work with both White and Black Popes. Some names like "Rothschild" you recognize (because they have been set out as bait), but some have been purposely obscured from your vision: Borja, Breakspeare, Orsini, Conti, Colonna, Farnese, Medici and Aldobrandini, give or take a few.

It can only be drawn by inductive reasoning and inference (rather than an overwhelming amount of empirical data) that such people are under the partial or complete control of malignant, interdimensional agencies. Their wealth has placed them in a realm of life experience that is literally alien to the average human being and they are, therefore, innately hostile to the common man, and they fear him as well.

"Fossil Fuel"

"Fossil Fuel" is not derived from living matter as there have not been enough living organisms since the foundation of life to account for all of the fuel pulled from the Earth and consumed to date.

The deepest fossil has been recovered at 16,000 feet yet oil has been drilled as low as 30,000 feet.

The labeling of this resource was done for the sole purpose of creating a false paradigm of scarcity in order to price-gouge this critical commodity.

SOURCES:

The Origins of Oil and Petroleum, July 1999, Prouty.org
http://www.prouty.org/oil.html

Jerome Corsi: The Great Oil Conspiracy, theDoveTV YouTube
https://www.youtube.com/watch?v=_NvuR8wlHkE

These people are whom author William Dean Garner has labeled "The First Sphere of Influence".

"Sphere of Influence" is a strategic descriptor.

> *In the field of international relations, a sphere of influence (SOI) is a spatial region or concept division over which a state or organization has a level of cultural, economic, military, or political exclusivity, accommodating to the interests of powers outside the borders of the state that controls it.* ~ Sphere of Influence, Wikipedia[1829]

It is this "First Sphere of Influence" that is behind the Counter-Reformation agenda to kill America's Middle Class.

> *The U.S. used to be the most industrialized nation on the planet.*
>
> *China now holds that distinction, and for good reason: ... The First Sphere of Influence (TFSI), a deeply hidden and dark cabal of men that controls the House of Rothschild and the planet... has systematically transferred manufacturing from the U.S. to China, effectively crushing the ability of the U.S. to build its own infrastructure. Now we must rely on an adversary for basic parts and supplies even for our high-tech military aircraft and ships.*
>
> *Recently, it was revealed that a 30-foot-tall granite statue of Dr. Martin Luther King, Jr., now on prominent display next to the Washington Monument, was Made in China.* ~ Who Really Owns Your Gold? William Dean A. Garner[1830]

Destroying nations via a long, calculated agenda of parasitic bloodletting (while simultaneously further-adding to their already-overflowing coffers) is where the Rothschilds excel.

> *An engineering feat, the destruction of a once-strong and proud Germany in the early 20th century has visited the world dozens of times since the late 1770s. Curiously, this was shortly after Meyer Amschel Bauer founded his little banking institution in Frankfurt, Germany, and after The First Sphere of Influence was unceremoniously banished from certain ecclesiastical halls by Pope Clement XI and then later resurrected, only to begin a new reign of terror across the world but especially in the United States. ...*
>
> *Bauer's father, Amschel Moses Bauer, hung a red shield outside his five-story house, signifying he was the go-to man for money changing and lending in town, a skill he passed on to Meyer*

Amschel. In short order, Bauer the younger's business flourished, and he wished to be more closely associated with it, so he changed his name to Rothschild. In German, rot means red; schild is shield. The Red Shield. ~ Your Gold, Garner[1831]

But regardless of how well the Rothschilds have bled mankind by central banks, they are still the accountants of Rome.

In 2011, a Vatican press release repeated the agenda for total world economy. The future design for this "One World Order" is one central authority over all of the other national central banks.

They've decided that it's time to cut out the middle-man.

In perfect Hegelian form, the Luciferian Elite intend to use the corruption and instability *they* created as excuse for the final One World System. [italics suspended]

> The Vatican called on Monday for an overhaul of the world's financial systems, and again proposed establishment of a supranational authority to oversee the global economy, calling it necessary to bring more democratic and ethical principles to a marketplace run amok.
>
> In a report issued by the Pontifical Council for Justice and Peace, the Vatican argued that "politics — which is responsible for the common good" must be given primacy over the economy and finance, and that existing institutions like the International Monetary Fund had not been responding adequately to global economic problems. ...
>
> "The time has come to conceive of institutions with universal competence, now that vital goods shared by the entire human family are at stake, goods which the individual states cannot promote and protect by themselves," Cardinal Peter Kodwo Appiah Turkson, the president of the pontifical council, said as he presented the report on Monday. ...
>
> The language in the document, which the Vatican refers to as a note, is distinctively strong. "We should not be afraid to propose new ideas, even if they might destabilize pre-existing balances of power that prevail over the weakest," the document states.
>
> ..."To function correctly the economy needs ethics; and not just of any kind, but one that is people-centered," the document states, paraphrasing an encyclical that Pope Benedict XVI issued in 2009

calling for greater social responsibility in the economy.

> In the United States, the report was embraced by politically liberal Catholics who are concerned about the widening gap between rich and poor. Vincent J. Miller, a professor of Catholic theology and culture at the University of Dayton, wrote, "It's clear the Vatican stands with the Occupy Wall Street protesters and others struggling to return ethics and good governance to a financial sector grown out of control after 30 years of deregulation." ~ Elisabetta Povoledo, NY Times[1832]

Did you follow that logic? To address the excesses of "the rich", we must give complete and total control of our already corrupt, centralized, corporate financial system to a single, authority.

The Seed of the Serpent

After Adam and Eve fell in disobedience, YHWH pronounced judgment that most Bible readers don't read carefully enough.

> The Lord God said to the serpent,
>
> "Because you have done this,
> Cursed are you more than all cattle,
> And more than every beast of the field;
> On your belly you will go,
> And dust you will eat
> All the days of your life;
> And I will put enmity
> Between you and the woman,
> And between your seed and her seed;
> He shall bruise you on the head,
> And you shall bruise him on the heel." ~ Genesis 3:14-15

The Bible explains that there are *spiritual* allegiances a human has that make either God or the Adversary his or her "father". [John 3:3, John 8:31-47, Romans 6:16]

But is there a *literal* "seed of the serpent"?

Endnotes

[1754] *Secret Counsels of the Society of Jesus*, Robert Breckinridge, Baltimore: Edward J. Cole & Co. (1835), p. 99

[1755] *"Gold Is Money, Everything Else Is Credit" JP Morgan*, Bill Holter, 30 June 2014, Miles Franklin Brokers
http://blog.milesfranklin.com/gold-is-money-everything-else-is-credit-jp-morgan

[1756] *3 Reasons to Repeal 1913*, Topher Morrison, 6 February 2012, AMTV
http://www.greenewave.com/3-reasons-to-repeal-1913/

[1757] *The Law That Never Was*, Bill Benson, Constitutional Research Associates
http://www.thelawthatneverwas.com/

[1758] *The Great IRS Scam*, Johnny Cirucci YouTube
https://www.youtube.com/watch?&v=d4jrbkCJwTM

[1759] *USA Today Ad*, We the People, GiveMeLiberty.org
http://www.givemeliberty.org/features/taxes/usatoday.htm

[1760] *IRS Whistle Blower Acquitted of Tax Fraud Charges*, Peymon Mottahedeh, 23 February 2012, Freedom Law School
http://freedomlawschool.org/victories/former-irs-agent's-victory.html

[1761] *Ex-IRS Agent Sherry Jackson Shows Why She Was Jailed & Disappeared*, Johnny Cirucci YouTube
https://www.youtube.com/watch?v=V6tXsUvsX0s&

[1762] *Sherry Peel Jackson, IRS Whistleblower, Sentenced to 4 Years in Prison, Atlanta, GA*, the Cathy Harris Show, 4 October 2007, blog talk radio
http://www.blogtalkradio.com/thecathyharrisshow/2007/10/04/the-cathy-harris-show

[1763] *What Ron Paul Did For Me*, Sherry Jackson, 18 April 2012, Sherry Peel Jackson.org
http://www.sherrypeeljackson.org/newsletter/april-2012/

[1764] *Kent Hovind*, Creation Science Hall of Fame
http://creationsciencehalloffame.org/inductees/living/kent-hovind/

[1765] *Is IRS Persecuting Kent Hovind For Creationism?* Peter J. Reilly, 8 February 2013, Forbes
http://www.forbes.com/sites/peterjreilly/2013/02/08/is-irs-persecuting-kent-hovind-for-creationism/

Although I'm grateful to Forbes for covering Kent's case, this guy is an asshole who puts up straw-man arguments like "Is the IRS targeting Creationists?"

No, *moron*. Not *all* Creationists. Just powerful Christian voices who are a threat to government hegemony.

[1766] *Not Income Tax Evasion - Structuring - That's How They Got Kent Hovind*, Peter J. Reilly, 30 January 2013, Forbes
http://www.forbes.com/sites/peterjreilly/2013/01/30/not-income-tax-evasion-structuring-thats-how-they-got-kent-hovind/

[1767] *Santa Rosa County Jail — More Criminal Charges*, Dr. Kent Hovind's Blog
http://www.kenthovindblog.com/?p=1078

[1768] *Aaron Russo*, Wikipedia
https://en.wikipedia.org/wiki/Aaron_Russo

[1769] *Traitors to the American Revolution*, Thomas DiLorenzo, 12 September 2006, LewRockwell.com

http://www.lewrockwell.com/2006/09/thomas-dilorenzo/traitors-to-the-american-revolution/
[1770] *A History of Central Banking in the United States*, the Federal Reserve Bank of Minneapolis
https://www.minneapolisfed.org/info/mail/mail.cfm
[1771] *Aaron Burr Arrested for Treason*, Richard Cavendish, History Today, Volume: 57; Issue: 2, 2007
http://www.historytoday.com/richard-cavendish/aaron-burr-arrested-treason
[1772] *Coinage Clause*, Todd Zywicki, The Heritage Guide to The Constitution
http://www.heritage.org/constitution/#!/articles/1/essays/42/coinage-clause
[1773] *History of Central Banking in the United States > First Bank of the United States*, Wikipedia
https://en.wikipedia.org/wiki/History_of_central_banking_in_the_United_States#First_Bank_of_the_United_States
[1774] *Private Banks (Quotation)*, Monticello.org
http://www.monticello.org/site/jefferson/private-banks-quotation
  Note the "UNESCO" lable at the bottom of each web page—because that's who we need to govern our knowledge of Thomas Jefferson: the ____ing United Nations.
[1775] *Andrew Jackson: His Life and Times*, H.W. Brands, Doubleday (2005), p. IX
[1776] *ibid*, pp. 4, 5-6
[1777] *ibid*, p. 61
[1778] *ibid*, p. 37
[1779] *Andrew Jackson > Military Career*, Wikipedia
https://en.wikipedia.org/wiki/Andrew_Jackson#Military_career
[1780] *Andrew Jackson*, Brands, pp. 309-310
[1781] *ibid*, p. 418
[1782] *ibid*, p. 450
[1783] *ibid*, p. 456
[1784] *ibid*, p. 458
[1785] *The Creature from Jekyll Island: A Second Look at the Federal Reserve*, G. Edward Griffin, American Media (1994), pp. 347-348, 350
[1786] *Andrew Jackson > National Bank Controversy*, Wikipedia
https://en.wikipedia.org/wiki/Andrew_Jackson#National_bank_controversy
[1787] *56,662,169 Abortions in America Since Roe vs. Wade in 1973*, Randy O'Bannon, Ph.D., 12 January 2014, LifeNews.com
http://www.lifenews.com/2014/01/12/56662169-abortions-in-america-since-roe-vs-wade-in-1973/
[1788] *Abortion Methods Described*, Pro-Life America
http://www.prolife.com/ABORMETH.html
[1789] *Abortion: Opening the Gates of Hell!* L.A. Marzulli, 4 October 2011, L.A. Marzulli's Blog
http://lamarzulli.wordpress.com/2011/10/04/another-sample-chapter-from-l-a-marzullis-new-book-the-cosmic-chess-match/
[1790] *The Book of the Law*, III, 24, "Aiwass" via Aleister and Edith Crowley
[1791] *Andrew Jackson*, Brands, p. 469
[1792] *ibid*, p. 470

[1793] *The Synagogue of Satan*, Andrew Carrington Hitchcock, RiverCrest Publishing (2007), pp. 18, 19-20, 21-23
[1794] *The Creature from Jekyll Island: A Second Look at the Federal Reserve*, G. Edward Griffin, American Media (1994), p. v
[1795] *Eustace Mullins' on FED, Ron Paul, Rockefeller & G. Edward Griffin*, globalbeehive YouTube
https://www.youtube.com/watch?v=FiUGrlLccDc
   Excerpt from an interview of Eustace Mullins by Jan Irvin.
[1796] *The Creature from Jekyll Island*, p. 4
[1797] *The Secrets of the Federal Reserve*, Eustace Mullins, Bankers Research Institute (1983), pp. 13-14
[1798] *Jekyll Island*, p. 18
[1799] *Jekyll Island*, p. 6
[1800] *The Secret Bailout of J. P. Morgan: How Insider Trading Looted Bear Stearns and the American Taxpayer*, Ellen Brown, 30 December 2012, Global Research
http://www.globalresearch.ca/the-secret-bailout-of-j-p-morgan-how-insider-trading-looted-bear-stearns-and-the-american-taxpayer/8974
[1801] *J.P. Morgan - Savior—The Panic of 1907*, Brian Trumbore, President/Editor, StocksandNews.com
http://www.buyandhold.com/bh/en/education/history/2000/122499.html
[1802] *Jekyll Island's Hidden Past*, Ray Crook, The Society for Georgia Archaeology
http://thesga.org/2009/12/jekyll-island%e2%80%99s-hidden-past/
[1803] *Ghosts of Jekyll Island, Georgia*, Dale Cox, 22 October 2014, ExploreSouthernHistory.com
http://www.exploresouthernhistory.com/jekyllghosts.html
[1804] *Jekyll Island*, pp. 11-12
[1805] *Secrets of the Federal Reserve*, p. 18
[1806] *Jekyll Island*, pp. 16-17
[1807] *Secrets of the Fed*, p. 19
[1808] *Jekyll Island*, p. 20
[1809] *Famous Actor Rails Against Difficulty of Opening a Small Business in California*, Erica Ritz, 29 August 2013, The Blaze
http://www.theblaze.com/stories/2013/08/29/famous-actor-rails-against-difficulty-of-opening-a-small-business-in-california/
[1810] *Small Businesses Hit Hard by Weak Job Gains*, Elizabeth Laderman, 9 September 2013, the Federal Reserve Bank of San Fransicko
http://www.frbsf.org/economic-research/publications/economic-letter/2013/september/small-business-job-growth-employment-rate/
[1811] *Inflation Watch: $245,000 to Raise a Child in United States*, 19 August 2014, EconoMatters
http://www.econmatters.com/2014/08/245000-to-raise-child-in-united-states.html
[1812] *5 Reasons One Parent Should Stay At Home*, Brian Reed, 25 January 2012, Investing Answers
http://www.investinganswers.com/personal-finance/savings-budget/5-reasons-one-parent-should-stay-home-4026
[1813] *Two-Paycheck Couples Are Quickly Becoming The Norm*, E.J. Dionne Jr., 18 April 2012, the Washington Post

http://www.washingtonpost.com/opinions/two-paycheck-couples-are-quickly-becoming-the-norm/2012/04/18/gIQALSzIRT_story.html
[1814] *Ouch: Obama Claims America Doesn't Want Stay-At-Home Moms*, Sarah Jean Seman, 31 October 2014, Townhall.com
http://townhall.com/tipsheet/sarahjeanseman/2014/10/31/ouch-obama-claims-america-doesnt-want-stayathome-moms-n1912706
[1815] *Secrets of the Fed*, p. 25
[1816] *Secrets of the Fed*, pp. 26-27
[1817] *"An Independent Destiny for America": Charles A. Lindbergh on Isolationism*, History Matters
http://historymatters.gmu.edu/d/5163/
[1818] *"Megan's Law" Killer Escapes Death Under N.J. Execution Ban*, 17 December 2007, CNN
http://www.cnn.com/2007/POLITICS/12/17/death.penalty/index.html
[1819] *Nation's Longest Serving Death-Row Inmate Dies in Florida*, Dan Sullivan, 21 May 2013, the Tampa Bay Times
http://www.tampabay.com/news/publicsafety/crime/nations-longest-serving-death-row-inmate-dies-in-floirda/2122196
[1820] *The Lindbergh Baby Kidnapping Mystery*, James Perloff, 23 April 2012, the New American
http://www.thenewamerican.com/culture/history/item/10966-the-lindbergh-baby-kidnapping-mystery
[1821] *Secrets of the Fed*, p. 36
[1822] *ibid*, pp. 38-39
[1823] *ibid*, p. 50
[1824] *Alan Greenspan: The Federal Reserve Does NOT Answer to the American People*, Johnny Cirucci YouTube
https://www.youtube.com/watch?v=gWtzT0ldkmQ
[1825] *The Federal Reserve, a Privately Owned Banking Cartel, Has Been Given Police Powers, with Glock 22s and Patrol Cars*, Pam Martens, 17 September 2012
http://www.alternet.org/economy/federal-reserve-privately-owned-banking-cartel-has-been-given-police-powers-glock-22s-and

If you check this source you'll see that it's friendly to the Occupy Wall Street kids who, before they were bought out by George Sores-os, had a startling amount in common with the Tea Party...and still do.
[1826] *The Fed's $16 Trillion Bailouts Under-Reported*, Tracey Greenstein, 20 September 2011, Forbes
http://www.forbes.com/sites/traceygreenstein/2011/09/20/the-feds-16-trillion-bailouts-under-reported/
[1827] *Richest 1% Of People Own Nearly Half Of Global Wealth, Says Report*, Jill Treanor, 14 October 2014, the Guardian
http://www.theguardian.com/business/2014/oct/14/richest-1percent-half-global-wealth-credit-suisse-report
[1828] *Big Oil's Secret Strategy to Gush Profits Exposed*, Joe Kovacs, 8 September 2005, WorldNetDaily
http://www.wnd.com/2005/09/32227/#!
[1829] *Sphere of Influence*, Wikipedia

https://en.wikipedia.org/wiki/Sphere_of_influence
[1830] *Who Really Owns Your Gold?* William Dean A. Garner, Adagio (2014), pp. 9, 16-17
[1831] *ibid*, p. 21
[1832] *Vatican Calls for Oversight of the World's Finances*, Elisabetta Povoledo, 24 October 2011, NY Times
http://www.nytimes.com/2011/10/25/world/europe/vatican-calls-for-global-oversight-of-the-economy.html?_r=0

Chapter 20

King Ghidorah: the Dragon from Outer Space

*"For as it was in the days of Noah,
so shall the Return of the Son of Man be."* ~ Matthew 24:37

And I saw coming out of the mouth of the dragon and out of the mouth of the beast and out of the mouth of the false prophet, three unclean spirits like frogs; for they are spirits of demons, performing signs, which go out to the kings of the whole world, to gather them together for the war of the great day of God, the Almighty. ~ Revelation 16:13-14

Is there an organization powerful enough to pull together the religions of the world and point them to the feet of mankind's newly-disclosed alien brethren...and creators?

Is there a dragon approaching Earth from outer space?

The Devil Will Have His Due

One would think that a Faustian bargain with malignant interdimensional beings for wealth and power would have powerful consequences...and one would be right.

It has been the goal of men like Aleister Crowley, Jack Parsons, L. Ron Hubbard and perhaps even John Dee and mystics like him, to commune with such entities. But what are the goals of the entities?

In times past, they have been called the Archons—powerful beings who once ruled over man and who are predicted to return.

Theodotion, a Hebrew scribe that translated the Book of Daniel into Greek for the Septuagint[1833], used the term 6 times in Daniel 10 to describe the archangel Michael and his foes, the princes of Persia and Greece.[1834]

If the Archons were eager to return and regain ascendency over man, could they do it as fallen angels?

Could they do it as "aliens"?

What if those "aliens" were part of an elaborate scheme to claim themselves as the progenitors of man?

In Steven *Spielberg's Close Encounters of the Third Kind* (1977), a group of well-wishing rednecks waits patiently for the arrival of "ET" with signs that proclaim "Stop and be friends!" (or something like that) but the distant lights of UFOs on the horizon loom into threatening military helicopters, instead.

When the aliens arrive in *Independence Day* (1996), everything goes well until bombers drop out of the mothership and start strafing everyone.

But it was all explained decades before in the seminal classic *Invasion of the Astro-Monster* (1965) later retitled *Godzilla vs. Monster Zero*.

A new moon of Jupiter has emerged, named "Planet X" and astronauts Fuji and Glenn are sent to investigate. While there, they are kidnapped by an alien race called "Xians" who apologize for the kidnapping and are attempting to prove their good intentions to the two astronauts when the intergalactic 3-headed space dragon King Ghidorah (whom the Xians call "Monster Zero") attacks.

The damage is considerable but they survive.

> ### They Have Rules
>
> Why is it that the vast majority of animals involved in unexplainable mutilations are cattle?
>
> The entities who conduct these "experiments", though completely evil, have rules—just as their human followers do.
>
> I know of no examples of a beloved household pet being found in such a condition.
>
> Is it possible that mankind, via the barbarism of his own lust for flesh, has signaled that cattle and even horses are "fair game" because his heartless processing of those advanced, feeling mamals is just as brutal?
>
> Who is more guilty for the crimes of these beings?

The Xians tell Fuji and Glenn they wish to make a deal—they will give Earth the formula for a drug that will cure all disease, if Earth will let them borrow Godzilla and Rodan to help put Ghidorah in his place.

Fuji and Glenn return to Earth to find the Xians are already there—they've been hiding underground and under water.

When it comes time to deliver the miracle drug they double-cross humanity and loose all three monsters on Japan.

"Stop and Be Friends!"

Author Nick Redfern has been telling audiences for years that, unlike the extremely popular Tommy Lee Jones/Will Smith series of movies from Columbia "Men in Black", the real "Men in Black" are far more sinister and, perhaps, not even fully human.

"Men in Black" is made by Columbia Pictures.

"Columbia" is a woman holding a shining torch of knowledge like Isis[1835], or like the statue of Liberty. Lady Liberty is modeled after the Colossus of Rhodes but with the face of Apollo[1836]/Osiris/Nimrod (Lucifer) thereby making one of our greatest landmarks a beacon of transgender pagan worship.

In 2010, Redfern published *Final Events and the Secret Government Group on Demonic UFOs and the Afterlife*, the premise of which is nothing short of chilling. [italics suspended]

> Ray Boeche, an Anglican priest who served as the Rector of the Celebration Anglican Church in Lincoln for nearly a decade ... was also the founder and former director of the Fortean Research Center, a former Nebraska State Director for the Mutual UFO Network, and the recipient of a B.A. from Peru State College and a Th.M. degree from St. Mark's School of Divinity. [Boeche was contacted by] two Department of Defense physicists who would reveal to him what they claimed was the dark and disturbing truth at the heart of the UFO mystery.
>
> [Boeche told Redfern] "I found it interesting because they had contacted me at work; and I have no idea how they tracked me down there. ..."
>
> And thus it was that Boeche was plunged headlong into a strange and surreal world of classified Department of Defense projects, secret meetings and follow-up dialogues with Deep Throat-style sources, and stories of very disturbing encounters with what were described to him as NHEs, or Non-Human Entities, which many within the UFO research community believe are aliens, but that certain elements of the DoD believe are nothing less than the deceptive minions of Satan. The story told to Boeche is both provocative and startling, as are its implications, if they are genuine, of course. ...
>
> [Boeche told Redfern] "Both men were physicists. I'd guess they were probably in their early-to-mid fifties, and they were in a real moral dilemma. Both of them were Christians, and were working on a Department of Defense project that involved trying to contact

the NHEs. In fact, this was described to me as an 'obsessive effort.' And part of this effort was to try and control the NHEs and use their powers in military weapons applications and in intelligence areas, such as remote-viewing and psychotronic weapons."

They came to believe that the NHEs were not extraterrestrial at all; they believed they were some sort of demonic entities. And that regardless of how benevolent or beneficial any of the contact they had with these entities seemed to be, it always ended up being tainted, for lack of a better term, with something that ultimately turned out to be bad. There was ultimately nothing positive from the interaction with the NHE entities. They felt it really fell more under the category of some vast spiritual deception instead of UFOs and aliens. In the course of the whole discussion, it was clear that they really viewed this as having a demonic origin that was there to simply try and confuse the issue in terms of who they were, what they wanted, and what the source of the ultimate truth is. If you extrapolate from their take that these are demons in the biblical sense of the word, then what they would be doing here is trying to create a spiritual deception to fool as many people as possible.

As to how elements of the DoD were engaging the NHEs in some form of contact, Boeche was given a truly strange and alarming story. "From what they told me, it seemed like someone had invoked something and it opened a doorway to let these things in. That's certainly the impression they gave me. I was never able to get an exact point of origin of these sorts of experiments, or of their involvement, and when they got started. But I did get the impression that because of what they knew and the information that they presented, they had been involved for at least several years, even if the project had gone on for much longer. They were concerned that they had undertaken this initially with the best of intentions, but then as things developed they saw a very negative side to it that wasn't apparent earlier. ...

The story became even more complex when the reasoning behind, and the goals of, the project were revealed to Boeche: "Most of it was related to psychotronic weaponry and remote viewing, and even deaths by what were supposed to be psychic methods." Certainly, the NHEs, it was deduced by those attached to the DoD project, possessed extraordinary, and lethal, mental powers. And, as a result, deeper plans were initiated, using nothing less than ancient rites and black rituals, to actually try and contact the NHEs with two specific—some might say utterly crackpot—goals in mind:[1] controlling them and[2] exploiting their extraordinary mental powers in the form of devastating weaponry.

While contact was apparently wholly successful, as were the attempts to use the mental powers of the NHEs, Boeche said the two physicists believed that those in the DoD working on this project were being utterly deceived and lulled into a false sense of security. They thought that "the project personnel were allowed to assume they had somehow technologically mastered the ability to do what the NHEs could do: remote-viewing and psychotronics. But, in actuality, it was these entities doing it all the time, or allowing it to happen, for purposes that suited their deception. With both psychotronic weapons and remote-viewing, I was told that the DoD had not really mastered a technology to do that at all; they were allowed by the NHEs to think that this is what they had done. But the NHEs were always the causal factor. ~ *Final Events*, Nick Redfern[1837]

They called themselves "the Collins Elite" because, when they first got started some 60 years ago, one of their researchers was a Quaker from Collins, NY and an expert in "Devil worship".[1838]

Even worse than the usual "alien abduction" stories, Redfern devotes an entire chapter[1839] to how secret military units appear to be tag-teaming the aliens with *their own* abduction and surveillance programs for similar purposes; to use average citizens as human guinea pigs.

But what are they testing...or creating?

Zeta Homunculi

In Jewish folklore there is a creature known as a "golem" which can be fabricated by gnostic rabbinical adepts and animated to do the rabbi's bidding.

One of the most famous was the golem of Rabbi Judah Loew ben Bezalel of 16th century Prague who created a guardian to defend the Jewish inhabitants from persecution until the creature began to kill indiscriminately and had to be "deactivated".

Benjamin Kerstein of *Jewish Ideas Daily* made this fascinating comment regarding golems:

The roots of the legend are ancient: the Talmud claims that Adam himself—and thus, theologically speaking, all of humanity—was a golem until God breathed a soul into his nostrils.[1840]

Repeatedly in Genesis, it states that Elohim created plants and animals to reproduce "after their kind". In the first chapter, alone, the phrase is repeated ten times just as the phrase "—and God said..." is also repeated 10 times.

In Scripture, the number 10 has been associated with *order* and *government*.

It is important not to be seduced by numerology, however, seemingly insignificant things in the Bible are actually quite significant. [Matthew 5:18]

Is there a Divine Order to reproduction? It would seem that as long as a created being reproduces "after its kind", a soul enters a human or the spirit of a lion enters the lion.

What would happen if that process were interrupted?

"And There Were Giants In The Land..."

There is a shocking agenda that can be found in your Bible, one the majority of pastors are not teaching their flocks. Yet it is an agenda that is critical to apologetics and understanding the Christian world view: fallen angels have used genetic experimentation to create human hybrids with super-human traits. These *gibborim* [ppp] (Hebrew for "mighty men") were golems, organic portals for unclean spirits to inhabit. The Hebrew term for them is "Nephilim": "fallen ones".

> *Now it came about, when men began to multiply on the face of the land, and daughters were born to them, that the sons of God saw that the daughters of men were beautiful; and they took wives for themselves, whomever they chose. Then the Lord said, "My Spirit shall not strive with man forever, because he also is flesh; nevertheless his days shall be one hundred and twenty years." The Nephilim were on the Earth in those days, and also afterward, when the sons of God came in to the daughters of men, and they bore children to them. Those were the mighty men who were of old, men of renown.* ~ Genesis 6:1-4, NASB

The Septuagint (Greek translation of the Old Testament) calls them

---

[ppp] This word is apparently not exclusive to hybrids in Scripture.

gigantes, which the King James sometimes mistranslates as "giants" but actually should be translated as "Earth-born" because, like golems, they are animated in an unnatural way.

Job 26:5 tells us:

> *Dead things are formed from under the waters,*
> *and the inhabitants thereof.*

The Latin Vulgate agrees with the Septuagint and uses *gigantes*[1841] but the Hebrew calls them the *rephaim*— רְפָאִים —"shades", "wraiths", "ghosts of the dead".

In 1884, Edwin Abbott published his satirical short novel about the lives of geometric figures in their two-dimensional world titled *Flatland*[1842]. A three-dimensional being can enter into Flatland wherever he wants and will only appear as the outline of what he is.

Christians may have a Biblical facsimile.

After His Resurrection, Jesus Christ was able to suddenly appear in a room with His disciples which frightened them terribly [Luke 24:36-37]. He offered to have Thomas put his hands upon the wounds of His ordeal [John 20:27-28], then eat a piece of fish [Luke 24:41] and disappear. There was a depth to His dimensions human beings are not normally capable of.

The Bible implies that loyal angels have full freedom of movement between the realms for their missions [Hebrews 13:2], while disloyal entities need to trick humans into giving permission which allows them to cohabit that person's body.

From an angelic perspective, this can be quite unfulfilling if the host has no temporal power or authority. All that work to trick someone and they turn out to be the school janitor.

But what if a living organic portal could be created? Then the creators could imbue that portal with superhuman qualities to guarantee their place as generals and kings.

This tampering with the genome is almost certainly the reason why YHWH destroyed the entire Earth with a flood. If the lineage of the Messiah were in any way not fully human, the redemption of all humanity would either be nullified or would be forcibly extended to fallen angels.

The King James Version has interesting wording for why Noah was chosen to survive the Flood.

> *Noah was a just man and perfect in his generations, and Noah walked with God.* ~ Genesis 6:9

That word "perfect" is *tā·mîm*, in the Hebrew and implies a *physical* perfection of Noah's genealogy. We see the word appears again in Exodus 12:5 describing the physical perfection required of the Passover lamb!

Noah was chosen for two reasons;

1. He loved the Lord.
2. His bloodline was not tainted by the Watchers.

"The Watchers" show up in several Apocryphal books like the book of Enoch, the book of Jasher, the Book of the Giants and more.

Many of these documents are actually mentioned in Canon but not included. Jashar is mentioned in Joshua 10:13 as well as II Samuel 1:18 while Jude 14-15 (Jude is a 1-chapter Book) recounts the prophecy of Enoch found in I Enoch 1:9 (some editions have this passage as Chapter 2 verse 1).

> *It was also about these men that Enoch, in the seventh generation from Adam, prophesied, saying, "Behold, the Lord came with many thousands of His holy ones, to execute judgment upon all, and to convict all the ungodly of all their ungodly deeds which they have done in an ungodly way, and of all the harsh things which ungodly sinners have spoken against Him."* ~ Jude 14-15

Have Christians missed important information by not having these books included in their Bibles?

Part of the concern stems from reliability.

What is now called "Enoch" or "Jashar" or "Jubilees" may not be the same as what the Bible is mentioning. Often, unscrupulous authors would put famous names to their work to increase circulation.

Another question is, "Which version of Enoch is this?"

The Protestant Bible has a startling number of manuscripts behind it with very little change between them.[1843]

Regardless of their reliability, the Apocryphal and Deuterocanonical sources on the Watchers all agree on the malignant nature of the Archons.

This is not the message coming from Hollywood and the 2014 movie *Noah* is an excellent example. Although the movie offers fresh, realistic and respectful insights into the Biblical narrative, its chief downfall is complete inversion of who the Watchers were. Jewish writer/director Darren Aronofsky turned them from the reason for the Flood into the saviors of mankind who ultimately get redeemed.[1844]

Far from the idea of Prometheus the giver of fire, punished for his compassion, or Lucifer the bearer of light and knowledge, man's increase in technology and understanding only exacerbated his predicament. As with the aggregation of wealth; the more powerful man becomes, the more concentrated his evil with fewer checks upon it.

Not content to simply "watch", the Archons forced genetic experimentation on humans by raping women and then ruled mankind with their perverse offspring.

They had an insatiable appetite, slaughtering and eating animals at first (created by God as companions for Adam [Genesis 2:18-19]) and eventually eating men. [italics suspended]

> And it came to pass when the children of men had multiplied that in those days were born unto them beautiful and comely daughters. And the angels, the children of the Heaven, saw and lusted after them, and said to one another: "Come, let us choose us wives from among the children of men and beget us children." And Semjaza, who was their leader, said unto them: "I fear ye will not indeed agree to do this deed, and I alone shall have to pay the penalty of a great sin." And they all answered him and said: "Let us all swear an oath, and all bind ourselves by mutual imprecations not to abandon this plan but to do this thing." Then sware they all together and bound themselves by mutual imprecations upon it. And they were in all two hundred; who descended in the days of Jared on the summit of Mount Hermon, and they called it Mount Hermon, because they had sworn and bound themselves by mutual imprecations upon it. ...
>
> And all the others together with them took unto themselves wives, and each chose for himself one, and they began to go in unto them and to defile themselves with them, and they taught them charms and enchantments, and the cutting of roots, and made them acquainted with plants. And they became pregnant, and they bare great giants, whose height was three thousand ells: Who consumed all the acquisitions of men. And when men could no longer sustain them, the giants turned against them and devoured mankind. And they began to sin against birds, and beasts, and reptiles, and fish, and to devour one another's flesh, and drink the blood. Then the

Earth laid accusation against the lawless ones.

And Azazel taught men to make swords, and knives, and shields, and breastplates, and made known to them the metals of the earth and the art of working them, and bracelets, and ornaments, and the use of antimony, and the beautifying of the eyelids, and all kinds of costly stones, and all colouring tinctures. And there arose much godlessness, and they committed fornication, and they were led astray, and became corrupt in all their ways. Semjaza taught enchantments, and root-cuttings, Armaros the resolving of enchantments, Baraqijal (taught) astrology, Kokabel the constellations, Ezeqeel the knowledge of the clouds, Araqiel the signs of the earth, Shamsiel the signs of the sun, and Sariel the course of the moon. And as men perished, they cried, and their cry went up to heaven ... ~ excepts from I Enoch, Chapters 6, 7 and 8[1845]

Even when they taught seemingly benign skills like writing, it only helped man be led further astray. They reveled in debauchery and furthered the practice by teaching women how to kill their unborn children. [italics suspended]

> The name of the fourth is Penemue: he discovered to the children of men bitterness and sweetness;
>
> And pointed out to them every secret of their wisdom.
>
> He taught men to understand writing, and the use of ink and paper.
>
> Therefore numerous have been those who have gone astray from every period of the world, even to this day.
>
> For men were not born for this, thus with pen and with ink to confirm their faith;
>
> Since they were not created, except that, like the angels, they might remain righteous and pure.
>
> Nor would death, which destroys everything, have effected them;
>
> But by this their knowledge they perish, and by this also its power consumes them.
>
> The name of the fifth is Kasyade: he discovered to the children of men every wicked stroke of spirits and of demons:

The stroke of the embryo in the womb, to diminish it; the stroke of the spirit by the bite of the serpent, and the stroke which is given in the mid-day by the offspring of the serpent, the name of which is Tabaet. ~ I Enoch Chapter 68 (some editions show 69)[1846]

Unfortunately, the Flood didn't end their agenda. As Genesis 6:4 tells us, the giants were on the Earth in those days, *and also afterward.*

Once the lineage of the Messiah was secured, the Fallen Ones gave up on that agenda and turned their attentions to the Promised Land.

Most Bible readers do not know why the Children of Israel were condemned to wander the desert for 40 years until an entire generation died off. It was because when they arrived in Palestine after YHWH rescued them from slavery in Egypt, 12 spies were sent out, one from each Tribe. When they returned, 10 spies frightened the people with their report.

> *"We are not able to go up against the people, for they are too strong for us." So they gave out to the sons of Israel a bad report of the land which they had spied out, saying, "The land through which we have gone, in spying it out, is a land that devours its inhabitants; and all the people whom we saw in it are men of great size. There also we saw the Nephilim (the sons of Anak are part of the Nephilim); and we became like grasshoppers in our own sight, and so we were in their sight."* ~ Numbers 13:31-33

Only Joshua and Caleb had the courage to continue on. They, alone, survived the 40 years in the desert and returned full of virility to re-engage their hybrid foes.

It was that generation that began systematically wiping out the Nephilim and driving them out of Palestine.

For eons since, critics of the Bible have mocked a God who would give instructions to wipe out every man, woman and child in warfare. Yet that is exactly what must be done when dealing with genetic aberrations.

There are even specific instructions that show it was only particular tribes who were fully condemned in such a manner—the Hittite and the Amorite, the Canaanite and the Perizzite, the Hivite and the Jebusite. [Deuteronomy 20:17]

In the cities that "are far from you" [Deuteronomy 20:15], the women, children and animals were to be spared because they hadn't been experimented on.

But once the giants started falling, things changed.

"Discretion is the better part of valor." ~ Henry IV

It would appear that this was the frame of mind of the hybrids when their numbers were dwindling and more than a few almost certainly used their superior intelligence and abilities to escape to the New World. Evidence of non-human entities has been suppressed for generations but it has become so prevalent that Darwinian evolutionists are now forced to discuss it openly, though their paradigm falls far short of providing reasonable explanations.

> *Updated genome sequences from two extinct relatives of modern humans suggest that these 'archaic' groups bred with humans and with each other more extensively than was previously known.*
>
> *The ancient genomes, one from a Neanderthal and one from a member of an archaic human group called the Denisovans, were presented on 18 November at a meeting on ancient DNA at the Royal Society in London. The results suggest that interbreeding went on between the members of several ancient human-like groups in Europe and Asia more than 30,000 years ago, including an as-yet-unknown human ancestor from Asia.*
>
> *"What it begins to suggest is that we're looking at a Lord of the Rings-type world — that there were many hominid populations," says Mark Thomas, an evolutionary geneticist at University College London who was at the meeting but was not involved in the work. ~* Ewen Callaway, Nature[1847]

Beings with 6 fingers and 6 toes [II Samuel 21:20], elongated skulls, unusual red hair and massive size have been found by researchers like L.A. Marzulli in both South and North America.[1848]

With each successive generation—from David's miraculous victory over Goliath, on—the hybrids began to die out.

—Until mankind pulled them out of the grave.

> *"The Awakening," J. Seward Johnson Jr.'s 15-foot-high sculpture of a giant struggling to emerge from the earth, is soon to leave a site near the National Mall that millions of tourists have visited since the work's installation in 1980.*

Although it stood for 27 years on public parkland at Hains Point in the southwest section of the city, "The Awakening" did not belong to the National Park Service. It was the property of the Sculpture Foundation, a group that promotes public art. Mr. Johnson, of the Johnson & Johnson pharmaceutical family, gave the foundation a collection of his work to oversee. ~ Sarah Abruzzese, NY Times[1849]

William F. Yurasko – Wikimedia Commons

The "Gift" of Technology

Technology is the "gift" that filled the gap for the Watchers when their chief practitioners were imprisoned for gross genetic manipulation. [Jude 6, II Peter 2:4]

If the news media is covering "scientific ethicists" questioning whether to clone human beings or not, what is actually true is that they are already in the 2nd or 3rd generation of human clones and it's been decided to warm humanity to the reality. [italics suspended]

150 Human Animal Hybrids Grown in UK Labs: Embryos Have Been Produced Secretively For The Past Three Years

Scientists have created more than 150 human-animal hybrid embryos in British laboratories.

The hybrids have been produced secretively over the past three years by researchers looking into possible cures for a wide range of diseases.

The revelation comes just a day after a committee of scientists warned of a nightmare "Planet of the Apes" scenario in which work on human-animal creations goes too far.

Last night a campaigner against the excesses of medical research said he was disgusted that scientists were "dabbling in the grotesque".

Figures seen by the Daily Mail show that 155 "admixed" embryos, containing both human and animal genetic material, have been created since the introduction of the 2008 Human Fertilisation Embryology Act.

This legalized the creation of a variety of hybrids, including an animal egg fertilised by a human sperm; "cybrids", in which a human nucleus is implanted into an animal cell; and "chimeras", in which human cells are mixed with animal embryos. ~ the Daily Mail[1850]

Of course, it's always couched in positive terms like "curing disease" but that's just the cover.

The only way "life extension" technology will be offered to the common man will be as a way to further enslave him/her. It will be the ultimate deal with the devil and one such scenario will include an implant that changes your DNA until your consciousness is gone and a Rephaim has taken over your body as the "aliens" did in *Invasion of the Body Snatchers* (1956).

"Deep Underground Bases" are a fact of "Continuity of Government" plans[1851]. Imagine what the world's most powerful people along with the most unscrupulous scientists are doing in such bases to achieve these ends.[1852]

Long have rumors swirled around the blogosphere of Island of Dr. Moreau horrors chained and caged deep underground at the mercy of literal demons and figurative ones.

"Brother Astronomer to Brother Alien...Come In!"

On top of the highest mountain in all of the state of Arizona sits some of the most advanced astronomical observatories in the world.

Mount Graham is named after a friend of the Army topographer who mapped the area in 1846.[1853]

But it's not just the mountain's height that has attracted scientists—the mountain has long since been revered by Apache Indians as a portal to the spirit world.

> *Apaches in the West, particularly those of the San Carlos and White Mountain tribes, have considered Mount Graham (known as* Dzile Nchaa Si'An *or Big Seated Mountain) as one of their sacred mountains since time immemorial.*

Once a part of the original San Carlos Apache reservation, the mountain was taken from the tribe by the federal government in 1872, notwithstanding the fact that Apaches considered it a portal to the spirit world with the belief that spirits known as Gaahn, guardian spirits of the Apache, reside there and provide health, direction, and guidance. The mountain is also an ancestral Apache resting place [and] *a ceremonial site...* ~ Lee Allen, Indian Country Today [1854]

Perhaps, not surprisingly, Executive Orders have been used to confiscate this prized real estate.

Executive Orders of 1872 or 73 are often cited but none of Ulysses Grant's EO's remain in relation to Mt. Graham. [1855,1856]

However, there is an interesting EO from Grant forbidding the sale of cartridge-based ammunition to "hostile Indians of the Northwest". [1857]

Later, in 1906, Teddy Roosevelt would issue "Executive Order 515":

It is hereby ordered that all that part of the military reservation of Fort Grant, Arizona, as declared by Executive Order of April 17, 1876, which lies northerly and easterly of the following-described lines, shall become a part of the Mt. Graham Forest Reserve, to be protected and administered as forest-reserve land, but that the same shall remain subject to the unhampered use of the War Department for military purposes, and to insure such use, the land shall not be subject to any form of appropriation or disposal under the land laws of the United States... ~ Wikisource [1858]

This would be amended by William Howard Taft, a founding member of Yale's Skull and Bones [1859], to have Graham taken from the military and given to the Department of the Interior. [1860]

Graham boasts one of the most advanced optical devices in the world; the "Large Binocular Telescope".

The Large Binocular Telescope (LBT) is an optical telescope for astronomy located on Mount Graham (10,700-foot (3,300 m) in the Pinaleno Mountains of southeastern Arizona, and is a part of the Mount Graham International Observatory. The LBT is currently one of the world's most advanced optical telescopes; using two 8.4 m (27 ft) wide mirrors, with a 14.4 m center-center separation, it has the same light gathering ability as an 11.8 m (39 ft) wide single circular telescope and detail of a 22.8 m (75 ft) wide one.[4] *Either of its mirrors would be the second-largest optical telescope in continental North America, behind the Hobby–Eberly Telescope in West Texas; as of summer 2014, it would still be the largest non-segmented mirror in an optical telescope. Optical performance of the telescope is excellent, and Strehl ratios of 60–90% in the infrared H band and 95% in the infrared M band have been achieved by the LBT.[5]* ~ Wikipedia[1861]

The location is labeled as an "International" Observatory managed by the University of Arizona.

The Jesuits manage them both.

The VATT facility is really the brainchild of Jesuit George V. Coyne, who became director of the Vatican Observatory in 1978. In addition to his duties as a Jesuit, he was an adjunct professor in the University of Arizona's astronomy department, as well as associate director of the Steward Observatory. As a darling of the atheist community he appeared with Richard Dawkins advocating a deistic form of Darwinism and stunned the high priest of atheism by also promoting a radical form of pluralism, the idea that all religions lead to the same God.[61] Of course, to those familiar with the radical revisionism of Vatican II (Second Vatican Council), it was no big surprise, but Coyne stretches the bounds of orthodoxy even given Rome's embrace of postmodernism. He profaned the film Religulous hosted by atheist Bill Maher, claiming that the Scriptures are scientifically inaccurate obscurantisms to the cheers of secularists and pagans universal. ...it seems that just as Malachi Martin lamented in The Jesuits: The Society of Jesus and the Betrayal of the Roman Catholic Church *(1987), this sort of reductionist postmodernism has become the stock and trade of third- millennium Jesuitism. ~ Exo Vaticana*, Tom Horn and Cris Putnam[1862]

Few know that the Vatican has its own observatory and the Jesuits run all locations.

In fact, the current director of the Vatican Observatory is Father José Gabriel Funes[1863]. He's a Jesuit from Argentina just as is Pope Francis, Jorge Mario Bergoglio.

The Vatican Observatory has two locations; Castel Gandolfo in Italy and Mt. Graham in Arizona.[1864]

The "VATT" is stunningly capable.

> *The 1.8 meter Alice P. Lennon Telescope and its Thomas J. Bannan Astrophysics Facility, known together as the **Vatican Advanced Technology Telescope (VATT), is a Gregorian telescope observing in the optical and infrared which achieved 'first light', the first starlight to pass through the telescope onto a detector, in 1993. ...*
>
> *The heart of the telescope is an f/1.0 honeycombed construction, borosilicate primary mirror. The VATT's mirror is unusually "fast", f/1, which means that its focal distance is equal to its diameter. Because it has such a short focal length, a Gregorian design could be employed which uses a concave secondary mirror at a point beyond the primary focus; this allows unusually sharp focusing across the field of view.*
>
> *The unusual optical design and novel mirror fabrication techniques mean that both the primary and secondary mirrors are among the most exact surfaces ever made for a ground-based telescope. In addition, the skies above Mount Graham are among the most clear, steady, and dark in the continental North America. Seeing of better than one arc-second even without adaptive optics can be achieved on a regular basis. ~ Wikipedia*[1865]

The heart of the "Large Binocular Telescope" is a super-cooled near-infrared spectrometer named L.U.C.I.F.E.R.

The designers went to great lengths to arrive at such an acronym.

> *Large (binocular telescope near-infrared) Utility with Camera and Integral Field unit for Extragalactic Research*

When Chelsea Schilling of WorldNetDaily called the German research facility that created L.U.C.I.F.E.R. to find out why the name was given, the Catholic inventor (at his secular facility) waxed a theological explanation of how "Lucifer" isn't who we think he is.

> *WND contacted German astronomers at the Center for Astronomy of Heidelberg University who gave LUCIFER its diabolical name.*
>
> *Professor and astronomer Andreas Quirrenbach, who also identified himself as a Catholic, told WND there's a common misconception about the term "Lucifer."*

> *"The origin of the name is Latin, meaning 'bearer of light,'"* Quirrenbach said. *"Whereas today most people may associate the name with a mythical fallen angel, who is also frequently identified with the devil, this is by no means the only and also not the original use of the name.*
>
> *"In fact the designation 'Lucifer' was used in antiquity to designate the 'morning star,' i.e., the planet Venus when it is visible in the morning sky. This is the first use of the name, and so its occurrence in astronomy precedes any religious connotations."*
>
> *Quirrenbach also told WND, "[T]he only biblical connotation of 'Lucifer' is the astronomical reference to the morning star, which in turn is used to symbolize the Babylonian rulers (probably because the Babylonians identified constellations with gods). The downfall of the morning star is then a powerful picture for the end of Babylonian rule over Israel, as prophesied by Isaiah. Several authors have linked the name 'Lucifer' in the Bible to the devil, but this is due mostly to a misreading of the relevant biblical verses. However, these misreadings have propagated into folklore."* ~ Chelsea Schilling, WND[1866]

Astronomers like this have more in common with agnostic Freemasons than with fellow scientists.

It was "LUCIFER" that Scottish Rite Master Mason Albert Pike dedicated his most famous work *Morals and Dogma* to.

> *LUCIFER, the Light-bearer! Strange and mysterious name to give to the Spirit of Darkness! Lucifer, the Son of the Morning! Is it he who bears the Light, and with its splendors intolerable blinds feeble, sensual or selfish Souls? Doubt it not!*[1867]

The Communist rabble-rouser who had such an influence on Barack Obama's views of "community organizing" in Chicago[1868], Saul Alinsky, wrote this in his *Rules for Radicals*.

> *Lest we forget at least an over-the-shoulder acknowledgment to the very first radical: from all our legends, mythology, and history (and who is to know where mythology leaves off and history begins—or which is which), the first radical known to man who rebelled against the establishment and did it so effectively that he at least won his own kingdom—Lucifer.*[1869]

Alinsky was, himself, another "court Jew" propped up by Catholic organizations like the United States Catholic Bishops for the purpose of propagating Communism[1870]; once again, putting the Jew up front to be identified as the enemy. To explain the *millions* of Catholic dollars flowing to Alinsky, both duped Catholic conservatives and Papal coadjutors of deception have woven the ridiculous yarn that Alinsky has even conquered the Church[1871,1872] when, in reality, "the Church" and the Jesuits *created* Communism. How else could Phyllis Schlafly uncover how the Church had paid for Barack Obama to attend Alinsky's "Industrial Areas Foundation" in 1986[1873]? What did "the Church" know about Obama's future that no one else did...?

The Light Bearer

Isaiah 14 has long been considered by both Jewish and Christian scholars to have a double meaning toward both the king of Babylon and the devil. As "Babylon" was the first rebellion against YHWH it is a metaphor in Scripture for all rebellion in general which gives it a triple meaning.

Similarly, Ezekiel 28:12-19 appears to be a lament over the evil of the king of Tyre yet the wording is unusual and shows more than one meaning. Clearly, the Adversary is being addressed indirectly in both respect for what he once was and derision for his self-centered apostasy.

> *Again the Word of the Lord came to me saying, "Son of man, take up a lamentation over the king of Tyre and say to him, 'Thus says the Lord God,*
>
> *"You had the seal of perfection,*
> *Full of wisdom and perfect in beauty.*
> *You were in Eden, the garden of God;*
> *Every precious stone was your covering:*
> *The ruby, the topaz and the diamond;*
> *The beryl, the onyx and the jasper;*
> *The lapis lazuli, the turquoise and the emerald;*
> *And the gold, the workmanship of your settings and sockets,*
> *Was in you."*
>
> [This is likely a Hebrew euphemism describing a being of dazzling multi-colored light.]
>
> *On the day that you were created*
> *They were prepared.*
> *You were the anointed cherub who covers,*
> *And I placed you there.*
> *You were on the Holy Mountain of God;*

You walked in the midst of the stones of fire.
You were blameless in your ways
From the day you were created
Until unrighteousness was found in you. ..."'"
~ Ezekiel 28: 12-15, NASB (some capitalization added)

Quirrenbach went on to explain that L.U.C.I.F.E.R. was named after a politician—whose name was actually "devil".

The lead institution for the construction of the LUCIFER spectrographs is the Observatory of the German State of Baden-Württemberg, which is now part of Heidelberg University, he explained. When a German partnership was formed to join Arizona's Large Binocular Telescope project, funding became problematic. At that point, then-Prime Minister of Baden-Württemberg Erwin Teufel stepped in and ensured state funding was available.

"Now, as it happens, the name of this governor is Teufel, which is the German word for 'devil,'" Quirrenbach explained. "Again, absolutely no offense to anyone; this is a fairly common name in Germany. So to those familiar with the local state politics in Southwest Germany, it is plainly obvious that the two Lucifer instruments are named in honor of Teufel, who helped the state observatory become a member of the LBT."

He added, "It's as simple (or complicated, as you will) as that. Nobody thought of the possibility that anybody could take offense at the name 'Lucifer.' ..." ~ Chelsea Schilling, WND[1874]

The official Vatican statement on L.U.C.I.F.E.R. seems just as evasive.

There was another strange phone call today. Somebody was apparently just recently hurt by a misinformation which has been circulating on the web for two or three years. This calumny claims that the Vatican astronomers named some instrument or telescope "Lucifer".

It is fairly clearly a typical case of degradation of information. The truth of the matter is that the Vatican Observatory is a member of the Mount Graham International Observatory (MGIO) consortium, together with a number of other institutions from Europe and the USA. The MGIO comprises a large number of stake holders, most of whom have nothing to do with the Vatican Observatory or its telescope.

How does this work? It is quite similar to share holders in a company. Supposing you had a six percent share in a company, while Mr XYZ had a four percent share. What could you do if Mr XYZ decided to name his pet hamster "Demon"?

One of the stake holders in the MGIO is a group of European institutes who built an infrared camera and spectroscope, and named it "Lucifer". So what happened? First, somebody reported that an instrument called "Lucifer" was installed on Mt Graham. Then somebody remarked that Mt Graham also hosts the Vatican Advanced Technology Telescope, and that it is somewhat amusing that Mt Graham has both Vatican and Lucifer. Then the information somehow degraded and the slur was born: Vatican astronomers are supposedly friends with Lucifer... ~ Vatican Observatory.org[1875]

Baptizing ET

One of the Jesuit's star astronomers is Guy Consolmagno.

With Darwinian Evolution flatlining in every serious empirical venue, Consolmagno is a staunch ally and critic of scientists who are defending the Christian concept of a Designer.

Consolmagno is a friendly peer of vehement atheist Stephen Hawking.

Aliens might have souls and could choose to be baptized if humans ever met them, a Vatican scientist said today. The official also dismissed intelligent design as "bad theology" that had been "hijacked" by American creationist fundamentalists.

Guy Consolmagno, who is one of the pope's astronomers, said he would be "delighted" if intelligent life was found among the stars.
...

The Pontifical Academy of Sciences, of which Stephen Hawking is a member, keeps the senior cardinals and the pope up-to-date with the latest scientific developments. Responding to Hawking's recent comments that the laws of physics removed the need for God, Consolmagno said: "Steven Hawking is a brilliant physicist... ~ Alok Jha, the Guardian[1876]

Check Your Brain

The topic of "aliens" is just as religious as that of evolution. There are "believers" and "skeptics" and little room for clear-minded empirical examination of the facts without a bias towards the outcome.

> *I believe that UFOs are physically real. They represent a fantastic technology controlled by an unknown form of consciousness. But I also believe that it would be dangerous to jump to premature conclusions about their origin and nature, because the phenomenon serves as the vehicle for images that can be manipulated to promote belief systems tending to the long-term transformation of human society. I have tried to identify some of the manipulators and to highlight their activities, which range from apparently harmless hoaxes such as the false professor George Adamski's meetings with Venusian spacemen to bloody expeditions that have littered the American landscape with the carcasses of mutilated animals. I have found disturbing evidence of dangerous sectarian activities linked to totalitarian philosophies. The ease with which journalists and even scientists can be seduced into indiscriminate promotion of such deceptions is staggering. In the context of an academic attitude that rejects any open investigation of paranormal phenomena, such fanatical conversions must be expected. For me, that is only one more reason for an independent thinker to remain vigilant against false ideas and simplistic political notions planted by those I have called the "Messengers of Deception." ~ Messengers of Deception*, Jacques Vallée[1877]

On April 6th 2013 the Biography Channel showed its first episode in a new documentary series titled *Alien Encounters*. Two alien abduction victims told their stories and they were re-enacted for the audience; Audrey Hewins and Whitley Strieber.

Strieber is the author of a series of books about his experiences that have been hugely successful starting with the religiously-named *Communion* in 1987.

In that pilot episode of *Alien Encounters*, Strieber recounts the horrors of being forcibly abducted from his bed, receiving an "implant", having a needle thrust into his brain while he watched and being fully aware of something getting shoved into his rectum.

He later states that he was shown the deathbed of his father, whom he was very close to, a vision of his son being harmed and/or abducted and an apocalyptic explosion of a weapon of mass destruction in an unknown city.

Unbeknownst to him, this was the same agenda of fear that was being imposed on those who come upon mutilated animals that have been purposefully left to be seen: fear is what the "aliens" feed off of. Not very "advanced" of them.

Later in the episode, the actor depicting Strieber is shown using a Hindu meditation technique to entice the entities—whom Strieber is very careful not to strictly label as "aliens"—to return.

Beast Forgotten?

For centuries, Protestants have seen Rome as Babylon and the Pope as the anti-Christ.

Several of Martin Luther's original Theses were based upon Church policies that were clearly unbiblical. They betrayed the trust Catholics had in their church leadership to steward their souls because of their lust for political influence.

> *28. It is certain that when money clinks in the money chest, greed and avarice can be increased...*
>
> *32. Those who believe that they can be certain of their salvation because they have indulgence letters will be eternally damned, together with their teachers.*
>
> *33. Men must especially be on guard against those who say that the pope's pardons are that inestimable gift of God by which man is reconciled to him.*
>
> *34. For the graces of indulgences are concerned only with the penalties of sacramental satisfaction established by man.*
>
> *35. Any truly repentant Christian has a right to full remission of penalty and guilt, even without indulgence letters.*
>
> *36. Any true Christian, whether living or dead, participates in all the blessings of Christ and the church; and this is granted him by God, even without indulgence letters.*[1878]

The exploitation of the confessional was explicitly taught to Jesuit insurgents in their guidebook *Secreta Monita*.

> *Let our members take care to provide, in places where they reside, a physician who may be faithful to the society, whom they should especially commend to the sick, and extol above others; that in turn, he commending us in preference to other religious orders, may cause that every where we will be called to them that are sick and dying, and especially to such as are persons of great distinction. ...*

> *If any confessor should hear, from a strange woman, that she has carnally known some member of the society, he must not absolve her, unless besides her confession, she reveals the name of her paramour, nor even then, until she shall solemnly swear never to disclose it again to any mortal, without the society's consent.*[1879]

Such abuse continues to this day, and has no basis in Christian doctrine. [Mark 2:1-12, James 5:16]

> *Most of Rome's wealth has been acquired through the sale of salvation. Untold billions of dollars have been paid to her by those who thought they were purchasing heaven on the installment plan for themselves or loved ones. The practice continues to this day- blatantly where Catholicism is in control, less obviously here in the United States. No greater deception or abomination could be perpetrated. When Cardinal Cajetan, sixteenth-century Dominican scholar, complained about the sale of dispensations and indulgences, the Church hierarchy was indignant and accused him of wanting "to turn Rome into an uninhabited desert, to reduce the Papacy to impotence, to deprive the pope ... of the pecuniary resources indispensable for the discharge of his office."[12] ~ A Woman Rides The Beast*, Dave Hunt[1880]

In Daniel Chapter 7, the reader is taken past the reign of Nebuchadnezzar to his grandson, Belshazzar, proven by secular documents to have been an actual sovereign.

> *Belshazzar, Neo-Babylonian Bel-shar-usur, Greek Baltasar, or Balthasar (died c. 539 bc), coregent of Babylon who was killed at the capture of the city by the Persians.*
>
> *Belshazzar had been known only from the biblical Book of Daniel (chapters 5, 7–8) and from Xenophon's Cyropaedia until 1854, when references to him were found in Babylonian cuneiform inscriptions. Though he is referred to in the Book of Daniel as the son of Nebuchadrezzar, the Babylonian inscriptions indicate that he was in fact the eldest son of Nabonidus, who was king of Babylon from 555 to 539 BC...* ~ Encyclopædia Britannica ["Son of" was a Hebrew euphemism for the lineage of a prominent person, hence one can be a "son" of his grandfather or great-grandfather, etc.][1881]

Here, Daniel receives a vision of the Four Beasts and the End of the Age. Disturbed and perplexed by what he sees, he asks his angelic guide for help.

> *"Thus he said: 'The fourth beast will be a fourth kingdom on the Earth, which will be different from all the other kingdoms and will devour the whole earth and tread it down and crush it. As for the ten horns, out of this kingdom ten kings will arise; and another will arise after them, and he will be different from the previous ones and will subdue three kings. He will speak out against the Most High and wear down the saints of the Highest One, and he will intend to make alterations in times and in law...'"* ~ Daniel 7:23-25

The four kingdoms/beasts of Daniel's vision mirror the four kingdoms of different metals related to Daniel in Nebuchadnezzar's dream of the great statue in Chapter 2—a statue representing man's rebellion.

The vast majority of Christian scholars have always accepted that the "legs and feet of iron" in the statue was Rome—so why not understand the Fourth Beast as the same?

Today, Rome is, indeed, a kingdom and a force unlike any other in history.

Setting the Stage

The Jesuit Crusader for Darwinian Evolution, Pierre Teilhard de Chardin, ironically did much to set the stage for acceptance of our "alien brethren" with his unconventional teachings on Original Sin.

> *...original sin, taken in its widest sense, is not a malady specific to the earth, nor is it bound up with human generation. It simply symbolizes the inevitable chance of evil (*Necesse est ut eveniant scandala*)[8] which accompanies the existence of all participated being.* ~ *Christianity and Evolution*, de Chardin[1882]

"Evolution" proved that there was nothing special about the Earth and, therefore, at best the redemption of mankind by Jesus Christ was not singular to the third planet from the sun. According to de Chardin, our alien brethren from Andromeda will be part-and-parcel to our eventual hive-mind collective consciousness.

> *If the earth may be conceived as "unica", or at least as "singularis" in* natura rerum,[16] *then our co-existence in time and space with Christ is no more extraordinary than our own personal coexistence with the earth and the present. The new Adam was made man, rather than anything else, for a reason intrinsic to mankind.*
>
> *That may be perfectly true; but the whole problem is to find out*

> *whether in order to retain this supreme geocentrism, so comforting a concession to our weakness, we are not obliged to resist the truth. A mankind which proclaims that it is alone, or in a special position, in the universe reminds us of the philosopher who claims to reduce the whole of the real to his own consciousness, so exclusively as to deny true existence to other men.*
>
> *... the hypothesis of a special revelation, in some millions of centuries to come, teaching the inhabitants of the system of Andromeda that the Word was incarnate on earth, is ... ridiculous.* ~ de Chardin[1883]

When "Evolution" conflicts with the "rust" of Scripture, clearly it is the Bible that needs to be oiled and tweaked.

> *...the representation of original sin has been borrowed almost literally from the rust chapters of Genesis. It is apparent that today we are being irresistibly driven to find a new way of picturing to ourselves the events as a consequence of which evil invaded our world.*
>
> *... as a result of* [supposed evolutionary evidence] *Christian thought is being gradually obliged to abandon its former ways of conceiving original sin.*
>
> [It is de Chardin's aim t]*o indicate certain directions in which believers would now appear to be turning in their attempt to present the dogma of the Fall in a way that can be reconciled with what is least hypothetical in the evidence of experience and history.* ~ de Chardin[1884]

Rather than question Evolution, we must see "inconsistent" Biblical narratives as metaphor and allegory as they are obviously beyond comparison to accepted scientific theory such as the changing of one species into another.

> *Since there is no room in the scientific history of the world for the point at which original sin marks a retrogression; since, in the series **known to our experience**, everything happens as though there were no Adam and no Eden; then it must be that the Fall, as an event, is something which cannot be verified or checked. For some reason the traces of the initial tragedy necessarily escape our analysis of the world.* ~ de Chardin [emphasis his][1885]

Perhaps in de Chardin's hive mind collective we all worship the same creator...but who will it look like?

One World Religion

When the Archons return, lead by the Anti-Christ, will all be required to worship them?

Ecumenicalism is the movement for a One World Religion and it's an agenda Rome is pushing hard, even if it is upsetting some Christians to do it.

> *The Pope has struck a surprisingly conciliatory tone towards atheists and agnostics, saying that God will "forgive" them as long as they behave morally and live according to their consciences.*
>
> *The unprecedented gesture came as his incoming number two, the Vatican's newly-nominated secretary of state, said that the rule that priests should be celibate was not "a dogma of the Church" and could be open for discussion.*
>
> *Francis, who has won praise for spontaneous and unusual moves during his six month papacy, wrote a lengthy letter to a newspaper, La Repubblica, which the Italian daily printed over four pages, including page one, under the simple byline "Francesco".*
>
> *"God forgives those who obey their conscience," he wrote in the unprecedented letter, the latest example of the markedly different tone and style from his predecessors that he has set since being elected in March.* ~ Nick Squires, the Telegraph[1886]

In 2007, Martinus Petrus Maria "Tiny" Muskens, the Bishop of the Diocese of Breda, Netherlands, stated that one man's "Allah" is another man's "YHWH".

> *"Allah is a very beautiful word for God. Shouldn't we all say that from now on we will name God Allah? ... What does God care what we call him? It is our problem," Muskens told Dutch television.* ~ FoxNews[1887]

In November of 2014, the first Jesuit Pope made an historic trip to Istanbul, Turkey, where he bowed before Orthodox Patriarch Bartholomew and beseeched his blessings in an "extraordinary display of Christian unity."[1888]

While there, Francis took off his shoes, entered Istanbul's Blue Mosque, faced Mecca and bowed his head in silence in "joint adoration" of

"God".

> *A group of school children waving Turkish and Vatican flags chanted "Long live Pope Francis" in Italian as the Muslim call to prayer rang out across the Sultanahmet square, the heart of Istanbul's historic quarter.* ~ Newsweek[1889]

The Turkish soldier on guard inside the Mosque recognized the Pope's temporal authority and smartly saluted him.[1890]

After his trip to Turkey, Pope Francis defended Islam, guided by the Koran, which he called "a prophetic book of peace." Equating Christian Biblical literalists with jihadists, Jorge Bergoglio had an apologetic "we all have to put up with them" approach.

> *The Argentine pope ... said it was wrong for anyone to react to terrorism by being "enraged" against Islam.*
>
> *"You just can't say that, just as you can't say that all Christians are fundamentalists. We have our share of them (fundamentalists). All religions have these little groups," he said.* ~ Philip Pullella, Reuters[1891]

In Malaysia, the Jesuits have a fascinating tradition; whenever they pray, it is to "Allah". Recently, some "fundamentalist" muslims have started to take offense. Fortunately, the Society of Jesus is steadfast in their worship of the moon god being synonymous with the G-d of Avraham, Yitzak, Yakov and Yeshua.

> *Malaysian police recently suggested that Fr. Lawrence Andrew SJ, the Editor-in-Chief of the national Catholic newspaper* Catholic Herald, *be called in to answer to charges of sedition. This was after the Sultan of Selangor, one of Malaysia's thirteen states, decreed that non-Muslims could not use the name "Allah" any more as a reference to God. But Fr. Andrew said in a statement that Selangor's parishes will continue to use it, just as they have done for the past 1600 years.* ~ Marco Tosatti, the Vatican Insider[1892]

Try as the Jesuits might, Allah does not stack up well against YHWH. If one understands the brutality of warfare against genetically-altered human/demon hybrids, the disparity becomes overwhelming.[qqq]

[qqq] Never forget that the Bible was written for *Eastern* minds and an *Eastern* culture, in place thousands of years ago.

> *The only reward of those who make war upon Allah and His messenger and strive after corruption in the land will be that they will be killed or crucified, or have their hands and feet on alternate sides cut off, or will be expelled out of the land. Such will be their degradation in the world, and in the Hereafter theirs will be an awful doom; Save those who repent before ye overpower them.* ~ Quran 5:32-33

Nor does YHWH promise you for reward, 72 virgins, untouched by man or fallen angel.

> *Reclining upon the couches lined with silk brocade, and the fruits of the Gardens will be near at hand. Then which of the Blessings of your Lord will you deny? Wherein will be those houris, restraining their glances upon their husbands, whom no man or jinn has opened their hymens with sexual intercourse before.* ~ Quran 55:54-56

If a dutiful muslim is worried that 72 virgins will wear him out, there have been provisions made for him, as well.

> *Priapism is a potentially painful medical condition, in which the erect penis or clitoris[1] does not return to its flaccid state, despite the absence of both physical and psychological stimulation, within four hours. The name comes from the Greek god Priapus, a fertility god often represented with a disproportionately large and permanent erection.[2][3] ...*
>
> *According to Islamic scripture, all Muslim males that are admitted to Paradise will technically suffer from priapisms. A hasan hadith[5] from Ibn Majah (one of the six canonical hadith collections) concerning the 72 virgins provides this detail on the physical attributes given to men by Allah to sustain them (Muslim males "will have an ever-erect penis").[6] Al-Suyuti (one of the latter-day authorities of the Shafi'i School of fiqh) also wrote that the "penis of the Elected never softens. The erection is eternal".[7]*
> ~ WikiIslam[1893]

Much less covered in mainstream examination of Islam, is the encouraged predation of young boys. Such pedophilia (common amongst Luciferians, politicians and priests) is actually promised by the Quran as a "reward".

> *And there will go round boy-servants of theirs, to serve them as if they were preserved pearls.* ~ Quran 52:24

They will be served by immortal boys. ~ Quran 52:24

And round about them will (serve) boys of everlasting youth. If you see them, you would think them scattered pearls. ~ Quran 76:19

These are the fruits of those who "slay the unbeliever" [Quran 2:191].

In June of 2014 Pope Francis hosted Jewish, muslim and Christian prayers at the Vatican[1894]. These efforts included ensnaring Orthodoxy.

> *Patriarch Bartholomew, the spiritual head of the Orthodox Church, is also attending. Francis invited him to show that the two main branches of Christianity that split in 1054 can work together for peace.* ~ Reuters[1895]

Pope Francis is building religious bridges as if he were "purpose-driven" and Rick Warren is helping him do it.

> *In a new video, megachurch leader and author Rick Warren is calling for Christians to unite with Roman Catholics and "Pope Francis," who Warren recently referred to as the "Holy Father"— a move that is raising concerns among Christians nationwide and is resulting in calls for Warren to repent.*
>
> *Warren made the comments following his visit to the Vatican last month, where he spoke at an interfaith conference...*
>
> *"We have far more in common than what divides us," he said in the two-minute video released by the Catholic News Service on Wednesday, described as being an outline for "an ecumenical vision for Catholics and Protestants to work together..."*
>
> *The author of the bestselling book "The Purpose Driven Life" then sought to defend Catholics from those who take issue with the practice of seeking the intercession of Mary and the various deceased persons that have been sainted by the Vatican.*
>
> *"Sometimes protestants think that Catholics worship Mary like she's another god, but that's not exactly Catholic doctrine," Warren contended. "People say, 'What are the saints all about? Why are you praying to the saints?' And when you understand what they mean by what they're saying, there's a whole lot more commonality* [that we have with Roman Catholics]*."* ~ Heather Clark, Christian News[1896]

One group interested in building bridges amongst religions is the

Council on Foreign Relations.

The CFR was founded by Carnegie lawyer Elihu Root, the same Root who spearheaded the passing of the 17th Amendment.

At best, the CFR and its members have been considered as frequently losing sight of the interests of Americans in favor of global concerns and, at worst, purposely subverting American institutions to install a One-World Order.

Not only is Rick Warren a member of the CFR[1897], he's actively working with a Cardinal who was educated by Jesuits and ordained by Francis Cardinal Spellman[1898], Theodore McCarrick.

Standing next to them is Richard Land, the leader of the Southern Baptist Convention who recently wrote Barack Obama, encouraging him to further his efforts on "gun control".[1899]

> ***Religion and Foreign Policy Meeting Series***, *in New York and Washington, on the impact of religious doctrine on foreign policy. In recent months, the Council has hosted Richard Land, president of the Southern Baptist Convention's Ethics & Religious Liberty Commission; Rick Warren, founding pastor of Saddleback Church and author of The Purpose Driven Life; Cardinal Theodore McCarrick, archbishop of Washington; and Vali R. Nasr, adjunct senior fellow for Middle Eastern studies at the Council and professor of national security affairs at the Naval Postgraduate School. The National Program teleconferences and/or webcasts these sessions to members outside of New York and DC.* ~ Ongoing Programs, the Council on Foreign Relations[1900]

Self-esteem guru Joel Osteen is also a fan of the Pope. Osteen was invited to speak to Josh Zepps of the Huffington Post[rrr] about his new book *Break Out: 5 Keys to Go Beyond Your Barriers and Live an Extraordinary Life*. During the interview, Osteen called Francis "fantastic" and he bragged that both his and Bergoglio's churches are "open" because "God is big".[1901]

Jorge Mario Bergoglio has become a rockstar amongst the Left and the news media. They're so excited, they hope even Jesus measures up to him. [italics suspended]

[rrr] Osteen's gospel of "me!" is easily consumed by the Huffington Post audience.

Like Pope Francis? You'll Love Jesus.
Pope Francis's viral quotes on wealth, abortion, atheists, war and gay Catholics.

Months before Time magazine blessed Pope Francis as its 2013 "Person of the Year," the secular media's love affair with the Argentine pontiff was well underway.

"We love him," swooned the Huffington Post.

"Our cool new pope," declared Gawker.

"You know who I freakin' love?" gushed MSNBC's Chris Hayes, who said he grew up Catholic but stopped attending church during his freshman year at Brown. "This new pope. Pope Francis. . . . Are you watching this guy? Because you should be. It's early, but I'm thinking . . . *best pope ever.*"

...that's the Francis Effect. No surprise, then, that Time took the final, logical step: Slapping Francis on the cover of its "Person of the Year" issue is a sort of secular canonization.

"In a matter of months, Francis has elevated the healing mission of the church — the church as servant and comforter of hurting people in an often harsh world — above the doctrinal police work so important to his recent predecessors," Time's profile said. "John Paul II and Benedict XVI were professors of theology. Francis is a former janitor, nightclub bouncer, chemical technician and literature teacher."

These are the forces that see Francis as a progressive reformer, a long-awaited Catholic antidote to the religious right. None of that theological or doctrinal stuff, thank you. Just give us the humble pontiff, not like the other guy with his high-church pomp and fancy red shoes. Francis — the pope who kissed a man disfigured by a gruesome disease! The one who lives in humble quarters! The pope who took it to trickle-down economics! By critiquing the excesses of religion and politics — a criticism that resonates in media circles — Francis has given the press permission to change its narrative about the church. ~ Elizabeth Tenety, the Washington Post[1902]

This cult of personality has become a siren song of ecumenicalism to "Evangelicals".

> *When it was reported that Pope Francis chose public transportation over limo service as a cardinal, the world smiled. When he spent ... Thursday washing the feet of incarcerated women at a local prison, it touched our hearts. When he embraced a disfigured man, it left us flat-out speechless. Francis is not your father's Pope.*
>
> *But among the most surprising fans of the Pope are Protestants, a group that has often had a less-than-amenable relationship with Catholics historically. But somehow Francis–who some have called the "evangelical Pope"–has begun prying open their arms and sneaking into their hearts. Protestant evangelist Luis Palau has prayed with Francis and even defended his faith. Timothy George, a respected Baptist theologian, has written an article claiming the Pope is "Our Francis, Too." And a writer for "The Catholic Herald" opined that the Argentine Jesuit is "stirring the hearts of evangelicals all over the world."* ~ Jonathan Merritt, Religion News Service[1903]

By carefully re-examining an obscure prophecy of Irish Catholic Saint Malachy Morgair (1094-1148), authors Tom Horn and Cris Putnam believe that Jorge Bergoglio could very well be the "Final Pope" before the End of the Age.[1904]

Are they right?

The Return of the Archons

There is something odd about the last kingdom in Nebuchadnezzar's vision—it has "NHE's" (Non-Human Entities) in it.

> *Then there will be a fourth kingdom as strong as iron; inasmuch as iron crushes and shatters all things, so, like iron that breaks in pieces, it will crush and break all these in pieces. In that you saw the feet and toes, partly of potter's clay and partly of iron, it will be a divided kingdom; but it will have in it the toughness of iron, inasmuch as you saw the iron mixed with common clay. As the toes of the feet were partly of iron and partly of pottery, so some of the kingdom will be strong and part of it will be brittle. And in that you saw the iron mixed with common clay, they will combine with one another in the seed of men; but they will not adhere to one another, even as iron does not combine with pottery.* ~ Daniel 2:40-43

There are questions surrounding the official story of just who *either* of Barack Obama's parents were.

When Obama first toured Egypt, he spent most of his time apologizing for America[1905]. Several observers remarked how he looked like some of the ancient Pharaohs. One blogger actually asks, "*Is Obama the Clone of Akhenaten?*[1906]"

Even the Egyptian face on the Shriner emblem (p. 731) seems to resemble him.

Many of humanity's ancient Nephilim rulers had physical anomalies that set them apart like elongated skulls.[1907]

Was Barack Obama's skull originally misshapen and then surgically altered? He has the scars that make some wonder.[1908]

Who is the Anti-Christ?

What advantages does the devil have by existing outside our space-time continuum?

Theologians have suggested that angelic beings can see the continuum of time as looking through a glass, darkly. It is an advantage but not an overwhelming one. There is still much they do not know.

As a result, world leaders have been positioned throughout history to step in to the role of the "Man of Sin" should the circumstances suddenly fall into place.

Is Barack Obama a pre-positioned Anti-Christ?

Endnotes

[1833] *Theodotion*, Jewish Encyclopedia
http://www.jewishencyclopedia.com/articles/14361-theodotion
[1834] *Archon > Judaism and Christianity*, Wikipedia
https://en.wikipedia.org/wiki/Archon#Judaism_and_Christianity
[1835] *The ISIS Ploy: Illuminati Sorcery and Sacrifice*, Zen Gardner, 14 June 2014, Zen Gardner.com
http://www.zengardner.com/isis-ploy-illuminati-sorcery-sacrifice/
[1836] *What Brad Meltzer's Decoded Missed About The REAL Meaning of the Statue of Liberty's Symbols*, Mark Dice, 20 December 2010, Infowars
http://www.infowars.com/what-brad-meltzers-decoded-missed-about-the-real-meaning-of-the-statue-of-libertys-symbols/

The jury's still out on whether Mark Dice is a "coadjutor" or not. He frequently mocks his own "Truther" (hate that word) audience regarding "conspiracies" that are sometimes actually accurate.

So far, I see the reason as because he's just an arrogant jerk, but there may be something more to it.

[1837] *Final Events and the Secret Government Group on Demonic UFOs and the Afterlife*, Nick Redfern, Anomalist Books (2010), pp. 9-14
[1838] *ibid*, p. 75
[1839] *ibid, Chapter 19: Project Abduction*, pp. 238-249
[1840] *The Golem: Universal and Particular*, Benjamin Kerstein, 14 September 2010, JewishIdeasDaily.com
http://www.jewishideasdaily.com/718/features/the-golem-universal-and-particular/
[1841] *Job 26*, Sacred Texts
http://www.sacred-texts.com/bib/cmt/clarke/job026.htm
[1842] *Flatland*, Edwin Abbott Abbott (parents were first cousins—freakin Limeys!), Seely & Co. (1884)
[1843] *The New Testament Compared to Classical Literature*, Wayne Jackson, undated, Christian Courier
https://www.christiancourier.com/articles/1441-new-testament-compared-to-classical-literature-the
[1844] *Noah: The Review You Need To Read*, Johnny Cirucci, Friday, 22 August 2014, the Patriot Press
http://johnnycirucci.com/wp/entertainment-reviews/noah-the-review/
[1845] *The Book of Enoch*, Sacred Texts
http://www.sacred-texts.com/bib/boe/
[1846] *The Book of Enoch, Chapter LXIX*, Sacred Texts
http://www.sacred-texts.com/bib/boe/boe072.htm
[1847] *Mystery Humans Spiced Up Ancients' Sex Lives*, Ewen Callaway, 19 November 2013, Nature
http://www.nature.com/news/mystery-humans-spiced-up-ancients-sex-lives-1.14196

How big an asshole do you have to be to write a moronic headline like this?
[1848] *On The Trail of the Nephilim II*, L.A. Marzulli, 26 September 2014, L.A. Marzulli's blog
https://lamarzulli.wordpress.com/2014/09/26/on-the-trail-of-the-nephilim-ii-sample-chapter/

[1849] *After 27 Years, a Popular Sculpture Moves From a National Park Into Private Hands*, Sarah Abruzzese, 29 December 2007, NY Times
http://www.nytimes.com/2007/12/29/arts/design/29awak.html?_r=2&
[1850] *150 Human Animal Hybrids Grown in UK Labs: Embryos Have Been Produced Secretively For The Past Three Years*, Daniel Martin and Simon Caldwell, 22 July 2011, the Daily Mail
http://www.dailymail.co.uk/sciencetech/article-2017818/Embryos-involving-genes-animals-mixed-humans-produced-secretively-past-years.html
[1851] *Interview with Paul Fritz Bugas, Former On-site Superintendent, The Greenbrier Bunker*, The American Experience, PBS
http://www.pbs.org/wgbh/amex/bomb/sfeature/interview.html
[1852] *The Alien Agenda: Myth, Underground Bases & The Extraterrestrial Presence*, Dr. Rita Louise, 29 June 2013, Ancient Origins
http://www.ancient-origins.net/myths-legends-unexplained-phenomena-news-mysterious-phenomena-opinion-guest-authors/alien-agenda#_methods=onPlusOne%2C_ready%2C_close%2C_open%2C_resizeMe%2C_renderstart%2Concircled%2Cdrefresh%2Cerefresh%2Conload&id=I0_1415062298217&parent=http%3A%2F%2Fwww.ancient-origins.net&pfname=&rpctoken=23031588
[1853] *History Road Trip: Mount Graham Observatory*, John Stanley, 8 June 2014, The Republic
http://www.azcentral.com/story/travel/road-trips/2014/06/07/history-road-trip-mount-graham-observatory/10168173/
[1854] *Pray for Arizona's Mount Graham During National Sacred Places Prayer Days*, Lee Allen, 18 June 2012, Indian Country Today Media Network
http://indiancountrytodaymedianetwork.com/2012/06/18/pray-arizonas-mount-graham-during-national-sacred-places-prayer-days-119122
[1855] *Executive Orders, 1872, Ulysses S. Grant*, The American Presidency Project
http://www.presidency.ucsb.edu/executive_orders.php?year=1872&Submit=DISPLAY
[1856] *Executive Orders, 1873, Ulysses S. Grant*, The American Presidency Project
http://www.presidency.ucsb.edu/executive_orders.php?year=1873&Submit=DISPLAY
[1857] *Ulysses S. Grant, Executive Order November 23, 1876*, The American Presidency Project
http://www.presidency.ucsb.edu/ws/index.php?pid=70548
[1858] *Executive Order 515*, Wikisource
https://en.wikisource.org/wiki/Executive_Order_515
[1859] *The 15 Most Powerful Members Of "Skull And Bones"*, Thornton McEnery, 20 February 2011, Business Insider
http://www.businessinsider.com/skull-and-bones-alumni-2011-2?op=1
[1860] *Executive Order 1397*, Wikisource
https://en.wikisource.org/wiki/Executive_Order_1397
[1861] *Large Binocular Telescope*, Wikipedia
https://en.wikipedia.org/wiki/Large_Binocular_Telescope
[1862] *Exo-Vaticana: Petrus Romanus, Project L.U.C.I.F.E.R. and the Vatican's Astonishing Plan for the Arrival of an Alien Savior*, Cris Putnam and Thomas Horn, Defender Publishing (2013), p. 38
[1863] *José G. Funes, S.J.*, Vatican Observatory.org

http://vaticanobservatory.org/about-us/personnel-and-research/73-personnel-and-research/jose-funes/318-jose-funes
[1864] *Vatican Observatory*, Wikipedia
https://en.wikipedia.org/wiki/Vatican_Observatory
[1865] *Vatican Advanced Technology Telescope*, Wikipedia
https://en.wikipedia.org/wiki/Vatican_Advanced_Technology_Telescope
[1866] *What the Devil? Scientists Tap Power of "Lucifer"*, Chelsea Schilling, 20 January 2013, WorldNetDaily
http://www.wnd.com/2013/01/what-the-devil-scientists-tap-power-of-lucifer/#!
[1867] *Morals and Dogma of the Ancient and Accepted Scottish Rite of Freemasonry*, Albert Pike, self published (lame-ass!) (1871)
[1868] *How Saul Alinsky Taught Barack Obama Everything He Knows About Civic Upheaval*, AWR Hawkins, 14 March 2012, Breitbart.com
http://www.breitbart.com/Big-Government/2012/03/14/How%20Saul%20Alinsky%20Taught%20Barack%20Obama%20Everything%20He%20Knows%20About%20Civic%20Upheaval
[1869] *Rules for Radicals*, Saul D. Alinsky, Random House (1971), dedication
[1870] *Economic Justice for All: Pastoral Letter on Catholic Social Teaching and the U.S. Economy*, 1986, United States Catholic Bishops
http://www.usccb.org/upload/economic_justice_for_all.pdf
[1871] *The CCHD and Saul Alinsky*, RealCatholicTV YouTube
https://www.youtube.com/watch?&v=481bgi5Du0s
[1872] *Saul Alinsky, Barack Obama linked to Catholic Church*, Jo Scott, 18 February 2012, Colorado Coalition for Life
http://coloradocoalitionforlife.com/saul-alinsky-barack-obama-catholic-church
[1873] *New Book's Ironic Claim: Catholic Church Paid to Send Obama to an Alinsky-Founded Group's Community Organizing Training (See the Documents)*, Billy Hallowell, 23 July 2012, the Blaze
http://www.theblaze.com/stories/2012/07/23/new-books-ironic-claim-catholic-church-paid-to-send-obama-to-an-alinsky-founded-groups-community-organizing-training-see-the-documents/
[1874] *Scientists Tap Power of "Lucifer"*, Chelsea Schilling, WND
http://www.wnd.com/2013/01/what-the-devil-scientists-tap-power-of-lucifer/#!
[1875] *Vatican and Lucifer*, Super User, 10 October 2012, Vatican Observatory.org
http://vaticanobservatory.org/vo-news/news-archive/98-news-archive/vatican-lucifer/515-vatican-lucifer
[1876] *Pope's Astronomer Says He Would Baptise An Alien If It Asked Him*, Alok Jha, 17 September 2010, the Guardian
http://www.theguardian.com/science/2010/sep/17/pope-astronomer-baptise-aliens
[1877] *Messengers of Deception UFO Contacts and Cults*, Jacques Vallée, Daily Grail (2008), p. vi
[1878] *The 95 Theses* (English), Luther.de
http://www.luther.de/en/95thesen.html
[1879] *Secret Counsels of the Society of Jesus*, Robert Breckinridge, Baltimore: Edward J. Cole & Co. (1835), pp. 69, 92
[1880] *A Woman Rides The Beast*, Dave Hunt, Harvest House (1994), p. 75
[1881] *Belshazzar*, Encyclopædia Britannica

http://www.britannica.com/EBchecked/topic/60121/Belshazzar
[1882] *Christianity and Evolution*, Pierre Teilhard de Chardin, Harcourt (1971), p. 40
[1883] *ibid*, pp. 43, 44
[1884] *ibid*, p. 45
[1885] *ibid*, p. 47
[1886] *Pope Francis Reaches Out to Atheists and Agnostics*, Nick Squires, 11 Sep 2013, the Telegraph
http://www.telegraph.co.uk/news/worldnews/the-pope/10302850/Pope-Francis-reaches-out-to-atheists-and-agnostics.html
[1887] *Roman Catholic Bishop Wants Everyone to Call God "Allah"*, unattributed, 16 August 2007, FoxNews
http://www.foxnews.com/story/2007/08/16/roman-catholic-bishop-wants-everyone-to-call-god-allah/
[1888] *Pope Francis Bows, Asks For Blessing From Ecumenical Patriarch Bartholomew In Extraordinary Display Of Christian Unity*, Nicole Winfield and Suzan Fraser, 30 November 2014, AP via Huffington Blows
http://www.huffingtonpost.com/2014/11/30/pope-francis-ecumenical-patriarch-bartholomew-_n_6243414.html
[1889] *Pope Francis Prays in Istanbul's Blue Mosque*, Reuters, 29 November 2014, Newsweek
http://www.newsweek.com/pope-francis-prays-istanbuls-blue-mosque-288014
[1890] *Pope Francis Appeases The Religion Of The Antichrist, Enters A Mosque, And Prays Toward Mecca During The Islamic Call To Prayer*, Theodore Shoebat, 29 November 2014, Shoebat.com
http://shoebat.com/2014/11/29/pope-francis-appeases-religion-antichrist-enters-mosque-pays-toward-mecca-islamic-call-prayer/
[1891] *Pope Says It Is Wrong To Equate Islam With Violence*, Philip Pullella, 30 November 2014, Reuters
http://uk.reuters.com/article/2014/11/30/uk-pope-turkey-mideast-idUKKCN0JE0AB20141130
[1892] *Malaysia: Jesuit Priest Under Fire For Use of the Name "Allah" in Reference to God*, Marco Tosatti, 23 January 2014, the Vatican Insider
http://vaticaninsider.lastampa.it/en/world-news/detail/articolo/malesia-malasia-malaysia-allah-31481/
[1893] *Priapism (Permanent Erection)*, WikiIslam.net
http://wikiislam.net/wiki/Priapism_-_Permanent_Erection
[1894] *First Ever Jewish, Muslim, Christian Prayers at Vatican*, Reuters, 8 June 2014, the NY Post
http://nypost.com/2014/06/08/first-ever-jewish-muslim-christian-prayers-at-vatican/
[1895] *ibid*
[1896] *Rick Warren's Call for Christians to Unite With Catholics, "Holy Father" Raising Concerns*, Heather Clark, 2 December 2014, Christian News
http://christiannews.net/2014/12/02/rick-warrens-call-for-christians-to-unite-with-catholics-holy-father-raising-concerns/
[1897] *Membership Roster; W*, Council on Foreign Relations
http://www.cfr.org/about/membership/roster.html?letter=W
[1898] *Theodore Edgar McCarrick*, Wikipedia

769

http://en.wikipedia.org/wiki/Theodore_Edgar_McCarrick
[1899] *SBC Leader Supports Gun Control*, Bob Allen, 24 January 2013, Baptist News
http://baptistnews.com/culture/social-issues/item/8158-sbc-leader-supports
[1900] *Ongoing Programs*, the Council on Foreign Relations
http://www.cfr.org/world/role-religion-us-foreign-policy-focus-new-council-initiative/p9771
[1901] *Joel Osteen Talks Pope, Gays And Why You Should "Pray For Big Things"*, Josh Zepps, 2 October 2013, Huffington Blows
http://www.huffingtonpost.com/2013/10/02/joel-osteen-pope_n_4031530.html
[1902] *Like Pope Francis? You'll Love Jesus.* Elizabeth Tenety, 11 December 2013, the Washington Post
http://www.washingtonpost.com/opinions/like-pope-francis-youll-love-jesus/2013/12/11/cf2d4fd8-610d-11e3-8beb-3f9a9942850f_story.html
[1903] *Why do Protestants Love Pope Francis? EWTN's Raymond Arroyo weighs in.* Jonathan Merritt, 2 December 2013, Religion News Service
http://jonathanmerritt.religionnews.com/2013/12/02/why-evangelicals-love-pope-francis-raymond-arroyo/
[1904] *Pope Francis History's "Final" Pontiff?* 13 March 2013, WND
http://www.wnd.com/2013/03/pope-francis-historys-final-pontiff/#!
[1905] *Barack Obama's Massive Middle East Mea Culpa*, Nile Gardiner, 4 June 2009, the Telegraph
http://blogs.telegraph.co.uk/nile_gardiner/blog/2009/06/04/barack_obamas_massive_middle_east_mea_culpa
[1906] *Is Obama The Clone of Akhenaten?*, Kemal Ottoman (cute), no idea what the correct date is (comments go back on the *Turkish* calendar 2 years), Gizlimi.com
http://gizlimi.com/ingilizce-makaleler/is-obama-the-clone-of-akhenaten-barackhenaten
[1907] *DNA Results For The Nephilim Skulls In Peru Are In And The Results Are Absolutely Shocking*, Michael Snyder, 10 February 2014, The Truth Wins.com
http://thetruthwins.com/archives/dna-results-for-the-nephilim-skulls-in-peru-are-in-and-the-results-are-absolutely-shocking
[1908] *Mystery Scars on Obama's Head Prompt Another Question From Conspiracy Theorists - Has the President Had Brain Surgery?* A unattributed, 6 April 2011, the Daily Mail
http://www.dailymail.co.uk/news/article-1373780/Mystery-scars-Obamas-head-begs-question--President-brain-surgery.html

Chapter 21

#ResistanceRising

> *Judah went up, and the Lord gave the Canaanites and the Perizzites into their hands, and they defeated ten thousand men at Bezek. They found Adoni-bezek in Bezek and fought against him, and they defeated the Canaanites and the Perizzites.*
>
> *But Adoni-bezek fled; and they pursued him and caught him and cut off his thumbs and big toes.*
>
> *Adoni-bezek said, "Seventy kings with their thumbs and their big toes cut off used to gather up scraps under my table; as I have done, so God has repaid me."*
>
> *So they brought him to Jerusalem and he died there.* ~ Judges 1:4-7

"They rule the world."

"They have captured America."

"They want one-world government, one-world commerce, one-world religion and a One World Order."

Who are "they"?

We have so far answered that question with; a handful of unspeakably wealthy families in league with the Vatican. The shock troops of Rome are the Jesuits who have become so powerful that they now "run the Pope". The Company of Loyola *is* "the Vatican" and now more than ever with a Jesuit White Pope who stands alongside the Jesuit Black Pope.

Are there forces behind even these?

To answer that question, one must be open to things unseen.

Openness of that nature may offend logical thinking, but such offense is actually quite dangerous.

> *"My dear brothers, never forget, when you hear the progress of enlightenment praised, that the most cunning wile of the devil is to persuade you that he doesn't exist."* ~ *The Generous Gambler*, Charles Pierre Baudelaire, 1869

Nimrodded

Was Nimrod the author of the first great rebellion against God? Was he genetically-altered to be a half human/half spirit anti-Christ?

Such a world leader, a "mighty hunter before the Lord", seems an unstoppable force yet tradition has it that Shem (son of Noah), filled with righteous indignation, rose up and punished the demigod hybrid.

The execution of this great rebel has echoed throughout the ages via several mythological legends but in those legends the antagonist is twisted to become an innocent victim. In these myths, the rebel was not apprehended by authorities and judged but secretly betrayed and subdued. [italics suspended]

> The death of the great ringleader of the apostasy was not the death of a warrior slain in battle, but an act of judicial rigour, solemnly inflicted. This is well established by the accounts of the deaths of both Tammuz and Osiris. ... From what is related of the Egyptian Hercules, we get very valuable light on this subject. It is admitted by Wilkinson that the most ancient Hercules, and truly primitive one, was he who was known in Egypt as having, "by the power of the gods" * (i.e., by the SPIRIT) fought against and overcome the Giants.
>
> * The name of the true God (Elohim) is plural. Therefore, "the power of the gods," and "of God," is expressed by the same term.
>
> Now, no doubt, the title and character of Hercules were afterwards given by the Pagans to him whom they worshipped as the grand deliverer or Messiah, just as the adversaries of the Pagan divinities came to be stigmatised as the "Giants" who rebelled against Heaven. But let the reader only reflect who were the real Giants that rebelled against Heaven. They were Nimrod and his party; for the "Giants" were just the "Mighty ones," of whom Nimrod was the leader. Who, then, was most likely to head the opposition to the apostasy from the primitive worship? If Shem was at that time alive, as beyond question he was, who so likely as he? In exact accordance with this deduction, we find that one of the names of the primitive Hercules in Egypt was "Sem."
>
> If "Sem," then, was the primitive Hercules, who overcame the Giants, and that not by mere physical force, but by "the power of God," or the influence of the Holy Spirit, that entirely agrees with his character; and more than that, it remarkably agrees with the

Egyptian account of the death of Osiris. The Egyptians say, that the grand enemy of their god overcame him, not by open violence, but that, having entered into a conspiracy with seventy-two of the leading men of Egypt, he got him into his power, put him to death, and then cut his dead body into pieces, and sent the different parts to so many different cities throughout the country. The real meaning of this statement will appear, if we glance at the judicial institutions of Egypt. Seventy-two was just the number of the judges, both civil and sacred, who, according to Egyptian law, were required to determine what was to be the punishment of one guilty of so high an offence as that of Osiris, supposing this to have become a matter of judicial inquiry. ~ *The Two Babylons*, Alexander Hislop[1909]

Tradition holds that this event fell on a "day of infamy" for the Luciferians.

...Shem came to Egypt and, being a very eloquent person, convinced a group of seventy two powerful and influential Egyptians to assist him in the execution of the wicked ruler. Nimrod's loyal followers and spies immediately gathered his forces and attacked the forces of Shem and his Egyptian allies. The numbers favored Nimrod, but the command to execute Nimrod had been given by God through Noah. Nimrod's forces were defeated, God giving the victory to Shem's smaller forces.

When Nimrod saw his forces defeated, he fled for his life and went into hiding in Italy. But Shem and his followers followed him there, found him and executed him. His dead body was cut into pieces, and the pieces sent to different areas, including Egypt, as a warning of what would happen to the apostates if they followed Nimrod's God-defying practices. According to ancient tradition his death took place in the summer of 2121 [BC[sss]] on the 17th day of the month of Tammuz.

Slaying of Nimrod sent shock waves and fear among the rebels, and any who would worship the Sun-fire-serpent god, or sacrifice humans or their own children in the fire. They would no longer worship the Sun-fire-serpent god openly, but had to invent mysteries to continue their pagan worship. ~ *Satan vs. God*, Herman Saini[1910]

[sss] This *Christian* used the convention of "BCE", "Before 'Common Era'". It is both ridiculous (the dates don't change, Christ is still the Source, just relabeled to obscure Him) and blasphemous.

And go underground they did.

The month of Tammuz is from the Assyrian/Babylonian calendar and adopted by the Hebrews—named after the child of Semiramis and deified in myth.

Did Semiramis come up with the elaborate story of impregnating herself with the phallus of her dead husband (which is now the centerpiece of America's capital) because she was impregnated by means which created another hybrid?

In the National Theatre of Miskolc, Hungary sits a statue of Tammuz by artist Imre Schrammel; its appearance is that of a classic Minotaur.

Mythological beasts that are part human/part animal appear to imply a technology for creating living creatures that can easily be inhabited by malignant interdimensional beings.

But even in their rebellion, they only seek to imitate the Divine.

Tammuz—the chosen son of the Queen of Heaven—is a figure of untimely death and mourning, executed before his time. Whether we speak of Nimrod or the son of Semiramis, the two are joined in mythology.

Szalax – Wikimedia Commons

Tammuz worship was the first "secret society".

Great judgment was brought down upon Israel because the elders (men in authority) worshipped demon deities "in the dark"—

"...they say, 'The Lord does not see us...'" ~ Ezekiel 8:12

—and the women mourned for Tammuz openly. [Ezekiel 8:14]

In Exodus 32, we read of how Moses came down from Sinai with the tablets of the Law only to find his own people in orgies of sex magick and drunken revelry, worshipping before a golden calf of whom his own brother had crafted for them and said blasphemously:

"This is your god, O Israel, who brought you up from the land of Egypt!" ~ Exodus 32:4

Apis, the Egyptian bull deity was sometimes depicted as a Minotaur-like creature with the head of a bull and the body of a man.[1911]

Moses smashed the Law at their feet. He ground the golden icon to fine powder, cast it upon the waters and made them drink it. [Exodus 32:20]

Still they refused to cease their revelry.

So Moses called to the men of Israel, "You who are for the Lord, rally to me!" The sons of Levi heard the call and came to Moses who told them to gird themselves with a sword and cut down the revelers, every man and his brother.

Jewish tradition holds that this also occurred on the 17th of Tammuz.[1912]

Perhaps we now see the "magic" of IMF Managing Director Christine Lagarde's numerology promise to the National Press Club being fulfilled in the downing of Malaysian Airlines flight MH-17 (downed on July 17th of 2014[ttt]) and the subsequent framing of Russia.

Did they expect World War III to have resulted? By being so obtuse, they avoid the humiliation of their failure except to those in the know or the few who have deciphered their "code".

Don't worry, they'll keep working towards war. It's their best and favorite method of killing us and enriching them.

Like many other significant pagan dates, "All Hallows' Eve" (Halloween) was appropriated by Rome for celebration[1913] (along with the "Easter"/Ishtar/Isis festival[1914]).

It was on October 31st, 1517[1915] that Martin Luther nailed his 95 theses on the door of the *All Saints Church* in Wittenberg. 17 years later, Ignatius Loyola first assembled his Company while in France in 1534.

In 2015, the 17th of Tammuz falls on the 4th of July.

Full-Spectrum Christianity

Where is America in the Bible?

Pious and sanctimonious preachers rail against the USA in King James Shakespearian as the Whore of Babylon (if anything, we have been the Beast

---

[ttt] This was the 19th of Tammuz in the Hebrew year 5774.

for the Whore). In essence, they do the devil's work for him by convincing their sheep that we live in a no-win situation. Just wait for the Rapture, there's nothing else we can do.

But the reality is that there's a *Divine Reason* America isn't in Scripture.

Our demonic enemies have an advantage on us in their ability to see what we can not see, either through an earthly intelligence network or an ethereal perspective on the river of time.

But even they only see through a glass darkly.

The Divine Chessmaster has purposely left America out of the Bible to keep her destiny in play. Can she be ripped from the clutches of evil by a handful of the righteous? Of course! All it takes is for them to get inspired.

A journey of a thousand miles begins with a single step...
~ Lao Tzu from the *Tao Te Ching*, Chapter 64

I'm excited to see what happens on July 4th, 2015.

Perhaps nothing.

Perhaps nothing you are allowed to be privy to.

There is no such thing as a completely "secular state" and the best examples of what comes close to that ideal were the Soviet Union and today's "People's Republic" of China who, combined, slaughtered nearly one hundred and fifty million of their own citizens.

Christians will often eschew their responsibility to speak out against injustice because Christ said before Pilate, *"My Kingdom is not of this world."* [John 18:36]

Yet they neglect the context.

The context is that mankind was forbidden from partaking of the Glory of God by sin. The Sin Offering was made by Christ who was both High Priest *and* the sacrifice!

Like Melchizedek, Christ is both priest *and* king. Please see *Hebrews 7:17*.

It was important for Pilate's own guilt that Jesus not allow Himself to be perceived as a political threat, and to fulfill His first mission.

The Kingdom of the Son of God being "not of this world" is a technicality as the *entirety* of Creation is His [Colossians 1:16]. It is up to the stewards He left behind to accept His Authority or reject it.

Christians who accept the pluralism woven by Jesuit agents such as the Carrolls are like the servant who buried the one talent he had.

He ended up being assigned a place with the heathen where there is great "weeping and gnashing of teeth".

Some religious *are* better than others.

A nation receives its legitimacy based upon the foundation of its culture and laws. At one time, despite the influence of Luciferians, Jesuits and their secret society henchmen, America proudly held Christianity as that foundation and it was the source of all other freedoms.

> *"It can not be emphasized too strongly or too often that this great nation was founded, not by religionists, but by Christians; not on religions, but on the Gospel of Jesus Christ. For this very reason peoples of other faiths have been afforded asylum, prosperity and freedom of worship here."* ~ Patrick Henry, March 23rd, 1775 at the Second Virginian Convention given at St. John's Church in Richmond, Virginia

Within *three days* of telling Pontius Pilate "My Kingdom is not of this world," Jesus Christ sat down at the Right Hand of the Father and received His full Authority. [Mark 16:19]

Dominion Theology

> **Dominion Theology** or **Dominionism** *is the idea that Christians should work toward either a nation governed by Christians or one governed by a conservative Christian understanding of biblical law. At least under this name, it exists primarily among non-mainstream Protestants in the United States. It is a form of theocracy and is related to theonomy, though it does not necessarily advocate Mosaic law as the basis of government. Prominent adherents of Dominion Theology are otherwise theologically diverse, including the Calvinist Christian Reconstructionism and the charismatic/Pentecostal Kingdom Now theology and New Apostolic Reformation. ...*
>
> *The term "Dominion Theology" is derived from the King James Bible's rendering of Genesis 1:28, the passage in which God grants humanity "dominion" over the Earth.*

> *And God blessed [Adam and Eve], and God said unto them, "Be fruitful, and multiply, and replenish the earth, and subdue it: and have dominion over the fish of the sea, and over the fowl of the air, and over every living thing that moveth upon the earth."*
>
> *In the late 1980s, several prominent evangelical authors used the phrase Dominion Theology (and other terms such as dominionism) to label a loose grouping of theological movements that made direct appeals to this passage in Genesis.[1] Christians typically interpret this passage as meaning that God gave humankind responsibility over the Earth, but the distinctive aspect of Dominion Theology is that it is interpreted as a mandate for Christian stewardship in civil affairs, no less than in other human matters.* ~ Wikipedia[1916]

Some will call the desire to see Christian virtue returned to guide America as "Dominionism". If "Dominion Theology" is consistent with the above definition, so be it. It is neither heresy nor misguided. It is the ultimate outcome of a Believer who gives in proportion to what they have received.

"Christians" who fear putting their faith to power often harbor secret sins they wish to remain uninterrupted. Like fleshly Israelites with the choices of *war* or *slavery* before them, they long for the leeks and cucumbers of Egypt...even if it means a taskmaster puts his foot on their neck and the necks of their children.

If America does not have Christianity as her compass, alternatives will be substituted—and have already been.

The secular hedonism imposed on America by unaccountable agents of the Papal Luciferian Elite has taken a terrible toll. [italics suspended]

> Education expert William Jeynes said on Wednesday that there is a correlation between the decline of U.S. public schools and the U.S. Supreme Court's 1962 and 1963 decision that school-sponsored Bible reading was unconstitutional.
>
> "One can argue, and some have, that the decision by the Supreme Court – in a series of three decisions back in 1962 and 1963 – to remove Bible and prayer from our public schools, may be the most spiritually significant event in our nation's history over the course of the last 55 years," Jeynes said.
>
> On June 25, 1962, the United States Supreme Court decided in

Engel v. Vitale that a prayer approved by the New York Board of Regents for use in schools violated the First Amendment because it represented establishment of religion. In 1963, in Abington School District v. Schempp, the court decided against Bible readings in public schools along the same lines.

Since 1963, Jeynes said there have been five negative developments in the nation's public schools:

- Academic achievement has plummeted, including SAT scores.
- Increased rate of out-of-wedlock births
- Increase in illegal drug use
- Increase in juvenile crime
- Deterioration of school behavior

"So we need to realize that these actions do have consequences," said Jeynes, professor at California State College in Long Beach and senior fellow at the Witherspoon Institute in Princeton, N.J., "When we remove that moral fiber—that moral emphasis – this is what can result." ~ Penny Starr, CNS News[1917]

They do plan to replace it with a religious authority, however. But it won't be a Christian one.

> *This study* [of 50 American court cases] *evaluates published appellate legal cases that involved "conflict of law" issues between Shariah (Islamic law) and American state law. For every case in this sample drawn from published appellate legal cases, there are innumerable cases at the trial level that remain unnoticed except by the participants. Thus, this report is a only a sample of possible cases—a "tip of the iceberg"—of legal cases involving Shariah in local, state and federal courts.*
>
> *Our findings suggest that Shariah law has entered into state court decisions, in conflict with the Constitution and state public policy. Some commentators have said there are no more than one or two cases of Shariah law in U.S. state court cases; yet we found 50 significant cases just from the small sample of appellate published cases. Others state with certainty that state court judges will always reject any foreign law, including Shariah law, when it conflicts with the Constitution or state public policy; yet we found 15 Trial Court cases, and 12 Appellate Court cases, where Shariah was found to be applicable in the case at bar. The facts are the facts: some judges are making decisions deferring to Shariah law*

even when those decisions conflict with Constitutional protections. This is a serious issue and should be a subject of public debate and engagement by policymakers. ~ The Center for Security Policy[1918]

Said "Dominionism" should not be confused with any post millennial heresy which states Christians must *create* Christ's Kingdom to usher in His Return. The Divine Sovereign acts completely independent of anything humanity does.

This isn't about developing Christ: it's about developing *you*. Fighting the Machine may be insurmountable but, as a Christian, *you are required to act*.

Critics of the desire to utilize Christian teachings as the basis for public policy will point toward the many failures of the Jerry Falwell "Moral Majority".

The failures, however, were the result of the Elite skillfully co-opting that movement with Jesuit actors.

Tim LaHaye's *Left Behind* series has been a veritable narcotic, anesthetizing Christians from their civic duty lest they invest too much before the Rapture whisks them from experiencing challenge, trial, trauma or tribulation.

It is interesting to note that, in LaHaye's imaginary series, a future "Pope John XXIV" is also a beneficiary of the *raptura*.[1919]

LaHaye founded the Council for National Policy during the "hayday" of the Moral Majority (1981) to help steer "Conservative Christian" policy initiatives.

> *Marc J. Ambinder of ABC News said about the Council: "The group wants to be the conservative version of the Council on Foreign Relations." The CNP was founded in 1981. Among its founding members were: Tim LaHaye, then the head of the Moral Majority, Nelson Bunker Hunt, T. Cullen Davis, William Cies, and Paul Weyrich.*[4]

> *Members of the CNP have included: General John Singlaub, shipping magnate J. Peter Grace, Edwin J. Feulner Jr of the Heritage Foundation, Rev. Pat Robertson of the Christian Broadcasting Network, Jerry Falwell, U.S. Senator Trent Lott, Southern Baptist Convention activists and retired Texas Court of Appeals Judge Paul Pressler, and the Reverend Paige Patterson,*[5] *Senator Don Nickles, former United States Attorneys General Ed*

Meese and John Ashcroft, gun-rights activist Larry Pratt, Col. Oliver North, and philanthropist Elsa Prince, mother of Erik Prince, the founder of the Blackwater private security firm.[6] ~ Wikipedia[1920]

Nelson Hunt was part of the coalition that had targeted John F. Kennedy as a Communist sympathizer. When Kennedy arrived in Dallas the day of his murder, a Hunt attack-ad blazed across the Dallas papers.

Nelson Bunker Hunt was behind the hostile ad that confronted Kennedy in the November 22 edition of the Dallas Morning News (23 WH 690), an ad which, at a sponsor's insistence (5 WH 507-09) attacked the CIA for "arranging coups [i.e., against Diem[uuu]] *and having staunch Anti-Communist allies of the U.S. bloodily exterminated" (18 WH 835).* ~ Deep Politics and the Death of JFK, Peter Dale Scott[1921]

The CNP was completely infiltrated by Catholic agents and Knights of Malta.

The secretive Council for National Policy was formed in 1981 by Tim LaHaye, author of the "Left-Behind" series, with funding from Texas billionaires Nelson Bunker Hunt, Herbert Hunt and T. Cullen Davis. ...

The agenda of a meeting in Colorado Springs in 1982 listed [Richard] Viguerie and fellow Catholics Terry Dolan, Pat Buchanan, Phyllis Schafley, Jeane Kirkpatrick (US Ambassador to the UN) and Frank Shakespeare—Knight of Malta, former president of CBS Television, director of Radio Free Europe, vice president of Westinghouse, vice chairman of RKO General and member of the board of trustees for the Heritage Foundation—as speakers. Maj. Gen. John Singlaub ret. (a WACL operative on special operations in El Salvador at the time), Philip Trulock of the Heritage Foundation, and Joseph Coors were also listed as members of the Council. Other realy supporters of the CNP included Fr. Charles C. Fiore, chairman of the National Pro-Life PAC, Knights of Malta J. Peter Grace and Lewis Lehrman, Howard Phillips and Lt. Col. Oliver North. ~ The Neo-Catholics, Betty Clermont[1922]

[uuu] Ngo Dinh Diem, the Catholic President of South Vietnam who was overthrown and murdered.

Resistance Rising

The centerpiece of the Vatican's efforts for one-world religion are through the Pentecostal and Charismatic Protestant sects. It is here that church-goers are more likely to *feel* direction rather than test it as the Bible requires. [Acts 17:11, I Thessalonians 5:20-21, I John 4:1-3]

Controversial[1923,1924] televangelist Kenneth Copeland gathered together a massive room full of Charismatics in February of 2014 so that they could receive an intimate message recorded for them in secret[1925] by the Pope's personal emissary—International Ecumenical Officer for the Communion of Evangelical Episcopal Churches, Bishop Tony Palmer.[1926]

In the message, Palmer told his audience, "...the Protest is over!" "The glory binds us together, not the doctrine..." and "we'll sort out the doctrine later."

As the Jesuits well know, it's an axiom of assassination that "'accidents' work best" and operating a small, fast craft make "accidents" look good.

Former Director of the CIA William Colby died in a "boating accident".[1927]

While looking in to a Nebraska pedophile sex slave ring, private investigator Gary Caradori died in a small plane crash with his son.[1928]

Rolling Stone reporter Michael Hastings died in a fiery car wreck[1929]. Subsequent investigations have proven that *any* of today's processor-ridden vehicles can be remotely hacked and controlled to speed up and crash as his did.[1930]

If there was one man critical to bringing Protestants together under Rome it was rising star, Anglican Bishop Tony Palmer. Charismatic (by character, not belief) and knowledgeable, he was making great strides in ecumenism for Pope Francis.

These efforts all came to a screeching halt on the back of a motorcycle.[1931]

Tony Palmer, Who Captured Pope Francis' Bid For Christian Unity With A Cellphone, Dies After Motorcycle Crash

Bishop Tony Palmer, a charismatic preacher who used a cellphone camera to record Pope Francis issuing an appeal for Christian unity between Catholics and evangelicals, died Sunday (July 20) after a motorcycle crash in the United Kingdom.

In January, Palmer held the smartphone that recorded Pope Francis calling on all Christians to set aside their differences. Palmer, a bishop and international ecumenical officer with the independent Communion of Evangelical Episcopal Churches, also helped coordinate the pope's meeting with televangelists in June.

In the video, Pope Francis referred to Palmer as "my brother, a bishop-brother," saying they had been friends for years. "Let us allow our longing to increase so that it propels us to find each other, embrace each other and to praise Jesus Christ as the only Lord of history," Francis said. ~ Sarah Bailey, the Washington Post[1932]

Is there a Counter-Counter Reformation playing by the Company's ruthless rules?

Complex assassinations of that caliber require substantial assets and serious players. Who around the world is capable?

While covering the conflict in Ukraine, a VICE News journalist was apprehended by pro-Russian rebels. The behavior of several western journalists lead the rebels to believe that they were being exploited as intelligence gatherers. As a result, they arrested VICE reporter Simon Ostrovsky.

Ostrovsky was later released in one piece with just bumps and bruises but something he observed and later relayed in an interview was very interesting.

There were two sort-of groups of guards that we had, maybe even three.

There were our caretakers who were unarmed and wearing civilian clothing. Then there were a group of guards who were definitely locals from Slovyansk—the town itself—who had rag-tag camouflage clothing that they'd managed to put together themselves.

And then there was a higher group of what everybody in the cellar [detention area of the captured SBU building] *called "the Special Ops guys"—*спецый*—and they were...they're what's also called "the Little Green Men" everybody suspects to have some kind of ties to Russia but nobody's been able to prove it yet.*

To me, I couldn't verify 100% for myself if they were Russian or not. They sounded like they had southern accents, to me, which could be Ukrainian or from Southern Russia.

My true feeling about the people who were dealing with us is that they were members of—that they were military veterans who had been member[s] of some kind of organization together, even before this conflict began.

They had this sort of nationalist/religious/fundamentalist/Orthodox/Christian ideology that they kept talking about.[1933]

"Be Strong and of Good Courage!"

In I Samuel 14 is a thrilling story of how Jonathan, the son of Israel's first king, Saul, was filled with a fiery spirit to turn the tables on the oppressive Philistines. He encouraged his armor-bearer to come with him and challenge an entire Philistine outpost. When the Philistines heard his challenge, they were surprised and mocked him, "Look at the Hebrews popping up out of the holes where they were hiding!" [I Samuel 14:11]

Jonathan even gave his enemies the choice, come to him or invite him to them. They did the latter.

Even so, he cunningly picked key terrain for his fight, between two crags. The passage actually gives you their names; *Bozez* and *Seneh*.

Jonathan routed the entire outpost and quickly scattered 20 slain enemies across a ½ acre of land as the Philistines eventually fled in terror. Like a keen warrior, Jonathan had his armor bearer cover behind them and even he felled foes. [I Samuel 14:13]

A literal "fear of God" overcame the entire Philistine camp, helped along by an earthquake. The Philistines panicked and fled and the turncoat Hebrews who had been fighting for them turned again and attacked them in their own camps. [I Samuel 14:21]

What do *Bozez* and *Seneh* mean? According to the International Standard Bible Encyclopedia, Bozez means "shining" and Seneh means "thornbush". Thornbushes are symbolic of the curse of sin, the impediment to a hard day's work of tilling the soil. A thornbush on fire means "sin: judged, vanquished." It was out of a burning bush that Moses heard the Voice of the Lord. Yeshua ha Nazareth identified Himself as that Voice [John 8:58] and it was the Mashiach who vanquished sin for those who believe in Him. Did Jesus Christ stand with Jonathan that day?

To make earth-shattering changes, the God of the Bible doesn't need an army, just 300 good men.

The battle of the pass at Thermopylae between Greece and Persia has echoed through the ages to become greatly embellished by Hollywood, recently. The movie 300 (2006) portrayed 300 Mr. Universe-bodied Spartans holding off innumerable Persians until they all perished. However, even the Greek historian Herodotus lists the Greek numbers as having started at 7,000 and then dwindling to 1,000 Thespians and Spartans. The 700 Thespians are now today's most invisible heroes.[1934]

The Bible tells of an *actual* "300"...and they won.

In Judges 7, the unlikely son of a prostitute (Gideon), had been made general over the armies of Israel in a desperate plea to stave off oppressors like the Midianites. As Gideon assembled his men, a Word from the Lord came, "You have too many. Weed out the weak." [Judges 7:2]

Gideon made the announcement, that any soldier afraid for his life was invited to leave the encampment. 22,000 left and 10,000 stayed. [Judges 7:3]

The Lord gave special instructions that were very insightful. He had Gideon take his men to water, those that lowered their whole body to drink with abandon, he was to reject. Those who lifted the water to their mouths and kept situationally-aware, he kept. They numbered only 300. [Judges 7:4-6]

It takes but a few sheepdogs to protect the sheep and rouse the rams.

Magnificent Conclusion

Today, the Luciferian Elite have it all. Political Parties, judges and generals; all follow the agenda of enslavement and domination for the destruction of America.

When the people speak overwhelmingly, their voice is countered by a single Federal Judge, their upstart newly-elected representatives are immediately mitigated and marginalized in Congress by entrenched insiders.

Every mega-corporation is on board, every billionaire, every key leader have all been vetted, blackmailed and/or bribed.

Even local Police departments have been outfitted with drones and armored military vehicles.

Americans have been poisoned, dumbed down, and inundated with foreigners hostile to their values and way of life.

But it's all a house of cards.

All it will take is one spark when the wrong citizen is killed; when the wrong child is kidnapped by "Social Services"; when the wrong family dog is shot during a "no-knock" warrant or the wrong piece of property is confiscated.

Author William Dean Garner says the Jesuits use "celestiophysics"[vvv] to time their agenda and 2012 was a year of over-reach for them. In an e-mail to me, Garner wrote:

> *When a significant celestiophysical event occurs, the Jesuits must then accurately time their actions and events on Earth just right to produce the largest possible event, say, collapse of financial markets or increased rainfall in a certain region. The Jesuits overestimated the magnitudes of celestiophysical events in 2012 and thus appear to have carried out their own attacks using too much force and overkill and thus expended or wasted energy, which is something they hate to do. Celestiophysical energy is a precious resource, not a commodity.*

Even the most powerful angelic enemy is still a created being with flaws and limitations.

Do-nothing Christians claim as their writ for inaction, that our enemies are incorporeal.

> *For we wrestle not against flesh and blood, but against principalities, against powers, against the rulers of the darkness of this world, against spiritual wickedness in high places.* ~ Ephesians 6:12, KJV

What they fail to deduce is that not only are our enemies angelic, but so are our allies—and they outnumber them $2/3^{rds}$ to $1/3^{rd}$! [Revelation 12:4]

In *The Magnificent Seven* our mercenary cowboys put up a great fight defending the village. The banditos are stung hard, several die, and they are forced to retreat.

[vvv] A term used by Garner to mean study of trends and cycles (many of which are precipitated by heavenly bodies) and the strategic exploitation of their effects upon the Earth. See also *Cycles: The Mysterious Forces That Trigger Events*, Edward R. Dewey, Prentice-Hall (1971)

But they don't go away. They can't. They have no food. They must conquer the village or perish in the cold of winter.

When the villagers learn of this, they are distraught. Traitors betray their defenders. Leaders in the village are imprisoned and the cowboys are captured. The banditos respect them, however, and give them the option to leave unharmed and never return.

But something compels them all to throw care to the wind and return to the village to free it of its oppressors. The motto of the United States Special Forces is *De Oppresso Liber*; "to the burdened—freedom."

Now the mercenaries must assault and the banditos defend.

It is an axiom in Infantry tactics that, to attack on a fortified, waiting enemy, the assault must have a 3 to 1 advantage in numbers yet our heroes started the fight already outnumbered.

Slowly, they begin to fall in battle.

"Lee" (Robert Vaughn) is the man who wrestles with fear the most and he commits himself to one act of bravery: free the three village Patriots who were imprisoned for organizing the town defense.

When they are freed, they rush into the streets, picking up axes, scythes, clubs and rocks to join the outnumbered cowboys.

It starts an avalanche of town support and even the turncoats are compelled to help rout the Banditos.

When the Patriots run into the streets in America...where will you be?

Illuminati Unmasked

Endnotes

[1909] *The Two Babylons; or the Papal Worship: Proved to be the Worship of Nimrod and His Wife*, Loizeaux Brothers (1916), pp. 56-57
[1910] *Satan vs. God, Volume II*, Herman Saini, Xulon Press (2009), p. 354
[1911] *Ancient Egyptian Gods – Apis*, Art Fctory.com
http://www.artyfactory.com/egyptian_art/egyptian_gods/apis.htm
[1912] *Chodesh Tammuz—A Month of Tragedies and Mourning*, John Parsons, Hebrew4Christians
http://www.hebrew4christians.com/Holidays/Rosh_Chodesh/Tammuz/tammuz.html
  I love these covetus assholes who protect their pages so that you can't copy and paste what's on them, as if that will forever keep their words from being plagiarized—and a "religious" one at that.
[1913] *History of All Hallows' Eve*, Jennifer Gregory Miller, 2003, Catholic Culture.org
http://www.catholicculture.org/culture/liturgicalyear/overviews/months/10_2.cfm
[1914] *Happy Easter, Ishtar, Isis Goddess of Fertility, Sex and War Wife of Satan*, osiris mann YouTube
https://www.youtube.com/watch?v=KQ7WiAC9-ul
  This jerkoff did his video with the assumption that Christians actually worship his pagan whore instead of Christ thanks to Rome. Don't bother watching the semi-accurate video, you get the point. Look up the connections yourself.
  But I had to leave this comment:
Actually, the answer to all of this is simple: ROME.

The Catholic Church is NOT pagan, much like Islam (a "religion" enabled by the White and Black Popes), it is a SYSTEM of total CONTROL and it appropriated your pagan ritual and handed it to Christians for power and emphasis.

The pagans knew Spring was a time of rebirth but they didn't know why: it was the culmination of the Sacrifice of the Son of God which gives us SPIRITUAL rebirth.

As to your snarky attitude of ignorance that assumes real "Christians" unknowingly worship your sex whore...piss off.
[1915] *The 95 Theses and their Results (1517-1519)*, KDG Wittenberg 1997
http://www.luther.de/en/anschlag.html
[1916] *Dominion Theology*, Wikipedia
http://en.wikipedia.org/wiki/Dominion_Theology
[1917] *Education Expert: Removing Bible, Prayer from Public Schools Has Caused Decline*, Penny Starr, 15 August 2014, CNS News
http://www.cnsnews.com/news/article/penny-starr/education-expert-removing-bible-prayer-public-schools-has-caused-decline
[1918] *Shariah Law and American State Courts*, 21 June 2011, The Center for Security Policy, Johnny Cirucci Scribd
https://www.scribd.com/doc/249686778/American-Courts-Acknowledging-Sharia-Law
[1919] *The Authorized Left Behind Handbook*, Tim LaHaye and Jerry Jenkins, Tyndale House (2004), p. 209
[1920] *Council for National Policy > Meetings and Membership*, Wikipedia

http://en.wikipedia.org/wiki/Council_for_National_Policy#Meetings_and_membership
[1921] *Deep Politics and the Death of JFK*, Peter Dale Scott, University of California Press (1993), p. 214
[1922] *The Neo-Catholics: Implementing Christian Nationalism In America*, Betty Clermont, SCB Distributors (2011), online digital copy with no frigging page numbers
 This woman is a prize moron (doubtless a diarrhea-brained Leftist) who dug up great dirt yet thought these Catholic insurgents were working for "Christian Nationalism in America".
[1923] *Kenneth Copeland*, Apostasy Watch
http://www.apostasywatch.com/Wolves/WolfReports/KennethCopeland/tabid/87/Default.aspx
[1924] *Kenneth Copeland*, Deception In The Church
http://www.deceptioninthechurch.com/kcopeland.html
[1925] *Pope Francis to Pentecostal Conference: Tears of Love, Spiritual Hugs*, Kathy Schiffer, 20 February 2014, Patheos.com
http://www.patheos.com/blogs/kathyschiffer/2014/02/pope-francis-to-pentecostal-conference-tears-of-love-spiritual-hugs/
[1926] *Pope Francis Sends Video Message to Kenneth Copeland - Lets Unite*, Prove All Things YouTube
https://www.youtube.com/watch?&v=uA4EPOfic5A
[1927] *William Colby > Death*, Wikipedia
https://en.wikipedia.org/wiki/William_Colby
[1928] *Special Report, FBI Killed Franklin Scandal Investigator from Wayne Madsen Report*, Roseanne Barr, 20 June 2014, Roseanne World
http://www.roseanneworld.com/blog/2014/06/special-report-fbi-killed-franklin-scandal-investigator-wayne-madsen-report/
 Clearly, I'm not a fan of Roseanne Barr but she's a wayward soul who fights her rabid Leftism with a portion of the Red Pill that she has yet to fully ingest (because she's afraid of waking up completely).
 But I do appreciate her re-posting the excellent work of NSA whistleblower-turned-journalist Wayne Madsen who, himself, is a flaming Leftist and who charges for access to his work which is an excellent way to insure no one sees it!
 Asshole.
[1929] *Rolling Stone Journalist Feared Prior to Crash His Car Was Tampered With: Report*, unattributed, 22 August 2013, FoxNews
http://www.foxnews.com/us/2013/08/22/michael-hastings-asked-to-use-neighbor-car-night-his-death-report/
[1930] *Researchers Hack Cars to Remotely Control Steering and Brakes*, James Vincent, 26 July 2013, the Independent
http://www.independent.co.uk/life-style/gadgets-and-tech/researchers-hack-cars-to-remotely-control-steering-and-brakes-8733723.html
[1931] *Bishop Tony Palmer, Champion of Unity, Dies in Motorcycle Accident*, Jennifer LeClaire, 21 July 2014, Charisma News
http://www.charismanews.com/us/44726-bishop-tony-palmer-champion-of-unity-dies-in-motorcycle-accident
[1932] *Tony Palmer, Who Captured Pope Francis' Bid For Christian Unity With A Cellphone, Dies After Motorcycle Crash*, Sarah Bailey, 22 July 2014, the Washington Post

http://www.washingtonpost.com/national/religion/tony-palmer-who-captured-pope-francis-bid-for-christian-unity-with-a-cellphone-dies-after-motorcycle-crash/2014/07/22/89a52fd0-11d9-11e4-ac56-773e54a65906_story.html

[1933] *Simon Ostrovsky Describes His Kidnapping: Russian Roulette In Ukraine (Dispatch 31)*, VICE News
https://www.youtube.com/watch?v=tQGRJN4Radk

[1934] *Battle of Thermopylae in Popular Culture*, Wikipedia
http://en.wikipedia.org/wiki/Battle_of_Thermopylae_in_popular_culture

Appendix A

The Secret Jesuit Leadership Oath

The following has been taken from the European Institute of Protestant Studies[1935]. [italics and indentation suspended]

When a Jesuit of the minor rank is to be elevated to command, he is conducted into the Chapel of the Convent of the Order, where there are only three others present, the principal or Superior standing in front of the altar. On either side stands a monk, one of whom holds a banner of yellow and white, which are the Papal colours, and the other a black banner with a dagger and red cross above a skull and crossbones, with the word INRI, and below them the words *IUSTUM NECAR REGES IMPIUS*. The meaning of which is: *It is just to exterminate or annihilate impious or heretical Kings, Governments, or Rulers.*

Upon the floor is a red cross at which the postulant or candidate kneels. The Superior hands him a small black crucifix, which he takes in his left hand and presses to his heart, and the Superior at the same time presents to him a dagger, which he grasps by the blade and holds the point against his heart, the Superior still holding it by the hilt, and thus addresses the postulant:

(The Superior speaks:)

My son, heretofore you have been taught to act the dissembler: among Roman Catholics to be a Roman Catholic, and to be a spy even among your own brethren; to believe no man, to trust no man. Among the Reformers, to be a Reformer; among the Huguenots, to be a Huguenot; among the Calvinists, to be a Calvinist; among other Protestants, generally to be a Protestant; and obtaining their confidence, to seek even to preach from their pulpits, and to denounce with all the vehemence in your nature our Holy Religion and the Pope; and even to descend so low as to become a Jew among Jews, that you might be enabled to gather together all information for the benefit of your Order as a faithful soldier of the Pope. You have been taught to plant insidiously the seeds of jealousy and hatred between communities, provinces, states that were at peace, and to incite them to deeds of blood, involving them in war with each other, and to create revolutions and civil wars in countries that were independent and prosperous, cultivating the arts and the sciences and enjoying the blessings of peace; to take sides with the combatants and to act secretly with your brother Jesuit, who might be engaged on the other side, but openly opposed to that with which you might be connected, only that the Church might be the gainer in the end, in the conditions fixed in the treaties for peace and that the end justifies the means.

You have been taught your duty as a spy, to gather all statistics, facts and information in your power from every source; to ingratiate yourself into the confidence of the family circle of Protestants and heretics of every class and character, as well as that of the merchant, the banker, the lawyer, among the schools and universities, in parliaments and legislatures, and the judiciaries and councils of state, and to be all things to all men, for the Pope's sake, whose servants we are unto death.

You have received all your instructions heretofore as a novice, a neophyte, and have served as co-adjurer, confessor and priest, but you have not yet been invested with all that is necessary to command in the Army of Loyola in the service of the Pope. You must serve the proper time as the instrument and executioner as directed by your superiors; for none can command here who has not consecrated his labours with the blood of the heretic; for "without the shedding of blood no man can be saved". Therefore, to fit yourself for your work and make your own salvation sure, you will, in addition to your former oath of obedience to your order and allegiance to the Pope, repeat after me:

(Text of the Oath:)

I_____, now in the presence of Almighty God, the blessed Virgin Mary, the blessed St. John the Baptist, the Holy Apostles, St. Peter and St. Paul, and all the saints, sacred host of Heaven, and to you, my Ghostly Father, the superior general of the Society of Jesus, founded by St. Ignatius Loyola, in the pontification of Paul the Third, and continued to the present, do by the womb of the Virgin, the matrix of God, and the rod of Jesus Christ, declare and swear that His Holiness, the Pope, is Christ's Vice-Regent and is the true and only head of the Catholic or Universal Church throughout the earth; and that by the virtue of the keys of binding and loosing given to His Holiness by my Saviour, Jesus Christ, he hath power to depose heretical Kings, Princes, States, Commonwealths, and Governments, and they may be safely destroyed.

Therefore to the utmost of my power I will defend this doctrine and His Holiness's right and custom against all usurpers of the heretical or Protestant authority whatever, especially the Lutheran Church of Germany, Holland, Denmark, Sweden and Norway, and the now pretended authority and Churches of England and Scotland, and the branches of same now established in Ireland and on the continent of America and elsewhere and all adherents in regard that they may be usurped and heretical, opposing the sacred Mother Church of Rome.

I do now denounce and disown any allegiance as due to any heretical king, prince or State, named Protestant or Liberal, or obedience to any of their laws, magistrates or officers. I do further declare the doctrine of the Churches of England and Scotland of the Calvinists, Huguenots, and others of the name of Protestants or Masons to be damnable, and they themselves to be damned who will not forsake the same.

I do further declare that I will help, assist, and advise all or any of His Holiness's agents, in any place where I should be, in Switzerland, Germany, Holland, Ireland or America, or in any other kingdom or territory I shall come to, and do my utmost to extirpate the heretical Protestant or Masonic doctrines and to destroy all their pretended powers, legal or otherwise. I do further promise and declare that, notwithstanding, I am dispensed with to assume any religion heretical for the propagation of the Mother Church's interest; to keep secret and private all her agents' counsels from time to time, as they entrust me, and not to divulge, directly or indirectly, by word, writing or circumstances whatever; but to execute all that should be proposed, given in charge, or discovered unto me by you, my Ghostly Father, or any of this sacred order.

I do further promise and declare that I will have no opinion or will of my own or any mental reservation whatever, even as a corpse or cadaver (*perinde ac cadaver*), but will unhesitatingly obey each and every command that I may receive from my superiors in the militia of the Pope and of Jesus Christ. That I will go to any part of the world whithersoever I may be sent, to the frozen regions north, jungles of India, to the centres of civilisation of Europe, or to the wild haunts of the barbarous savages of America without murmuring or repining, and will be submissive in all things, whatsoever is communicated to me.

I do further promise and declare that I will, when opportunity presents, make and wage relentless war, secretly and openly, against all heretics, Protestants and Masons, as I am directed to do, to extirpate them from the face of the whole earth; and that I will spare neither age, sex nor condition, and that will hang, burn, waste, boil, flay, strangle, and bury alive these infamous heretics; rip up the stomachs and wombs of their women, and crush their infants' heads against the walls in order to annihilate their execrable race. That when the same cannot be done openly I will secretly use the poisonous cup, the strangulation cord, the steel of the poniard, or the leaden bullet, regardless of the honour, rank, dignity or authority of the persons, whatever may be their condition in life, either public or private, as I at any time may be directed so to do by any agents of the Pope or Superior of the Brotherhood of the Holy Father of the Society of Jesus.

In confirmation of which I hereby dedicate my life, soul, and all corporal powers, and with the dagger which I now receive I will subscribe my name written in my blood in testimony thereof; and should I prove false, or weaken in my determination, may my brethren and fellow soldiers of the militia of the Pope cut off my hands and feet and my throat from ear to ear, my belly be opened and sulphur burned therein with all the punishment that can be inflicted upon me on earth, and my soul shall be tortured by demons in eternal hell forever. That I will in voting always vote for a Knight of Columbus in preference to a Protestant, especially a Mason, and that I will leave my party so to do; that if two Catholics are on the ticket I will satisfy myself which is the better supporter of Mother Church and vote accordingly. That I will not deal with or employ a Protestant if in my power to deal with or employ a Catholic. That I will place Catholic girls in Protestant families that a weekly report may be made of the inner movements of the heretics. That I will provide myself with arms and ammunition that I may be in readiness when the word is passed, or I am commanded to defend the Church either as an individual or with the militia of the Pope.

All of which I,_____, do swear by the blessed Trinity and blessed sacrament which I am now to receive to perform and on part to keep this my oath. In testimony hereof, I take this most holy and blessed sacrament of the Eucharist and witness the same further with my name written with the point of this dagger dipped in my own blood and seal in the face of this holy sacrament.

(He receives the wafer from the Superior and writes his name with the point of his dagger dipped in his own blood taken from over his heart.)

(Superior speaks:)

You will now rise to your feet and I will instruct you in the Catechism necessary to make yourself known to any member of the Society of Jesus belonging to this rank. In the first place, you, as a Brother Jesuit, will with another mutually make the ordinary sign of the cross as any ordinary Roman Catholic would; then one crosses his wrists, the palms of his hands open, and the other in answer crosses his feet, one above the other; the first points with forefinger of the right hand to the centre of the palm of the left, the other with the forefinger of the left hand points to the centre of the palm of the right; the first then with his right hand makes a circle around his head, touching it; the other then with the forefinger of his left hand touches the left side of his body just below his heart; the first then with his right hand draws it across the throat of the other, and the latter then with a dagger down the stomach and abdomen of the first. The first then says *Iustum*; and the other answers *Necar*; the first *Reges*; the other answers *Impious*. The first will then present a small piece of paper folded in a peculiar manner, four times, which the other will cut longitudinally and on opening the name *Jesu* will be found written upon the head and arms of a cross three times. You will then give and receive with him the following questions and answers:

From whither do you come? Answer: The Holy faith.

Whom do you serve? Answer: The Holy Father at Rome, the Pope, and the Roman Catholic Church Universal throughout the world.

Who commands you? Answer: The Successor of St. Ignatius Loyola, the founder of the Society of Jesus or the Soldiers of Jesus Christ.

Who received you? Answer: A venerable man in white hair.

How? Answer: With a naked dagger, I kneeling upon the cross beneath the banners of the Pope and of our sacred order.

Did you take an oath? Answer: I did, to destroy heretics and their governments and rulers, and to spare neither age, nor sex, nor condition; to be as a corpse without any opinion or will of my own, but to implicitly obey my Superiors in all things without hesitation or murmuring.

Will you do that? Answer: I will.

How do you travel? Answer: In the bark of Peter the fisherman.

Whither do you travel? Answer: To the four quarters of the globe.

For what purpose? Answer: To obey the orders of my General and Superiors and execute the will of the Pope and faithfully fulfill the conditions of my oaths.

Go ye, then, into all the world and take possession of all lands in the name of the Pope. He who will not accept him as the Vicar of Jesus and his Vice-Regent on earth, let him be accursed and exterminated.

Appendix B

Correspondence Between Reverend George Washington Snyder and President George Washington[1936]

Frederick-Town (Maryland) Augt 22. 1798

Sir,

You will, I hope, not think it a Presumption in a Stranger, whose Name, perhaps never reached your Ears, to address himself to you the Commanding General of a great Nation. I am a German, born and liberally educated in the City of Heydelberg in the Palatinate of the Rhine. I came to this Country in 1776, and felt soon after my Arrival a close Attachment to the Liberty for which these confederated States then struggled. The same Attachment still remains not glowing, but burning in my Breast. At the same Time that I am exulting in the Measures adopted by our Government, I feel myself elevated in the Idea of my adopted Country. I am attached both from the Bent of Education and mature Enquiry and Search to the simple Doctrines of Christianity, which I have the Honor to teach in Public; and I do heartily despise all the Cavils of Infidelity. Our present Time, pregnant with the most shocking Evils and Calamities, threatens Ruin to our Liberty and Goverment. Secret, the most secret Plans are in Agitation: Plans, calculated to ensnare the Unwary, to attract the Gay and irreligious, and to entice even the Well-disposed to combine in the general Machine for overturning all Government and all Religion.

It was some Time since that a Book fell into my Hands entituled "Proofs of a Conspiracy &c. by John Robison,"[1] which gives a full Account of a Society of Freemasons, that distinguishes itself by the Name "of Illuminati," whose Plan is to overturn all Government and all Religion, even natural; and who endeavour to eradicate every Idea of a Supreme Being, and distinguish Man from Beast by his Shape only. A Thought suggested itself to me, that some of the Lodges in the United States might have caught the Infection, and might cooperate with the Illuminati or the Jacobine Club in France. Fauchet is mentioned by Robison as a zealous Member: and who can doubt of Genet and Adet? Have not these their Confidants in this Country? They use the same Expressions and are generally Men of no Religion. Upon serious Reflection I was led to think that it might be within your Power to prevent the horrid Plan from corrupting the Brethren of the English Lodge over which you preside.2

I send you the "Proof of a Conspiracy &c." which, I doubt not, will give you Satisfaction and afford you Matter for a Train of Ideas, that may operate to our national Felicity. If, however, you have already perused the Book, it will not, I trust, be disagreeable to you that I have presumed to address you with this Letter and the Book accompanying it. It proceeded from the Sincerity of my Heart and my ardent Wishes for the common Good.

May the Supreme Ruler of all Things continue You long with us in these perilous Times: may he endow you with Strength and Wisdom to save our Country in the threatening Storms and gathering Clouds of Factions and Commotions! and after you have completed his Work on this terrene Spot, may He bring you to the full Possession of the glorious Liberty of the Children of God, is the hearty and most sincere Wish of Your Excellency's very humble and devoted Servant

G. W. Snyder

---

25 Sept.: Sir, Many apologies are due to you, for my not acknowledging the receipt of your obliging favour of the 22d Ulto, and for not thanking you, at an earlier period, for the Book you had the goodness to send me.

I have heard much of the nefarious, & dangerous plan, & doctrines of the Illuminati, but never saw the Book until you were pleased to send it to me. The same causes which have prevented my acknowledging the receipt of your letter, have prevented my reading the Book, hitherto; namely—the multiplicity of matters which pressed upon me before, & the debilitated state in which I was left after, a severe fever had been removed. And which allows me to add little more now, than thanks for your kind wishes and favourable sentiments, except to correct an error you have run into, of my Presiding over the English lodges in this Country. The fact is, I preside over none, nor have I been in one more than once or twice, within the last thirty years. I believe notwithstandings, that none of the Lodges in this Country are contaminated with the principles ascribed to the Society of the Illuminati. With respect I am Sir Your Obedt Hble Servt Go: Washington

---

1 Oct. from Frederick:

Some Weeks ago I sent you a Letter with Robison's Proof of a Conspiracy which I hope you have received. I have since been more confirmed in the Ideas I had suggested to you concerning an Order of Men, who in Germany have distinguished themselves by the Names of Illuminati—German Union—Reading Societies—and in France by that of the Jacobine-Club, that the same are now existing in the United States. It also occurred to me that you might have had Ideas to that Purport when you disapproved of the Meetings of the Democratic-Societies, which appeared to me to be a Branch of that Order, though many Members may be entirely ignorant of the Plan. Those Men who are so much attached to French Principles, have all the Marks of Jacobinism. They first cast off all religious Restraints, and then became fit for perpetrating every Act of Inhumanity. And, it is remarkable, that most of them are actually Scoffers at all religious Principles. It is said that the 'Lodge Theodore in Bavaria became notorious for the many bold and dangerous Sentiments in Religion and Politics that were uttered in their Harangues, and its Members were remarkable for their Zeal in making Proselytes'; (and no Wonder since the Order was to rule the World.) Is not there a striking Similarity between their Proceedings and those of many Societies that oppose the Measures of our present Government? Even in this small Place the French-Faction is very numerous—their Expressions are like those of Bloody-Lutetia [Lutetia Parisiorum, or Paris]: their Sentiments in exact Unison with those of the Jacobine Club: their Hearts panting for Faggots and Guillotines. The Foundation of their Sanctuary is laid with Lies, and every Stone of the Superstructure reared with Falsehood. They are laboriously employed to excite Discord—to extinguish public Virtue—to break down the Barriers of Religion—to establish Atheism, and work the Downfall of our Civil—and Religious Liberty. Should their perfidious Schemes succeed (I tremble even at the Imagination of the Consequences) what would become of our Columbia?

---

10 Oct.: Sir: It is more than a fortnight since I acknowledged the receipt of your first letter, on the subject of the Illuminati and thanked you for Robinson's account of that society. It went to the post office as usual addressed to the Rev'd Mr Snyder, at Frederick Town Maryland. If it had not been received before this mishap must have attended it, of which I pray you to advise me, as it could not have been received, at the date of your last, not being mentioned. I am, &c. G. Washington

17 Oct. Snyder wrote GW: Your Excellency's Favour of the 25th of Septr last I had the Pleasure to receive on the 3d Current. My Pleasure, however, was interrupted, because I had sent another Letter [dated 1 Oct.] for your Excellency to the Post-Office about an Hour before I received Your's." After further pleasantries Snyder goes on to write: "I should be very happy in your Excellency's good Opinion, that the Contagion of Illuminatism or Jacobinism had not yet reached this Country; but when I consider the anarchical and seditious Spirit, that shewed itself in the United States from

the Time M. Genet and Fauchet (who certainly is of the Order) arrived in this Country and propagated their seditious Doctrines, which the illuminated Doctor from Birmingham has been zealously employed to strengthen, I confess I cannot divest myself of my Suspicions: yet I trust that the Alwise and Omnipotent Ruler of the Universe will so dispose the Minds of the People of these United States that true Religion and righteous Government may remain the Privileges of this Nation! I cannot conclude without acquainting your Excellency that I have made Extracts from 'Robison's Proofs of a Conspiracy,' and arranged them in such a Manner as to give a compendious Information to the Public of the dangerous and pernicious Plan of the 'Illuminati or Jacobins,' and by some Remarks to caution them against it. I had them published in 'Bartgis's Federal Gazette' of this Place, from which they were copied and inserted into the 'Baltimore Federal Gazette[']' of the 9th Inst. I write under the Signature of Cicero. Whether my Endeavours shall benefit the Public Time alone can evince. Harm I am conscious I do not design. Should your Excellency have Leisure to peruse the Piece, I shall deem it a peculiar Favour to receive your Opinion upon it

---

GW's response from Mount Vernon on 24 Oct. brought the exchange to a close: "Revd Sir I have your favor of the 17th instant before me; and my only motive to trouble you with the receipt of this letter, is to explain, and correct a mistake which I perceive the hurry in which I am obliged, often, to write letters, have led you into.

It was not my intention to doubt that, the Doctrines of the Iluminati, and principles of Jacobinism had not spread in the United States. On the contrary, no one is more fully satisfied of this fact than I am.

The idea I meant to convey, was, that I did not believe that the Lodges of Free Masons in this Country had, as Societies, endeavoured to propagate the diabolical tenets of the first, or the pernicious principles of the latter (if they are susceptible of seperation). That Individuals of them may have done it, and that the founder, or instrument employed to found, the Democratic Societies in the United States, may have had these objects—and actually had a seperation of the People from their Government in view, is too evident to be questioned.

My occupations are such, that but little leisure is allowed me to read News Papers, or Books of any kind; the reading of letters, and preparing answers, absorb much of my time. With respect—I remain Revd Sir Your Most Obedt Hble Ser. Go: Washington

Appendix C
A Defense of Intelligent Design

DNA is a self-correcting *digital* information database.

> *As scientists began to decode the human DNA molecule, they found something quite unexpected—an exquisite 'language' composed of some 3 billion genetic letters. "One of the most extraordinary discoveries of the twentieth century," says Dr. Stephen Meyer, director of the Center for Science and Culture at the Discovery Institute in Seattle, Wash., "was that DNA actually stores information—the detailed instructions for assembling proteins—in the form of a four-character digital code"...*
>
> *It is hard to fathom, but the amount of information in human DNA is roughly equivalent to 12 sets of The Encyclopaedia Britannica— an incredible 384 volumes" worth of detailed information that would fill 48 feet of library shelves!*
>
> *Yet in their actual size—which is only two millionths of a millimeter thick—a teaspoon of DNA, according to molecular biologist Michael Denton, could contain all the information needed to build the proteins for all the species of organisms that have ever lived on the earth, and "there would still be enough room left for all the information in every book ever written"* ... ~ *DNA: The Tiny Code That's Toppling Evolution,* Mario Seiglie[1937]

Mutation is the *loss* of information from the DNA code and there are *no* substantive examples of dramatically-beneficent mutation. The X-Men are x'ed out of reality.

Further advances have proved that the phrase "junk DNA" shows a startling ignorance of genetics. There is no such thing.[1938]

The very premise of Darwinian Evolution is false; the idea that life arose from the simple to become complex. The 2nd Law of Thermodynamics[1939] states that all unattended systems migrate from order to chaos. Nothing in nature contradicts this, save the "theory" of Evolution.

> *If it could be demonstrated that any complex organ existed, which could not possibly have been formed by numerous, successive, slight modifications, my theory would absolutely break down.* ~ *On the*

Origin of Species, Charles Darwin[1940]

Thanks to the electron microscope, it is now a fact that there is no such thing as a "simple, single-celled organism". The "simplest" bacterium is a miraculous factory of processes and functions.

The more we look, the more we see processes that can not be reduced in simplicity and still be of use.

Noting this, Dr. Michael Behe of Lehigh University has coined the phrase "irreducible complexity" and illustrates it thus: a simple mouse trap composed of a hammer, spring, bar, platform and catch that loses one of its 5 components doesn't catch $1/5^{ths}$ fewer mice, it catches *no mice at all* because it ceases to operate.

As we examine an apparatus like the flagellum that propels bacteria, we see shocking symmetry and complexity—basically, a bioelectric outboard motor.

> *By itself, the rotor is able to turn at a speed between 6,000 and 17,000 rotations per minute (rpm) but* [nominally] *achieves a speed of 200 to 1000 rpm when the flagellar filament (that is, the propeller) is attached. Its forward and reverse gears allow the motor to reverse direction within a quarter turn.*
>
> *The bacterial flagellum, which has been described as a "nanotechnological marvel" (Berg, 2003), has long been championed as an icon of the modern intelligent design movement and the flagship example of "irreducible complexity" (Behe, 1996). But even biologists outside of this community have been struck by the motor's engineering elegance and intrinsic beauty. As one writer put it, "Since the flagellum is so well designed and beautifully constructed by an ordered assembly pathway, even I, who am not a creationist, get an awe-inspiring feeling from its 'divine' beauty," (Aizawa, 2009). ~ The Bacterial Flagellum,* Jonathan McLatchie (B.Sc, M.Res)[1941]

The process of random mutation bringing about beneficial change to an organism would theoretically require millions of tries (if, indeed, it's possible *at all*). Millions of such "transitional forms" should be overflowing at every dig yet there are *none*. Every fossil in the record is a fully-functioning organism, not a failure transitioning into one.

There is an anomaly in the fossil record, though: an explosion of fossils in the Cambrian period that defies an evolutionary explanation.

When faced with the facts, Darwinians simply restate the damning evidence as proof of their fanciful paradigm. We have termed that here, "Gaslighting".

> *The transition between the Precambrian and the Cambrian period (about 550 million to 500 million years ago) records one of the most important patterns of fossils in all the geological record. Complex animals with a suite of shells, intricate body plans and associated movement traces appeared for the first time, suddenly and unambiguously, in sequences all over the world during this interval. This "Cambrian explosion" remains one of the most controversial areas of research in all of the history of life, and one of the most exciting. Palaeontological data like this is definitive in its support for evolutionary theory, the relative sequence of first appearances in the fossil record over the past several billion years ties very closely with what we would expect from evolutionary theory.* ~ Jonathan B. Antcliffe, Paleontology Online[1942]

The Scopes "Monkey Trial" was a propaganda ploy designed to sensationalize a common-sense piece of Tennessee legislation that treated evolution as no more a scientific "theory" than the account of Creation in Genesis.[1943]

In the 1960 movie version of this sophistry *Inherit the Wind*, Christians are lampooned as close-minded, superstitious zombies, allergic to the rationality of "science".

In reality, the reverse is true.

Macro evolution doesn't even qualify as a legitimate "theory" based upon empirical evidence via the scientific method. It's not observable, testable or repeatable. You can't isolate the variables and replicate it.

Darwinian evolution does not qualify as a scientific hypothesis yet it is taught in all public schools with Jesuitical rigor. Any true scientist that allows even open debate is at least ridiculed and worst (and, most often) fired.

> *Dr. Guillermo Gonzalez is an astrophysicist and assistant professor of Astronomy at Iowa State University (ISU). To Gonzalez's credit, he boasts some 68 peer review articles, co-authored the standard astronomy textbook used even by fellow faculty members of ISU, was instrumental in the discovery of two new planets and his research has led to what is now known as the galactic habitable zone (GHZ). In fact, GHZ is a term coined by Gonzalez and as he*

puts it, "Our star, the Sun, is one of the few stars in the Galaxy capable of supporting complex life. The sun is composed of the right amount of "metals," and its orbit about the galactic center is just right. Our solar system is also far enough away from the galactic center to not have to worry about disruptive gravitational forces or too much radiation. When all of these factors occur together, they create a region of space now known as a Galactic Habitable Zone." However, despite Gonzalez's impressive record, in April of 2007 Iowa State University (ISU) denied him tenure.

Why? Many are saying that the reason for the denial was because of a book co-authored by Gonzalez called "the privileged planet" in 2004, which is a position which supports intelligent design (ID) and is at odds with ISU's evolutionary fundamentalism. ~ Matthew C. Statler, Trinity Law School[1944]

Prof Suggests Answering Creationism Questions, Gets Fired

A scientist who suggested creationism be discussed in school science classes as a "worldview" if students raise questions has been banished from his UK Royal Society job for advocating the open exchange of information.

According to a report in the London Telegraph, the Royal Society, the world's oldest scientific body, declared that Professor Michael Reiss, who was director of education at Britain's scientific academy as well as an ordained Church of England minister, had "damaged its reputation" and had to leave his post. ~ WND[1945]

NASA Scientists Claims He Was Harassed, Demoted Over Intelligent Design Beliefs

Supervisors at the Jet Propulsion Laboratory harassed and demoted a high-level computer systems administrator who as a self-described evangelical Christian expressed his belief in intelligent design to co-workers, the plaintiff's attorney told a judge Tuesday.

Lawyer William Becker, on behalf of David Coppedge, delivered his opening statement to Los Angeles Superior Court Judge Ernest Hiroshige in trial of the religious discrimination lawsuit his client filed in April 2010.

Coppedge maintains he was fired nine months later in retaliation for bringing the suit. Becker said his client was treated different because of his interest in religion. ~ FoxNews[1946]

Intelligent Design Film Shut Down By Museum

A decision at a popular museum in Los Angeles to shut down debate over Darwin's theory of evolution has prompted a lawsuit alleging officials violated the First Amendment rights of supporters of a documentary exploring Intelligent Design.

The lawsuit was filed by the American Freedom Alliance, which said the California Science Center inappropriately canceled an event that was to feature films exploring both evolutionary theory and Intelligent Design.

Intelligent Design challenges the fundamental foundation of evolution, arguing the incredible complexities of life bear evidence of a designer.

The complaint alleges free speech rights violations occurred when the science facility abruptly reversed a decision to allow the showing of the films at the museum's IMAX Theater. ~WND[1947]

With as much faith as Darwinian Evolution now requires, in light of real science, one would think Creationism[www] could get equal time, but this has been ruled by the United States Supreme Court to be forbidden in the school room, not even as an elective.

For 15 years, in defiance of a Supreme Court ruling, Larry Booher taught creationism in his high school biology class. He even compiled a textbook of sorts and passed out copies in three-ring binders. The school superintendent didn't know what was going on. Neither did the school board president. Then, they got an anonymous tip.

Booher has agreed to revise his lesson plan, though he maintained that he handed out the book, titled "Creation Battles Evolution," to his Biology 2 students only as a voluntary, extra-credit option. "He told the students, 'You may read this. You don't have to. It has some Bible references in it,'" said Alan Lee, superintendent of Washington County schools. "This teacher felt like he wasn't doing anything wrong."

The Supreme Court ruled in 1987 that creationism, the belief that God created the universe as explained in the Bible, is a religious

---

[www] "Intelligent Design" simply acknowledges a Designer. Creationism specifically acknowledges the God of the Bible as the Designer.

belief, not science, and may not be taught in public schools along with evolution. "Creationism is not biology and has no place in a biology class," said Kent Willis, executive director of the American Civil Liberties Union of Virginia. "What makes it wrong is not the theory of creationism, but the teaching of creationism as part of a science class." ~ Associated Press[1948]

Endnotes

[1935] *The Jesuit Oath Exposed*, Professor Arthur Noble, 5 April 2000, the European Institute of Protestant Studies
http://www.ianpaisley.org/article.asp?ArtKey=jesuit
[1936] *To George Washington from G. W. Snyder, 22 August 1798*, The Washington Papers, Founders online archive
http://founders.archives.gov/documents/Washington/06-02-02-0435
[1937] *DNA: The Tiny Code That's Toppling Evolution*, Mario Seiglie, undated, UCG.org
http://www.ucg.org/science/dna-tiny-code-thats-toppling-evolution/
 —a religious site but the information is solid and there's no such thing as "secular" science.
[1938] *"Junk DNA" Concept Debunked By New Analysis Of Human Genome*, David Brown and Hristio Boytchev, 5 September 2012, the Washington Post
http://www.washingtonpost.com/national/health-science/junk-dna-concept-debunked-by-new-analysis-of-human-genome/2012/09/05/cf296720-f772-11e1-8398-0327ab83ab91_story.html?hpid=z4
[1939] Second Law of Thermodynamics, Wikipedia
https://en.wikipedia.org/wiki/Second_law_of_thermodynamics
[1940] *On the Origin of Species*, Charles Monkeyman, John Murray (1859), p. 173
[1941] *The Bacterial Flagellum*, Jonathan McLatchie (B.Sc, M.Res), September 2012, Scribd
https://www.scribd.com/doc/106728402/The-Bacterial-Flagellum
[1942] *Patterns in Palaeontology: The Cambrian Explosion – Paradoxes and Possible Worlds*, Jonathan B. Antcliffe, 8 September 2012, Paleontology Online
http://www.palaeontologyonline.com/articles/2012/the-cambrian-explosion-paradoxes-and-possible-worlds/
[1943] *The Monkey Trial* (fact vs. Hollywood), Monkey Trial.com
http://www.themonkeytrial.com/
 This is a great resource listing just how outrageous this farce was.
[1944] *Guillermo Gonzalez v. Iowa State University. Discrimination and Intelligent Design*, Matthew C. Statler, 31 July 2007, Trinity Law School
http://trinitylawschool.wordpress.com/2007/07/31/guillermo-gonzalez-v-iowa-state-university-discrimination-and-intelligent-design/
[1945] *Prof Suggests Answering Creationism Questions, Gets Fired*, 18 September 2008, WND
http://www.wnd.com/2008/09/75620/#!
[1946] *NASA Scientists Claims He Was Harassed, Demoted Over Intelligent Design Beliefs*, 14 March 2012, FoxNews
http://www.foxnews.com/scitech/2012/03/14/nasa-scientists-claims-was-harassed-and-demoted-over-intelligent-design-beliefs/
[1947] *Intelligent Design Film Shut Down By Museum*, Bob Unruh, 26 November 2009, WND
http://www.wnd.com/2009/11/117203/#!
[1948] *Creationism Teacher Told To Stop*, 10 June 2005, the Associated Press
http://www.sullivan-county.com/deism/booher4.htm

About the Author

Johnny Cirucci is a career military man whose deployment to Iraq changed his perspective. Upon returning home, he began to see that America's greatest enemies were within her own most critical institutions. He started a relentless search to unmask who those enemies were.

Johnny recalled his experience in debate and writing columns for the University paper at college and immersed himself in alternative media and journalism.

His unique writing style and signature phrase "[italics suspended]" derive from his efforts to use mainstream open sources to overwhelmingly convince his readers of the very unconventional reality they live in.

Unlike other public figures, Johnny welcomes your input and will do his damnedest to respond in kind.

web site: www.johnnycirucci.com

blog: www.johnnycirucci.com/wp

e-mail: johnny@johnnycirucci.com

Facebook personal: www.facebook.com/JohnnyCirucci

Facebook fan page:
www.facebook.com/The.Johnny.Cirucci.fanpage

Twitter: @Johnny_Cirucci

YouTube: https://www.youtube.com/user/THEJohnnyCirucci

Printed in Great Britain
by Amazon